Occasional Papers
Department of Anthropology, University of Manitoba
No. 1

LIFE, LAND AND WATER

Proceedings of the 1966 Conference on Environmental Studies of the
Glacial Lake Agassiz Region.

EDITED BY
WILLIAM J. MAYER-OAKES

University of Manitoba Press
Winnipeg, 1967

Published with financial support from the National
Research Council.

Clothbound SBN 88755 101 7

Paperbound SBN 88755 601 9

Library of Congress Catalog Card Number 72-83105

First Printing 1967

Second Printing 1969

PREFACE

It is particularly satisfying to the editor to have experienced both the Conference and the pleasures and problems of the subsequent publication process. Details of the Conference itself are presented in Part I. Here we wish to record and acknowledge the various kinds of help and support that made the Conference, and this volume, possible.

In the early years of archeological work at the University of Manitoba we were substantially encouraged and supported in our emphasis on Glacial Lake Agassiz by the President, Dr. H.H. Saunderson and the Dean of Arts and Sciences, Dr. William M. Sibley. Within the University, Dr. James C. Ritchie provided needed encouragement and example by his on-going botanical work. Outside the University, we are particularly indebted to John Elson, R.S. MacNeish, William E. Taylor and William N. Irving, as well as Elden Johnson who with his archeological work on Glacial Lake Agassiz in Minnesota was a good example to us. The first archeological survey of Glacial Lake Agassiz was carried out by Matthew H. Hill with the assistance of Eugene Gryba and Leo Pettipas.

At the 1965 INQUA sessions we learned how really broad were the possible horizons of Glacial Lake Agassiz and are deeply indebted to John Brophy, Earl Christiansen, Lee Clayton, Jim Ritchie, Jaan Terasmae and Sam Tuthill for the advice and encouragement they provided. This really amounted to the "inspiration" for a Conference -- all else was more or less perspiration.

While in the planning stage, the Conference idea was strongly supported by Harry Duckworth with shaping to final dimensions shared by a willing and helpful committee -- John Elson, Al Hochbaum, Zenon Pohorecky, Jaan Terasmae and Steve Zoltai. Here, and in the final planning, our department secretary Carole Johnstone was of invaluable assistance.

In the actual Conference operation a large number of people were involved. From our department came the help of several staff members: Jim Chism, Joan de Peña, Virginia Gerelus, Carole Johnstone, Kathryn Sutton, Morgan Tamplin and Joan Townsend all pitched in for assigned or obvious tasks with enthusiasm. Our graduate students took on important parts of the job, ranging from chauffering participants around to operating the tape recorders. Dennis Joyes, Jonathan Maas, Mary Lou Miller, Bill Morgan, Leo Pettipas, Peter Priess and Leigh Syms each did yeoman service while keeping a successful Conference going and some of these were even taking notes on the side!

Several University of Manitoba staff members helped greatly by chairing sessions. Bruce Wilson also hosted the first session in his geology building. We are pleased to record jobs well done and express the gratitude of the Conference to the other chairmen: Wilson Laird, Earl Christiansen, Roy Waygood, Harold Welch,

iii

Elden Johnson and Herbert Wright. The socializing and creature
comfort aspects of the Conference were supported by several
agencies. The Manitoba Department of Mines and Resources not
only welcomed the group through the Minister, the Honorable
Gurney Evans, but also hosted a luncheon. The University of
Manitoba was host to the Saturday night banquet, courtesy of the
President, Dr. Saunderson. Two highlights were clearly the buffet
banquet at the home of Roy Waygood and the Delta field trip. Mrs.
Waygood and Mrs. Mayer-Oakes were co-hostessess for the first event,
which will long be remembered for its charm and abundance of good
food. The Delta Waterfowl Research Station and Al Hochbaum were
hosts for the final afternoon's field trip and supper. The large
roaring fire and Ian Cornwall's guitar and singing made a fitting
finale to the Conference.

     The "fallout" after the Conference was substantial, much of
it you will find in the remaining pages of this volume. Hard work
at the typewriter by Mrs. James Ross brought the tapes of the
Conference and the pages of this volume into being. Both Susan
Foley as editorial assistant and Carole Johnstone as "special
effects" typist and general helper were also fundamental to the
process of publication preparation. All three have the gratitude,
affection and admiration of the editor for all their help in so
many ways.

     In final appreciation and acknowledgement we want to emphasize
the role played by the National Research Council. From N.R.C. came a
grant that enabled us to hold the Conference and from N.R.C. has come
a grant that enables us to publish. For this support, the Conference
members, the University and all interested in Glacial Lake Agassiz
are deeply grateful.

WELCOMING REMARKS

Mr. Chairman, Ladies and Gentlemen, it is a pleasure for me to express the welcome of the University to the members of this Conference. In fact the extent of my desire to be here can be gauged by the fact that I left the November meeting of the National Research Council a day early in order to return to Winnipeg last night, notwithstanding the fact that an application of my own for the support of a Conference on Atomic Masses is coming up for consideration today. If I may quote from Scripture, "Greater love hath no man than this, that he forsake his own conference for that of his friends".

Nevertheless, I am delighted to be here and to be participating in this affair, even if only superficially, because I have followed with special interest the emerging recognition by the members of this group of their common interest in Glacial Lake Agassiz. I believe that the 1965 International Quaternary Conference (INQUA) was an important stage in this recognition. Incidentally, another significant result of the strong Canadian participation in this Quaternary Conference was the establishment by the National Research Council of Canada of an Associate Committee on Quaternary Research, with a membership possibly to be decided today, either before or after action is taken on the Duckworth application for support on the Conference on Atomic Masses. But even more, I am pleased to be here because the study that is represented by this Conference is held in very high esteem by the University, and on several counts.

To begin with, ancient Glacial Lake Agassiz is a subject of unusual inherent interest, lending itself without difficulty to the type of scholarship appropriate to a University. In the second place, it is a subject that not only lends itself to interdisciplinary study but, indeed, cannot be tackled most effectively without bringing several disciplines into the act. This University in common with many others has come to appreciate the unique advantages that emerge from a correlated, many-faceted approach to some problem of common interest. The cumulative total achievment of the members of such a cross-disciplinary group is greater than the sum of the separate parts, and invariably things are got at that would have been inaccessible to the practitioners of one discipline alone. And, in the third place, the University is interested in this particular study because of its special relevance to the Province of Manitoba. Presumably an increased knowledge of the state of affairs a few years ago will help us to realize more fully our present potentialities.

Our appreciation of the value and significance of this Conference is naturally reflected in appreciation towards those who have made it possible. On the grant-awarding side we are grateful to the National Research Council and, on the arrangement side, we are grateful to the members of the Conference Committee and to those who have worked with them. Two members of the Committee, Dr. Hochbaum and Mr. Zoltai, although not regular members of the

University staff, are intimately involved in many of our activities and we have come increasingly to rely upon them. Dr. Terasmae, an occasional visitor to the campus from the Geological Survey of Canada, is viewed by us as sort of a one man, self-contained, interdisciplinary group. Dr. Pohorecky from the University of Saskatchewan and Dr. Elson from McGill University have been interested in this area of study for some time, and I know they have been in touch intermittently with members of our own staff. Finally Dr. Mayer-Oakes, the principle ring-leader, has worked very hard and obviously very effectively for the success of this meeting. I don't know when his wife sees him, but I understand that she derives what pleasure she can from the thought that since he is an archeologist, the older she gets the more he becomes interested in her.

Finally, may I welcome especially to the campus those who have come from a distance to be here, from other Canadian Universities and laboratories, from the United States and, in the case of the keynote speaker, from the United Kingdom. I speak for the University when I express the hope to you all that the Conference will be successful, and the further hope that your stay on campus will be as pleasant to you as your presence here is agreeable to us.

Thank you very much.

Henry E. Duckworth,
Vice-President,
University of Manitoba.

CONTRIBUTORS

John A. Brophy
North Dakota State University

Reid A. Bryson
University of Wisconsin

Ian W. Cornwall
University of London

Alan M. Cvancara
University of North Dakota

John A. Elson
McGill University

H. Albert Hochbaum
Delta Waterfowl Research Station

Walter O. Kupsch
University of Saskatchewan

Paul W. Lukens, Jr.
Wisconsin State University

Charles L. Matsch
University of Minnesota

William J. Mayer-Oakes
University of Manitoba

John H. McAndrews
Royal Ontario Museum

James C. Ritchie
Trent University

Creighton T. Shay
University of Manitoba

Morgan J. Tamplin
University of Manitoba

Jaan Terasmae
Geological Survey of Canada

Samuel J. Tuthill
Muskingum College

John Warkentin
York University

Wayne M. Wendland
University of Wisconsin

Thomas C. Winter
United States Geological Survey

Herbert E. Wright, Jr.
University of Minnesota

Stephen C. Zoltai
Canada Department of Forestry and Rural Development

CONTENTS

FOR CORRIGENDA, PLEASE SEE PAGES 415 - 416.

CONTENTS--<u>Continued</u>

TABLES

TABLES--Continued

FIGURES

FIGURES--<u>Continued</u>

Part I

The 1966 National Research Council
Conference

THE 1966 NATIONAL RESEARCH COUNCIL CONFERENCE

William J. Mayer-Oakes

History

In this introductory part of the Conference proceedings, we wish to record very briefly some of the major steps leading up to publication.

Because of the editor's bias, being so close to the entire affair, we begin our account with his 1962 personal entry into the Glacial Lake Agassiz region. Early in the first academic year of my residence in Winnipeg (1962-63), it became clear that a local focus for archeological attention should be this outstanding Pleistocene and Recent feature -- the great glacial lake -- with all its implications for contextual or "environmental" archeology. By correspondence and later in person, I contacted John Elson for advice and information. This exchange worked two ways. Elson had for some years not returned to his scene of earlier work in Manitoba, but now with promise of local interest, he renewed his activities in the area. My initial proposals (1963 and 1964) for long range environmental archeological work on Glacial Lake Agassiz were largely unsuccessful. Encouragement and financial support from the National Museum of Canada (especially R. S. MacNeish and W. E. Taylor) was followed by strong general support from the University of Manitoba. A full-time research post in our department was established in 1965.

The year 1965 was a pivotal year in many respects. This was the first year of Elson's serious and intensive return to field work in the region. He continues this annually and as this is written in August, 1967, is now in the field. Also in the field now is the University of Manitoba's field party (under Morgan Tamplin) carrying out the third full field season of the Glacial Lake Agassiz Archeological Survey. This program was initiated in 1965 with support of both the University and the National Museum. It has carried on in 1966 and 1967 with strong support from the National Research Council.

Of perhaps outstanding importance during 1965 was the series of events that occurred at the INQUA sessions in Boulder, Colorado. A number of scholars interested and active in Glacial Lake Agassiz studies attended this meeting in early September, 1965. A highlight for me was the informal breakfast and lunch sessions in the University dormitories. Here, I became more completely aware of the many contributions already made by scholars from Wisconsin, Minnesota and North Dakota. At these sessions I was somehow persuaded to help "get the ball rolling" on an informal workshop or conference which seemed needed. Lee Clayton of the University of

North Dakota, John Brophy of North Dakota State University and
Earl Christiansen of the University of Saskatchewan were
particularly persuasive and helpful at this stage.

    In our innocence we barged ahead, sending out a questionnaire
in early fall of 1965 to some forty-odd names. During the
academic year 1965-66 results from this survey were digested. By
the summer of 1966, with advice and encouragement from a conference
steering committee (Elson, Hochbaum, Terasmae, Pohorecky and Zoltai),
it was clear that a November 1966 conference at Winnipeg would
probably be a welcome and useful event. A request for financial
assistance was supported by N.R.C. Strong encouragement and support
was offered by the University. With the active support of a good
many local people, University staff and students and others, the
Conference was held on November 3, 4, 5 and 6. During the last
three weeks before the Conference, it became clear that we had
underestimated serious interest in the subject. From a planned
"workshop" type conference of some thirty or so active field workers,
our participants swelled to nearly one-hundred. Fortunately, the
weather was reasonable, our facilities and conference staff
adequate, and a lively session became part of history, unrecorded
except for the audio tapes made of the papers and discussions.

    Below we reproduce the printed program of the Conference.

PROGRAM

CONFERENCE ON ENVIRONMENTAL STUDIES OF THE GLACIAL LAKE AGASSIZ REGION [*]

NOVEMBER 3 - 6, 1966

UNIVERSITY OF MANITOBA

WINNIPEG, CANADA

* Supported by a grant from the National Research Council of Canada.

PROGRAM

CONFERENCE ON ENVIRONMENTAL STUDIES

OF THE

GLACIAL LAKE AGASSIZ REGION

THURSDAY, NOVEMBER 3, 1966 7 P.M. - 10 P.M.

Coffee and Registration at Anthropology Laboratory

FRIDAY, NOVEMBER 4, 1966

MORNING SESSION   Room 211, Geology Building

9:30   Opening Remarks:
       Welcome: H. E. Duckworth, Vice President, University of
                                                              Manitoba.
                    The Honorable Gurney Evans, Minister of Mines &
                                                  Natural Resources.
       Address: "MAN IN HIS ENVIRONMENT" - Ian W. Cornwall,
                                                 University of London.

COFFEE BREAK

11:00 Opening Theme: H.D.B. Wilson,
                              University of Manitoba, CHAIRMAN.

                    A summary of Glacial Lake Agassiz Studies -
                    Morgan J. Tamplin, University of Manitoba

12:00 Luncheon: Montcalm Hotel   (Manitoba Department of Mines
                                         and Natural Resources, host.)

AFTERNOON SESSION   Anthropology Laboratory

1:30   "GLACIAL LAKE AGASSIZ"   --   W. M. Laird,
                              University of North Dakota, CHAIRMAN.

                    Geological Deposits   --   J.A. Elson,
                                                     McGill University.
                    Discussant: J.A. Brophy,
                                          North Dakota State University.

                    Eastern Outlet   --   S.C. Zoltai,
                                          Canada Department of Forestry.
                    Discussant: B.B. Bannatyne,
                    Manitoba Department of Mines & Natural Resources.

Post-glacial uplift   --   W.O. Kupsch,
University of Saskatchewan.
<u>Discussant:</u> L. Clayton, University of North Dakota.

Coctail Party: Faculty Club
(Laboratory of Anthropology, host)

Buffet Supper: --   Eraway Farm

EVENING SESSION   Anthropology Laboratory

8:00   "GLACIAL LAKE AGASSIZ"   (cont'd)
-- E.A. Christianson,
University of Saskatchewan, CHAIRMAN.

Drainage History   --   A.M. Cvancara,
University of North Dakota.
<u>Discussant:</u>   R. W. Klassen,
Geological Survey of Canada.

Contemporary Drainage   --   H.A. Hochbaum,
Delta Waterfowl Research Station.
<u>Discussant:</u>   W.J. Brown, University of Manitoba.

SATURDAY, NOVEMBER 5, 1966

MORNING SESSION   Anthropology Laboratory

9:00   "PALEO-ECOLOGY"   --   E.R. Waygood,
University of Manitoba, CHAIRMAN.

Vegetation History - Sourthern area -- C.T. Shay,
Colorado State University.
<u>Discussant:</u> M.L. Heinselman, U.S. Forest Service.

Vegetation History - Northern area --J.C. Ritchie,
Trent University.
<u>Discussant:</u>   J.H. McAndrews, Cornell College.

Paleo-climate   --   R.A. Bryson,
University of Wisconsin.
<u>Discussant:</u>   J. Terasmae,
Geological Survey of Canada.

AFTERNOON SESSION   Anthropology Laboratory

1:30   "PALEO-ECOLOGY" (cont'd)   --   H.E. Welch,
                               University of Manitoba, CHAIRMAN.

                       Paleo-zoology and Molluscan Paleontology   --
                               S.J. Tuthill, Muskingum College.
                           Discussant: A.M. Cvancara,
                               University of North Dakota.

                       General Considerations   --   J. Terasmae,
                               Geological Survey of Canada.
                           Discussant: J.C. Ritchie, Trent University.

Dinner, 6:00   Paddock Restaurant   (University of Manitoba, host.)

EVENING SESSION   Anthropology Laboratory

8:00   "HUMAN ASPECTS OF LAKE AGASSIZ AREA"   --
                               E. Johnson, University of Minnesota, CHAIRMAN.

                       Grand Rapids Site Fauna   --   P.W. Lukens, Jr.,
                               Wisconsin State University.
                           Discussant: H.A. Hochbaum,
                               Delta Waterfowl Research Station.

                       Human Population History   --   W.J. Mayer-Oakes,
                               University of Manitoba.
                           Discussant: J.H. Warkentin, York University.

                       SUNDAY, NOVEMBER 6, 1966

MORNING SESSION   Anthropology Laboratory

9:30   "PRESENT STATUS AND FUTURE DIRECTIONS"   --
                               H.E. Wright Jr., University of Minnesota,
                                                          CHAIRMAN.

AFTERNOON   Depart for Field trip at 1:00.
                       Visit Delta Waterfowl Research Station.
                       Buffet Supper
                               (Delta Waterfowl Research Station, host.)
                       Return to Winnipeg by 9:00 P.M.

The program printed above was not carried out exactly as scheduled. Aircraft malfunctions delayed Ian Cornwall's departure from London, so that he arrived in Winnipeg only after the conclusion of the Friday evening sessions. His "keynote address" was thus not given until Saturday evening, when it replaced the session on "Human Aspects of Lake Agassiz Area". This latter session was held Sunday morning, prior to the scheduled session on "Present Status and Future Directions". The Sunday field trip was made memorable by delightful hospitality, glacial age weather, and Ian Cornwall's singing of English folk songs.

Proceedings

At the final formal session of the Conference there was a general consensus that proceedings should be published if papers were available. Several participants left final versions of papers with me at the time of the Conference. By January 1, 1967 I had eight papers on hand, plus encouraging word from the remainder of the authors. Thus, we planned to publish and commenced our search for funds. We also began transcriptions of certain papers from the tape recordings. Really serious full-time effort at editing and arranging began in May, the last two papers (not counting the editor's which really was last) arrived at the end of June, as did notification that N.R.C. would give financial assistance to the publication. A final unexpected hurdle was the need to change printers; a problem primarily financial in nature. This last barrier to publication was surmounted with the help of Vice-President Duckworth and the re-constituted University of Manitoba Press.

Having now indulged your editor by allowing him this exercise in historic recounting of secondary matters, we can now move on to the fundamental contributions made by the Conference and its participants.

Part II

Man in His
Environment

MAN IN HIS ENVIRONMENT

Ian W. Cornwall

You may be asking yourselves why I, formally an archaeologist, should have been brought from London to Winnipeg to introduce the subject of environmental studies, as applicable to man, to an audience including workers in so many different fields of Science.

All I can say is that in London we had, from 1937 to 1963, the late Frederick E. Zeuner, the first, and for long the only, Professor of Environmental Archaeology in the world. I was his student and colleague for 18 of those 26 years and represent here the Department founded by Zeuner and the ideas which have there been made available to all post-war students of the University of London Institute of Archaeology.

Zeuner was, first and foremost, a palaeontologist and geologist, but also a very good all-round natural scientist, with biological preferences. From Pleistocene palaeontology, geology and chronology, studied for their own sakes, his interest later turned to the origin, evolution and relation to his natural environments of early, especially Palaeolithic and Mesolithic, man in the Old World. With his early purely scientific background, he never concealed the fact that man, having reached the Neolithic and early Metal-Age stages of culture, ceased to command his full interest, whereas, for most of our colleagues at the Institute -- the real Old World archaeologists, with an Arts training as foundation -- this was where the subject seemed properly to begin!

Zeuner would never have denied that the influence of natural environment on human societies continued beyond the Neolithic -- indeed, his last book, *A History of Domesticated Animals*, (1963) dealt with almost exclusively post-Neolithic human achievements -- but, in writing it, the palaeontologist and mammalian ecologist were always uppermost, despite his scholarly references to ancient historic sources and illustrations largely derived from his personal collection of early coins bearing animal representations.

Gordon East (1965) wrote an admirable little book entitled *The Geography behind History*. Had he lived, Zeuner might equally well have written one called *The History behind Geography*, putting the time-dimension back into human geography, which the geographers themselves (with honourable exceptions) too often tend to leave out. In the past there were clear-cut distinctions between the Faculties of Arts and Science in many of the older European Universities. The boundaries of these are, fortunately, now becoming

somewhat blurred, but the gulf between the Two Cultures was due
to faults on both sides. Archaeologists had never, until the last
50 years, felt that it was their business to concern themselves
with anything beyond the work of men's hands, their artifacts.
Scientists, for their part, felt that the study of past human
cultures was properly part of history, rather than having anything
to do with them.

Zeuner was a scientist working among colleagues who were,
therefore, almost exclusively arts-based, but he took the trouble
to inform himself about the content of archaeology, as they understood it. He expected them and their students, in their turn, to
consider the human artifacts, and the people who made them, in
their natural environmental context. In this at least with some
of his younger colleagues and students, he succeeded. No archaeologist trained by the Institute since the end of the War, at least,
has gone out into field or museum without certainly some conception
of the importance of environmental considerations in his studies.
Some few scientists, also, have turned, under Zeuner's teaching
and influence, to applying their specialities in archaeological
contexts -- geographers, geologists and zoologists, for the most
part -- but even one nuclear physicist wrote his thesis in our
department, on carbon fourteen dating; a meteorologist, on Pleistocene climatology; one anthropologist, on Postglacial sea-levels
and another on the weathering changes on the surfaces of Neolithic
axes; a bronze-age archaeologist on mineral studies in pottery
thin-sections. I myself, a linguist and prehistorian originally,
gained a Ph.D. in Arts, examined by Zeuner and Wooldridge, both
scientists, my thesis being on the application of methods of soil-
science to archaeological deposits!

Among this "omnium gatherum" of scientific interest, it may
be supposed that any individual practitioner must tend to be a
Jack-of-all-Trades -- and, it follows, Master of None. This would,
of course, be inevitable if any one of us aspired to cover the
entire field of science for the archaeologist equally. In practice,
each of us acquires a working knowledge of a limited area of science
beyond our original specialities and, since we have to impart some
appreciation of the whole vast field to students who, generally,
are still not scientifically minded, we need at least a theoretical
grasp of some other parts of it.

Thus, for instance, my present Professor, G.W. Dimbleby, is
fundamentally a botanist with ecological leanings, who uses pollen-
analysis and soil-science as his chief tools. On the side of
archaeological applications, he tends to interest himself in the
ecological impacts of human societies on their biological (especially plant) environments and in early agriculture. My specialities
meet his in the investigation of ancient soils and sediments from
archaeological, mainly pre-Neolithic, sites and I continue to cover
the geological, palaeo-zoological and chronological fields which
formed Zeuner's focus of interest. We have, for example, two
current Ph.D. students, both B.Sc.'s in zoology, the one special-
izing in land and freshwater shells and the other in small terrestrial and aquatic arthropods, as environmental indicators in archae-

ological contexts. Neither subject is new in archaeological studies, but there are very few active practitioners in either field and we hope that these two men will fill the gaps.

If we get archaeological questions about specialities beyond the department's academic and technical resources, we act as inter-mediaries to put the inquirer into touch with the appropriate spec-ialists. This is especially the case when it is a question of one of the more modern physical or chemical investigations, such as carbon 14 or potassium-argon dating, thermoluminescence or palaeo-magnetism, for instance, or, on the geological side, petrology and heavy-mineral analyses.

With Zeuner's backing of enthusiasm for Pleistocene palaeon-tology, the study of human and animal bones from archaeological sites has always formed an important part of our teaching and research. Each generation of young archaeologists has had some instruction in bone-determination and several zoologists with spec-ial interests in Pleistocene mammals have gained higher degrees in the department under his supervision.

In the course of time, we have been able to build up a large (though still incomplete) comparative osteological collection. With this elementary technical foundation, the students have gone on, in their second year, to a short course in Human Palaeontology and to Zeuner's own lectures on Pleistocene faunas and the relation of the animals to early man, right up to historic times.

With Dimbleby succeeding Zeuner in the Chair, now re-named "Human Environment", the department's interests and activities have considerably widened into the botanical and plant ecological fields. The microscopic determination of timbers and charcoal from archaeological sites, the study of plant-remains, both macro-and microscopically, has been extended to fruits and seeds, leaves, bud-scales, hairs, epidermal and other tissues, stems, grass-opals and even to non-flowering plants such as ferns and mosses.

Dimbleby lectures on plant ecology, with special reference to the influence of prehistoric and early historic communities on their plant and soil environments, plant cultivation and early agri-culture. As a pollen analyst, he has applied those techniques to the study of pollen in soils, rather than in peats, not only in soils still evolving at the modern surface, which, by a stratifica-tion of their pollen-content may show the past changes in plant-communities at that site, but in buried soils beneath earthworks and other structures erected by man, which still show the features of their times. The comparison of the changing assemblages in such profiles has thrown light on prehistoric land-use and human influ-ence in changing the soils and natural plant environments.

Both Dimbleby and I have for some time been associated, with others, as members of a British Association Research Sub-Committee on Field experiments, which has now constructed two bank-and-ditch earthworks on contrasting soils (chalk and sand), in imitation of prehistoric examples. (Dimbleby 1963)

In these we have set up various experiments under strictly recorded and controlled conditions. The intention is to investigate, by periodical excavations over the next hundred years, the natural changes undergone by these structures and their buried contents -- flints, sherds, bones, timber and pollen, textiles, leather etc. Our colleagues on the Committee include archaeologists, a geographer, a geomorphologist, a zoologist, a meteorologist, a chemist, and we have all the support and help of the Nature Conservancy's specialists, on two of whose Reserves these "monuments" have been erected. The results, as they come in over the succeeding years, will be of interest to a far wider spectrum of sciences than to archaeology only, though the Committee does owe its first conception and organization to Section H (Anthropology) of the British Association, and the fundamental work of Charles Darwin.

The only other scientific Department of the Institute is concerned with teaching and research in Prehistoric technology and conservation of archaeological materials -- cleaning, repair, reconstruction and reproduction of objects; research into materials and processes used in antiquity. This work is also environmentally orientated, for it is concerned, not only with the material resources of ancient macro-environments but with the conditions in the micro-environments to which buried materials have been exposed since their loss or abandonment. It is important to know something about these when prescribing treatment for cleaning and preventing the further deterioration of antiquities under museum conditions.

In this direction, the work of the Conservation Department links with our own interests in the materials, inorganic and organic, available to ancient man in different natural environments and at different times, so we work closely together.

These examples, from my own first-hand knowledge and experience, may serve as an introduction to the more general consideration of what form co-operation should, and could, take between anthropology (including, as it does in North America, archaeology) and other branches of natural science. Since this is only my second, very brief, visit to Canada, I would not out of my ignorance, presume to apply more than the most general principles and recommendations to the situation of anthropology in this particular environment.

In their enthusiasm for excavating ancient settlements and studing the artifacts which they expose and collect, archaeologists sometimes tend to forget that they are really concerned with people. Physical anthropologists, similarly, are likely to consider their osteological materials with an absorption that allows them, at times, to overlook that these are remains of once-living, sentient and self-conscious men and women, whose history and way of life were bound up with their contemporary environments and the material potentials of those surroundings.

Properly to take into account all the relevant natural evidence which may have a bearing on their people and the sites that they chose for occupation, anthropological and archaeological field-workers must be prepared to lift their eyes out of their trenches and excavations and look about them at the surrounding country, as far as possible not only with vision of the present state of that country, but with some insight of how it may have appeared to the people whom they are studying.

Where, as in Great Britain, man has been occupying and modifying the natural environment for thousands of years, this may present considerable difficulties, but in this Province, where the land has been much less changed by its shorter history of human use, the present state of affairs must still be much closer to the natural condition than it is with us.

In this connection, it may be interesting to investigate to what extent the great impoverishment and acidification of northwest European boreal forest and moorland, and their soils, is due, not only to Nature, but to man's millennial interference with his natural environment.

The natural Postglacial history of the Yorkshire or Scottish moors must be essentially the same as that of the Lake Agassiz Basin. Admittedly, there are natural environmental differences to be taken into account -- notably that, in Canada you have a markedly continental type of climate, while that of Britain or the Baltic lands is, in comparison, oceanic and mild. This means that while, with us, chemical and microbiological soil-processes, if not plant-growth, continue through the winter, in your climate the prolonged winter freeze-up brings such activity to an almost complete halt for nearly half of each year. This would suggest that your soils are little more than half as mature, in chemical terms, as are ours! Nevertheless, with you, Nature has had an almost free hand in forming the environment as we see it today, while, in Europe, prehistoric and historic men have occupied it in increasing numbers and intensity for at least the last ten thousand years. To judge by the photographs which I have seen, even today man has not interfered appreciably with Nature in the northern part of Manitoba, so that here we have a very good control for studying the European human influence in boreal forest surroundings.

In one other aspect the two environments seem to differ appreciably. In Scotland and Norway -- even on the Yorkshire Moors -- there is considerable variety of relief. Admittedly, most of what I have so far seen of Canada has been from an aeroplane so that my idea of the topography of Alberta, Manitoba and Saskatchewan is, perhaps, unduly, foreshortened. Nevertheless, the distribution of land and water, even as seen from the air, shows that much of the country is, by our standards, fairly flat. This absence of steep slopes and, even more, of bare peaks and eminences subject to frost-weathering, must have an important influence on the current-velocity and transporting power of drainage streams, on rates of erosion and indeed, on the mere volume of sediments available to form Postglacial accumulations. This it is, perhaps, which governs the comparative rarity of well-stratified recent geological and archaeological deposits and so will make the establishment of an archaeological chronology, even a relative one, much more difficult for you than it has proved for us.

The further we go back in time, the greater are the natural geographical, geomorphological and biological changes which must be taken into account in reconstructing the past landscape, so that the anthropologist must needs call on geologists and geographers, botanists and zoologists -- and, at times, for chronological purposes, even nuclear physicists and astronomers! -- to help him piece together the evidences of past times in which his ancient folk had their being and of the environments on which their living depended.

A couple of examples from my own experience may serve to illustrate these generalizations. I was once called to a site by an excavator to help him to interpret the stratification exposed by his trenches. He was greatly puzzled by a thick deposit filling a prehistoric ditch, clean and almost devoid of occupation debris or human artifacts. He was inclined to interpret it as artificial filling by the ancients or as "hill-wash", until I pointed out, as to the latter explanation, that his site was on level ground, far away from any appreciable slope which might have afforded an origin for such material. The fill was clearly quite natural and, as such, could only have come from the walls of the ditch itself and its immediate surroundings, including, latterly perhaps, some contribution from the adjacent mound, to construct which the ditch had originally been dug. This shows how an archaeologist can sometimes so concentrate on his restricted trenches as to remain oblivious of their surroundings, and undertake the excavation of a ditch without much idea of how such artificial features come, in time, to be modified and almost obliterated by natural processes.

My second illustration is from a remoter period of the past. Palaeolithic implements are often found in gravels of ancient river terraces, sometimes at considerable heights above the talwegs of the present day rivers. In such a situation, the implements are inevitably derived, for these are river bed deposits containing the re-worked materials of a more or less contemporary, but now vanished, flood plain, the land surface on which the makers of the implements doubtless once lived. In order to visualize the local surroundings as they were in those times, we have, in imagination, to undo the erosive and aggradational work of the river through the hundreds of thousands of years which have since elapsed, relying on the terrace fragments and their reconstructed longitudinal profiles up and down stream in order to do so. This calls for a geological and geomorphological effort of restoration of which, at least in the recent past, few collectors of palaeoliths were capable, so that their ideas of the Palaeolithic topography, based only on what can be seen today, were frequently much mistaken. I remember during my school days hearing an imaginative account by one such collector of a vast river in Palaeolithic times, filling with water the entire modern valley from bluff to bluff and rolling in its mile-wide channel the hand-axes and elephant teeth which its ancient terraces today afford. He was, perhaps, following Dean Buckland, visualizing in part the retreat of Noah's Flood and in part James

Geikie's deglaciation! We now know that a stream no larger than
the present modest tributary can, in the time available, achieve
the erosive effects that we see and that in a manner no more spectacular than by the processes that can, in any modern year, be
observed at work, and that the fossiliferous terraces represent
fragments of old, high level flood plains.

        Thus, while it is obviously advisable that every field archae-
ologist should have some background ideas relating to environment
from several branches of Natural Science, it is not to say that he
need become a specialist in any of them. He may, in fact, do so,
out of interest for a subject closely related to his own study,
but where his own knowledge is deficient he should call in specialist advice to help in the solution of his environmental problems.
Often he will find that something about his site which seems to
him to present insoluble difficulties has a ready and satisfactory
explanation when seen by a colleague with a different technical
outlook, knowledge and skills. Such a solution may well depend on
sampling and analysis, or a least closer examination in the consultant's laboratory, by techniques and with equipment not accessible to most archaeologists. At the same time, it is important
that the archaeologist should have some idea of what can, and
cannot, be done for him by other specialists and this is necessary
so that he may intelligently inform his consultant of the nature,
scope and meaning to himself of a technical investigation and its
results. Proper cooperation thus, on occasion, involves a meeting
in the field of excavator and consultant, to view the problems
together and for each to communicate his own thoughts about them.

        Ideally, it might be supposed that every excavation project
should be accompanied by a body of scientific specialists in a
variety of disciplines. In most cases, this is clearly not economic in term of either time or money and though, as I have said,
it is all important for an excavator to get the man on the site, a
short visit by a specialist, arranged when the progress of the
excavation has exposed some sections likely to be of interest to
him, is all that is necessary. I was recently invited, by the
leader of a proposed American archaeological expedition to the
Near East, to accompany them for a matter of months as a soil
consultant. I suppose that I enjoy foreign travel as much as the
next man, but, quite apart from the difficulty of finding the time
to accept this invitation I had, in all honesty, to turn it down
because, under the circumstances, I could not foresee that I should
be able to make any contribution commensurate with the cost of my
permanent attendance at a late Classical site. A short flying
visit at a late stage in the work would be another matter, and
possibly useful to both sides.

        Without the man seeing the site, being able to look about
him at the present country and form his own opinion about its
condition at the relevant period, his view may be put in blinkers.
Samples on his bench, sent by someone else, are necessarily
divorced from their context, however well documented, and though,
if adequately described, they may yield results of some interest,
they are still best supported by a personal visit to the site, if
at all practicable.

It is probably true to say that, in the New World, archaeology has not been as closely identified with the art-historical, non-scientific, approach that still, to some extent and in some branches, fetters the subject in the Old World. For one thing, archaeology in the New World is taught at University level as a branch of Anthropology and this, though it may have other drawbacks, ensures that no archaeologist can complete his training without making contact on a wide front with several branches of Natural Science. The result is that the inter-disciplinary approach, taking all the aspects of the environment into account as well as the purely human phenomena, has developed to a far greater extent here than is usual with us. One of the most striking recent examples of success in this direction has been Richard MacNeish's work at the Tehuacan caves, (1962) with the environmental study of which a whole galaxy of specialists was concerned. The point I want to make with this example is that, if it was the archaeological excavation that brought them together in the first place, and if their joint labours have greatly contributed to illuminate archaeological and human environmental questions, the benefits have been reciprocal also. To take only a single instance: the corn cobs from the dry cave deposits have been of great value to Mangelsdorf in elucidating the history and chronology of maize cultivation.

Thus, if the archaeologist hopes to gain information of value to his own study by the work of associated specialists, in their turn it is from datable archaeological sites that the various specialists can most readily obtain materials enabling them to view their own subjects in relation to a scale of times past. Without the excavation, carried out by the archaeologist for his own purposes, the beneficiaries would, in most cases, never have had the opportunity to examine the materials thus disclosed -- materials of intrinsic interest to their own subjects, apart from their possible bearing on archaeology.

In addition, therefore, to excavations carried out by the archaeologists, for primarily archaeological purposes, which may, quite incidentally, uncover non-archaeological materials of interest, there is a strong case for the techniques of archaeological excavation to be more widely used by other specialists, or groups of different specialists, to give a time-scale to their studies.

This is, of course, often done by geologists, palaeozoologists and palaeobotanists, who are primarily interested in phenomena of times past, but it could be much more widely used, for instance, by soil-scientists, geomorphologists and geographers seeking for the time dimension in relation to their field materials. This should be the case not only on sites of human occupation, which are chosen primarily because they may contain concentrations of artifacts, but at places considered to be most likely to yield the special chronological evidence sought, in which archaeological materials, if present at all, would be subsidiary, and provide only a check on the chronology, I have in mind as an example, the studies on Postglacial soils and valley deposits and their contained assemblages of land mollusca, used by Dr. M. Kerney, of Imperial College, London, to investigate the climatic and ecological changes of the Chalk Downland in Kent, in which the evidence of the influence of Neolithic and later human interference with the environment has emerged only as a by-product. From time to time he sends us potsherds from his sections, for determination and dating, much as an enlightened archaeologist might send him the snails from his site for their ecological interpretation.

Such inter-disciplinary field and laboratory investigations are profitable and instructive for all participants. Dr. Kerney is at present helping one of our Ph.D. students who is studying land mollusca and has been to address our archaeological students on the results of his work.

In another place I have (following Jenny's 1941 example in *Factors of Soil-Formation)* listed the factors of human environment as follows:

1. Place

2. Climate

3. Land-forms

4. Rocks and Minerals

5. Soils

6. Plants

7. Animals (including man)

8. Time

This serves to show how, in the study of a site in the entirety of its natural environmental context, geographers, climatologists, geomorphologists, petrologists and mineralogists, pedologists, botanists, zoologists and physical anthropologists and the numerous specialist chronologists may all be able to add something to the total knowledge about the ancient people concerned, the influence of the natural environment on them and their culture and, indeed, their influence on it.

While, as I have already suggested, pre-colonial hunting, fishing and collecting man in Canada may not have affected the fundamental character of his natural environment to anything like the same extent as did the sedentary Neolithic and post-Neolithic inhabitants of Europe over the last 5-6 thousand years, it is certain that his presence had some effect. and perhaps a larger one than might, at first glance, be supposed. One calls to mind Sauer's theory that the open prairies were largely man-made and man-maintained through the Indians' use of fire for game-driving,

apart from accidental fire-damage, which is not uncommon. Such a
periodical artificial disturbance of the natural climax vegetation
is clearly as much of interest to the plant ecologist and the geographer as it is to the archaeologist. The soil, the hydrography
and much else may be affected, generally adversely. The disturbance would, of course, be most marked and most permanent in a zone
of climatic stress, where a comparatively feeble causative agency,
such as wanton or accidental human damage, could upset the equilibrium, if not permanently, at least for a very long time. In such
circumstances, both physical and organic degradation of an environment tends to be progressive and, what is often forgotten, natural
regeneration becomes impossible if key species, whether plant or
animal, have become locally extinct.

     In animal ecology, the beaver is a good example of a key
species. Beaver dams in the headwaters of a catchment, by slowing
drainage, conserve water, prevent catastrophic spates and prolong
stream flow even in high-summer drought. The ponds which they
maintain provide a habitat for large populations of fishes, waterfowl and other vertebrates and invertebrates and so encourage also
the predators of these species, among whom may be counted primitive
man. Remove the beaver, and the rest of the animal environment is
disproportionately impoverished as a direct consequence and, within a very short time, may become incapable of supporting the human
hunter.

     Such are influences directly due to human occupation, evid-
ence of which should be sought at the sites themselves. If un-
considered as ecological effects, they may, quite mistakenly, be
attributed to climatic change. Evidence for any important climatic
cause of historic desiccation in the Near East, for example, is
very slender. It is more and more being realized that increasing
human populations clearing land and their uncontrolled browsing
domestic animals have been the most potent influence in degrading
the Mediterranean environment, barely poised as it was to resist
the stress of summer drought, and with a vegetation-type incapable
of rapid natural regeneration. The timer-bearing species, which
we know from literary sources to have been present in early Classical times, if not extinct, are no longer locally represented. Even
the soil that once supported them has in many areas since been
washed away, so that their natural re-establishment is today
impossible.

     Archaeology, like the biological and earth-sciences, started
by being almost entirely descriptive. It will have to continue to
describe new phenomena, qualitatively, but more and more it must
try to gain precision by quantifying its results.

     Co-operation with representatives of allied disciplines,
working in the same field, makes available to archaeologists, not
only the different materials and outlooks of scientific colleagues,
but also the tools and methods which they use to study them and
present their results.

It is one thing to say, for instance, that a type of artifact is much more numerous at Site A than at Site B. It is far more convincing to be able to say that it is three times as numerous, and this finding may be important in framing archaeological and anthropological conclusions, about Sites A and B at first, with C, D and E to be compared additionally at a later stage.

The intention eventually to express results quantitatively will, to some extent, affect policy at an early stage of the work in the field. Good statistics depend on material well sampled in the first place. Valid sampling consists, not, as too often in the past, in selecting the better and more showy pieces and discarding the "rubbish" -- a subjective judgement, this! -- but in having available total assemblages of adequate size from given archaeological horizons. With such a study in view, the extent of the excavation and the method of collecting the material will be different from that required for taking a qualitative sample only.

The same principles apply to studies of human and animal bones, plant remains, geological specimens or soil samples and, indeed, to mapping archaeological distributions and drawing human geographical conclusions therefrom. Of course, the very partial and fragmentary nature of what is known about an area or of what has chanced to be preserved is often the limiting factor to making an adequate collection. One knows of plenty of instances from the past in which mere quantity was sufficient, but the methods of collection, recording and documentation of the finds so deficient as to render the material practically valueless for modern purposes.

Long ago, now, I had the sobering, but instructive, experience of assisting the late Frank Addison, one-time Director of Antiquities to the Sudan Government, to study and publish a large collection of archaeological material made 35 years previously at the Wellcome excavations in the Sudan. The material had been brought home literally in shiploads, but so little attention (because of the scale and pace of the work) had been paid to the stratification and recording when it was excavated that quantitative treatment was in most cases a waste of time. This is no reflection on the competence of the archaeologists concerned, among whom, as a young man, was the late O.G.S. Crawford. They were simply too few and too overworked to do their job as they knew it ought to have been done. Fifty years on, our excavation-techniques have, too, also improved on 1914, but alas most fieldwork is no longer so lavishly financed as it was in the days of Sir Henry Wellcome!

Besides, even if (as A.J. Arkell wrote in his review of our eventual publication): "A few cubic metres of occupation-debris... excavated with knife and brush will tell more of the history of the village than tons of debris put through sifting-machines", the material might be an insufficient sample for statistical treatment of the finds.

The Wenner-Gren Symposium (Viking Fund Publications, No. 28, 1960) on Quantitative Methods in Archaeology is a fund of

information on many aspects of the subject. Though I, who was a
contributor, say it, both archaeologists and workers in related
sciences could (and, perhaps, do!) read it with profit. The "Bible"
of our subject, in the Department of Human Environment in London,
is also due in great part to the Wenner-Gren Foundation symposium:
"Man's role in changing the face of the Earth". (Thomas, W. 1956)

Finally, may I say how happy and how honoured I feel to have
been asked to contribute to this Conference. There is no more
important cause in Science today than to encourage and assist
specialists in different disciplines to get together, pool their
knowledge and get to understand each other's attitudes to common
problems. This is especially true in the study of Human Environment, and I expect that the exchange of ideas here will be most
fruitful.

Part III

Glacial Lake Agassiz

A BRIEF SUMMARY OF GLACIAL LAKE AGASSIZ STUDIES

Morgan J. Tamplin

Introduction

The purpose of this paper is to present a brief general introduction to the previous research which has been conducted within the basin of Glacial Lake Agassiz. As a comparative new-comer to this area, I approached this assignment with some mis-givings, for I realized that most of my audience would have far more experience in the field and would be much more familiar with the pertinent literature than myself. In fact some of you are even preparing bibliographies on this topic.

As an anthropologist by formal training, an archaeologist by experience and an environmentalist by choice, I can only hope to outline what seem to me to be the important or significant trends in the history of research on the problem of Glacial Lake Agassiz. Many of you, listening to my account, may relive your own first experiences as you attempted to track down the more obscure pub-lications (such as the appendix to the report of the Chief of Engineers of the United States Army) or tried to pry the relevant data from a particular groundwater study or soil survey publication. While this paper has afforded a unique (but traumatic) opportunity for me to become familiar with the literature on this vast subject, I can only hope it will bring one or two new fragments of inform-ation to most participants, or possibly jolt the better-informed into rebuttal. It may also serve to pinpoint the relevant material and such irrelevant information as a novice invariably digs out to amuse himself need not be mentioned later but can be left here where it will not clog the more constructive discussions to follow.

Nineteenth Century Studies

The pioneer explorers in this area who recognized beach structures related to Lake Agassiz include Keating (1825), Owen (1852), Palliser (1863), Hind (1859), Dawson (1875) and Warren, (1868). Of these, it appears that Hind first realized the extent of the body of water which formed these ridges, although he saw it only as an enlargement of Lake Winnipeg, caused by damming of glacial ice to the north. General Warren (most of whose articles are tucked away in the Government Reports mentioned previously) enlarged and confirmed these observations by tracing the south-ward drainage of this lake to the Minnesota River, but he rejected the glacial damming hypothesis as, "Unsupported, and barren of any fruit."

Thus, by the late 1870's the existence of an early lake was known and its boundaries and channels roughly sketched. In 1879, Warren Upham joined the Minnesota Geological Survey and during the summer of that year had amassed sufficient field information to define the southern limits of the lake in considerable detail. In the *Annual Report of the Minnesota Geological Survey* for that year proposed the name Lake Agassiz, in honor of Louis Agassiz, the father of Pleistocene Geology.

The director of the geological survey, N.H. Winchell, writes in the same report with some pride that

> *Mr. Warren Upham, late of the New Hampshire Geological Survey, has been occupied nearly the whole season in studying the geology of the drift-covered counties in the central and western portions of the state, with special reference to the topography, glacial geology and economic resources of those counties. With a horse and wagon he has travelled about 3,300 miles and has in his note-books the necessary information for reporting in full on twenty-two counties, or an area of 16,000 square miles.*

Although some may find it difficult to accept that this area could be covered adequately in such a short time with the primitive facilities available, surely the fact that a large area was covered quickly must have been instrumental in crystallizing Upham's concept of the Lake, where a more detailed survey in the initial stages would have restricted his view. Upham continued his exploration of the Lake Agassiz shore lines during the latter half of the 1880's, this time working more slowly on foot with a rodman, doing levels, advancing three to ten miles a day. He continued the survey as far north as Riding Mountain in Manitoba in 1888 under the auspices of the Geological Survey of Canada. The results of this latter survey were published in the *Geological Survey of Canada Annual Report* for 1888-89, section E. When he began levelling in Canada Upham experienced some difficulties, for an error in the initial government survey had created a difference of 24 feet between elevations on the east side of the Red River and those on the west.

The culmination of this research (which represented six year's field work) appeared in 1896 as *Monograph 25 of the United States Geological Survey*, Upham's "The Glacial Lake Agassiz". While this work has many factual and theoretical shortcomings, it certainly is an impressive beginning for research in any area especially considering the rugged nature of the terrain and working conditions.

Upham concluded that the lake was formed in front of a single retreating ice front, and that each beach-stage could be correlated to a particular terminal moraine. T.C. Chamberlain (1895) writing an alternative hypothesis to that presented in Upham's monograph, points out the difficulties of the Upham hypothesis, citing the example of the Herman beach, thought by Upham to be a single unit

formed by the lake during the formation of three moraines, all of
which thus must have been formed after the moraines were deposited.

Upham also concluded that the silts of the Red River Valley
were of fluvial origin and deposited after retreat of the Lake.
He recognized the multiplication of the strandlines to the north
and ascribed their upward slope to uplift following glacial
retreat.

Canada's first contribution to this research was made by J.
B. Tyrrel of the Geological Survey, who, during 1888 to 1890,
explored the Manitoba lake system by canoe, working inland on
horseback or by horse and buggy from the south end of Riding
Mountain to Red Deer Lake and beyond. He traced Agassiz beaches
to the north end of the Duck Mountains. Tyrrel, with his equally
energetic assistant Dowling, also managed to cover an impressive
amount of territory in a comparatively short time despite the
fact that he was suffering from typhoid fever during much of the
survey!

I recently had an opportunity to read portions of Tyrrel's
field notes and ran across such daily entries as "had a touch of
fever this morning so only went 20 miles." Perhaps as an archeologist, I seem to be over-impressed by the work of early geologists,
but a reminder of their tremendous pioneer efforts is a useful
counterbalance to any criticisms which we may have of their conclusions. We can only make such criticisms by the way, with the
benefit of hindsight.

Tyrrel published a preliminary report and map in the *Geological
Survey of Canada Annual Report* (no. 3) for 1887-88, while his final
report is in the *Annual Report* (no. 5) for 1890-94, (section E).
He published his theories in 1896 in the *Journal of Geology* (possibly in response to Upham's monograph). Because he was more
familiar with the vacant beaches and more northern moraines, he
saw the genesis of Lake Agassiz in the coalescence of two lobes of
ice which blocked the Lake outlets from the north. To him, the
southern portion of the Lake was never invaded by ice while it
was in existence. It has taken many years to resolve these apparently diametrically opposed views of Upham and Tyrrel. The possibility of more than one Wisconsin re-advance associated with a
second stage of the Lake was only dimly conceived. In 1909,
Leverett saw two substages of the Wisconsin, which he termed
"Earlier" and "Later" and in 1912 related these to the early stages
of Lake Agassiz. (He later considerably expanded these stages in
the 1930's).

Twentieth Century Studies

Apart from Leverett, there seems to be a lessening of interest
(in the literature, at least) in the Lake Agassiz problem during
the first years of the 20th century. This may be historically
linked to other interests in the history of geological research.
In Canada, certainly exploration was directed towards the northern territory. On the other hand, I may be doing an injustice to
relevant studies which have not yet come to my attention.

Interest was renewed with the publication of Johnston's paper
in the *Journal of Geology* of 1916 entitled, "The Genesis of Lake
Agassiz -- a confirmation". The confirmation was, in part, for
Tyrrel's view that the glacial activity had been centerd at the
northern end of the Lake. There was a rebuttal in the *Bulletin
of the Geological Society of America* next year by Upham, who
adhered to his previous theory. But Johnston had also found stratigraphic evidence for a discontinuity in the Lake deposits at
Lake of the Woods, showing that the level had radically fallen and
then risen.

He also advanced his concept of a "hinge-line" in the isostatic
uplift of the beaches, although at this time he felt that this uplift took place only after the glacier had completely receded.

Johnston continued his research in the Lake Agassiz area with
the Geological Survey of Canada for many years publishing on the
Whitemouth and Winnipegosis area in 1921 and on the Winnipeg map
area in 1934. The culmination of his investigations came with the
publication of a slim *Geological Survey of Canada Bulletin* in 1946,
"Glacial Lake Agassiz with Special Reference to the Mode of Deformation of the Beaches".

In this article we have the most detailed total small-scale
mapping of the beaches (with selected altitudes) which has appeared
in print to date. The mapping is presented together with longtitudial
profiles and an amplification of his hingeline concept.

Johnston's views on the timing of the uplift had undergone
considerable revision for he now saw five stages of uplift and
stability correlated to the recession of the ice and beach-stages.
His chronology, however is too extended, for he dates the Campbell
Beach at about 14,000 B.C. (10 to 11 thousand is more acceptable)
and the last beach at about 1000 A.D., which is too early.

Despite the reservations one may have about these correlations,
the uplift and bifurcation of beaches must still be systematically
accounted for, and correlations with glacial phases refined.

Perhaps the most original hypothesis was that advanced by
Nikoforoff, (1947) who was intimately acquainted with the Agassiz
beaches through his detailed Soils Survey of Minnesota. He saw
the genesis of Lake Agassiz in the coalescence of a number of lakes,

thus accounting for variable beach levels and eliminating the need for isostatic uplift. This hypothesis however, has not been generally accepted*

In 1931, Ernst Antevs produced a *Geological Survey of Canada Memoir* entitled "Late-Glacial Correlations and Ice Recession in Manitoba", in which he attempted to correlate varved clays to the European sequence which had been previously established.

In doing a historical review of this sort, one is always tempted to set up "early, middle and late" periods of research. The studies on Lake Agassiz do not readily lend themselves to this type of analysis, however. Although one can confidently assign Upham and Tyrrel to an early period and Leverett and Johnston and Antevs to more extended middle phase, the boundaries are blurred because the workers at this time publish their results in soil surveys, groundwater studies and glacial monographs. It is fairly obvious that the history of Lake Agassiz is inextricably linked with the later glacial history of this continent but I do not propose to embark on a history of glacial research except to recall Leighton's revised nomenclature of the Wisconsin which first appeared in *Science* in 1933 and more revised versions have been published in the *Journal of Geology* in 1958 and 1960.

The Soils, Groundwater and Geological Survey of North Dakota and Minnesota are probably the most fruitful sources of data during this period (20's and 30's). Soil surveys have afforded us, to date, the best large-scale maps of beaches, although it must be remembered that they are not mapped primarily as beaches but as soils, and neither their altitudes or morphology are recorded. Beach structures are even more peripheral to groundwater studies. Both soil and groundwater research flourished in the 1930's.

Moving on to what could be called the "Late period" of Lake Agassiz Research, one enters the post-war years of specialization. In addition to the traditional geological, pedological and hydrological studies, newcomers have appeared on the scene.

The study of aerial photographs has enabled the morphologist and glacial geologist to see vast areas of territory comparatively quickly but in much greater detail than before. Both lake and glacial features can be spotted and later checked on the ground, and maps are far easier to prepare. This is the modern equivalent of covering 16,000 square miles by horse and wagon during a single field season.

Aerial photographs also introduced new problems into the study, such as the minor intersecting ridges, not visible from the ground, which have been variously interpreted as due to wave action, periglacial activity, bedrock fracture, glacial action and dragging of lake ice on the lake bottom.

---

*Reference to Nikoforoff's contribution was included in this paper at H.E. Wright's suggestion.

Another newcomer is Carbon-14 dating, which has introduced some measure of absolute chronology into a system which formerly had to rely on a beach, moraine and stratigraphic correlation without any real chronological basis at all.

Probably the most frequently quoted paper in the recent literature is that by Elson in *Science,* 1957, "Lake Agassiz and the Mankato-Valders Problem", which employs the most recent Carbon-14 dates and the data derived from a study of aerial photographs to correlate moraines and beaches dates with glacial advances, retreats and the formation of Lakes Agassiz I and II.

Briefly, Elson postulated that during intermittent northern retreats of the Mankato ice, Lake Agassiz I was formed. It discharged southward until the outlet was eroded down to the Tintah or Norcross Level, at which time the Lake Superior ice had retreated, opening an eastern outlet which was subsequently blocked by a major readvance. Further erosion at the southern outlet resulted in formation of the Upper Campbell beach from which the Lake retreated when the eastern outlet reopened. The Lake subsequently drained prior to crustal uplift. Lake Agassiz II was formed by the Valders readvance and discharged eastward until the outlet was blocked by the glacier. As it was also blocked by the alluvial fan at the southern end of Brown's Valley the lake rose again to Norcross or Tintah level but then subsided to the Lower Campbell level. During the Valders retreat stage, the lake discharged to the east again through outlets which have been described and traced by Zoltai. Beaches below the Campbell stage were formed as the Lake drained. Final drainage occurred when Keewatin ice split from the Laurentian glacier and residual ice in the Nelson River spillway had melted.

It can be seen that both Upham and Tyrrel were correct in their hypotheses but that each was, in a sense, seeing a different lake.

Another new discipline which has contributed to the study of Lake Agassiz is Soil Mechanics. In 1952, in the *Journal of Geology,* Rominger and Rutledge reported on their studies from borings in North Dakota. Using such qualitative data as liquid limit, plastic limit, water content and preconsolidation stress they established five stratigraphic units in previously undifferentiated sediments and also established the presence of a drying surface denoting a short interval of drainage for the lake.

One of the older disciplines, botany, is also actively engaged in the Lake Agassiz problem. The first studies were mainly descriptive accounts of the present vegetation, but were quickly followed by phytogeographical studies which attempted to plot the present day distribution of eastern, western or northern plant "types" in the drained and deglaciated areas in order to deduce their temporal distribution as the Lake and glacier receded. A count of the bibliographies on this topic reveals that most of the articles quoted are of post-war origin and most of the research has been done since 1950 in this field.

The most comprehensive of these papers is Love's "The Post-glacial Development of the Flora of Manitoba -- A discussion", *Canadian Journal of Botany*, 1959, which postulated a marsh-grassland, followed by riverine spruce phase after the Lake Agassiz I draining, and an initial deciduous forest following Lake Agassiz II, with pine-oak savannah to the north and a south west-ern prairie flora covering the bottom of the draining lake. Spruce from west and east encroached upon the deciduous zone which in turn entered the prairie.

Wright and others, in a study of pollen spectra in Minnesota (*Bulletin of the Geological Society of America*, Vol. 74, 1963) offers the most recent stratigraphic approach. This line of re-search holds the most promise for future studies and for the most accurate correlation dating of Lake Agassiz deposits with each other and with the ecological history of the area.

The pollen changes show a shift from spruce to pine or hard-wood and this is postulated as the end of the Wisconsin Glaciation. On the basis of these pollen zones, Wright also tentatively in-ferred their climatic analogs. In a later paper in the *Journal of Geology*, 1964, entitled, "The Classification of the Wisconsin Glaciation", Wright integrates this stratigraphical-palynological information with the latest proposals for the subdivision of the Wisconsin, although defending many of the previous subdivisions of Leighton from the proposed lumping of the recent stratigraphic column.

Archeological Studies

I would now like to say a brief word on the archeological research within the framework of Lake Agassiz, and a brief word is all that is necessary, for compared to the geological data, archeology is a poor third or fourth. Material is scarce and difficult to locate in the lake context.

Although Upham (1895) records archeological sites (mostly late mounds on the beaches) in an appendix to his monograph, and Tyrrel (1893) reports a few isolated finds, the earliest discovery of any importance from the point of view of Lake Agassiz (in some ways the most important) was the discovery of lanceo-late projectile points with oblique, parallel flaking associated with a human skeleton near Brown's Valley, Minnesota.

The burial was intrusive into gravel, which was correlated with the Tintah/Norcross level, by Leverett (1936) but was below undisturbed humus. In other words it postdated the gravel but it was felt, not by very much. Although dating is still uncertain, the find is of considerable antiquity and probably not less than 8,000 years old.

The work of MacNeish (1958) on sites in the Whiteshell in
Manitoba during the first half of the 1950's, revealed an industry
designated as the Whiteshell focus in the lowest level of the
Cemetery Point site, on an early beach of Lake Nutimik or, alternatively a late beach of Lake Agassiz. A date of 3,500 to 5,000
years ago was postulated. The industry consists of narrow lanceolate points with concave bases, various scrapers and one multi-
barbed harpoon point. This was followed by the Larter focus,
whose characteristic points were ovoid or triangular; some were
corner-notched and a few were side-notched. Scrapers predominate
the assemblage. This was dated 2,500 to 3,500 years ago.

The recent interest in the problems of Lake Agassiz has
resulted in two research programs. In Minnesota, Elden Johnson
conducted a survey of the Glacial Lake Agassiz basin under an
N.S.F. grant, and the University of Manitoba has embarked on a
long-term Lake Agassiz Survey with support from National Research
Council and the National Museum of Canada. Neither of these
surveys has yet definitely established human occupation in direct
association with the beaches although in Manitoba surface finds
of Paleo-Indian material have been reported, mainly from the
western perimeter of the Lake.

The idea of the 1966 Conference on Environmental Studies of
the GLAS Region was conceived at the 1965 INQUA conference in
Boulder, Colorado, where workers actively engaged in problems of
Lake Agassiz met informally to discuss their mutual interests.
The task of organizing a conference was taken on by William J.
Mayer-Oakes under the auspices of the University of Manitoba,
with financial support from the Canadian National Research Council.
It may be thought odd that a department of Anthropology should
presume to bring together geologists, botanists, zoologists,
geographers and archeologists, but such an interdisciplinary
fusion is essential to understand the early human occupation and
its relationship to the environment of the lake basin and how it
relates to the present environment. That, essentially is what
an environmental archeologist is trying to do.

In the broad topics discussed in the other papers in this
volume, participants are expressing their interest in problems of
stratigraphy (both geological and palynological), paleontology,
drainage, climatic patterns, isostatic uplift and human occupation.

Conclusions

My brief study of the literature has left me with a few
distinct impressions which may be erroneous, but which I would
like to pass on. Study of Lake Agassiz begins fairly systematically but this is not surprising as there were only two workers in
the field. Since then, work has been sporadic and rarely Lake-
oriented; most of the data have been compiled for other studies.
In the 1950's interest in Lake Agassiz reawakened and considerably
more papers from more divergent disciplines have emerged.

I get the impression that there has been very little geomorphological research on the lake by geomorphologists.* This may be because geomorphologists generally work within a framework of existing processes of erosion or agradation rather than what might be termed the "fossil geomorphology" of Pleistocene beaches, and these problems have been left to geologists.

I am ever more painfully aware of an immediate need for a comprehensive bibliography of Lake Agassiz research. Some participants have already expressed an interest in such an undertaking and some have even prepared bibliographies with this idea in mind, so I have not presumed to prepare a bibliography at this time. Such a compilation would have to be annotated because much of the literature has no immediate relevance to persons outside a particular field of specialization. For example, a groundwater paper of considerable significance to a geologist might have little relevance to a botanist or archeologist, unless the relevant data are abstracted in some way. Information in local and frequently unobtainable publications would be given much wider circulation if it could be placed in such a collection.

I would be interested to see some sort of meeting of persons concerned with this problem take place during this conference so that we can pool resources and card files. Until this bibliography is published however, a few works have appeared which have extremely comprehensive lists of references. Upham's monographs lists all the relevant data known before 1895, although this is mainly of historical interest and appears as footnotes rather than any systematically bibliographic form. The most recent general paper to date is by Laird (1964). The most comprehensive geological bibliography is by Elson (1961). The most comprehensive botanical bibliography is by Löve (1959).

---

*Some North American geologists disagree with this statement claiming that geologists also do geomorphological research. Classic geomorphology which deals with the "evolution" of land-forms, is usually done by geographers. The essential difference is the respective emphasis placed by geologists and geomorphologists on structure as opposed to surface features. I would still hold to my original statement that very little geomorphological research has been conducted by geomorphologists.

Editors Note:

Figure 1 (overleaf) is a generalized rendition of Glacial Lake Agassiz and environs based on a silk screen print made by John Elson. The adaptation made for Fig. 1 and the copy used on the book cover were prepared by Ian Cameron. We are grateful to Dr. Elson for letting us use this and to Miss Cameron for her skillful art work and draftsmanship.

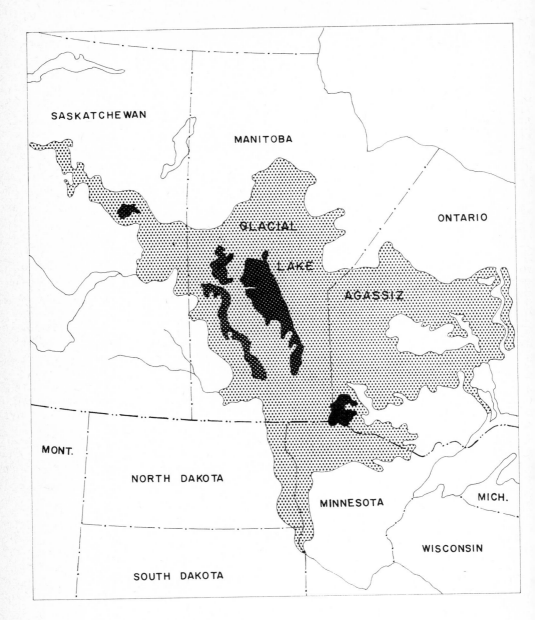

Figure 1. Schematic drawing, Glacial Lake Agassiz.

GEOLOGY OF GLACIAL LAKE AGASSIZ*

John A. Elson

Introduction

Evidence of Glacial Lake Agassiz occurs in an area of roughly 200,000 square miles in the provinces of Ontario, Manitoba, and Saskatchewan, and the states of Minnesota, North Dakota, and a small portion of South Dakota. The history of our knowledge of this Lake is summarized by Morgan Tamplin (this volume). It should be emphasized that the recent work of V.K. Prest (1963) and S.C. Zoltai (1965a, 1965b) in northwestern Ontario has added much information essential to new interpretations of the Lake's history. Also, the Surveys and Mapping Branch of the Department of Energy, Mines, and Technical Surveys has nearly completed (late 1966) a series of maps at the scale 1:250,000 with 100 foot contours covering the Lake basin in Canada. Similar maps for the part within the United States have been available for about ten years. These maps make possible the delineation of water planes and the search for related ice margins and outlets. The completion of aerial photographic coverage and construction of new highways extending into parts of the basin hitherto reached only by aircraft and canoe, also have aided greatly.

Although Lake Agassiz sediments occur within an area of 200,000 square miles, that area was not all submerged at any one time. As the ice margin retreated, the southern outlet eroded deeper causing the lake to become shallower and hence to contract in the south while it expanded in the north. Subsequently, new, still lower outlets opened into other drainage basins, mainly to the east. The surface areas of most phases of Lake Agassiz probably did not exceed about 80,000 square miles, at any one time.

General Features of the Glacial Lake Agassiz Basin

Boundaries

The accuracy of the boundaries of Glacial Lake Agassiz (Fig.2) varies considerably. In western Minnesota and along the escarpment extending from South Dakota into northern Saskatchewan the strandlines are well developed beach ridges and wave cut scarps and

---

*This preliminary report is based on the presentation made in Winnipeg in November, 1966 with substantial revisions. Because of rapid evolution of thought while new data were being incorporated, several minor inconsistencies in the historical part of the text have appeared.

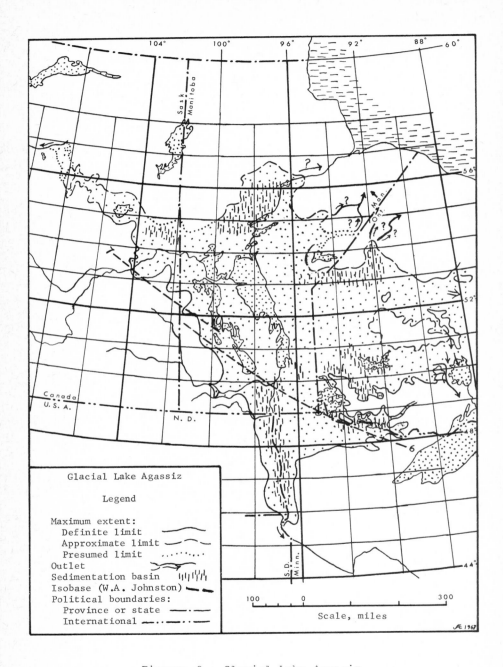

Figure 2. Glacial Lake Agassiz.

terraces. In the western part of Northern Ontario, however, the boundary is particularly difficult to map because the coast was mainly an archipelago of drift-covered bedrock islands that inhibited wave action. The positions of former water planes there are marked by strandline features (such as wave formed scarps and terraces) only on thick drift deposits such as end moraines and eskers. Elsewhere they are defined by the limits of areas of well-sorted sand resting on till (which itself is sandy) or on bedrock. Both Prest and Zoltai interpret the Lake boundary to be where this washed deposit has an upper limit at a consistent altitude. Other evidence is less direct. The crests of some eskers and moraines are flat (wave washed) whereas others are hummocky and have kettles (not washed). From these it is possible to determine upper limits of wave action and to extrapolate the presumed water plane to its intersection with the topography.

The northern Lake limit in Ontario and Manitoba is based on scattered geological reports containing references to: (1) varved clays, (2) the presence of washed eskers, and (3) several end moraines which have wave-formed terraces on one side whereas the other sides have knob and kettle topography and therefore were not subjected to wave action.

A basin area north of latitude 56° in the vicinity of longitude 100° in northern Manitoba has previously been included as part of Lake Agassiz but is excluded from it in this report in concurrence with Antevs (1931:46). This area is excluded because the basin, which is in the Churchill River drainage basin, is separated from the rest of Lake Agassiz (about 50 to 100 miles to the southeast) by high ground and an end moraine that is unwashed on the west side but has wave-formed features on the east side. The lake formerly present in the Churchill drainage does not seem to have been confluent with Lake Agassiz according to present information, although it may have been contemporary.

Between longitudes 100° and 104°, intensely folded metamorphosed Precambrian rocks form topography with a relief of several hundred feet and the lake basins enclosed by the rock ridges do not appear from air photograph interpretation to contain lacustrine clays. The geological literature for that area is of little assistance in determining the northern Lake Agassiz boundary. Farther west the rock basins do appear to contain clays. The boundary shown (Fig.2) is in part based on the intersection of a water plane (defined by the well-marked strandline on the escarpment that formed the south side of the lake -- Wapawekka Hills) with the topography on the north side of the basin at and west of Lac LaRonge, Saskatchewan (longitude 105°).

A previously unreported outlet of Lake Agassiz near longitude 109° is shown (Fig. 2). The strandline on the south side has been traced a few miles east of longitude 106°. If the sloping water plane inferred from the strandline is extrapolated westward it intersects the topography at Flatstone Lake (longitude 108°, just north of latitude 56°). There the lake discharged through four channels west from Flatsone Lake and possibly also through the Aubichon arm of

Lac Ile a la Crosse, into the Churchill Lake basin. The Churchill
Lake basin is comparatively small and formerly contained a lake
that discharged northwestward through anomalously large channels
into the Clearwater River system. Clearwater River flows westward
to join Athabasca River where it turns north toward Lake Athabasca.
Thus there may have been a waterway extending from the Arctic Ocean
by way of the MacKenzie River, through Lake Agassiz and south by
the Mississipi River system to the Gulf of Mexico for a short time
(possibly several decades) roughly 10,000 years ago. The possibility
of nearby Methy Portage serving as an outlet was considered by Upham
(1895:231-232) and rejected because of its high altitude. The
present interpretation is based on new topographic data.

Topography

     Local relief in the Lake Agassiz basin ranges from about a
foot or two per square mile in parts of the southern (Red River)
clay belt to several hundred feet per square mile in areas of Precambrian rock in the eastern and northwestern parts of the basin.
A generalized topographic map (Fig. 3) showing the general configuration of the basin was compiled from the 1:250,000 maps mentioned
above.

     The east-facing escarpment that defines the west side of the
Lake is known as the Coteau des Prairies in the south, and as the
Manitoba escarpment farther north. It increases in height above
the lake floor from about 400 feet in the south to more than 1100
feet at Riding and Duck mountains, decreases to about 800 feet
south of Lac LaRonge, and fades out from there toward the northwest.
Seven major reentrants in the escarpment were formed by preglacial
river systems and divide it into a series of cuestas each from
20 to 100 miles long. From south to north these are: Pembina
Mountain at the International Boundary; Riding Mountain; Duck
Mountain; Porcupine Hills; Pasquia Hills; Cub Hills; and Wapawekka
Hills, southeast of Lac LaRonge. The escarpment is formed by
Mesozoic rocks, primarily the Cretaceous Riding Mountain formation
which is a silicious shale (equivalent to the softer Bear Paw
formation and the Pierre shales elsewhere).

     The reentrants are now drained by river systems, from south
to north respectively, Assiniboine River (between Pembina and
Riding Mountain), Valley River, Swan River, Red Deer River,
Saskatchewan River, Bear River and Montreal River. Of these,
the Saskatchewan is largest and the Assiniboine is next largest.
Both of these last systems are parts of extensive preglacial
drainage systems that extended across the Great Plains from the
Rocky Mountains and discharged northeastwards into the Hudson Bay
region. They formed major drainage lines during deglaciation.

     The low-lying, low relief terrain that forms the part of the
Lake Agassiz basin occupied by the present-day lakes Winnipeg,
Manitoba, Winnipegosis and Cedar Lake, extends west to Lac LaRonge
and is underlain by Paleozoic dolomite and limestone formations
that dip west or southwest at a few feet per mile. In the south

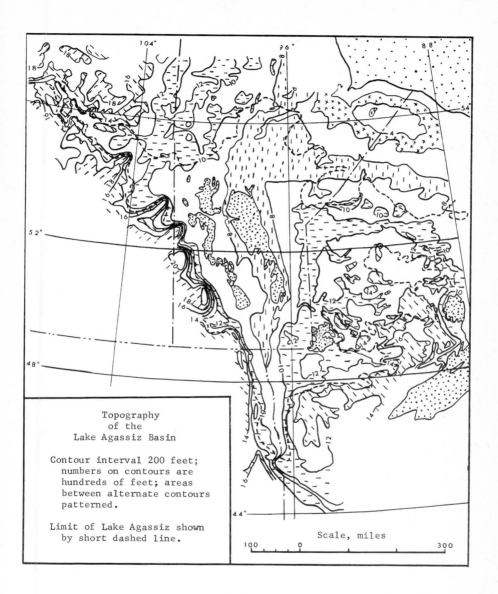

Topography
of the
Lake Agassiz Basin

Contour interval 200 feet;
  numbers on contours are
  hundreds of feet; areas
  between alternate contours
  patterned.

Limit of Lake Agassiz shown
  by short dashed line.

Scale, miles

Figure 3. Topography of the Lake Agassiz Basin.

and west most of this rock plain is concealed under glacial and
lacustrine sediments. But in the north, extending almost as far
west as the Wapawekka Hills from Lake Winnipeg and Lake Winnipegosis, are many low cuestas with the scarps facing north and northeast.

On the north and east sides of this elongate lowland, the
Precambrian rocks have a diversified topography. Along latitude
54°, west of longitude 100°, intricately folded belts of Precambrian
metamorphic rock have a local relief of roughly 200 feet. From this
area southeast to the angle in the boundary between Manitoba and
Ontario, the cover of drift is relatively thick and preglacial relief of the Precambrian rocks must have been low. Much of it is an
exhumed erosion surface from which Paleozoic rocks have been stripped.
The relief in most of this region is usually on the order of a few
tens of feet with some outcrops projecting higher. The low relief
Precambrian area extends south along the east side of Lake Winnipeg
in a belt extending east from the lake to longitude 96°. A straight
portion of the 800 foot contour just east of Lake Winnipeg (Fig. 3)
trends south southeast and joins a similar straight portion extending east from the north end of that lake. A similar straight section
forms part of the 600 foot contour trending southeast just east of
longitude 96°, latitude 54°. These straight contours probably
represent the pre-Paleozoic erosion surface. Flat-lying Paleozoic
rocks underlie the Hudson Bay lowland for roughly 100 miles or more
southwest of Hudson Bay.

The topography on the Precambrian rocks in western Ontario is
too diversified for summary description. In the south are belts
of folded metamorphic rocks with relief as great as 500 feet. In
the area north of Lake Superior and west of Lake Nipigon, through
which extend several of the outlets of Lake Agassiz, are tablelands
comprising Keweenawan sills and flows resting on nearly horizontal
interbedded red shales and sandstones that lie unconformably on older
Precambrian intrusive and metamorphic rocks. Here local relief is
as great as 500 feet, although 200 to 300 feet is more general. In
the region south of latitude 52°, centered around longitude 92°,
local relief is generally less than 100 feet. In this area, more
or less homogeneous intrusive rocks tend to form the high ground,
and minor folded metamorphic rock series form lower ground. Some
local relief here is due to moraines and eskers, but most of it
represents bedrock.

End moraines and interlobate moraines form most of the highest
ground in the area north of latitude 53° along longitude 92° and
in a belt extending 100 miles west and 200 miles southeast from
there (Fig. 4). A moraine forms the peninsula on the west side
in northern Lake Winnipeg and extends west to form the divide between
Cedar Lake and Lake Winnipegosis (Fig. 4).

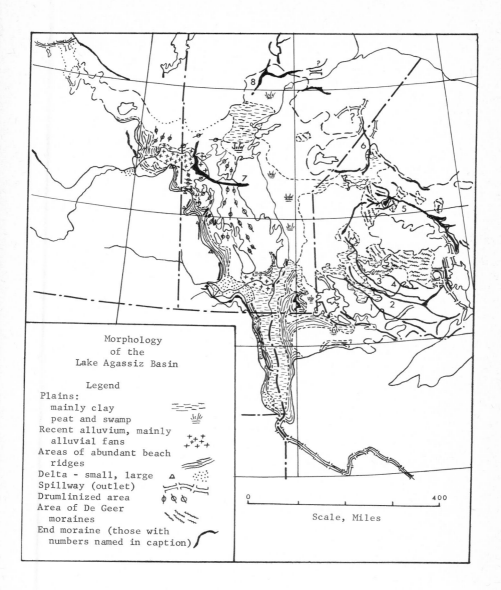

Figure 4. Morphology and surface deposits of the Glacial Lake Agassiz basin.
Numbered moraines are: 1, Eagle-Finlayson; 2, Hartman; 3, Lac Seul; 4, Sioux Lookout; 5, Agutua; 6, Sachigo; 7, The Pas; 8, Burntwood - Etawney.

Outlets

The positions of most outlets of Lake Agassiz are indicated
in Figures 2 and 4. The southern outlet (via the Minnesota River
Valley) crosses the Continental Divide near Lake Traverse where the
states of North and South Dakota and Minnesota meet. It is called
the River Warren (Upham 1895) was named in 1884 and probably
functioned longer than any other single outlet. The divide between
Mackenzie River drainage and Hudson Bay drainage in the northwest
at latitude 55°, longitude 108° developed into the Clearwater outlet mentioned previously. Discharge of the Lake to the east was
blocked by the high ground west of Lake Nipigon until the ice margin
had retreated nearly to the north end of Lake Nipigon. The outlets
in this area are the Kaiashk, Pillar-Armstrong, and Pikitigushi
systems from south to north and are described elsewhere in this
volume by S.C. Zoltai. Subsequent northward withdrawal of the ice
sheet opened other outlets around the north side of high ground in
western Ontario outlined by the 1200 foot contour and the lake was
confluent with Glacial Lake Barlow-Ojibway to the east for a short
time. Lake Agassiz drainage must have been through channels represented now by cross-axial stream systems draining north into
Hudson Bay, such as Sachigo River, Echoing River (?) Hayes River,
Bigstone River, and perhaps finally in the north, the east-flowing
Limestone River (latitude 56°35', longitude 95°).

Having now discussed briefly the major features of limits,
topography and outlets of Glacial Lake Agassiz, the remainder of
the paper will be devoted to more detailed description of geological
evidence for the Lake. Finally, radiocarbon dates tabulated below
make possible a synthesis of the history of Glacial Lake Agassiz.

Sedimentary Basins -- Offshore Sediments

The bedrock topography forms a number of partially closed
basins in which most of the deep water sediments of Lake Agassiz
accumulated (Fig. 2). Maximum water depths generally ranged from
200 to 700 feet. The sediments were deposited generally within
less than 100 miles of the ice margin even though more remote areas
were also submerged. The most important of the sedimentary basins
is the Red River Valley in the south. Counterclockwise from this
the basins include the Lake of the Woods-Rainy River area, the
Wabigoon basin which is separated from the Lac Seul basin by the
Hartman moraine, and the Berens River basin of which little is
known. The Sandy Lake basin straddles the Ontario-Manitoba boundary
at latitude 53° and is connected to the Sachigo basin a little farther
north. North of Lake Winnipeg is an extensive area of sedimentation,
the Grass River region (Antevs, 1931) which is really the northern
part of the Red River-Lake Winnipeg-Nelson River lowland. It is
roughly the same size as the Red River basin in the south from which
it is separated by 300 miles of glacial drift with very little lacustrine cover. To the west between longitude 103° and 104° is the
Sturgeon-Weir River basin.

All the basins have characteristic sediments related to certain events in the history of Lake Agassiz because they were tilted toward the ice sheet during the episode of sedimentation, and record fluctuations in water level that occurred across their ranges of altitudes (Fig.5). For instance, the sediments in the Red River basin should provide the most complete historical record of Lake Agassiz because all fluctuations between the highest Herman and the Grand Rapids phases of Lake Agassiz should be recorded somewhere in the sedimentary sequence in the area between Lake Winnipeg and the Lake Traverse outlet. Events between the Norcross and Hillsboro phases should be recorded also in the Rainy River basin and in part, at least, in the Wabigoon-Lac Seul basins if the ice had retreated from that area. Other basins record various later events and have their own characteristic sedimentary sequences, examples of which are described below (Tables 1 to 4).

Red River basin

The part of the Red River basin that contains deep water lake sediments is about 300 miles long, from north to south, and from 30 to 60 miles wide; the north part is widest. Maximum water depths ranged from less than 200 feet south of Fargo to about 700 feet near Winnipeg. The basin was elongate more or less radially from the ice margin and discharged across a drift barrier distal to the ice sheet. The lake was thus relatively stable compared with lakes that drain along the ice margin as did some later phases of Lake Agassiz; it received appreciable sediment from land areas, particularly to the west.

Dawson (1875) recognized that an upper light brown silty clay unit overlay a thicker grey clay unit. Later, Upham (1895) noted an upper silty unit in Minnesota and North Dakota at the bottom of which "turf" (peat) was often found in wells and excavations. He interpreted the silt as alluvium deposited by the Red River after the final drainage of Lake Agassiz. He, too, observed a thicker grey clay underlying the silt.

More recent work connected with ground water investigations e.g., Dennis, Akin, and Worts (1949) has extended our knowledge of the silt and clay units, and the unconformity between them has since been radiocarbon dated at several localities as about 10,000 years old. The silt unit is usually about 20 feet thick, though it varies between 10 and 30 feet and contains a higher proportion of clay-size material than the name suggests. The underlying grey clay is usually about 50 feet thick but ranges from 40 to more than 100 feet in thickness. In an area where it was not easily recognized by other means, Rominger and Rutledge (1952) identified a dessication surface (by means of soil mechanics techniques) that probably is the disconformity between the silt and clay units. Work still in progress indicates that the sedimentary sequence may be more complex than the two-unit concept implies (Lee Clayton, personal communication). Local interfingering of shallow and deep water sediments in the southern part of the basin may be expected if the Lake's history is as complex as evidence elsewhere is beginning to suggest. On the other hand, the

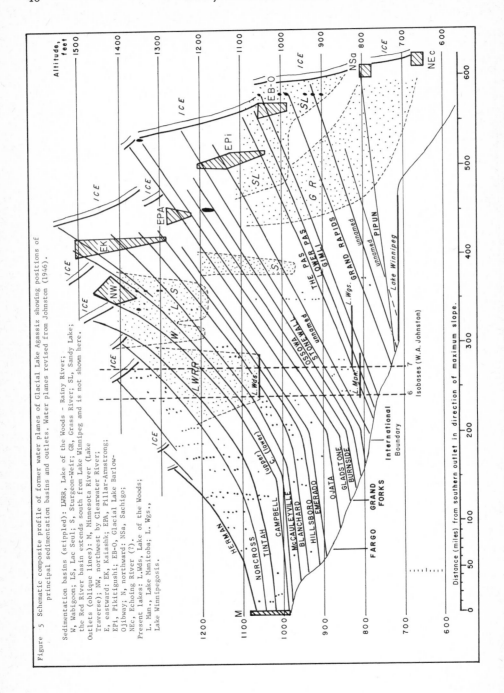

Figure 5　Schematic composite profile of former water planes of Glacial Lake Agassiz showing positions of principal sedimentation basins and outlets. Water planes revised from Johnston (1946).

Sedimentation basins (stippled): LWRR, Lake of the Woods – Rainy River; W, Wabigoon; LS, Lac Seul; S, Sturgeon-Weir; GR, Grass River; SL, Sandy Lake; the Red River basin extends south from Lake Winnipeg and is not shown here.

Outlets (oblique lines): M, Minnesota River (Lake Traverse); NW, northwest by Clearwater River; E, eastward: EK, Kaiashk; EPA, Pillar-Armstrong; EPi, Pikitigushi; EB-O, Glacial Lake Barlow-Ojibway; N, northward: NSa, Sachigo; NEc, Echoing River (?).

Present lakes: L.Wds, Lake of the Woods; L. Man., Lake Manitoba; L. Wgs., Lake Winnipegosis.

silt-clay unit subdivision is not readily made south of Fargo (J.A. Brophy, personal communication).

There are several bands of gravel (reported from drill-hole data) that trend transversely across the western part of the basin near the International Boundary, underlying the lower clay unit and apparently resting on stony clay or till. Data are insufficient to decide if these are sub-lacustrine morainal features or some other form of ice-contact stratified drift. The improbable possibilty that they are subaerial stream deposits cannot be wholly refuted, although the generally accepted picture of ice recession in this region militates against the idea. Excavations have exposed considerable thicknesses of laminated stony lake clays, described below, which are not usually distinguishable from till in disturbed drill core samples (Lee Clayton, personal communication).

Because of its low relief topography the central part of the basin is a poor region to find natural exposures. A few cuts occur around the south end of Lake Winnipeg. In these, sandy-silty till is commonly overlain by undulating to openly folded layers of material resembling till in grainsize distribution but much less compact than till. The layers of "stony clay" are 2 to 6 cm. thick and are usually separated by thinner layers of grey stone-free clay less than 1 cm. thick. Usually the clay layers become thicker upward in the section and the till-like "stony clay" layers become thinner. More normal lake clay usually overlies these stony lake clays with a disconformable contact. Similar stony lake clays occur in the Rainy River-Lake of the Woods region (Johnston 1915:46).

From the south end of Lake Winnipeg to Winnipeg and east as far as the Winnipeg River a layer of yellowish brown, sandy-clayey silt about 0.5 to 2.0 feet thick occurs about 8 to 13 feet below the surface. Earlier this was interpreted as the bottom of the silt unit recognized in North Dakota (Elson 1961:67) but observations since then show that it is within the upper part of the underlying clay unit, in which it is conformable. It is probable that the upper silt unit north of Winnipeg is not the same upper silt unit recognized in North Dakota. The silty "yellow clay" bed is well known around Winnipeg because of its weak structural properties which make foundation conditions difficult. It seems to represent an event of relatively short duration when there was an influx of sediment coarser than clay size into the northern Red River basin. Two interpretation possibilities are: (1) opening of a new basin in the eastern part of Lake Agassiz as a result of ice margin retreat -- the resulting rapid discharge eastward would have transported sediment derived by wave action from newly exposed shorelines; or (2) a lowering of lake level by a few tens of feet causing incision by rivers and active wave erosion along newly exposed shores or a subsequent rise of level which would have accelerated erosion (Schwartz 1967). The lake bottom in the area in question could have been several hundred feet below water level even during such a fluctuation. The second hypothesis is better than the first which should have given a continuing effect visible throughout the overlying sediments.

A section exposed at the Provincial campsite just below the
north end of the Pine Falls hydro-electric dam on the Winnipeg
River (Table 1) illustrates the stratigraphy typical of the Red
River basin (except for the laminated stony lake clay, which is
absent). The stratigraphy can be interpreted as representing the
following sequence of events:

(1) Gravel and till were deposited underneath the glacier.

(2) Silt with clay laminae was deposited in open water not
     far from the ice margin.

(3) Thin clay laminae indicate a remote source or a small
     supply of sediment; probably an ice margin retreat
     occurred.

(4) There followed a long episode of abundant sediment with
     density currents strong enough to erode into unit 2;
     the papery laminae in the upper part suggest a remote
     ice margin and deep water at the end of this eposode.

(5) An influx of relatively coarse material (the yellow
     silty clay) occurred, possibly caused by fluctuation
     of lake level causing shore erosion that provided a
     source of sediment; the water was still deep at Pine
     Falls though the Lake level may have fluctuated more
     than 100 feet.

(6) Thin laminated clay was deposited in deep water from
     a remote ice margin.

(7) The water level at Pine Falls dropped low enough so
     that the surface was eroded either subaerially or in
     shallow water with strong wave action.

(8) The lake level rose and the silt unit was deposited;
     the deepening seems to have been gradual as the silt
     unit (unit 7) grades from sandy silt at the base to
     clay at the top. The ice margin was remote.

(9) Water level dropped and the surface was again eroded
     either by wave action or by subaerial agencies.

(10) Fine sand was deposited in fairly shallow quiet water.
     This may have involved minor rise of water level, but
     it could also have resulted from delta construction or
     other shore processes without much change in water level

The water level fluctuations suggested above were caused by
opening and closing of outlets other than the River Warren outlet at
Lake Traverse, Minnesota.

TABLE 1

PINE FALLS SECTION[a]
(Latitude 50°34', Longitude 96°11')

Unit	Thickness	Description
8	0.0'-2.5'	Sand, fine to very fine grained, yellowish brown, horizontally bedded with laminae as thin as 2 mm. Modern soil profile developed in upper half, not present everywhere.
--------	Erosional contact with at least 2 feet of relief ------	
7	5.0'-7.0'	Silt unit: basal 3 feet is sand, very fine grained, and silt, yellowish brown, in laminae and beds from 1 to 3 cm. thick with sand partings. Grades upward into silty clay, greyish brown in couplets 1 to 2 cm. thick with sandy parting layers changing to silt and silty layers changing to silty clay. Partings thin upwards and disappear. Upper part of the unit is a massive greyish brown silty clay.
--------	Erosional contact with at least 2 feet of relief ------	
6	3.0'-5.0'	Upper half is clay, massive, drying to a blocky structure, olive brown. Lower half is clay, moderate olive brown in layers 1 to 3 mm. thick with silty interbeds 1 to 2 mm. thick, drying to a papery product. Probably varved.
5	0.5'	Silt, clayey, yellowish brown.
4	10.0'-12.0'	Clay, greyish brown, gritty with numerous granules and sand grains. Beds 7 to 12 cm. thick are apparent on drying. Upper part dries to paper-like platy fragments.
	15.0'-20.0'	Clay, fine grained, moderate olive brown, in beds 1 to 6 cm. thick separated by layers 0.5 to 2.0 cm. thick containing angular and rounded fragments of light grey compact silt. Locally the silt fragments form horizontal lenses of silt breccia with a clay matrix. Several lenses of sand and silt, upper surface convex, lower surface broadly V-shaped. The silt fragment layers are more abundant in the lower part of the section. The breccia is near the base. Cobbles and boulders present, deform underlying bedding.

TABLE 1--<u>Continued</u>

Unit	Thickness	Description
3	1.0'	Clay, laminated in layers 3 to 4 mm. thick. Moderate olive brown with grey yellowish brown silt partings. The laminae thin to 1 to 2 mm. at the base.
2	2.0'	Silt, sandy yellowish brown. Upper part in beds 5 to 10 mm. thick with clay thinner and more widely spaced. It forms only a thin line 5 cm. below the top. Upper half of silt is laminated, lower half in beds 3 to 5 cm. thick with a few angular to sub-rounded stones. Lowest 8 cm. is clayey silt, may grade downward into till in some places.
1	1.0'	Gravel, coarse sand to cobbles. Bedrock.

ªAltitude of top about 750' MSL or a little lower (25' contour map) base about 715' or a little higher. Units are described from top to bottom.

Lake of the Woods-Rainy River basin

The Lake of the Woods - Rainy River basin extends about 150 miles
southeast from Lake of the Woods to Steeprock Lake (Glacial Lake
Johnston of Antevs 1951) and is about 60 miles wide. All the northern
boundary and the eastern third of the basin are in part of the Precambrian shield that has 100 to 300 feet of relief, hence those
margins are very irregular and rarely have strandline forms. The
basin is roughly outlined by the 1200 foot contour, although the
north side is about 100 feet higher due to crustal warping. This
basin is separated from the Red River basin by high ground west of
Lake of the Woods but there was a connection across a broad divide
northwest of Lake of the Woods until the water level there dropped
below about 1100 feet. Events prior to the McCauleyville beach
formation back in time to the formation of Norcross or lower (late)
Herman beaches should be recorded in the sediments of this basin.

The average maximum depths of Lake Agassiz here ranged from
about 150 feet on the south side to about 250 feet on the north
side. There were locally much deeper areas, still occupied by lakes.
The main basin was oblique to the ice margin for most of its history
and received glacial sediments mainly from the east. A broad valley
trending northeast from the northeast corner through Lac de Mille
Lacs connected with the margins of ice lobes in the Lake Superior
basin. The relatively shallow depth of this basin, and the comparatively small increment of glacial "milk" it received due to separation from the ice margin by high ground for much of its history
resulted in water that was warm for a glacial lake. As a result,
mollusk fossils are common. Clear waters must have been common
also, as they are indicated by numerous occurrences of marl, an algal
deposit requiring clear, warm shallow water.

A stratigraphic section just east of Lake of the Woods (Table 2)
records events during the early part of the deglaciation of this
basin. Proximal varves having thick sandy layers and thin clay
layers in the bottom of the section suggest deep water not far from
an ice margin. This was followed by deposition from a more distant
source producing "normal" varves with light and dark layers of about
equal thickness. The next sediments must have been supplied from a
distant source as the couplets are thin and mainly clay. In all
probability the ice margin had retreated from the high ground northeast of Lake of the Woods and this sediment moved in from the Red
River basin to the west. This was followed by shoaling water during
which sand was deposited; the uppermost gravelly sand was probably
derived by wave attack on the drift that covered the bedrock hills
at this locality. In summary, this section represents an unbroken
period of deposition mostly well below wave base. It seems to have
happened before the Campbell strandline formed, and if the couplets
are true varves (annual layers) the episode may have lasted roughly
500 years.

A section at Frontier, Minnesota, about 500 feet below the
Campbell water plane (Table 3) records events that occurred late
in the history of this basin, as well as some of the earlier events.
The basal, stony laminated lacustrine clays were probably deposited

TABLE 2

CALIPER LAKE, ONTARIO SECTION[a]
(Latitude 49°00', Longitude 93°51')

Unit	Thickness	Description
4	1.5'	Sand, medium grained, well sorted with pebbles and small cobbles in upper part.
	4.0'	Sand, very fine grained, and interbedded silt. Moderately dark yellowish brown (10YR 5/4), in layers 6 to 8 mm. thick. Some clay layers near base. About 100 layers.
	ca. 3.0'	Clay, unctuous, varved, light layers are pale yellowish brown (10YR 6/2), dark layers are greyish brown (5YR 3/2). Varves are 2.5 to 5 mm. thick, estimated about 200 present.
3	0.1'	Clay, poorly exposed, part of unit below.
	1.0'	Clay, varved, 44 couplets, 1 to 2 cm. thick at base, thinning to 4 to 8 mm. at top; dark layers greyish brown, light layers yellowish grey, about equal thickness.
2	1.5'-4.5'	Sand, fine, silty, light olive grey (5Y 5/2) in beds 1.5 to 15 cm. thick, separated by clay layers 2 to 4 mm. thick. Ice-rafted stones present. 22 couplets. Rusty brown sandy layer top 1 to 10 cm. thick.
1	1.0 +'	Till, sandy, compact, abundant stones. Bottom of ditch.

[a]Altitude at top of section about 1180' MSL (estimated from 1:250,000 map with 100 foot contour interval). Section exposed in a new road cut on east side of Highway 71 about 4.75 miles south of Caliper Lake provincial camp ground entrance. Described from top to bottom.

TABLE 3

FRONTIER, MINNESOTA SECTION[a]
(Latitude 48°39', Longitude 94°15')

Unit	Thickness	Description
5 (?)	6.0'	Probably silt or sand, but not exposed.
5	1.0'	Silt, brownish grey, laminated with very fine sand. Contains numerous shells of Sphaerium and a large Naiad too fragile to collect.
	1.3'	Sand, very fine, brownish grey, silt interbeds; sand siltier near base. Sphaerium abundant in lower half.
4	0.2'	Silt, clayey, containing Sphaerium and Naiads.
	0.2'-2.5'	Sand containing pebbles and small cobbles; brown, oxidized, lenticular. Upper contact gradational, lower contact sharp.

-------------------- Erosional unconformity ------------------

Unit	Thickness	Description
3	1.0'	Clay, slightly sandy, massive, greyish brown at top to brown near base. Oxidized along vertical fractures. Decomposed carbonate pebbles in upper 0.5 feet.
2	5.0'	Stoney sandy loam, greyish brown, in layers 2 to 4 cm. thick separated by layers of grey clay about 7 mm. thick. Loam not compact, beds undulating.
1	2.0 +'	Till, sandy, silty, greyish brown.
		Base not exposed.

[a]East side of gully, about 25 feet deep, south side of Route 11, 1 mile east of Frontier, described from top to bottom. Altitude at top about 1085 feet ± 20 feet MSL (estimated from 100 foot contours).

under the floating margin of the ice sheet and are overlain by normal
glacial lake clays. Elsewhere these clays are in couplets but at
Frontier, weathering (mainly drying), has destroyed the primary
structures. Perhaps the ice margin was at or beyond the north side
of the basin at this time so that the light layers were thin, hence
easily obliterated. The next event was the lowering of the lake
so that this locality was either in the zone of wave action or was
subaerially exposed. After an erosional interval the locality was
inundated again by water, forming a suitable habitat for mullusks.
The depth increased to and exceeded the lower limit of wave action
(roughly 30 feet). Unfortunately, the uppermost part of the section
is concealed.

     Not far from Frontier (about three miles southwest of Pinewood,
Ontario, on the north side of Rainy River) a gravel pit exposes about
2.5 feet of clay, massive at the top but interbedded with silt and
sand near the bottom, and having a thin layer of marl at the base,
resting on well sorted granule gravel and sand containing shells of
Sphaerium and *Helisoma trivolvis*. The gravel and sand was first
interpreted as a beach deposit in the field, but more recent study
of air photographs reveals that it is part of a delta deposited by
Rainy River when the lake level stood at or below about 1080 feet.
The overlying clay must have been deposited in water more than about
30 feet deep and was derived from a fairly distant source.

     A layer of red clay in the Steeprock Lake basin was reported
by Antevs (1951); its distribution was mapped later by Zoltai (1961).
West of Rainy Lake the clay is massive and only from 3 to 6 inches
thick. North of Rainy Lake the thickness increases from about 10
inches in the west to 24 inches at Steeprock Lake in the east and
it comprises distinct couplets (varves). According to Zoltai the
red clay in the Lake of the Woods - Rainy River basin is usually
overlain by about two feet of grey clay. Where I have observed red
clay just east of the crossing of Seine River on Route 11, (latitude
48°14', longitude 92°17') there were about 85 grey clay couplets
overlying about 58 red clay couplets (an unusual number) which in
turn overlay two feet of massive grey clay. Usually there are fewer
than 25 red couplets. In the Steeprock Lake basin, closer to the
source, Antevs found 177 grey clay couplets overlying 24 red clay
couplets which in turn overlie several series of varves totalling
1044 couplets and including one layer of till above the lowest 125
varves. Zoltai (1963) showed that the red clay was derived from
the east when glacial Lake Kaministikwia was formed by an advance
of ice in the Lake Superior basin to the Marks moraine, about 25
miles west of Fort William.

     To review, then, the Lake of the Woods - Rainy River basin
contains evidence for the middle part of the history of Lake Agassiz.
An erosional unconfromity indicates a major fluctuation in Lake level,
related to retreat and advance of an ice margin that opened and
closed an eastern outlet. The red clay is a useful time marker. Its
position near the top of the offshore sediments shows that it is
related to the readvance that closed the eastern outlet and caused
the final rise of water level. This probably resulted from Marks
moraine episode in the Lake Superior basin. There still are gaps

in the evidence. For example, the red clay layers have not yet been observed in the same exposure as the unconformity and their relationship to it is an inference.

Wabigoon - Lac Seul basins

The Wabigoon - Lac Seul basins are part of the watershed of English River which flows west to join Winnipeg River near the Manitoba-Ontario boundary. They are separated from the Lake of the Woods - Rainy River basin by a broad ridge with a summit at roughly 1400 feet that trends southeast from north of Lake of the Woods. The basins are roughly outlined by the 1200 foot contour (Fig. 3) and together have the pattern of the capital letter "H" tilted so that the long members trend northwest-southwest. The lower, southern limb forms the Wabigoon basin and the upper limbs and cross bar are the Lac Seul basin. The Lac Seul basin is about 125 miles long from northwest to southeast and is roughly 40 miles wide. The southern portion of the basin is a little shorter and narrower. The margin is irregular in detail. The long limbs were parallel to ice fronts which are indicated by prominent end moraines including the Eagle-Finlayson, Hartman, and Lac Seul moraines. The reason for separating the basins into two is the contrast in the sediments on the opposite sides of the Hartman moraine, which is the dividing ridge. The west end opened into the main part of Lake Agassiz (Red River - Lake Winnipeg lowland) while the eastern end of the Lac Seul basin leads to an outlet eastward through the Kaiashk valley into the Lake Nipigon basin.

The position of these basins with respect to the waterplanes of Lake Agassiz (Fig. 5) shows that events from about the time of the Norcross water plane to the Emerado water plane could be represented in the sediments. The ice, however, may not have retreated from the basin until the time of the Campbell water plane and thus some of the earlier events may not be represented, especially in the Lac Seul basin.

The sediments of the Wabigoon basin are grey varved clays with a band of red clays (Rittenhouse 1934, Zoltai 1961) similar to those in the eastern part of the Lake of the Woods - Rainy River basin, except that there are usually about 24 couplets south of the Eagle-Finlayson moraine and 15 couplets north of it. Road cuts on Route 72 north of Dinorwic south of the Hartman moraine show a sequence of layered sediments indicating continuous sedimentation (Table 4). A cut 0.7 miles north of the junction with Route 17 has roughly 270 grey varves above the red clay band, here 14 layers thick, and about 360 below it, the lower part of the latter being clayey silt and sand (proximal varves).

Zoltai (1961) has not observed the red clays north of the Hartman moraine, and new road cuts on Route 72 between Dinorwic and Sioux Lookout confirm his observations in that area. He reported that varved clays are from 60 to 20 feet thick in the Lac Seul basin and contain more silt and sand than the clays of the Wabigoon basin. Hurst (1933) and Zoltai (1961) both observed till resting on varved clay in the Sioux Lookout area.

TABLE 4

A STRATIGRAPHIC SECTION IN THE WABIGOON BASIN,
NORTH SIDE OF ROUTE 72, SIX MILES NORTHEAST OF ROUTE 11 JUNCTION[a]
(Latitude 49°46', Longitude 92°27')

Unit	Thickness	Description
	1.0'-3.0'	Back fill (mainly till).
4	4.6'	Silt and clay, varved. Couplets in lower 2.5 feet decrease from 2.5 cm. thick at base to 1.5 cm. at top. Silt forms 80% of each varve. In upper 2 feet, thickness of couplets decreases from 10 mm. near base to 7 mm. near top. Upper part disturbed by soil formation. Total 145 varves.
3	1.7'	Silt and clay, varved, clay red, silt grey. Couplets 2 to 5 cm. thick, 15 to 30% of thickness is silt. Minor distortion and channeling with silt replacing clay. Total 15 varves.
2	4.9'	Silt and silty clay, varved, grey. Thickness of varves variable but generally increases from 8 mm. near base to 25 mm. at top. Middle varves are about 25 mm. thick and are sandy. Varve Number 32 above base has 10 cm. sand (a "drainage varve"). Silty layer is about 80% of thickness of most varves. Several ice-rafted pebbles observed. Total 67 varves.
1	5.0'	Till, sandy, stony, abundant cobbles and boulders. Base of exposure.

[a]Altitude about 1350 ± 40 feet, estimated from 100 foot contour map and one barometric observation. Described from top to bottom.

In review then, the deep water sediments of the Wabigoon Lac Seul basin indicate continuous sedimentation following the ice retreat, with an episode of red clay deposition similar to that in the Lake of the Woods - Rainy River basin that apparently lasted longer south of the Eagle-Finlayson moraine than it did between the Eagle-Finlayson moraine and the Hartman moraine. Rittenhouse (1934) counted 440 varves below 24 red varves and 360 above. Red clay sedimentation apparently ceased before the ice withdrew very far from the Hartman moraine. One or more readvances of the ice margin occurred in the Lac Seul basin but the extent is not yet known.

Sturgeon-Weir basin

The Sturgeon-Weir sedimentation basin is along the edge of the Precambrian shield mainly in Saskatchewan west of Flin Flon. It includes the area from Ballantyne Bay of Deschambault Lake east to Amisk Lake and might be extended to include Athapapuskow Lake and the Goose River drainage basin (longitude 101°20'). Thus its length from west to east is roughly 90 miles and its width about 30 miles, less at the west end. There is little or no closure of the south side of the eastern half of this area, as a result of crustal warping. Geological reports on the region north of the Saskatchewan River here are few and information on surface deposits is sparse. Where they have been exposed in the new road cuts, the lake sediments are thin.

The altitude of this basin ranges from about 965 feet (Amisk Lake) to about 1200 feet. Hence, if free of ice, it could have recorded events from the time of the Ojata water plane to the time of an unnamed water plane between the Stonewall and The Pas levels (Fig. 5), during which the Pikitigushi outlet probably functioned.

Shallow road cuts and borrow pits along Route 106 (Hanson Lake Road), and on Route 167 from Flin Flon southwest to Denare Beach on Amisk Lake, expose 6 to 10 feet of lake sediments. Between latitudes 54°40' and 54°50' the stratigraphic sequence has at the top contorted clay with abundant stones, or else a sandy till from 2 to 3 feet thick, overlying 2 to 3 feet of varved clay comprising as many as 80 couplets. The varved sediments tend to be coarse and are sandy near the base. In exposures at an altitude of about 1050 feet or lower the varves rest on stratified sand and till. At altitudes above about 1100 feet (for example about two miles west of the Sturgeon-Weir River crossing on the Hanson Lake Road) the varves grade downward into well sorted sand with ripple marks and a few pebbles. The altitude here is about 1200 feet. In places pebbles are concentrated at a horizon 1.5 to 3 feet below the surface; many are faceted ventifacts. The upper part of the sand has been reworked by wind action, though dunes are rare.

The Sturgeon-Weir basin appears to have functioned for a relatively short time if the couplets observed are true varves. Initially proximal varves were laid down and these were overridden by an ice readvance. Evidently there was little or no deep water sedimentation when the ice retreated so this basin may have been drained when the retreat occurred. Furthermore, present observations

have not entirely eliminated the possibility that some or all of
the upper till-like layers are the result of periglacial soli-
fluctuation when the lake floor was first exposed. Early in the
history of this basin there was a rise of water level, perhaps from
about 1100 feet to 1200 feet.

Sandy Lake basin

The Sandy Lake basin is mainly in northern Ontario and trends
west to east across the Manitoba-Ontario boundary just north of the
angle; an arm extends north at the east end. The basin comprises
the valley of Cobham River, Sandy Lake, and the headwaters of
Sachigo River. The eastern limit is uncertain. The west-east
portion is about 145 miles long, extending east from longitude
95°30' to Sakwaso Lake (an enlargment of Windigo River). It is
between latitudes 53° and 53°20' and is mostly about 30 miles wide.
The west end opens into the Lake Winnipeg-Nelson River basin at an
altitude of a little below 1000 feet. The north-trending part of
the basin at the east end is about 80 miles long and 25 miles wide.
It descends from about 1000 feet altitude in the south to 800 feet
in the north. In all probability the northern part around Sachigo
Lake became separated from the main body of Lake Agassiz when the
water level dropped below the altitude of the divide at the west
end of the Cobham River watershed. Strandlines on the moraine west
of Sachigo Lake, however, represent an earlier water plane that
stood above the divide. The south side of the basin slopes gently
and is ill-defined.

The position of this basin (Fig. 5) shows that it functioned
from about the time of the unnamed waterplane between the Stonewall
and The Pas water planes until shortly after the Gimli waterplane.
It must have been a strait connecting Lake Agassiz with Glacial
Lake Barlow-Ojibway for a time.

There is only general information on the nature and distribution
of the lake sediments in the Sandy Lake basin with little detail.
Derry and MacKenzie (1931) reported varved clays along the Manitoba-
Ontario boundary where it crosses Cobham River valley, a traverse
about 50 miles long, oblique to the basin. In the lower part of
the valley the varved clay is as thick as 80 feet; most varves seen
were about one inch thick and comprised sand and clay layers of equal
thickness, but there is great variation. Farther east Hurst (1930)
observed stratified clay as thick as 30 feet but averaging 10 feet
in part of the Severn River watershed (including Angekum and Sandy
Lakes). The varves average one inch in thickness but are paper
thin near the top; in several localities 100 varves were counted.
The total thickness of the clay increases from west to east.

Satterly (1937) mapped an area that straddles the Sachigo
moraine in the north-south limb of the Sandy Lake basin. He found
varved clays on both sides of the moraine and named Glacial Lake
Ponask on the west side and Glacial Lake Sachigo on the east side.
He was able to correlate an 18-layer section in the basins on both
sides of the moraine showing that they were contemporaneous. The

varves were mostly 0.8 to 2.7 inches thick and occur in cliffs from 10 to 30 feet high. The clay portions of the varves form only a quarter of their thickness. Satterly estimated that there were 280 varves in the Ponask basin and a similar number in the Sachigo basin. Thicker varves were found farther north on Little Sachigo Lake where "winter" portions (clay) were about 1.5 inches thick and the "summer" portions as thick as 6 inches. Varves were also found on Kistigan Lake which straddles the interprovincial boundary at longitude 92°30'. The little Sachigo Lake basin and the area north of it may not have been part of Lake Agassiz.

Grass River basin

The Grass River basin is roughly the shape of a parallelogram, bounded by latitude 54°30' between longitudes 98° and 100° and latitude 56° between longitude 96° and 98°; its average length is about 130 miles and the average width about 60 miles. It includes much of the watersheds of Burntwood and Grass Rivers and a part of the Nelson River system between them. The limit of the basin in the southwest, west, and northwest is about at the 1000 foot contour. To the southeast and east it is at the 700 foot contour, with the lowest area in the northeast in the Nelson valley at about 650 feet. The region between this sedimentation basin and Lake Winnipeg is swamp and perhaps should be included in it. At this time no information is available on the surficial deposits here.

Its altitude limits show that the Grass River basin functioned from about the time of the unnamed waterplane between the Stonewall and The Pas waterplanes until the final drainage of Lake Agassiz.

Lake clays in this basin were described by Antevs (1931) who examined at least 60 cuts in order to date the recession of the ice by varve counting. He counted 374 varves. Sedimentation was continuous and unmodified by any major changes of water level. In general the couplets are thin in the southwest (remote from the ice margin) and thick in the northeast. Variations in thickness and grain size can be attributed to differences in distance from the ice margin. All varieties of varves are present.

New sections have been exposed recently on Manitoba Route 391 giving access to Thompson. Most cuts reveal 5 to 10 feet of varved clay but in several valleys the clay is as thick as 30 feet.

A stratigraphic section between the western limit of the Grass River basin and the eastern end of the Sturgeon-Weir basin about a mile east of the town of Snow Lake, on the south side of Route 392 in a borrow pit (latitude 54°52.5', longitude 100°00'). The top of the section has an altitude of about 930 feet. Varved clay about 3 feet thick, comprising approximately 100 silty clay and sand varves, overlies 10 feet of well sorted fine to very fine sand. The sand is coarser near the base and has ripple marks. This section represents a deepening of the lake as the well sorted basal sands resemble sediments of a shallow water environment rather than sediments deposited close to an ice margin.

Other areas of offshore sedimentation

There are several smaller areas of sedimentation which owe
their existence either to topographic basins, proximity to an ice
margin, or the opening in the western escarpment of reentrants
still separated from each other by the ice sheet. These have not
been studied enough yet to be fitted into the general sequence of
Lake Agassiz events. The "basins" include the headwaters of Berens
River in western Ontario for which no references are available.
Silt and clay occur along the Saskatchewan River between Cedar Lake
and Lake Winnipeg where Tyrrell (1893:146E) reported till overlying
varved clay, and where borrow pits for the Grand Rapids hydro-
electric project exposed silt and clay on the surface as thick as
10 or 15 feet. The reentrant in the Manitoba Escarpment occupied
by Saskatchewan River and Carrot River contains thinly bedded clays.
At the crossing of Route 35 over Carrot River about 13 feet of clay
and sand in couplets overly about 7 feet of horizontally bedded sand
and silt, which rests on at least 7 feet of clay and silt couplets.
There is at least one erosional unconformity in this sequence. The
altitude here is roughly 1150 feet.

Other reentrants containing offshore sediments include the
Red Deer valley, Swan Valley, the Valley River valley, and the
Assiniboine valley where a delta covers deep water sediments.

Intersecting ridges and grooves

Ridges and grooves with a relief of 0.5 to 5 feet, widths
ranging from 50 to 200 feet, and lengths of from a few hundred
feet to several miles are abundant in the northern part of the
Red River basin (Horberg, 1951) and in the lowland occupied by
Lakes Winnipeg, Manitoba, and Winnipegosis as far north as the
southern parts of the Grass River and Sturgeon-Weir basins. They
are in areas of till where they are superimposed on drumlin-like
forms as well as ground moraine, and in areas of lake clay and
silt. The pattern resembles that of fractures and joints typical
of Precambrian shield rocks, but north-northwest and northwest trends
dominate in much of the region, especially in the northwest. Similar
features occur in other glacial lake basins and formerly submerged
areas.

References on these features are listed by Clayton *et al* (1965)
and the literature is not reviewed here. Clayton *et al* recognize
multiple origins of the ridges and grooves but emphasize the hypothesis that many are "signatures" of wind driven ice pans which were
partly grounded in a shallow lake, a phenomenon that has been
observed in Great Bear Lake. Other ridges are caused by differential
settlement (compaction) of lake clays over underlying topography
(Lee Clayton, personal communication). My own view is that some (not
all) ridges result from upward seepage of ground water through joint
and fracture planes in the subjacent bedrock which retards compaction
of the sediment above the fracture. The source of the water pressure
head may be the landward side of the basin or the glacier itself.
This hypothesis will be tested by field observations.

The importance of the ridges to this discussion of Lake Agassiz is that some of them have a form that superficially resembles a beach ridge. Several have been erroneously identified as beaches. The Niverville beaches at the type locality, about 25 miles south of Winnipeg (Upham 1895:471) are an example.

Near-shore Deposits

Around the sides of the Lake Agassiz basin, particularly along the Manitoba Escarpment, an apron of silt a few feet thick and a dozen miles wide occurs down slope from areas of wave action as indicated by beaches and terraces. It represents the silt fraction of the eroded till, but includes some deltaic material and probably some alluvium, although the alluvium generally is more poorly sorted. This is not the same as the silt unit in the central part of the Red River basin.

Deltas and Alluvial Fills

Deltas are the first features that record former water levels to form in glacial lakes. They may provide the only evidence of water levels where conditions were unfavourable for the formation of beach ridges and terraces by wave action. Deltas form quickly because newly deglaciated ground with little or no vegetative cover is highly erodable and provides abundant sediment to streams. Later, when water levels fall, the deltas in turn are readily eroded by the streams that formed them, pauses during the lowering are recorded by terraces.

Major deltas described by Upham (1895) were the Buffalo and Sand Hill deltas in Minnesota, in North Dakota from south to north the Sheyenne, Elk Valley and Pembina deltas and in Manitoba the Assiniboine delta. Smaller deltas (Table 5) occur farther north on the Cretaceous escarpment. The Saskatchewan River deposited a large delta, but whether it formed in Lake Agassiz or in an earlier glacial lake in the Saskatchewan valley is uncertain at this time.

Upham thought that the sediments in the deltas were of glacial origin, and that the volume of material in them was too great to have been derived from erosion of the valleys feeding them. Leverett (1932) went so far as to suggest that they were bodies of outwash deposited in the reentrant between the ice margin standing in Lake Agassiz and the escarpment, and challenged the appropriateness of the word "delta". He thought that the steep northeast slopes of the western deltas were ice-contact faces. The Elk Valley Delta is confined on the east by part of the Edinburg moraine, which supports his hypothesis. However more recent studies have failed to confirm the ice-contact origin of the northeast slopes of the other deltas. Though retreating ice margins must have had some influence in shaping the large deltas, the action of waves from the direction of storm

winds of greatest fetch was probably more important. The sediments
in the northeast part of the Assiniboine delta are silt rather than
the coarser, poorly sorted material deposited near an ice margin.
Recalculation of delta volumes and the volumes of the source valleys
shows that these are nearly commensurate and that the contribution
from glacial sources was smaller than suggested by Upham.

Buffalo and Sand Hill River deltas

Most relict deltas are conspicuous topographic benches on an
escarpment, or if of "estuarine" form are paired valley terraces
that end abruptly or splay out of the end of the valley to form a
bench. Neither the Buffalo or the Sand Hill deltas (Upham 1895:
290-292 and 298-299 respectively) have these typical forms. Leverett
(1932:126-127) found the sand deposits of the deltas to be thinner
than Upham's estimate by a factor of 10. Soil maps by Nikiforoff
et al (1939) show sandy soils in the areas mapped as deltas by
Upham, but they appear to have been widely dispersed by wave action.

Sheyenne delta

The Sheyenne delta (Upham 1895:315-317) is an area of about
800 square miles centered around latitude 46°30' longitude 97°15'
at the point where the trench-like Sheyenne valley debouches from
the western escarpment. It is being studied in detail by J.A. Brophy
who has presented some of his results elsewhere in this volume. The
following brief description is given to avoid a gap in this account.

The delta forms a terrace about 20 miles wide and roughly 40
miles long from north to south. Its surface slopes from about 1090
feet altitude in the west near the apex to about 1040 feet in the
east at the top of the "foreset" slope which has been modified by
shore processes subsequent to deposition. The northeast front of
the delta is straight and steep compared with other parts and was
interpreted by Leverett (1932) as an ice-contact face. The delta
was formed by glacial meltwater discharging through the Sheyenne
valley. This valley has the form of a trench about a mile wide and
100 to 200 feet deep in the escarpment near the delta. It was an
outlet of glacial Lake Souris and is about 240 miles long. Its
volume is roughly five cubic miles; Upham's estimate of the volume
of the delta was six cubic miles. Considering the decrease in
density in the change from till and bedrock to delta sediment,
little glacial increment need be added to that supplied by erosion
to build the delta.

The Sheyenne River crosses the north part of the delta in a
trench trending east-northeast after following a course northward
along the west side for about 10 miles from the apex. The river
is sinuous and there are terraces including some formed on a valley
fill. Dr. Brophy (personal communication) thinks that the valley
across the delta was cut during a low phase of Lake Agassiz and that
the alluvial fill was deposited during later higher phases. Because
of the low overall gradient of this part of the river and the plain

it crosses beyond the delta the problem of distinguishing between the effects of base level changes and effects of changes in regimen is difficult.

Elk Valley delta

The Elk Valley delta (Upham 1895:333-336) is a narrow triangle about 60 miles long trending south southeast with the apex in the north and the base, about 12 miles wide, in the south. Its apex is between the Edinburg moraine and the Cretaceous escarpment west of Grand Forks. No major drainage system feeds into the apex of this delta, so it can only be of glacial origin. The southern part of this mass of outwash is drained by the Goose River system, the central part by Turtle River and the northern part by Forest River. Terraces in these valleys have not been linked to fluctuations of Lake Agassiz as yet. The altitude of the delta surface ranges from about 1225 feet in the north to 1040 feet in the south. The northern part is mainly sand and gravel but this grades into sand and silt at Larimore (due west of Grand Forks). According to Upham the delta was formed during the early Herman phases of Lake Agassiz.

Pembina delta

The Pembina delta (Upham 1895:pl.XXX;357-363) forms a terrace against Pembina Mountain south of the International Boundary. It is triangular with its apex at the north end. It is about 16 miles long from north to south and about 8 miles wide in the south. Its surface slopes from about 1250 feet altitude at the apex to about 1150 feet at the front (top of the "foreset" slope). The foot of the "foreset" slope is about at the 1000 foot contour. The north-east front is straight and steep for about eight miles centered at Walhalla. Sand dunes are abundant on the distal part of the delta, mainly below 1150 feet.

Pembina River now occupies a trench-like valley that trends east across the north part of the delta. The floor of the valley emerges from it at about 975 feet altitude. There are two or three terraces above 1100 feet altitude in this valley, obviously related to levels of Lake Agassiz. At the time of my field observations detailed contour maps of this region were not available, and the altitudes of these terraces are still unknown. On the south side of the valley south of Walhalla is a terrace formed by a valley fill, with an altitude of 1025 feet (average of six aneroid traverses) about 50 feet above the valley floor. A cut exposed the upper 35 feet which is fossiliferous, horizontally-bedded silty sand and silty clay. Fragments of a large clam shell (Naiad) and the columnella of a lymnaeid snail, neither identifiable, were found. The terrace is approximately at the level of the Campbell water plane (Fig. 5) but the sediments suggest that the water was a few to several tens of feet deep when they were deposited. This valley fill is similar to one in the Assiniboine delta (described below). The level of Lake Agassiz here must have fallen below the present altitude of 990 feet and risen higher than about 1035 feet before the final lowering resumed.

Assiniboine delta

The Assiniboine delta was first described by Upham (1895: 370-381, pl. XXXIII) and later mapped by Johnston (1934) and Elson (1960). It occupies part of a valley eroded through the Manitoba escarpment by the preglacial Missouri River between latitudes 49°35' and 50°15' and longitudes 98° and 100°. The apex is just east of Brandon and the delta extends eastward about 85 miles. Its maximum width from north to south is about 45 miles. With Johnston, I consider it to be smaller than did Upham, who included part of an older lake to the west and some recent alluvium in the east.

The delta is divided into two parts by the Campbell strandline which trends northwest in a curve following approximately the 1050 foot contour. This contour delineates the eastern third of the delta. The older, higher part (topset beds) in the west, slopes from about 1250 feet near the apex eastward to about 1200 feet at the top of the delta "front". This higher part is mainly a primary depositional slope. The upper delta also slopes south from about 1275 feet in the north to about 1225 in the south as a result of crustal warping. As might be expected the modern Assiniboine valley now crosses the low southern side. The northwest front of the delta north of the Assiniboine River slopes as much as 150 feet in 3 miles. Locally it is a straight cliff about 100 feet high but mostly it is a belt between the 1200 and 1050 foot contours much dissected by gullies. The gullies are part of valley systems that formed as consequent streams flowing northeast on the emerged delta front and were subsequently dismembered by the retreat of the scarp under wave attack. Several of the gullies, which are mostly broad, flat-floored features, are blocked by advancing sand dunes, now stabilized. Several have beaches built across them where they emerge from the upper delta.

The sediments of the upper delta range from gravelly sand near the apex to clayey silt near the front. A thickness of 240 feet was recorded in one test hole that seems to be representative. A large proportion of the sand has been blown into dunes from 10 to 50 feet high and locally it has migrated across the silt.

The lower, younger part of the delta is a north-south belt in the east about twelve miles wide where clayey bottomset beds of the older delta have been extensively covered by sands eroded from the front as a result of wave action. This younger part of the delta slopes northeast or east from the 1050 foot contour down to the 850 foot contour. A large proportion of this sand southeast of the Assiniboine River is now in the form of sand dunes. Several dune belts are aligned parallel to the contours apparently because wave action concentrated medium grained sand along the shore, (fine grained sand retains capillary water giving cohesion and thus preventing dune formation). These sediments grade into those of the Red River basin to the south.

Most of the delta was deposited during the Herman phase of
Lake Agassiz. The sediment in it was derived mainly from the
erosion of the Assiniboine and Qu'Appelle glacial spillway systems
and their tributaries. These spillways, which average about a
mile wide and about 250 feet in depth, total roughly 800 miles in
length. Meltwater from a retreating ice front and areas of stagnant
ice west of the escarpment eroded the valleys, deposited the delta,
and no doubt transported some sediment directly from the glacier.
The sediments of the delta proper, and for that matter, all the
deposits of early Lake Agassiz, seem to be barren of Pleistocene
fossils because of the cold, turbid nature of the water and the
unvegetated margin of the early Lake (Tuthill 1963:97, Upham 1895:
237-238).

Other Deltas

In all, thirty-three deltas (Table 5) have been identified
on the margins of Lake Agassiz, including those described above.
Most are small deltas deposited by short, steep-gradient streams
on the face of the Manitoba Escarpment. As yet not all have
been examined in the field, but most are easily recognized on
air photographs and approximate altitudes are available for many
contoured topographic maps and by photogrammetric measurements.

The highest parts of deltas 19 and 23 to 25 (Table 5) were
probably deposited in a glacial lake in the Swan River reentrant
that discharged west into the Assiniboine glacial spillway and
which pre-dated Lake Agassiz. The lower parts of these deltas
formed in Lake Agassiz. Some small deltas formed a little later
than adjacent larger ones. The delay may be related to wastage of
stagnant glacier remnants on the tops of the various "mountains"
of the escarpment. Probably each delta was deposited in only a
few years.

Delta 18, Swan River, and 33, Bear River, were deposited in
bays cut off from the main body of the lake by bayhead beaches.

The Saskatchewan delta (number 32) has been mapped by
pedologists but has not been studied in a geological context as
yet.

No valley fills similar to those in the Sheyenne, Pembina,
or Assiniboine deltas have been found so far within any of deltas
8 to 33 (Table 5), nor has other evidence of lake fluctuation
been discovered. Probably delta deposition was followed by rapid
uplift out of the range of later fluctuations.

Several deltas (8, 14, 15 in Table 5) have ice-contact
topography in the apicies. These formed on the east (proximal)
sides of moraines along the face of the escarpment just after

TABLE 5

PRINCIPAL DELTAS OF LAKE AGASSIZ

Name or designation (P)-presumed delta	Latitude		Longitude	
	deg.	min.	deg.	min.
Southern deltas				
1 Buffalo	46	52	96	25
2 Sand Hill	47	--	96	--
3 Rainy River	48	41	94	15
4 Sheyenne	46	30	97	15
5 Elk Valley	48	00	97	40
6 Pembina	48	50	97	50
7 Assiniboine	50	--	99	--
Riding Mountain				
8 Scott Creek	50	47	99	39
9 Ochre River	50	54	99	49
10 Edwards Creek (P)	50	59	100	04
11 Vermillion River	51	01	100	10
Duck Mountain				
12 Fork River	51	32	100	33
13 Garland River, S. branch	51	37	100	33
14 Garland River, main	51	40	100	35
15 Pine River	51	47	100	37
16 Duck River	52	01	100	45
17 Roaring River	52	01	101	14
18 Swan River (P)	51	58	101	37
Porcupine Mountain				
19 Bowsman River	52	16	101	23
20 Kematch River	52	20	101	14
21 Birch River	52	24	101	10
22 Bell Lake road (P)	52	27	101	08
23 6 mi. N. Birch R. town	52	28	101	08
24 Bell River	52	35	101	05
25 Steeprock River	52	42	101	10
26 2 mi. W. of Baden	52	47	101	16
27 Homestead Creek	52	49	101	23
28 3 mi. SW of Barrows	52	47	101	29
29 Little Woody River	52	46	101	34
30 Armit River	52	44	101	35
Others				
31 Bainbridge River	53	34	102	07
32 Saskatchewan River (P)	53	15	104	15
33 Bear River	54	35	104	15

TABLE 5--Continued

Approx. Area, square miles	Altitudes, etc. (K-Kettles in apex, f-front, t-terrace, a-apex)
3.0 (?)	1100 - 1075 (Upham)
5.0 (?)	1130 - 1100 (Upham)
2.0	1080, later submerged
800.0	a 1090, f 1040
300.0	a 1225, f 1040
150.0	a 1250, f 1150
2500.0	a 1250, f 1200, tilted S
2.0	K, a 1500, f 1250
5.0	a 1450, t 1350, f 1300
1.0	a 1500-1600, f 1400-1425
.05	t 1350, f 1250
2.0	a 1400, t 1350, f 1325
1.0	t 1350, f 1325
1.0	K, t 1375, f 1325
4.0	K, t 1375, f 1350
1.5	altitudes not measured
2.0	t 1300, f 1275
5.0-8.0	t 1375
1.5	t 1425, t 1410, f 1340
0.3	f 1375
1.0	f 1375
0.1	f 1425
0.15	t 1475, f 1425
1.5	f 1475, a 1350-1375, f 1275
2.0 (+)	f 1500, t 1250
0.01	altitudes not measured
2.0	" " "
0.5	" " "
0.5	" " "
1.0	" " "
1.0	a, t 1320, f 1260
100.0 (+)	a - f 1400 - 1200
7.0	a - f 1400 ±

the ice withdrew from it, so quickly that blocks of ice were
buried and later melted to produce kettles. This is the closest
approach to the termination of a strandline against the ice margin
that has yet been observed.

Assiniboine Valley

     The Assiniboine valley is so vital to understanding the
history of Lake Agassiz that some detailed description is necessary.
Upstream from its confluence with the Souris River, as far as the
end of the trough-like valley just east of Brandon, the Assiniboine
valley is broad and shallow, yielding little information from cut
banks and terraces. Similarly, in the younger part of the delta
east of the 1050 foot contour, the valley is V-shaped with some
narrow terraces and yields little data. However, between the
confluence of Souris River (longitude 99°35') and the Campbell
strandline (1050 foot contour) north of Rathwell (longitude 98°30'),
the valley is a trough averaging about a mile in width, 100 to 200
feet deep, with a sinuous course about 60 miles long. It contains
five or six sets of terrace systems graded to various phases of
Lake Agassiz. Most are cut terraces, but several are covered by
sand dunes. There are some non-paired terraces, mostly low in the
valley and generally in the eastern part of this segment. One
set of terraces is on a valley fill similar to the one in the
Pembina delta (described above), and contains abundant fossil
material. An older, higher, fossiliferous unit is also present,
and forms the upland at the top of the south valley wall at Treesbank Ferry.

Treesbank Ferry section

     At the upper end of the trough-like part of the valley
across the delta, on the south side of the Treesbank Ferry crossing (latitude 49°47', longitude 96°16'), is a road cut with its
top at an altitude of 1160 feet. This elevation is at or just
above the Norcross waterplane. Fine sand, six feet thick which
contains near the base abundant shells of *Amnicola, Valvata,
Pisidium,* a few *Planorbis arcticus,* and fragments of a *Naiad,*
overlies about ten feet of fine sand, silt, and silty clay in beds
ranging from 0.2 to 0.4 feet thick, containing *Amnicola* and *Valvata*
in the upper two feet. Below this is about five feet of clay in
beds 0.7 feet thick with sandy interbeds from 0.5 to 1.0 inches
thick, overlying fine sand. Till is exposed lower in the cut.
Slumping of the bank has concealed the lower contacts.

The following events are interpreted from this section:

(1) Lowering of Lake Agassiz by an unknown amount below
     about 1140 feet in this locality and erosion of a
     valley across the south side of the delta. This
     must have been after the erosion of the Assiniboine
     and Qu'Appelle spillway systems because erosion had
     replaced desposition in the delta. The glacial source
     of water west of the escarpment was remote or had
     vanished and the land was protected by vegetation.

(2) A rise of Lake Agassiz caused the valley to be flooded
     to a level somewhat higher than 1160 feet. Clays
     were deposited followed by silt and sand.

(3) The water level dropped and it became shallower again
     during the silt and sand deposition. At this time con-
     ditions were suitable for an invasion by a molluskan fauna.

(4) Water level dropped still further, permitting the river
     to cut down through the deposit.

Another occurrence of molluskan fossils just above the Norcross
water plane in Minnesota (latitude 48°47', longitude 96°16') was
described by Tuthill (1963). Almost all other occurrences of
fossiliferous sediments in Lake Agassiz are related to the Campbell
water plane or younger features.

Below the altitude of the Treesbank section and downstream from
it are several terrace systems, some of which are parts of former
channels that can be traced across the delta several miles away from
the present Assiniboine valley.

The 1050-foot valley fill (Steels Ferry to Rathwell)

In the lower 45 miles of the segment of the valley crossing
the upper delta a conspicuous paired terrace system is formed by
remnants of a valley fill. Its surface slopes from about 1060 foot
altitude at Steels Ferry (longitude 99°15') to about 1050 feet
north of Rathwell (longitude 98°32'). Tributary gullies on the
north side of the Assiniboine valley in the lower ten miles of this
valley segment contain valley fills graded to the one in the
Assinibloine valley proper.

At the east end, the fill sediments are typical of a lacustrine
environment. They grade westward into sediments deposited in a
shallow lake or river environment, possibly a digitate delta. Sections
exposed in gullies in the fill at the east end generally have at the
top about ten feet of clay in beds two to four inches thick overlying
about ten feet of silt and fine sand in beds of similar thickness.
The silt overlies as much as forty feet of medium-grained sand.
Fossils are abundant at the top of the sand and in the base of the

silt and include freshwater and some terrestrial snails, clams
(Naiads, probably *Lampsilis* as well as *Sphaerium)*, fragments of
wood, and some cones (probably tamarack). The number of both
species and individuals of mollusk fossils decreases upward with
the increase of clay content of the silt. The upper clay unit
contains only large fragile clam shells, probably *Anodontoides;*
unfortunately they are too decomposed (leached) to collect for
laboratory identification. Clam shells from the top of the sand
unit gave a radiocarbon date of 11,230 years ago (Table 6, Y-166)
and wood of the same general age from a fill in a gully near Lavenham,
about seven miles west, was dated as 10,550 years old (Table 6,
Y-411).

    Near Steels Ferry (longitude 99°14'), north of Glenboro, about
35 miles upstream from the upper delta "front", sediments exposed
in a river cut through the terrace on the south side of the valley
have at the top one to three feet of sandy silt with abundant
acquatic snail shells, mostly *Lymnaeids* This overlies and in part
grades into a lenticular bed of pure marl as thick as 1.5 feet
and several hundred feet long with abundant aquatic snail shells
(mainly *Lymnaeids)* of relatively large size. Below the marl is about
eight feet of interbedded sand and silty clay with thin lenses of
coarse sand. Several clay beds have mud cracks filled with sand.
Shells of *Amnicola* and *Valvata* are common in the sand. These beds
are underlain by two feet of medium to fine grained pebble gravel
containing a few *Sphaerium* shells. Underneath this, extending
down to river level (about 10 to 15 feet) is grey unfossiliferous
clay and silt, probably part of the older delta. Marl, believed
to be the same age as that in the upper part of this section, overlies the wood (Y-411) in the gully near Laveham mentioned above,
and gave a radiocarbon age of 10,600 years (Table 6, GSC-383). The
sequence of sediments and fossils indicates that shallow water with
good but gentle circulation (shown by *Valvata* and *Amnicola*) gave
way to conditions of alternate flooding and drying (mud cracked clay
interbedded with sand), followed by shallow, clear water (suitable
for the growth of marl-secreting algae and hospitable to *lymnaeid*
snails) such as delta ponds behind natural levees.

    Because of its position lower in the valley, the nature of the
sediments and the much greater number of species in its fossil fauna,
this valley fill is no doubt younger than the fossiliferous deposits
at Treesbank Ferry. The lower valley was eroded when the level of
Lake Agassiz at the east end of the fill dropped to or below an
altitude of 990 feet and then rose to about 1060 feet 10,600 years
ago. This fluctuation must have resulted from the opening and closing of an eastern outlet, probably the Kaiashk, as shown by relationships in Fig. 5.

Souris confluence section

    An important stratigraphic sequence is exposed on the north
bank of the Assiniboine River 0.8 mile east of the mouth of the
Souris River (latitude 49°40', longitude 99°33'). The altitude of
the river here is about 1090 feet and the top of the section ranges

TABLE 6

RADIOCARBON DATES[a]

Sample Number	C14 Age Years Ago	Location Lat.	Long.	Notes
				I. Dates directly related to Glacial Lake Agassiz.
Y-165	12,400±420	49°47'	98°35'	Rossendale, Man., peat in alluvial fill. Science 122, 457.
Y-1327	11,740	–	–	Below Herman beach in NW Minn. Wright & Frey, 1965, Quaternary of U.S.A., p. 39.
Y-166	[11,230±480]	49°44'	98°34'	Rossendale, Man., clam shells in alluvial fill. Science 122, 457.
W-723	10,960±300	47°56'	97°22'	Grand Forks, N.D., wood in sand overlying till. Radiocarbon Supplement 2, 152.
GSC-383	10,600±150	49°46'	98°45'	Lavenham, Man., marl from valley fill. Publication pending; Radiocarbon 9.
Y-411	10,550±200	49°46'	98°45'	Lavenham, Man., wood from valley fill, locality of GSC-383. Science 126, p. 912.
GX-498	10,310±260	48°05'	93°30'	Koochiching Co., Minn. Peat from base of raised bog. Radiocarbon 8, p. 144.
W-900	10,080±280	47°50'	97°20'	Grand Forks, N.D., wood in sand. Radiocarbon Supplement 3, 88.
W-1005	10,050±300	47°46'	97°07'	Thompson, N.D., wood in gravel. Radiocarbon 6, 47.
L-563c	10,000±1000	48°49'	91°39'	Steeprock Lake, Ont. disseminated carbonate in varved clay. Radiocarbon Supplement 3, p. 145.
GSC-391	9,990±160	49°00'	95°14'	Buffalo Point, Man., wood in gravel. Publication pending; Radiocarbon 9.
W-388 C-497	9,930±280 [11,283±700]	– –	– –	Moorehead, Minn., wood in clay. Science 127, 1478. Libby, 1955, Radiocarbon Dating, p. 121.
W-993	9,900±400	46°55'	96°45'	Fargo, N.D., wood below 28 ft. clay and silt. Radiocarbon 6, 45.
W-1361	9,820±300	47°37'	97°10'	Blanchard beach, N.D., wood. Radiocarbon 7, p. 378.
W-1360	9,810±300	47°38'	97°05'	Hillsboro beach, N.D., wood. Radiocarbon 7, 378.

TABLE 6-- Continued

Sample Number	C14 Age Years Ago	Location Lat.	Location Long.	Notes
GSC-384	9,580±220	48°33'	93°29'	Roddick Tp., Ont., carbonaceous matter in marl under beach gravel. Publication pending.
W-1057	9,200±600	48°53'	95°03'	Lake of the Woods, Minn., wood from beach. Radiocarbon 6, 44.
Y-415	9,110±110	49°40'	99°33'	Treesbank, Man., wood. Science 126, 913.
GSC-9	8,860±250	51°26'	93°43'	Nungesser Lake, Ont., gyttja below alt. 1335'. Radiocarbon 4, 18.
Y-416	8,020±100	49°37'	99°26'	Stockton, Man., wood and peat. Science 126, 913.
SM-696-2	7,861±423	49°02'	94°18'	Morson, Ont., organic carbon from antler in wave-formed terrace. Can. Jour. Earth Sciences 2, 238.

II.   Minimum age for the drainage of Glacial Lake Agassiz.

Sample Number	C14 Age Years Ago	Location Lat.	Location Long.	Notes
GSC-92	7,270±120	58°11'	95°03'	Churchill, Man., marine shells from emerged beach, Radiocarbon 6, 170.

III.   Dates in alluvium younger than Glacial Lake Agassiz.

Sample Number	C14 Age Years Ago	Location Lat.	Location Long.	Notes
W-860	6,200±320	49°48'	97°12'	Winnipeg, Man., wood from silt above till. Radiocarbon Supplement 2, 175.
W-862	6,750±320	"	"	
GSC-215	3,650±140	49°45'	97°08'	Winnipeg, Man., shells and wood respectively beneath 25' silt. Radiocarbon 7, 30.
GSC-216	3,660±130	"	"	
C-723	[2,684±200]	48°35'	98°10'	Robbin, Minn., charcoal, Libby, 1955, Radiocarbon dating, p. 126.
C-722	[2,150±400]	48°35'	98°10'	Robbin, Minn., charcoal, Libby, 1955, Radiocarbon dating, p. 125.
W-1185	2,540±300	46°32'	97°14'	Sheyenne R., Richland Co., N.D., wood. Radiocarbon 7, 378.
Y-11	2,830±130	49°30'	99°04'	Cypress River, Man., wood, Science 122, 457.
Y-64	[2,560±200]	49°30'	99°04'	Cypress River, Man., wood, Science 122, 457.

TABLE 6--Continued

Sample Number	C14 Age Years Ago	Location Lat.	Long.	Notes
S-94	3,200±70	49°42'	98°50'	Holland, Man., wood from landslide. Radiocarbon 4, 71.
GSC-346	1,670±130	51°02'	100°31'	Grandview, Man., charcoal, Radiocarbon 8, 107.
S-178	770±50	53°34'	102°07'	Bainbridge Creek, Sask., wood, Radiocarbon 7, 231.

IV. Dates from peat deposits in or near the Glacial Lake Agassiz basin.

W-562	4,360±160	48°27'	94°00'	Lindford, Minn., Radiocarbon Supplement 2, 148.
GX-429	3,160±75	48°05'	93°30'	Koochiching Co., Minn., Radiocarbon 8, 144.
S-129	9,570±130	50°43'	99°38'	Riding Mtn. Nat. Park, Man., Radiocarbon 4, 75.
Y-418	1,400±80	51°10'	100°15'	Ashville, Man., Science 126, 913.
GSC-10	4,670±130	52°53'	99°08'	Grand Rapids, Man., Radiocarbon 8, 107.
WIS-1	2,380±90	54°07'	101°17'	Root Lake, Man., Radiocarbon 7, 405.
S-122	5,050±80	55°36'	105°17'	La Ronge, Sask., Radiocarbon 4, 73.
WIS-72	6,530±130	56°50'	101°03'	Lynn Lake, Man., Radiocarbon 8, 531.

[a]Square brackets indicate dates made by the solid carbon method.

from 1150 to 1165 feet. The cut is about 500 feet long and is mostly slumped. The following composite section is based on observations made in 1955 and repeated in 1964. The upper five to twenty feet is medium grained sand of dunes which have masked the original surface morphology of the locality, but are now stabilized. Below this is a relict soil profile -- developed mainly on horizontally bedded sand -- a dark grey humified "A" horizon about two feet thick overlies a "B" horizon composed of an iron oxide-cemented zone 1.5 feet thick at the top containing reddish brown sand with caliche tubes formed around root openings. This grades downward into brown sand mottled with red and grey about one foot thick overlying horizontally bedded brown sand. Fossil terrestrial snail shells are abundant in the cemented part of the "B" horizon. Beneath the relict soil are lenticular silty and sandy beds containing abundant fossil wood fragments, chiefly transported logs, some of which have insect borings. Locally, peat is present in a thin layer. Bones, most probably *Bison*, were also found. The organic material is most abundant in a layer about two feet thick in the upper part of these beds. No complete section could be observed because of the slumping, but these beds appear to be from three feet thick at the east end to twelve feet at the west end of the exposure. Wood from near the base of this layer gave a radiocarbon age of 9,110 years (Table 6, Y-415). Underlying the fossiliferous sand and silt are up to five feet of sand and gravel resting on till. The contact is erosional and the surface of the till has a relief of fifteen feet.

A tentative interpretation of this sequence can now be presented After an episode of downcutting and erosion of the till, the river aggraded and shifted its course so that the fossiliferous silt and sand was laid down in relatively quiet water. Deposition was followed by some downcutting and lowering of the water table, in order for the soil profile to develop. The soil, formed in a humid to slightly subhumid climate, was followed by an episode of eolian action, possibly resulting from a drier climate. This interpretation is compatible with climatic events that caused the transition from pollen zone 1 of Ritchie (1964) to pollen zone 2 in the southern part of the Riding Mountain area that occurred sometime after 9,570 years ago (Table 6, S-129). However, the geological data are insufficient to discriminate among three possible hypotheses of aggradation. The cause may have been (1) a change of base level resulting from a fluctuation of Lake Agassiz, (2) downstream extension of the river by delta growth, or (3) a result of climatic events. This deposit is younger than the Treesbank Ferry deposits and does not appear to correlate with the valley fill farther downstream which is radiocarbon-dated at 1500 years older. Contemporaneity, assuming an aberrant date, would require an unreasonable and unaccountable river gradient of 4.5 feet per mile between this point and Steels Ferry. Perhaps this enigmatic aggradation episode may be explained by temporary blocking or diversion of the river as a result of a landslide or sand dune activity.

Rossendale gully

Some gullies on the eastern front of the older delta, such as one about three miles south-southeast of Rossendale at latitude 49°47', longitude 98°35', also contain alluvial fills. In this area silty sand at least thirteen feet thick overlies peat exposed in a dugout (reservoir) now filled with water. The silt and sand are interbedded, poorly sorted and contain wood fragments below about seven feet (as observed in an augur hole). The buried peat is at an altitude of about 1055 feet and gave a radiocarbon date of 12,400 years (Table 6, Y-165). This single date is considerably older than was expected and interpretation has been held in abeyance. However, recently J.C. Ritchie (personal communication) has obtained a date of a similar order from a lake south of the delta which adds weight to the possible validity of date Y-165.

Strandlines, Including Beaches

The term "beach" is often used loosely by geologists to designate any indication of a former shore. In the strict sense it means only the sand and gravel ridge deposited by waves at the shore. The word "strandline" includes all forms that can be used as indicators of the boundary between land and water. The principal waterplanes of Lake Agassiz represented by well developed strandlines are listed in succession from oldest (top) to youngest (bottom) in Fig. 6.

Beaches

Beach ridges are the most common strandline forms in Lake Agassiz and are abundant on both sides of the Red River basin and along the Manitoba Escarpment north to latitude 55° (Fig. 4). Their usual form is a ridge two to fifteen feet high, but locally as high as about thirty feet where spits have extended across embayments. Width ranges from about 150 to 500 feet but commonly several are grouped together into complexes a half-mile or more wide. Their lengths between gaps (such as embayments and deltas), are mostly tens to scores of miles. Where coastal slopes change, beaches may change into terraces or wave-cut cliffs. Many beaches are partly buried under alluvial fans near the foot of the Manitoba Escarpment. Some have been destroyed by erosion of younger, lower shores. Beach ridges are easily traced on air photos because they have a vegetation that contrasts with growth on adjacent deposits. For beach formation, waves must attack a material (generally till) that will yield sand and gravel-size particles. Locally, longshore transport or migration has extended sand and gravel beaches beyond their parent sources into areas of silt and clay.

LIFE, LAND AND WATER

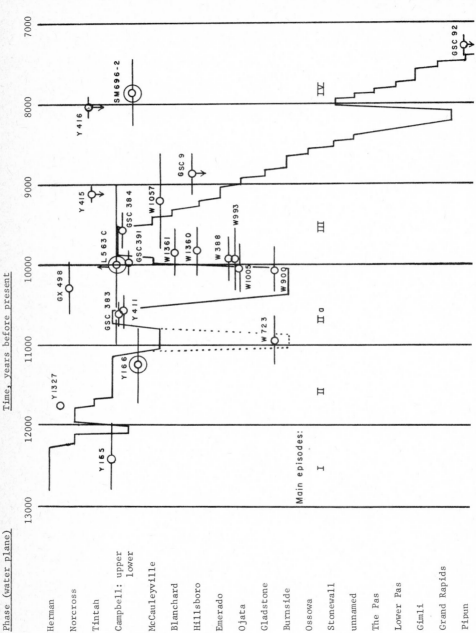

Figure 6. Hypothetical sequence of water levels of Glacial Lake Agassiz. (Note: This figure has been revised since the accompanying text was written and shows five main lake

Strandline Morphology

In addition to beaches, strandline forms include low scarps five to fifteen feet high, where waves attack silt and clay or gently sloping coasts. Sand may be moved in, laterally, by beach drift. Some low scarps that have sand at the base also have it at the top, thrown up by violent wave action. At least one such scarp (at Elm Creek, Manitoba) has been misinterpreted by Johnston (1946) as representing two water levels. He interpreted both sand bodies to be beaches. The low scarps are common in the Swan River and Carrot-Saskatchewan River reentrants.

Higher scarps, from 25 to more than 100 feet high are common only along the Campbell strandline, apparently because insufficient time was available for their formation at other levels. The scarp of the Campbell water plane has a sand beach at the base and stands highest in the silts of the Assiniboine delta. Lower scarps (25 to 40 feet) occur in till. In some places, the Campbell strandline follows bedrock scarps but these are exhumed preglacial, lithologically controlled features.

Wave-cut terraces armoured with a lag concentrate of boulders are common on the southern part of the Cretaceous escarpment.

Although ice-pushed ridges resulting from the pressure of floating ice driven by the wind are common around the modern lakes of the region, they have not been certainly identified among the Lake Agassiz strandlines except on the crest of the Eagle-Finlayson moraine in Ontario. There, boulders averaging 2.5 feet in diameter form ridges from 3 to 10 feet high and as wide as 75 feet and several miles long.

Factors influencing the form of strandlines cannot be discussed in detail here but they include:

(1) the slope of the coast -- this determines whether eroded detritus will remain in the zone of wave action to form a beach or will be deposited in deep water out of reach;

(2) the depth of water as determined by the slope governs the width of the area across which wave energy is dissipated;

(3) the fetch, and hence the size, of the waves depends on the wind direction as well as the size and shape of the lake;

(4) the type and erodability of material attacked by the waves, e.g., till, clay, or sand;

(5) the direction of wave attack which depends on both the effective storm wind directions and the configuration of the coast;

(6) the duration of the water level;

(7) the frequency of storms.

The identification of a water level represented by relict strandlines is basic to tracing them across gaps, as well as basic to theorizing about crustal uplift. Usually the points measured by levelling are the crests of beach ridges and the toes of scarps, but Upham (1890:90E) used the base of the lakeward slope and recognized that the crests were five to fifteen feet above the lake level. According to Bagnold (Bascom 1964:198-199) the crest of a beach ridge is generally 1.3 time the deep-water height of the wave that built it above the water level. However, the toe of a wave-cut scarp is less consistent and may be above or below water level, depending on wave height and also on the geological structure of the coast. Hence, tracing strandlines across gaps is not a simple matter of extrapolating the crest of a beach, especially if the beaches form changes.

Duration of water levels

Radiocarbon dates bracketing Lake Agassiz indicate a duration of roughly 4,500 years. About 55 water planes are represented by strandlines (not including five or more water planes that existed during low-water phases). Hence the maximum average duration of the waterplanes was less than 80 years, not allowing for the time taken for the water levels to change. Wide departures from this hypothetical average are certain.

The duration of the Campbell water planes (the lowest phase of Lake Agassiz to discharge south through the Minnesota River valley) was obviously longer than any others because the massive beach (and the escarpment behind it), which together can be followed for about 1500 miles, required more energy for their formation. The properties of the sediments in beaches is indicative of the wave energy expended on them, hence their duration. At any given locality, the sands and gravels of the Campbell beach are well rounded and well sorted compared with other beaches in the vicinity. The degree of rounding of pebbles may be indicative of duration. Sorting involves, as well, the violence (energy) of individual storms and may be more related to wave height, hence fetch.

A preliminary study of roundness of three samples of beach gravel from 4 to 32 mm. in size gave the following results:

(1) Herman beach, Larimore, N.D. -- roundness 0.56, fetch
    150 miles;

(2) Campbell beach, Dauphin, Man. -- roundness 0.62 fetch
    250-300 miles;

(3) Burnside beach, Amaranth, Man. -- roundness 0.58 150-200
    miles.

The scale of roundness ranges from 0.1 for a sharply angular particle to 1.0 for a sphere.

Effect on beaches of lake size, shape and orientation

Some relationships between wind velocity, duration, fetch, waves and beaches are shown in Table 7. An index of wave energy and the minimum water depths for which these relationships hold are also given. In speculating on the form of coastal features it is assumed that the effective storm wind directions were mainly from the northeast and northwest as at present.

The variation in the effectiveness of waves on various segments of a given strandline is illustrated by combining the information in Table 7 and Fig. 9 (Campbell phase). Waves attacking the Pembina, Riding and Duck mountains had a fetch of 200 to 300 miles. The energy index of these ranges from 90 to 180 and beaches 12.5 to 17 feet above water level were formed. In this region the Campbell scarp is well developed and the beach is massive. On the west side of the Red River basin south of latitude 48°, the fetch for the same winds (from the northeast) was 25 to 100 miles, the energy index only from 4 to 30, and corresponding beach heights are from 2.5 to 7 feet. In marked contrast, waves generated by northwest winds with a fetch of 400 to more than 500 miles attacked the east side of the Red River basin north of latitude 48° in Minnesota. These were no doubt somewhat impeded by shallow water offshore and interference of an island in southeastern Manitoba, but for part of the coast the energy index was greater than 275 and beaches 21 feet high could have been formed. In this area the Campbell beach is a spectacular ridge system 90 miles long.

The effects of the lowering of lake level are apparent if Table 7 is examined in conjunction with Figs. 7 to 10. For example, consider the west shore at latitude 48° which was attacked mainly by waves from the northeast. The fetch changed from about 150 miles during Herman time to 200 miles or more during Norcross and Campbell times, although then partly impeded by an island in the east; it was then reduced to 50 miles in McCauleyville time. The energy index was initially 60, increased to 100 and then decreased to 10. Corresponding beach heights are 10, 13, and 4 feet respectively. This locality is obviously not one in which to compare beach characteristics for purposes of estimating duration of various waterplanes, except for the highest ones. A suitable locality for comparing beaches is along Riding Mountain where the basin was deep and the fetch was more than 200 miles during most of the lake's existence. Unfortunately, alluvium covers much of the beaches there, but Duck Mountain beaches are not covered so extensively and are in almost as strategic a position. A study of them is in progress.

TABLE 7

CONDITIONS OF WAVE AND BEACH FORMATION

1 Fetch Miles	2 Wave height feet	3 Beach height feet	4 Energy index	5 Wind Velocity mph	6 Generation time hours	7 Deep water limit feet
25	2	2.5	4	14	4.5	14
50	3	4	10	18	7	22
100	5.5	7.5	33	24	11	40
150	7.5	10	59	27	14	54
200	9.5	12.5	94	30	17	68
250	11.5	15	132	32	19.5	80
300	13.5	17.5	177	34	22	93
350	15	19.5	225	35	24.5	102
400	16.5	21.5	275	36.5	26.5	116

Notes:

This table was prepared by converting data given by Bascom (1964:53, Table III) from nautical to statute miles and plotting them as graphs. The figures above are interpolated from the graphs and rounded off to the nearest half or whole number. They are, thus, orders of magnitude, not precise data.

The column headings refer to the following facts.

(1) Fetch is the distance the wind blows across water in creating waves.
(2) Wave height is vertical distance between the trough and the adjacent wave crest.
(3) Beach height is measured from the mean water level to the crest of the ridge.
(4) The energy index is dimensionless, equal to the square of wave height, and is proportional to the amount of kinetic and potential energy stored in a wave.
(5) The velocity given in miles per hour is that which if acting on the corresponding fetch would produce waves of the height given. No greater waves could be produced by this wind.
(6) The time in hours required for the given wind to generate its maximum wave height. (5 and 6 together are relevant to frequency and duration of storms effective in beach construction.)
(7) Minimum depths of water necessary for development of these waves. In shallower water waves are impeded by drag on the bottom.

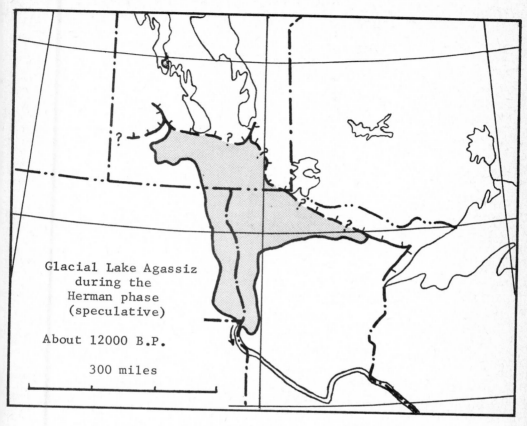

Glacial Lake Agassiz
during the
Herman phase
(speculative)

About 12000 B.P.

300 miles

Figure 7. Glacial Lake Agassiz -- Herman phase.

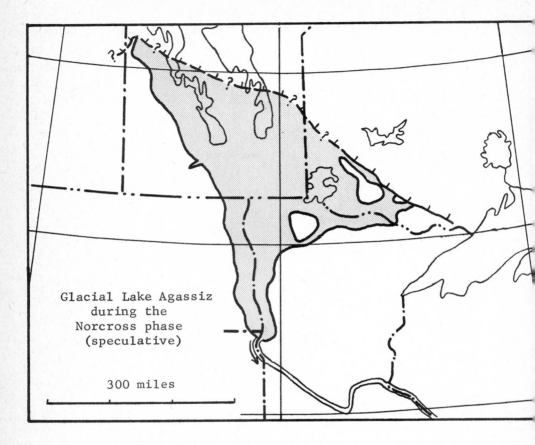

Glacial Lake Agassiz
during the
Norcross phase
(speculative)

300 miles

Figure 8. Glacial Lake Agassiz -- Norcross phase.

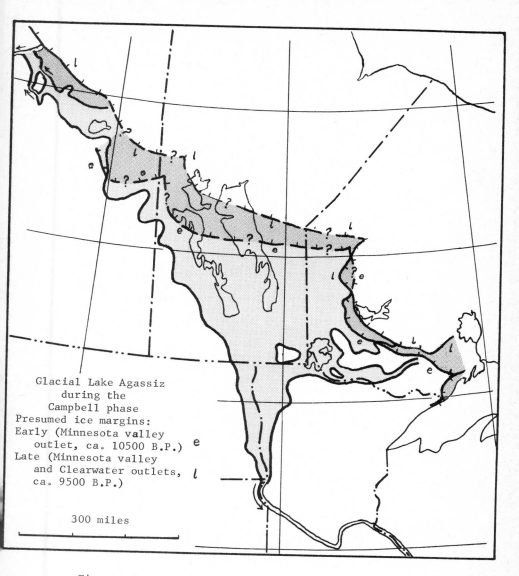

Glacial Lake Agassiz
during the
Campbell phase
Presumed ice margins:
Early (Minnesota valley
   outlet, ca. 10500 B.P.) e
Late (Minnesota valley
   and Clearwater outlets, l
   ca. 9500 B.P.)

300 miles

Figure 9. Glacial Lake Agassiz -- Campbell phase.

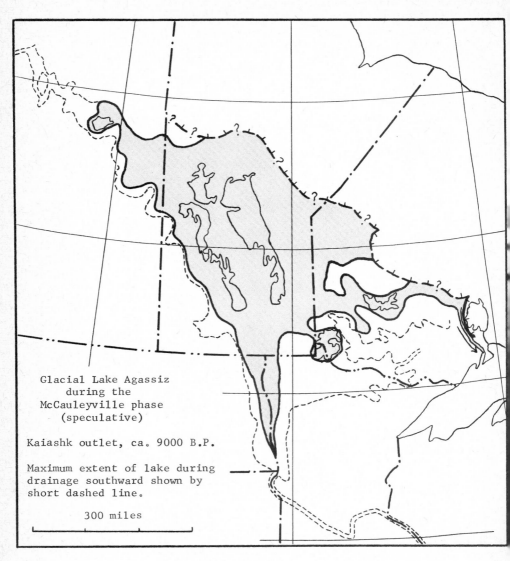

Glacial Lake Agassiz
during the
McCauleyville phase
(speculative)

Kaiashk outlet, ca. 9000 B.P.

Maximum extent of lake during
drainage southward shown by
short dashed line.

300 miles

Figure 10.   Glacial Lake Agassiz -- McAuleyville phase.

Deformation of water planes

Upham (1890, 1895) observed that the strandlines of Lake Agassiz slope southward. After finding from theory that gravitational attraction of the water by the ice sheet, and expansion of the earth's crust resulting from warming (after the ice disappeared) were negligible, he, with several others, attributed the tilting to crustal rebound following the disappearance of the load imposed by the glacier. Comprehensive investigations of post-glacial differential uplift began in the late 1880's and Upham's study was among the first. Leverett (1932) revised some of Upham's data in North Dakota and added new information from Minnesota. Some discrepancies between Leverett and Upham may be the result of the former measuring altitudes of the crests of beaches and the latter measuring the foot of the lake-side slope. During various projects from 1912 to 1929 Johnston (1946) measured altitudes of many beaches in Manitoba and Ontario.

The slope of former water planes is found by drawing contours (isobases) between points of equal altitude on a strandline that has been traced around both sides of a lake, bay or peninsula. Slope direction and degree are measured perpendicular to these isobases which usually are roughly concentric to the center of glaciation.

The highest Lake Agassiz water planes (Fig. 5) slope southwest at 2 to 3 feet per mile at the north (glacier) end, and their gradient decreases gradually to about 0.5 feet per mile near the southern outlet. The middle water planes slope at about 1.3 feet per mile in the north but at a zone of inflection from 150 to 200 miles north of the southern outlet the slope decreases to about 0.5 feet per mile. This so-called "hinge line" (really a belt about 10 to 20 miles wide) appears farther north, the lower the water plane. The lowest group of water planes have uniform southwest slopes of about 0.8 feet per mile throughout, except the youngest (here called the Pipun, previously unnamed) which slopes about 0.3 feet per mile. The different slopes reflect the thickness of the former glacier and its rate of retreat (Broecker 1966).

At the conference on Lake Agassiz in Winnipeg, November 4-5, 1966, Professor W.O. Kupsch severely criticised all work on relict strandlines and condemned the work done on Lake Agassiz, especially by Johnston (1946). He implied that no strandlines were traced continuously, but that they were merely interpolated between widely spaced sets of measurements, the relationship of which to the water planes represented was unknown. His further comments on the errors inherent in drawing isobases and on the interpretation of their tectonic significance are indeed well taken. However, the impression he created for the non-geologists of his audience was that sloping water planes are imaginary and not valid evidence for the interpretation of geologic history. This view would be contested strongly by a majority of geologists.

In defence of Lake Agassiz studies, Upham (1890:90E) specifically mentions continuous surveying of some strandlines. Johnston
produced several detailed maps (e.g., references 1921, 1931, cited
in his 1946 paper) on which strandlines are mapped for many miles.
That he was well aware of the problems of morphology is shown by
his reference to Goldthwait (1910). It is true that not every
strandline was traced, but enough were traced to establish trends
and to bracket the positions of intervening shorelines. There are
obviously some errors, and some lengthy extrapolations to the widely
scattered strandlines in the north of the basin will always be
necessary, but these weaknesses do not invalidate the general
relationships and principles involved.

An abstraction from strandline data to hypothetical water
planes must be made in the study of any large glacial lake, because
no former level can be designated simply by its present altitude.
Fig. 5, showing water planes, is revised from Johnston (1946: Fig.2).
As Professor Kupsch suggested, the lines representing water planes
should really be very thick (I would suggest ten to twenty feet in
Fig. 5) to take into account uncertainties resulting from interpretation of morphology and seasonal fluctuation. Furthermore, the
hypothetical former water planes are curved, and an even greater
thickness should be given if this were to be accommodated. In
addition they should be shown as wedges, thicker in the north (wider
part of the basin, thus more curvature). These constructions are
impractical for the present presentation and Fig. 5 merely provides
a framework for historical discussion.

Glacial Deposits

A summary of the glacial sediments in the Lake Agassiz region
was published earlier (Elson 1961). Only those pertinent to the
history of the Lake are mentioned here.

A layer of till rests on bedrock and underlies most of the
Lake sediments. It is the source of the material in most beaches.
In extensive areas, especially to the west of Lake Winnipeg, the
usual lake clays and silts are very thin or absent, presumably
because the glacial source was remote. In these regions a lag
concentrate of poorly sorted sand and gravel not more than a few
inches thick, overlain by a foot or two of silt and sand, covers
the till. This was formed by wave action during the late, shallow
phases of the lake.

Minor moraine ridges of the De Geer type -- washboard moraines
of Norman (1938) which form at or near ice margins standing in deep
water, are common west and northwest of Lake Nipigon, south and
southeast of the Sandy Lake basin, and in a small area northwest of
Lake Winnipeg. These ridges are useful in delimiting the lake where
other evidence is lacking or unreported.

End moraines representing important intervals of equilibrium of the ice margin have been mapped in northern Ontario by Prest (1963) and Zoltai (1965a, and b) and also occur in northern Manitoba and Saskatchewan. Some parts of these were deposited in the lake and other parts were probably deposited on land and subsequently reworked by wave action. In many places they are the only features on which strandline forms, mainly scarps and terraces, could develop. Several of the northern moraines (e.g., Sachigo, Island Lake and Burntwood-Etawney) have, in places, strandlines on one side and unmodified moraine topography at lower levels on the other, showing that the ice sheet was present on one side while strandlines formed on the other.

Small end moraines contemporary with early phases of Lake Agassiz trend obliquely down the slope of the Manitoba Escarpment. The Edinburg moraine in North Dakota joins the Darlingford moraine in southern Manitoba and descends from 1650 feet altitude on Pembina Mountain to about 1100 feet west of Grand Forks (latitude 48°). Other moraines occur on Riding, Duck, and Porcupine mountains; they are progressively younger toward the north. Their southern ends are in reentrants and all descend southward. The Pasquia Hills have southeast-trending drumlins on top but are without an end moraine similar to the others. All the "mountains" of the escarpment have some dead ice moraine on them. A large end moraine extends northwest from the Carrot-Saskatchewan River reentrant west of longitude 104°.

Younger (post-Lake Agassiz) Sediments

Recent sediments covering parts of the Lake Agassiz basin include alluvium mainly in the form of alluvial fans at the foot of the western escarpment, but also as fans or deltas of the Saskatchewan and Assiniboine Rivers (Fig. 4). Some fans along the escarpment have areas of several tens of square miles although most are small. In some areas they completely cover the strandlines. Landslides involving one to twenty square miles have destroyed segments of strandlines on Porcupine and Pasquia Hills. In deltaic areas extensive eolian activity has masked or destroyed some strandlines. Most of the recent deposits are a hinderance to Lake Agassiz research, but some alluvial fans have paleosols and other organic matter that can be radiocarbon dated (e.g., Table 6 (III): W-1185; Y-11; Y-64; GSC-346; S-178) and are useful in interpreting more recent events.

Radiocarbon Dates

Twenty-one radiocarbon dates on Lake Agassiz material and others relevant to the problem (published prior to June, 1966) are listed in Table 6 and many are shown graphically in Fig. 6. Space limitations preclude description of the occurences here but typical situations have been mentioned already in the discussion of the Assiniboine delta. The dates range from more than 12,000 years ago (Y-165)to about 9000 years ago (W-1057). Several within and beyond this range are of uncertain significance because their geological situations are not as clear as was originally thought (e.g., Y-165, Y-415, Y-416) or the characteristics of the dated materials (carbonate, antler) are inadequately known (Y-166, L-563C, SM-696-2). Some are limiting dates only (GSC-9, GSC-92). Organic materials associated with the unconformity in the Red River basin have given dates W-723, W-388, and W-993, all in the 10,000 to 11,000 year range; these, with the dates from the Assiniboine delta, are firm evidence for the major low water interval, but the latter dates seem to be too old. A minor fluctuation may have occured before the main low water phase (Fig.6).

History of Glacial Lake Agassiz

At the time of writing not all the data have been fully assimilated and the following history is tentative. It accounts for the position of the water planes, degree of development of beaches stratigraphy in the individual sedimentation basins and valley fills, and fits the radiocarbon dates. The history is shown graphically as a succession of water levels (Fig. 6) and as maps of different lake phases (Figs.7 to 13). The events were as follows:

(1)   The ice sheet receded from the south end of the Red River basin prior to 11,700 years ago and probably before 12,400 years ago while extensive areas of stagnant ice remained on the plains farther west. The highest beaches of Lake Agassiz began to form when the ice left the area north of the sediments that Upham interpreted as formed in a glacial lake he called the Milnor phase. Baker (1966) showed that the Milnor deposits were really outwash from the Sheyenne valley. The Herman phase (the first one) of Lake Agassiz expanded rapidly northward until the ice margin paused at or readvanced to the Darlingford-Edinburg-Erskine moraine. The southern outlet at Lake Traverse (the River Warren) stabilized because of the accumulation of a lag concentrate of boulders derived from the Big Stone moraine (Wright 1965). Differential crustal uplift resulted in the development of a succession of beach ridges in the north. The ice margin withdrew to the north of the north side of the Assiniboine delta during the later part of the Herman phase (Fig.7). The

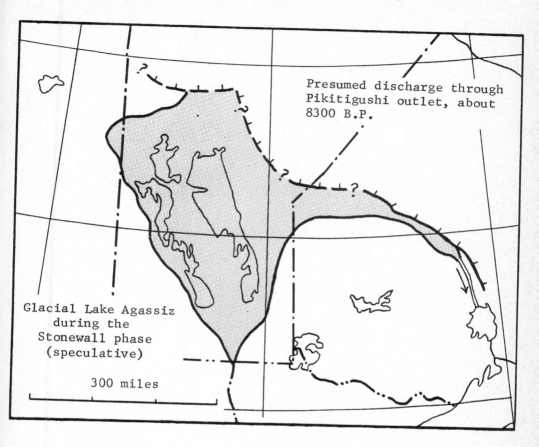

Figure 11. Glacial Lake Agassiz -- Stonewall phase.

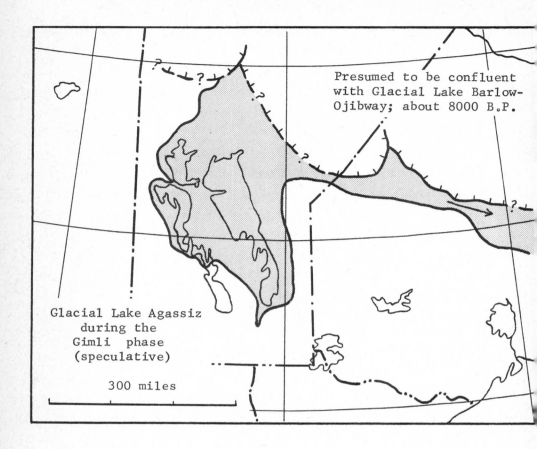

Presumed to be confluent
with Glacial Lake Barlow-
Ojibway; about 8000 B.P.

Glacial Lake Agassiz
during the
Gimli phase
(speculative)

300 miles

Figure 12.   Glacial Lake Agassiz -- Gimli phase.

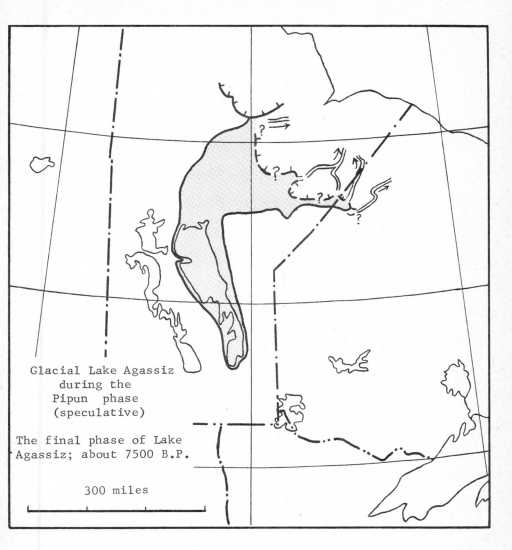

Glacial Lake Agassiz
during the
Pipun phase
(speculative)

The final phase of Lake
Agassiz; about 7500 B.P.

300 miles

Figure 13. Glacial Lake Agassiz -- Pipun phase.

Sheyenne, Elk Valley, Pembina and Assiniboine deltas were deposited in succession during Herman time. This was Lake Agassiz I.

An increase of discharge of uncertain origin caused the River Warren to erode through the boulder armour (Wright 1965) and cut down to the Norcross level (Fig. 8) The cause may have been climatic, or the result of a shift of glacial drainage in southwestern Saskatchewan and southern Alberta from the Big Muddy-Missouri system into the Souris-Lake Agassiz system about 12,000 years ago. This idea, however, conflicts with chronology as presently interpreted in some other parts of Saskatchewan (Christiansen 1965).

(2) Ice retreat in northern Ontario opened the west branch of the Dog River spillway at Coldwater Lake and Lake Agassiz briefly discharged into the Lake Superior basin while its level fell to about the Tintah water plane. Vegetation had covered the deglaciated region which was also inhabited by a molluskan fauna.

(3) Ice readvanced to the Dog Lake moraine and blocked the eastern outlet. Lake Agassiz rose again to the Norcross Level (Fig. 8). Fossiliferous beds were deposited in the Assiniboine valley at Treesbank Ferry. Numerous small deltas were deposited on the escarpment farther north and strandlines formed at lower levels as differential crustal uplift continued. This phase now may be called Lake Agassiz II (but see episode 9 below).

(4) Downcutting of the Lake Traverse outlet continued until a new boulder armour accumulated at the Tintah level (Wright 1965). This period of stability seems to have been brief as the Tintah strandlines system has a narrower vertical range than the Herman or Norcross systems and beaches are less well developed.

(5) Accelerated melting of the ice sheet caused the ice margin to retreat. The southern outlet again cut down through the lag concentrate to the Campbell water plane and Lake Agassiz expanded northward (Fig. 9). It may have discharged both through the Flatstone Lake-Clearwater River system as well as southward part of the time. The consequent reduction of flow through the southern outlet may have forestalled further down-cutting there, but exposure of a bedrock sill was also a factor.

(6) Recession of the ice sheet north of Lake Superior opened eastern outlets (probably in succession, lower from south to north) into Lake Superior by way of Lake Nipigon; the level of Lake Agassiz fell to about the Burnside water plane. The low water phase lasted long enough for vegetation to cover the newly exposed lake

floor and an abundant molluskan fauna to invade the
region. The Pillar-Armstrong outlet, which was at
this time about 100 feet lower than shown on Fig. 5
as a result of delayed crustal uplift, may have functioned at this time. This important low-level phase
may include several fluctuations involving eastern
outlets. The time range was 11,000 to 10,000 years ago,
but deciphering of events within this interval requires
more data. Radiocarbon dates suggest an episode of
fluctuation (Fig. 6, Episode IIa) before the main low
water phase.

(7) An important readvance of the ice margin resulting from
     climatic causes, or possibly from a reduction in the
     rate of wastage at the ice margin because the water
     became shallow, blocked the eastern outlets north of
     the Kaiashk spillway. The water level rose to the
     McCauleyville level (Fig. 10). Rainy River deposited
     its delta near Pinewood. Sediments in the Sturgeon-
     Weir basin reflect the deepening water.

(8) Further ice margin advance in the east blocked the
     Kaiashk outlet and reached the Hartman-Kaiashk moraine
     system and the Marks moraine in the Lake Superior basin.
     The water level again rose to the Campbell strandline,
     the lower one, (Figs. 9, 7) and the lake discharged
     southward. For a brief period red clay was discharged
     into the Wabigoon and Rainy River basins from the ice
     front at the Marks moraine. The glacier readvance was
     general and lake sediments in the Sturgeon-Weir basin
     and south of The Pas moraine, as well as the moraine
     itself, were overridden. Valley fills were deposited
     in the delta segments of Sheyenne, Pembina and Assiniboine
     valleys, though some or all may be the result of an earlier
     fluctuation.

     This, the second, Campbell phase of Lake Agassiz may
     have been stable for 200 to 500 years. It was previously
     referred to as Lake Agassiz II (Elson 1957). If the
     intra-Norcross low water phase (Episode II) is valid
     (Episode IV) should now be called Lake Agassiz III.

(9) Northward retreat of the ice margin west of Lake
     Nipigon opened a series of successively lower outlets
     and the level of Lake Agassiz dropped in a series of
     steps to about the Grand Rapids water plane. At the
     end of this time the lake was discharging eastward
     through the Sandy Lake basin, probably into glacial
     Lake Barlow-Ojibway (cf. Fig. 12, intermediate in
     these events). The low water resulted in erosion rep-
     resented by an unconformity at Pine Falls.

(10) An ice readvance (Cochrane ?) in the northeast blocked
     the outlet through glacial Lake Barlow-Ojibway and
     stabilized at the Agutua moraine. Lake Agassiz again
     discharged through the Pikitigushi spillway into Lake
     Nipigon (Fig. 11) and it rose to a level between the
     Stonewall and The Pas waterplanes. The upper silt unit
     was deposited at Pine Falls and the deepening and ice
     advance resulted in the deposition of varved clays over-
     lying sand at Snow Lake. This phase is here termed Lake
     Agassiz IV.

(11) Ice retreat reopened the eastern outlet to the Barlow-
     Ojibway basin -- the water level lowered to the Gimli
     strandline. Disintegration of the ice sheet in Hudson
     Bay opened new lower outlets such as Sachigo, Echoing,
     Hayes, and Bigstone rivers. The Lake level fell accord-
     ingly in a series of steps to the Pipun water plane.

(12) Disintegration of a remnant of the ice sheet lying
     across the Nelson River valley caused Lake Agassiz to
     drain into Hudson Bay prior to 7,300 years ago.

Conclusion

     In this paper, the topographic setting and deposits of Glacial
Lake Agassiz have been outlined and examples of stratigraphic and
geomorphologic evidence necessary to interpret the history of the
lake have been presented. From these, and a background of data too
extensive for inclusion, a hypothetical history of the lake involving
four high water phases separated by three low-water phases has been
presented. The weak links in the chain of evidence are mainly the
details of positions and continuity of water planes (as pointed out
by W.O. Kupsch) and the limited stratigraphic data. Many more data
will come to light in the future, but much evidence was destroyed
by glacier readvances.

     The sequence of events outlined here should be regarded by non-
geologists as an illustration of how evidence can be fitted together
to establish a continuous story of Lake Agassiz. This four episode
history is a substantial advance over the two phase concept (Johnston
1916, Elson 1957) but it still contains much speculation and undoubtedly some fiction.

     Lake Agassiz is vast, but the cordial cooperation, already long
manifest, of researchers involved in its many problems, is speeding
the evolution of a history with fewer weaknesses.

Acknowledgements

This contribution is the result of research supported by grants from the Geological Society of America in 1964 and by the Geological Survey of Canada from 1964 to 1967. I am grateful to these organizations for their generous assistance.

SOME ASPECTS OF THE GEOLOGICAL DEPOSITS OF THE SOUTH END
OF THE
LAKE AGASSIZ BASIN

John A. Brophy

Lake Deposits of the Fargo Area

Through a combination of surface exposures and subsurface data, the stratigraphy of Lake Agassiz deposits in the vicinity of Fargo, North Dakota (Fig. 14) has become reasonably well known. The nature and thickness of these deposits is shown in the following description of a composite section. The detailed description of Units 1, 2 and 3 and the upper 10 feet of Unit 4 was made from a Corps of Engineers high-water diversion cut on the Red River about 1 mile north of Fargo. The remainder of Unit 4 is known from large diameter auger holes dug to the top of the fill for emplacement of cast-in-place concrete pilings for high-rise buildings in Fargo (from the surface downward):

(1) Silt and clay, thin-bedded to laminated except in upper 10 feet where bedding is not evident (probably due to weathering), some minor, gently inclined cross-lamination, oxidized in upper 26 feet, unoxidized in lower 2 feet, no fossils observed------------28 feet

(2) Silt, laminated, unoxidized, containing abundant organic remains, predominantly wood, but including seeds, pollen, insects parts and mollusk shells------6 inches to 2 feet

(3) Clay and silt, thin bedded, locally faintly laminated, unoxidized, no fossils observed---------------- 3 feet

(4) Clay, massive, bedding obscure or lacking, unoxidized, highly plastic, no fossils observed, rests on unweathered drift, generally till----------------------70 feet.

C.O. Rosendahl (1948) identified 39 plant species from unit 2 above. See McAndrews (this volume) for a more recent paleobotanical study of this unit from the Seminary Site. The insect remains and mollusk shells recognized in this unit have not yet been identified.

Unit 4 is interpreted as a deep water Lake Agassiz I deposit, units 3 and 2 as shallow lacustrine and paludal accumulations of the Agassiz I - II interval and Unit I as the deposits of Lake Agassiz II. The wood of Unit 2, radiocarbon dated at about 9900 years ago. (W-388 and W-993) is believed to represent trees killed by the rising waters of Lake Agassiz II, thus providing a good date for the arrival of the transgressing lake.

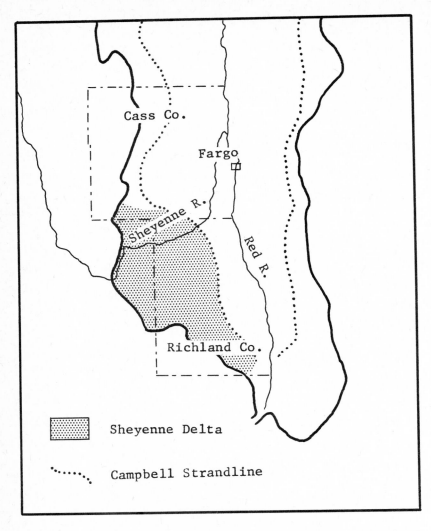

Figure 14.   Map of south end of Lake Agassiz basin in North Dakota
             and Minnesota. Dotted lines mark basin margin.

A subaerial Agassiz I - II interval in the southern basin is indicated also by two factors, first a desiccation zone in the upper part of Unit 4, a local disconformity between Unit 4 and overlying beds, and second linear sand bodies (interpreted as fluvial deposits) intercalated between units 1 and 4. How far this rather simple stratigraphy extends beyond the immediate environs of Fargo is not precisely known. There are some indications, however, that the two major units (1 and 4) can be recognized within an area of at least 100 square miles around Fargo and possibly much farther out. See for example Dennis, Akin and Jones (1950) and Paulson (1953). So far, no evidence of an earlier low-water phase, as recently proposed by Clayton (1966), has been found in the southern part of the basin.

The Sheyenne Delta

Origin

Upham (1895) and Leverett (1932) disagreed on the source of sediments of the Sheyenne Delta which occupies about 800 square miles at the southwest corner of the basin. (Fig.14). Upham believed the sediments were supplied by the Sheyenne River to Lake Agassiz in true deltaic fashion.

Leverett felt that the great size of the Sheyenne Delta (and other Lake Agassiz deltas) suggested that the material was not entirely supplied by inflowing streams. "On the contrary," he says (1932:126-27), "it appears probable that the greater part was contributed directly by the melting ice sheet as its border was receding across them. The Sheyenne area of sand has an abrupt northeast border, like an ice-contact face, rising 30 to 50 feet above the clayey plain to the northeast. The sand on this border is but a few feet thick and covers a highly calcareous, somewhat pebbly clay, which seems best interpreted as a glacial deposit in ponded water."

Upham's earlier view now seems strongly supported by the following recent findings:

(1) Exposures, shallow borings and deep test holes along the steep northeast delta front show only thin-bedded to laminated fine sands, silts and clays beneath an eolian sand veneer. In my studies of many surface exposures and shallow auger holes, none of Leverett's "pebbly clay" was found, though the deltaic beds frequently have abundant pebble-size calcareous concretions. For deep hole data, see Baker (1966). These deposits, which seem best interpreted as deltaic in origin, continue downward about 50 feet below the base of the delta front. Both they and the lake beds to the northeast lie upon a glacial drift surface which has about the same elevation under both (Fig.15).

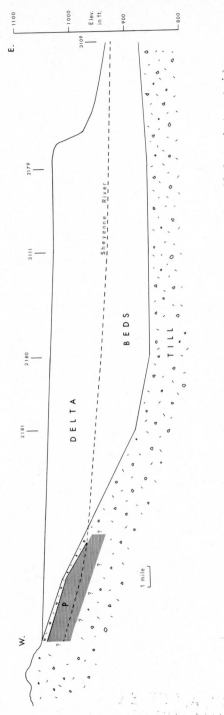

Figure 15. Generalized east-west cross-section of Sheyenne Delta parallel to but outside of Sheyenne River trench. Dashed line is projected water surface curve of descent for Sheyenne River. Numbers above section refer to U.S.G.S. test holes.

(2) New topographic maps (contour interval 5 feet) show that the delta surface declines gently from the Herman level on the west to the Campbell level on the east. This would be the expected gradient for a delta built by the Sheyenne River entering Lake Agassiz from the west, but would be hard to explain as a depositional surface built by a northeastward-retreating ice front.

(3) Map and field studies of the steep northeast-facing edge of the delta show that the morphology and elevation of the steepest break are consistent with origin as a Campbell wave-cut feature.

(4) Though a detailed discussion would not be appropriate here, it now appears that Leverett's evidence for a lake-laid end moraine looping southward across the basin as a correlative continuation of his delta-edge ice-contace face was tenuous at best, and that no truly reliable criteria for a stationary ice-front exist along that line. Leverett considered this moraine a lake-laid extension of his Erskine moraine. On *Glacial Map of the United States East of the Rocky Mountains*, it is labeled "Wahpeton."

Stratigraphy

The description of stratigraphic sequence presented below is the outgrowth of studies of surface exposures along the trench which the Sheyenne has excavated across the northern part of the delta, plus somewhat limited data from various borings and drill holes. Because of great distances between good exposures and a general lack of reliable criteria for correlation, the stratigraphy should be considered tentative.

The oldest unit so far recognized is a series of non-fossiliferous, thin-bedded to laminated fine sands, silts and clays known only from outcrops in the Sheyenne trench near the landward (western) edge of the delta. The texture and bedding of this unit and its position beneath a thin till suggest that it may be a pro-glacial lacustrine deposit. (Fig. 15). If so, it may correlate with sub-till lacustrine deposits recognized elsewhere in the southern part of the Agassiz basin. Sub-drift silt and clay units interpreted as possible older lake beds have been described from Northern Cass County by Brookhart and Powell (1961) from central Cass County by Dennis, Akin, and Worts (1949) and in southern Richland County by Paulson (1953). Its extent, thickness and absolute age are not yet known.

Immediately above these beds in most outcrops is a thin till (Fig. 15), and in several places a north-south striated cobble pavement lies at the contact between the two. The till can be traced westward to the ground moraine behind the delta where it is the surface deposit, locally separated from a lower till by a similarly north-south striated cobble pavement. Eastward the thin till disappears beneath the floor of the Sheyenne trench, but it probably correlates with at least the upper portion of the till known from drilling farther east.

Next youngest are the deltaic deposits, or perhaps more accurately a deltaic-lacustrine complex, which forms an eastward thickening wedge of sediments lying on the till. (Fig. 15). Typically, these sediments are non-fossiliferous, well-bedded (often thin-bedded or laminated), well-sorted, sands, silts and clays. At the head of the delta, where the glacial Sheyenne river entered, these beds coarsen to gravel and coarse sand.

Outside of the Sheyenne trench the delta beds, or eolian sands derived from them, form the surface. Discounting the eolian increment, this surface, traced northeastward from the delta head, slopes gently downward from the elevation of the Herman Beach (about 1070 feet) to its lakeward terminus in an escarpment at about the Campbell Beach level (about 990 feet). The delta beds thus were deposited during the early, high stages of the lake and can therefore be correlated with the lower part of the massive clay unit (Unit 4) of the lake deposits near Fargo.

Eolian sands derived from the sandy delta beds form a cover over much of the delta plain and parts of the Sheyenne trench as well. As a stratigraphic unit the eolian beds are strongly time-transgressive, for while the most intense eolian action was probably early in the subaerial history of the delta (before vegetation was established), new eolian deposits are still being derived from locally exposed sandy delta beds. Morphologically the sand cover varies from a thin, low-relief veneer to highly irregular hills rising as much as 60 feet above the delta surface. Locally a paleosol is found in the top of the delta beds beneath the eolian sand, and multiple paleoregosols occur within the eolian sequence itself.

Within the Sheyenne trench and restricted to it, there are several additional stratigraphic units all of which are younger than the deltaic sequence (Fig. 16). A series of fluvial deposits underlies a series of terraces standing at various levels above the present river. These terraces probably represent the attempts of the Sheyenne river to regrade the delta to the various base levels imposed by the fluctuation of Lake Agassiz, and the best developed of them is graded to the Campbell level. The fluvial deposits which veneer these terraces contain a molluscan fauna and vary in texture from gravel to clay.

At two places in the trench, thin-bedded to laminated fine sand, silt and clay units were found which resemble the deltaic-lacustrine beds except that they contain a sparse fauna of small mollusks. At the top of one of these sequences there is a marly peat, a sample of which from the Mirror Pool site is analyzed paleobotanically by McAndrews (in this volume). Wood from this peat has been dated at 9130 ± 150 years ago (I-1982), a date which is close to the time that Lake Agassiz II is presumed to have dropped from the Campbell level. Both of the known occurrences of these beds lie below the Campbell level in the trench. Considering their position, their nature and the Carbon-14 date, these beds are interpreted as a deltaic-lacustrine fill laid down in the "estuary" created by invasion of Lake Agassiz II water into the

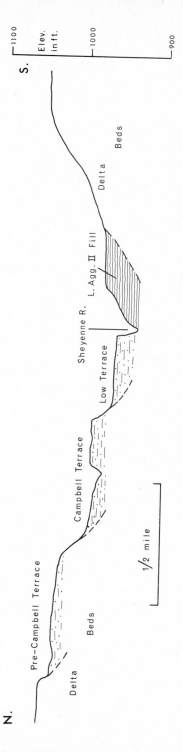

Figure 16. North-south cross section across Sheyenne River trench about five miles west of outer edge of delta.

deep trench cut by the Sheyenne River during the Agassiz I-II low water interval. If this interpretation is correct, they should correlate with the lower part of the silt and clay unit (Unit 1) in the lake sequence near Fargo.

The youngest beds in the trench underlie a low terrace, the top of which is about 18-20 feet above normal stream levels. This terrace apparently was a flood plain until a few hundred years ago, but is seldom reached by modern floods, which in general are confined to the main channel and a series of deep meander-scar channels which cut the low terrace. As shown by Carbon-14 dating, the upper 20 feet of beds under this terrace has been deposited since about 2500 years ago. Wood from about 20 feet below top of terrace (W-1185), dates to 2540 ± 300 years ago. Deposition of sediments near the top of the terrace has occurred as recently as about 235 years ago (I-2093, 235 ± 90 years ago charcoal from one foot below top of terrace). Lithologically this latest increment of deposition is largely fine sand, silt and clay.

History

The following sequence of geologic events is proposed for the delta area:

(1) A proglacial lake was ponded between a southward-advancing late-Wisconsin ice front and high ground to the south, with the ice eventually overriding the lake deposits.

(2) Ice retreat reopened the southern Lake Agassiz basin to lake-water accumulation. The Sheyenne River deposited a delta during the Herman, Norcross and Tintah stages.

(3) During Campbell I stability, the Sheyenne River trenched the delta until it was graded to the Campbell level. Concurrently the northeast edge of the delta was steepened by wave attack.

(4) During the Lake Agassiz I-II sub-aerial phase, the Sheyenne River adjusted to its lower base level by further trenching, probably to below present trench-floor levels.

(5) The rising waters of Lake Agassiz II invaded the trench and a lacustrine-deltaic complex was deposited. Local peat accumulation marked the end of this phase as Lake Agassiz fell from the Campbell II stand about 9100 years ago.

(6) Sheyenne River again cut downward in its trench adjusting to a falling base level and removing much of the Lake Agassiz II fill.

(7) At least one aggradational episode has resulted from
     post-Agassiz readjustment of the Sheyenne, with
     fluvial filling of a somewhat deeper trench up to
     the level of the present low terrace which bounds
     the stream.

(8) At present the Sheyenne appears to be slowly dissecting
     the low terrace.

(9) Eolian activity, which probably began as soon as sandy
     delta beds stood above water, continues at present,
     primarily as blow-out activity in delta beds and
     previously deposited eolian sands.

     Study is continuing on the nature of the various sedimentary
units and their organic contents.

Acknowledgements

The support of the National Science Foundation (Grant GP-1347)
is gratefully acknowledged.

EASTERN OUTLETS OF LAKE AGASSIZ

Stephen C. Zoltai

Introduction

Glacial Lake Agassiz occupied large areas in Manitoba and Ontario, extending southward into North Dakota and Minnesota and westward into Saskatchewan. In the initial high water stages it drained south into the Mississippi River system through Lake Traverse in Minnesota. As ice recession uncovered lower outlets, the lake drained east into the Lake Superior drainage basin (Upham 1896; Leverett 1932; Johnston 1946; Elson 1957). Evidence shows that two, or possibly three high level lakes existed (Elson 1965), separated by significantly lower water stages. It is assumed that the intervening low stages and the initial final low water stages drained to the east (Elson 1957; Laird 1964). Eslon (1957) located the possible eastern outlets, the Brule, Kaministikwia, Kaiashk, Pillar and Pikitigushi channels from erosional features recognized on aerial photographs, but subsequent field observations failed to confirm this function of the Brule and Kaministikwia channels (Zoltai 1963). The other eastern outlets were discussed by Zoltai (1965), but the sill elevations were not determined. This paper describes these eastern outlets and relates their opening and closing to fluctuating ice movements.

Elevation of outlet sills and wave-cut terraces occurring at high altitudes were determined by A.H. Aldred. This was done by interpolation of the Canada Department of Forestry and Rural Development, Forest Management Research Section, Ottawa, Ontario using National Topographic Series maps showing 100-foot contours. The elevations were checked on aerial photographs (scale approx. 1:70,000), using a parallax bar with a graphical correction method, as outlined by Moffitt (1959). The elevations are believed to be accurate within 25 feet. This method was adopted because of the inaccessibility of this heavily wooded area.

The Eastern Outlets

The outlet channels were recognized from erosional and depositional features. Most channels originated in moderately rolling areas of Precambrian bedrock hills having a thin till mantle. The upper reaches of the channels are located in valleys between these bedrock hills or in fault valleys which are now occupied by underfit streams or lakes. The erosive action of water removed the loose material from valley floors, leaving only large boulders. The downstream parts of the channels were cut through lacustrine

107

or outwash sand plains, leaving well defined troughs which are
often floored by gravel. Most channels end in deltaic deposits.
Figure 17 shows the location of these outlet channels, and the
elevation of sills are given in Table 8.

The Kaiashk outlet

This outlet originated in three distinct branches, here named
the Roaring River, Pantagruel and Rabelais Creek channels (Nos. 1a,
1b and 1c in Fig. 17   and Table 8).   A fourth branch, the Awkward
Lake channel (1d), initially entered into the main Kaiashk channel,
but later it assumed an easterly direction, possibly after eroding
a drift barrier. The main Kaiashk channel ends in a lacustrine
and outwash sand plain of later origin which obliterated any deltaic deposits that may have existed.

The sill elevations show that initially all four branches
functioned simultaneously, eroding the thin drift cover in their
beds to bedrock in all but the Pantagruel channel. Later the
sill of this channel was also eroded to bedrock, which, being at
a lower elevation, reduced the volume of water in the other channels. The Pantagruel channel is the largest and broadest of the
tributaries comprising the Kaiashk outlet.

Pillar and Armstrong outlets

The main channel of the Pillar outlet was composed of four
narrow branches, the Chief Lake, Track Lake, Badwater Lake and
Little Caribou Lake Channels (Nos. 2a, 2b, 2c, and 2d). The tributaries followed valleys and faults among bedrock, but the main
Pillar channel was eroded in outwash sand and gravel of the nearby Nipigon moraine, ending in a large delta.

The main Pillar channel follows the Nipigon moraine, nowhere
crossing it in spite of the presence of low passes. The little
Caribou branch, however, crossed the moraine before joining the
main channel, and later it established a direct easterly route,
independent of the Pillar channel, after eroding the Armstrong
outlet (No. 3). The courses taken by the channels suggests that
the Chief, Track and Badwater lakes channels functioned first,
forming the main Pillar channel after becoming confluent. Ice at
the Nipigon moraine caused the Pillar channel to flow to the south,
but later a partial withdrawal of ice opened the Little Caribou
channel, joining the well entrenched Pillar channel. Further ice
withdrawal then permitted the Armstrong channel to drain directly
to the east.

Big Lake outlet

Farther north the Big Lake outlet (No. 4) was eroded across
the Nipigon moraine at lower elevations than the Pillar and Armstrong outlets. The channel is often scoured to bedrock and

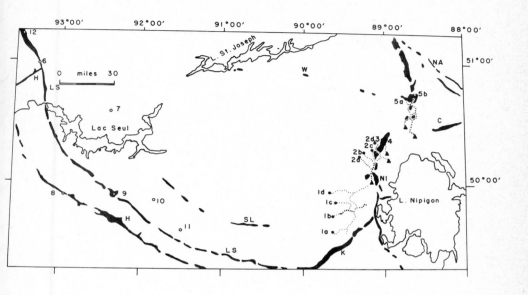

Figure 17. Map of area containing the eastern outlets of Lake
Agassiz, showing moraines and location of wave-cut
bluffs. Outlets are dotted and numbered 1 to 5, as
in text. Land features with bluffs are numbered 6
to 12. Deltas are shown by triangles. Moraines are
identified by letters: H, Hartmann; LS, Lac Seul; SL,
Sioux Lookout; NI, Nipigon; W, Whitewater; NA, Nakina
moraines; C, Crescent moraine; and K, Kaiashk interlobate moraine.

TABLE 8

PRESENT ELEVATIONS OF OUTLET SILLS

Outlet	Channel	Elevation (feet)	Location Longitude	Location Latitude
1. Kaiashk	1a. Roaring R.	1375	89°38'30"	49°37'30"
	1b. Pantagruel Cr.	1375	89°37'00"	49°44'15"
	1c. Rabelais Cr.	1420	89°34'15"	49°49'45"
	1d. Awkward L.	1425	89°39'30"	49°57'30"
2. Pillar	2a. Chief L.	1265	89°20'00"	50°16'00"
	2b. Track L.	1245	89°14'45"	50°16'30"
	2c. Badwater L.	1252	89° 8'30"	50°18'45"
	2d. Little Caribou L.	1256	89° 7'30"	50°23'30"
3. Armstrong	3. Little Caribou L.	1256	89° 7'30"	50°23'30"
4. Big Lake	4. Big Lake	1175	88°58'30"	50°24'00"
5. Pikitigushi	5a. Raymond R.	1125	88°44'00"	50°44'30"
	5b. Clearbed L.	1125	88°39'00"	50°46'30"

contains numerous large boulders, and ends in a small delta.
Although this channel is well defined, it appears to be too small
to accommodate the outflow of Lake Agassiz.

Pikitigushi outlet

This outlet system originated in two channels, the Raymond
River and Clearbed Lake channels (Nos. 5a, 5b). These channels
followed an intricately forked course through the Nipigon moraine
and among tablelands, ending in a large delta.

Shore Features

Shore features are of limited occurrence in the area (Fig.
17) because materials suitable for the formation of these features
rarely occurred at elevations exposed to wave action. The terraces
at locations 6, 8, 9 and 12 occur on high portions of moraines and
the others on high, isolated kames. Examination of aerial photographs shows that the highest portions of these moraines and kames
were inundated only at location 11. Deep kettles occur on the
unmodified parts of these moraines and kames. All these high drift
hills show four to six lower strandlines, but their elevation was
not determined. Prest (1963) noted that the highest parts of the
Lac Seul moraine in the northwestern part of the map (Fig. 17)
escaped modification by the lake. The most northerly of these
ridges is at location 12.

The present elevations of the wave-cut terraces (Table 9)
show that they were cut by a high level stage of Lake Agassiz.
The scarp at location 11 is at a lower elevation than the other
terraces, and records a lower stage of the Lake, having been
completely submerged in the high water stage.

Correlation of Outlets and Shore Features

The water plane indicated by shore features at high altitude
was reconstructed in the assumed direction of uplift, N30°E, and
the outlet levels were plotted normal to this line (Fig. 18).
This direction of uplift was based on Johnston's (1946) work who
found it to be between N27°30'E in the main Lake Agassiz basin,
and on Farrand's (1960) work who established it to be N30°E in
the Lake Superior basin.

Figure 18 shows that the terraces at high altitudes correlate
well with a beach at Emo, Ontario, about 85 miles southwest of the
map area, which is believed to be an Upper Campbell beach (Johnston
1946). The completely submerged kame at location 11 falls below
this water plane, but is well above the Kaiashk outlet. The

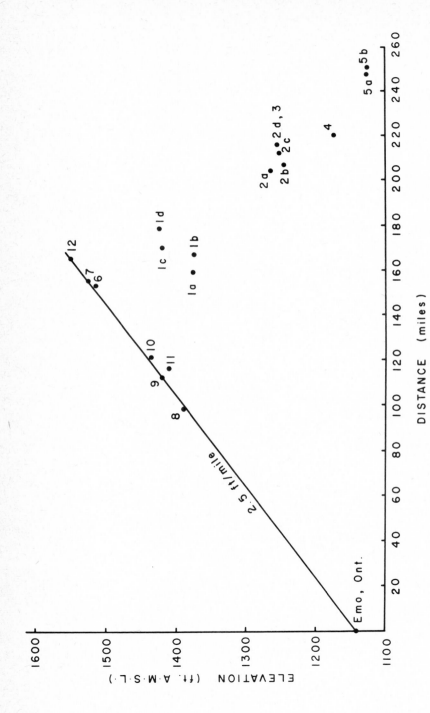

Figure 18. Water plane reconstructed in the assumed direction of uplift, N30°E, based on present elevations of shore features and outlet elevations. Bluffs (Nos. 6 to 12) and outlets (Nos. 1 to 5) are shown by dots.

TABLE 9

PRESENT ELEVATIONS OF HIGH TERRACES

Number Fig. 17	Elevation (feet)	Location	
		Longitude	Latitude
6	1515	$93^{\circ}11'00''$	$50^{\circ}57'00''$
7	1525	$92^{\circ}25'15''$	$50^{\circ}39'45''$
8	1390	$92^{\circ}54'00''$	$49^{\circ}53'30''$
9	1420	$92^{\circ}18'30''$	$49^{\circ}55'15''$
10	1435	$91^{\circ}48'30''$	$49^{\circ}52'15''$
11	1410	$91^{\circ}27'30''$	$49^{\circ}39'15''$
12[a]	1550	$93^{\circ}00'00''$	$51^{\circ}11'45''$

[a]Data from Prest (1963).

indicated rate of uplift is about 2.5 feet per mile, a rate higher than that obtained by Johnston (1946) in the main Lake Agassiz basin. Johnston's data show that the rate of uplift increases to the northwest, thus the greater rate of uplift indicated by the water plane is acceptable and appears to be of the right order of magnitude.

The Kaiashk outlet elevations fall about 160 feet below the high shore features, as shown in Fig. 18.   The sill elevations of the Pillar outlet are about 220 feet lower than the Kaiashk outlet, indicating a considerably lower lake level. Because of the great distance between these outlets and lower beaches of Lake Agassiz, the correlation of these outlets with lake stages is not possible. The highest beaches occurring on the Windigo moraine at 1350 feet elevation, some 110 miles north of Lake St. Joseph (Prest 1963) may be related to the Pillar outlet system.

It is unlikely that the Big Lake channel represents an outlet of Lake Agassiz. A lowering of the lake level of 85 feet from the Pillar to the Big Lake outlet would have elevated the land above the lake level, severing any connection with the main part of Lake Agassiz. This channel probably served as an outlet of a small ice-marginal lake.

The outlet elevations of the Pikitigushi channels at 1125 feet are on the estimated level of Glacial Lake Nakina (Zoltai 1965), a long, narrow ice-marginal lake. The outlet elevation of the Jellicoe outlet of Lake Nakina farther to the southeast is 1130 feet (Zoltai in press), showing that the Pikitigushi channel was another, perhaps later outlet of Lake Nakina. However, Lake Agassiz may have drained into Lake Nakina farther north (Prest, personal communication).

Correlation of Outlets With Ice Movements

Outlets of the first high water stage of Lake Agassiz were not found in the east. The lowest stable water level of this lake was at the Norcross beach (Elson 1965), and the lake drained to the south through the Lake Traverse outlet. The lake was confined in the north by a receding ice front and in the east by Precambrian highlands. Field observations (Zoltai 1961) showed that the ice front became stationary at the Hartmann moraine in the west. A more extensive retreat may have occurred in the east, possibly through more rapid wastage in glacial lakes in the Superior and Nipigon basins. This could have uncovered lower outlets in the east, possibly in the Kaiashk area. Any such outlets, however, were obliterated by the subsequent Valders readvance which built the Kaiashk interlobate moraine and the Dog Lake moraine (Zoltai 1965).

The second high stage of Lake Agassiz was created by the advancing Valders ice, blocking the eastern outlets (Elson 1957). The lake level rose to the Norcross beach, but was later lowered to the Upper Campbell beach (Elson, personal communication). At this stage the lake was confined in the northeast by ice at the Hartmann moraine (Zoltai 1965). The ice then receded and later readvanced to the Lac Seul moraine. The extent of this retreat is not known, but a retreat and readvance of at least 20 miles is indicated by overridden varved clays in the Lac Seul area. A retreat of similar extent in the east would have opened outlets in the Kaiashk area. If an outlet was indeed opened, then the level of Lake Agassiz was first lowered and later raised to the Upper Campbell level as this outlet was closed by the readvance to the Lac Seul moraine. This lake level was maintained until the resumption of ice retreat following a recessional pause at the Sioux Lookout moraine (Fig. 19).

Ice retreating from the Sioux Lookout moraine again became stationary a short distance farther north, after uncovering the Kaiashk outlet of Lake Agassiz (Fig. 20). Further ice retreat of unknown magnitude followed. If the ice retreated far enough, the outlets in the Pillar area would have been opened. Any further lowering of the lake levels through lower outlets would have exposed so much land above lake levels, that an eastern outlet in the map area would be improbable.

Ice then advanced from the east to the Nipigon moraine, abutting on the stagnant ice mass of the northern ice lobe which was stationary at the Whitewater moraine. This readvance deflected the main channel of the Pillar outlet along the ice front at the Nipigon moraine (Fig. 21).

Further ice retreat followed, accompanied by uplift of the land as the weight of the ice was removed, and large areas, including the Pillar outlet emerged as dry land. A further renewal of glacial activity resulted in a readvance to the Nakina moraine in the south (Zoltai 1965) and to the Agutua moraine in the north (Prest 1963). Lake Agassiz possibly inundated a long, narrow bay in front of the Agutua moraine (Fig. 22) to an elevation of 1200 feet (Prest, personal communication). Lake Nakina, a long, narrow lake was formed in front of the Nakina moraine. This lake was initially confluent with a high water lake stage in the Superior basin, but crustal uplift severed connection with the Superior basin and the independent Lake Nakina was established (Zoltai in press), consisting of two basins separated by shallows. One basin drained from the east into the Lake Nipigon basin through the Jellicoe outlet (Zoltai in press), and the other through the Pikitigushi outlet. Lake Agassiz may have drained into Lake Nakina along the ice front, possibly through several channels as the melting ice uncovered lower areas. Upon the resumption of the final ice retreat lower outlets may have become available in the north, but continuing uplift makes it improbably that these drained to the east.

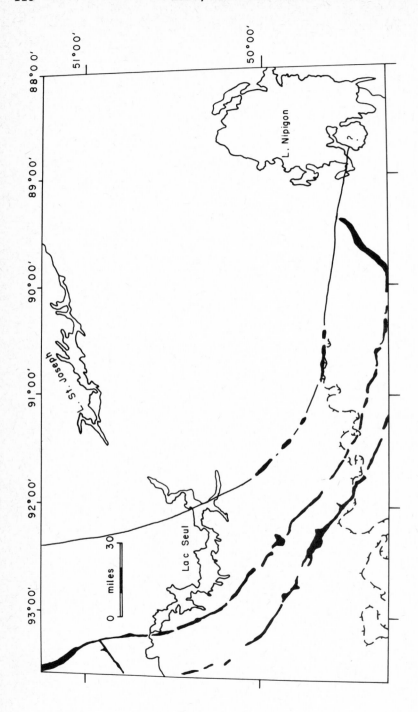

Figure 19. Eastern extent of Lake Agassiz during the Upper Campbell stage, with ice front at the Sioux Lookout moraine.

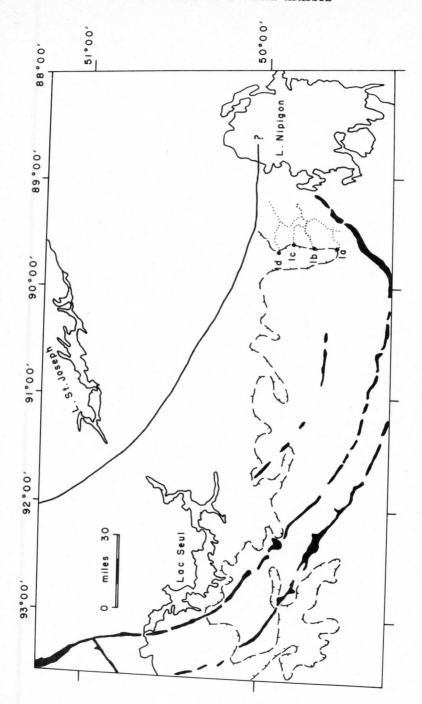

Figure 20. Eastern extent of Lake Agassiz during the Kaiashk outlet stage.

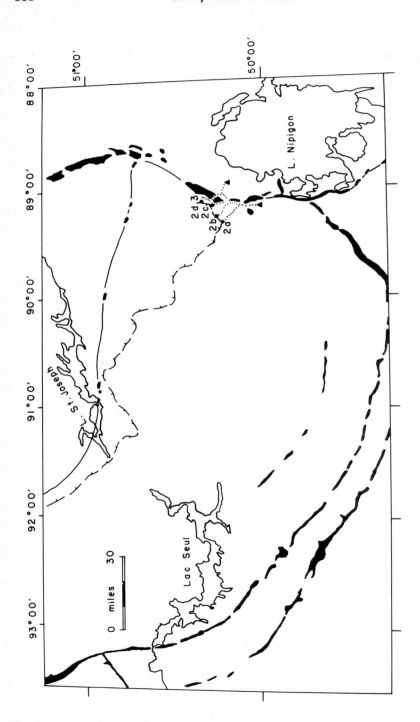

Figure 21.   Eastern extent of Lake Agassiz during the Pillar outlet stage.

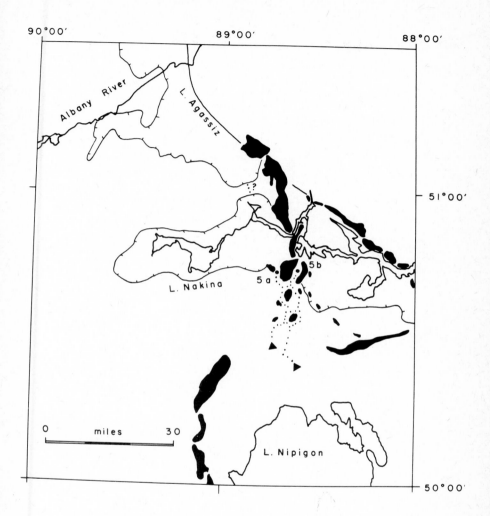

Figure 22. Eastern extent of Lake Agassiz with Lake Nakina during the Pikitigushi outlet stage.

Summary Conclusions

1. No outlets were found in the east which drained Lake Agassiz
   when the lake level stood at or above the Campbell beaches.

2. On two occasions ice retreats and readvances may have opened
   and closed eastern outlets prior to the final lowering of the
   lake, but the readvances which closed these outlets also
   obliterated any evidence of them. Consequently, there is no
   direct evidence of these early eastern outlets, and indications
   of two early low water stages of Lake Agassiz should be obtained
   in the undisturbed part of the main Agassiz basin.

3. The early eastern outlets were closed by the Valders readvance
   and by the ice readvance to the Lac Seul moraine. The indication
   that lake levels reoccupied the beaches the lake built before
   the opening of the lower outlets implies that little crustal
   uplift took place during the low water intervals, and that these
   intervals were of short duration.

4. The early eastern outlets may have lowered the lake level by as
   much as 380 and 160 feet, respectively, but complete drainage
   of the lake could not have taken place at this time.

5. Direct evidence indicates three eastern outlets of Lake Agassiz
   at a later stage, namely the Kaiashk and Pillar outlets, and a
   possible indirect drainage through the Pikitigushi outlet. Lake
   levels controlled by the Pillar outlet may have preceded by a
   lower water stage, followed by a rise to this outlet as ice
   readvanced to the Nipigon moraine.

THE SOUTHERN OUTLET OF LAKE AGASSIZ

Charles L. Matsch and Herbert E. Wright, Jr.

Introduction

In 1868 General G.K. Warren, Chief of Engineers, United States Army, ascribed the wide Minnesota River Valley to the erosive effects of a great river that drained Glacial Lake Agassiz, which had been recognized since 1823. This southern outlet stream, named Glacial River Warren by Upham in 1884, was abandoned when the level of Lake Agassiz dropped below the elevation of the outlet gorge as glacier ice melted from the basin and opened lower outlets in the northeast.

Careful mapping by Upham (1895), Leverett (1932), and others showed that before the southern outlet was abandoned the lake stood at four successively lower levels, long enough to produce extensive, well-developed strand features. These strands and their elevations near the outlet are the Herman (1060 feet), Norcross (1040 feet), Tintah (1020 feet), and Campbell (980 feet). The intervals between successive strands represent periods when the lake level dropped too rapidly for such features to develop.

The major southern outlet channel of Glacial Lake Agassiz begins as a wide, shallow trough just north of White Rock, South Dakota. At White Rock it is a distinctive channel 50 feet deep and almost three miles wide, trending southwest. As it enters the north-facing slope of the till upland that forms the southern rim of the Red River Lowland, the channel becomes deeper and narrower -- the segment now occupied by Lake Traverse. Two miles north of Browns Valley, where it crosses the Big Stone Moraine, the channel floor is 175 feet below the moraine crest and just a half mile wide. This deep and narrow stretch turns southeastward and continues for 16 miles through high terrain to Hartford Beach, where it bends to the east and then southeast to Ortonville. In this stretch, now occupied by Big Stone Lake, the channel widens to over two miles, then constricts to one mile at Ortonville.

From Ortonville the regional upland slope is southeasterly, and the channel, following this trend, shallows and widens as it crosses successively lower topography. Two miles east of Odessa, the valley floor is almost 5 miles wide and 100 feet deep, and it is dotted with small bedrock hills that once were islands in the outlet river. Downstream from this point the valley branches into a wide system of narrow channels, which coalesce into a single channel again at Montevideo.

121

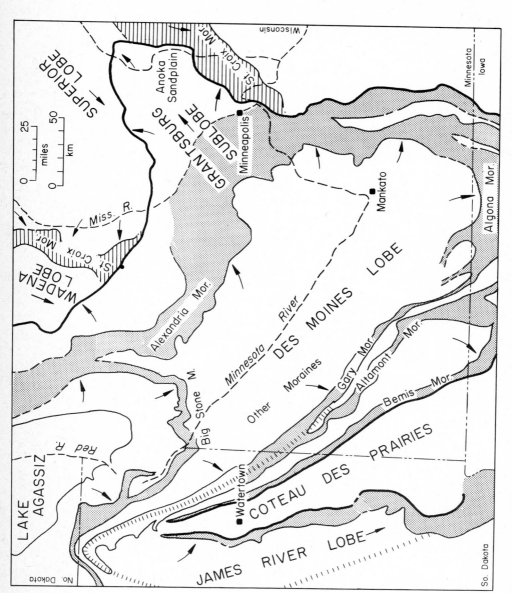

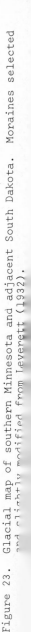

Figure 23. Glacial map of southern Minnesota and adjacent South Dakota. Moraines selected and slightly modified from Leverett (1932).

At Granite Falls the regional slope reverses, and the relief between the valley floor and adjacent upland surface heightens. Eleven miles northwest of Redwood Falls the valley breaches a high moraine-mantled bedrock ridge, beyond which the upland slopes to the southeast and east.

In this 125-mile stretch between White Rock and Redwood Falls, the landforms hold the record of several thousand years of glacial recession and Lake Agassiz history. Because the strandlines are perhaps the most distinctive geomorphic feature of Lake Agassiz, and because their levels are controlled by the activities of the outlet stream, it is important to understand the history of the River Warren. This paper describes the morphology of the outlet valley and summarizes the probable sequence of events in the valley area just before the formation of Lake Agassiz and while the lake was being drained by River Warren. This study, under consideration for several years, has only recently been made possible by the completion of topographic maps of the region by the U.S. Geological Survey. Field work was supported by the Minnesota Geological Survey. Discussions with Raymond T. Diedrick, Soil Conservation Service, and his unpublished manuscript, called attention to otherwise unnoticed features in parts of the area.

Glacial Retreat in Western Minnesota

The dominating topographic control on the Wisconsin glaciation of western Minnesota was the Red River bedrock lowland, which now drains to the north. Its continuation to the southeast is the Minnesota River lowland. To the west is the flat-topped Coteau des Prairies, which presents a steep east-facing slope almost 1000 feet high. This wedge-shaped upland, pointing north, served to split the southward-moving ice sheet into two prominent lobes, the James Lobe on the west and the Des Moines Lobe on the east. Lateral moraines of these two lobes were piled on the top and flanks of the Coteau during successive phases of glaciation, leaving a wedge-shaped area between that became progressively wider during recession of the ice.

The Des Moines Lobe reached its terminus about 14,000 years ago (Wright and Ruhe 1965) at the Bemis Moraine, whose type locality is on the west side of the lobe on top of the Coteau (Fig.23). The position of the east margin of the Des Moines Lobe at this time was not marked by a prominent moraine but rather by a thin overlap on older drifts.

Shrinkage of the Des Moines Lobe, followed by a stillstand or readvance, led to the construction of the broad Altamont Moraine along the eastern edge of the Coteau (western side of the ice lobe). On the east side of the Des Moines Lobe the correlative position is not certainly identified, but it may be at the Alexandria Moraine complex.

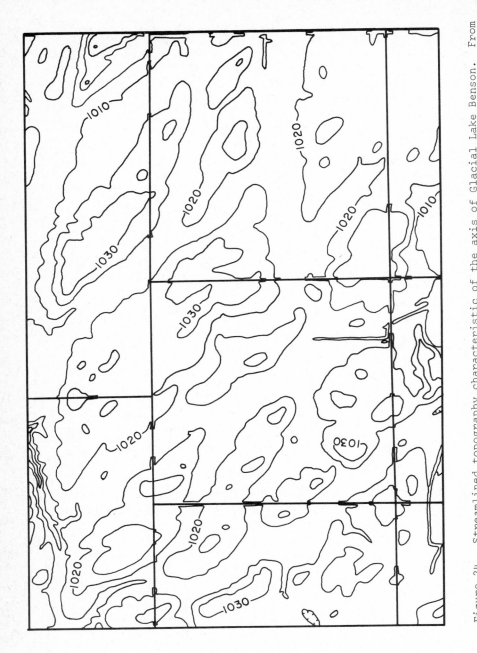

Figure 24. Streamlined topography characteristic of the axis of Glacial Lake Benson. From the Montevideo, Minnesota quadrangle, 7½-minute series.

Further withdrawal produced additional lateral moraines on the eastern escarpment of the Coteau, as well as end moraines in the lowlands, until the narrowed lobe was destroyed through much of southern Minnesota, probably by 13,000 years ago. A major marker in this retreatal phase is the wide Big Stone Moraine, which was built across the present divide between the Red River and the Minnesota River. As the lobe wasted from this position, water was ponded between the ice front and the Big Stone Moraine, marking the beginning of Lake Agassiz.

Glacial Lake Benson

As the ice melted to its position at the Big Stone Moraine north of Ortonville, a small, roughly triangular basin was exposed. This basin, whose major axis trends southeast, stretched from Ortonville nearly to Redwood Falls, a distance of approximately 75 miles. A broad, shallow bay reached eastward beyond Benson, Minnesota.

It was flanked on the southwest by the moraine-draped Coteau, on the north by the Big Stone Moraine, and on the east partly by the Alexandria Moraine and partly by other recessional moraines of the Des Moines Lobe. The highest closed contour on the perimeter of this basin, between 1050 and 1070 feet, crossed the present Minnesota River Valley 11 miles northwest of Redwood Falls along a minor moraine that lay athwart a high bedrock ridge. The deepest part of the basin lay generally between Granite Falls and Odessa, with lowest elevations below 1000 feet.

Diedrick (1967), concluded on the basis of extensive soils surveys that the basin was occupied by a lake to an elevation of about 1050 feet. For this lake he proposed the name Glacial Lake Benson. Independent geomorphic and stratigraphic work by the authors supports his conclusion.

Although now deeply entrenched by the waters of River Warren, the axis of this basin is preserved in a few places and marked by a belt of streamlined hills. These drumlin-like features are confined to a 2- to 4-mile belt on the upland margins of the present valley. They are especially well developed near Granite Falls and Montevideo (Fig.24). At Appleton they are partially subdued because outwash from the Pomme de Terre River was later deposited among them.

Typically the hills, composed of till, are arranged *en echelon* with a strong northwest-southeast orientation. They are 3 to 6 times longer than they are wide, ranging in length up to 2 miles. The hills are separated by narrow, flat-floored channelways surfaced with boulders or with sand and gravel. This streamlined topography is restricted to elevations below 1030 feet, and it contrasts sharply with the more irregular topography at higher elevations.

This distinctive ensemble of hills and channels is not a small drumlin field, despite the superficial appearance, nor is it a series of lateral moraines on the sides of a very narrow ice lobe (Leverett 1932, p. 105; Leighton 1957, p. 1037). Instead, the hills were fashioned by strong currents generated during rapid drainage of Glacial Lake Benson. This lake did not last long, because it left only weak and discontinuous strandlines and a thin veneer of bottom sediment. When the lake reached 1050 feet or slightly higher, it spilled over its dam near Redwood Falls and cut rapidly through the moraine, which may still have been cored with dead ice. The rapid outflow of the lake streamlined the irregular bottom topography along the axis of the basin and per-haps flushed out some of the sediment that had been deposited. Small bodies of water continued to occupy deeper portions of the basin. Meltwater streams draining from the retreating ice front had probably formed deltas in Lake Benson, and when the lake drained the streams continued to pour outwash fans into the basin, partially filling the shallow channels between the streamlined hills or completely burying lower ones to form a graded surface. The fan of the Whetstone River, for example, grades from 1050 feet at Ortonville to 1010 feet near Appleton, where it joins the fan of the Pomme de Terre River.

Big Stone Moraine

The Benson basin constricts northward and closes rather sharply against the south side of the upland that forms the southern rim of Lake Agassiz. The crest of this upland is the Big Stone Moraine, with elevations exceeding 1200 feet. The ice-marginal Little Minnesota River crossed the upland obliquely through a long, low intermorainic sag (perhaps segmented into small lakes) now occupied by Big Stone Lake, finally entering the much lower Benson basin, where it joined with the Whetstone and Pomme de Terre Rivers.

Formation of Lake Agassiz

As the Des Moines Lobe retreated from the Big Stone Moraine between Browns Valley and Ortonville, water became ponded in the newly exposed Red River Basin. At first there was a narrow lake named Lake Milnor (Fig.25), which had an elevation of 1100 feet. The South Dakota portion drained across low points in the Big Stone Moraine, which may still have carried stagnant ice blocks, and it incised several small channels, including Cottonwood Slough. Near Browns Valley the overflow waters joined the Little Minnesota River, which thereupon cut into its outwash surface, leaving a terrace at 1100 feet. The Minnesota portion of Lake Milnor formed no strand and left only small patches of lake sediment, but in spilling across the moraine it cut the small channel of Fish Creek, which joined the Little Minnesota River at about 1070 feet. From Browns

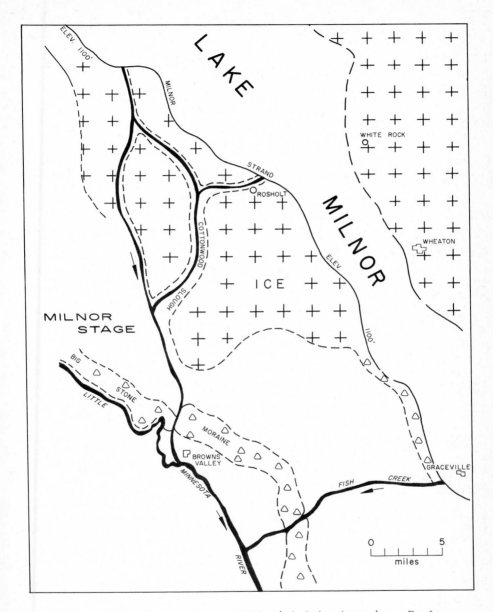

Figure 25. Lake Milnor stage of Glacial Lake Agassiz. Early outlets drained through stagnant ice blocks to the incipient Little Minnesota River.

Valley the now erosive waters flowed across the till upland to
Ortonville and into the Benson basin, trenching the outwash fans
of the Whetstone and Pomme de Terre Rivers.

Continued wastage of the ice allowed the small Lake Milnor
to enlarge into Lake Agassiz proper and to occupy two lower spillways, one near Wheaton and the other at Cottonwood Slough (Fig.26).
Both outlets were deepened to form small gorges, and the earlier
outlets (such as Fish Creek) were abandoned. Below Browns Valley
the Big Stone Moraine was entrenched more deeply, uncovering large
boulders in the drift, which began to form a lag deposit on the
channel floor. From Odessa southward the waters of this outlet
stream (River Warren) were dispersed throughout a wide system of
auxiliary channels which eventually entrenched 20 to 30 feet into
the Pomme de Terre outwash (Fig.27). Several of these were guided
by the streamlined till hills of the old Lake Benson floor. These
waters joined to form a single course below Montevideo, following
the axis of the small Benson basin. The waters of several small
lakes, remnants of Lake Benson, drained through outlets graded to
River Warren at this stage. One such channel now is occupied by
the lower course of the Chippewa River.

When Lake Agassiz had spread north around both sides of the
wasting ice lobe, the outlet channel between Browns Valley and
Ortonville was armored by a boulder pavement, so the lake became
stabilized at the Herman strand (1060 feet), dated by Carbon-14
as 11,700 years ago. Four miles south of Browns Valley the boulder-
paved terrace is at 1050 feet. Farther downstream, as at the Ortonville Fish Hatchery, similar terraces occur between 1040 and 1000
feet. The higher level probably represents the bed of River Warren
at the Herman stage of Lake Agassiz.

Subsequent retreat of the ice allowed the Lake to enlarge into
Canada. The outlet stream deepened and widened its channel, and
the Cottonwood outlet was abandoned (Fig.28). Dissection of the
channel-bottom pavement may be attributed to increase in the volume
and thus the competence of the outlet stream as Lake Agassiz enlarged. Subsequent lake stabilizations occurred at 1040 feet
(Norcross), 1020 feet (Tintah), and 980 feet (Campbell), in response
to halts in downcutting of this southern outlet. Boulder pavements
at elevations lower than 1050 feet in the gorge below Browns Valley
are remnants of the floors of the successively lower outlet channels.

As the lake waters dropped from the Herman shoreline, River
Warren between Odessa and Milan deepened its course, abandoning many
branches of the former drainageway. Erosion after the Tintah shoreline had been developed resulted in the formation of a single channel in this stretch (Fig.29). The river split around a large island southeast of Milan, then it converged again to a single channel
at Montevideo. During this period of lake drainage (to the Campbell
strand at 980 feet), the channel below Ortonville was being excavated partially through bedrock. Finally, about 9200 years ago, ice
retreat uncovered lower Canadian outlets, and River Warren was beheaded.

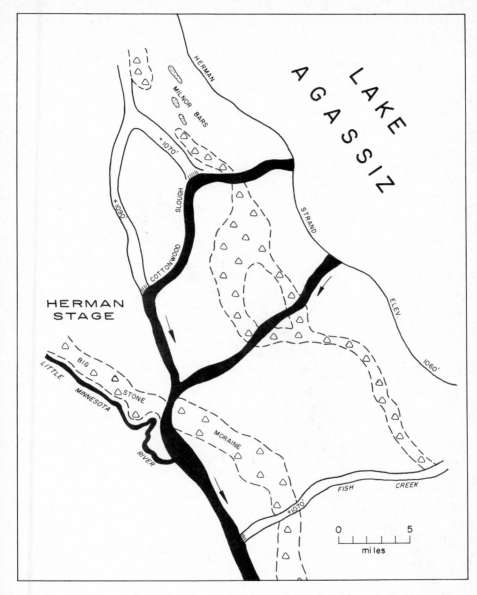

Figure 26.   Herman stage of Lake Agassiz.   Some earlier outlets
are abandoned.   Lake level is stabilized by development
of a boulder pavement in the gorge downstream from the
Big Stone Moraine.

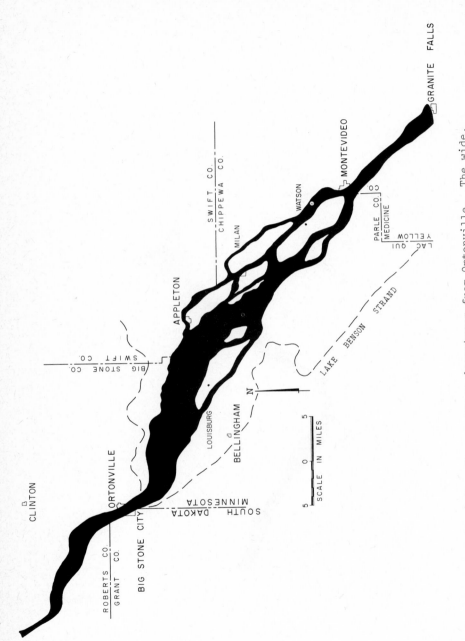

Figure 27. Herman stage downstream from Ortonville. The wide, shallow river flows along the axis of the just-drained Glacial Lake Benson, branching around islands of drift.

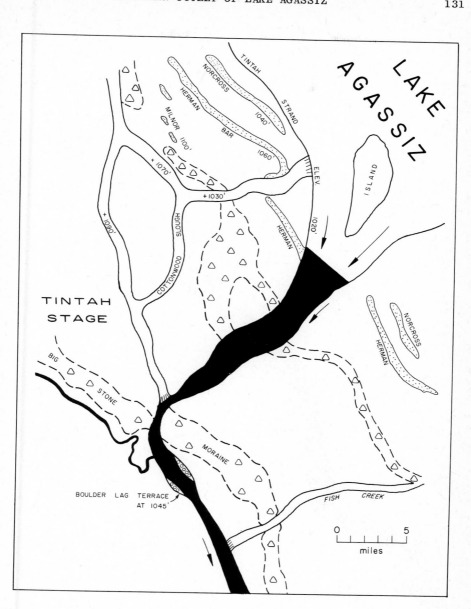

Figure 28.   Tintah stage of Lake Agassiz. Cottonwood Slough is
abandoned during deepening and widening of the outlet
stream.

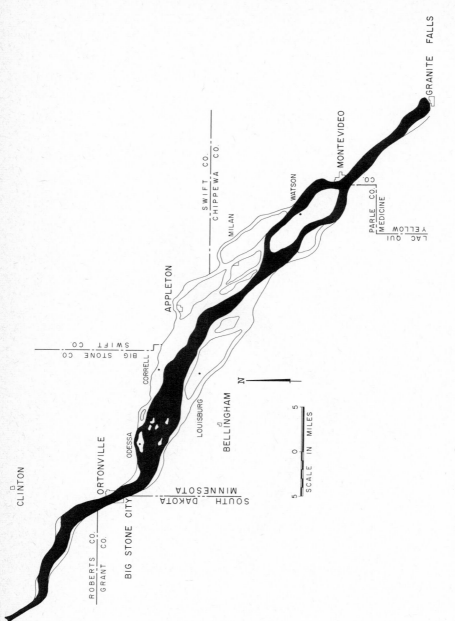

Figure 29.   A post-Tintah stage downstream from Ortonville. The
auxiliary channels are abandoned as the river trenches
more deeply. A few islands, some of bedrock, appear in
the channel near Odessa.

Tributary streams thereafter deposited alluvial fans in the abandoned gorge, segmenting the floor of the gorge into a series of long, shallow lakes. The alluvial fan of the little Minnesota River dams Lake Traverse (Fig.30), the fan of the Whetstone River dams Big Stone Lake, and that of the Lac Qui Parle River dams Lac Qui Parle Lake (Fig.30).

Summary and Discussion

The distinctive features of the southern outlet area of Lake Agassiz partly predate Lake Agassiz itself. The drainage of Lake Benson caused the formation of streamlined hills on its floor -- a kind of miniature scabland. The lower (western) channels among the hills were later partially filled with outwash of the Little Minnesota, Whetstone, and Pomme de Terre Rivers, leading from the Big Stone Moraine. As the ice retreated north of this moraine, Lake Milnor and finally Lake Agassiz discharged waters through some of the same channels. Successive lowering of the outlet level, apparently determined by formation and then breaching of boulder-paved floors in the narrow segments of the outlet valley, ultimately led to the confinement of the river to a single channel. Subsequent history of the river, after diversion of the Lake Agassiz outlet to the north, has involved a slow alluviation of its floor, largely through deposition of alluvial fans by tributaries and sedimentation in lakes between the fans. Ultimately alluviation may cause the once-branched channels to join again, as they have far down the river near St. Paul at Grey Cloud Island as a result of this post-glacial regime of alluviation.

Lake Agassiz strandlines, so well defined and continuous at least in the United States portion of the basin, clearly record long periods of stable lake level, and their subsequent southward tilting provides the evidence for crustal uplift caused by glacial unloading. Because the Herman, Norcross, Tintah, and Campbell strandlines all relate to events at the southern outlet, further discussion on the factors controlling stability of lake level may be pertinent.

The Lake Milnor stage of Lake Agassiz was probably quite temporary -- or at least the level was not stable very long. This small proglacial lake was crowded between the retreating ice front and the Big Stone Moraine. It may actually have consisted of two separate bodies, one in South Dakota draining through Cottonwood Slough and other outlets, the other in Minnesota draining through Fish Creek. The lake had simply risen until it overflowed the moraine at these several points, and the outlets immediately began to cut down, probably at different rates. Lake Milnor formed no good strandlines, so it probably did not persist at any level very long. It is recorded only by patches of lake sediment above the Herman level and by the outlets themselves.

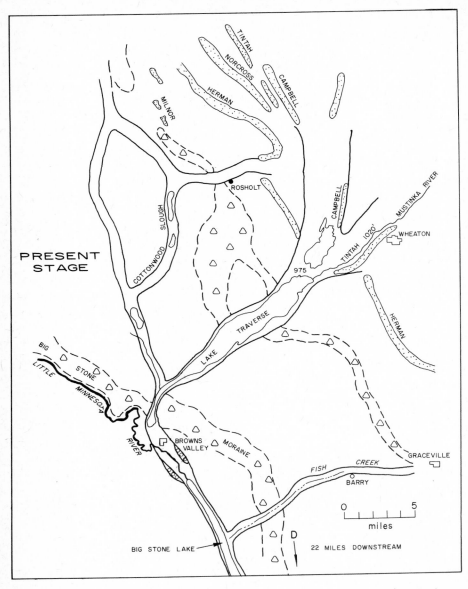

Figure 30.   Lake Agassiz outlet area at the present time.   An
alluvial fan at the mouth of the Little Minnesota
River dams Lake Traverse.

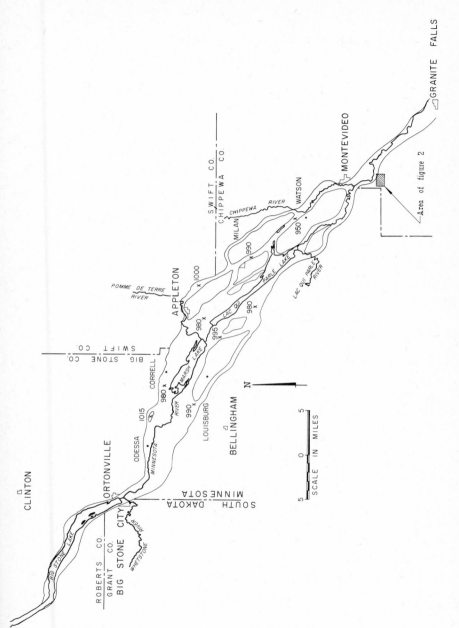

Figure 31. Present valley below Ortonville. Alluviation by tributaries has segmented the valley into a series of long, shallow lakes.

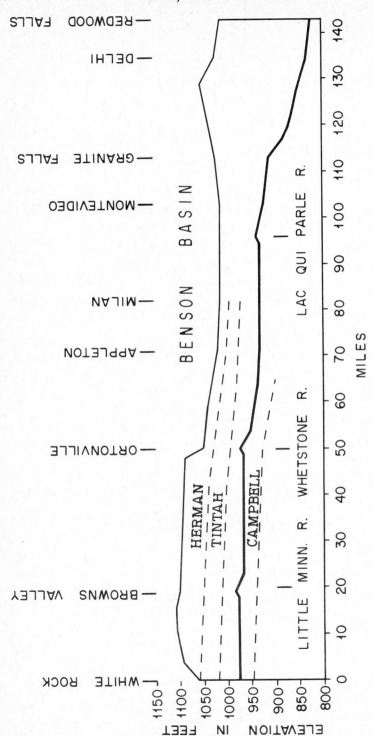

Figure 32. Top profile is the pre-River Warren topography. Dashed profiles are inferred channel floors of River Warren at various lake stages. Heavy line is present valley profile showing segmentation by tributary alluviation.

As the ice retreat continued, Lake Agassiz became larger, and the volume and erosive power of the outlet streams increased. Adjustments continued, with abandonment of smaller outlets, until finally only Cottonwood Slough and the Wheaton channel were occupied. In time, however, deep erosion through the broad Big Stone Moraine had freed so many large granite boulders from the till that the channel floor became paved with them, and incision of the floor ceased. The spillway thus became stabilized, and the Herman strandline was formed as far north as the Canadian boundary. The center of the Red River lowland may still have been filled with ice at this time, although the prominence of the strandline implies strong waves and thus a broad lake.

Lake Agassiz was lowered below the Herman strandline about 11,700 years ago, according to a radiocarbon date on the basal sediment of a small beach pond that began to form as soon as the strandline was abandoned (Shay, 1965). Several explanations may be offered for the lowering of the lake level -- all related to the activity of the outlet stream.

(1) Upham (1895) suggested that after the ice sheet had retreated the outlet area was rhythmically uplifted, and that the outlet stream was eroded immediately to the same degree. Strandline formation marked pauses in this uplift. Subsequent study of the beaches has shown that the uplift is primarily far north of the outlet area and that most of it is long delayed after ice retreat rather than immediate.

(2) Chamberlin (in Upham 1895, p. 244) suggested that the lowering of the outlet by stages might be attributed to a stoping process, as the result of the river's encounter with alternating material of unequal resistance. The drift as exposed between Browns Valley and Ortonville does not seem to have the complexity of structure necessary for such a mechanism to be effective.

(3) Knickpoints on the River Warren could migrate upstream to the spillway, which could thus be lowered abruptly. The only knickpoint on the river profile clearly available for this process is the one originally at the head of the Lake Benson basin. Here, the initial river gradient was probably as high as 40 feet per mile in contrast to a few inches per mile in the segment upstream through the Big Stone Moraine. The upstream migration of this knickpoint could not have resulted in the breaching of the boulder pavement of the Herman terrace because the toe of the initial debouchment slope (the fan-head surface of the Glacial Whetstone River at 1050 feet) was higher than the subsequent downstream segment of the outlet floor (1040 feet, Fig.32). However, the rapid upstream migration of this break in slope probably contributed to the rapid development of the sharp gorge across the drift upland and to the subsequent production of the boulder pavement on the channel floor. Other knickpoints from positions farther downstream can not be easily identified. Certainly knickpoints represented by waterfalls over the flat-lying Paleozoic beds 200 miles downstream are too far away to have had the necessary effects.

(4) Retreat of the ice front may have enlarged Lake Agassiz so that the volume of discharge was increased enough to breach the boulder pavement on the channel floor. Such an explanation is used by Bretz (1951a,b) to explain the various lake stages in the Saginaw Basin, Michigan, and the lowering of the Glenwood stage of Lake Chicago in the Lake Michigan basin. There the increased discharge resulted from the abrupt addition of water from the Lake Huron basin, when the ice front retreated enough to open the Grand River between the two basins. This explanation seems to be the most satisfactory for the periodic erosion by the River Warren through successive boulder pavements. It probably requires ice retreat in three distinct stages. Such periodic ice retreat is indicated by the several moraines in Ontario north of Minnesota (Zoltai 1961, 1963, 1965), but the relation between these moraines and the strandlines in question is unknown at present.

By the time of the Campbell stage (980 feet), Lake Agassiz extended far into Canada, and its strandline is strong and easily traced, at least along the western side of the lake and along the Minnesota portion of the eastern side. The spillway level can not easily be determined because of subsequent alluviation of the floor. The swampy floor at White Rock is 976 feet. Lake Traverse (975 feet) has at least 30 feet of water and sediment, so the Campbell level in this segment is below 945 feet. The base of the alluvial fan of the Little Minnesota River at Browns Valley is at least 25 feet deep and thus is at an elevation below 940 feet. Farther downstream, just below Ortonville, where the Whetstone River has deposited 30 feet or more of fill, the floor is below 920 feet. Much farther downstream, in the Mississippi River below St. Paul, River Warren at its Campbell stage flowed in a channel 250 feet below the outwash terraces of the Des Moines Lobe (Zumberge 1952).

The Campbell strandline of Lake Agassiz was abandoned when the ice front retreated far enough to the north to uncover a lower outlet to the east into Lake Superior. This event occurred after 9200 years ago, according to a radiocarbon date for wood in a Campbell beach ridge in northern Minnesota. The southern outlet was thereby beheaded, and tributary streams immediately began to segment the valley with alluvial fans, forming a series of long lakes. These are gradually being filled with sediment, and eventually the valley floor will once again have a smooth gradient with a continuous river.

The stratigraphy of the Lake Agassiz sediments has led several investigators to postulate at least one "drying interval" -- a time when the southern outlet was abandoned before the lake returned once again to the Campbell level. The principal evidence for the drying interval is the occurrence of plant detritus and shore sediment buried by deep-water lake deposits. Such an interval was elaborated first by Johnston (1946). Clayton (1966) proposes two intervals to account for the wide range of radiocarbon dates.

Such drying intervals left no record at the southern outlet. In order to explain some radiocarbon dates on the Assiniboine delta of Lake Agassiz in Manitoba, Elson (1957) proposed that after the drying interval the lake returned not only to the Campbell level but to the Norcross level. He postulated that during the drying interval the Little Minnesota River had built a fan across the outlet near Browns Valley, thus allowing Lake Agassiz to rise to a higher level before spilling over in the south. Field study of the area around Browns Valley and the Little Minnesota River has revealed no geomorphic or stratigraphic features that can be attributed to such a high earlier damming.

The lack of evidence for a drying interval (between Lake Agassiz I and II) in the southern outlet does not, of course, deny that such a low lake level occurred or that the Campbell strandline was occupied two or three times several hundred years apart. Perhaps the Campbell strandline itself might hold such evidence in its detailed stratigraphy or morphology. Also, if at least 1000 years intervened between first and last occupations of this level, the strandline might be expected to split northward, as a result of crustal tilting in the interim.

On the other hand, perhaps Lake Agassiz I had its lowest southern outlet at the Norcross strandlines. Ice retreat into Canada could open an eastern outlet. Modest readvance could close this outlet and divert the lake once again to the south, up to the Norcross outlet a second time; but with the larger volume of water at this time the outlet river could breach the boulder pavement and cause dissection to the Tintah level. If the lake had two drying intervals, the Tintah boulder pavement could be breached in the same way, for dissection to the Campbell level. Final retreat of the ice then brought abandonment of the Campbell level.

It should be emphasized that the southern outlet area holds no positive evidence for such a complex history. The relations at the outlet are compatible with hypotheses for only one drying interval, or several, or none at all. The proof for drying intervals might better rest on the stratigraphy of the lake sediments themselves.

Conclusion

Lake Agassiz was the largest Pleistocene proglacial lake in North America, and through the River Warren it fed the largest river system on the continent. The massive features of the River Warren valley, when compared to the size of the modern Minnesota River that occupies it today, provide as strong a reminder of the great events of glaciation as does Lake Agassiz itself. By means of this great outlet stream, the indirect effects of glaciation were carried far from the glaciated area -- for 1500 miles to the Gulf of Mexico -- and many of the features of erosion and deposition in the middle and lower reaches of the Mississippi

River owe their origin to this great epoch of valley entrenchment
and to subsequent filling that reflects the adjustment in river
regime since the beheading of River Warren. Clarification of
the controlling factors and the chronology in the source area
should lead to a greater understanding of the sequence of events
far downstream and of the processes that control river regime.

Acknowledgements

     This paper is Contribution No. 53 from the Limnological
Research Center, University of Minnesota.

LINEAR SAND AND GRAVEL DEPOSITS IN THE SUBSURFACE

OF GLACIAL LAKE AGASSIZ

Thomas C. Winter

Introduction

The history of Glacial Lake Agassiz has been interpreted largely from surficial glacial deposits. Test drilling for ground water has revealed complexities in the subsurface that add new perspectives to the interpretation of the history of the Lake.

Hydrologic studies in Minnesota by the U.S. Geological Survey have resulted in the discovery and delineation of several unconnected linear sand and gravel deposits in the subsurface of Glacial Lake Agassiz. Besides their obvious importance as aquifers, the deposits are of interest to the glacial geologist for two reasons:

1. they indicate the size and form of the ice-contact and outwash deposits within the lake deposits and the relation of these to the surrounding finer-grained lake sediments, and

2. they indicate the relative volume of sediments deposited by Lake Agassiz I and Lake Agassiz II.

The units all lie within the area covered by the Campbell stage of Lake Agassiz (Fig. 33). Unit A, in Kittson and Marshall Counties, is four to six miles wide and forty miles long. Unit D, in Marshall County, is about one-fourth mile wide and five miles long. Unit C, in Clay and Wilkin Counties, is about one-half to one mile wide and thirty miles long. Unit B, in Traverse County is about a half mile wide and six miles long.

The geology of part of Unit A (Halma and Lake Bronson area) was discussed by Schiner (1963). Unit C was mentioned by Dennis *et al.* (1949), on the basis of a few drill holes east of Moorhead, but its extent was unknown. Unit D (near Stephan, Minnesota) was described by Maclay and Schiner (1962), but the interpretation of its origin is somewhat modified in this report.

The Linear Sand and Gravel Deposits

Unit A

Unit A is a complex deposit of interbedded clays, silts, sands, and gravels that lie in a linear depression (Fig.34). In general, the coarsest sediments in the unit are in the Halma-Lake Bronson area (sections C and B), where sand and gravel extend from the surface to depths greater than 150 feet. These coarse materials

141

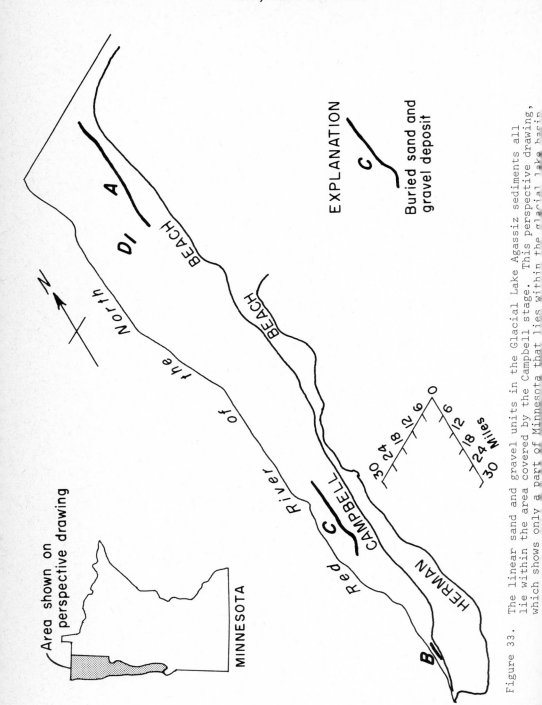

Figure 33.   The linear sand and gravel units in the Glacial Lake Agassiz sediments all
lie within the area covered by the Campbell stage. This perspective drawing,
which shows only a part of Minnesota that lies within the glacial lake basin,

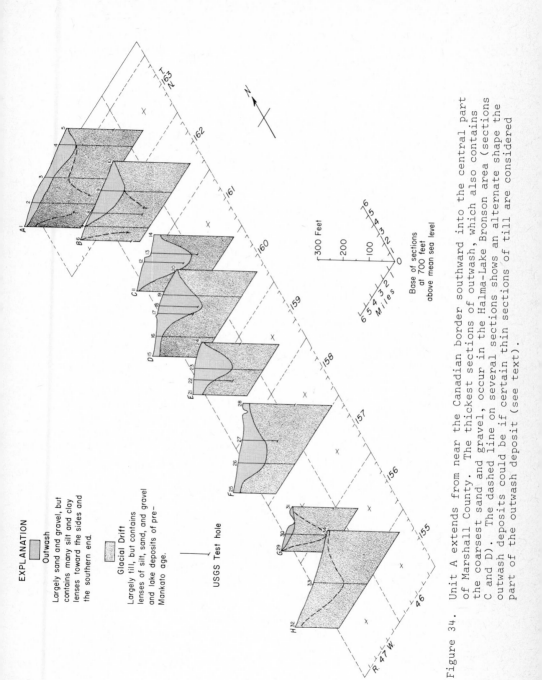

Figure 34. Unit A extends from near the Canadian border southward into the central part of Marshall County. The thickest sections of outwash, which also contains the coarsest sand and gravel, occur in the Halma-Lake Bronson area (sections C and D). The dashed line on several sections shows an alternate shape the outwash deposits could be if certain thin sections of till are considered part of the outwash deposit (see text).

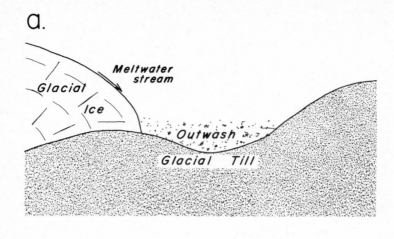

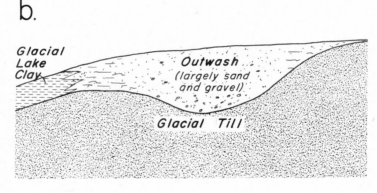

Figure 35.   Generalized sections of unit A shows the origin of the
             deposit.

        a.   Meltwater streams flowing from the glacial ice,
             which lay in the central part of the Red River
             lowland, deposited outwash adjacent to the ice.
             The sediment was prevented from spreading eastward
             by the high bank of till on the east side of the
             channel.

        b.   With melting of the glacial ice, the outwash became
             interfingered with the Lake Agassiz sediments to the
             west.

grade to finer sediments -- fine sands, silts, and clays -- toward the edges and sides. The eastern boundary of the linear depression is till, which is exposed at the surface or is buried by thin deposits of clay and/or fine sand. The elevation of the east bank is about 1,000 feet above mean sea level. The western side is also bounded by till, but here it is covered by a thicker section of Lake Agassiz clays and silts. The elevation of this edge generally is between 850 and 930 feet above mean sea level. The base of the linear deposits is at about 800 feet elevation. Northward from the Halma-Lake Bronson area the linear depression becomes shallower and section A has only a hint of a channel on its eastern side. The enclosed sediments, although finer, are still largely sand. Here, too, the sediments are finer toward the edge of the depression. Southward from the Halma-Lake Bronson area the depression also becomes shallower and is nearly non-existent in section G, here the sediments are considerably more fine grained than those to the north, being largely clay to fine sand.

Unit A is believed to be outwash deposited along the east side of the glacial ice lobe as a kind of kame terrace by a superglacial meltwater stream (Fig. 35). The linear depression probably already existed, possibly as an inter-morainal lowland, but the bottom could have been scoured slightly during the early stages of stream flow. The stream emitting from the glacier was prevented from spreading eastward by the high bank of glacial till on the east side of the depression, so it flowed along the edge of the ice until it could enter the pro-glacial lake at the south end of the ice. Most of the coarse material was dropped by the stream in the Halma-Lake Bronson area, and as it flowed southward toward the lake the decreased velocity caused finer and finer material to be deposited.

The coarse outwash reaches a higher elevation than the western edge of the linear till depression, so ice must have been present to the west. Also, the source of the outwash must have been a glacial stream because there is no known evidence of a source area to the east of the deposit.

The subsurface geology of the area is complicated by the presence of multiple sections of older (pre-Mankato) Lake Agassiz deposits and till. The outline of the channel on the various sections was drawn at the top of the uppermost till in each hole. According to this interpretation the channel deposit would be post-Mankato in age, formed when the Mankato ice was receding from the Red River lowland.

Thick sections of water-laid material underlying till in several holes suggest an alternate interpretation. In holes 2 and 3 along Section A about thirty feet of sand underlie thin sections of till, and in hole 2 this is underlain by a very thick section of clay. Likewise, in holes 7 and 8 in section B very thick sections largely of clay are separated from the linear depression by thin sections of till. The same is true for hole 30 in section G and hole 33 in section H. The shape of the channel along the section, if the thin amounts of till are disregarded, is shown by the dashed line on the various sections. If the channel were to be interpreted

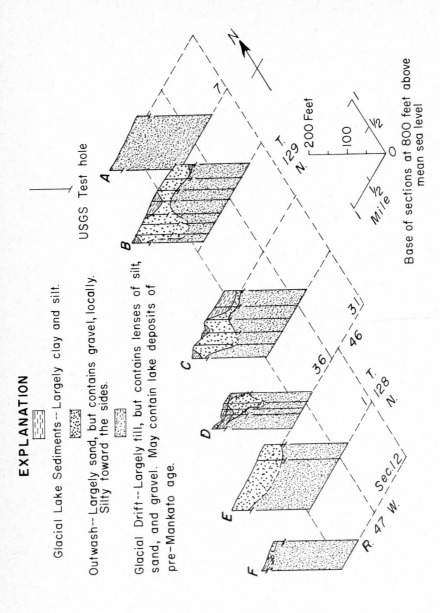

EXPLANATION

Glacial Lake Sediments--Largely clay and silt.

Outwash--Largely sand, but contains gravel, locally. Silty toward the sides.

Glacial Drift--Largely till, but contains lenses of silt, sand, and gravel. May contain lake deposits of pre-Mankato age.

USGS Test hole

Base of sections at 800 feet above mean sea level

Figure 36.   Unit B consists of over 100 feet of sand where it lies in a linear depression in the underlying till. The unit is generally less than a mile wide and about six miles long.

with these relations it would change the age to at least pre-Markato,
assuming the till is from the last glacial advance. This age is
supported to a certain degree by a radiocarbon date of greater than
36,000 years ago on wood from a drill hole in the village of Lake
Bronson, supposedly from the channel deposits. (The laboratory
number of this radiocarbon sample could not be located, nor could
the exact location.)

The difficulty in this second interpretation, where certain
tills are disregarded, lies in deciding which till, if any, should
be included within the outwash deposits and which actually form
the boundary of the outwash deposits. The complexities of the
subsurface in this area (see Schiner, in press) could not be shown
on sections at the scale shown on Fig. 34 but the outwash channel
could take on many different shapes, or not be a channel at all.
It was because of these uncertainities that it seemed most logical
to draw the boundary of the outwash at the top of the uppermost
till.

Unit B

The axial portion of unit B consists largely of fine to medium
sand, locally, with some coarse sand (Fig.36). The sand grades to
very fine sand and silt both eastward and westward along its length.
The absolute depth of the sand deposits is unknown because the
power auger used to drill the holes has a limit of 100 feet. The
bulk of the linear deposit lies above the general level of the
underlying till, but where the sand is thickest it lies in a narrow
linear depression. Section A is drawn on the basis of two holes
about one mile apart and both penetrated till only. It is possible
that the deposit extends northward between the two holes, but if it
does it must be smaller than it is farther south and probably fine-
grained. The southern limit of the deposit probably is between
sections E and F, but it could possibly swing westward into South
Dakota somewhere between the two sections.

Unit C

Unit C consists of fine sand to gravel (Fig. 37). In general,
the coarser material, mostly medium to coarse sand, is in the axial
and lower part of the unit. The few occurrences of gravel are in
several holes in section C, the central and lower part of section J,
and the western side of section K. The sand in unit C grades, both
eastward and westward, into very fine sand, silt, and clay. It is
difficult to determine in small-scale subsurface relationships
whether the material grades into or interfingers with the fine-
grained, lacustrine silts and clays. The internal structure of the
sand body itself, as best as can be determined by drilling, is very
complex, with much interfingering of fine sands with medium and
course sands and silts. This vertical and lateral variation suggests
an alluvial origin of the sand unit itself. The main body of unit
C is above the general level of the underlying till at most places,
but in section A through F a narrow steep-sided linear depression

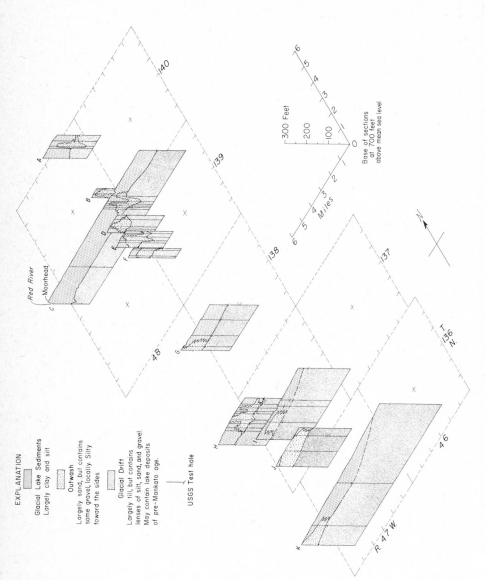

EXPLANATION

Glacial Lake Sediments
Largely clay and silt

Outwash

Largely sand, but contains
some gravel, locally. Silty
toward the sides

Glacial Drift

Largely till, but contains
lenses of silt, sand, and gravel
May contain lake deposits
of pre-Mankato age.

USGS Test hole

Figure 37.   Unit C is a narrow ridge of sand generally less than a
mile wide and over thirty miles long.   The sand contains
much gravel in the area east of Moorhead (T.139N.)

in the underlying till is filled with sand. This depression may actually extend the full length of the unit, as suggested by section H, but the control is not so close in the southern part of the deposit as in the northern, and it was not found in four of the five southern sections. Throughout most of its length the unit is covered by silt and clay, but in a few localities it comes close to the surface, and near section D there are a few gravel pits in it. The unit is longer than is shown in this report, but the absolute length is unknown. Section A indicates that unit C becomes smaller to the north and probably does not extend much beyond here. The drilling was stopped with this section because of the reduced size of the deposit. The southern extent is also unknown, but might extend into North Dakota. Further test drilling is needed in this area.

I believe that units B and C are similar in origin, although they might not have been contemporaneous. They are bounded by silt and clay on both sides. Because there is no indication of a source area for the sand from the highlands to the east, the source must have been from the glacial ice. If the ice lobe lay along the axis of the Red River valley, it must have been relatively narrow in the case of both units, because they are both less than ten miles from the Red River. As the lobe narrowed the pro-glacial lake probably extended up the lowland along its sides (Fig. 38). Small meltwater streams and/or sheetflow flowing from the glacial ice into the pro-glacial lake would have dropped the coarse-grained materials first and carried the fine materials further into the lake. This would explain the separation of the sand from the shore-line deposits of the lake. With further reduction in the size of the ice lobe, the western side of the sand unit would have been exposed to open water and the sand then became interfingered with the fine-grained lacustrine sediments being deposited. The generally fine-grained texture of the sand unit suggests that the meltwater streams flowing from the ice had a fairly low competence. Unit B may have been the result of one stream, but Unit C was probably the result of several. The occurrence of sand and gravel in sections C and D suggest a relatively larger stream in the area east of Fargo-Moorhead.

A modification to the above interpretation should also be considered. The sand and gravel deposits could be ice-crack fillings. If this were the case, it would be necessary to have ice on the eastern as well as the western side of the deposits. Instead of the meltwater streams flowing from the glacial ice into a pro-glacial lake, they would flow into an ice crack where the sand and gravel would be deposited. Upon melting of the adjoining ice, the deposits would be in the waters of Glacial Lake Agassiz, where their edges would become interfingered with the clays and silts being deposited in the lake (Fig. 39).

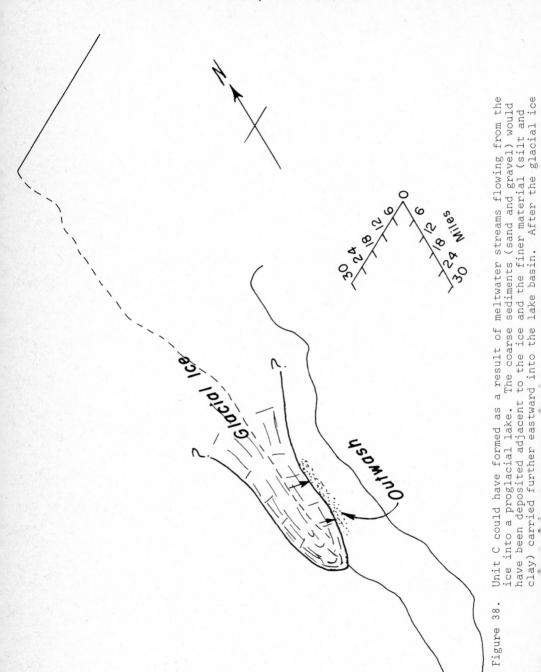

Figure 38. Unit C could have formed as a result of meltwater streams flowing from the ice into a proglacial lake. The coarse sediments (sand and gravel) would have been deposited adjacent to the ice and the finer material (silt and clay) carried further eastward into the lake basin. After the glacial ice

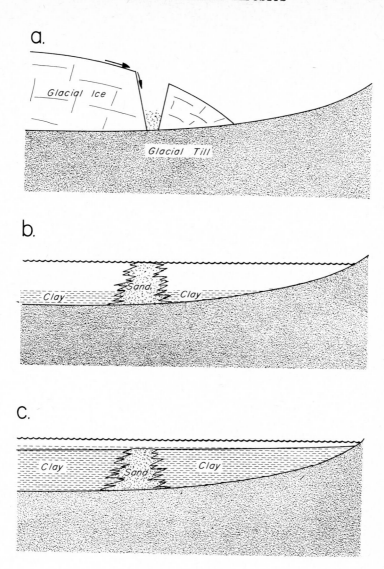

Figure 39.   Unit C could also have formed as a result of an ice
             crack filling process: (a) meltwater streams flowing
             from the glacier would have deposited sand in a large
             crack in the glacial ice; (b) after the ice melted
             lake clays would have accumulated on both sides of the
             sand ridge during an early stage of Glacial Lake Agassiz;
             (c) a later stage of Lake Agassiz (probably Lake Agassiz
             II) would then have deposited a thin layer of clay over
             much of unit C.

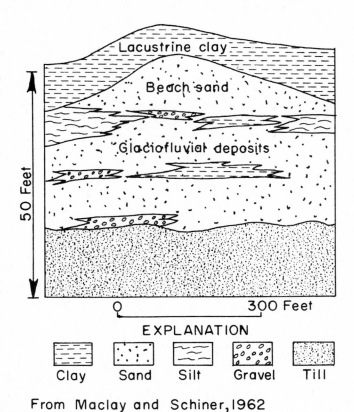

From Maclay and Schiner, 1962

Figure 40.   Generalized section across unit D shows sand overlying
              till with the upper part formed into a beach ridge. The
              sand was probably deposited in much the same way as
              described for units B and C.

Unit D

Unit D is not so thick or extensive as units A, B, and C - the thickest section of sand is about seventy feet in the northern part of section 27, T.157 N., R.48., about four miles south of Stephan, Minnesota.

This deposit was described by Maclay and Schiner (1962) and was interpreted as a beach ridge overlying glacial fluvial sediments which were deposited contemporaneously with the Mankato till (Fig. 40). According to their interpretation the upper part of the large body of glacio-fluvial sand was exposed along the shoreline of a low stage of Glacial Lake Agassiz and was reworked into a beach deposit. Nearly the entire sand deposit is covered by lacustrine clays, which were deposited during a subsequent higher stage of the lake. This seems like a logical interpretation of the origin of the deposit, but I suggest an alternative based on both a re-examination of the data and indications the other deposits described in this report. Most drill holes in the deposit indicate that the sand described as glaciofluvial and intimately associated with the Mankato till largely overlies the till and actually could just as likely be interbedded with the lake deposits (Fig. 40). If this is true, the formation of the deposit could be identical as that for units B and C. The beach deposit in the upper part of the sand could have occurred in either case as the receding shore line of Lake Agassiz I reached the location of the sand deposit. The lake clays overlying the sand were probably deposited by Lake Agassiz II, which extended to the Campbell beach about fifteen miles east of this deposit.

Relationships to the History of Glacial Lake Agassiz

The form and sedimentary relationships of the sand and gravel deposits described above suggest that each was deposited as a single unit along a different segment of the east side of the ice lobe. It is unlikely that the fluctuating ice front came to a standstill and that sand-laden meltwater streams flowed from the ice at exactly the same place more than once. Furthermore, all the units rest directly on till, so they must have been deposited with the first sediments in the early stages of Lake Agassiz, probably while the Herman beach (and possibly later beaches) were being formed. If this is the case, nearly the entire thickness of Lake Agassiz sediments, which are contemporaneous with the sand and gravel units as shown by the gradational changes of sediment types, was deposited during the existence of Lake Agassiz I. Only a thin section of the sediments would be attributed to Lake Agassiz II, the clay overlying the sand and gravel in much of units C and D. Sediments of Lake Agassiz II are difficult to detect in units A and B, which are situated in the shoreline section of Lake Agassiz II, where clays do not overlie the sand. Lake Agassiz II probably merely reworked the uppermost sediments of these sand and gravel units.

Summary

     Four linear sand and gravel deposits have been mapped in the
subsurface of Glacial Lake Agassiz. Unit A, in Kittson and Marshall
counties, consists of over 150 feet of materials ranging from silt
through course gravel, deposited in a depression parallel to the
east side of the ice lobe and bounded on the east by till. Units
B and C in Traverse, Wilkin, and Clay counties, consists of over 100
feet of silt through medium gravel, deposited by streams flowing
from the ice sheet into a pro-glacial lake, where the coarser sediments were deposited adjacent to the ice front. As the ice front
retreated to the west the sand interfingered with clays in the centra
part of the Red River lowland. An alternate interpretation is that
the sediments in streams flowing from the ice were deposited in large
ice cracks. Upon melting of the ice bounding the cracks the sand
became interfingered with the clay being deposited on both sides of
it in the proglacial lake.

     Unit D, in Marshall county, consists of about ten to seventy
feet of silt and sand. This unit was described briefly and interpreted by Maclay and Schiner (1962) to a beach ridge overlying
glaciofluvial material contemporaneous with the till. However, I
believe its origin is similar to that of units B and C.

     The units were deposited at an early stage of Glacial Lake
Agassiz. The great thickness of the units, with the associated
silts and clays on one or both sides indicates that the bulk of
Lake Agassiz sediments was deposited during the existence of Lake
Agassiz I. The silt and clay overlying units B, C and D were
probably deposited by Lake Agassiz II which extended over all the
units.

POSTGLACIAL UPLIFT -- A REVIEW

Walter O. Kupsch

Introduction

Postglacial uplift is a broad subject dealt with in introductory geology classes as prime evidence for the reality of isostasy and isostatic compensation, "An equilibrium condition in which elevated masses such as continents and mountains are compensated by a mass deficiency in the crust beneath them. The compensation for depressed areas is by a mass excess." (Howell, *et al* 1960:156)

It should be stated that I have never done any research on either the concept of isostasy or glacial uplift and that the following review is based on secondary sources only. The literature on the topic is voluminous and within the short time available to me it has been possible only to scan some of the more comprehensive works. The present paper is therefore not to be regarded as a review of any substance but only as a collection of some questions which arose when reading general accounts, mainly on the textbook level, dealing with postglacial uplift. I am raising these questions at the peril of exposing my own ignorance. Persons with a better knowledge of the subject may very well be able to answer most of them or to show that some are based on a misunderstanding on my part of the basic concepts and working methods involved.

General Concept

Because I am using Arthur Holmes' (1965) textbook for classes in general geology, it appears appropriate to start the review with the following quotation:

> *During the recession of the continental ice-sheets of Europe and North America conditions were highly favourable to the development of widespread marginal lakes* [such as Lake Agassiz] *(Fig. 515)* [here reproduced as Fig.41]. *At the time of maximum extension of the ice the less mountainous parts of the underlying floor were depressed into a shallow bowl by the isostatic effect of the load of ice. The thickness of the ice reached 8,000 feet or more, tapering off towards the margins. The corresponding subsidence of the crust, where the load was greatest, would therefore be over 2,000 feet; sufficient, that is, to depress vast areas of the rock surface well below sea-level. Such is the condition of Antarctica today. During the retreat of the ice the crust was gradually unloaded*

155

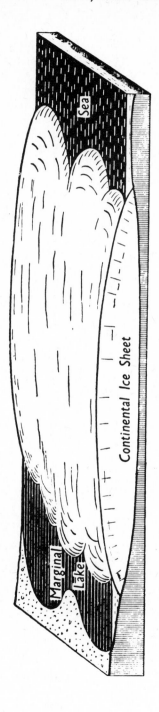

Figure 41. Crustal depression. The diagram illustrates the isostatic
depression of a land surface loaded by a continental ice
sheet and the consequent development of marginal lakes,
such as Lake Agassiz, during the recession of the ice.
Vertical scale and slopes are greatly exaggerated. The
diagram fails to show the earth's curvature which on this
scale (the North American ice sheet having covered as
much as 40° of arc in its longest dimension) should have
been taken into consideration. After Holmes (1965:684).

*and isostatic recovery worked in from the margins, though
with a considerable lag. Consequently, for thousands of
years there were large tracts, abandoned by the ice, that
sloped towards and beneath the receding ice-front. Many
of these became giant lakes while others were invaded by
the sea. The isostatic recovery already achieved since
the disappearance of the ice is clearly demonstrated by
the emergence of beaches now locally preserved at various
heights above sea-level, and by the tilted attitude of
many lake terraces. Moreover, the fact that the shores
of Hudson Bay and the Gulf of Boothia are steadily continuing to rise shows that the process of restoring
isostatic equilibrium is still going on (Holmes 1965:
683-684).*

The general concept of the earth's crust depressed under the
weight of a continental glacier and readjusting itself after the
disappearance of the ice follows a discussion on isostasy and
isostatic readjustment which in part reads as follows:

*It may happen that certain processes disturb the pre-
existing isostatic balance much more rapidly than it
can be restored by deep-seated rock-flowage in the
mantle. For example, when the last of the thick
European and North American ice-sheets melted away
between, say, 11,000 and 8,000 years ago, these regions
were quickly relieved of an immense load of ice. The
resulting uplifts which then began are still actively
in progress. Far above the shores of Finland and
Scandinavia there are raised beaches which show that
a maximum uplift of nearly 900 feet has already occurred
(Fig. 40) [this is also evident from Fig. 42 this paper],
and every twenty-eight years another foot is added to
the total all around the northern end of the Gulf of
Boothia. The region is still out of isostatic balance,
and it can be estimated that it has still to rise another
700 feet or so before equilibrium can be reached.*

*Similarly around the northern shores of Hudson Bay new
rocky islands have appeared within the memory of the
older Eskimos, and the land is known to have risen at
least 30 feet since the Thule Eskimos first established
themselves there, indicating an average uprise of not
less than three feet per century (Holmes 1965:59).*

In the following sections we will consider the varied evidence
on which the concept of isostatic readjustment following continental
glaciation is based.

Hudson Bay

The "emergence of beaches" (Holmes 1965:684) was observed in Hudson Bay as early as 1631 by Captain Luke Foxe (Warkentin 1964: 13-14). His explanation that the abandoned strandlines represent extraordinarily high-tide storm beaches is no longer acceptable now that it is known that some strandlines are as high as 900 feet (Innes and Weston 1966) above the average present level of Hudson Bay. Many textbooks in geology (see quotations from Holmes presented above) leave the impression that the abandoned beaches of Hudson Bay are above present sea-level solely because of isostatic movements following deglaciation, that they would be even higher above the water of the bay were it not for the eustatic rise in sea-level which resulted from the melting of the continental glacier, and that the out-pacing in vertical rise of the land over the sea is still going on today. A direct analogy with the much more intensely studied Fennoscandian region is generally suggested.

However, when we consider isostatic readjustment as the sole cause of the high-level beaches around Hudson Bay, no account is taken of the preglacial geological history of this sedimentary basin. King (1965: 837) stated: "Beneath Hudson Bay the Precambrian rocks of the Canadian Shield are extensively covered by Paleozoic strata, downwarped into a shallow basin . . . . The bay owes its submergence largely to effects of the last glaciation, but it has been a long-persistent negative area as well." A review of the geology of the Hudson Bay Basin (Nelson and Johnson 1966) suggests that the basin, which was a strongly negative element in Paleozoic time, became land sometime in the late Jurassic or early Cretaceous. It is interesting to note that some Russian geologists maintain that Fennoscandia was being uplifted before glaciation (Coulomb and Jobert 1963:122).

Although, therefore most of the Hudson Bay region was probably no longer below sea level just prior to the first Pleistocene glaciation, it was lower in elevation than western Canada. It is generally held that the preglacial drainage from that part of the North American continent was to the northeast toward the lowland now covered by the sea water of Hudson Bay (Barton *et al* 1965:195, 197; Flint 1957:170). It follows from this that a depression of the topographic surface of the earth's crust already existed between western Canada and the Hudson Bay region before the continental glacier developed. The weight of the ice emphasized this bowl-shape but did not create it. To show the position of the crust before loading by glacier ice as a level line is therefore misleading, at least in the case of a cross section between western Canada and Hudson Bay (Fig. 52).

The "fact that the shores of . . . the Gulf of Boothia are steadily continuing to rise shows that the process of restoring equilibrium is still going on." (Holmes 1965:684) This is based on observations of level changes as recorded by tide-gauges at several places where long term records are available. Gutenberg (1941: 733-739), who constructed a map showing the present rate

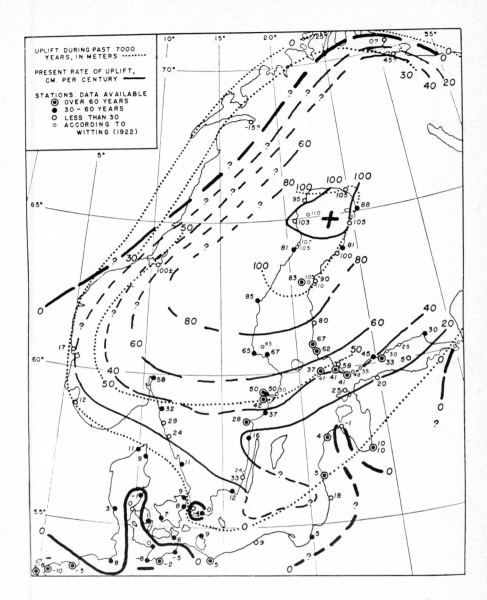

Figure 42.   Fennoscandian postglacial uplift. The map shows the
             postglacial uplift which has taken place during the
             past 7000 years in meters as well as the presently
             continuing uplift expressed in centimeters per century.
             After Gutenberg (1941:738).

of uplift in Fennoscandia (Fig. 42), used observations from 98
tide-gauge stations with records extending over time periods
varying in length from less than 30 years to as much as 126 years.
Calculations of the presently continuing uplift in the Great Lakes
region of North America are based on fewer (19) lake-level gauge
stations of which nine exceed a 60-year observation period
(Gutenberg 1941:742).

The "fact that the shores of Hudson Bay . . . are steadily
continuing to rise . . . " (Holmes 1965:684) is based on limited
local evidence. In Hudson Bay only one control point is available,
a tide gauge, at Churchill, Manitoba, for which records have been
kept since 1928, suggesting a present rate of uplift exceeding 1
meter per century (Gutenberg 1941:717). Other historical evidence
has been used both to refute and to substantiate the contention
that the land around Hudson Bay is still rising. Tyrrell (1896:
205) concluded from the position above the water-level of inscrip-
tions on rocks made by sailors in the eighteenth century near
Churchill that "post-glacial uplift of this portion of the shore
of Hudson Bay has virtually ceased." He thus refuted Bell's
(1880:21C) earlier contention that "the relative level of the sea
and land in this vicinity is changing at the rate of about seven
feet in a century." The problem was again investigated in the
field by Johnston (1939:97) who agreed with Tyrrell in concluding
that ". . . the prime cause of post-glacial uplift was the
removal of the weight of the ice sheet; but . . . this cause has
apparently long ceased to act at Hudson Bay . . . ." He went on
to suggest by analogy that ". . . the recent uplift of the Great
Lakes basins is due to some recent and local cause, and is not a
direct continuation of post-glacial tilting due to glacial
melting." (Johnston 1939:98) A re-evaluation of the field-evidence
was made by Gutenberg (1941:749) who regarded the information as
uncertain, supported Bell's earlier contention that the land is
still rising, and added that this conclusion was ". . . confirmed
by the very recent tide-gauge data", referring to the one station
at Churchill. It is worth mentioning here that the Churchill tide
gauge is "located on a wharf within the harbor" (Gutenberg 1941:
747), which does not appear to be a particularly stable place on
which to locate such a reference point.

From the above it follows that the evidence on which the
"fact" of continuing uplift of Hudson Bay is based is slender,
that it may be unreliable, that it has been disputed by some,
and that statements implying presently continuing uplift are based
largely on analogy with other regions, particularly Fennoscandia.
The rate of the implied present uplift is arrived at either by
extrapolation of rates in the better-studied Great Lakes region
or by regarding it as being of the same order as the values
obtained in Fennoscandia. Some geophysicists attempted to
calculate the prevailing rate of uplift of the land around Hudson
Bay by assuming that isostatic balance prevailed before the
Pleistocene glaciers developed, that depression of the crust
resulted entirely from the weight of the ice, and that uplift
will halt on re-establishing crustal equilibrium. The precepts
in any such calculations appear to be tenuous, however, as they
ignore the possibility of earth movements having no connection
with glaciation.

Lake Agassiz

The "tilted attitude of many lake terraces", mentioned by Holmes (1965:684) as evidence for isostatic recovery already achieved after disappearance of the continental glacier, has been recognized since the end of the last century in the Glacial Lake Agassiz region.

> *The successive shore-lines of Lake Agassiz are not parallel with each other and with the present levels of the sea and of Lakes Winnipeg and Manitoba, but have a gradual ascent from south to north, which is greatest in the earlier and higher beaches and slowly diminishes through the lower stages of the lake, being at last only slightly different from the level of the present time (Upham 1885:474).*

In explaining the present non-horizontality of the abandoned shorelines of Lake Agassiz, Upham asked himself the question if the water level was tilted upward at the time the shoreline features were formed because of the gravitational attraction of the large ice mass on the water in front of it. Based on some calculations made for him by R.S. Woodward of the United States Geological Survey he came to the conclusion that such an effect had existed but that it could account for a tilting factor of only about six inches per mile at the most, whereas his average tilt measurements showed values of as much as one and one-half feet per mile (Upham 1885:490). "A quarter part, or probably less, of the changes in the levels of these beaches is therefore referable to ice attraction, while the remaining three-quarters, or a larger part, . . . belongs to a differential elevation of the land" (Upham 1885:490-491).

If gravitational pull would indeed account for as much as 25% of the total tilt, as Upham believed, it is a factor that should not be ignored. However, Flint (1957:242) states that such a distortion "is minor if not negligible" because, as he points out, not even the fraction calculated by Woodward is "actually attributable to gravitative attraction of the glaciers, because subsidence of the crust beneath the weight of the ice reduces the mass effective for distorting water levels."

There is also another reason why the water surface of Lake Agassiz may not have been level at the time the lake existed. There was a gradient of the surface of the lake from the ice, in front of which the water ponded, to its outlet through which the lake drained. How much was this gradient and did it have any appreciable effect on the now apparent non-horizontality of the strandlines?

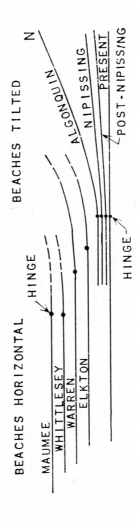

Figure 43. Great Lakes region, postglacial uplift. This generalized
diagram shows the tilting of shorelines of successive
lakes across the central part of the Great Lakes region
and the northward displacement of the zero isobases
(hinges). Older lakes are above and to left, younger
lakes below and to right. After King (1965:834).

The "differential elevation of the land" to which Upham (1885: 491) attributed 75% of the tilting effect was regarded by him as the result of (a) the imposed weight of the ice-sheet and its removal, or (b) earth movements independent of glaciation (Upham 1885:487). As far as the relative importance of these two suggested causes of uplift is concerned, Upham (1885:521) believed that "All the movements . . . , as recorded by the changes of levels of the beaches, seem to have resulted from the tendency of the earth's crust to regain equilibrium, after the ice melted away."

When the abandoned shorelines of the Great Lakes region were studied in detail during the beginning of this century it became apparent that the shorelines of each lake stage are horizontal in their southern parts, but beyond a zero isobase (or hinge-line) they rise northward (Fig. 43). Mapping of many of the Glacial Lake Agassiz beaches in Manitoba and adjacent parts of Saskatchewan and Ontario by Johnston (1946), who incorporated earlier work, made possible the drawing of isobases (Fig. 44), or lines of equal deformation, which are drawn through two or more points of equal elevation of an abandoned beach, believed to have been formerly level, but now deformed. By means of such isobases and a profile of the beaches drawn perpendicular to their isobases (Fig. 45) the mode of uplift of the Glacial Lake Agassiz region was shown. The question of the mechanics uplift was also raised by Johnston, who tried to determine whether warping on a large scale or only tilting of blocks of the earth's crust had occurred. Johnston (1946:13) recognized at least seven hinge lines of deformation of which he regarded the first and fifth as major ones.

Before the hinge lines drawn by Johnston are accepted as well-substantiated features, it is well to review his fieldwork and his presentation of the data obtained. The basic assumption that the former water planes, and therefore their line of intersection with the land surface, were level may be correct as already pointed out above. Moreover, the field determination of the present position of these water levels meets with several operational difficulties.

The bases of eroded cliffs cut by wave action into the largely unconsolidated drift deposits surrounding a glacial lake are probably the most accurate indicators of the position of the former water level. At least, this is the opinion expressed by Upham (1885:277) but according to Johnston (1946:5) "Elevations of cut terraces, the bases of old shore cliffs . . . , as a rule, . . . are not so reliable in determining the ancient lake levels as are the elevations of the beach ridges." However, divergent opinions on the reliability of wave-cut cliffs do not really matter much in the Lake Agassiz region where only a small portion of the shores consist of wave-cut slopes of till (Upham 1885:198) and where nearly all altitude determinations represent the crests of beach ridges (Johnston 1946:5).

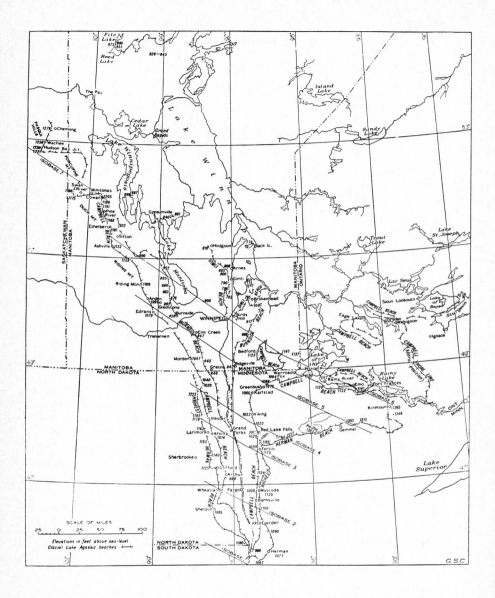

Figure 44.   Lake Agassiz beaches, map.   The map shows elevations in
             feet above sea-level of Glacial Lake Agassiz beaches and
             selected isobases (hinge lines).   After Johnston,
             (1946: Fig. 1).

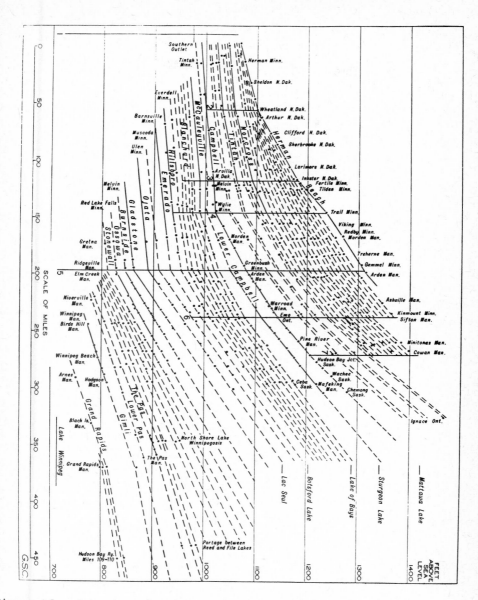

Figure 45.   Lake Agassiz beaches, profile. The profile shows the
present attitude of the Lake Agassiz beaches. The
selected isobases (hinges) are numbered as in Fig. 44.
After Johnston (1946: Fig. 2).

In most places the ancient shores of Lake Agassiz are marked
by a smoothly rounded beach ridge of gravel and sand. They

> *vary considerably in size, having in any distance of 5
> miles some portions 5 or 10 feet higher than others
> . . . ; waves driven toward the shore by storms gathered
> the beach gravel and sand from the deposit of till or
> other drift which was the lake bed . . . ; the most
> massive and typical beach ridges [are] often continuous
> [for] several miles with remarkable uniformity of size
> . . . ; under the influence of irregular contours of
> the shore, however, the beach deposits assume the form
> of bars, spits, hooks, loops, and terraces (Upham
> 1885:199).*

The tracing of the beach ridges of Glacial Lake Agassiz is
now much facilitated by the use of air photographs not available
to Upham and not mentioned as having been used by Johnston. Some
of the geomorphological mapping problems encountered by earlier
workers may now be solved by the use of air photos and photo
mosaics. More serious difficulties arise if it is realized that,
even in the case of a well-defined, continuous beach ridge such
as the Campbell Beach, which is uniformly and strongly developed
in the north and in the south, the height determinations of the
crest will give only an approximation of the former water level.
Upham (1885:277) realized this when he wrote: "From these descriptions of the beach ridges and eroded shores of the old lake, its
levels at the time of formation of these shorelines are deducible
approximately [*italics mine*]. The elevation of the crests of the
beach ridges . . . are commonly 5 to 10 feet, or rarely 15 feet
or more, above the level held by the lake when the beaches were
heaped up by the waves, chiefly during storms." Where the sand
and gravel ridges are bars, spits, and other similar features,
they were below the water level and, moreover, not at a constant
depth below that level. Yet, the elevations used by Johnston
(1946) do not take these uncertainties into account. If a reasonable margin of error of plus or minus 10 feet would have been
allowed, the definite elevation values represented by a point in
Fig. 45 would become indefinite values within limits and would be
represented by short vertical lines, proportionate to the greatly
exaggerated vertical scale of that figure. Then, if the curves
representing the present attitude of the beaches are drawn, some
of the "knick points" in the curves, indicating hinge lines, may
become rather indefinite.

As far as representation of data in the map view is concerned
it is hard to understand why only those isobases which are believed
to be hinge lines are shown. A more objective manner of showing
isobases would be to treat these lines of equal elevation like other
contour lines by using a regular interval. A steepening of the
gradient of the deformed surface would then be evident only where
the lines become more closely spaced. As a change in gradient can
then be seen to occur within a more or less broad zone rather than
along one narrow line arbitrarily placed within that zone, it is

easier for the reader to come to realize that, even if the presence of gradient changes has to be assumed within the margins of error of the data, the position of such hinges in the plan view is by no means as definitely and narrowly defined as shown in Fig. 44.

It should also be pointed out that most of the selected isobases (hinge lines) shown in Fig. 44 are straight lines drawn through two control points, the distance between these points varying from 60 to as much as 200 miles. To draw a straight line is all that can be done, but it should not be assumed that this is the only possible trace of the contour lines, which may well be curved between the two points. This consideration again introduces a margin of error (but now in the horizontal direction) in the position of the points shown in Fig. 45, which is a cross-section, drawn perpendicularly to the isobases but of unrecorded position in the map view and on which the elevation points have been projected, presumably by a straight line projection along the isobases. Considering both the vertical and horizontal margins of error it becomes clear that the control points shown in Fig. 45 would have been presented best not by points, nor by vertical lines, but by rectangles. (Because of the greatly exaggerated vertical scale, however, the rectangles would be much higher than wide and in practice come close to a vertical line.) It also means that where three or more control points are available which do not have a straight line relationship, the assumption made by Johnston (1946:13) that there are ". . . lateral hinge lines trending in the direction of tilt and passing through points on the isobases where these show marked changes of course . . ." may be invalid. It is possible that the surface, instead of being faulted into blocks, is warped and, moreover, even if it is "laterally hinged" the assumption that such a hinge passes through the aberrant control point is unwarranted.

Regarding the question if the Lake Agassiz region is still undergoing uplift, an admittedly cursory search of the literature failed to reveal any information. Apparently no long-term lake-level data are available for the large remnant lakes of Lake Agassiz.

Most maps of the Fennoscandian area which show the recovery of the crust in postglacial time present a picture of continuous warping in that the isobases are regularly spaced (Fig. 42). That no hinge lines are suggested on these regional maps by a closer spacing of the contour lines is mainly the result of the small scale and large contour interval used on these maps which obliterates local detail. According to Flint (1957:246) the majority of students of Baltic strandlines agree on the general sequence and attitudes of the strandlines as interpreted from the field evidence but he adds that

> *There are, however, other opinions, such as that strand-lines steepen abruptly at one or more points along their sloping profiles, and that this implies inward shifting, with time, of the outer limit of doming. That opinions*

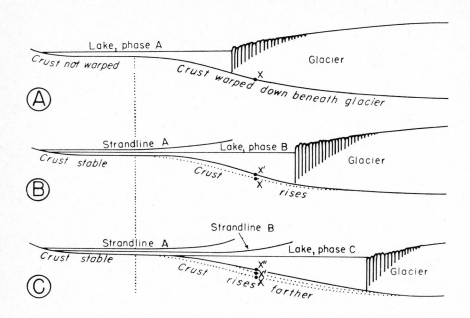

Figure 46.   Progressive upwarping. The three idealized sections
              show progressive upwarping of the earth's crust during
              deglaciation. (A) Glacial lake (phase A) has formed
              between the receding glacier margin and higher ground
              to left. (B) Uplift has affected the area to the right
              of the vertical dotted line, bending the strandline of
              phase A to a higher position. Point x has been lifted
              to position x'. A new lake phase, B, has formed at a
              lower level. (C) Renewed uplift has affected the area
              to the right of the vertical line, bending the strand-
              line of phase B, and warping a little more the extreme
              righthand end of A. Point x has been lifted to position
              x". A third phase, C, has formed at a still lower level.
              After Flint (1957:252).

*on such a matter can differ is less surprising than it
seems at first, because the field evidence in many places
is obscure and confusing. In some areas strandlines are
so numerous and so closely spaced that piecing together
a single one from discontinuous remnants is very difficult. In others the strandlines are so faint that the
error of altitude measurement is large. In consequence
universal agreement can hardly be expected until virtually
the entire region has been measured in minute detail
(Flint 1957:246-247).*

Geophysics

If, as some contend, changes in the rate of uplift are abrupt
and hinge-lines are the surface traces of faults, an expression of
this fracturing may be noticeable in the field and movement along
the hinges may have caused historically recorded earthquakes.
Moreover, if the hinges resulted from the periodic retreat and
intervals of halting or readvance of the glacier margin (Fig. 46)
the fracture pattern in the lacustrine and marine areas should
show some correlation with the glacial deposits recording that
history on the land areas. That the history of postglacial uplift
as determined from water-covered areas is intimately intertwined
with the late glacial and postglacial history of land areas and
that attempts at correlation between the two are imperative is
suggested by King (1965:834) follows from the following:

*The perfection of some of the shorelines suggests that
they were formed during lengthy interludes between times
of tilting, as though regional uplift alternated with
stillstand, perhaps because unloading was interrupted
by pauses in ice wasting or by renewed ice accumulation.*

In the Lake Agassiz region where Johnston (1946:13) recognized
at least seven hinge lines of deformation of the beaches there are
no apparent topographical or geological features which indicate that
the location of the hinge line was influenced by a line of weakness.
"The absence of any such feature suggests that the earth crustal
movements were very deep seated in origin." (Johnston 1946:13)
However, a future more detailed study of the topography and surficial geology using airphotos may reveal some subtle features
which escaped the attention of previous workers.

As far as seismicity is concerned, the area of maximum postglacial uplift in the interior of the Canadian Shield appears to
be almost completely aseismic (Gutenberg and Richter 1949:91) and
the thinly-covered Shield, to which the Lake Agassiz region belongs,
shows only a very low to low frequency of occurrence of earthquakes
which, moreover, have no direct discernible relationship to any
hinge lines.

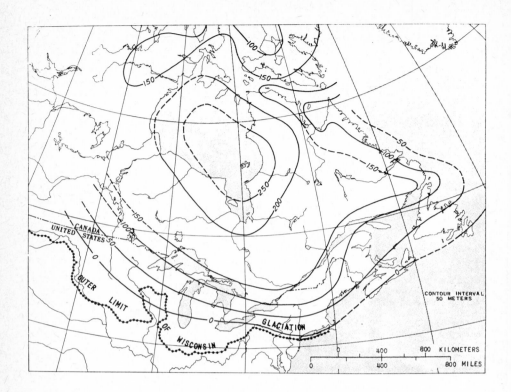

Figure 47.   North American postglacial uplift.   The map of north-
             western North America illustrates postglacial uplift
             by means of contours (isobases) on the highest observed
             marine and lacustrine strandlines indicating the minimum
             amount of uplift which has taken place since deglaciation.
             The contour interval is 50 meters.   After King (1965:836,
             Fig. 4A).

As shown in Fig. 47, the zero isobase or first hinge line of North American postglacial uplift closely corresponds to or roughly approximates the position of the outer limit of Wisconsin glaciation (King 1965:836). That there is no closer correspondence between the limit of glaciation and the zero isobase is the result of various factors such as the impossibility to determine uplift, or lack of it, where there are no indications of former levels preserved in beaches or other suitable features. It should also be kept in mind that in the Great Lakes Region, for instance, the Maumee zero isobase represents only the outer limit of measurable crustal warping in that region (Fig. 43 and Fig. 47). This is so because, as Flint (1957:244) points out

> . . . as soon as the ice began to thin, the crust began to rise. But actual displacement of the glacier margin had to take place, permitting lake or sea water to occupy part of the region formerly covered with ice, before shoreline-making could start. Hence it is inevitable that some recovery of the crust by upwarping must have occurred before even the earliest strandlines were fashioned. As there are no means of measuring the amount of this early recovery, the value of total measured recovery . . . is a minimum and total actual recovery was greater than this by an unknown amount.

The discovery of negative isostatic anomalies in Fennoscandia, suggesting that the land there still has to rise about 200 metres before equilibrium has been restored, led to gravity investigations in Canada designed to determine if analogous conditions exist in the Hudson Bay region (Innes and Weston 1966:171). The separation of the gravitational effects due to deep-seated sources from those arising from near-surface mass distributions is a difficult problem and usually an intractable one. Nevertheless it is clear that gravity variations due to density changes within the upper parts of the crust are superimposed upon strong regional trends in which the anomalies are systematically more negative in the vicinity of Hudson and James Bay and reach minimum values in an area believed to have been the locus of maximum glacial loading (Innes and Weston 1966). Although gravity studies support the contention that postglacial and presently continuing uplift resulted from the removal of an ice load, Innes and Weston (1966:175) recognized ". . . that both the Canadian and Scandinavian Shields were rising prior to the onset of glaciation, as the result of some fundamental but unknown process. It may be concluded, therefore, that their recent uplift is the combined result of short term glacio-isostatic effects of large amplitude, superimposed upon tectonic events having a much longer time-scale." The same thought is also expressed by King (1965:837): "All the Quaternary isostatic movements were superposed on a much greater, long-term trend of epeirogenic movements in the Canadian Shield and its surroundings."

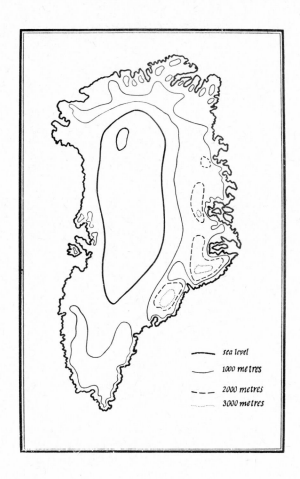

sea level
1000 metres
2000 metres
3000 metres

Figure 48.   Greenland, bedrock topography. The map is a contour map
in meters of the ice-rock interface showing a large
central part below sea level. After Hamilton (1958:121).

The failure to recognize processes other than glacio-isostatic uplift to account for raised and tilted strandlines may lead to misinterpretations of the postglacial history, particularly in places where anomalously high uplift conditions exist within deglaciated and risen regions. Sim (1961) in describing high-level marine shells from Ellesmere Island, mentioned the possibility that there, marine submergence may extend well above the elevations usually suggested. He did not discuss the possibility that local or regional earth movements other than glacio-isostatic uplift could account for this anomaly and other abnormally high levels in Greenland and Ellesmere Island.

Analogies

A contour map of the ice-rock interface presented by Hamilton (1958:121), here shown as Fig. 48, shows that a large part of Greenland lies below sea level. If a cross section through this part is presented (Fig. 49) it clearly shows the present bowl-shape. Similarly, parts of central Antarctica are below sea-level (Fig. 50) in places as much as 750 meters, comparable in value to local depression under the thickest ice in Greenland. The cross-section used to illustrate this does not show such a pronounced regional down-bending as the Greenland one. It has to be kept in mind, however, that a direct comparison between the two cross-sections can not be made because of differing scales. The original sections have about the same vertical scale; the Greenland section has a vertical exaggeration of 40 times. The Antarctic section having a horizontal scale almost half that of the Greenland section has therefore a vertical exaggeration of about 80 times.

The ice-bedrock interface in both Greenland and Antarctica was determined during traverses across the ice caps, determining their topography, and by seismic reflection shooting their thicknesses. Because only a limited number of shot points can be established under the difficult conditions of travel, details of the ice thickness profiles are filled in with measurements of the gravity field which is particularly sensitive to changes in ice thickness because of the large density contrast between ice and rock (Bentley et al 1964:1). The chief source of error in the seismic method, because of the absence of velocity surveys in drill holes penetrating the ice from surface to bottom, is an uncertain variation in seismic wave velocity with depth in the ice sheet. Where the ice near the base may have a large load of debris the seismic velocity may approach that of the rock underneath. If in such places the first change in velocity is regarded as indicating solid rock the ice thickness may actually be greater than calculated. Such difficulties described by Hamilton (1958: 115-116) from south Greenland where " a layer of frozen moraine underlies the ice and that the reflections normally obtained are from the interface between the ice and the moraine" are mentioned here only to demonstrate that a certain amount of interpretation (rather than direct observation as is the case with the topography

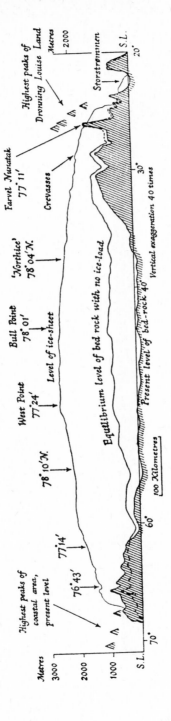

Figure 49.   Greenland, profile. This cross-section of North Greenland shows the present shape of the ice sheet and the
estimated profile of the land without a glacial load.
Note that in this calculated equilibrium level the
western margin of Greenland is expected to sink, whereas
the central part is to rise on deglaciation. After
Hamilton (1958:119).

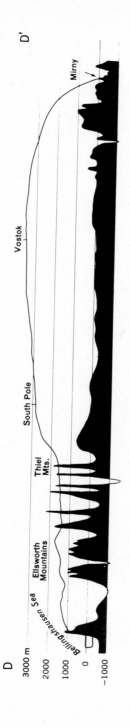

Figure 50. Antarctica, profile. This cross-section from the Bellinghausen Sea across the South Pole to Mirny shows the present topography of the ice sheet and the ice-rock interface. After Bentley *et al.*, (1964: plate 2, section D-D').

of the ice) goes into the reconstruction of the ice-rock
interface. It should not be assumed, however, that such errors
are large enough to invalidate the regional reconstruction of
that interface.

Even if the existence of low topographic basins below the
ice caps of Greenland and Antarctica is accepted on the basis of
the seismic and gravity evidence it does not necessarily follow
that it is soley the result of a loading phenomenon caused by the
ice. The possibility of independent earth movements should be
considered as well as the possible effects of deep erosion as
shown in Fig. 51, if the model presented by Dapples (1959:407)
is correct. It is generally held, however, that ice-loading
has been the main cause of the depression of Antarctica and that
any erosional effect, if present, has been only a minor contributing factor because the continent is now essentially in isostatic
equilibrium as determined from seismic and gravity data (Innes and
Weston 1966:175).

Mechanics

If the cross-section of Greenland (Fig. 49) is studied it
can be seen that whereas the central part would rise in the event
that the ice-load were removed it is held, in this particular
reconstruction, that the margins of Greenland would sink. In this
view the margins are regarded as having been bowed up too high at
present and thus the concept of a forebulge underneath the ice-cap
margin is introduced. It is mainly in this respect that an analogy
between Greenland and North American Pleistocene glaciation does
not hold. As already mentioned above, in the Great Lakes region
the postglacial movements are either up or non-discernible (Fig.43),
the presently continuing movement is positive. No negative movements have so far been found distributed in a systematic manner
surrounding the region of postglacial uplift. In Europe super-
elevation of southern Denmark, northern Germany, The Netherlands,
and the floor of the North Sea (regions which by now have "snapped
down" nearly to their original preglacial positions but are still
sinking at present as suggested by tide-gauge measurements) has
been assumed by some authors (Daly 1926:200; Gutenberg 1941:738).
Recent studies in The Netherlands cast doubts on the interpretation
that downsinking of the Dutch coast is to be regarded as solely a
negative glacio-isostatic movement. A large part, if not all, of
the downward movement may be the result of compaction ("inklingking"
in Dutch) of the unconsolidated sediments characteristic of the
Danish, German, and Dutch coasts and of the North Sea Basin. Non-
glacial epeirogenic movements may also be involved in this sedimentary basin. For instance, it has been suggested by some that downward movements have resulted from solution of the Permian Zechstein
salts.

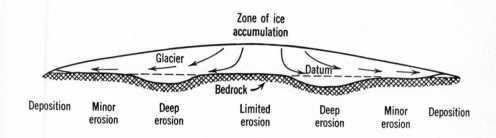

Figure 51.   Ice sheet model. This conceptual illustration of an
             ice cap shows zones of accumulation, deep erosion, minor
             erosion and deposition. After Dapples (1959:407).

The absent or tenuous evidence for any presently negative earth movements in the marginal area of former continental glaciers should be kept in mind when the mechanics of crustal response to glacial loading are considered. Although it is generally stated that crustal uplift in formerly glaciated tracts is due to horizontal flow of subcrustal material tending to restore equilibrium following the melting of the ice (Innes and Weston 1966:175) it should also be pointed out that "the question of what happened to the displaced substance remains unanswered" and that although "displacement of rock material at depth is implied, evidence of compensating uplift during glaciation is negative." (Flint 1957:257).

It can be demonstrated for the Great Lakes region that the rate of crustal uplift during glaciation changes sensitively with variations in mass of the glacier. In this region an inward shift of the outer limit of deformation with time can be noticed. If Fig. 43 is studied it can be seen that the outer limit of warping for each of the successive beaches lies north of its predecessor. If time determinations of the beaches are taken into account a northward migration of 160 miles during about 8,000 years becomes evident (Flint 1957:254). In North America it is believed that very likely the same sort of migration took place all around the center of glaciation, although not exactly contemporaneously. In Fennoscandia such a migration is, however, not clearly demonstrable:

> *There the zero isobases of successive water bodies seem to occupy nearly the same position. The difference between North America and Fennoscandia may be a result of the fact that in Fennoscandia the water bodies lay nearer the center of the ice sheet than did the North America lakes. Therefore they did not form until a greater proportion of the maximum volume of the ice had wasted away, and hence a greater proportion of the total crustal adjustment had taken place, than had occurred in North America before the great glacial lakes appeared. (Flint 1957:254)*

The mechanics of the postglacial uplift as the result of the removal of the continental glaciers in Europe and North America are discussed at length by Daly (1934:119).

> *The rocky floor under any of the Pleistocene ice-caps sank for two different reasons: because of the earth's elasticity, and also because of the earth's plasticity . . . . Under the weight of each meter of ice added to an extensive ice-cap, the whole planet is immediately elastically, distorted a little. If without delay that meter of ice be removed, the earth immediately takes on its original shape. Both reactions are those of an almost ideally elastic body. But against extensive loads of prolonged application the earth's materials flow and the crust is basined, plastically, under the load.*

Suppose, on the other hand, that an extensive ice-cap completes its basining of the earth's crust and then melts away. The uncovered region rises, at first by elastic response of the earth, and later by a plastic response. The rise is the greatest in the central region where the ice was thickest, so that the ultimate result is an updoming of the glaciated tract.

Two theories about the mode of plastic recoil are reviewed by Daly (1934:120-126). They can be summarized as follows:

Bulge or wave hypothesis

Basining is believed to have been accompanied by outward, horizontal flow in the substratum and just beneath the crust (Fig. 52). A comparatively narrow bulge is formed and horizontal flow takes place at small depth, not far from the 100 kilometer level. The bulge hypothesis demands pure bending of the crust, but not localized zones of vertical fracturing.

Punching hypothesis

Outward horizontal flow is believed to have taken place at great depth, below the 1000 km. level. The plastic basining is supposed to have been accompanied by an extremely slight uplift of the continent surrounding the glacial tract. The low, broad peripheral bulge is of a much smaller order of magnitude than that assumed in the bulge theory (Fig. 53). The crust, on unweighting by the melting of ice, yields to the stress and rises plastically. The floor of the ice-cap is punched up along a circumferential zone of vertical fractures, the "hinge-zone"

Daly (1934:123-124) prefers the second hypothesis of the develeling of the earth's crust because it is "supported by the discovery of actual hinge zones in both North America and Europe." He believed that in the hinge zones "the individual displacements in the vertical sense should be small and not represented by conspicuous fractures and 'faulting' at the surface of the earth." (Daly 1934:147)

Whichever theory is preferred, "the disposition of the displaced rock material during glacial maxima remains a mystery". (Flint 1957: 241) Both theories require some uplift outside the glaciated tract during times of glaciation. They differ only quantitatively in this respect. But the evidence for any peripheral elevation is "wholly negative, even where shore features and stream terraces should reflect such movement and afford a basis for measuring it." (Flint 1957:241)

To substantiate his contention that the punching hypothesis, which implies sudden displacements in the outer shell of the earth, is to be preferred over the wave hypothesis, Daly (1934:127-128) calls attention to the position of earthquake centers in Denmark and also states that" . . . occasional earthquakes centering in the Province of Quebec may possibly be connected with . . . postglacial

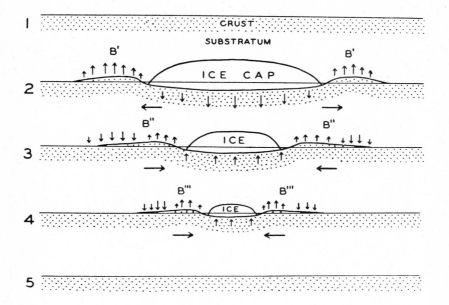

Figure 52.   Bulge Hypothesis. The sections illustrate the bulge
             or wave hypothesis to explain the plastic upwarping of
             a deglaciated tract. After Daly (1934 [1963]: 121).

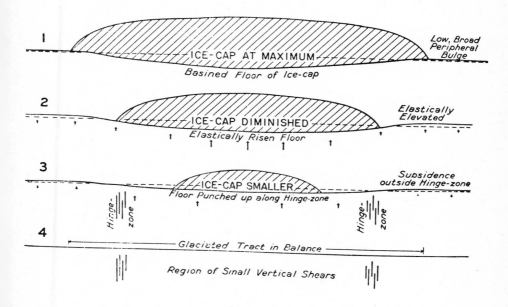

Figure 53.   Punching hypothesis. The sections illustrate the
             punching hypothesis to explain the plastic upwarping
             of a deglaciated tract. After Daly (1934 [1963]: 122).

recoil." As far as seismicity in North America is concerned it should be reiterated that most of the glaciated tract has few, if any, earthquakes and that those in the St. Lawrence valley are generally regarded as of tectonic origin unconnected with glacio-isostatic uplift. (Kumarapeli and Saull 1966:641)

Summary

        The idea that postglacial uplift of formerly glaciated tracts in Fennoscandia and North America is mainly the result of the removal of the superimposed weight of ice on the crust is not criticized in principle but a review of the observations on which this idea is based shows that in places detailed information is still lacking, and that other possible causes are generally not considered.   The various observations and conclusions are summarized in the following series of statements.

1. Field evidence of postglacial uplift is provided by abandoned strandlines substantially above present ocean or lake levels.

2. Altitude determinations on these abandoned strandlines show that they are higher above the present level surface where, according to other independent evidence, the continental glaciers were thickest than near the margins of those glaciers. Regionally, contour lines drawn on the elevated strandlines are therefore concentric to the area where the ice was the thickest (Fig. 42; Fig. 47).

3. In both Fennoscandia and North America the zero contour of uplift lies generally north of and approximately parallel to the limit of the latest glaciation.

4. The elevated strandlines are believed to have been originally level surfaces and any gravitational attraction of the water by the ice mass and any possible surface gradient of flowing lake water is regarded as being quantitatively negligible.

5. The height of the abandoned strandlines above the present level surface is believed to provide only a minimum measure of the actual uplift which has taken place for various reasons: (a) when the ice thinned some uplift took place already but the covering of the land by water and the attendant creation of strandlines had to await the total disappearance of the ice, and was possible only because of a time lag between water invasion and full recovery; (b) postglacial uplift and deleveling was accompanied by an eustatic rise in sea-level.

6. Postglacial uplift data are most complete for the Fennoscandian region. Fewer data are available for North America where the most detailed work has been done in the Great Lakes area. The well-developed raised beaches of Hudson Bay and the Canadian Arctic Archipelago await further study and even in the Lake

Agassiz region some necessary detail is still lacking. "Of
the strandlines of Lakes Regina, Souris and Agassiz . . .
we can say that they are warped up toward the north and east,
the highest ones the most steeply in the case of Agassiz. But
the unraveling of the discontinuities awaits detailed measurements that have not been made." (Flint 1957:255)

7. In the Lake Agassiz region and elsewhere detailed studies are
    beset by uncertainties in tracing wave-cut cliffs and beaches,
    and by relating such shore line features to the former water
    level. Introduction of reasonable margins of error in height
    determinations of former water level may eliminate or weaken
    the evidence for some hinge-lines. The question ". . . whether
    warping on a large scale or only tilting of blocks of the
    earth's crust occurred" (Johnston 1946:1) has not yet been
    answered. It is possible that only in some localities actual
    failure of the crust along hinges occurred whereas in others
    a slight bending or warping took place.

8. Surface expressions of hinge lines have not been recognized
    and the record of earthquakes in North America does not suggest
    any movement along such hinges in historical times. The Can-
    adian Shield is the region of lowest seismicity on the conti-
    nent and earthquakes in other more mobile regions, such as
    the St. Lawrence valley, are generally attributed to earth
    movements unconnected with develeling following removal of
    the weight of an ice sheet. An area of higher than average
    seismicity in Denmark has been related to the position of a
    hinge line by Daly (1934:128).

9. Detailed study of the region surrounding the Glacial Lake
    Agassiz basin is required to establish if the postulated
    hinge lines in the basin can be related to ice marginal
    positions in the land area. A correlation of the postglacial
    history of the lake basin and that of the surrounding land
    area is needed to determine if the hinges resulted from the
    periodic retreat and intervals of halting or readvance of the
    glacier margin.

10. Although the weight of the continental ice sheet depressed
    the crustal surface in North America, that surface was not
    perfectly level before the glacier developed. The preglacial
    drainage pattern indicates a gradient sloping from western
    Canada down to what is now Hudson Bay.

11. The deep erosion by the continental ice sheet peripheral to
    its areas of accumulation probably contributed only insignif-
    icantly to the bowl shaped surface of the earth underneath
    the ice.

12. Field evidence of continuing uplift of formerly glaciated
    regions is provided mainly by level gauges along the present
    shores of the ocean or lakes.

13. Abundant data of continuing upward movement are available
     for Fennoscandia; fewer data are available for the Great
     Lakes area; minimal data, including, besides one gauge station,
     some historical records, are available for Hudson Bay.

14. Data suggesting that the land surrounding Hudson Bay is at
     present still rising are slender, may be unreliable, and have
     been disputed by some investigators.

15. A rate of present uplift of about 1 meter in 100 years has been
     calculated for Fennoscandia (Fig. 42) and the average rate of
     warping of the Great Lakes area in North America is given by
     Flint (1957:249) as "a little less than 1 mm/100 km/yr, not
     quite as much as the rate in the Baltic region." In the
     absence of reliable data for Hudson Bay the present rate of
     uplift of that region can be given only by analogy with the
     better studied regions of Fennoscandia and the Great Lakes
     region.

16. The contention that the Hudson Bay region is not yet in isos-
     tatic balance, and therefore still subject to rising until
     that balance is restored, is supported by gravity measurements.
     However, the observed negative anomaly which increases toward
     the locus of greatest former ice thickness may be interpreted
     as the combined result of short term glacio-isostatic effects
     of large amplitude, superimposed on tectonic events having a
     much longer time-scale.

17. The failure to recognize the influence of earth movements other
     than glacio-isostatic uplift may lead to misinterpretations,
     particularly where anomalous uplift conditions exist within
     formerly glaciated regions.

18. Cross-sections used to illustrate that interior parts of
     Greenland and Antarctica are below sea level and that the
     land underneath the ice is presently bowl-shaped are based
     on seismic and gravity measurements. Possible errors in the
     ice thickness determinations are not believed to be of such
     an order of magnitude that they invalidate the concept of a
     presently downwarped surface underneath the glaciers.

19. The effects of glacial erosion on the present position of the
     bedrock below sea level are believed to be minor in the
     interior regions of Greenland and Antarctica but probably had
     a profound influence on the depths of fiords occupied by outlet
     glaciers in the marginal areas (Fig. 50).

20. Ice-loading is believed to be the main cause of the depression
     of Antarctica because the continent is now essentially in
     isostatic equilibrium.

21. The results of future unloading of Greenland can be anticpated
     as shown in Fig. 49, which presents a prediction introducing
     the concept of a fore-bulge, where on deglaciation negative
     earth movements would take place. In some geology textbooks
     (Zumberge 1958:73) post-glacial uplift of Greenland, accom-
     panied by an eustatic rise of sea level, is shown without
     any change in shape from the presently prevailing one under-
     neath the ice (Fig. 54).

22. The evidence for presently continuing downward movements out-
     side the glaciated tract in Western Europe is weak. The
     interpretation that subsidence resulted as a compensating
     movement to glacial unloading is controverted by some
     investigators.

23. Evidence for negative movements in North America outside the
     formerly glaciated area is absent and the question as to what
     happened to the supposedly displaced crustal material has not
     yet been answered.

24. Theoretical considerations of the mechanics of glacial load-
     ing and postglacial uplift are only in part supported by
     acceptable field evidence. The main points still being
     disputed are, (a) the importance of hinge lines, and (b) the
     presence and size of a fore-bulge.

                            Acknowledgements

     Attendance of the Lake Agassiz Conference and the consequent
preparation of the paper were made possible from grants by the
National Research Council and the Saskatchewan Research Council.

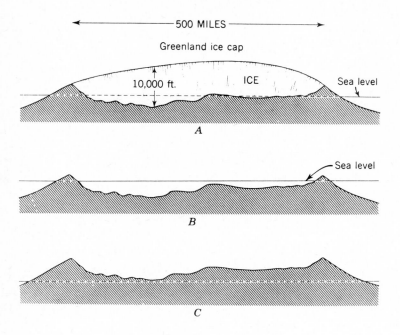

Figure 54.   Eustatic and isostatic rise. (A) The land beneath
              Greenland is depressed below sea level because of the
              weight of the overlying ice. (B) If the ice melted,
              the crust would begin to rise, but would lag behind
              the sea-level rise caused by return of glacier ice to
              the hydrologic cycle. (C) Final isostatic balance,
              reached long after the ice melted, would raise the
              entire land surface above sea level. In these diagrams
              only the effects of an eustatic rise of sea level and
              an isostatic rise of Greenland without a change in shape
              from a bowl to that of a dome are considered. After
              Zumberge (1958:73).

MUSSELS OF THE RED RIVER VALLEY IN NORTH DAKOTA AND MINNESOTA
AND THEIR USE IN DECIPHERING DRAINAGE HISTORY

Alan M. Cvancara

Introduction

The purpose of this paper is to synthesize the knowledge of the mussels in the Red River Valley of North Dakota and Minnesota, and suggest their application to deciphering drainage in the Valley. A detailed account of the distribution and ecology of Red River Valley mussels will appear in a forthcoming paper.

Field work for this study was done during the summers of 1965 and 1966. Mussels were collected by a combination of two methods, hand-picking and the use of an eight-foot crowfoot dredge.

The Red River and eighteen of its tributaries were checked for mussels at 119 stations, thirty of which are on the Red River (Fig. 55). Usually, five stations were selected for each tributary, including generally one or two stations just outside of the lake plain.

Physical characteristics of the river were noted at each station. About one dozen chemical tests of the water were made at most stations, in the field, with a Hach Chemical Company portable chemical kit.

Mussel Species

Thirteen species of mussels are known to occur in the Red River Valley of North Dakota and Minnesota (Fig. 56). Dawley (1947: 679) also reported two additional species living in the Red River, *Obliquaria reflexa* and *Actinonaias carinata*. I have not been able to verify these occurrences from my own fieldwork.

Four species -- *Lasmigona complanata*, *Anodonta grandis*, *Anodontoides ferussacianus* and *Lampsilis siliquoidea* -- occur in most rivers. The other species are relatively erratic in their distribution. Two species, *Lasmigona costata* and *Proptera alata*, have been collected alive only from the Red Lake River.

187

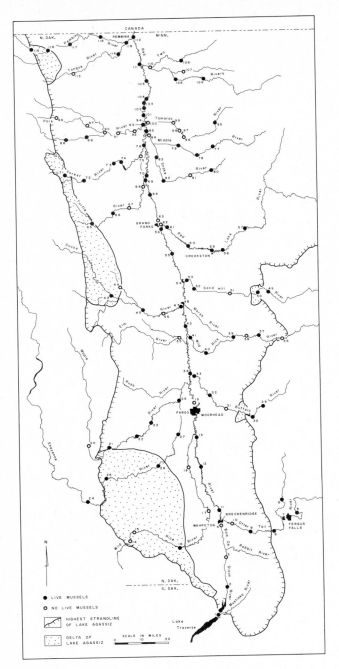

Figure 55. Map of Red River Valley in North Dakota and Minnesota show-
            ing mussel collecting localities. The highest strandline
            of glacial Lake Agassiz is taken from Leverett (1932) and
            Colton, Lemke and Lindvall (1963). The deltas of glacial
            Lake Agassiz are taken from Upham (1895).

● LIVE MUSSELS
○ EMPTY SHELLS
⊕ FOSSIL SHELLS

MUSSELS \ RIVERS	RED	OTTER TAIL	WILD RICE	SHEYENNE	MAPLE	BUFFALO	WILD RICE	GOOSE	SAND HILL	RED LAKE	TURTLE	FOREST	SNAKE	MIDDLE	PARK	TAMARAC	TWO RIVERS	TONGUE	PEMBINA
Fusconaia flava	●	●		●	○	●	●		●	●	⊕						○		
Amblema costata	●	●		●		○	●			●									
Quadrula quadrula	●			⊕						●									
Lasmigona compressa		○		●			○		●		⊕	●					○		●
L. costata		○								●									
L. complanata	●	●	○	●	●	●	○	○	●	●	●	●				○	●	●	●
Anodonta grandis	●	●	●	●	●	●	●	●	●	●	●	●	●	●	○	●	●	●	●
Anodontoides ferussacianus		●		●	●	●	●	○	●	●	●	●	●	●	●	●	●	●	●
Strophitus rugosus	○	●		●		○	○		●	●	⊕	●					○		●
Proptera alata	○			⊕			○			●									
Ligumia recta latissima	●	⊕		⊕			○		○	●									
Lampsilis siliquoidea	●	●	○	●	○	●	●	○	●	●	●	●		●	○	●	●	●	●
L. ventricosa	●	●		●			○		●	●							○		

Figure 56. Mussels occurring in the Red River and eighteen of its tributaries. Indicated are those species collected alive, those represented only by empty shells and those from river terrace sediments interpreted as fossils. Tributaries, as read from left to right, are arranged from south to north.

Generally, the larger the river, the greater is the number of mussel species. The Red Lake River has yielded the most species (10); the Red River has only eight living species. The other tributaries have from one (Park River) to nine species (Sheyenne River). *Lasmigona compressa* apparently does not occur within the studied part of the Sheyenne River, but has been taken above station 24 (Figs. 55, 56). In the Forest River, *Strophitus rugosus* was collected, after this study was completed, at a single station approximately half way between stations 72 and 73.

Five species -- *Amblema costata, Quadrula, Proptera alata, Ligumia recta latissima,* and *Lampsilis ventricosa* -- have been taken from only the larger rivers in the Valley (Fig. 56). Three species -- *Quadrula quadrula, Proptera alata,* and *Ligumia recta latissima* -- were collected from only the two largest rivers, the Red and Red Lake The presence of these three species in terrace sediments would therefore suggest greater discharge in a particular river at some previous time.

Two species, *Lasmigona compressa* and *Anodontoides ferussacianus,* are generally indicative of smaller rivers in the Valley, or the upper reaches of larger rivers.

Ecology

Physical factors

Bottom type and turbidity show a close relationship in the rivers of the Red River Valley. The bottom varies from gravel to sand at or near the margin of the lake plain and is silty clay or clayey silt near the axis of the Valley. Turbidity in the tributaries increases downstream as the bottom sediment becomes finer (Tables 10 to 15). The water of the Red River is highly and consistently turbid (80 to 240 ppm). Secchi disk readings are correspondingly low, with values of 0.50 to 1.0 feet.

River discharge appears to be a significant physical factor, because rivers with higher discharges generally have greater numbers of mussel species. Rivers with low or sporadic discharge generally have few or no live mussel species. This is discussed further under "Factors limiting mussel distribution."

Chemical factors

Water was analyzed for dissolved oxygen, free carbon dioxide, pH, total chloride, nitrate and nitrite content, phenolphthalein and total alkalinity, calcium and total hardness, and iron and phosphate content. Only total alkalinity, and total chloride for six selected rivers are given here (Tables 10 to 15).

TABLE 10

TOTAL ALKALINITY, TOTAL CHLORIDE, TURBIDITY, AND LIVE MUSSEL
SPECIES WITH STATION IN THE PEMBINA RIVER, NORTH DAKOTA.
VALUES, IN PPM, WERE DETERMINED ON AUGUST 3, 1966.

Station	Total Alkalinity	Total Chloride	Turbidity	Live Mussel Species
115	244	14	31	4
116	250	14	18	4
117	270	16	37	1
118	292	16	68	3
119	266	16	138	3

TABLE 11

TOTAL ALKALINITY, TOTAL CHLORIDE, TURBIDITY, AND LIVE MUSSEL
SPECIES WITH STATION IN TWO RIVERS, MINNESOTA. VALUES,
IN PPM, WERE DETERMINED ON AUGUST 4, 1966.

Station	Total Alkalinity	Total Chloride	Turbidity	Live Mussel Species
106	256	6	28	4
108	302	20	28	3
107	260	4	38	0
109	304	8	28	4
110	310	22	72	1

TABLE 12

TOTAL ALKALINITY, TOTAL CHLORIDE, TURBIDITY, AND LIVE MUSSEL
SPECIES WITH STATION IN THE TURTLE RIVER, NORTH DAKOTA.
VALUES, IN PPM, WERE DETERMINED ON AUGUST 27, 1965.

Station	Total Alkalinity	Total Chloride	Turbidity	Live Mussel Species
65	290	18	13	4
66	340	24	15	4
67	330	260	78	0
68	270	2180	43	0

TABLE 13

TOTAL ALKALINITY, TOTAL CHLORIDE, TURBIDITY, AND LIVE MUSSEL
SPECIES WITH STATION IN THE RED LAKE RIVER, MINNESOTA.
VALUES ARE IN PPM; THOSE FOR STATION 61 WERE
DETERMINED ON AUGUST 21, 1965, AND
ALL OTHERS WERE MADE ON
AUGUST 20, 1965.

Station	Total Alkalinity	Total Chloride	Turbidity	Live Mussel Species
58	250	4	40	8
59	220	4	35	9
60	210	4	57	2
61	240	5	57	2

TABLE 14

TOTAL ALKALINITY, TOTAL CHLORIDE, TURBIDITY, AND LIVE MUSSEL
SPECIES WITH STATION IN THE SHEYENNE RIVER, NORTH DAKOTA.
VALUES ARE IN PPM; THOSE FOR STATION 25 WERE
DETERMINED ON JULY 26, 1966, AND
ALL OTHERS WERE MADE ON
JULY 27, 1966.

Station	Total Alkalinity	Total Chloride	Turbidity	Live Mussel Species
24	300	30	73	3
25	270	23	66	6
26	260	22	105	3
27	260	21	138	2
28	260	31	180	1

TABLE 15

TOTAL ALKALINITY, TOTAL CHLORIDE, TURBIDITY, AND LIVE MUSSEL
SPECIES WITH STATION IN THE OTTER TAIL RIVER, MINNESOTA.
VALUES, IN PPM, WERE DETERMINED ON JULY 14, 1966.

Station	Total Alkalinity	Total Chloride	Turbidity	Live Mussel Species
5	250	6	11	5
7	250	5	33	2
8	280	4	30	8
9	290	4	65	1
10	250	6	88	0

Generally, the variability of chemical factors is related to discharge with smaller rivers showing greater chemical variability. In comparison, the water chemistry of the Red River exhibits relatively little variability.

Of those chemical factors measured, chloride content appears to be ecologically significant for mussels. It is relatively high in the lower reaches of the Turtle, Forest and Park rivers of North Dakota (Fig. 55 and Table 12). These high chloride values are probably the result of seepage of saline water from Cretaceous rocks of the Dakota Group. Upham (1896: 527) was perhaps the first to suggest this possibility. Few, if any mussels occur where total chloride values are high (Table 12). In the other tributaries, chloride values are low and appear to have little relationship to mussel distribution (Tables 10, 11, 13 to 15). Total chloride values for the Red River are also relatively low and show little variability.

Biologic factors

Biologic factors have been only partially considered in this study, but may be as important, or more important, than the physical and chemical factors. The fish host, for example, may be particularly significant in regulating the local distribution of mussels. Other factors, such as predation by muskrat and raccoon, may be of secondary importance.

Factors Limiting Mussel Distribution

Those factors presently considered most significant in limiting mussel distribution in the Red River Valley are: chloride content, long periods of no flow, pollution, and possibly turbidity. The importance of high chloride content has already been mentioned as affecting the mussel fauna of the lower Turtle, Forest and Park Rivers.

Long periods of no flow may restrict or exclude mussels from certain rivers. Possible effects are the increased concentration of salts, low dissolved oxygen, and increased predation. The factor of long periods of no flow may be significant in the lower reaches of the Tamarac, Middle and Snake Rivers. There, no flow may be expected for continuous periods longer than seven and eight months (MacLay, Winter and Pike, 1965).

Pollution -- industrial, municipal or domestic -- appears to affect mussel distribution in parts of the Valley. Notable examples exist just below Grand Forks and Fargo.

Turbidity may affect mussel distribution in some rivers or parts of rivers. Turbidity increases downstream in most of the tributaries (Tables 10 to 15). However, several species of mussels can live successfully in highly turbid water, as is indicated by the mussel fauna of the Red River.

Mussels as Aids in Deciphering Drainage History

Mussels may be used as aids in deciphering drainage history in at least two ways: (1) to indicate changes in river discharge, and (2) to suggest former drainage connections.

The finding of large-river mussel species in the terrace sediments of a presently small river suggests that the river had a greater discharge in the past. This hypothesis has been tested in the Sheyenne River with some tentative results. The shells of three mussel species -- *Quadrula quadrula, Proptera alata* and *Ligumia recta latissima,* -- have been collected from a lower terrace of the Sheyenne River, and have not been found alive in that river. These three species are apparently presently living only in the Red Lake and/or Red Rivers, the largest rivers in the Valley. Evidence of similar changes occur for the Otter Tail and possibly Turtle Rivers. The Pembina River would be another river where on might apply this approach.

The use of mussels in suggesting the connection of former drainages that are now separate has been applied in Michigan (Van der Schalie 1962) and elsewhere. Further study is necessary to determine if this approach can be applied in the Red River Valley.

Summary

Thirteen species of mussels are known to live in the rivers of the Red River Valley of North Dakota and Minnesota. High chloride content, long periods of no flow, pollution, and possibly turbidity are considered to be the most significant factors limiting present mussel distribution in the Valley. By applying these factors to past times, mussels may be useful as aids in deciphering Red River Valley drainage history.

Acknowledgements

This work was supported by the North Dakota Water Resources
Research Institute with funds provided by the U.S. Department
of Interior, Office of Water Resources Research under P.L. 88-379.

I wish to acknowledge Dr. Lee Clayton, Department of Geology,
University of North Dakota, for reviewing the manuscript.

CONTEMPORARY DRAINAGE WITHIN TRUE PRAIRIE OF
THE GLACIAL LAKE AGASSIZ BASIN

H. Albert Hochbaum

Introduction

The broad, shallow Glacial Lake Agassiz Basin is a region of gentle contours and poor drainage. Few regions of North America are so richly endowed with standing waters. East and north, within the PreCambrian Shield, the basin is littered with bogs and acid lakes. On its southern and western prairies are countless marshes and alkaline lakes that have had a profound influence on the welfare of man settling there. Because of the size and complexity of the Glacial Lake Agassiz Basin as a whole, my discussion is limited to the range now most heavily occupied by man, the tall-grass, True Prairie of southern Manitoba (Weaver 1954), southeastern Saskatchewan, northwestern Minnesota and northeastern North Dakota. This rich agricultural region is distinguished on any road map by its many towns and villages. Human habitations are less frequent in the forested PreCambrian Shield and on the shortgrass, Mixed Prairie of the west.

General Considerations

The largest waters of the Glacial Agassiz watershed are the great lakes of Manitoba, remnants of the vanished inland sea. One of these, Lake Manitoba is virtually closed. Indeed, MacKay (1965:6) found that "evaporation losses from Lake Manitoba are much larger than the runoff from the incremental drainage area." Lake Winnipegosis and Lake Dauphin, both with small drainage basins, are nearly closed in drought years. Some of the smaller lakes, such as Dog Lake and the three Shoal Lakes, are without outlets most years and may be drying up in our time. Lake Winnipeg, the largest of the Manitoba lakes, is fed by three major rivers draining a massive watershed. It also receives water from its large sister lakes in Manitoba. Hence Lake Winnipeg is at the very bottom of the Glacial Lake Agassiz Basin and, in the long run of time, must be the region's most permanent body of water.

Great marshes are associated with each of the large prairie lakes, having become established in lagoons behind points, spits, bars and beaches. The beach marshes of Lake Manitoba and Lake Winnipeg are among the largest and most famous in the world, renowned as gathering and molting places for migratory waterfowl of many species. Wooded beach ridges protect these marshes from direct wind and wave, creating conditions favorable for the growth of

marsh plants (Walker 1959;1965). Seiches, or wind tides, flowing
through openings in the beaches, provide a gentle ebb and flow
that serves to maintain the individual pattern of each marsh.

On some Lake Manitoba marshes, as on the Delta Marsh, long
narrow channels reach back several miles into the prairie. Some
of these shallow, marshy "creeks" may have been formed by the
force of seiche currents during high water years, perhaps in the
same manner as the fenland meres of Norfolk, England (Hutchinson
1957:119). Marshes of deltaic origin may be found near the mouth
of the Red River. Aerial maps of the Delta Marsh show some deltaic
formations, as where an earlier mouth of Portage Creek entered
Cadham Bay. But this marsh, as a whole, exists because of the
protective beach built by Lake Manitoba wind and wave.

In its decline, Glacial Lake Agassiz left conspicuous beaches
that now stand out as long, narrow ridges of sand or gravel (Dowling
1901). Some extensive marshes remain in the poorly drained regions
adjacent to these ridges, especially in the lowlands west of the
Burnside Beach near Langruth and Amaranth, Manitoba. Hind (1859:27),
describing his explorations there, complained that "for thirty
miles we had to wade through marshes and bogs, separated by low
ridges; in fact the distance named may be said to be made up of
marsh, bog, ridge, marsh, bog, ridge in most wearisome succession."

River marshes, some of them broad, shallow lakes in wet years,
were conspicuous features of the Glacial Lake Agassiz lowlands in
pristine times. Lateral levees, typical of prairie rivers in their
lower courses, withheld some local spring runoff from the river
every year. In times of flood, river water spilled over these
levees to become entrapped. Most of these marshes, however, have
now vanished as the levees have been built up artificially and runoff carried downstream by ditches.

Oxbow lakes and marshes are frequent along the permanent rivers
and streams of the Glacial Lake Agassiz prairie. In both the lowlands and uplands of this basin there are frequent meandering
drainage channels that carry flowing water only during wet years.
Along the courses of these dry creeks there are deeper pockets
gouged out by runoff currents. These hold water most years, thriv-
ing as small, narrow marshes known widely as "sloughs". Oak often
grows on the slough bank. Indeed, when the White Man arrived, the
only groves of oak over wide regions of prairie were near the
sloughs. These places were favored as campsites by the native
Indians and became the farmsteads of early settlers.

Kettle lakes and marshes probably comprise the most numerous
small prairie waters within the Glacial Lake Agassiz watershed.
These were formed where glacial outwash was studded with masses of
ice. When the ice melted, a depression remained and a lake was
formed. Most of the kettle lakes in the Glacial Lake Agassiz
region are relatively small, less than two acres in extent. They
usually have marshy borders and are widely known as "potholes".
Such small pothole marshes are typical of the boulder till plains
in the southwestern portion of the Glacial Lake Agassiz Basin

(Bird 1961:1). In some regions, as near Minnedosa, Manitoba, there are as many as 150 potholes within a square mile; and this Minnedosa range is but a part of a vast region of kettle marshes extending over 4,000 square miles. These potholes, like the sloughs, are closely associated with agriculture through most of their range, often cultivated to their edges. They receive their water from miniature drainage basins, sometimes only a few hundred feet across. Most years they hold water through the autumn, and it is clear that they thrive as wet places because of long winters and short summers. Although annual precipitation is light (about 21 inches at Winnipeg according to Munro, 1963:106) snow accumulates from November through March. The local runoff available to a pothole is enlarged by snow-drifts caught by shoreline clumps of willow and marsh vegetation. Meyboom (1966:33) suggests that willow-ringed potholes he studied near Davidson, Saskatchewan, are the result of outcrops of ground-water.

Besides these ice-formed kettle lakes and marshes of the upland prairie, there are many wetlands formed by irregularities in the ground moraine. Hutchinson (1957:94) points out that these are often difficult to distinguish from the kettle lakes, but the latter may be deeper. There are also many basins on the lowlands established by irregularities of the poorly drained prairie. Originally, some of these closed basins were extensive marshes, long since drained. But there remain many shallow depressions on farmland, showing as wet places in early spring, usually drying out in time for cultivation. In wet years, however, they survive the spring and summer, producing marshy edges of emergent vegetation growing from seeds that have lain dormant through dry seasons.

Contemporary Drainage Activities

The most conspicuous contemporary drainage within the prairie of the Glacial Lake Agassiz Basin is that now being caused by man himself. Certainly the wet and dry patterns of this country are being changed by human activity at a speed and in a volume never known to occur in our time as the result of natural forces.

It is reasonable, of course, that man should wish to interfere with the natural conditions of the prairie; drainage to improve land is one of man's oldest cultural activities. Within the Glacial Lake Agassiz Basin, drainage was certainly in the minds of the front-iersman, as it was started by the earliest settlers. Hind, consid-ering the marshes behind the Burnside Beach, exclaimed that "if the drainage of many thousand square miles of swamp and marsh in this part of the country should ever become a question of national interest, I know of no enterprize of the kind which could be executed with so little cost and labour, and promise at the same time such wide spread beneficial results." (Hind 1859:27)

As communities became organized, so were the drainage programs. Now there is no region in the world where agricultural drainage is so intensive as within the prairie watershed of Glacial Lake Agassiz.

This move to break through the lips, the rims and the seals holding back the shallow prairie waters has been followed in nearly every portion of this region and in some localities all of the original lakes and marshes are now permanently removed.

Wetland drainage is essentially an agricultural activity. It has two major objectives: (1) to improve farmland by hastening the flow of spring runoff from the fields; (2) to create new cropland by removing the water from lakes and marshes.

Extensive drainage to improve agricultural land began in 1907 within the United States watershed of the Glacial Lake Agassiz Basin. Spring runoff was carried from farmland by way of long, deep, legal ditches, these fed by smaller branching veins that reached out and divided until nearly all the tillable land of a region was accessible to the main drain. Then upland landowners could easily and inexpensively tip the water from their fields, rushing it down the drains to the river bottoms.

This drainage away from the uplands continued at a steady pace in the United States until 1917. Then it came to a halt and even the maintenance of ditches was neglected through the stretch of years leading to the drought of the 1930s. By the early 1940s, however, heavy drainage activity had been resumed. By 1955, it was considered that about one-half of the large legal drains required for upland flood control had been completed in the United States portion of the Red River Valley (Augustadt 1955:575).

A similar pattern of drainage was carried forward in Manitoba within the Red River Valley and elsewhere on broad prairie. This has advanced steadily since World War II and main drains are now conspicuous features of the southern Manitoba countryside. In Manitoba this drainage accomplished considerably more than the protection of farmland from spring runoff. The long, deep ditches permanently dried out some of the large river marshes and removed water from several large glacial beach marshes opening new land for farms. Hind's dream for the drainage of the marshes behind Burnside Beach came true; but his promise of prosperity there so far has been ill-founded.

Shortly after World War II, drainage of kettle lakes and marshes to increase the realm of agriculture gained momentum in the United States prairie of the Glacial Lake Agassiz Basin. It has advanced rapidly since. In Manitoba and Saskatchewan, such drainage did not become intensive until the middle 1950s; then it increased as the natural drying-up of potholes during drought made ditching simpler and cheaper. Recently, drainage efficiency has been enchanced by refined techniques and new machinery, such as the back-hoe, a small scoop-shovel that may be operated by a farm tractor. Near Minnedosa, Manitoba, 2 - 4% of the small kettle lakes and marshes have been drained each year since 1959. On some individual sections of land, most of these potholes have been removed. In the United States, drainage of marshes has been even more complete. In 1960 I examined pothole drainage in Mahmomen County, Minnesota, finding about 50% of small lakes and marshes drained -- drainage continues there to the present.

Drainage programs in the United States and in Canada now aim to complete the system of ditches by which spring runoff is hastened from upland fields and most of the slough and pothole marshes dried. Recently, in both countries, there have been moves to curb pothole drainage because of the importance of marshes to waterfowl and other wildlife. Purchase of some wetlands with state, federal and private funds is now underway in the United States. In Canada there are plans to protect pothole marshes in agricultural regions by way of cash agreements drawn up between the landowner and the government (Munro 1965). As yet, however, the number of lakes and marshes saved by purchase or agreement is small in both countries.

Through all the years of drainage, some types of marshes have survived. The small scattered oxbows offer little to agriculture and are not easily drained. Most remain in pristine condition. The few deltaic marshes of the prairies have not been drained. (It is worth noting that some important deltaic marshes within the Glacial Lake Agassiz Basin have been lost to flooding, as the marshes of the Delta of the Saskatchewan River, covered by the rising waters of Cedar Lake, held back by the dam at Grand Rapids, Manitoba.)

Lake marshes have not been drained because they are dependent on lake water levels. Recently, however, control structures have been established at the outlet of Lake Manitoba, where it enters the Fairford River, and the level of this lake is now being held as close as possible to 811.5 feet above sea level. The result is that some important Lake Manitoba marshes are withering.

The Effects of Contemporary Agricultural Drainage

The local successes of drainage have been widely acclaimed, the mistakes and expensive failures passed over lightly. The steady advance of ditching within the Glacial Lake Agassiz prairie seems to imply that the overall results have been profitable. Most of this removal of water from the prairies of Canada and the United States has been paid in part or in full by the public at large, often for the benefit of individual landowners. So far, however, little serious consideration has been given to the long-term influences of drainage beyond the farms. What have been the results of drainage elsewhere within this watershed? Beyond the farmlands, what has there been of gain and loss? In his text, *Modern Hydrology*, Kazmann (1965:235) tells us that

> *"from the standpoint of hydrology and geomorphology, drainage and the subsequent change in land use has two principal results. The concentration times of ever-larger areas of watershed are decreased, thus increasing the likelihood of downstream floods and raising the probable stages. The erosion from the land surface is increased due to the operation of*

> *plows and other earth-scratchers which reduce the*
> *cohesion of the formerly swampy soils and release*
> *fine particles into the stream channel.*

It seems reasonable that if water is dumped from upstream regions during spring flood, downstream flood must be increased. Thomas agrees with Kazmann on this point: "drainage of many natural depressions has aggravated the flood capabilities of streams by providing an outlet for surplus runoff which, prior to drainage, has been held within the area." (Thomas 1956:554) MacKenzie and his committee, in their examination of Red River floods, reject this view. They consider that the removal of upstream waters by drainage leaves "the area in a condition to absorb spring precipitation and snowmelt. The net effect of the drains on either the magnitude or the frequency of flood flows is insignificant, but they accelerate the draining of the land after flooding." (MacKenzie, *et al*,1953:39)

None of these authors present evidence in support of their conflicting conclusions. Nor, indeed, have studies been carried out within the Glacial Lake Agassiz Basin to answer the question one way or another. Floods are inevitable -- rich valley soils have been founded in flood. Now, as we appraise the complex problem of human occupancy of entire watersheds, we must begin to learn more about the influence of upstream ditching on the degree of downstream flood. This is not the place to discuss flood control reservoirs or diversions, which are now being constructed on some major rivers of this region. And yet, it is reasonable to point out that while drainage may add land to agriculture upstream (some of it submarginal) reservoirs and other downstream treatments remove rich bottomlands permanently from cultivation. Moreover, these reservoirs gather the sediment of upstream soils, hence are relatively shortlived.

There have been no studies directly relating drainage to soil erosion and lake sedimentation within the Glacial Lake Agassiz Basin. Many new ditches in Manitoba, carrying heavy burdens of suspended sediment, act as troughs leading almost directly from field to lake. Surely this must accelerate sedementation in some lakes. The south lobe of Lake Manitoba may be undergoing bottom changes, although this is suggested by casual rather than by scientific evidence. Fishermen claim the bottom was once hard; now it is soft and muddy in some places. Cottage owners at the south end of the lake recently have found soft, muddy bottom where it was once hard and sandy. The abundance of carp and sauger at the south end of Lake Manitoba may reflect the influence of mud bottom.

Studies of the waters feeding the south end of Lake Manitoba and their influence on this lake are urgently needed, especially in view of a new inflow which will come with the Portage Diversion. Measurements of suspended sediment of the Assiniboine River at Portage la Prairie reveal that some years, as in 1957, the silt load carried by this river in April and May amounts to more than 600,000 tons (Anon. 1964:17). With spring diversion of the Assiniboine River to Lake Manitoba, much of this suspended sediment may come to rest in the lake.

Lake Winnipegosis and the northern lobe of Lake Manitoba are fed by waters relatively silt-free. But Lake Dauphin, like the south end of Lake Manitoba, is shallow and its inflow is from heavily drained farmland. Measurements taken at Selkirk show that the Red River carried 2,327,700 tons of suspended sediment to its mouth in April and May of 1956 (Anon. 1964:30). Some of this would have dropped at the delta, but much must have been carried out into the lake. Is this a normal load of silt? Is the lake bottom being changed? So far, there are no answers.

If ditches carry silt to the lakes more quickly and in greater volume, might this not also be true for materials in solution? Lake Manitoba, as already noted, is closed some years. It is the only one of Manitoba's Great Lakes within the saline lakes zone (Frey 1963:454). More than one-half of its watershed is within heavily drained agricultural land. Is there the possibility that its salinity may be steadily increased by the rush of drainwater it now receives? What is the role of contemporary drainage in transporting agricultural fertilizers, pesticides and herbicides to the rivers and lakes of the Glacial Lake Agassiz Basin? Surely the lake is in delicate balance with its surroundings and further modifications must be carried forward with care and understanding.

It is clear that drainage dries upland lakes and marshes, speeds spring runoff to the lowlands. It thus seems reasonable to expect that ditches might alter the reserves of sub-surface water. Thomas (1955:77) explains that groundwater has been decreased in some localities by drainage, "to the detriment of agricultural use of the land or municipal use of the water." He also suggests that "in many places in the United States the drainage has not been as beneficial as anticipated. Some drains have made land suitable for plowing earlier in the spring but have also reduced the available water supplies for crops in the critical late-summer months. Commonly, the effects of drainage have extended considerably beyond the troublesome swampy area, and the water table has been lowered to the disadvantage of surrounding areas."(Thomas 1956:554) Ellis (1957:27) says simply: "the more runoff, the less water there is penetrating into the soil . . ." Manson, however, who has had an important influence on drainage policy in the Red River watershed within the United States, says that "the only water removed by drainage is free, or gravitational water. It is this free water that literally drowns a plant if it remains too long in the root zone . . ." (Manson 1957:6)

Agricultural drainage races ahead without our being sure, or often without our even wondering if it is always good for the land and its people.

Conclusions

We know that very little in our environment is permanent.
Especially subject to steady, constant change are the streams,
the rivers and lakes which from the beginning of civilization
have been the centres for man's cultural development. Our Glacial
Lake Agassiz country now abounds with lakes and yet "lakes are not
permanent features of the landscape. Once a lake has formed, and
indeed even while a newly formed basin is being filled, an array
of forces operate to level the shoreline, to fill the basin with
sediments, and to erode an outlet. The impermanence of lakes is
a basic principal of limnology. Lakes are ephemeral . . . 'Lakes
are born to die.'" (Reid 1961:44)

In the face of this inevitability of change, we are curious
about the evolution of changes. Now here, in our midst, by the
grace of massive public funds, and with machinery that moves,
grinds and digs with the force of a glacier, we men are making
changes to our land that normally would require thousands of years.
Some of these changes benefit a few people in an instant of the
present. Let us be sufficiently curious to learn if there might
come some harm to many people over a long period of time by the
subtle, indirect results that follow our moments of force.

Part IV

Paleo Ecology of
Glacial Lake Agassiz

PALEOECOLOGY: A PRACTICAL VIEWPOINT AND
GENERAL CONSIDERATIONS

Jaan Terasmae

Introduction

Paleoecology is not a new science in the same sense as is, for example, space research. It has a long tradition but it has experienced a tremendous surge of revitalization in recent years. As claimed by G.Y. Craig (1966), "in recent years palaeoecology has become fashionable." In this discussion I propose to search for reasons behind the renewed, and rather sudden resurgence of interest in paleoecology. The writer believes that it is not because paleoecology has become suddenly fashionable, but more likely owing to a number of serious practical problems, related to the environment in which we live, that attention has been focused on paleoecology for finding practical solutions which require coordinated research efforts. It was gratifying to note that in his opening remarks for this conference The Honorable Gurney Evans, Minister of Mines and Natural Resources of Manitoba, expressed his optimism about the practical value of the research carried on by the conferees.

In the proposed search for reasons it seems appropriate to start with the rather fundamental question, "why have the studies reported at this meeting been made?" They are all concerned with the general subject of environment, within the broad limits of Glacial Lake Agassiz. Some help can be forthcoming from a synthesis of widely ranging subject matters discussed, including glacial history, Quaternary geology, geomorphology, archaeology, geography, paleoecology and several aspects of biology. Although in most of the reports presented the primary objective has been an academic one, the writer intends to show that there are also important practical implications evident in these investigations and futhermore, that the scientific studies are essential for drawing meaningful practical conclusions.

The following discussion will be restricted to the field of paleoecology, which is in itself of an interdisciplinary nature. Particular reference will be made to problems related to management of our natural resources, pollution and conservation. An attempt will be made to show how the techniques and methods employed in paleoecology can be utilized to suggest possible solutions for the basically environmental problems facing us at the present time in these three fields. Some examples will be taken from the reports presented at this conference and others from the available published data.

        After an assessment of the fundamental question of "why",
some suggestions will be offered towards the somewhat naturally
following question of how future studies could be implemented
with the greatest benefit to both scientific and practical
problems.

        Ecology has been defined as a branch of biology concerned
with studies of relationships between living biota and their
environment.   Paleoecology, on the other hand, has been defined
as a branch of geology dealing with ancient biota and their
contemporary environment (Imbrie and Newell 1964).   Although both
disciplines have many similarities in their approach to problems,
there are also some important differences.   In paleoecology one
is dealing with fossil biota and hence, their life processes
cannot be observed.   The chemical and physical factors of the
ancient environments cannot be studied directly, and the fossil
assemblages found have been subject to both post-mortem and diagenetic (post-depositional) changes.   Two important conclusions
can be drawn from the above statements.   First, ecology including
biota and their physical environment (Fig.57), operates at a
higher level of precision than is available in paleoecology and
second, paleoecology is more inclusive than ecology owing to the
depositional circumstances and diagenetic processes affecting
the fossil assemblages.   As pointed out in this conference by
W.J. Mayer-Oakes, the importance of man in the total ecosystem
cannot be ignored.   The profound influence of human activities
on the existing ecosystems has been well documented and has
gradually increased to become a dominant factor in ecological
considerations.

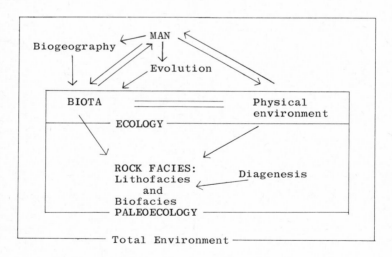

Figure 57.   Causal relationships in biology and geology, as related
             to ecology, paleoecology, and Man in the total ecosystem.
             Modified in part after Imbrie and Newell (1964).

Quaternary paleoecological interpretations rest on the fundamental assumption of uniformitarianism. This principle presupposes that the living equivalents of fossil biota have the same or closely similar ecological requirements and tolerance ranges. That the paleoecologist and ecologist should work closely together is clearly evident because both disciplines are supplementary to and more or less dependent on one another in several aspects.

The Myth of Unlimited Resources

From the times of early explorers to North America, accounts of limitless natural resources abound. These impressions were amply reflected by an English sea captain Arthur Barlowe shortly after 1584 when he wrote that, "I think in all the world the like abundance is not to be found," (Farb 1966). Today, in North America, only about one tenth of one per cent of the eastern woodland remains in primeval condition, as a pitiful remnant of the once magnificent forests. In a recent issue of *Geotimes* (1966) John C. Frye wrote,

> *During most of the history of our country we have operated on a theory of superabundance -- that is, we have assumed that we had unlimited area in which to expand, unlimited rock, mineral, and hydrocarbon resources to exploit, unlimited water to use or pollute, and unlimited time in which to plan for the future. Suddenly we are realizing . . . that none of these old assumptions is true.*

When the famous pine forests were logged along the Ottawa River the people who worried about the future were assured that these forests were so huge in extent that they could never be exploited completely, and that they would, after all, naturally grow back soon after logging. We know now that these forests certainly could be exploited to destruction, and they never have grown back beyond a miserable brush stage. The greed for the immediate economic gain greatly outweighed any reasonable attempts of management and conservation. Similar attitudes have prevailed throughout the following years with frequently devastating results. Having reached the end of the road of ignorance, we are now faced with an urgent need for improved management practices, hopefully forthcoming in part through paleoecological and ecological research.

We have been forced to the conclusion that instead of wasting and indiscriminately exploiting our natural resources we have to turn to sensible management and conservation of the wealth of natural resources which we still possess. In reference to the earlier posed question of "why", it is clearly evident that our knowledge of environmental factors is still inadequate, especially where such factors are an integral part of our natural resources (e.g.,

forestry, agriculture and fisheries). A much greater volume of
additional basic paleoecological data is required for an intelli-
gent appraisal and understanding of the dynamics of ecosystems
with which we are dealing, including the impact and results of
introduced human disturbances which are affecting these ecosystems.
Without an adequate paleoecological background it is commonly
difficult to separate the effects of the natural factors from
those of the introduced ones in the ecosystems studied. For example, in the boreal forest of Ontario where regeneration of black
spruce growing on a muskeg substrate has deteriorated, it has been
difficult to decide whether this deterioration of sites is due to
(1) recent forest management practices through fire prevention,
or (2) is caused by a natural development of this particular
ecosystem influenced by a possible change in climate. Paleoecological studies (including paleoclimatology) of the history of this
forest environment might well contribute useful data towards
solution of this important economic problem.

The Water Crisis and Pollution

Up until very recently people in most of North America have
been content with the optimistic assumption that good, clean water
has always been, and will be, plentiful and cheap. We have for a
long time dumped our wastes into the convenient rivers and lakes
without much concern. Now, this uncontrolled pollution has reached
a point where it cannot be ignored any longer. The bitter truth
has dawned upon us that there is hardly an unpolluted stream or
lake left in the whole of the United States and much of southern
Canada. A water crisis has resulted from the misuse of one of our
most plentiful natural resources. Decisions have been made at
different levels of government to seek ways and means for correcting
the situation. It has become obvious, however, that this is more
easily said than done. As so many times in the past, people are
looking for new sources of water first rather than to management
and conservation of existing sources. Grandiose schemes have been
proposed, including bringing water for the south from huge reservoirs dammed up in the Yukon and Alaska.

As reported in *Geotimes* (1966), R.L. Nace of the U. S. Geological Survey (while discussing the proposed $100 billion North
American Water and Power Alliance-NAWAPA-at the August 25-26, 1966,
International Water Quality Symposium in Montreal,) raised several
important questions about this water development plan. The proposed huge reservoirs along 400 miles of the 900-mile Rocky Mountain Trench would place a new stress on this geological structure
and we might wonder about the effects of this loading. Large
volumes of water would be dammed up over permafrost areas. Great
quantities of water would be introduced into the now semi-arid
regions. Nace emphasized the possibilities of "unwanted, unfore-
seen and undesirable side effects."

It would seem possible that paleoecological and geological studies of large ice-dammed lake basins, such as that of the Glacial Lake Agassiz, will yield useful data on the effects of such lakes on the regional climate and crustal loading. This information, in turn, could be helpful in estimating the effects of the planned huge reservoirs.

Some of the water development schemes proposed have bordered nearly on fiction, as pointed out by Lloyd (1966): "A seaway for shipping is also proposed to James Bay, where as is well known, the off-shore waters are so shallow that even a canoe cannot be assured of getting within sight of land at low tide." The writer agrees with Lloyd that such imaginative plans underline the danger of allowing armchair planning and wishful political thinking to replace sound scientific knowledge and acquaintance with the land (see also Deevey 1966). Lloyd (1966:16) concluded that, "there is room for concern that too often the conclusions of the scientists and engineers are liable to be overridden by the demands of the politician -- who may be sensitive to the pressures of local, short-term interests, rather than to those of the country as a whole."

Our current knowledge of the dynamics of lakes, rivers and groundwater is inadequate for defining the limits and tolerances of pollution (as became evident at the Great Lakes Research Conference at Chicago, in the spring of 1966), which are required before the situation can be controlled by formulating meaningful and efficient laws. In this field, paleoecology can make a very substantial contribution by helping to distinguish the natural factors at work from the artificially introduced ones. Paleoecological evidence forms an essential part of case histories outlining the processes of pollution. In cases where the natural regime of a lake or river has been destroyed and changed beyond recognition, it is only through paleoecological studies that the pre-existing conditions can be reconstructed.

Water crises can result also from limited natural resources in semi-arid regions and in the prairies where large seasonal fluctuations occur in the water balance. Paleoecological studies coupled with knowledge of paleoclimatology are essential for establishing the periodicity and past fluctuations of the water and moisture regime. This information can be used, in turn, to predict the possible future trends in the water balance.

Furthermore, the development and dynamics of our extensive muskeg in areas of apparent overabundance of water can be better understood and more efficiently managed through improved paleo-ecological knowledge of that particular ecosystem.

The Problems of Pesticides and Conservation

The use of pesticides has increased enormously during the
last twenty years. It has become gradually fashionable to spray
with some potent chemical poison any of the plant and animal species
which create a nuisance or hinder man's exploitation of the biological world. A good example of such rather selfish action on
man's part was described recently by Bryan (1966) concerning
"cleaning" of a lake near Ottawa, in Quebec.

In spite of the warnings for caution which are overshadowed
by advertising, or brushed aside by the promoting agencies of the
chemicals used, the use of pesticides has continued on an ever
increasing scale. As the pests become resistant to available
poisons, more potent ones are created in abundance (van de Vanter
1965), and as claimed by Lisk (1966) thousands of new compounds
are being tested each year. However, large scale sprayings of
the whole landscape for one pest or another have commonly turned
out to have been singularly ineffective, and consequently unecon-
omical, for the intended eradication of a particular pest whereas
in the heat of battle an unknown multitude of other species were
destroyed. It is interesting to note that the suppliers of pesticides invariably assure the user that when handled and applied
according to label instructions these poisons are not dangerous.
One might wonder why several of these supposedly "safe" pesticides
have been removed from the market recently. It appears that
economic interests have once again replaced the sound ecological
principle of testing of these chemicals in relation to their
cumulative effects in time. This whole matter was brought into
sharp focus by Rachel L. Carson (1964) when she published her
book, "Silent Spring." Although both praised and ridiculed, this
book did stimulate research concerned with pesticide residues.
The analytical methods for these studies were summarized by Lisk
(1965). Recent studies have already established the presence
of pesticide residues or metabolites in all ecosystems. As pointed
out by Gripp and Ryugo (1966), in Lake County, California, some
100 to 300 lbs of actual DDT per acre have been applied in pear
orchards during the past 20 years. Analyses showed that 94% of
the DDT had remained in the upper 12 inches of soil. This example
emphasizes the importance of the time factor and cumulative effect
in the use of pesticides. These are factors frequently underestimated or inadequately understood both by the users and suppliers
of these chemicals.

Similar findings elsewhere strengthen the reasons for concern
expressed by Carson in her book. We still know little about the
long-term effects of pesticides. Cumulative effects of residues
or metabolites may take many years before the symptoms can be
observed in the biological systems and their significance recognized. It is important to develop improved chemical detection
methods for studies of pesticide residues in our various ecosystems.
It is equally important to explore further the possible pest control measures through biological research and techniques which
will leave no harmful residues.

Paleoecological studies may prove to be the only means by which the effects of pollution and pesticides on environment and biological systems can be followed and studied from the time of their initial large-scale introduction into different ecosystems. For example continuously accumulating lake bottom sediments may be one of the best sources of information for these studies.

Peter Farb (1966: 174) summarized the need for conservation as follows, "Now we stand at the end of the long wilderness road that has plowed through the great eastern forests, crossed the rippling sea of grasses, hurdled the great mountain barriers. The only extensive sweep of unspoiled America that remains is the northern roof of the continent, the coniferous forests and tundra of Canada and Alaska." Unfortunately, however, both the conifer forest and tundra are already beginning to suffer under the influence of man. If we despoil these areas, too, we cannot claim any longer that there is more wilderness beyond the next mountain range because this is where the wilderness ends.

It is gratifying to see the increasing attention given to problems of conservation. The setting aside of smaller and larger areas in many parts of the United States and Canada is not only important in view of recreation and historical values. It has become increasingly difficult to find suitable test areas for ecological studies as indicated in the paper by A.M. Cvancara, presented in this volume. Such study areas, however, are essential for investigations of the existing ecosytems and their natural dynamics through time. The disturbances created by human activities have hindered many botanical and zoological investigations. The practical and economical value of conservation on a long-term basis should not be underestimated.

In Search of Untapped Natural Resources

Having run into difficulties and facing complex problems on land -- as related to supplies of food and natural resources -- man is again trying to look for new areas to exploit. The "limitless" oceans and our large inland lakes seem to be the escape hatch this time. However, the enthusiasm and optimism for this new and relatively little known and understood resource was rather badly shaken by reports presented at the second international oceanographic congress (Moscow, 30 May - 9 June, 1966). It was agreed that a modern fishery cannot afford to overlook the fact that the sea is not an inexhaustible supplier. In fact, the top limit seems to have been reached in both Atlantic and Pacific oceans (Charlier 1966). T.S. Rass from the U.S.S.R. disclosed that some fishing grounds in the Far East will be exhausted within a few years. J. Strickland (Scripps Institution of Oceanography) questioned the popularly held view about the ocean as a vast cornucopia, an untapped reserve of food and mineral resources. He seriously doubts that we will have the requisite ability to describe, or sufficient understanding to manipulate, the marine environment by the time

mankind is faced with the ultimate need for large-scale aquaculture
and waste disposal. Unless we bring about a revolution in our
approach to the study of the ecology of the open sea both in technique of study and the magnitude of manpower and financial resources
required (Dietz 1966), we may never achieve these ends.

The need for paleoecological studies of marine and also fresh
water ecosystems was clearly evident from statements made by many
participants of the Moscow congress. It seems that our hopeful,
optimistic and fond dreams about the "limitless" ocean have been
crudely shattered by the harsh realism of factual evidence. The
above discussion is also quite applicable to attitudes frequently
expressed in regard to our large inland lakes and their proposed
exploitation for the benefit of human population. It is again
clear that we have to resort to improved long-term management
through environmental research rather than to unplanned exploitation on a short-term basis.

The Final Diagnosis

My final analysis of the existing situation can be illustrated
by a comparison adopted from the medical field. The symptoms observed by the doctor examining a patient can be compared with ecological studies. The case history leading up to the existing symptoms
would be equal to paleoecological studies. Only in simple cases
will the observed symptoms be sufficient for prescribing the drug
or treatment. In more complex ones both the case history and the
observed symptoms have to be considered and diagnosed. It may be
necessary to make several lab tests and call on specialists for
consultation before arriving at the final diagnosis. Similarly,
in paleoecological studies it may be both necessary and beneficial
to call on the help of experts from different fields before arriving at a diagnosis and suggesting the cure.

In the foregoing I have dealt with chiefly the symptoms of the
patient, which are the observable facts in our complex environment.
Coming back to my proposed search for reasons for the increased
interest in paleoecology, the following reasons seem to stand out
rather prominently.

As in the medical field where man has been both fearful and
yet fascinated in a curious sort of way by fatal and little known
or incurable diseases, the problems of pesticides and pollution
appear to be a comparable category. We can observe the sometimes
rather terrifying symptoms in our ecosystems but the case histories
are lacking or insufficiently known. We have realized that man is
very much a part of the ecosystems, not above and outside of them
where he can observe the happenings with indifference. The need
for finding a cure for our environmental diseases has become urgent
because of the apparent advanced stage of many cases of these ills.
As emphasized by Barnes (1966), "Erring economists and false econ-
omies cannot conceal the simple fact that we cannot afford NOT to

control air and water pollution, to preserve and restore beauty
to our environment." Chemists have been blamed for helping to
precipitate the pesticide predicament, but we must also realize
that the only conceivable help may be forthcoming through chemical
research coupled with paleoecological studies.

A further comparison with medical problems is interesting.
It is important not to ignore the psychological aspects of this
diagnosis. Anxieties, fears and superstitions commonly exist
because of insufficient knowledge of the apparent causes of the
symptoms observed. Perhaps we have been mislead at times about
the matters of pollution and pesticides by commercial interests.
It is almost frightening to learn how we have been, and are being
influenced and manipulated quite easily by techniques developed
through motivational research and depth research in advertising.
(Packard 1957). In some measure we may be suffering from psycho-
somatic illnesses, but to sort out the imagined and factual reasons
urgently requires more basic information than is available now.
Ben Bagdikian (1966) published a very illuminating review of one of
such case histories concerning air pollution. He found that when-
ever control measures were enforced the initial response of the
offenders was "as predictable as religious ritual." They claimed
that clean up was technically impossible, it was economically ruinous, they threatened to move away from that particular area, and
finally resorted to political pressures. However, it has been
amply demonstrated that clean up is technically possible and not
ruinous to the industries concerned. In fact, some of the control
measures can be turned into profit by further utilitization of
waste products. The last two objections by industries are eliminated by a successful solution of the first two. Persistence,
persuasion and a firm stand by the administrative and/or govern-
mental agencies are necessary attributes for reaching successful
solutions.

These agencies can be helped by providing them with paleoecological "ammunition" and other available and necessary facts as
well as by establishing closer cooperation between the research
and administrative organizations, as pointed out at this conference
by W.M. Laird. It is in this regard that studies such as those
reported in this volume and at the Glacial Lake Agassiz conference
can attain very real practical importance. They may suggest
possible ways for correcting the existing environmental mismanage-
ment of the surroundings in which we live.

Although I am optimistic about the outcome of the intended
therapeutic measures, it will take many years of intensive research
to build up the required case histories through co-ordinated studies.
Only then can the final diagnosis be sufficiently accurate to suggest meaningful solutions to our environmental problems. We can
only hope that we will not be too late to save the "patient".

HOLOCENE VEGETATION OF THE NORTHWESTERN PRECINCTS OF THE
GLACIAL LAKE AGASSIZ BASIN

James C. Ritchie

Introduction

I propose to discuss the contribution of work in the Western
Interior of Canada to the topic of the Holocene vegetation and
ecology of the precincts of the Lake Agassiz basin. This will
restrict my attention to the region west of the Lake basin, within
Canada.

Our inquiry sets out to accumulate an inventory of the plant
sub-fossils (pollen, seeds and organ fragments) preserved in
Holocene limnic sediments in appropriate geological situations.
These data are interpreted in terms of vegetation, thereby establishing whatever regional sequence of vegetation can be detected.
Finally, the findings will be correlated with data from other
disciplines, to draw up an ecological conspectus for the region
during the Holocene.

The area of our enquiry (Fig. 58) encompasses entirely that
natural geographical region referred to appropriately by Warkentin
(1964) as the Western Interior of Canada. This is a region of
considerable uniformity in geomorphology, climatic and vegetational
zonation, and floristics. The first objective was to select sites
in similar landform regions, where primary limnic deposits of
Holocene age are found. Cores have been taken from small closed
lakes or ponds in the hummocky disintegration moraine or related
glacial deposits throughout the Western Interior. The sites along
the western periphery of Glacial Lake Agassiz are of most relevance
to this symposium, and the results from a few of these will be
considered. The main tool in the work is pollen analysis. Some
of the essential preliminary studies, undertaken to assure some
validity in the application of this technique, will be discussed
briefly.

Prerequisites For The Interpretation Of Pollen Diagrams

It has been found that the surficial sediment of lakes is an
appropriate repository for the pollen rain of a particular region.
It would appear useful therefore to establish any quantitative
relationships between the pollen spectrum from surficial sediment
samples and the vegetational composition of the surrounding landscape. However, as is well-known, several factors preclude this
simple procedure. Anemophilous species of trees, shrubs and herbs

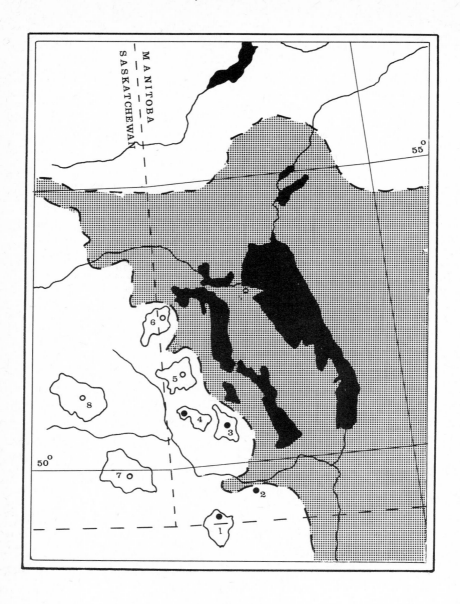

Figure 58. A sketch map of the northwestern precincts of the Glacial
            Lake Agassiz basin showing the site regions from which
            Holocene data have been obtained. (1) Turtle Mt.; (2) Tiger
            Hills; (3) Riding Mountain; (4) Russell. Currently being
            investigated: (5) Duck Mt.; (6) Pasquia Hills; (7) Moose
            Mt.; (8) Touchwood Hills. The approximate maximum extent
            of the Glacial Lake basin is shown (light shading).

vary enormously in their pollen production, in the efficiency of dispersal of the pollen, and in the relative preservation of pollen in sediments. To take a specific example from the Western Interior of Canada, the pollen of poplar is produced in large quantities each spring. Our studies of atmospheric samples indicate that the relative amount of poplar pollen is in proportion to the representation of the tree in the landscape. However, poplar pollen is rarely found in contemporary sediments, and it appears that its extraordinarily thin outer wall breaks down very quickly in most limnic situations.

This problem is illustrated by the data in Table 16, which compares the relative frequencies of the main pollen types recorded in top sediments from small lakes in the Riding Mountain uplands with the forest composition of the entire area expressed in terms of basal area. (These data were abstracted from Manitoba Forest inventory Report No. 4). The values for *Pinus* (pine) and *Populus* (poplar) illustrate the extreme discrepancies which can be found between values for pollen frequency and forest composition.

The most serious problem in establishing relationships between present day vegetation and the pollen spectra accumulating in lake sediments, or any other suitable repository, is that the areal extent of the source of pollen is indeterminable. Therefore inherent problems are posed in any quantitative studies of the relationship between the spectrum and the surrounding vegetation. Our approach to this problem, which is really an attempt to establish prerequisites for adequate interpretation of Quaternary pollen spectra, rests on the proposition that if the theory of pollen analysis has even partial validity, it should be possible to characterize landform-vegetation regions in terms of pollen spectra. On this basis we have explored the relations between pollen spectra of top sediments and the general character of the landform-vegetation regions of selected parts of west-central Canada. The plant cover of the Western Interior falls into certain distinctive assemblages on particular landform units. For example, the vegetation cover of southern Manitoba can be classified rationally into units whose distinguishing features are, on one hand landform, and on the other the structure and composition of the vegetation. Thus we have a distinctive assemblage on the deltaic deposits of the Carberry Spruce Hills, on the rolling Newdale till plain, on the Riding Mountain upland, in the Red River Valley Region, and so on.

Our procedure has been to sample a large number of surficial lake sediments in these landform-vegetation regions from the grasslands to the tundra in the Western Interior. Currently we are completing the analysis and collation of the data from some two hundred sites of this kind. To aid our present discussion, we offer here some of the general results of this study. Fig. 59 shows the frequencies of the main pollen types from the nine major vegetation regions in the Western Interior. It should be stressed that within each large vegetation region there are distinct units of landform-vegetation, and we have investigated their pollen spectra, but for our present purposes we will examine only this simplified general summary of the data.

TABLE 16

RELATIVE FREQUENCIES OF THE MAIN POLLEN TYPES FROM TOP
SEDIMENTS OF FIVE SMALL LAKES IN THE RIDING MOUNTAIN
COMPARED WITH THE PERCENTAGE BASAL AREAS
OF THE FOREST SPECIES (V).

	Pollen Sum					$\bar{X}$	V%
	Lake 1	Lake 2	Lake 3	Lake 4	Lake 5		
Pinus	14.4	12.2	23.9	9.4	24.2	16.8	1.1
Picea	24.6	26.6	10.4	18.6	16.8	19.4	13.9
Larix	1.6	0.6	-	0.3	0.5	0.6	<0.5
Betula	19.4	14.6	26.1	33.7	26.1	23.9	3.4
Populus	1.6	2.0	-	1.0	1.6	1.2	81.1
Quercus	0.6	0.2	1.4	1.3	1.4	0.9	<0.1
Ulmus	0.4	-	0.4	0.3	0.2	0.3	<0.1
Fraxinus	0.4	1.0	0.1	-	0.2	0.3	<0.1
Alnus	5.8	12.0	22.0	15.0	12.5	13.4	
Corylus	2.6	0.8	3.9	1.0	1.3	1.9	
Salix	2.8	3.0	1.0	2.8	2.4	2.2	
Gramineae	5.6	5.8	2.6	2.3	3.1	3.8	
Chenopodiineae	1.4	4.4	0.7	3.1	0.8	2.3	
Ambrosieae	0.8	1.6	1.6	1.3	1.1	1.3	
Artemisia	9.2	9.8	5.1	8.2	5.7	7.6	
Tubuliferae	3.2	1.4	0.4	2.5	0.8	1.6	

Tundra sites, lying not less than 100 kilometers north of the northern limit of trees, but still within the low arctic region, show a high proportion of tree pollen. The tundra sites summarized in Fig. 59 might be distinguished tentatively by the high proportion of *Betula* pollen, in this case of the dwarf shrub species, a high frequency of Cyperaceae, and consistent amounts of neath and grass pollen. Because these gross characteristics of the pollen spectrum are not striking, our conclusion to this point is that the positive identification of tundra spectra will require in addition the records of specifically arctic species whose pollen occurs quite rarely in lake sediments. The pollen spectra from forest tundra sites are characterized by a high frequency of spruce pollen associated with alder, the absence of broad leaved tree species, and low frequencies on non-arboreal pollen. The remaining Boreal zones, the open conifer and closed conifer forests can be distinguished only with difficulty, being characterized by larger relative amounts of pine, a frequent species in the Boreal forest following disturbance, and consistent amounts of alder and birch. The southern fringe of the Boreal forest, the mixed conifer-deciduous forests, are characterized by more or less equal proportions of spruce, pine and birch pollen, with consistent though relatively small frequencies of non-arboreal pollen. The broad leaved forests on upland sites in the Western Interior of Canada yield spectra with relatively high amounts of birch and oak pollen associated with increased amounts of non-arboreal species. The Aspen Parkland Region is distinguished with difficulty from grassland sites, due mainly to the almost complete absence of poplar pollen. Grassland sites show high frequencies of non-arboreal pollen, chiefly of grasses, chenopods, ragweed and sagebush pollen.

It is now clear, from this preliminary presentation, that there are serious difficulties facing an attempt to characterize even such broad geographical regions in terms of pollen spectra. We would suggest that any adequate interpretation will require, in addition to these kinds of studies, critical and careful studies of these pollen grains of highly indicative species which occur in sediments in low frequencies. Further, it is clear that the data from analyses of macrofossils will be of value in refining interpretation.

Pollen Assemblages From the Tiger Hills Region

A long core of lake sediment taken from a small lake in the Tiger Hills region of Manitoba has been analyzed both for pollen and macrofossils. From this core we now have available several Carbon-14 dates from various levels. As the studies of Elson (1955) have shown, the Tiger Hills consist of rolling morainic uplands; the site reported here lies at the edge of a region of end moraine, just south of a drift plain with associated outwash. The vegetation of this region, which has been disturbed greatly by agricultural activities, consists of a closed forest made up of

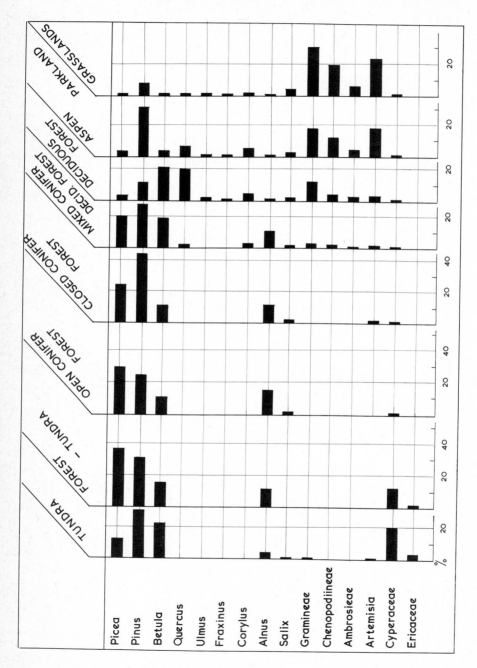

Figure 59. A summary of the average frequencies, expressed as percentages of the total pollen sum, of the main pollen types for the major vegetation zones of the Western Interior.

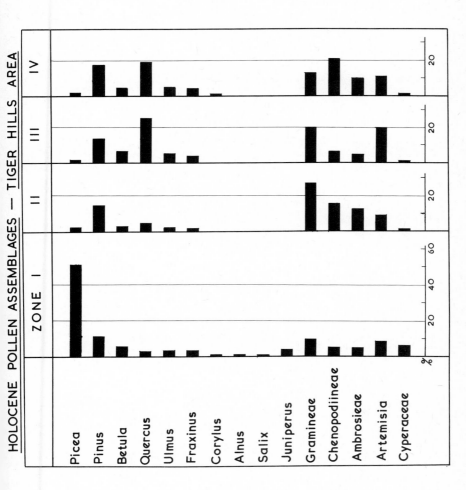

Figure 60. Typical pollen spectra from the four main pollen zones of a pollen diagram from Holocene sediment in the Tiger Hills.

roughly equal proportions of poplar, birch and oak. A somewhat
generalized version of the detailed pollen diagram of this site
is given in Ritchie (1966). Our sample from this site (the
Glenboro site) consists of ten metres of limnic sediment spanning
approximately 12,500 years of Holocene time. Initially we suggest
that there are four main assemblages of pollen recorded in these
sediments. The lower assemblage has relatively high frequencies
of spruce associated with *Artemisia* (sagebush) and, although not
shown on this diagram, consistent but small quantities of various
shrub and herb species which are proving to be characteristic of
these early Holocene sediments. The second Holocene assemblage
is dominated by non-arboreal pollen, the third shows a marked
increase in the pollen of deciduous tree species, especially oak.
Near the top of the diagram (this feature is characteristic of all
pollen diagrams from settled regions of the Western Interior) are
certain changes in the frequencies of non-arboreal species indicating human settlement.

Now, if we abstract from this diagram the characteristic
assemblages of these four zones presenting them as average relative
frequencies of the main pollen types (Fig. 60), and if, by direct
comparison, we attempt to find spectra from present day sediments
which match even approximately these Holocene assemblages, we will
have taken a useful first step in reconstructing the vegetation
which might have prevailed in this region throughout the Holocene.
The first point to be noticed (and this has been recorded by other
workers throughout the mid-western United States) is that the zone
I assemblage (early Holocene or late glacial) differs markedly
from all present-day spectra. While the high relative frequency
of spruce coincides well with the spectra from, for example,
forest tundra sites, the consistent or small quantities of pollen
of deciduous species, characteristic today of more or less temperate regions, and the consistent though relatively small frequencies
of non-arboreal pollen types set off this assemblage from modern
spectra. In addition one should point out that certain less
frequent pollen types are recorded with remarkable consistency
throughout all zone I Holocene assemblages examined so far in the
Western Interior. These have not been found in any modern assemblage.

This zone I assemblage poses one of the main problems in the
paleo-ecology of midwestern Quaternary sites, and we shall return
to this shortly. This zone II assemblage shows reasonable similarity to the grassland spectra from modern day deposits, with
the possible exception of the pine representation. To this point,
our reconstruction of the vegetation of zone II has been grassland
vegetation. This zone III spectra differ from the zone II mainly
in the increased relative amount of oak and birch pollen, and this
is in accord with the difference between modern grassland sites
and sites on uplands with deciduous forest in the Western Interior.
For this reason we have suggested tentatively that spectra of this
type indicate a landscape whose vegetation was primarily a mixed
deciduous forest dominated by oak, birch, and one supposes aspen
poplar. The upper Holocene zone is of interest only in the shift
in relative amounts of non-arboreal pollen especially that of the
pigweed family and the ragweed family, suggesting the effects of
human settlement in the region.

In summary, and simplifying the botanical details, the
Glenboro site suggests a succession of floral assemblages, starting with a mixed assemblage dominated by spruce with temperate
and boreal associates, and thus difficult of interpretation.
Next, an assemblage suggesting a grassland, then a zone interpreted in terms of deciduous forest, and finally a change in the
late Holocene induced by settlement.

Early Holocene Spectra From the Russell Region

To explore further the problems of early Holocene interpretation, we offer some very recent data compiled from an analysis
of a core of limnic sediment extracted from a small pond in hummocky disintegration moraine near Russell, Manitoba. The diagram
(Fig. 61) is from only a small slug of this core, some 30 cm. in
length. The complete diagram will be made available elsewhere.
Briefly we have found that these small ponds and lakes in this
morainic terrain yield approximately four meters of sediment, the
lowest metre of which is a laminated organic gyttja, above which
there is approximately two meters of heavy, largely inorganic clay,
overlain by one metre of loosely compacted somewhat flocculent
sediment. The lowest sediment has yielded the assemblages shown
in this diagram and a short slug from approximately the 390 cm.
level has been Carbon-14 dated at 10,350 years ago.

This diagram suggests that about 10,500 years ago there was a
shift from a pollen assemblage zone dominated by *Picea* and *Artemisia* (sagebush), associated characteristically with *Shepherdia
canadensis* (soapberry), and what we suggest tentatively is *Juniperus*.

The pollen assemblage zone which follows immediately can be
identified satisfactorily with the grassland spectrum type, as we
have pointed out earlier. However, the assemblage zone from the
early Holocene level at Russell, and at approximately one dozen
sites we have now examined in the Western Interior of Canada, as
well as many sites reported by others in the midwestern United
States (e.g. Cushing 1965), presents a problem of interpretation.
The characteristic pollen types of the assemblage appear to be
spruce, in some sites poplar, an assemblage of broad leaved trees
characteristic of temperate regions, never occurring in large
quantities in the diagrams, *Shepherdia canadensis* and a significant
fraction of non-arboreal pollen dominated usually by sagebush,
associated with ragweed pollen types. What vegetation did this
pollen assemblage represent? It is clear from all studies throughout North America that no contemporary pollen spectrum has been
detected which represents even approximately this assemblage. As
we saw earlier neither tundra, forest tundra nor open coniferous
forest spectra can be matched satisfactorily with the early Holocene
spectra. However, some consideration of the individual species
involved might throw light on the problem.

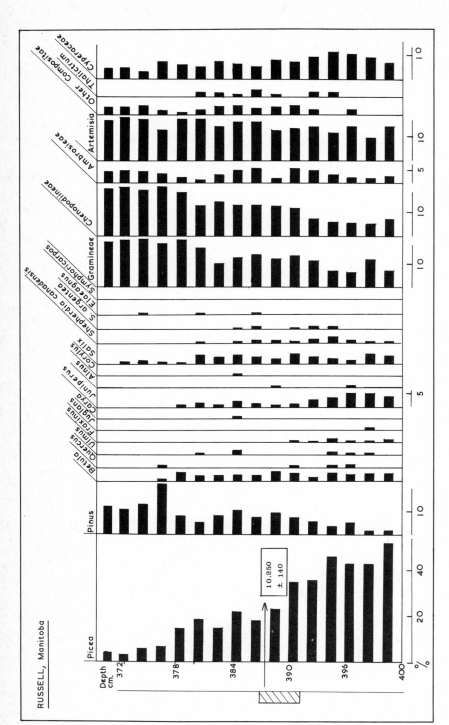

Figure 61.   A pollen diagram constructed from analysis at 2 cm. intervals of a 30 cm. core of sediment taken from a small lake near Russell, Manitoba. The percentages are based on the total pollen sum (excluding aquatics); a pollen sum of 1000 was recorded at each level. The Carbon-14 date of 10,250 ± 140 years ago for the short slug shown was determined by Isotopes Inc. (I – 2106).

We have shown elsewhere that long distance dispersal of certain pollen types, particularly such southern temperate deciduous trees as oak, ash, elm, walnut and others can be demonstrated conclusively for a subarctic location (Ritchie and Lichti-Federovich 1967). If we assume tentatively that the occurrence of pollen of these types in early Holocene sites is an expression of dispersal distances of perhaps 500 km. from the site of deposition, then we have circumvented one ecological problem. The remaining pollen types which fit somewhat unconformably into the concept derived from present day studies can be considered separately. If we examine the present day landscape of boreal and subarctic regions of Canada it is possible to find local communities of plants which, were they present on a regional scale, might be expected to produce a pollen rain of this type. Certain habitats in the boreal region of Canada do in fact bear communities which bring together some of the main species recorded in these early Holocene spectra.

For example, the pioneer forest vegetation found on alluvial deposits of the Hudson Bay lowlands is dominated by poplar and white spruce, associated with substantial quantities of *Shepherdia canadensis*, while such opportunist herbs as *Artemisia* are found frequently on gravel bars and river bank slip-off slopes, (Ritchie 1960). A *Picea-Shepherdia* association in the plains region of North America is characteristic of relatively recent mineral soils. It has been pointed out recently by Tisdale *et al* (1966) that *Shepherdia* and spruce, in this case Englemann spruce, are among the first woody pioneers on very recent morainic soils at the periphery of retreating glaciers in both Alaska and British Columbia. Further when we look at the present day distribution of *Shepherdia canadensis* we find that it occurs in southern and middle boreal forest situations only as scattered individuals within the forest, achieving significant structural proportions only on unusual edaphic sites.

We envisage this early Holocene vegetation as a mosaic of trees, shrubs and herbs dominated by highly mobile opportunist species such as white spruce, poplar, soapberry and others rapidly re-immigrating into recently deglaciated areas and later in middle Holocene times, becoming restricted in extent under the influence of a variety of factors including possibly climatic change. In the present day boreal forest, communities of this type are rare. Their diminution and local elimination can perhaps be explained in terms of changing soil conditions over 10 millennia, disturbance favouring the fire tree species such as pine, birch, while the elimination of fresh mineral soils by peat formation diminished a favourable sub-strate.

The assemblage of plants found on the sandy deltaic deposits of the upper Agassiz delta, as West (1961) has suggested earlier, bears some resemblance to what might have been the early Holocene vegetation of the midwest. However, it should be pointed out that the edaphic conditions prevailing here are of a rather specialized nature, and one cannot assume that they were widespread throughout the Western Interior. A related deposit close to Winnipeg is the sands and gravels of the Birds Hill Region, where in spite of the evident recent disturbance one can find an unusual mixture of

boreal and temperate plants, plants characteristic on the one hand
of the boreal forest and on the other of the grasslands, including
several of the species recorded in the early Holocene assemblages.

Within the boreal forest on such special edaphic sites as a
fault ridge on Laurie Lake, Ritchie (1956) has described a highly
localized but characteristic spruce-*Shepherdia canadensis*-poplar
community.

Concluding Comments

These suggestions regarding the vegetation history of the
uplands to the west of the main part of the Glacial Lake basin
might be summed up as follows in Table 17, on the basis of our
unpublished data from the Turtle Mountain, Tiger Hills and Russell
area, and cores from the Riding Mountain area (Ritchie 1964).

TABLE 17

VEGETATION HISTORY OF UPLANDS WEST OF GLACIAL
LAKE AGASSIZ BASIN

Approximate time in years ago	Areas occupied today by deciduous forest or aspen parkland	Areas occupied today by mixed deciduous-conifer forest
2,000	oak-birch-poplar forest, as at present	spruce-birch-poplar forest as at present
4,000		birch-poplar-oak fore
6,000	grassland	grassland
8,000		
10,000		
12,000	spruce-soapberry-sagebush assemblage	spruce-soapberry-sagebush assemblage

With the important proviso that the cores we have examined so far (although they all reach the underlying till) might not record the first communities to occupy deglaciated ground, it appears that most of the Western Interior of Canada was occupied in early Holocene times (12,500 to 10,500 years ago) by a vegetation yielding typical pollen assemblage dominated by spruce, soapberry and sagebush. We reconstruct the vegetation for this period as follows: a spruce-soapberry forest on mesic sites; poplar and willow stands as seral communities on young sites; treeless communities dominated by sagebush, grasses and locally juniper on the most xeric sites. As we have pointed out elsewhere (Ritchie 1966), the present day geographical affinities of the species of this assemblage are both boreal-subarctic and temperate, precluding a cold continental climate like that of the present northern coniferous forest or forest-tundra, but suggesting rather a warmer climate perhaps resembling that of the southern mixed coniferous-deciduous forest of the Western Interior.

At about 10,500 years ago all our diagrams record a change in spectra suggesting that at the latitudes of 49° N to approximately 51° N the western precincts of the lake basin were occupied predominantly by treeless vegetation of the grassland type. Such a change suggests strongly a climatic amelioration, involving perhaps a decrease in precipitation and increase in temperature during the summers, and a decrease in temperature and increase in precipitation during the winters. (These suggestions are frankly speculative; the subject is dealt with authoritatively elsewhere in this volume by Bryson and Wendland).

Finally, there is some evidence that about 3500 to 4000 years ago there was a change in vegetation involving a diminution in the extent of grassland with a concomitant spread of forest from northern and southeastern areas into the area. It is possible that this change was influenced primarily by climate, but it should be emphasised that three factors, separately or in interaction, might have caused changes in vegetation during the late Holocene in this area. These three factors are climatic change, the activities of aboriginal man and large herbivores, and the relative rates of immigration of the dominant species from southern and northern refugia.

Acknowledgements

I wish to thank my colleague, Mrs. S. Federovich, for permission to use certain of her unpublished data in this paper. The original investigations of the author referred to above were supported by grants from the National Science Foundation (GB 3821) and the National Research Council of Canada (T-1443).

VEGETATION HISTORY OF THE SOUTHERN LAKE AGASSIZ BASIN

DURING THE PAST 12,000 YEARS

Creighton T. Shay

Introduction

The Lake Agassiz basin south of the International boundary in northern and northwestern Minnesota, eastern North Dakota and extreme northeastern South Dakota covers an area of approximately 22,000 square miles. Today, the central axis of the basin comprises the Red River Valley, one of the world's richest agricultural regions. Prior to modern agriculture, however, this broad lake plain supported expanses of tall grass prairie grazed by bison, elk and deer. Prairie was broken in places by isolated stands of trees around wet depressions and along the Red River and its tributaries. Morainic uplands on the west also originally supported prairie but those on the east were characterized by a variety of forest types roughly aligned in north-south zones. From west to east these zones consisted of marginal oak and aspen forests and groves, deciduous forest and mixed coniferous-deciduous forest. North of Red Lake extensive peat lands have developed on the bed of Lake Agassiz.

The vegetation and flora of the Agassiz basin have been of interest to ecologists and plant geographers because of their transitional nature between the forested eastern area and the grasslands of the Great Plains to the west. The prairie-forest border on the eastern basin margin has been investigated with regard to its composition and the possible factors responsible for its position (Ewing 1924, Buell and Cantlon 1951, Buell and Facey 1960). The factors usually stressed are climate, soil and fire. The prairie-forest border also forms the boundary of three floristic provinces: the Northern Conifer Forest and the Eastern Deciduous Forest on the east and the Grassland Province on the west (Gleason and Cronquist 1964).

The transitional nature of the region has provided fertile ground for hypotheses regarding postglacial plant migration and vegetation development (Rudd 1951, Löve 1959). Until recently, however, paleobotanical evidence of vegetation history has been largely lacking except for a few plant macrofossils identified by Rosendahl (1948) and several tree pollen diagrams from the pine-hardwood forest (Potzger 1946, Erdtman 1954). More recent studies commenced with the comprehensive investigation by McAndrews (1966) of the pre-settlement vegetation and pollen rain coupled with four pollen profiles (in a transect across the prairie-forest transition) spanning the last 12,000 years. Other studies in the region include three complete or truncated pollen diagrams from ponds between Lake Agassiz beaches (Shay in press) and a detailed pollen and macrofossil sequence from a lake on the Prairie Coteau in northeastern South Dakota (Watts and Bright in press). This paleobotanical evidence

231

combined with a series of radiocarbon dates from pond sediments and
plant remains associated with Lake Agassiz deposits provides useful,
if incomplete, data for reconstructing the regional vegetation and
flora during the past 12,000 years. Plant nomenclature used in this
paper follows Fernald (1950).

Physiography, Soils and Climate

        The basin is a relatively flat lobate depression surrounded by
Late Wisconsin morainic uplands rising 500 to 1,000 feet above the
basin floor. The slopes to these uplands are especially steep along
the Pembina escarpment on the northwest and to the Prairie Coteau on
the southwest. Streams originating in most of the uplands empty into
the northward-flowing Red River which bisects the basin. Runoff in
the extreme south, however, and from the eastern flank of the Prairie
Coteau, flows into the Minnesota River. Drainage on the flat lake
plain is poorly developed, but it has been accelerated by drainage
ditches.

        Soils of the southern basin can be grouped according to their
parent material and its mode of deposition (Elson 1961). A transect
outward from the center of the basin reveals several intergrading
soil parent materials: (1) alluvial silt to gravel on the floodplain
and terraces of the Red River; (2) deep-water deposits of calcareous
clayey silt; (3) littoral deposits of calcareous silt and fine sand
(4) beach ridges of well-sorted sand and gravel; (5) moraines of
silty to sandy calcareous till. In addition, extensive tracts of
deltaic silts, sands and gravels occur. Post-Agassiz eolian activity
has produced dune areas within these deltas, e.g., along the Sheyenne
River. North of Red Lake, extensive tracts of peat overlie clays,
sands and gravels and lake-washed till (Heinselman 1963).

        Climate is sub-humid with warm summers, cold winters and a
warm-season precipitation pattern. Annual precipitation ranges from
18 inches in the northwest to 24 inches in the southeast, approximately 75% of it falling during April through September (USDA 1941)
July mean temperatures from north to south range from 66°F. to 72°F.
January means range from -2° to 12°F. Isotherms are parallel across
the basin but dip southward over the surrounding uplands. Red River
Valley has several climatic features contrasting it with the forested
eastern uplands (McAndrews 1966) and the peatlands north of Red Lake
(Heinselman 1963). In contrast to these areas the basin has less
overall precipitation, less winter snow cover, less continuous snow
cover and higher summer temperatures.

        Climatic gradients appear to be steepest where elevation
differences between the basin floor and uplands are greatest
(McAndrews 1966). One might consider the general prairie-forest
border as a climatically controlled tension zone similar to that
outlined for Wisconsin (Curtis 1959) with soil conditions controlling
specific vegetation boundaries. In any case, the combined effects
of climate and soil have led to distinctive vegetation histories in the
basin and surrounding eastern uplands for the past 10,000 to 11,000
years.

Natural Vegetation

The composition and distribution of plant communities prior to their alteration or destruction through recent agricultural activities can be partially reconstructed by reference to early plant collections and descriptions, maps, land survey records and subsequent studies of remaining stands of forest and prairie. The land survey records containing brief descriptions of vegetation and identifications of bearing trees along survey lines have been used to construct a veg- etation map for Minnesota (Marschner 1930). Figure 62 is based upon McAndrew's (1966) generalized version of Marschner's map. Forests along water courses and lakes in the prairie follow the maps of Upham (1896) and Ayers (1899). The tree species characterizing each forest vegetation type shown on the map are listed in Table 18. (Infrequent or rare tree species recorded for the region include: *Acer saccharinum, Prunus serotina, Betula lutea, Ulmus thomasii, U. rubra, Pyrus americ- ana, P. decora, Carpinus carolinana* and *Quercus ellipsoidalis Q.alba.* In the vegetation descriptions and historical reconstruction to follow, attention will be directed to those upland plant taxa important in the fossil pollen and macrofossil record. References to more detailed vegetation and fossil studies are cited throughout the discussion.

Prairie

At the end of the 19th Century, prairie was the most widespread vegetation type within the basin and westward. West of the basin, on the drift plains of central North Dakota, the taller grasses of the east gradually declined in importance and were replaced by the mid- and short grasses (Whitman *et al* 1941). Prairies on the eastern edge of this transition zone have been recently described in detail by Dix and Smeins (1966). Within the basin, floristic composition of the prairie varied according to slope, exposure, soil texture and drainage. On well-drained medium-textured soils, extensive stands of tall and mid-grasses e.g., *Andropogon gerardi, A.scoparius, Koeleria cristata, Stipa spartea,* dominated, according to Whitman *et al* (1941) and Ewing (1924). Coarse-textured soils on dry sites in delta and outwash areas as well as exposed slopes and bluffs of river valleys supported a prairie flora rich in species more characteristic of the grasslands to the west (Wanek and Burgess 1965).

Wet meadows and marshes contained such grasses as reed grass *(Phragmites),* together with arrowhead *(Sagittaria latifolia),* cattail *(Typha latifolia),* sedges *(Carex* spp.) and bulrushes *(Scirpus* spp.). On alkali flats grew species of Chenopodiaceae *(Chenopodium, Atriplex, Salicornia, Suaeda)* together with other salt-tolerant plants (Upham 1892). In addition to the grasses, species of the composite (Compositae), sedge (Cyperaceae), pulse (Leguminosae), rose (Rosaceae) and lily (Liliaceae) families make up most of the flora.

Shrub communities were scattered throughout the prairie in a variety of habitats. Low shrubs such as prairie-clover *(Petalostemum)* and lead-plant *(Amorpha canescens)* occurred throughout the prairie formation. Extensive colonies of silverberry *(Elaeagnus commutata),* wolfberry *(Symphoricarpos occidentalis)* and chokecherry *(Prunus*

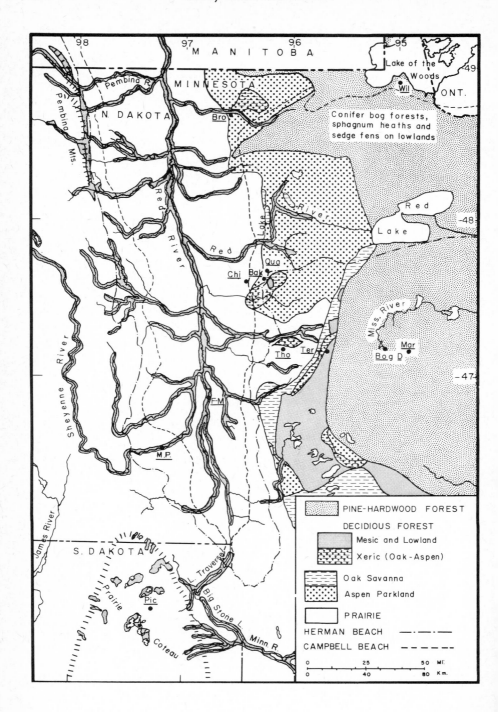

Figure 62.   Major beaches and vegetation types in the southern Lake
             Agassiz basin. Herman and Campbell beaches after Leverett
             and Sardeson (1932); vegetation units based on McAndrews
             (1966), Ayers (1899), and Upham (1896). Paleobotanical
             sites include: Bog D, Tho (Thompson Pond), Mar (Martin
             Pond), Ter (Terhell Pond), McAndrews (1966); M.P. (Mirror
             Pool), McAndrews (this volume); F-M (Fargo-Moorhead area
             including Seminary), McAndrews (this volume) and Moorhead
             (Rosendahl 1948); Pic (Pickerel Lake), Watts and Bright
             (in press); Qua (Qually Pond), Bak (Bakken Pond), Chi
             (Chicog Lake), Shay (in press); Wil, Williams (Heinselman
             1963); Bro (Bronson interglacial site) Rosendahl (1948).

virginiana) were prevalent on dry prairie slopes and knolls (Ewing 1924). On the driest sites, especially in dune areas, creeping savin *(Juniperus horizontalis)* was common. These species (except *Juniperus* together with hazel *(Corylus americana)*, smooth sumach *(Rhus glabra)* dogwood *(Cornus* spp.), arrowwood (*Viburnum* spp.), currant, gooseberry (*Ribes* spp.) and members of the rose family *(Amelanchier, Crateagus, Prunus, Rubus)* occurred at forest and stream margins along with willows *(Salix* spp.) and also within oak and aspen groves (Ewing 1924, Moore 1958, Buell and Facey 1960). Willows and bog birch *(Betula pumila* var. *glandulifera)* grew on the edges of marshes and the central depressions of aspen groves.

The most conspicuous change in the prairie since the late 19th Century when fire frequency was reduced, has been the expansion of forests, especially along the eastern margin of the basin. Succession of prairie to forest is usually accomplished through an intermediate shrub community on ground exposed through headwater erosion of streams (Weaver 1960), on moist sites in small valleys (Moyer 1910) or by expansion from margins of marshes and wet depressions within the prairie (Ewing 1924). Once established, forest groves spread over upland prairie through a marginal thicket or, occasionally, seedlings (oak) or shoots from underground roots (aspen) will become established directly in the prairie. Increased soil moisture and fewer fires can accelerate this succession whereas drier conditions and increased fire frequency can reverse it (Curtis 1959).

The tree species important in this early phase of succession vary within the basin. Aspen (*Populus tremuloides*) is most important in the north, aspen and bur oak (*Quercus macrocarpa)* in the central portion and bur oak along with pin oak (*Quercus ellipsoidalis* in the southeast. Succession associated with stream erosion may involve species of the lowland deciduous forest. The composition of the resulting communities -- aspen parkland, oak savanna and deciduous forest -- will be described in turn.

Aspen Parkland and Oak Savanna

In the northern part of the basin and into Canada, aspen groves surrounded by shrub thickets ranged in size from small isolated patches surrounding wet depressions in the prairie to extensive tracts of dense stands (Bird 1961). Balsam poplar (*Populus balsamifera)*, paper birch (*Betula papyrifera)* and bur oak were associates of aspen. Aspen may invade prairie through its root systems by suckers, although frequent fires may cut back such sprouts (Buell and Buell 1959).

In the central and southern parts of the basin, open-grown bur oaks with a ground cover of prairie occupied extensive areas. This vegetation type was maintained by fire (Curtis 1959) for, since the cessation of fires, stunted shruby oaks or "grubs" have had an opportunity to mature into trees. In a stand studied by McAndrews (1966) near TerhellPond, oak savanna has succeeded to oak forest dominated by bur oak, and including aspen, box elder *(Acer negundo)* and ash (*Fraxinus pennsylvanica)*. These even-aged forest stands with enclosing scattered open grown oaks can be considered one type of xeric forest, although several other types were also present in the central basin.

Xeric Deciduous Forests

Other xeric deciduous forests ranged from stands of mixed close-grown bur oak and aspen (McAndrews 1966) to groves in which either was dominant. Ewing (1924) considered this type to be successional, with oak eventually replacing aspen. Although not noted on Fig. 62, aspen and oak also were important in the vegetation along the Pembina escarpment in North Dakota (Stevens 1950), and also in the Turtle Mountains to the West (Potter and Moir 1961). Since the late 19th Century, in the absence of fires, several of these xeric forest stands have succeeded to mesic deciduous forest with the invasion or increase of elm (*Ulmus*), birch and ash (McAndrews 1966).

In Minnesota southeastward of the region considered in Fig. 62 the xeric deciduous forests consisted chiefly of bur, pin and white oak (*Quercus alba*) together with small amounts of red oak (*Quercus rubra*) according to Daubenmir (1936).

Mesic and Lowland Deciduous Forests

Elsewhere in the prairie area groves of decidous species occurred throughout the basin along stream margins, on river flood-plains, surrounding lakes and in moist habitats along escarpments and beach ridges. The species were principally those of the upland deciduous forests to the east along with aspen and oak. On flood-plains, species included box elder, green ash (*Fraxinus pennsylvanica* var. *subintegerrima*), basswood (*Tilia americana*), ironwood (*Ostrya virginiana*), american elm (*Ulmus americana*), cottonwood (*Populus deltoides*), peach-leaved willow (*Salix amygdaloides*) and hackberry (*Celtis occidentalis*). See Stevens (1950) and Burgess (1965).

Along the prairie forest transition extensive stands of upland deciduous forest occurred in mesic situations between the oak and aspen communities on the west and pine-hardwood forests on the east. On the basis of land survey data McAndrews (1966) noted an elm-basswood (*Ulmus-Tilia*) type and a more mesic maple-basswood (*Acer-Tilia*) type; the latter has tended to succeed the elm-basswood type since settlement time, about 1900. Other characteristic species of the mesic deciduous forests are listed in Table 18.

Pine Hardwood Forests

East of the deciduous forest zone was a series of conifer and deciduous communities designated as the "pine-hardwood" forest by McAndrews (1966). On well-drained, medium-textured soils decid-uous species of mesic forests occurred with various admixtures of conifers. Among the latter, white pine (*Pinus strobus*) was most important, especially in the western portion. White pine was also associated with red pine (*Pinus resinosa*) on these soils.

TABLE 18

FOREST TYPES

Species	Conifer Bog	Pine-Hardwood Forest	Deciduous Forest Mesic	Deciduous Forest Lowland	Deciduous Forest Xeric	Oak Savanna	Aspen Parkland
Abies balsamea / Balsam fir	X	X					
Picea mariana / Black spruce	X	X					
P. glauca / White spruce		X					
Larix laricina / Larch	X	X					
Thuja occidentalis / White cedar	X						
Pinus strobus / White Pine		X					
P. banksiana / Jack Pine		X					
P. resinosa / Red Pine		X					
Fraxinus nigra / Black ash	X	X	X				
Populus grandidentata / Large-toothed aspen		X	X				
Acer rubrum / Red maple		X					
Betula papyrifera / Paper birch		X	X		X		X

Species	Conifer Bog	Pine-Hardwood Forest	Deciduous Forest Mesic	Deciduous Forest Lowland	Deciduous Forest Xeric	Oak Savanna	Aspen Parkland
Populus balsamifera / Balsam poplar		X	X		X		X
Populus tremuloides / Quaking aspen		X	X		X	X	X
Quercus macrocarpa / Bur oak		X	X		X	X	X
Acer saccharum / Sugar maple		X	X				
Quercus rubra / Red oak		X	X				
Ostrya Virginiana / Ironwood		X	X	X			
Ulmus americana / American elm		X	X	X			
Acer negundo / Box elder		X	X	X			
Tilia americana / Basswood		X	X	X			
Fraxinus pennsylvanica including F. pennsylvanica var. subintegerrima / Red and Green ash		X	X	X			
Populus deltoides / Cottonwood				X			
Salix amygdaloides / Peach-leaved willow				X			
Celtis occidentalis / Hackberry				X			

On coarser-textured soils, red pine formed pure stands or was mixed
with jack pine (*Pinus banksiana*). Stands of jack pine mixed with
balsam poplar, aspen and paper birch had developed on recently
burned sites. The boreal conifers, such as balsam fir (*Abies
balsamea*) and white spruce (*Picea glauca*), associated with paper
birch, also contributed to the vegetation (Buell and Niering 1957).

Throughout the pine-hardwood forest, peat deposits have accumulated in depressions and around lakes and on the flat bed of Lake
Agassiz, north of Red Lake. The forests on these bogs were dominate
by black spruce (*Picea mariana*), larch (*Larix laricina*) and northern
white cedar (*Thuja occidentalis*). See Conway (1949) and Heinselman
(1963). Black ash (*Fraxinus nigra*) and balsam fir were common trees
on both lowland mineral soils and in upland forests. Common bog
shrubs included willows, bog birch, alder (*Alnus rugosa*) and species
of the heath family (*Ericaceae*).

Vegetation History

The foregoing summary of prairie and forest communities implies
a rich and diversified flora within the region. The map of Gleason
and Cronquist (1964:174) shows the southern basin enclosing parts
of three floristic provinces: Northern Conifer, Eastern Deciduous
and Grassland. The basin's floristic diversity was recognized by
Upham (1892) and later further documented for North Dakota (Rudd
1951) and Manitoba (Löve 1959). The latter two authors presented
late- and post-glacial vegetation histories for their respective
regions based on modern plant distributions, glacial fluctuations,
Lake Agassiz events and limited fossil evidence. At present, howeve
additional pollen and macrofossil studies (McAndrews 1966 and this
volume, Watts and Bright in press, Shay in press) are available
for reconstructing the vegetation history during the past 12,000
years.

Before turning to the discussion of vegetation history a
cautionary note should be inserted here concerning the accuracy
and completeness of vegetation reconstructions based on pollen and
macrofossils. The reasons for this caution are twofold. The first
concerns the relationship between the local and regional vegetation
and the recovered fossil pollen or seed assemblage. Wide disparities exist between production of both pollen and seed from plant
to plant (Watts and Winter 1966). In addition, variations in
preservation result in over- and under-representation of various
plant species or, for much of the flora, probably no representation
at all. Although several studies which relate modern pollen spectra
to contemporary vegetation in the region (McAndrews 1966, Janssen
1966) provide a reasonable basis for interpreting later postglacial
assemblages, no close modern analogs have been found for the earlier
spruce and pine-dominated pollen zones. Studies relating the modern
vegetation to contemporary seed "rain" are only beginning (Watts
and Winter 1966).

The second reason for caution involves the identification of fossil pollen or seeds to ecologically or phytogeographically significant taxonomic units. Many pollen taxa cannot yet be identified beyond the level of genus (oak) and some not beyond the family level (*Gramineae*). Macrofossils offer more detailed taxonomic information. This is usually limited to aquatic and damp-ground plants because upland plants are not often represented. For purposes of brevity this summary will deal primarily with the history of upland vegetation. Interpretations of fossil aquatic and damp-ground plants can be found in the studies cited.

The sites used in the summary (Figs. 62 and 63) include information drawn from three pollen diagrams from the present prairie (Pickerel, Thompson, Chicog), two from the aspen parkland (Qually, Bakken), one from the mesic deciduous forest (Terhell) and two from the pine-hardwood forest (Bog D, Martin). All of these sites are ponds or lakes in morainic topography except for Qually, Bakken and Chicog which are ponds associated with beach ridges of Lake Agassiz. Complete post-glacial sequences are lacking for the center of the basin although fossiliferous deposits in the Fargo-Moorhead area (Seminary, Moorhead) and Mirror Pool (Rosendahl 1948, McAndrews this volume) provide information about short intervals associated with Lake Agassiz I and II. An interglacial site -- Bronson -- is included in this summary also. (Rosendahl 1948).

The summary of vegetation history of the last 12,000 years in the basin has been divided into four time intervals, each characterized by one or more distinct combinations of pollen types recognized in diagrams within the region (Fig. 63). A series of radiocarbon dates of selected pollen horizons and macrofossil deposits furnishes chronological control. The four intervals are:

I. 12,000 to 10-11,000 years ago -- assemblage dominated by *Picea*.

II. 10-11,000 to 9,000-8,500 years ago -- assemblages dominated by *Pinus* and deciduous trees.

III. 9,000-8,500 to 4,000 years ago -- assemblages dominated by *Quercus* and herbaceous pollen, chiefly Gramineae and Compositae.

IV. 4,000 years ago to present -- assemblages dominated by various pollen taxa including herbs, deciduous trees, and *Pinus*

Interglacial Vegetation

Near Bronson in northern Minnesota ("Bro" in Fig. 62) wood and other plant remains were recovered from lake clays that underlie till and Lake Agassiz clays between 88 and 137 feet below the surface. Radiocarbon dates on several wood samples yielded dates greater than 38,000 years. The remains were of plants that grew in and around a

Thousands of Years B.P.	Prairie Coteau — Pickerel	Lake Agassiz Lowland — Mirror Pool, Fargo-Moorhead sites	Eastern Margin — Qually, Chicog, Bakken, Thompson	Morainic Upland — Terhell	Morainic Upland — Bog D, Martin
0	Prairie with local developing Deciduous Forest (Tilia, Fraxinus, Quercus, Ulmus, Populus, Salix)	Prairie with Deciduous Forest along streams	Prairie, Aspen Parkland and Oak Savanna (Quercus, Populus)	Deciduous Forest	Pine-Hardwood Forest Pinus banksiana and P. resinosa expand
-1					
-2			Prairie		Pinus strobus expands
-3				Deciduous Forest (Ulmus, Betula, Acer, Tilia, Ostrya)	
-4					
-5	Prairie (Gramineae, Artemisia Petalostemum, Amorpha)	Prairie	Prairie (Gramineae, Artemisia Petalostemum, Amorpha)	Oak Savanna with local Deciduous Forests (Quercus, Gramineae, Artemisia)	
-6					
-7		– Final Drainage –	— Maximum aridity — Ambrosia Peak ————		
-8			Prairie	Oak Savanna	
-9	Prairie expanding Deciduous Forest (Ulmus, Betula, Quercus, Acer, Pteridium)	Retreat from Campbell Stage	Prairie and Forest (Betula, Populus, Ulmus)	Pine and Deciduous Forest (Pinus banksiana, Populus, Betula, Pteridium)	
-10		Lake Agassiz II Low Water Stage			
-11		Retreat from Herman Stage		Spruce Forest (Betula, Fraxinus, Shepherdia canadensis)	
-12	Spruce Forest	Lake Agassiz I	(Picea, Larix, Populus)		

Figure 63. Summary of the vegetation history of the southern Lake Agassiz basin region. Characteristic pollen types for each interval are enclosed in parentheses. Based on paleobotanical evidence and radiocarbon dates from sites shown in Fig. 62.

lake that preceded the last glacial cover. The algae, *Chara*, several species of fungi, 21 species of mosses, the fern ally *Equisetum* and 49 species of seed plants make up the flora. Upland forest species include *Larix*, *Picea glauca*, *Picea mariana*, *Populus*, *Acer spicatum*, *Prunus pennsylvanica* and *Corylus cornuta*, all common in the pine-hardwood forests of today.

Interval I. 12,000 to 10-11,000 years ago

About 12,000 years ago Lake Agassiz I formed when the Des Moines Lobe in the basin retreated. Several minor ice advances as the lake formed are recorded by low moraines looping across the northern part of the basin (Clayton 1966: Fig. 3). The mapped border of the southernmost loop, Edinburgh-Holt, (Leverett 1932) is just five miles west of the Herman beach. These advances are estimated by Clayton to have occurred about 12,000 years ago. The highest Herman shoreline was abandoned shortly thereafter. This is indicated by a date of 11,740 ± 200 years ago (Y-1327) on organic sediments near the base of Qually Pond which is situated within the Herman beach complex mapped by Upham (1896). Subsequently, the lake dropped to low levels at least once between 11,000 and 10,000 years ago (Clayton 1966). During this time Agassiz I clays were subjected to drying and erosion while plant debris washed into the basin (Elson 1962).

The most extensive pollen record from this interval (130 cm. in length of core) is preserved at Qually whereas Pickerel, Thompson, Terhell, Bog D and Martin contain only the uppermost 20-30 cm. of the sequence. Pollen spectra are dominated by *Picea* (60-80%) along with varying amounts of other trees and shrubs. Herb pollen makes up less than 20% of the pollen sum.

Macrofossils include needles and seeds of *Picea* and *Larix laricina* (Pickerel, Qually and Martin). Bracts of *Betula papyrifera* occur at Martin associated with declining *Picea* values at the end of the interval. At Moorhead and Seminary in the center of the basin, plant remains washed in from the surrounding lake margin dating to the end of the interval (10,000 years ago) include *Picea glauca* (wood), *Larix* (wood, needles), *Populus balsamifera* and *Fraxinus pennsylvanica* (Rosendahl 1948, McAndrews this volume).

Although no macrofossils of *Juniperus* or *Thuja* have been found in the basin, *Juniperus communis* needles are recorded in Saskatchewan (Ritchie and deVries 1964) and in south-central Minnesota (Watts and Winter 1966) in deposits of similar age and pollen composition.

The pollen and macrofossil aspect of these *Picea* assemblages is similar to those at sites elsewhere in Minnesota and the Great Lake region (Watts and Winter 1966, Cushing 1965) as well as in Manitoba and Saskatchewan (Ritchie 1966) in central North Dakota (McAndrews *et al* 1967) and in the sandhills of south-central South Dakota (Watts and Wright 1966). Compared to central Minnesota the sites west and north of the basin have a smaller proportion of temperate deciduous trees while macrofossils and pollen of *Larix*

are absent (Manitoba, Saskatchewan, South Dakota). *Picea mariana*
and *Fraxinus nigra* are also thought to be absent from the sandhills
area (Watts and Wright 1966). Their absence may represent a lag in
migration of these trees from southern or eastern areas.

The major vegetation components of the Agassiz region were
Boreal and Great Lakes -- St. Lawrence forest species including
Picea (probably both *Picea glauca* and *P. mariana)*, *Populus
balsamifera* (and probably *P. tremuloides)*, *Fraxinus nigra*, and,
late in the interval, *Fraxinus pennsylvanica* and *Betula papyrifera*.
Both *Juniperus* and *Thuja* may have been present. *Abies* pollen is
recorded only at Qually and Pickerel. The small amounts of other
tree pollen suggest that *Pinus* and most deciduous trees were outside
the basin.

The habitats in the region available to these forest species
undoubtedly included a variety of soil texture and moisture conditions
involving beach ridges, outwash areas, morainic ridges and stream
banks. Glacial meltwater no doubt collected in upland depressions
and between beaches because drainage was probably still poorly
developed. Although all of these species now occur in a variety of
habitats within their present ranges (Fowells 1965), well-drained
upland sites were probably dominated by white spruce and *Populus*
mixed with birch, and in certain areas, fir. Poorly drained sites
around depressions and along streams accommodated larch, ash, black
spruce, and northern white cedar.

In areas adjacent to the Lake new habitats became available
as water levels fell. Pioneer communities colonizing beaches
around Lake of the Woods in northern Minnesota today (McMillan 1896)
include *Salix, Artemisia* and *Chenopodium* followed by *Juniperus
communis* and *Populus tremuloides*. Beach ridges and openings may also
have supported species of *Ambrosia* and *Euphorbia*. Shrub and herb
communities around depressions, along stream banks and in upland
forests consisted of *Salix, Alnus, Rubus* cf. *pubescens, Shepherdia
canadensis, Cornus canadensis* and, on drier sites, *Juniperus*.
Species of primarily northern distribution that do not occur in the
region today include *Saxifraga* cf. *oppositifolia* (pollen) at Qually,
Selaginella selaginoides (spores) at Qually and Pickerel and
Vaccinium cf. *uliginosum* (macrofossils) at Pickerel. The latter
two species now occur in extreme northeastern Minnesota (Butters and
Abbe 1953).

Vegetational trends recorded at Qually apparently favored the
expansion of tree vegetation. Although *Fraxinus* declines in percent,
Larix, Betula and *Populus* increase at the expense of NAP, suggesting
a continuous succession to forests in the vicinity. Forests may not
have completely colonized the emerging bed of Lake Agassiz, however.

The end of the sharp decline of spruce in the Agassiz region
has been dated at 11,000 ± 90 years ago (Y-1418) at Bog D and 10,670
± 140 years ago (Y-1361) at Pickerel. Wood associated with high
values of *Picea* pollen has been dated at the Seminary Pond site at
9,900 ± 400 years ago (W-993) and at Moorhead at 9,930 ± 280 years
ago (W-338). See McAndrews (this volume).

Interval II.   10-11,000 to 9,000-8,500 years ago

From the low water stage that ended about 10,000 years ago, Lake Agassiz rose to the Campbell strandline which was effective until about 9,000 years ago. Dates for the retreat from this second lake stage in the southern basin include 9,200 ± 600 (W-1057) at Williams, Minnesota, on *Larix* wood underlying a low beach ridge seven miles inside the main Campbell beach and 9,130 ± 150 (I-1982) at Mirror Pool in the Sheyenne River trench where plant remains are incorporated in marl overlying Agassiz II clays (Brophy 1967, McAndrews this volume). Paleobotanically, this second interval is characterized by maxima of *Pinus* and deciduous tree pollen. It ended sometime between 9,000 and 8,500 years ago. The short sequence at Mirror Pool immediately post-dating the Campbell stage shows declining tree and rising herb pollen values at the top. A similar sequence is recorded at Chicog situated just below the main Campbell beach. At Chicog, lithologic and fossil evidence suggests a change to a shallow pond at this time (Shay in press). At Bog D on the eastern uplands, the end of the pine maximum dates to 8560 ± 120 (Y-1419).

The abrupt decline of spruce to low values is accompanied by increases and subsequent maxima of *Betula*, *Populus*, *Ulmus*, *Pinus*, *banksiana resinosa* type and *Quercus*, although not necessarily everywhere in that order. These increases may reflect the arrival of several of these genera in the region from eastern refuges (Wright 1964). Most of these trees reach maxima as *Picea* declines to low levels. Herb percentages, chiefly Gramineae, *Artemisia* and *Ambrosia* rise, particularly near the end of the interval.

Macrofossils of trees and shrubs within the region include *Picea* needles at Qually, *Larix* needles at Mirror Pool, Pickerel and Qually and wood at Williams. *Betula papyrifera* bracts occur at Pickerel and Martin and bracts or bud scales of *Betula pumila*, *Alnus rugosa* and *Salix* at Mirror Pool. At Nicollet Creek Bog in Itasca Park, near Bog D, several cones of *Pinus banksiana* occur associated with pollen spectra similar to Bog D (Shay 1967). In the Assiniboine Valley near Treesbank, Manitoba, wood of *Picea*, *Fraxinus cf nigra* and *Ulmus americana* has been dated at 9,110 ± 110 years ago (Y-415) according to Löve (1959).

In contrast to the preceding interval, distinct sub-regional differences can be recognized on the basis of the relative amounts of *Pinus*, *Ulmus*, *Quercus*, and *Betula* pollen. Bog D and Martin have pine maxima of 55% and 75% respectively, *Betula*, 10-20%, *Ulmus*, less than 10% and *Quercus*, 5%. At Qually, Chicog, Thompson and Mirror Pool, pine reaches about 30-40%, *Betula*, 5-15%, *Ulmus*, 5-15% and *Quercus* less than 5%. Terhell is similar to the above three sites except that *Quercus* values rise throughout the interval to 15%. Pine is lowest at Pickerel, with peak values of less than 20%. *Betula* and *Ulmus* maxima are over 20% and *Quercus* peaks at about 15%.

The interpretation of these differences is confounded by the fact that *Pinus*, *Betula* and, to a certain extent, *Quercus* are copious pollen producers and disperse their pollen widely.

Consequently, these genera are often over-represented, particularly in areas where the local vegetation does not produce much pollen (McAndrews 1966, Janssen 1966). Pine trees undoubtedly expanded somewhere in the region but their abundance and distribution is difficult to deterime. West and north of the basin in central North Dakota (McAndrews *et al.* 1967) and Manitoba (Ritchie 1966), *Pinus* values range between 15% and 20%; *Betula* is 10% or less. At Madelia, southeast of the basin, *Pinus* is less than 5% and *Betula* rises to 40% (Jelgersma 1962). In central Minnesota *Pinus* and *Betula* values are comparable to those at Bog D (Cushing 1965). Altogether, these data, taken in conjunction with the macrofossil evidence, may mean that pine expansion was concentrated approximately within its present range in Minnesota and had not yet migrated into Manitoba. The dominant pine species involved in this expansion in the Agassiz region was probably jack pine. On the other hand, birch and other deciduous trees appear to have been widely, if unevenly, distributed in the basin.

Although the initial forests were largely replaced by pine, deciduous trees and prairie plants, in parts of the basin spruce, fir and larch, persisted. Spruce and larch apparently persisted in greater abundance in the areas adjacent to Lake Agassiz. In the present pine-hardwood area, jack pine (and possibly also red pine), paper birch and *Populus* dominated upland forests with a ground cover that included bracken fern, *Pteridium aquilinum*, in openings. Ash and elm occurred on both upland and lowland sites. These pine forests may not have extended west of the present limits of pine in the region (McAndrews 1966), although pine may have had an outlier in the Sheyenne Delta (McAndrews this volume).

Between the pine forests and Lake Agassiz, stands of *Populus*, birch, elm and oak grew along with prairie openings. These prairie areas expanded rapidly in the later part of the interval on the lowlands adjacent to the lake. On the eastern flanks of the uplands, increasing oak and herb pollen percentages at Terhell indicate the incipient development of oak savanna in that area.

South and west of the basin on the Prairie Coteau, spruce forests were replaced by primarily deciduous forests of balsam fir, paper birch, sugar maple, elm and oak with a shrub cover including *Corylus*. The occurrence of hickory *(Carya)* pollen in small but nearly consistent percentages (up to 1% may indicate the presence of *Carya* in the area. Comparable percentages were obtained in modern surface samples in a region of deciduous forest in south-central Minnesota that contained *Carya* (Janssen 1966). Today, the nearest *Carya* species, *C. cordiformis*, is 150 miles east of Pickerel Lake in Minnesota (distribution map in Fowells 1965, records of University of Minnesota Herbarium). Forest openings are indicated by moderate pollen percentages of Gramineae and *Artemisia* and the occurrence of *Shepherdia argentea* and *Pteridium*.

Interval III. 9,000-8,500 to 4,000 years ago.

After the retreat from the Campbell strandlines, the Lake continued to recede, completely draining into Hudson Bay before 7300 years ago (Elson this volume).

The rise in herb pollen (chiefly Gramineae, *Artemisia* and *Ambrosia*) continues in this interval reaching strong maxima in the prairie region, whereas *Quercus* is dominant at the eastern sites in the present pine-hardwood and deciduous forests. These spectra when compared to modern analogs in the region, can be interpreted as indicating prairie and oak savanna respectively (McAndrews 1966). In addition to oak, other deciduous forest species such as *Populus*, *Fraxinus pennsylvanica*, birch, elm, maple and ironwood occurred in the east on favorable sites on the morainic uplands around lakes and along stream courses. Low pollen values indicate that pine and other conifers were not abundant in the region. Macrofossils include *Populus balsamifera* (6200 ± 320 years ago -- W-860) and *Fraxinus* wood (6750 ± 320 years ago -- W-862) recovered from alluvial deposits along the Red River near Winnipeg.

Macrofossils of upland prairie plants at Pickerel include *Amorpha canescens*, *Petalostemum candidum*, *Panicum cf. capillare*, *Chenopodium hydridum* var. *gigantospermum*, *Polygala verticillata*, *Helianthus cf. laetiflorus*, *Verbena bracteata*, *cf. Ratibida pinnata*, *cf. Oenothera biennis*, *Lactuca canadensis* type, *Artemisia ludoviciana*, *Erigeron*, *Aster*, *Potentilla millegrana* (Watts and Bright in press). Pollen of *Lilium philadelphicum* occurs at Qually (Shay in press). Shrubs throughout the basin included *Corylus*, *Salix*, *Vitis* and particularly in the prairie area, *Juniperus*.

About 7-8,000 years ago a distinct peak of *Ambrosia* pollen is recorded in most of the diagrams in the prairie region reaching its maximum at Thompson (60%). This zone suggests a period of maximum aridity when *Ambrosia* colonized disturbed areas around ponds and on the upland (McAndrews 1966). This period roughly coincides with the final drainage of Lake Agassiz and species of *Ambrosia* and *Chenopodium* could also colonize the exposed lakebed. Although paleobotanical evidence from the center of the basin is lacking, it is inferred that marsh vegetation developed in areas of impeded drainage on the lake plain while prairie spread over better drained sites.

Interval IV. 4,000 years ago to the present

Radiocarbon dates marking this transition (all in years ago) are 3930 ± 100 (Y-1328) at Bog D and 4,270 ± 100 (Y-1329) at Terhell Pond. The onset of peat growth in the bog area north of Red Lake began 4,360 ± 160 (W-562). *cf.* Heinselman (1963). During this interval, several rivers in the basin underwent readjustments in their regimes. Filling episodes beginning sometime before 2,700 years ago are recorded in the Sheyenne (Brophy 1967) and Red Rivers (Libby 1955).

Beginning about 4,000 years ago a major change in pollen assemblage at sites in the eastern glaciated uplands suggests a gradual change from oak savanna to closed forest. The forest contained various mixtures of paper birch, oak, elm, basswood, ash, sugar maple and the understory tree ironwood. Traces of box elder, red maple and hackberry pollen indicate that these species were also present. Conifer species, chiefly pine, also expanded in the eastern area. Beginning about 2,700 years ago (Y-1156), white pine appeared in the region and by 2,000 years ago its pollen dominated these assemblages. About 1,000 years later jack pine and red pine expanded as well. Macrofossils of all three pine species occur at Martin.

Westward in the Agassiz lowland, herbaceous pollen continued to dominate although in decreasing amounts. Oak, birch, *Populus* and pine expanded gradually to their present values, indicating the establishment of aspen parkland and oak savanna. Although a few native jack pine are recorded for this area in recent time, prior to settlement pine was probably confined to the eastern area.

Southwest of the basin on the Prairie Coteau, herbaceous pollen declined slightly with the increase in oak, birch, *Fraxinus pennsylvanica,* basswood and *Populus,* indicating the establishment of the present deciduous forests that surround lakes and grow in valleys of the Coteau.

The top 20-30 cm. of sediment in the pollen diagrams record the development of agricultural activity with the rise in *Ambrosia* and other weed types.

Lake History and Vegetation

During its lifetime, Lake Agassiz not only acted as a partial migration barrier for plants but may have also influenced climate and vegetation around its shores. Although several unknowns are involved in assessing this influence, a consideration of conditions around the modern Great Lakes is useful. Climatic records and recent meteorological studies indicate that the Great Lakes significantly modify climates, especially along their downwind shores. This lake-modified climate is characterized by smaller seasonal temperature ranges and greater annual precipitation, due mostly to lake-induced autumn and winter rain or snowstorms (USDA 1941, Day 1926, Lansing 1965, McVehil and Peace 1965). Fall and winter storms are produced when a large ice-free lake transfers heat and water vapor to cold air masses passing over it. The areal pattern and magnitude of these storms depend partly on the over-water distance of these air trajectories (McVehil and Peace 1965). Orographic influences are evident although precipitation increases (up to 0.2 inches per day) were as great along the relatively flat shores of eastern Lake Michigan as those in elevated areas in Upper Michigan adjacent to Lake Superior (Pettersen and Calabrese 1960). These storms extended ten to twenty five miles inland. Those

observed adjacent to Lakes Erie and Ontario occurred in single or
multiple bands each one to five miles wide (McVehil and Peace 1965).
Autumn lake-induced thunderstorms recorded by Lansing (1965) seldom
extended over 20 miles inland of Lake Ontario.

Vegetation differences resulting from the lake effect have
been noted for areas adjacent to Lakes Erie and Ontario (Bray 1930),
Lake Michigan (Curtis 1959) and Lake Superior (Curtis 1959, Maycock
1961). Bray noted the occurrence of southern hardwoods in an otherwise northern hardwoods area whereas both Curtis and Maycock attributed the distribution of boreal spruce-fir forests along the
Superior shore and the Door Peninsula of Lake Michigan to the lake
effect. The lakes thus may have different effects depending on
the prevailing regional climate and vegetation.

If we are to apply the foregoing conditions to Lake Agassiz,
we must assume that (1) atmospheric circulation over the region was
not drastically different from today, (2) Lake Agassiz was ice-free
in winter and (3) radiocarbon dates for lake events and pollen zones
are essentially correct. The first of these assumptions can be
substantiated only by analogy and reconstructions of air mass movements based on glacial, paleobotanical and paleontological evidence
(Bryson this volume). The second assumption is crucial to the
lake-effect hypothesis because it involves autumn and winter temperatures and precipitation. If the lake were frozen over for only
part of the fall and winter the effect would be proportionately
smaller. The minor ice advances recorded in the northern part of
the basin about 12,000 years ago when Lake Agassiz was forming
probably meant that winter temperatures were low enough to freeze
the lake. There is some evidence to indicate that ice formed in
parts of Lake Agassiz even during its late phases. Colton (1958)
interpreted low intersecting ridges in the central and northern
parts of the basin as crack fillings in lake ice formed near shore
during late Agassiz II. The center of the lake, however, may have
been free of ice. Until further evidence is offered, this assumption
can neither be proven nor disproven. The third assumption is shared
by other explanations of the inferred vegetation differences and can
be supported or refuted by further paleobotanical studies and radiocarbon dates. If these three assumptions are accepted, we can proceed to review the paleobotanical record for evidence of a lake
effect.

The paleobotanical sites (Fig. 62) can be divided into those
within five miles of the Herman beach (Qually, Chicog, Thompson,
Mirror Pool, Williams) and those over twenty miles from the Herman
Beach (Terhell, Bog D, Martin). The lake's effect on vegetation
should be expected for the first but not the second group of sites.

During Lake Agassiz I (12,000-10,000 years ago) significant
values of *Picea* and *Larix* pollen are present at Qually adjacent
to the lake until the low water stage at 10,000 years ago. By this
time, at the eastern sites and on the Prairie Coteau (Fig. 63), spruce
had largely disappeared from the pollen record and been replaced by
pine and other types. In Lake Agassiz II (10,000-9,000 years ago)
when *Pinus* rises to peak values, *Picea* pollen is represented at the

sites near the lake (Qually, Thompson, Chicog) in higher percentages
(10-15%) than at all of the eastern sites (less than 5%) except
Martin Pond. In addition, *Larix* macrofossils occur at sites adjacent
to the lake (Mirror Pool, Qually, Williams) until about 9,000 years
ago but are absent at Martin Pond. As Lake Agassiz II drained
(9,000-7,300 years ago), prairie rapidly expanded near the lake and
onto the exposed lakebed while oak savanna developed on the eastern
uplands.

These data can be interpreted in the following manner. The
persistence of *Picea* and *Larix* adjacent to the lake is due to the
lake effect. Deeper winter snow cover and cooler summer temperatures
are felt to have been responsible for this. During the fluctuations
of Lake Agassiz, this effect probably varied considerably, however.
As the lake effect disappeared with the final drainage of Lake
Agassiz, the climatic difference between the lake shore and eastern
uplands gradually became reversed so that the eastern uplands became
more humid with less extreme seasonal temperatures than the lowlands.
This difference was largely responsible for maintaining prairie
in the lowlands and oak savanna and later deciduous and coniferous
forests on the uplands.

Although the lake effect hypothesis is attractive, other
explanations for these inferred vegetation differences must be
considered. These include (1) a lag in the migration of *Pinus*
from the Bog D area westward and (2) conditions of soil or climate
near the lake (unrelated to the lake effect) favorable for *Picea*
and *Larix* but not for *Pinus*.

Summary

Within the past 12,000 years several major changes in floral
species composition and distribution have been noted for the southern Agassiz basin region. Paleobotanical evidence indicates that
during the formation and subsequent fluctuations of Lake Agassiz I,
forests consisting largely of spruce, larch, *Populus,* ash and,
somewhat later, paper birch, dominated the landscape. All of these
occur in the region today although several northern species also
present then (*Saxifraga oppositifolia, Vaccinium uliginosum* and
Selaginella selaginoides) do not. Climate during this time is
thought to have been cool and moist.

In response to climatic warming, *Populus,* birch, elm, pine
and oak expanded or migrated into the region between 10-11,000 years
ago. Pollen and macrofossil evidence indicates that these genera
were not uniformly distributed throughout the region. Pine was
confined largely to the present pine-hardwoods area whereas *Populus,*
birch, oak and elm were more widely distributed in the region, the
latter two genera especially in the south on the Prairie Coteau.
In addition, sugar maple and probably hickory appeared on the Coteau.

Beginning about 9,000 years ago this expansion of pine and deciduous forests in the region was interrupted by the increase of prairie suggesting a shift to drier conditions. By 8,500 years ago as Lake Agassiz was retreating from its second stage, prairie was becoming dominant on the lowlands around the lake and on the Prairie Coteau while oak savanna was developing on the eastern uplands. Forest elements, other than oak gradually became restricted in their distribution. Between 7,000 and 8,000 years ago, a period of maximum aridity is indicated by high values of *Ambrosia* at several sites in the lowlands and on the flanks of the eastern uplands. This period roughly coincides with the final disappearance of Lake Agassiz from the basin.

Shortly before 4,000 years ago climatic conditions apparently became favorable for the increase in deciduous forest elements including birch, elm, *Populus*, ash, ironwood, basswood and later sugar maple. These deciduous forests were concentrated on the eastern uplands and occurred only in moist situations around lakes and along streams on the Agassiz lowlands and on the Prairie Coteau. Oak persisted in the eastern area and at the forest margins and gradually expanded along with *Populus* and birch culminating in the present mosaic of oak savanna, aspen parkland and xeric forest. A further indication of a climatic change is the onset of peat growth in the lowlands north of Red Lake. These deciduous forests in the present pine-hardwoods area were invaded about 2,700 years ago by white pine. Jack pine and red pine expanded in the same area about 1,000 years ago.

The region presently includes a variety of floristic elements distributed among prairie and forest communities. A major vegetation and floristic transition on the eastern edge of the basin has apparently existed for the past 10,000-11,000 years. This vegetation difference is felt to be due largely to climatic contrasts between the Agassiz lowland and the eastern uplands. Although several unproven assumptions are involved, it is hypothesized that while Lake Agassiz existed, it significantly modified the climate especially adjacent to its eastern shores. This local climate permitted spruce and larch to persist near the lake after these genera had largely disappeared from the eastern uplands and the Prairie Coteau. As Lake Agassiz drained and this lake effect disappeared, climatic differences became reversed and prairie dominated the lowlands while oak savanna and then later, closed deciduous and coniferous forests, developed on the eastern uplands.

Acknowledgements

I am much indebted to J.H. McAndrews from whose work and discussion this summary is largely based. H.E. Wright offered encouragement and advice throughout my investigations. Both supplied valuable comments and criticisms of the text. R.C. Bright kindly made unpublished information from Pickerel Lake available. Rod Wickwar prepared the map.

This paper is Contribution No. 56 from the Limnological Research Center, University of Minnesota.

PALEOECOLOGY OF THE SEMINARY AND MIRROR

POOL PEAT DEPOSITS

John H. McAndrews

Introduction

In other papers of this volume concerned with the south end of the Lake Agassiz basin, John Brophy has summarized the geological deposits and C.T. Shay has reviewed the paleoecology. Brophy mentioned two buried peats, one in the Fargo-Moorhead area (Seminary site of this report and Moorhead Station No. 2 of Rosendahl 1948) that represents a subaerial interval between phases I and II of Lake Agassiz. The second buried peat, the Mirror Pool site, overlies Lake Agassiz II clay along the Sheyenne River in the Sheyenne delta region (Fig. 64). Both peat deposits have been Carbon-14 dated and contain pollen as well as plant macrofossils, especially wood and seeds. In this paper these data will be used to reconstruct the peat-forming communities that followed the drainage of phases I and II. This reconstruction will then be related to the contemporary upland vegetation.

The modern natural vegetation of the south end of the Lake Agassiz basin is a prairie grassland. The finer-textured soils are dominated by such grasses as big bluestem, little bluestem and porcupine grass along with such forbs (broad-leafed herbs) as white sage and purple prairie clover (Dix and Smeins 1967). On the sandy soils of the Sheyenne delta the chief grasses are needle-and-thread, sandhill bluestem, Kentucky bluegrass and junegrass, and among the principal forbs are the wind-pollinated white sage, perennial ragweed and narrow-leaved goosefoot (Wanek and Burgess 1965).

Forests occur along the Red and Sheyenne Rivers. Burgess (1964) reconstructed the natural presettlement vegetation in a township (T.136N., R. 52W.) in the Sheyenne delta using the notes of the land survey of 1870-71. Most of the township was prairie but a wooded belt one to two miles wide occurred adjacent to the river. Bur Oak savanna occupied well drained soils while less well drained and more fire protected sites adjacent to the river had a wholly deciduous forest of bur oak, american elm, green ash, cottonwood, basswood, ironwood, hackberry, willow and probably box elder.

Aquatic plant communities occur where surface water is present for part of the year (Stewart and Kantrud 1967, Dix and Smeins 1967). Wet meadows, dominated by northern reedgrass, sedges and spike rushes and containing rough cinquefoil, wild mint and waterhorehound, occur on saturated soils where surface water is present only for a few weeks in the spring. Marshes of emergent biennials and perennials grow on sites where several inches of water persists throughout

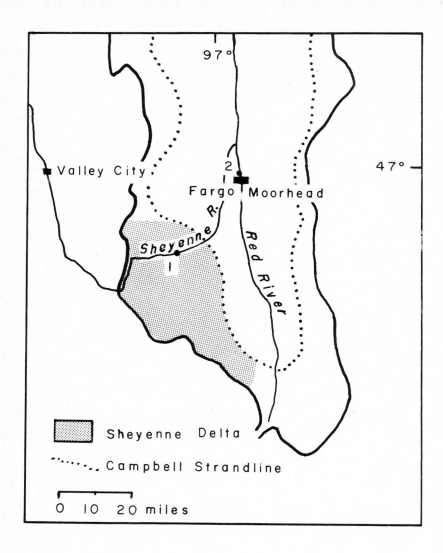

Figure 64.   Location of Mirror Pool site (1) and Seminary site (2).

the spring and summer; they are dominated by cat-tail, bulrush and spikerush. Where water is deeper, emergent aquatics are sparse and there occurs an open water community of such submerged aquatics as pondweed, mare's-tail and watermilfoil. During drought years when marshes and meadows dry out during the spring and summer there is formed a mud flat community dominated by such annuals as golden dock, red goosefoot and beggarsticks (see Table 19 for common names and their botanical equivalents). Our use of botanical nomenclature follows Fernald (1950).

Methods

Fossil pollen from the Seminary site and the Mirror Pool site was concentrated from about one cc samples (of each level) with successive treatments of HCl, KOH, HF and acetolysis solution, then mounted in silicon oil. The basic sum for the pollen percentages includes trees, shrubs and wind-pollinated upland herbs. Pollen types outside the basic sum were individually added to the basic sum before their percentages were calculated thus insuring that the percentages of locally abundant aquatic herbs did not exceed 100%. Percentages of the main pollen types are graphed in Fig. 65 and the minor types are given in Table 20.

Macrofossils were concentrated by treating the peat with 10% HCl and then sieving through a 0.5 mesh screen. Seeds were picked from the residue with a small brush and stored in a mixture of glycerine formalin and water. Identifications were made by comparison with documented modern material. The macrofossil data from the Moorhead and Seminary sites is given in Table 21. The number from the Seminary peat was obtained from a single sample of about 13,500 cc. Mirror Pool peat macrofossils (number per 100 cc. samples) are given in Table 22 and also listed in Table 21. The herb macrofossils are arranged according to their main habitat occurence, *i.e.*, open water, marsh, mud flat and beach, as given by Stewart and Kantrud (1967) and Fernald (1950).

Seminary Site

This peat layer is exposed at Fargo, Cass County, North Dakota, along the Red River in a diversion cut made in 1960 by the Corps of Engineers for flood control. It is on the grounds of the Catholic Seminary in the NW ¼, SE ¼, sec. 20, T. 140N., R. 48 W. The top of the cut has an elevation of 890 feet m.s.l. Twenty-seven feet of Lake Agassiz II silts and clays overly the 15 cm. layer of peat. Underlying the peat to a depth of about 70 feet (only the upper few feet are exposed in the cut) are silts and clays of Lake Agassiz I.

TABLE 19

COMMON NAMES AND BOTANICAL EQUIVALENTS OF GENERA AND
SPECIES REFERRED TO IN THE TEXT

TREES

Conifer

Pine .... Pinus

    jack .... P. banksiana

Spruce .... Picea

    black .... P. mariana

    white .... P. glauca

Tamarack .... Larix laricina

Hardwoods

Ash .... Fraxinus

    black .... F. nigra

    green .... F. pennsylvanica

Basswood .... Tilia americana

Box elder .... Acer negundo

Cottonwood .... Populus deltoides

Elm .... Ulmus

    american .... U. americana

Hackberry .... Celtis occidentalis

Ironwood .... Ostrya virginiana

Oak .... Quercus

    bur .... Q. macrocarpa

Poplar .... Populus

    balsam .... P. balsamifera

TABLE 19--Continued

SHRUBS

Alder .... _Alnus_

   speckled .... _A. rugosa_

Birch .... _Betula_

   dwarf .... _B. pumula_

Hazel .... _Corylus_

Soapberry .... _Shepherdia canadensis_

Wolf-berry .... _S. argentea_

Willow .... _Salix_

HERBS

Upland

Bracken fern .... _Pteridium aquilinum_

Goosefoot and Amaranth families .... _Chenopodiineae_

   goosefoot, narrow leaved .... _Chenopodium leptophyllum_

Grass .... _Gramineae_

   bluestem .... _Andropogon_

      big .... _A. gerardi_

      little .... _A. scoparius_

      sandhill .... _A. hallii_

   junegrass .... _Koeleria cristata_

   kentucky bluegrass .... _Poa praetensis_

   needle-and-thread .... _Stipa comata_

   porcupine .... _S. spartea_

Purple prairie clover .... _Petalostemon purpureum_

TABLE 19--Continued

HERBS (continued)

Ragweed .... Ambrosia

   perennial .... A. coronopifolia

Sage .... Artemisia

   white .... Artemisia

Aquatic

Arrowleaf .... Sagittaria

Beggarticks .... Bidens

Cat-tail .... Typha

Cinquefoil, rough .... Potentilla norvegica

Dock, golden .... Rumex maritimus

Goosefoot, red .... Chenopodium rubrum

Mare's tail .... Hippuris vulgaris

Marsh fern .... Dryopteris

Mint, wild .... Mentha arvensis

Pondweed .... Potamogeton

Reedgrass, northern .... Calamagrostis inexpansa

Sedge family .... Cyperaceae

   Bulrush .... Scirpus

   Sedge .... Carex

   Spikerush .... Eleocharis

Water horehound .... Stachys

Water milfoil .... Myriophyllum

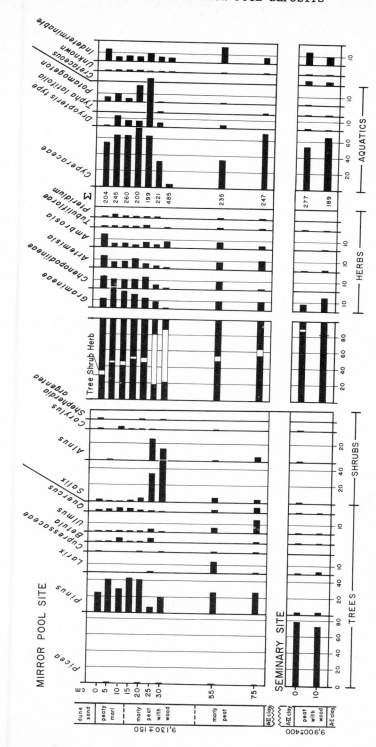

Figure 65. Pollen diagram of Seminary and Mirror Pool peat deposits.

TABLE 20

MISCELLANEOUS POLLEN AND SPORES FROM MIRROR POOL AND SEMINARY SITES

	Trees							Shrubs		Wind Pollinated Herbs			Miscellaneous Herbs											
depth (cm.)	Ostrya/carpinus	Fraxinus nigra	F. Pennsylvanica	Populus	Acer negundo	Tilia	Celtis	Vitis	Ephedra	Xanthium	Iva ciliata	Iva xanthifolia	Liguliflorae	Sarcobatus	Thalictrum	Galium type	Umbelliferae	Amorpha	Petalostemum purpureum	P. candidum type	Equisetum	Labiatae	Sparganium type	Sagittaria
Mirror Pool																								
1			0.5				0.5	0.5		0.4			1.5						0.5	0.5				
5	0.4				0.4		0.4		0.8		0.4	0.4	0.4						0.4	0.4				
10							0.5					0.4				0.4				1.0				
15																								
20												1.0	0.5	0.5					0.5					
25	0.9												1.0	1.0				1.0						
30	0.2																	0.2						
55	0.4					0.4						0.4	0.4	0.4		0.4		0.4	0.4		0.4		0.2	
75	0.4											0.4	0.4	0.4	0.8	0.4	0.5	0.4	0.4		0.8	0.8		0.4
Seminary																								
1				0.4									0.4	0.4					0.4		0.4	0.4		
10		0.7		0.4									0.4	0.4			0.5	0.4				0.4	0.5	

TABLE 21

COMPARISON OF MACROFOSSIL ASSEMBLAGES OF VASCULAR PLANTS FROM
LAKE AGASSIZ I-II INTERVAL PEAT IN THE FARGO-MOORHEAD AREA
AND THE POST LAKE AGASSIZ II PEAT AT THE MIRROR POOL SITE.
MOORHEAD FROM ROSENDAHL 1948; THE NUMBER OF SEEDS IN A
13,500 cc. SAMPLE IS GIVEN FOR THE SEMINARY SITE.
+ = PRESENT, - = NOT IDENTIFIED, * = UNCERTAINTY
WHETHER SEED, LEAF OR WOOD

	Moorhead	Seminary	Mirror Pool
TREES			
Picea glauca	*	-	-
Larix laricina	*	-	-
L. laricina needles	-	1	+
Picea-Larix wood	-	+	-
Fraxinus pennsylvanica	*	-	-
Populus balsamifera	*	-	-
SHRUBS			
Vaccinium angustifolium	+	-	-
Salix bud scales	-	-	+
Alnus rugosa bracts and seeds	-	-	+
Betula pumila bract	-	-	+
cf. Betula	-	-	+

TABLE 21--Continued

	Moorhead	Seminary	Mirror Pool
HERBS			
open water			
Najas flexilis	–	1	–
Potamogeton foliosus	+	–	–
P. richardsonii	+	–	–
P. zosteriformis	+	–	–
P. pectinatus	–	1	–
P. spp.	–	5	–
Ranunculus flabellaris	+	–	–
R. sect. Batrachium	–	2	+
Hippuris vulgaris	+	473	+
Myriophyllum sp.	–	8	–
marsh			
Typha sp.	–	–	+
Scirpus validus type	+	318	+
S. acutus	+	–	–
Sagittaria cuneata	+	3	–
S. latifolia	–	4	+
cf. Sagittaria	–	66	+
Eleocharis cf. palustris	+	1727	–
E. acicularis	+	–	–

TABLE 21--Continued

	Moorhead	Seminary	Mirror Pool
HERBS (continued)			
Carex cf. rostrata	+	485	+
C. sp.	-	-	+
Juncus canadensis	+	-	-
Sparganium eurycarpum	-	-	+
Polygonum amphibium	+	-	-
Ranunculus sceleratus	-	138	+
R. spp.	-	-	+
wet meadow			
Eleocharis intermedia	+	-	-
Potentilla norvegica	+	3	-
Lycopus americanus	-	6	+
Mentha arvensis	-	203	-
Ranunculus gmelini	+	-	-
Stachys sp.	-	-	+
Menyanthes trifoliata	-	1	-
Sium suave	-	2	-
Carex sychnocephala	+	-	+
C. cf. bebbii	+	213	-
C. cf. disperma	+	29	-

TABLE 21--Continued

	Moorhead	Seminary	Mirror Pool
HERBS (continued)			
mud flat			
Cyperus erythrohizos	+	-	-
Chenopodium sp.	-	3	+
Rumex maritimus	+	2	-
Bidens cernua	+	1	-
Polygonum lapathifolium	+	71	-
sandy beach			
Polygonum cf. ramosissimum	+	2	-
Coripsermum hyssopifolium	+	-	-
Equisetum arvense stem	+	-	-
unknown	-	20	+

MACROFOSSILS PER 100 cc. OF PEAT FROM THE MIRROR POOL SITE.

depth (cm.)	Open Water			Marsh									Wet Meadow			Mud Flat	Trees and Shrubs						Varia		
	Potamogeton sp.	Ranunculus sect. Batrachium	Hippuris vulgaris	Sparganium eurycarpum	Sagittaria latifolia	cf. Sagittaria	Typha sp.	Scirpus validus type	Carex rostrata	C. sp.	Ranunculus sceleratus	R. sp.	Carex sychnocephala	Lycopus americanus	Stachys sp.	Chenopodium sp.	Salix bud scales	Alnus rugosa	A. rugosa bracts	Betula/Alnus type	B. pumila bract	Larix needles	Unknown 1	Unknown 2	Miscellaneous unknown
0-10							5	13									6								3
10-20							1	741	226								5	22	14	14	1	8		16	9
20-30	1							20	5				2			1		2		2				9	21
30-40							2	200														1			
40-50								13																	3
50-60								1				7											178		
60-70			8		1	13	17	51	2			1					1			1		5			5
70-80		1	6	6	4	20	45	150	1	2		1		5	11									2	6

The peat layer is gray-black in color and can be traced for
100 feet or more along the cut. The most prominent element characteristic of this peat are pieces of wood up to 3 feet long which
lie parallel to the bedding plane. The wood tends to be flattened
while the smaller pieces have a grainy, weathered surface. The wood
cells contain pyrite. The peat is highly humified and mixed with
calcareous silt. Pollen are neither abundant nor well preserved in
contrast to the abundant wood and seeds.

Before further discussion it is necessary to correlate the
Seminary peat with the "vegetable stratum" of Moorhead Station No.2
(Rosendahl 1948). According to Brophy (personal communication 1967)
the Moorhead site was exposed at the Sewage Lift Station No.2 when
it was enlarged in the 1940's. The top of the excavation had an
elevation of about 895 feet but it is unclear from Rosendahl's
account whether the level of the peat stratum was 25 feet or 45 feet
below the top. Thus the Moorhead peat is either at an elevation of
870 feet or 850 feet. Both these elevations are comparable to the
863 feet elevation of the Seminary peat when possible local topographic irregularities are taken into consideration. In addition to
these elevation uncertainties a second difficulty in correlation
arises from diverse Carbon-14 dates. Three Carbon-14 dates have been
reported for these two sites, all on wood. From the Moorhead site
Arnold and Libby (1951) obtained a solid-carbon date of 11,283 ± 700
(C-497). A rerun of the same wood but with the more reliable gas-
carbon technigue gave a date of 9,930 ± 280 years ago (W-388, Ruben
and Alexander 1958).   A date by the gas-carbon technique on wood from
the Seminary peat was 9,900 ± 400 (W-993) years ago. Thus the dates
produced by gas-carbon technique are essentially identical for the
two sites.

The two spruce dominated pollen spectra indicate that the peat
was formed during late glacial times, a period characterized by boreal
type spruce forest domination. The woody plant pollen flora is dep-
auperate for it lacks appreciable poplar, black ash, willow and soapberry which are important in contemporaneous pollen assemblages in
northwestern Minnesota (McAndrews 1966) and central North Dakota
(McAndrews, Stewart and Bright 1967). Poplar and ash pollen could be
lacking because their relatively delicate grains were not preserved,
but an additional and more persuasive explanation for the lack of a
variety of tree and shrub pollen is that the peat was formed by a
treeless and shrubless marsh-meadow vegetation.

Rosendahl (1948) believed that the wood and other plant debris
was derived from beaches and moraines 15-20 miles distant from Fargo-
Moorhead. However, all the species represented by macrofossils (Table
21) except white spruce, green ash and blueberry are today found in
lowland sites where peat accumulates. Because most of the species
are part of treeless aquatic communities the evidence points to only
the wood being derived from the upland surrounding the lake. The terminal moraines of the uplands around the Agassiz basin were composed
of buried ice during the time of Lake Agassiz I (cfr Clayton 1967).
As the buried ice melted, the superglacial drift, which bore a spruce-
tamarack-poplar forest, collapsed and the forest disintegrated. Runoff
from meltwater and precipitation carried wood into Lake Agassiz I.
During the subaerial I-II interval the wood was stranded on the lake
bed, and the drying bed developed marsh and meadow vegetation.

Except for blueberry all identified seeds belong to species typical of aquatic or seim-aquatic habitats, all of which are native to eastern North Dakota and/or northwestern Minnesota. The most well represented communities, both in species and numbers of seeds, are from marsh and wet meadow habitats. The sandy beach habitat is least well represented probably because there were no local beaches. All these plant communities may have been contemporaneous in the immediate vicinity of Fargo-Moorhead or they may represent successional stages of drying and filling of the lake. While most of the species are adapted to fresh or slightly brackish water, there is no evidence of saline conditions (Stewart and Kantrud 1967).

The presence of balsam poplar, black spruce and tamarack cannot be excluded, but no rooted stumps were found and, except for one tamarack needle, no conifer needles were present in the Seminary peat sample.

Mirror Pool Site

The Mirror Pool site is an 80 cm. thick peat exposure on the south bank of the Sheyenne River in Ransom County, North Dakota, NE ¼, NE ¼, sec. 8. T. 135N., R. 52 W. The sequence of events (simplified from Brophy, this volume) leading to the formation, and burial and exposure of the peat begins with the deposition of delta sands in Lake Agassiz I by the Sheyenne River prior to 9,900 years ago. During the Agassiz I-II low water interval the river trenched its former delta. Rising waters of Lake Agassiz II deposited lacustrine clay in the trench and upon retreat of phase II, peat ceased to accumulate when aeolian sand of delta origin spilled into the trench, covered the peat-forming vegetation and preserved the peat. Subsequent river erosion has exposed the peat and about one foot of the underlying clay.

The moderately humified peat contains abundant wood, especially in the upper 50 cm., as well as bedded herb fragments. Pollen is not well preserved in this peat, particularly below 30 cm. The peat is gray in color due to the presence of marl. Because there is little inorganic material in the peat our interpretation is that there was no appreciable local aeolian or alluvial action while the peat was forming. A piece of wood from this peat has been Carbon-14 dated at 9,130 ± 150 years ago (I-1982).

The nine postglacial pollen spectra (Fig. 65) form an assemblage dominated by 20-40% line and 50% herbs and characterized by 2% bracken fern and occasional grains of wolf-berry. A similar assemblage, but with only 20% pine, centering around 9,000 years ago in northwestern Minnesota was interpreted as prairie (McAndrews 1966). However, in the Mirror Pool site peat the higher pine values suggest that jack pine in open stands with associated bracken fern may have grown on the sandy soil of the delta although most of the vegetation was typical of prairie.

The peat contains two distictive macrofossil assemblages, an earlier assemblage (from the 60-80 cm. levels) dominated by marsh species and a later assemblage centering around 25 cm. that is dominated by bog shrubs. The assemblage from the lower levels indicates an initial marsh community similar to that at the Seminary site except that cat-tail is abundant, sedge low and spikerush absent.

At 25 cm. and 30 cm. the relatively high pollen values of willow and alder correspond with the presence of willow bud scales and speckled alder seeds and bracts. Dwarf birch is present and together with willow and alder probably dominated a shrub bog community. These three genera still occur in the Sheyenne delta region (Stevens 1950). On the other hand, tamarack, whose needles occur at three levels, does not occur today in North Dakota. It was a member of the spruce-dominated late glacial vegetation (McAndrews, Stewart and Bright 1967) and apparently persisted in local bogs after the disappearance of spruce.

Discussion and Conclusions

Our pollen analyses herein reported show that the Lake Agassiz I-II subaerial interval occurred during the late glacial vegetation period, a period when upland sites had a boreal-type forest and type vegetation. Also indicated by our pollen analyses is the interpretation that the disappearance of the boreal-type forest and change to postglacial vegetation occurred during the time of Lake Agassiz II 9,900 to 9,100 years ago, Carbon-14 dates on lake mud deposited during the transition from late to postglacial vegetation are 11,000 years ago in northwestern Minnesota (McAndrews 1966) and 10,670 years ago in northeastern South Dakota (Watts and Bright 1967). The younger minimum age of the late-glacial (from the Seminary site) of 9,900 years is a date on wood. This wood date may be more accurate than the older mud dates because for mud may contain rock-derived pre-Pleistocene carbonate (cf. Ogden 1966, and Ogden personal communication 1967).

Our evidence indicates that the southern Lake Agassiz basin was never generally forested during the late glacial I-II interval nor during the early postglacial period of final lake shrinkage. On the widespread soils of slow drainage, marshes and meadows prevailed. During the earliest postglacial, late glacial plant species may have persisted on protected sites within the basin while pine, which was common on sandy soils east of the basin, may have occurred in the Sheyenne delta region. It is probable that the vegetation of the southern Lake Agassiz basin assumed a modern aspect some 7,000 to 9,000 years ago.

Acknowledgements

John Brophy discovered the Seminary and Mirror Pool sites and obtained their Carbon-14 dates. Field collection was aided by Brophy and William Code. The use of the facilities of Jamestown College, Bemidji State College, the University of Minnesota Itasca Forestry and Biology Station and Limnological Research Center is gratefully appreciated.

TENTATIVE CLIMATIC PATTERNS FOR SOME LATE GLACIAL
AND POST-GLACIAL EPISODES IN CENTRAL NORTH AMERICA

Reid A. Bryson and Wayne M. Wendland

The Modern Climatic Pattern

Before one attempts a reconstruction of past climates, it would appear necessary to have an appropriate knowledge of present climates. It is unlikely that there would be serious dissent to this statement among climatologists -- but in the context of the present discussion the key word of the statement is "appropriate". Clearly, we do have an adequate outline of the distribution of temperature, precipitation, wind, humidity, etc. for the present climate of North America, but is this the appropriate set of climatic fields for interpretation of the past with the current state of paleoclimatic knowledge? Evidences of past climate do not appear as readings of a thermometer, a rain-gauge, or a wind vane, but rather as natural phenomena which represent, usually, complexes of climatic parameters acting on soils, topography, or biota -- generally in rather vaguely understood combinations -- and often only in the sense of present or not present rather than as graded values that could be mapped with isopleths.

It would appear that an appropriate paradigm would be a description of the present distribution of climatic complexes, by naturally occuring categories, which were in turn meaningful in terms of the types of paleoclimatic evidences which are available. Here we must be careful to avoid circular reasoning. For example, the Köppen climatic classification scheme essentially starts with biotic distributions, for which arbitrarily selected climatic parameters are sought which best fit the boundaries of the biotic regions. Generally these are simple parameters, implying that single variables are limiting factors along the boundaries of the biotic regions. We have no *a priori* reason to assume this is true. These perhaps fortuitous parallelisms of, say, isotherms and biotic boundaries are then the basis for climatic regionalizations everywhere, ignoring the interactions of climatic parameters which might reasonably determine the suitability of the climatic environment for a particular biotic type. Use of such a system for a paleo-climatic reconstruction assumes that the same value of the same parameter that appears limiting today was also limiting in the past. The biotically defined climate is then used to describe the climate of the biotic region. It would seem philosophically more satisfying if one could identify natural climatic complexes which array themselves in natural climatic regions with distinct boundaries not arbitrarily chosen by the investigator, and which are congruent with the biotic regions and their boundaries. This might be regarded as wishful thinking if it were not for the

probability that biotic communities evolved in adjustment to
(or towards adjustment to) the climatic complexes present in their
region and extended as far as this complex extended without the
whole being absolutely limiting.

Naturally occuring atmospheric complexes with distinct
boundaries have been recognized for many decades and are generally
subsumed under the concepts of *airmass* and *front*. It has recently
been shown (Bryson 1966) that it is possible to delineate regions
bounded by the modal positions of distinct inter-airmass boundaries
(fronts) and occupied by a definite mean annual sequence of airmasses (Figs. 66 and 67).

As Figs. 68 and 69 indicate, these meterorologically defined
regions coincide quite well with certain major biotic regions of
about the same degree of generalization as the climatic regions.
Within the climatic regions there are mesoclimates and micro-
climates of scale comparable to the finer divisions of the biota.
(For purposes of climatic reconstruction, using biotic evidence,
it would be fruitful to identify the particular combinations of
plant or animal species that best fit the independently defined
climatic regions, rather than trying to find climatic regions that
fit the independently defined biotic regions. Similarly, the
identification of climatically significant combinations of pollen
taxa would make pollen profiles easier to use for paleoclimatic
purposes.)

It is on the basis of this correspondence between the independently derived climatic and biotic charts that the ideas of this
paper will be developed. It is assumed that the characteristic
airmass combination as it varies during the year at a given place
represents the significant climatic complex operating as an ecological control on the biotic community of that place.

Certain other considerations are involved in the following
paragraphs and several assumptions will be made. Most will be
identified as they appear, but it would seem appropriate to discuss
some of the major ones explicitly here. We will assume that climate
is the ultimate ecological control (Hare 1953). It is pointless
to argue the question of macroclimate versus microclimate in
relation to substrate at the scale of our present considerations.
After all, the macroclimate determines the modal microclimate, and
we are concerned at the present with "climata" and biota which are
regionally dominant. (The term *climata* is coined here as an
appropriate parallel to the term *biota*. We define it to mean the
naturally occurring complexes of meteorological parameters found
in the various climatic regions, much as the various biota occupy
biotic regions.) These clearly cut across geological substrate
distributions. Soils, on the other hand, depend on parent material,
plant cover, and climate and hence are not independent parameters.

A second assumption is that glaciers retreat in a "post-glacial"
climate. This seems obvious but is often not recognized in the
paleoclimatic literature. A corollary is that the time of retreat
from a terminal moraine marks the end of the "glacial" climate --
the presence of an extensive ice sheet does not indicate the presence

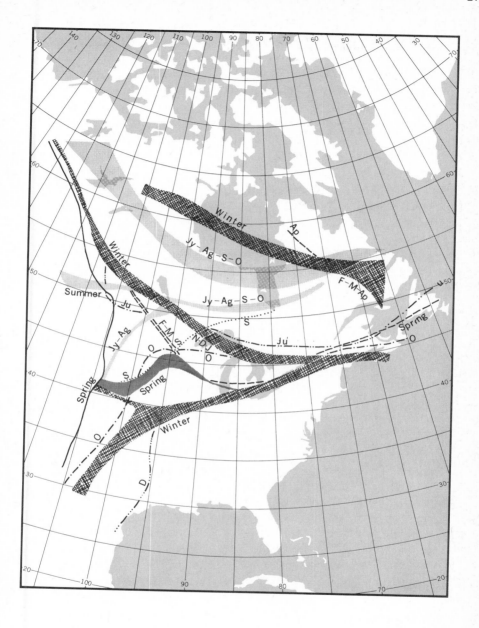

Figure 66. Composite chart showing the seasonal positions of mean
confluences between major airstreams, as determined from
the monthly surface resultant streamline charts. The
hatched bands give the total range of the monthly mean
position of the major confluences during the seasons
indicated. (Bryson 1966)

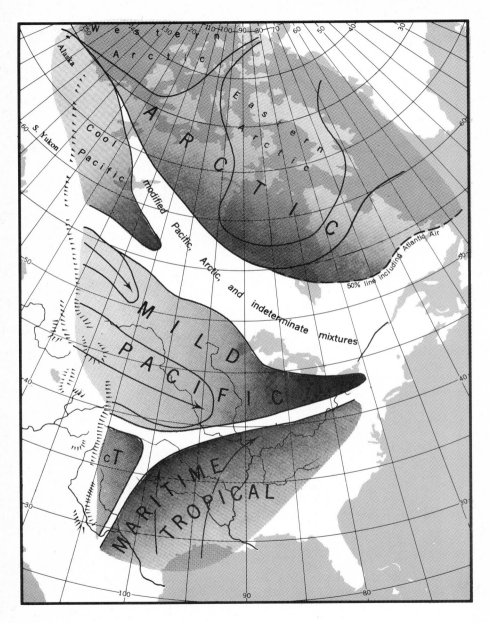

Figure 67. Composite chart of regions dominated by the various air mass types. The shaded regions are occupied more than 50% of the time by the indicated air mass. (Bryson 1966)

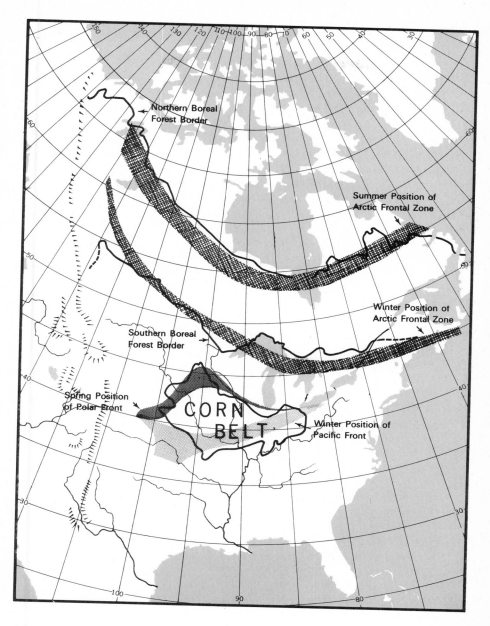

Figure 68. The coincidence of the "corn belt" and "boreal forest" biotic regions with meteorologically defined climatic (air mass) regions. Climatic regions are taken from Bryson (1966), Fig. 32: "corn belt" from "soils of the North Central Region of the United States" (1960): and the boreal forest generalized somewhat from Rowe (1959) and Larsen (1967).

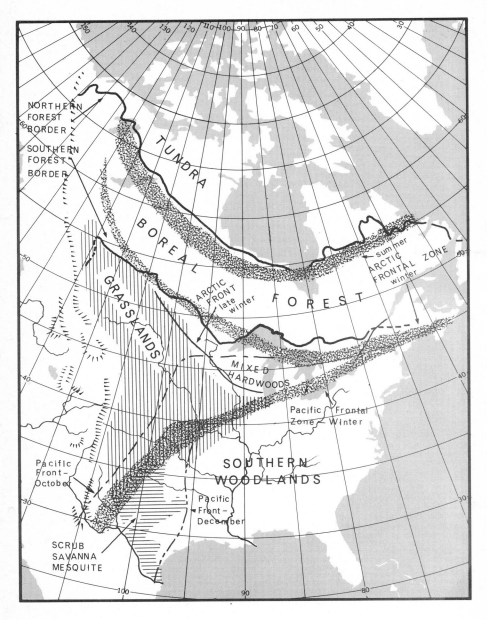

Figure 69.   The coincidence of biotic regions with meteorologically
             defined climatic regions. Climatic regions taken from
             Bryson (1966), Fig. 32: "grasslands" and "scrub savanna-
             mesquite" from Küchler (1964).

of a "glacial" climate. The rationale of this statement is easily
seen by use of an electrical analogy. If we think, for a moment,
of the sequence of climates as a square wave, an alteration of
"glacial" and "non-glacial" climates with abrupt changes from one
to the other, we can think of the accumulation of snow in glaciers
as the integral of this square wave (Fig. 70), which is a triangular
or "saw-tooth" wave unless limiting or "clipping" occurs. Qualitatively the sequence shown in Fig. 70 is as follows:

    (1)   During a "non-glacial" climate, (A), no glaciers
             accumulate.

    (2)   When the climate changes to "glacial" (B), ice
             starts to accumulate and continues to do so as long
             as the climate remains glacial unless the accumulation
             spreads to low enough altitudes or latitudes for
             wastage to equal supply, in which case the total
             glacial mass remains constant and the saw-tooth is
             "clipped" (B' in the diagram).

    (3)   When the "glacial" climate ends, the glacial mass
             starts to decline, and this retreat may extend well
             into the succeeding "non-glacial" climate (C). It
             should be noted that the glacial maximum is at or
             near the end of the "glacial" climate.

    (4)   The phase shifts of the climatic indicators (glaciers,
             sea level, vegetation, etc.) depend on their time-
             constants. Thus vegetation may show the presence of
             a "glacial" climate before the glaciers have grown to
             significant magnitude (B") and "post-glacial" charac-
             teristics before significant glacial retreat has
             occured (C").

    (5)   Even though there is evidence that climate does act
             somewhat like a square wave, i.e. with rather sudden
             shifts at the ends of successive climatic episodes,
             the general conclusions listed above would be equally
             applicable to a continuously varying climate.

    A third assumption is that within the past ten or fifteen
millenia a mix of airmasses occuring in the same frequency and
annual sequence as at the present would be associated with a similar
biotic system to that with which it is now associated. Similarly,
significant differences in airmass frequency or characteristics
should produce somewhat different biota, e.g. the boreal forest in
Valders time might have a different floristic composition if the
airmass characteristics in Valders time were different, even if the
general airmass frequencies and sequence were similar to the present.
This is equivalent to the geological concept of uniformitarianism,
namely, that the present is the key to the past. A corollary of
this assumption is that past climates differed from present climates
in quantity, but not in kind.

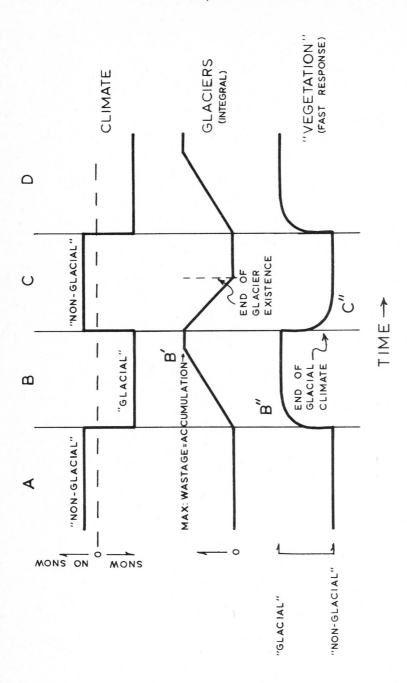

Figure 70. Suggested glacial and vegetative response to abrupt temperature changes with time.

Choosing the Episodes

The purpose of this paper is to present a few tentative reconstructions of past airmass regimes. Until more data are brought together in appropriate format and with good time control, these reconstructions will be necessarily rough and subject to improvement. Thus we have chosen to attempt partial reconstructions for three times: the late glacial period of about 13,000-10,000 years ago, the period around 9,000-8,000 years ago, and the period around 5,000-3,500 years ago plus some comments on the smaller fluctuations since that time. It appears that in the past five millenia the pattern has been sufficiently close to the present that climatic variations might best be discussed in terms of perturbations from the present.

The rationale for choosing these particular intervals is primarily that they are convenient and represent distinctly varied patterns. Secondarily they fit the world-wide sequence of climatic episodes. In principle, the climatologist knows that the atmosphere acts as a unit and that a major change in Europe cannot occur without a concurrent, though usually different, change in North America. Meteorological research papers too numerous to reference have established the hemispheric integrity of the atmosphere, and there is no reason to believe that the mechanics of the atmosphere were different in the past. Indeed, an analysis of radiocarbon dates and bog stratigraphy indicates that the dates applicable to the Blytt-Sernander European sequence are equally applicable in North America, though the relative effect of climatic changes in the two continents was different (Nichols 1967). For example, the end of the Atlantic period (*ca.*3,000 B.C.) appears more important in Europe than the end of the Early Sub-boreal (*ca.*1,500 B.C.) but the latter appears to have been more important in central Canada. There appears to be good reason for adopting the European terminology for North America as well (Baerreis and Bryson 1965; Bryson 1965) and this convention will be used in the remainder of this paper as far as possible.

With the limited precision possible, we may combine Mankato, Two Creeks, and Valders times and refer to them all as Late Glacial, for it is clear that these were more like each other than any one was like the pattern which followed the Late Glacial. Most of the pollen diagrams which reach back into the Lake Glacial show an abrupt and distinctive change into the postglacial. Evidently a rapid glacial retreat (in a postglacial climate) followed, but the Cochrane moraines of around 8,000 years ago (Falconer *et al.* 1965) indicate that a minor glacial episode intervened which terminated at about that time. This would appear to correspond to the Piori oscillation and our climatic reconstruction might then refer to Boreal time.

The third chart will be drawn for Early Sub-boreal time, 3,000-1,500 B.C., but it would appear that the chart for Atlantic time would not be much different on the warm side or the Sub-Atlantic on the cold side. Indeed though we will discuss the minor climatic changes of the past 2500 years, it is clear that we can differentiate these minor episodes because of a wealth of data rather than because they are as distinctive as the earlier episodes. The following table lists the more recent climatic episodes, as we recognize them at the University of Wisconsin Center for Climatic Research, though many authorities might class the later ones as minor details of the Sub-Atlantic.

TABLE 23

CLIMATIC EPISODES IN THE LAST 2500 YEARS

Episode	Rough Date
Recent	1850 - 1960 A.D.
Neo-boreal	1550 - 1850 A.D.
Pacific II	1450 - 1550 A.D.
Pacific I	1200 - 1450 A.D.
Neo-Atlantic	900 - 1200 A.D.
Scandic	400 - 900 A.D.
Sub-Atlantic	550 B.C. - 400 A.D.

(several sub-episodes identifiable)

It should be borne in mind that the shorter sub-divisions that may be recognized in the last few millenia may be too short for even the faster responding climatic indicators to reach full equilibrium with the climate though it is clear that locally significant changes did occur. Thus the vegetation should have a general Sub-Atlantic character through the last two millenia, but the concept of full climax must be used with caution and changes sought primarily in minor aspects of the floristic communities except in the vicinity of sharp ecotones. An examination of the literature suggests that the stability of the core of a biotic region compared to the instability of its borders in response to minor climatic oscillations is not widely recognized. (If we regard climate as limiting the biota, and also adopt the principle that climatic variation is <u>primarily</u> expressed as small displacements of the fields of climatic parameters -- the small perturbation approach -- then the impacts of that variation will be primarily at the boundaries of the biotic regions. In other words, ecotones are sensitive to climatic change and the heart of the biotic region is far less so.)

The Late Glacial Climatic Pattern

The accumulation of faunal remains in the New Paris sinkhole in western Pennsylvania may be divided into two layers: an upper stratum representing species presently living in the northeastern United States and particularly Pennsylvania, and a lower stratum of Late Glacial remains representing species currently living mostly in the boreal forest (Guilday *et al.* 1964). The maximum number of Late Glacial species from the lower stratum are presently found along an east-west axis just south of James Bay (Fig. 71) along what is presently the southern edge of the lichen woodland and the northern edge of tropical airmasses in summer (Fig. 66). Using our assumption that the present is the key to the past, this would suggest that the corresponding biotic and climatic boundary in Late Glacial time lay across central Pennsylvania.

The Late Glacial "Jones Fauna" of southwestern Kansas (Hibbard and Taylor 1960) is mostly found at the present time in the steppe area of the Dakotas and Montana (Fig. 72). This is just south of the boreal forest, i.e., in the region occupied by Pacific air in fall and winter, Arctic air in spring, and by Pacific air with incursions of Tropical air in summer. It is assumed that this sequence was characteristic of southwestern Kansas in Late Glacial time. If so, then Nebraska should have been in the boreal forest, and the pollen evidence indicates that it was (Wright 1964).

Since the frontal boundaries which delineate the airmass and airstream regions are anchored to the major breaks in the Cordillera as shown by Bryson (1966), and since the physics of climate requires that mean frontal boundaries follow broad, sweeping patterns, the information above is adequate to allow us to rough in the modal positions of certain climatic boundaries such as the southern edge

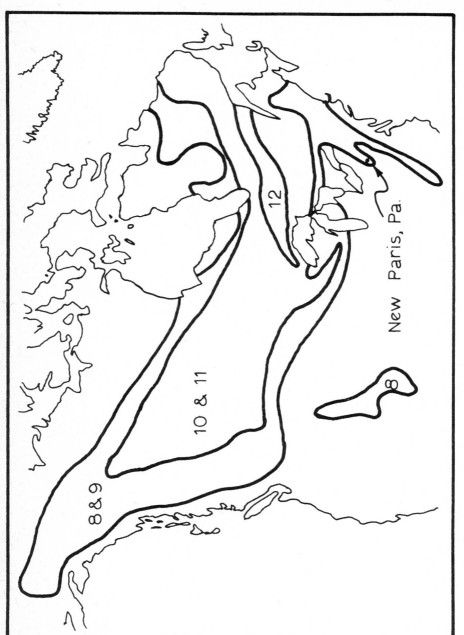

Figure 71. Present range overlap of the species of mammals found below 6 meters in the New Paris No. 4 site. Numbers within the areas indicate the number of species whose ranges overlap within the indicated area at the present

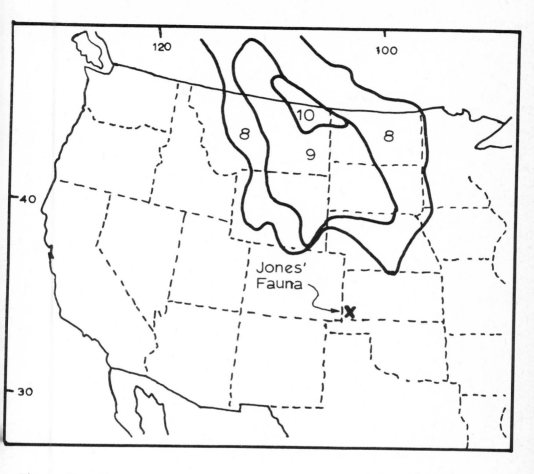

Figure 72.   Present range overlap of the nine species of mammals
              and one amphibian of the Jones' fossil fauna.   Numbers
              indicate the number of species whose ranges overlap
              within the indicated area at the present time. After
              Hibbard and Taylor (1960).

of "Arctic" air in winter. It must lie tangent to the east face of
the Rockies, run south of the Sand Hills of Nebraska but north of
southwestern Kansas, just north of or through the Dismal Swamp in
Virginia (Whitehead 1965), and along the boundary between the
Labrador Current and the Gulf Stream (Fig. 73). The northern edge
of Tropical air in summer should lie tangent to the mountains of
eastern Mexico, approach southwestern Kansas, then turn east to
cross central Pennsylvania. The summer position of the "Arctic"
front should lie along the edge of the glacier, probably north
of its terminus if we assume a dark, moraine covered surface.
(Ice fronts and the general slope of mountain fronts often have
slopes similar to frontal slopes. It is often observed that warm
fronts in particular will nearly coincide with mountain slopes
and tend to stagnate there. In any case the strong contrast of
ice to the north and darker land to the south should have held
the main baroclinic zone -- and therefore the mean front -- rather
close to the edge of the glacier in summer.) The position suggested
here fits nicely with the position in the North Atlantic reconstructed by Manley (1951) for the same time.

With ice in Canada and Tropical air to 40°N. the upper westerlies should have been strong along 40-45°N in summer, pushing
Pacific air eastward through northern Illinois, Indiana, Ohio and
Pennsylvania. Most of this air should have come through the
Wyoming Gap spreading southward as well as eastward so that southwestern Kansas should have had little continental Tropical air
from the Southwest.

In winter the continental glacier must have been a barrier
holding the very cold, low level Arctic air in the Arctic Basin,
forcing outbreaks of true Arctic air to be through the Bering Sea
and the North Atlantic.* Reasonable estimates of the height of the
ice sheet based on the characteristic peripheral slope profiles of
Antarctica and Greenland (Robin 1962) indicate a minimim height of
3,500 meters for the North American continental glacier. With all
cold airmasses shallower than this depth blocked from entering
southern North America, it is clear that the flow from the north
into the midwestern United States would have been Katabatic, with
adiabatic heating on the order of 30-35° Centigrade. Any reasonable
assumption of representative temperatures on the ice-cap averaging
higher than -60° Centigrade would mean air entering the United
States no colder than at present and usually warmer (The Late Glacial
ice cap was about the size and height of Antarctica. South Pole
temperatures in winter are about -60° Centigrade and Antarctic
coastal stations about -17° Centigrade which is about the same as
present day northern North Dakota in January. Remembering that
the North American ice cap was at much lower latitude than Antarctica, with shorter winters and more radiation, temperatures outside
the glacial terminus must have been somewhat warmer than Antarctic
coastal stations today.)

_____
*It is inconceivable in this circumstance that the Arctic Ocean
should have been ice-free or even partially open.

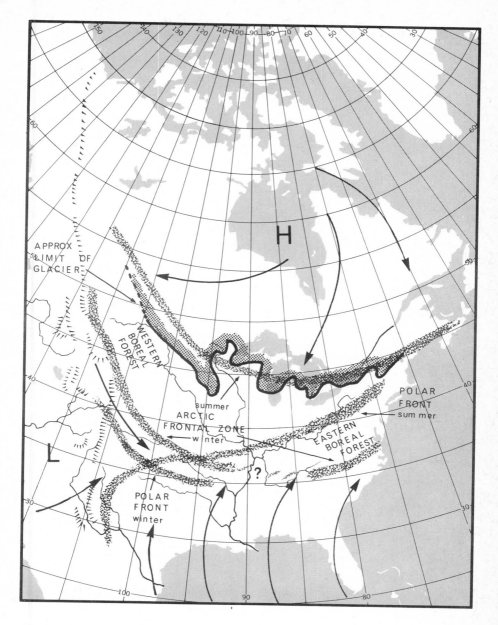

Figure 73. Partially reconstructed map of mean frontal zones during
            late glacial time (13,000 to 10,000 years ago). Southern
            glacial limit as shown is a summary of information found
            in Wright and Frey (1965).

Adiabatic warming of air from the west would be as great as at present, and air from the south would be about as warm as the present.

It is not very remarkable, therefore, that evidence from the faunal assemblages at Blackwater Draw (Sellards 1952) and the Domebo site (Leonhardy 1966) should indicate Late Glacial winters less severe than the present. (The Blackwater Draw Site is located in extreme east-central New Mexico. The Domebo Site is about 10 miles north of Lawton, Oklahoma.)

Assuming adiabatic compression of air coming from the ice cap, there should have been less cloud cover and very low relative humidity in outbreaks of air from the north flowing across the "boreal forest" of Late Glacial time. This difference in the characteristics of the airmass dominating the "boreal forest" in winter is why quotes have been used around "Arctic" air in the preceding paragraphs and "boreal forest" in this paragraph. The somewhat warmer, dry, clear air in winter and strong westerlies in summer should have made the climatic environment of the "boreal forest" somewhat more droughty in Late Glacial time, especially when coupled with the stronger radiation of its lower latitude. In turn one should not look for a "boreal forest" floristic community in the Late Glacial like that which is found today. On well drained sites and south-facing slopes spruce should have been supplanted by plants better adapted to drought; perhaps the *Shepherdia canadensis* reported by Ritchie (1966) as common in that community is one of these plants.

If one assumes strong northerlies along the North American west coast associated with the glacier-open Pacific temperature contrast, then deep lows should have been common in the southwest. This in turn would mean cloudy weather with abundant winter rain -- a situation optimum for widespread *Pinus ponderosa* over the basins of the southwest, or at least a greatly lowered treeline. The main tracks followed by cyclonic storms in winter should have been off the Gulf Coast along the winter jet stream and along the Colorado-Cape Hatteras track.

Certain significant details of the present day modal airmass-front pattern cannot yet be identified for Late Glacial time, for example the spring and autumn patterns. The northward bulge of the frontal zone between Arctic air and Tropical air in spring at the present, which delineates the northern edge of the corn belt (Figs 66 and 68), is an example. This bulge represents a mean warm sector of cyclones tending to stagnate over the prairie provinces of Canada in spring, and thus probably did not exist in Late Glacial time. One should not find evidence of a biotic community exactly equivalent to the tall-grass prairie in the Late Glacial, therefore.

Extending the Bjerknes circulation theorum to the case of an internal rather than an external boundary one finds that if the mean vorticity in a region is cyclonic, the circulation about a solid mass protruding up through the level being considered should be anti-cyclonic. Thus the circulation near the top of the ice cap should have been anticyclonic since the general vorticity must have been cyclonic. That this should be a cold-core anticyclone is indicated by the cold temperatures near the surface of the ice cap. A reasonable winter mean upper air flow pattern would indicate: (1) a cold-core anticyclone near the surface of the glacier, (2) reversal to a trough of low pressure above the surface anticyclone, (3) northerlies along the west coast, (4) a trough in the southwest United States, (5) cold outflow through the Bering Sea and North Atlantic and (6) the main jet stream over the Gulf Coast or northern Gulf. These features would imply frequent deepening of cyclones off Newfoundland which would provide an influx of moisture to maintain the glacier.

The Boreal Pattern

One of the striking features of pollen diagrams from central North America is the abrupt transition from Late Glacial to post-Glacial pollen assemblages (e.g., McAndrews 1966; Ritchie 1964; West 1961 and many others). Since the vegetation has a shorter time constant than a continental glacier, this is *prima facie* evidence for a quasi-square wave behavior of the climate, as suggested above, but the main significance to our present discussion is in the indication of an abrupt change in circulation pattern. Where adequately dated, the sudden collapse of the Late Glacial pattern of boreal forest appears to have occurred about 10,500 years ago to be replaced as far northward as southwestern Manitoba by grassland, and in northeastern Minnesota and Wisconsin by a jack pine-red pine forest similar to that of 400 years ago. (This is not meant to imply that the "jackpine" community of Boreal time in northwestern Minnesota was the same as in the later period. As pointed out by numerous authors, including McAndrews, we must bear in mind the effect of greater soils development as postglacial time progresses. This is one of several reasons why biotic details might be different even in two identical climatic episodes.)

This implies that a rapid change from boreal forest to grassland occurred over vast areas of the northern plains, an ecological event that could not have been without significant impact on the big game hunters of the plains and their cultures. The jack pine-red pine assemblage in turn disappeared rather abruptly about 8,500 years ago to be replaced by grassland (McAndrews 1966) in Minnesota or oak savanna characteristic of the forest-prairie ecotone in eastern Wisconsin (West 1961).

Around 8,000 years ago there was still a large amount of continental ice in the Cochrane ice sheet, but it must have been much thinner than during Valders time, producing less mountain effect on the circulation of the atmosphere. Some Arctic air must have flowed south between the Cordillera and the ice sheet in winter, and the main meridional temperature contrast in summer must have been at about latitude 50-55°N in mid-America. Strong westerlies must have prevailed across North America in mid-latitudes, extending the grassland climate of dry, subsident Pacific air far

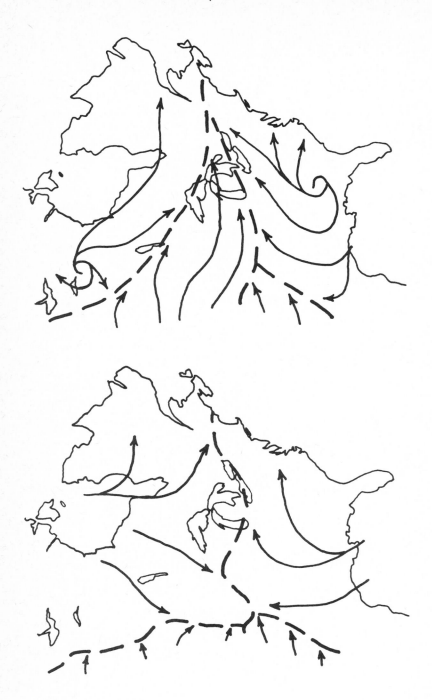

Figure 74. Schematic drawing showing the eastward penetration of Pacific air during times of low zonal index (left), and high zonal index (right).

eastward, almost to the edge of the ice in Manitoba -- in other
words somewhat farther east than at the present time. Under
these circumstances there should have been fewer deep lows over
the southwest and a much drier climate.

Some outlines of the climatic pattern during the Boreal can
thus be reconstructed by modifying the present day pattern to
reflect the winter position of the jet stream near the Gulf coast,
the summer position five to seven degrees farther south than now,
and with generally stronger westerlies across the northern United
States. The effect of stronger westerlies is shown schematically
in Fig. 74, and the reconstruction of those portions of the
tentative Boreal climate pattern which seem reasonable at present
are given in Fig. 75.

The significant feature of the climatic-biotic pattern for
Boreal time was the far northeast displacement of the forest-
grassland ecotone while the ice still existed far south into
Manitoba, effectively splitting the remnants of the boreal forest
into an eastern segment and a western segment in the Rockies. It
is possible that the present day distribution of boreal forest
floristic elements which overlap in the midwest (Larsen 1966) is
a heritage of this Boreal separation? If the pattern given in
Fig. 75 is correct, then the return of the *Pinus banksiana-Pinus
resinosa* community to northwestern Minnesota must have been from
the southeast as suggested by McAndrews (1966). If the close
proximity of grassland and ice front persisted through the wasting
of the Cochrane ice, then we also have a reason for extension of
the known range of Plano type projectile points as far north as
63° in the vicinity of the 100th meridian (William Irving, personal
communication).

The tentative sequence of events that then emerges at the
outset of post-glacial time is thus as follows:

(1)   An abrupt climatic change and rapid disappearance
       of a variety of boreal forest from large areas of
       the Dakotas, Nebraska, Iowa, Illinois, Wisconsin,
       Minnesota and eastward at the end of the Late
       Glacial.

(2)   Rapid shift to grassland in the western part of the
       area once occupied by *Picea* and to mixed woodlands
       dominated by *Pinus banksiana* in eastern Minnesota
       and Wisconsin, and probably Michigan during Pre-
       Boreal time.

(3)   In Boreal time, grassland extending nearly to the
       ice front in the Prairie Provinces, and to an oak-
       savanna-grassland boundary in central Wisconsin and
       eastern Minnesota, not far northeast of the present
       ecotone. It is probable that the *P. banksiana* mixed
       woods were found farther to the east during this time.

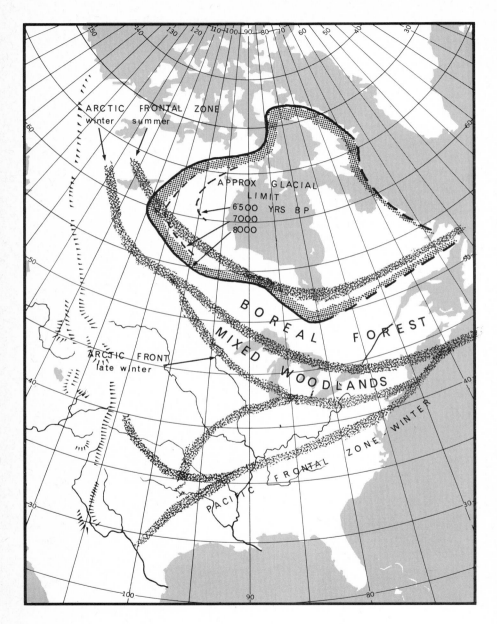

Figure 75. Partially reconstructed map of mean frontal zones during
            Cockburn-Cochrane time (*ca* 8,000 years ago). Glacial limit
            after Falconer *et al*. (1965).

Atlantic and Post-Atlantic Patterns

Rapid *in situ* wasting of the Cochrane ice must have occurred after about 8,000 years ago, as shown by the rough isochrones of the ice front in Fig. 75. These are based on field studies by the senior author and his colleagues who found that *Sphagnum* bogs started growing on the bottom of what had been pro-glacial Lake Kazan after its drainage about 6,000 years ago. Irving and Larsen (personal communication) found the apparent position of the ice front at that time in the vicinity of Dimma Lake. (61° 33' N lat., 101° 38' W long.) Nichols (1967) found necron mud farther south at Lynn Lake, Manitoba. (56° 50' N lat., 101° 03' W long.) Yet inside the Cochrane moraine which started to accumulate prior to 6,500 years ago. The large numbers of well-developed eskers with detailed features within the Cochrane moraine are strongly suggestive of *in situ* wasting. Even in a warm episode, such as the Atlantic was in central North America, there is a physical limit to the amount of net wastage in a year, and this limit is set by the amount of snowfall and the heat supply. It is possible that the snowfall in central Canada was as heavy in Atlantic time as in Valders time and even heavier than at present because more moisture could be present even with higher (though still below freezing) winter temperatures. Even neglecting the snowfall, if we take 70 Kcal/cm.^{2}-year as the total incoming radiation available, take the albedo over the glacier as .60, and the terrestrial back radiation as 20 Kcal/cm.^{2}-year, about 8 Kcal/cm.^{2}-year would be available for wastage. Assuming that 5 cm. of ice sublimated each year, there would be enough heat left to melt about 65 cm. of ice. Wasting at the rate of 70 cm./year, the Valders ice would last about 5,000 years, or until the end of Atlantic time!

Using a somewhat different calculation, we might reason that the available heat was considerably less than now, probably due to two reasons: (1) the altitude of the ice surface, and (2) the relatively high albedo of the ice. During the time of summer ablation, after the ice had been heated to 0° Centigrade at the surface, we calculate the net radiation to be about +15 Kcal available for ablation and heating. If convection and heating of the air are disregarded, the net radiation would be used soley for ablation. This simplified result would yield a maximum ablation rate. If 10% of the annual ice loss were sublimated, and the annual snowfall assumed to be 50 cm., the ice from Valders time would last about 3,500 years, or to at least 5,000 years B.C. Allowing some heat transfer to the air, more cloudiness, or heavier snowfall, still longer persistence of the ice might be expected.

The forest migrated northward as fast as the ice disappeared, probably even moving onto the moraine covered edges of the glacier. There is essentially no evidence for a tundra or treeless fringe between ice and forest (Nichols 1967). By early Sub-boreal time the forest border had migrated to a position about two degrees farther north in Keewatin than at the present (Bryson, Irving and Larson 1965) and there remained until about 1,500 B.C. Under the forest a podzol soil developed. The southern edge of the boreal

forest in mid-America continued to lie somewhat northeast of its
recent position through early Sub-boreal time (i.e., until 1,500
B.C.) (McAndrews 1966).

A reconstructed partial climatic map for early Sub-boreal
time (5,000 to 3,500 years ago) is given in Fig. 76. Note that
the most conclusive evidence for this time period is the position
of the northern forest border.

A word should be said at this point emphasizing that the
reconstructed maps are mean representations of the long term
climate. It will be noted that similar patterns can be found
in the modern series of daily or monthly mean charts (i.e., the
winter pattern of Figure 73 is very similar to the mean map of
February, 1952). This suggests that a change in the frequency of
"anomalous" patterns alone is sufficient to explain the reconstructed patterns of the past.

These rather small known departures of the forest borders
from the recent positions, and positions known for other more
recent times (Bryson *et al.*1965; Nichols 1967) indicate that from
Atlantic time on the most fruitful approach to the variation of
climate is in terms of small perturbations of the present climatic
distribution. Returning then to the Atlantic period we should
visualize the southern boundary of the boreal forest remaining
fairly stationary while the northern boundary moved north to a
position about two degrees north of its present position in central
Canada. The tree line position farther northwest near the mouth
of the MacKenzie River was probably nearly in its present position
for Atlantic and post-Atlantic time since the controlling frontal
zone is anchored there to the northern end of the Cordillera.
Around 3,500 years ago the boreal forest shifted southwestward
about two degrees, by migration in the south and by fire in the
north, after which the forest did not regenerate. This, along
with basal peat growth in Alaska [I (AGS) - 1, Heusser 1959]
and palynological evidence of cooler weather in Finland (1-776,
Trautman and Willis 1966) would suggest more meridional circulation
of the atmosphere. It has been suggested that reformation of the
permanent pack ice on the Arctic Ocean was associated with this
change (Brooks 1949). This would certainly be consistent with the
other evidence.

About 2,500 years ago, at the beginning of the sub-Atlantic,
a further change occurred. The position of the boreal forest did
not change much, but it became much wetter -- initiating the growth
of blanket peat or "upland-muskeg" (WIS-1, Bender *et al.* 1965). A
reasonable interpretation of the North American evidence, summarized
briefly by Baerreis and Bryson (1965a), would suggest that the
summers differed from the present primarily in the position of the
upper-air anticyclonic eddy normally found over the Great Basin in
summer. A displacement of this eddy northeastward would place the
isentropic moist tongue, which normally brings rains to Arizona in
summer (Bryson and Lowry 1955), along the Colorado Rockies, then
curving eastward across the boreal forest of the prairie provinces
and Ontario. Arizona should have been warmer under these circumstances (Woodbury 1961) and torrential thunderstorms should have

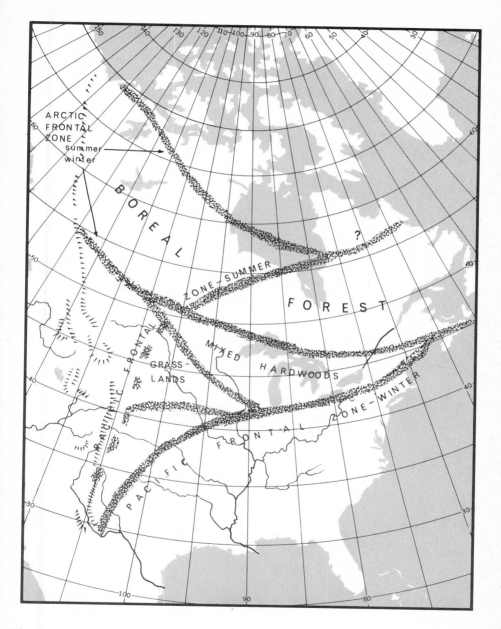

Figure 76. Partially reconstructed map of mean frontal zones during
            early Sub-boreal time (*ca.* 5,000-3500 years ago). Summer
            position of the Arctic front is the most certain feature
            of this time period.

denuded the slopes of the southern Rockies exposing more raw
material on which sage could better compete with grass. The
sediments from the slopes should have spread on the valley floors.
This is one interpretation that can be placed on an unpublished
pollen diagram by Maher (personal communication) for the Engineer
bog in the San Juan Mountains. The dry, eastern arm of the anti-
cyclonic eddy would then be displaced eastward to the east coast
rather than the eastern mid-west. The rapid rise of *Pinus strobus*
in the Sub-Atlantic in Minnesota (McAndrews 1966) is certainly
indicative of moister summers, for white pine is found only where
the precipitation exceeds the potential evapotranspiration (Fig.77).
Evidence of drought during the Sub-Atlantic should be sought on
the mid-Atlantic coast area, perhaps in the vicinity of Chesapeake
Bay, or the Dismal Swamp. The cloudier, wetter summers reduced
snow ablation and glaciers reformed in the Rockies south of 50°N
(Richmond 1965).

     The character of the winters in Sub-Atlantic time is not
clear at present, though it would seem likely on the basis of
European evidence that the Sub-Atlantic was a time of expanded
circumpolar vortex, the westerlies far south and the winters
stormier (Willett 1949). This would represent a partial return to
Late Glacial conditions.

     A return to conditions similar to the Atlantic started about
350-400 A.D. During the Neo-Atlantic, 900-1200 A.D., open water
appeared in the Canadian Arctic Archipelago, the tree-line readvanced into the tundra (Bryson *et al.* 1965), summer rains extended
farther into the southwest and corn-farming became practical across
the Great Plains (Bryson and Julian 1963). Glaciers disappeared
from the U.S. Rockies (Richmond 1965). These evidences suggest
weaker westerlies and more meridional circulation. The boreal fores
probably expanded both south and north, while prairies shifted west
at the expense of steppe. It would appear from a comparison of
summer rainfall with strong westerlies, and summer rainfall with
weak westerlies that a strip along the present forest-prairie ecoton
between northwestern Minnesota and southern Wisconsin was somewhat
drier (Fig. 78). There is pollen evidence for this in the *P. strobu*
and *Nuphar* decline in Minnesota (McAndrews 1966).

     The westerlies once again increased about 1200 A.D., termina-
ting the Neo-Atlantic (Baerreis and Bryson 1965a). The northern
edge of the boreal forest once more retreated southward (Bryson
et al. 1965). The prairie peninsula climate, carried by the westerlies, opened a wider wedge of prairie eastward across Illinois
and Indiana and the grassland communities were displaced eastward.
Antelope increased in importance in relation to bison in the diet
of the hunters of the western Dakotas (Lehmer 1966), bison became
more important than deer in the meat diet of the Mill Creek people
of northwestern Iowa (Baerreis and Bryson 1967), and some of the
drought-stricken upper Republican farming people of Nebraska moved
south to the Panhandle region of Oklahoma and Texas (Baerreis and
Bryson 1965b) where the summer rainfall had increased. It would
appear that the cultural impact of increased aridity in northern
Illinois might have caused a breakdown of the contact between

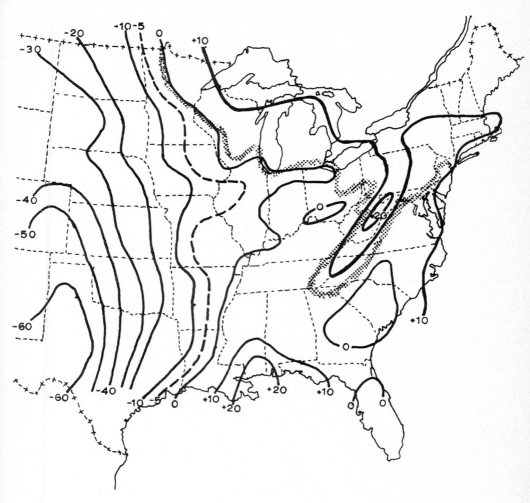

Figure 77.   Estimated distribution of precipitation minus potential
              evapotranspiration (annual). Stipples zone indicates
              approximate southern limit of *Pinus strobus* (Trees, the
              Yearbook of Agriculture, 1949).

Aztalan and Cahokia and the abandonment of that recently established
northern frontier outpost (Aztalan) of the Mississippian culture
(Baerreis and Bryson 1965a).

    At this point it might be noted that the climatic changes
being discussed are on a much shorter time scale than those associated with the earlier post-glacial climatic episodes. This does
not reflect an increased frequency of climatic change, but rather
an increase in the data available. There is also a change in the
character of the data, for pollen samples are most often taken at
intervals too gross to reflect the details of centuries.

    The Pacific episode (1200-1550 A.D.) of increased westerlies
was followed by an expansion of the circumpolar vortex and a return
to patterns more like the Sub-Atlantic. A far south jet stream in
winter associated with blocking highs over northwest Europe and a
reduced summertime penetration of Tropical air northward across
the United States and into Canada is. indicated by historical data.
It would appear that the boreal forest climate was broader: extending
this climate perhaps five degrees farther south in the Great Lakes
area is indicated (E. Wahl, personal communication), and is consistent
with Lamb's estimate for the corresponding frontal pattern in the
Atlantic sector (Lamb 1963). Summers were cool in the Neo-boreal
(1550-1850 A.D.) and autumns cold (about 4° F below normal) in the
eastern United States. Glaciers once again formed as far south as
New Mexico in the Rockies (Richmond 1965) and the summer precipitation in northern New Mexico seems to have been two or three inches
greater than the recent normal. Was this climatic deterioration
(from the farmer's viewpoint) in the northeastern United States,
more important in its impact on the life ways of the Indians than
the contact with the white man which occurred at the same time?

    The Neo-boreal closed in the mid-nineteenth century with the
well-documented climatic change which was associated with a return
to strong westerlies in mid-latitudes (Lamb 1966).

                    Conclusion and Caution

    The authors have attempted to demonstrate or at least suggest,
that an internally consistent matching of climatic pattern and
biotic evidence can be made for the past ten thousand years. The
treatment has been far from complete, for the material is voluminous,
but at least a few highlights and critical times have been indicated.
It is probably superfluous to caution the reader that many statements
contained in the preceding paragraphs are inadequately researched
and possibly premature. It is believed, however, that the general
pattern for North America is approximately as indicated. We hope
that the readers will supply more evidence, better interpretation,
and appropriate corrections.

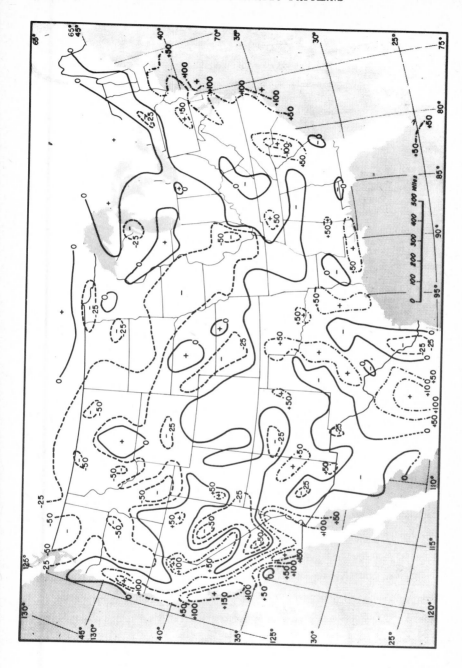

Figure 78. Precipitation with high zonal index minus precipitation with low zonal index. After Baerreis and Bryson (1967).

Acknowledgements

Research reported in this paper was supported by the National Science Foundation, Atmospheric Sciences Division, Grant GP-5572X, with some materials being supplied by Office of Naval Research, Geography Branch. Contract Nonr 1202(07).

PALEO-ZOOLOGY AND MOLLUSCAN PALEONTOLOGY OF THE
GLACIAL LAKE AGASSIZ REGION

Samuel J. Tuthill

Introduction

Three aspects of the paleo-zoology of the Glacial Lake Agassiz Region are discussed here. These are: (1) the nature of the fossil and modern invertebrate record with special emphasis on the mollusca, (2) the methods used in past molluscan studies and my recommendations for the future, (3) the data and rationale affecting paleoecologic reconstructions for the Region.

The Invertebrate Record

The records of fossil and modern Pleistocene mollusks, about which I know, are summarized in Table 24 in the form of a checklist. Only the most modern publications have been cited. The list of references cited in the checklist bibliography should be consulted for the original records. Molluscan occurences are frequently cited by political divisions rather than by physiographic divisions, thus making it impossible to employ some reports which may refer to the region.

The checklist is no doubt incomplete and is presented only as a summary which will provide a starting place for future studies. Despite their imperfections, the data summarized in the checklist permit some interesting and valuable considerations of the mollusks which have lived and are now living in the region formerly occupied by Glacial Lake Agassiz.

Molluscan Research Methods

Traditionally, analysis of species composition of faunas through time has been used as an operating technique. There are serious deficiencies in this method, about which more will be said in a later section, and it will be worthwhile to analyze the shifts in species composition of the Pleistocene molluscan fauna. Like the checklist, Fig. 79 is organized into three time units: Wisconsin, post-Hypsithermal, and Modern. Thirty-five species are listed for the Wisconsin, thirty-two species are listed for the post-Hypsithermal, and sixty-one species are listed for the modern fauna. Two mechanical elements of analysis must be considered here. First is the impact

TABLE 24

CHECKLIST OF PLEISTOCENE NON-MARINE MOLLUSCA FROM THE
GLACIAL LAKE AGASSIZ PLAIN[a]

Molluscan Taxa	Wisconsin Fauna	Post-Hypsithermal Fauna	Modern Fauna
	(Numers indicate reference in notes)		
NAIAD PELECYPODS			
Actinonaias carinata			2, 2b
A. ellipsiformis			2, 2b
Amblema costata			2, 2a, 2b
Anodonta grandis		1	1, 2, 2a, 2
A. decora			2
Anodontoides ferussacianus		1	1, 2, 2a
Fusconaia flava		1	2, 2b
Lampsilis anodontoides			2
L. luteolus (L. radiata siliquoidea and L. siliquoidea of other authors)	6, 7	1, 4	1, 2, 2a, 2
L. ventricosa			2, 2a, 2b
Lasmigona complanata			1, 2, 2b
L. compressa		1	2a
L. costata			2a, 2b
Leptodea fragilis			2
L. laevissima			2
Ligumia recta			2, 2b
L. recta latissima			2, 2a, 2b
Megalonaias gigantea			2
Obliquaria reflexa			2, 2a
Obovaria olivaria	6		2
Proptera alata			2
P. alata megaptera			2, 2a
Quadrula quadrula			2, 2a, 2b
Strophitus rugosus		1	2a
S. undulatus			2
Totals 23	2	6	23

TABLE 24--Continued

Molluscan Taxa	Wisconsin Fauna	Post-Hypsithermal Fauna	Modern Fauna
		(Numbers indicate reference in notes)	
SPHAERIID PELECYPODS			
P. casertanum	7		
P. compressum	7		
P. idahoense	7		
P. lilljeborgi	7		
P. nitidum	5, 7		
P. nitidum pauperdulum	7		
P. simile			2, 2b
Pisidium spp.	3	4	
Sphaerium striatinum	6, 7		2
S. sulcatum	6		2b
Sphaerium sp.		4	2b
Totals 10	9	2	4
BRANCHIATE GASTROPODS			
Amnicola binneyana	7	4	
A. emarginata			2b
A. limosa	5, 7	4	
A. lustrica	7		2
Valvata lewisi	3, 5		
V. sincera	7		
V. tricarinata	5, 7	4	
Totals 7	6	3	2
PULMONATE GASTROPODS			
Armiger crista	3		
Ferrissia shimekii	7		
Ferrissia sp.	4		2b
Gyraulus circumstriatus	7		
G. parvus	3, 5, 6, 7	4	2b
Gyraulus sp.		4	2b
Helisoma anceps	5, 7		
H. campanulatum			2
H. corpulenta	7		
H. trivolvis		4	2, 2b
Helisoma sp.	7	4	2b
Lymnaea bulimoides	7		
L. dalli	7		

TABLE 24--Continued

Molluscan Taxa	Wisconsin Fauna	Post-Hypsithermal Fauna	Mode Faun
	(Numbers indicate reference in not		
L. emarginata	7		
L. humilis (sensu Hubendick)	3,5	4	2, 2b
(sensu Baker)	7		
L. palustris	7		2b
L. parva	7		
L. stagnalis			2b
Lymnaea sp.		4	
Physa anatina	7		
Physa cf. P. ancillaria	3		
Physa cf. P. lordi			2, 2b
Physa cf. P. elliptica			2, 2b
Physa cf. P. gyrina			2, 2b
Physa sp.			2b
Totals 25	16	6	13
GASTROPODS-PULMONATES-TERRESTRIAL			
Carychium exiguum		4	2, 2b
Cionella lubrica		4	2b
Deroceras laeve			2, 2b
Deroceras sp.		4	
Discus cronkhitei		4	2, 2b
Euconulus fulvus			2, 2b
Gastrocopta armifera		4	2, 2b
G. contracta		4	2, 2b
G. holzingeri		4	2, 2b
Gastrocopta sp.		4	
Helicodiscus parallelus		4	2, 2b
Nesovitrea binneyana		4	2, 2b
Oxyloma retusa			2b
Strobilops sp.		4	
Succinea avara		4	2, 2b
Succinea sp.	3	4	
Vallonia cf. V. costata			2b
V. pulchella			2, 2b
Vallonia sp.		4	2b
Vertigo aurthuri			2

TABLE 24--Continued

Molluscan Taxa	Wisconsin Fauna	Post-Hypsithermal Fauna	Modern Fauna
	(Numbers indicate reference in notes)		
Vitrina alaskana			2
V. limpida			2, 2b
Zonitoides arborea	3	4	2, 2b
otals 23	2	15	19
rand Total, Number of Species	35	32	61
otal Number of Species for Pleistocene Molluscan fauna -- 88			

[a]The checklist above annotes published records of late Wisconsin, post-ypsithermal, and Modern mollusca collected in the parts of Manitoba, innesota, North Dakota and Ontario underlain by sediments deposited in lacial Lake Agassiz.

otes:

1. Cvancara and Harrison (1965).
2. Tuthill (1962, 1963a).
2a. Dawley (1947) lists the mussels which occur in the various drainages of Minnesota. Those she lists for the Hudson Bay drainage are noted in the above checklist by the designation "2a". Her reports sometimes form the basis for the inclusion of the taxon in Tuthill (1962).
2b. When I organized the material for the North Dakota checklist I mentioned the presence of specimens of a taxon in the University of North Dakota Department of Biology, Department of Geology, or my personal collection only when no previous published record of the taxon existed. Here I have designated taxa which I know to exist in these repositories by the notation "2b".
3. Tuthill (1963b).
4. Tuthill (1964).
5. Tuthill, Laird and Kresl (1964).
6. Upham (1895:237).
7. Zoltai, S. C., written communication to Tuthill, 15 November 1966, reporting mollusks "...collected from Lake Agassiz sediments... by S. C. Zoltai [,] identified by H. B. Herrington and H. von der Schalie."

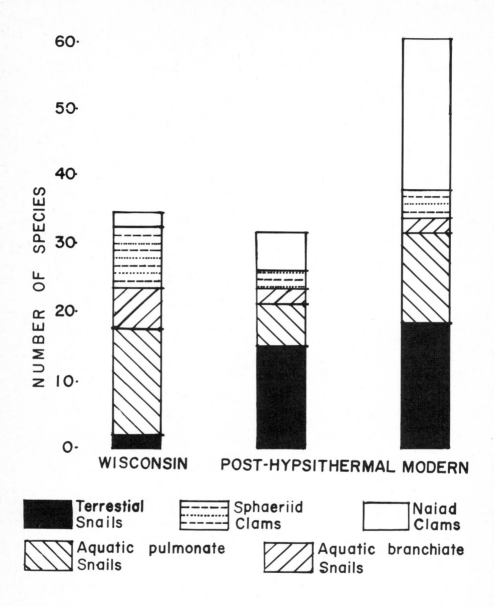

Figure 79. Pleistocene and recent -- molluscan fauna changes.

of the taxonomic skill of the author upon the diversity represented by any species list. More species of Sphaeriids appear in the Wisconsin faunal list than in the more recent lists because Herrington (Zoltai, personal communication) has a special skill in the identification of this family of clams. His work reported here has been entirely concerned with Wisconsin faunules. To interpret Table 24 as an indication that conditions favorable to *Sphaerium* and *Pisidium* have declined since the Wisconsin would be an error.

The second consideration is the state of taxonomy of any particular group. There was a tendency through the first third of this century to look at shells for differences rather than similarities. As a result a multiplicity of species became accepted in certain genera, which in the light of more modern studies, are not separated into species on shell characteristics alone. Excellent examples of this are the genera *Succinea, Lymnea,* and *Physa*. The complexity of the taxonomy of many of the groups of non-marine mollusca is so great that identification of fossils by non-specialists is not justified below the level of genus.

These mechanical problems are not beyond resolution. It is rather easy to determine whether an author was "splitting" or "lumping" and the specialties of the various authors are widely known. I raise the problems only as illustrations for the consideration of non-specialists who whould use fossil evidence as an element in the solution of a geologic problem.

By scrutinizing the checklist in greater detail a need for careful paleoecologic analysis can be illustrated. The species diversities below the level of class are worthy of note. The naiad pelecypods, for instance, show an interesting trend. In the Wisconsin fauna there are two, in the post-Hypsithermal there are six, and in the Modern there are twenty-three species. If we examine the source of these references we see that all of the Wisconsin occurrences are from beach sediments and all of the post-Hypsithermal and Modern occurrences are from fluviatile sediments and river environments, respectively. Thus we have a Wisconsin fauna and a post-glacial fauna which are not strictly comparable. With the draining of Glacial Lake Agassiz a new suite of environments became available and the diversity of the naiad fauna increased. Thus, while interesting to the study of biologic history, the analysis of species diversity gives no information about the geologic history of the region not already known from geomorphic studies.

The same is true of a comparison of the branchiate and pulmonate aquatic gastropod faunas. Branchiates, being organisms which breathe by gills, cannot survive fluctuations of water level so extreme as to include periodic or even occasional drying of the environment. Most pulmonates can withstand periodic drying of the environment. Thus with the draining of Lake Agassiz the stability of the available environments was reduced and pulmonates dominate the postglacial faunas.

The only pulmonate to disappear from the Pleistocene fauna is *Helisoma anceps*. Baker (1928a) regarded this species as typically a river and creek form, but we (Tuthill, Clayton, and Laird 1963) found it in a Minnesota lake which lacked either inlet or outlet. Why *H. anceps* no longer is found in the region may eventually be explained by the type of work reported by Cvancara and Harrison (1965) and by Cvancara (in this volume) or it may turn up in the living fauna as more thorough study of the modern mollusks of the region is accomplished.

The terrestrial gastropod faunas show a marked increase in the number of species in the post-Hypsithermal and Modern faunas. This is a reflection of the fact that the Wisconsin fauna is the result of the examination of fossils preserved in lacustrine sediments as opposed to the fluviatile sediments of the post-Hypsithermal and land surfaces of modern times. Of the fifteen genera found in the region, all but three were present in the area of the Sheyenne Delta as early as 2540 ± 300 years ago (W-1185, Tuthill 1964:154).

One final point intimated by the checklist is that very little paleontological work has been done in the Glacial Lake Agassiz region. Dr. Elson (personal communication) has reported that the southern portions of the Campbell beaches are abundantly fossil-iferous sites in the region.

The fossiliferous sites which have been studied in the Glacial Lake Agassiz region have, with one exception (Tuthill 1964), all been evaluated from "grab samples". Quantification of conclusion cannot be accomplished by quantification of sampling method alone. What is accomplished by a more precise method of collection is a greater permanency of data. La Rocque's (1960) method is clearly describable: later workers can know exactly what was done. By its use, much operator bias is removed from the data collection. It is obviously impractical for geologists, whose primary interest is not paleoecology, to conduct such time consuming studies, but paleontologic studies should employ the most precise methods avail-able. Collection of fossiliferous sites by non-specialists, however should continue to be made by the grab sample technique.

Thus far I have discussed only molluscan studies. Delorme (1965) and Guliov (1963) have demonstrated the great paleoecologic usefulness of studies of Pleistocene fossil ostracodes in Sask-atchewan. Their work also provides excellent reference literature for students of North American post-glacial ostracodes. As with mollusks, identification of ostracodes is an area where the non-specialist should tread cautiously.

Sponge spicules exist in some of the late Wisconsin super-glacial sediments and post glacial sediments of the Missouri Coteau district and no doubt will be found in the fossiliferous sediments of the Glacial Lake Agassiz region. They are parataxa and capable of being transported by wind, thus caution must attend their interpretation.

The presence of oögonia of *Chara* or a closely related genus of algae has been noted in several sites in the region. While these are not invertebrates, they are important to any paleoecologic study as they require light for success and could not occupy turbid waters.

In my opinion the greatest defect of methodology in paleontologic studies has been specialization. When only one kingdom or phylum is considered, we confine ourselves to the type of information that taxon can give about past environments and we ignore other types of information. The illustration of the usefulness of fossil algae mentioned above is an excellent example.

When paleoecologic interpretation is the object, I believe it is mandatory that all facets of a site be studied. The type of study which Shay (1967) is conducting at Itasca Park, Minnesota, is what is needed. From detailed population data, sequences of events may reveal themselves to be related to regional shifts in ecologic conditions which effected invertebrate populations sufficiently to make these changes stratigraphically useful.

One key interpretive aspect of fossil terrestrial and fresh-water invertebrates (with the exception of sponge spicules) is that even faunas contained in fluviatile sediments represent a more local situation than pollen or terrestrial vertebrates can be assumed to represent.

Paleoecologic Reconstruction

The basic rationale of paleoecology is descendant from Lyell's interpretation of the theory of the Uniformity of Nature. This is such common knowledge that we seldom consider its impact upon our conclusions. The basic assumption is that biologic responses to changes in the environment have always been the same as they are today. Scott (1963) has pointed out the possible inconsistency of maintaining this idea while at the same time accepting Darwin's theory of evolution with its dependence upon the acceptance of ecologic change as an element of the mechanism of speciation. There are three ameliorating factors in late Pleistocene non-marine molluscan paleoecologic studies with respect to this conundrum. These are: (1) the search for modern analogs to fossil populations, and I would emphasize the word populations, (2) the practice of suggesting the modern analog, not as an exact and bona-fide replica of the past environment, but as a possible interpretation of the past environment, and (3) the fact that in the Glacial Lake Agassiz Region no shell morphology-based speciation has been recognized since Wisconsin time. If paleoecology can be done at all, it surely can be done on late Pleistocene faunas of non-marine mollusca.

That we accomplish genuinely valid paleoecologic reconstruction
now is another matter. Taylor (1965) in reviewing the problems
faced by the North American paleocologist who employs Pleistocene
non-marine mollusca has cited La Rocque's (1952) need to rely solely
on Morrison's (1932) ecologic studies of the modern mollusca of
eastern Wisconsin as a source of water quality associated with
molluscan species.

Naiads had been studied by Coker and others (1919-1920), but
only from a natural history point of view for they were primarily
concerned with methods of propagation and conservation of commercially important mussels. Since 1952 Tuthill (1963), Tuthill and
Laird (1963) and Cvancara and Harrison (1965) have published
information about the ecology of modern molluscan populations in
Alaska, central North Dakota, and eastern North Dakota respectively.

It is readily apparent that the type of information published
by Baker (1928a, 1928b), which is widely used in North America,
is totally inadequate as a "knowledge of the Recent". The ecologic
data reported in Baker's work is the casual result of information
obtained by malacologists while they were collecting mollusks and
does not evaluate the seasonal variability of the environment. No
paleoecologic reconstruction can be more precise or more complete
than our knowledge of the Recent. The "quantitative" collecting
techniques recommended by La Rocque are beyond doubt an admirable
innovation in sampling methods. Any paleontologist wishing to
employ his time wisely will sample in this or a similar manner.
But the increased degree of precision of sampling techniques in
no way compensates for an imprecise, incomplete, or erroneous
knowledge of the present ecologic requirements of the living
members of the various molluscan taxa.

Assuming conditions which reason dictates to be required by
certain taxa, in the absence of real ecologic data can also be
dangerous. An example, regrettably from my own work, follows.
Because branchiate gastropods and all pelecypods respire by gills,
it seemed reasonable to me to assume that these mollusca could not
tolerate turbid water containing appreciable amounts of suspended
detritus. In 1964 in an article discussing a fossil molluscan
fauna taken from a marl beneath Campbell Beach sands, I stated,
"If the nine species of freshwater mollusks reported here lived
in Glacial Lake Agassiz, they are strong indicators that the lake
contained clear, seasonally warm, freshwater." My conclusion
about the presence of clear, warm water is valid, but not for the
reason which prompted me to reach it. The marl contained oögonia
of a genus of freshwater algae. These organisms require sunlight
and thus could not have lived in an aquatic environment incapable
of transmitting sunlight. Studies, of which I have had a part,
in Alaska during the period 1962-65 have shown that *Valvata siberica*
dominates the molluscan population of a lake in which values of
turbidity range around 50 ppm. In fact *V. siberica*, a close relative
of *V. lewisi*, was ten times more abundant in turbid lakes than in
clear lakes having about the same thermal and chemical characteristics. *Sphaerium,* a genus of small clams, was found only in turbid
environments.

Our work in central North Dakota and south-central Alaska has brought into question the practice of inferring the water quality of past environments from the water quality values stated for various species in Morrison's (1932) article. In the Missouri Coteau we found *Lymnaea humilis* (sensu Hubendick) in waters that contained from 830 to 15,800 ppm total dissolved solids, a pH range of 7.70 to 8.20 ppm, and a CO_2 range of 150 to 870 ppm. Morrison (1932:371) had given the ranges for *Fossaria obrussa*, which I believe to be comparable to the taxon discussed above, as pH 5.86 to 8.37 and CO_2 as 1.26 to 25.75 ppm. In Alaska we have found *Lymnaea humilis* in almost pure water having less than 1 ppm of dissolved solids, CO_2 of 0 to 7.8 ppm, and pH of 7.14 to 7.70. These disparities of water quality values certainly indicate the unreliability of our present ecologic knowledge. If an animal can exist and reproduce in such pure water as that found in Alaska I question its use as presumptive evidence of water quality. The lack of studies of a molluscan or an ostracode population throughout a single year is a great defect in our knowledge of modern inverteb-rate ecology. The Midwest Benthological Society 1966 *Bibliography of Taxonomy and Ecology of Benthic Macroinvertebrates* lists 166 titles on mollusks and 247 on benthic ecology published between 1956 and 1966 and not one is the report of a study of the ecology and structure of a molluscan population. Cvancara and Harrison (1965) are the only authors who have evaluated a naiad population from a Red River drainage system with respect to its physical and chemical environment, but even their work was confined to sampling during the summer. No extinctions among late Pleistocene mollusca are known in North Dakota, but marked and interpretively useful changes in the structure of molluscan populations can be seen. We desperately need to know the ecologic factors which influence the structure of natural populations.

Ecotypic shell forms offer a type of paleoecologic data which is perhaps the most reliable. The naiads are especially useful in this respect. When water temperature rises and/or water level is drastically lowered, mussels discontinue secretion of their shell. Numerous growth-interruption lines may be formed during a single year in this way. When such conditions exist in an environment containing species which are normally smooth-shelled, (e.g., *Lamp-silis* or *Anodonta)* increased external shell roughness is observed.

Lastly I believe that the Winnipeg area should house a regional, research-quality collection of Pleistocene non-marine mollusca and ostracodes. We need an "Old Home" for "happy" clams. The classifi-cation of habitat types, characteristic of distinct populations, in Great Britain by Boycott (1936) demonstrated a correlation between dissolved calcium and the distribution of certain taxa on nonmarine aquatic mollusks. The few studies of the ecology of these forms in North America discourages the idea that as simple and direct a classification can be looked forward to in the western hemisphere. The range of habitats in Britain is clearly less extreme than those available to mollusks on this continent and thus a regional approach to the paleoecology of nonmarine mollusca is required. The collection of both ecologic and paleontologic (especially those relating to taxonomy) data must be approached regionally here in order to diminish the effects of the adaptability of the molluscan species to different ecologic conditions through time and geography. Taxonomic and ecologic work will have much greater validity if it is regionally based.

While much of what I have discussed no doubt sounds gloomy, I do not have any doubts that molluscan and ostracode studies will eventually provide important information for understanding the history of the Glacial Lake Agassiz Region. Nor do I doubt that paleontologic work can be accomplished and reported in such a way as to be of permanent value. But at present I think we must be very careful what questions we ask our fossil faunas to answer. They are a bit like the lower school boy, equipped with a ready knowledge of the times tables. When asked questions about higher mathematics, he can be expected to give answers which are amusing fantasies, but noticeably inaccurate. If, with inadequate ecologic information, we insist upon detailed paleoecologic-paleolimnologic reconstructions we can be assured of failure. We can and should attempt to interpret the fossil populations, but we should not attempt to go beyond the limits of our knowledge of Recent ecologic information. Further, we should be very sure that the descriptive portions of our reports are clear enough to provide a basis for future interpretations, made when we know more about the various taxa.

At present the only information about the Glacial Lake Agassiz Region which can be inferred from the few invertebrate paleontologic studies which have been completed is that before the lake drained completely away it became colonized by mollusca, ostracodes, and calcareous algae. At the time of the formation of the upper Norcross, Campbell and Gladstone beaches molluscan populations of 9, 10, and 4 species respectively had colonized the lake and/or nearby land surfaces. Table 25 shows the distribution of these species with respect to the beaches mentioned. Fish were present in the lake because the naiads require them as hosts for their glochidial stage. The fish were probably species of the families Percadae and/or Centrarchidae. At the time the fossils found in the Norcross beach lived, terrestrial vegetation had colonized parts of the landsurface in Red Lake County, Minnesota, as evidenced by the presence of land snails. As mentioned previously, water clear enough to allow light penetration over a sufficient period of time to deposit ten inches of silty-marl existed in the region of Turtle River State Park, North Dakota, just prior to the formation of the upper Campbell beach. Organic detritus as well as aquatic plants no doubt existed concurrently with the mollusks, but more specific inferrences are not possible. Water temperature in the various molluscan habitats certainly rose 4°C seasonally and based on recent Alaskan studies of pro- and superglacial molluscan habitats (Tuthill 1966) probably ranged above 18° C in the summer. The water may have been very poor in dissolved solids (as little as 1 ppm) and may have been turbid seasonally at the Turtle River State Park site and throughout the year at the other sites studied. Changes in the available aquatic and terrestrial habitats since late Wisconsin time are, at present, better understood from sedimentologic and stratigraphic information.

TABLE 25

DISTRIBUTION OF MOLLUSCAN SPECIES IN SEDIMENTS FROM
BEACHES OF GLACIAL LAKE AGASSIZ

Molluscan Taxa	Beaches		
	Upper Norcross	Campbell	Gladstone
Pelecypods			
Naiads			
Obovaria olivaria		X	
Lampsilis luteolus			
Naiad fragments	X	X	X
Sphaeriids			
Sphaerium striatinum			
S. sulcatum			X
Pisidium nitidum		X	X
Pisidium sp.	X		
Gastropods			
Aquatic Pulmonates			
Armiger crista	X		
Gyraulus parvus	X	X	X
Helisoma anceps		X	
Lymnaea humilis	X	X	
Physa cf. P. ancillaria	X		
Physa sp.		X	
Terrestrial Pulmonates			
Succinea sp.	X		
Zonitoides arborea	X		
Aquatic Branchiates			
Amnicola limosa		X	
Valvata lewisi	X	X	
V. tricarinata		X	

Study of the development of the terrestrial gastropod fauna may eventually be the most significant contribution to the paleo-ecology of the region as their appearance in the sediments deposited after the draining of Lake Agassiz should tell us a great deal about the surface upon which they lived.

THE TAILRACE BAY SITE FAUNA

Paul W. Lukens, Jr.

Introduction

The Tailrace Bay site is located in west-central Manitoba about 225 miles north of Winnipeg, near the point where the Saskatchewan River empties into Lake Winnipeg (see Fig.80). The site lies near the foot of a series of large rapids, the Grand Rapids, and near the eastern end of a two and one-half mile portage that bypasses these rapids. A short distance upstream (west) from the Grand Rapids are located Cross and Cedar Lakes, both of which are natural impoundments of the lower end of the Saskatchewan River. To the north is Moose Lake. Cedar and Moose Lakes form the eastern limit of the Saskatchewan River delta, an alluvial flood plain which extends west to the Manitoba town of The Pas. The airline distance from Grand Rapids to The Pas is about ninety miles. Much of the region between Grand Rapids and The Pas is (or was) prime fish and wildlife habitat, for much of it was flooded with the completion of the Grand Rapids hydro-electric project in 1965.

The Grand Rapids site, a prehistoric habitation site called the Tailrace Bay site, was excavated during the summers of 1961 and 1962 by an archeological party from the University of Manitoba headed by Professor William J. Mayer-Oakes. The site yielded a wealth of cultural materials which connote at least four periods of occupation over a time span of about 4500 years. The dating of the earliest level of occupation, 2500 BC, is based on the presence of McKean Lanceolate points in the lower levels of the deposit. In general the cultural materials indicate increasing age with depth. The large quantity of scrap animal bone recovered constitutes one of the more important finds.

Both years the site was dug within a grid of 5-foot squares placed over the apparent zone of greatest concentration of cultural debris. All bone from each square was saved. Because of the limited depth of the sediments and the poorly defined stratigraphy, the bone was collected in 1961 from the arbitrary levels utilized. In 1962, however, an effort was made to excavate on the basis of natural stratigraphic zones. These zones were, from the top down, "sod", "plow", "gray" and "gravel". Thus the 1962 bones were segregated according to these four zones.

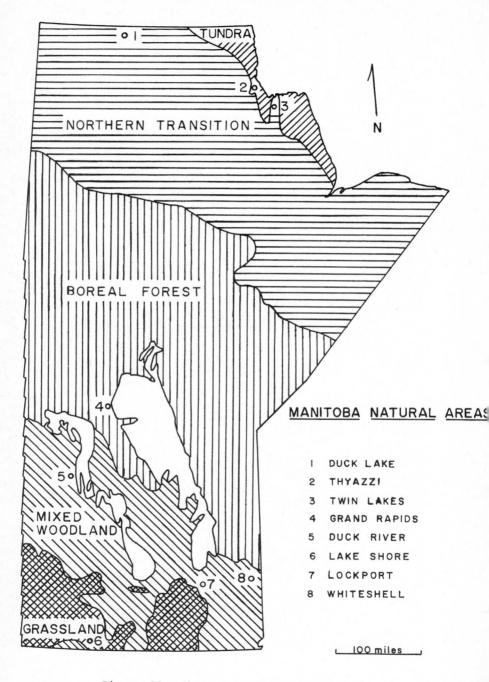

Figure 80.   Natural Areas of Manitoba.

Natural History

The Tailrace Bay site and its environs lie in the northern portion of a broad, fairly level plain known as the Manitoba lowland, a major physiographic division of Manitoba. The Manitoba lowland occupies much of the southern part of the Province and includes the three largest Manitoba lakes, Winnipeg, Winnipegosis, and Manitoba. Elevations in the lowland average 850 feet above mean sea level but do not exceed 1000 feet. Lake Winnipeg, at an elevation of 713 feet, is the lowest point in the Grand Rapids area.

The entire area has been glaciated and except for the clays, silts and very fine sands of the Saskatchewan Delta, the limestone bedrock of the north lowland is mantled with ground moraine of Wisconsin age. The calcareous till mantle, presumably derived from the underlying limestones, is relatively thin in most places but shows considerable depth variation. Usually it is deep enough to support vegetation. The present surface, a gently undulating till plain in which local relief is under twenty five feet, is interrupted by occasional bogs, swamps, and lakes. In the north lowland the lacustrine silts and clays that were laid down in the southern Manitoba lowland by Lake Agassiz are absent. However, a successive series of terraces and strandlines in the area do indicate the former presence of Lake Agassiz.

Vegetationally the Grand Rapids area lies within the northern coniferous forest. According to Rowe (1959) the area is situated in the Manitoba lowlands section of the boreal forest region. However, because of an admixture of broadleaved deciduous trees, this section of the boreal forest has been described by Ritchie (1962) as mixed forest.

Without going into detail suffice it to say that much of the forested portion of the Grand Rapids area consists primarily of closed stands of conifers but that there are numerous localized areas where, due to topography and soils, the forest cover is composed of mixed broadleaf and evergreen species. In many places forest succession has been altered by fire.

The Vertebrate Fauna

The vertebrate fauna from the Grand Rapids site consisted of more than 22,600 bones and bone fragments (Lukens 1966). Approximately 4/9 was fish bone, 4/9 was mammal bone and 1/9 was bird bone. A total of 59 vertebrate species was identified from the fauna. Included were 7 fish, 34 birds and 18 mammals (see Table 26 for the following discussion). About 3/8's (37%) of the total bone was identified to species.

TABLE 26

VERTEBRATES FROM THE GRAND RAPIDS SITE

FISH

Lake Sturgeon	*Acipenser fulvescens*
Lake Whitefish	*Coregonus clupeaformis*
Northern Pike	*Esox lucius*
White Sucker	*Catostomus commersoni*
Channel Catfish	*Ictalurus punctatus*
Walleye	*Stizostedion vitreum*
Freshwater Drum	*Aplodinotus grunniens*

MAMMALS

Snowshoe Hare	*Lepus americanus*
Woodchuck	*Marmota monax*
Least Chipmunk	*Eutamias minimus*
Red Squirrel	*Tamiasciurus hudsonicus*
Beaver	*Castor canadensis*
Muskrat	*Ondatra zibethicus*
Porcupine	*Erethizon dorsatum*
Dog	*Canis familiaris*
Red Fox	*Vulpes fulva*
Black Bear	*Ursus americanus*
Marten	*Martes americana*
Fisher	*Martes pennanti*
Mink	*Mustela vison*
Otter	*Lutra canadensis*
Lynx	*Lynx canadensis*
Moose	*Alces alces*
Woodland Caribou	*Rangifer tarandus*
Bison	*Bison bison*

BIRDS

Common Loon	*Gavia immer*
White Pelican	*Pelecanus erythrorhynchos*
Double-crested Cormorant	*Phalacrocorax auritus*
Great Blue Heron	*Ardea herodias*
Whistling Swan	*Olor columbianus*
Trumpeter Swan	*Olor buccinator*
Canada Goose	*Branta canadensis*
Blue or Snow Goose	*Chen* sp.
Mallard, Black Duck or Pintail	*Anas* sp.
Gadwall	*Anas* cf. *strepera*
Green Wing Teal	*Anas carolinensis*
Blue Wing Teal	*Anas discors*
Redhead or Canvasback	*Aythya* sp.

TABLE 26--Continued

BIRDS (Continued)

Lesser Scaup .... *Aythya* cf. *affinis*
Bufflehead .... *Bucephala albeola*
White-winged Scoter .... *Melanita deglandi*
Hooded Merganser .... *Lophodytes cucullatus*
Bald Eagle .... *Haliaeetus leucocephalus*
Osprey .... *Pandion haliaetus*
Spruce Grouse .... *Canachites canadensis*
Ruffled Grouse .... *Bonasa umbellus*
Whooping Crane .... *Grus americana*
Sandhill Crane .... *Grus canadensis*
Common Snipe .... *Capella gallinago*
Greater Yellowlegs .... *Totanus melanoleucus*
Glaucous Gull .... *Larus hyperboreus*
Herring Gull .... *Larus argentatus*
Ring-billed Gull .... *Larus delawarensis*
Bonaparte's Gull .... *Larus philadelphia*
Tern .... *Sterna* sp.
Passenger Pigeon .... *Ectopistes migratorius*
Raven .... *Corvus corax*
Crow .... *Corvus brachyrhynchos*
Common Grackle .... *Quiscalus quiscala*

The most abundant fish was the lake sturgeon; it represented 83% of the identified fish bone. The next most common fish, the northern pike, represented 15% of the identified fish bone. The other five species total only about 2% of the identified fish bone.

All seven of the fish from the Grand Rapids fauna occur today in Lake Winnipeg and the Saskatchewan River. However, there is a definite indication of an historic shift in the fish fauna and, possibly, of lake environments. Certainly commercial fishing is one reason for the shift. For example, the sturgeon, abundant at Grand Rapids prehistorically and still plentiful in early historic times, is now rare, a consequence of over-exploitation by man. Sixty years ago the freshwater drum fish was found only south of the narrows in Lake Winnipeg. Since then it has moved north and is now common at Grand Rapids. Only two fragments of the drum were recovered from the Tailrace Bay site.

Numerous species of Manitoba fish were not recovered in the archeological fish fauna. Perhaps the two most significant absences are the lake trout and the burbot. Lake Winnipeg is not lake trout habitat although occasional specimens have been taken there. The absence of the lake trout in the Grand Rapids fauna suggests either non-utilization or, more likely, prehistoric scarcity. Presumably Lake Winnipeg has not been suitable for lake trout throughout the period of human occupation at Grand Rapids.

The absence of the burbot from the site is further evidence for an historic change in the fish fauna, and it corroborates historic records. Since the mid-1930's the burbot has become abundant at Grand Rapids, and it is now common as far upriver as the Pas.

Considering the avifauna, important absences are noted. Three of the birds from the site, the passenger pigeon, trumpeter swan and whooping crane, are no longer found in Manitoba. The passenger pigeon is extinct, and the present ranges of the other two are limited in Canada to the western provinces. The other 31 species are still extant in Manitoba; most are presently common or abundant in the Grand Rapids area.

Only three of the 31 extant birds, the two grouse and the raven, are permanent residents in the Manitoba north lowland. All the other birds are migratory and hence resident only on a seasonable basis. Most of the migratory species are summer residents which nest in the Grand Rapids area. The rest are arctic nesters that pass through Grand Rapids on the way north in the spring and south in the fall.

The bulk of the birds from the Grand Rapids site are closely associated with aquatic habitats. Only six need not habitually occur near water: the two grouse, passenger pigeon, crow, raven and grackle. These six birds are basically inhabitants of varied forested habitats.

The birds do provide us with good information concerning the
season of occupation at the site. At present the earliest spring
migrants, certain of the water birds, arrive at or near Grand
Rapids in April, as soon as there is open water. The last of the
southbound migrants leave in early November with the freeze-up.
Thus some migratory species are resident for six or seven months.
Presumably the habits, and the habitats, of these birds have not
changed markedly during the period since the drainage of Glacial
Lake Agassiz and the initial human occupation of the Grand Rapids
area.

Numerous species of birds were not recovered at Grand Rapids.
The most notable are the grebes, hawks, ptarmigan, sharp-tailed
grouse, rails, coot, numerous shorebirds, owls and all the perch-
ing birds. The reasons for their absence from the site fauna are
uncertain, for all occur in Manitoba at present, and many have
been identified from other North American archeological sites.

Seventeen of the eighteen species of mammals from the site
are feral; the dog is the only domestic. Except for the bison,
all still occur in the Grand Rapids area.

The former status of the bison in the north lowland is uncertain. There are authentic accounts that place the bison not
far south and west of Grand Rapids in early historic times, and
bison bones have been recovered from Indian middens at the Pas.
However, I do not believe that the few bison bones at Grand Rapids,
fourteen fragments in all, justify the postulate that during this
period of time grasslands extended into west-central Manitoba.
The fauna as a whole simply does not exhibit a prairie character.
It is possible, however, that the Grand Rapids area may have been
much closer to the prairie several thousand years ago than it is
now.

There are about twenty-two kinds of recent Manitoba mammals
that were not represented in the Grand Rapids fauna. Fifteen of
these are small mammals and hence were probably of little util-
itarian value to the Indians. The other seven mammals not present
in the deposit include the wolverine, striped skunk, gray wolf,
coyote and three deer - the elk, whitetail and mule deer. The
wolverine is almost never found in archeological deposits, and
judging from other North American archeological faunas the absence
of the other three carnivores, skunk, wolf, and coyote is perplex-
ing.

The lack of whitetail and mule deer bone, however, is easily
explained. Neither immigrated to the north lowland until the early
1900's. Both moved north in response to man-made environmental
changes. More intriguing is the absence of the elk from Grand
Rapids. The archeological and recent records of the elk in Manitoba
tentatively suggest that it was not indigenous to the Grand Rapids
area and, possibly, that any abundance in Manitoba may be historic.

Discussion

The fossils from an archeological site have many uses. For the archeologist they provide valuable information about diet, season of occupation, habitat utilization and other cultural data. For the zoologist the animal remains furnish clues to past occurrences and distribution. However, the most important question as far as this conference is concerned is whether the Grand Rapids fauna, which covers a period of about 4500 years, shows any indication of a faunal change.

Comparison of the Grand Rapids archeological fauna with the recent terrestrial fauna of the Manitoba north lowlands suggests no major faunal changes and hence, by inference, no major environmental shifts during the period of human occupation. The obvious faunal differences are recent, the result of extirpation or envionmental alteration by the white man. Thus we can tentatively assume that the major habitats in the Grand Rapids area have not changed markedly during the past 4500 years. However, it is likely that vegetational succession has changed the relative proportions of the various habitats. The faunas in turn may be different, but the differences would be in distribution and abundance rather than kind.

There are now about eight general animal habitats in the Grand Rapids area. Three are aquatic, the other five are terrestrial or upland. All of the fossil vertebrates, except one, can be assigned with some degree of certainty to habitats now in existence in the Grand Rapids area. Among the mammals, for example, twelve come from forested habitats, either pure coniferous forest or an admixture of evergreen and deciduous trees. Four mammals are associated with aquatic habitats. The dog is domestic. The bison, the one exception, poses a special problem. Normally found in or near grassland situations, the bison may or may not have been taken locally. The fossil birds from the site can also be considered to have occupied habitats similar to those now present in the Grand Rapids area.

The Grand Rapids fauna as a whole is typically north woodland or boreal, and all of the animals were most likely killed locally, with the possible exception of the bison. The closest regular prehistoric occurrence of bison was probably to the west along what is now the Manitoba-Saskatchewan border. The bison bone from the site was too sparse to permit an estimate of the number of animals represented. However, the kinds of bones recovered, mostly from the distal ends of the limbs, seem to represent those portions of the carcass that would least likely be carried long distances. Hence the bison bone is probably from animal(s) killed locally rather than transported from elsewhere. These bones may represent an occasional stray that wandered into the Grand Rapids area, perhaps during a dry year or years of high population. The bison bones are intriguing also in that they imply a familiarity of the Grand Rapids people with this mammal. These people apparently knew what to do with a bison when they found one.

Since these conclusions are complicated by several considerations they are tenuous. First, the fauna as considered here
represents 4500 years compressed into one plane. From this standpoint the above inferences are superficial by being two-dimensional
rather than three-dimensional. The species composition of an area
may change through time. Second, habitats and hence animal species
are not evenly distributed. Some habitats are more productive and
hence support more species and a larger animal population than
others. Third, some animals may occupy different habitats at
different seasons. The moose, for example, a woodland inhabitant
during the cold season, moves into marshes and lake shores during
warm weather. Fourth, man himself need not be a permanent resident.
He may have been drawing on the animal resources only at certain
times of the year.

Finally, there is one other archeological fauna from the
Agassiz basin that invites comment. This is the fauna from the
Lockport, Larter and Cemetery Point sites in southeastern Manitoba
(MacNeish 1958a). The fauna from these three sites yielded evidence
of at least nine species of mammals together with numerous fish
and some bird bones. Bison bone was predominant. The archeological
horizons in the MacNeish report tentatively cover a time span of
nearly 5000 years, from 3000 BC to 1750 AD. The oldest Focus,
Whiteshell, contained McKean Lanceolate points and hence falls in
the same general time range as the oldest inferred dates for Grand
Rapids.

Perhaps the most interesting aspect of the fauna from these
southeastern Manitoba sites is the early abundance of bison bone
and the very evident decrease in the proportion of bison remains
from the earliest to the more recent levels of occupation. Presumably the bison population of southeastern Manitoba was declining.
Primarily on this basis MacNeish (1958a) infers an environmental
change from prairie to forest in southeastern Manitoba.

Certainly an ecological change is indicated, but how much
change is uncertain. Elk, deer, and bear, all indicative of wooded
habitats, were also recovered very early in the same stratigraphic
sequence as the bison. During the 1600's the plains bison penetrated deep into the deciduous woodlands of the eastern United
States, a long way from the home prairie of a supposedly typical
grassland mammal. Though it probably was never very abundant east
of the Mississippi River, the bison nevertheless did demonstrate
a tolerance for at least partially wooded habitats. Hence the
presence of bison in an archeological site, particularly a site
located in the zone of transition between two or three major vegetation types, is not necessarily certain evidence for a prairie
environment. On the other hand there are traces of prairie in
the soils and in the present flora of southeastern Manitoba and
western Ontario. This is one enigma that can be solved best by
a series of pollen diagrams from southeastern Manitoba and in
particular from the floor of Glacial Lake Agassiz.

Part V

Human Population History
of Glacial Lake Agassiz

HUMAN HISTORY OF THE GLACIAL LAKE AGASSIZ

REGION IN THE 19TH CENTURY

John Warkentin

Introduction

This discussion consists of a few remarks on the settlement of the Manitoban part of the Glacial Lake Agassiz Region in the 19th century. I won't attempt to give an account of the sequence of settlement because that is too long and complex a story for the few minutes at my disposal, and also not necessary because Professor W.L. Morton's (1957) excellent history of Manitoba is well known. What I will do is select some aspects of the settlement experience of the 19th century, and relate them, in some degree at any rate, to points made by Mayer-Oakes and Hochbaum elsewhere in this volume. The following factors will be considered: Site, Stability, Regionalization, and Sources of Data.

Site

For my present purpose, site refers to the local environmental conditions and to the advantages and disadvantages for human settlement of one locality over another. (This follows the usage of W.L. Morton (1951). The significance of a particular site to man will, of course, vary from one time period to another because of differences in technology, cultural attitudes and human goals. If you can tell what a group's technological attainments and what its social aims are, then you can tell what the resources of a site (or perhaps even of an extensive area) are for that group; that is, how that group perceives and utilizes a particular environment. Pertinent here is Erich Zimmerman's (1964) discussion of the functional concept of resources.

It is clear that in pre-European times different parts of the Glacial Lake Agassiz Region had specific site characteristics for the human inhabitants. Some of these site characteristics have already been described by anthropologists and archeologists, and as research continues, we can expect a great increase in our knowledge of the significance of site to the Indian. It is fairly evident that the Glacial Lake Agassiz clay plains were not ideal places for camping. There was little shelter, and the land was wet and often marshy. It is true, however, that by hunting bison, food could be obtained on the plains. The Indian camp sites were alongside the rivers or on redges as the anthropologists and archeologists have been demonstrating; that is, at a few special sites within the Glacial Lake Agassiz Region.

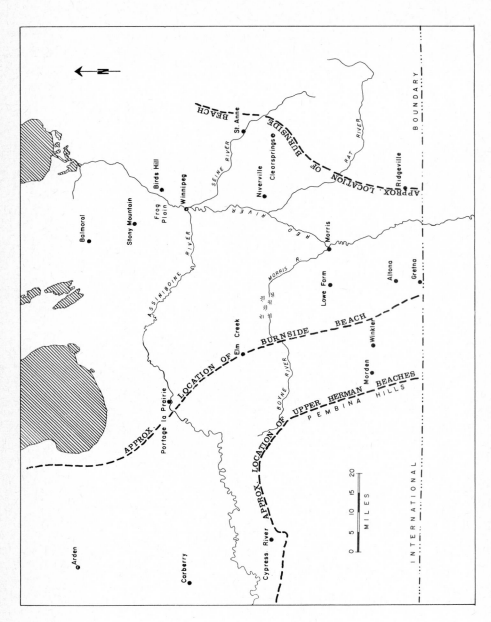

Figure 81.   South-central Manitoba: selected features and places.

The settlers who came to the Glacial Lake Agassiz Region in the 19th century had very different technologies and quite different aims from those of the Indians, so that in European times site took on new significance. For illustrative purposes, I will briefly refer to a number of components of site that are applicable to a study of the Glacial Lake Agassiz Region: beach ridges, vegetation, soil and water.

Beach Ridges

The beach ridges within the Glacial Lake Agassiz Region became important dry-point sites for farms in the 1870's when agricultural settlers from Eastern Canada and Europe came to Manitoba. Indians of course had used the ridges for travelling and for camping, but the farmers established permanent homes on the well-drained ridges. There are many easily recognized settlements associated with the ridges, for example at Ridgeville, Elm Creek, and Arden, but the less well-formed ridges (some of which are probably off-shore bars, such as the ridges near Niverville or Lowe Farm) also became desirable sites for farmsteads. (See Fig. 81)

Vegetation

Clumps of trees provided local shelter for European settlers, but I think it is fair to generalize that trees were not as critically important for survival in the agricultural colonization period as in pre-European times. This generalization needs careful qualification. There is plenty of evidence that in the early years of colonization lack of trees was a severe psychological as well as physical block to settlement, but the fact remains that with a new transportation technology, lumber for building material could be shipped into the grasslands from forested areas. To drive this point home with an extreme and almost ludicrous example, in one case in the 1870's, dressed timber was even shipped to the treeless plains west of Red River from the Ottawa Valley. I suggest, however, that in the long run trees assumed a vital role as an amenity, so that from the first days of settlement there have been persistent and valiant attempts to plant shelter belts on the prairies.

Soil

Once arable agriculture was introduced to the plains, soil took on a new significance. There may have been some cultivation in Indian times, and there was some during the fur trade period, but it was of slight importance. After 1870, with arable agriculture spreading quickly and widely on the prairies, certain soil qualities assumed significance: depth of soil, slope, stoniness, ease or difficulty breaking, and fertility. In the 1880's, the sandy-textured soils of the Carberry area (the Big Plain) were quickly brought under crop, partly because they could be easily broken. The rapid agricultural occupation of the Big Plain is actually a complex matter, because variables other than soil, such as proximity to the

railway, past experience of the farmers, and the capital they had
at their disposal, must be taken into account. It is revealing,
however, that in one municipality in the Carberry area over 125
acres were broken on the average farm in 1886, only five years after
the railway reached Brandon. An area of sandy loam to silty clay
such as the Portage Plain, where the land could be relatively easily
broken yet was of good fertility and was well drained, soon attained
wide recognition as an excellent farming district.

Water

      This was a site factor of very great significance, and I will
speak of it in a minute, because I want to use it as a special case
example under my remarks below on "stability".

      But first let me point out one very pertinent principle which
differentiates the significance of site in pre-European times, the
principle of commitment. By the principle of commitment in this
context I simply mean the tieing of an indiviual to a particular
parcel of land because of the social and economic systems which
were introduced by Europeans into the Western Interior of Canada
in the 19th century. Because a farmer has a "stake" in a particular
site, he is bound to that place. The Metis of Red River and indeed
some of the other settlers living there, were in a transition phase
between the Indian and the European attitudes to land, living partly
by farming and partly by hunting and other means (W.L. Morton's
"squatter" site), thus demonstrating, as an exception to the rule,
that there is some validity to the above generalization concerning
commitment.

      The European, after the first land surveys along the Red River
in the second decade of the 19th century, was committed to a particular plot of land. He carefully evaluated the potential of this
land, or at least he should have done so, and on the basis of this
appraisal was prepared to change the physical environment, or
"improve it" as the phrase goes, to suit his needs. His aim was to
make the holding, on which he wanted to establish roots, productive.
If economic advancement proved impossible because of a poor selection
of land (and in the early years of settlement when many would-be
farmers were inexperienced, this was all too frequently the case)
he abandoned the holding and moved on to try again elsewhere, or
try something else than farming.

      But even if a farmer had chosen land wisely, and remained on
his holding, the need for a constant appraisal and adjustment of
his farm enterprise remained. The evaluation and re-evaluation of
the land is an integral part of farming. It continues today and
will continue into the future. That is, when we are talking of
settlement, we are concerned with a dynamic process whose parameters
are always changing as man's needs, economic conditions, and technical capabilities change.

Stability

Man in occupying the land wants to achieve stability (in actual fact it will be a dynamic equilibrium) and he is willing to put forth a great deal of effort in order to achieve this stability.

In pre-European times in the Glacial Lake Agassiz Region, one of the great aims of the Indian, though not necessarily the only one, was survival -- subsistence. I am struck, when reading the life of John Tanner and the Journals of Alexander Henry the Younger, by the eternal restlessness of the people. Little groups moved in season to areas where food was available or the trapping was good, camped and hunted for a time, and then were off again. Frequently of course, this nomadism was carried out in definite patterns, with more or less regular return visits made to selected areas at certain seasons.

In or near the Glacial Lake Agassiz Region, as has already been suggested, there were some localities better suited for temporary occupance than others. Tanner (1956) describes how a small group of Indians travelled across the clay plains until it came to a site on the shores of Riding Mountain that suited its needs. Life was movement. Stability was adequacy of food supply and good trapping for a limited time within a region, not relatively permanent settlement on a selected square mile.

I have already suggested that in European times the concept of commitment to a specific piece of land became a critical social and economic factor -- the land became real estate and had a monetary value which hopefully would increase. This contained potential problems. In the Glacial Lake Agassiz Region one of the most important properties of a site is whether it has a sufficiency or deficiency of water. In fact, water is so important that it can be used as a common unifying theme in discussing the region as a whole. The point is that man had to come to terms with water in order to achieve stability in this environment, and in saying this, I don't deny the importance of other factors, such as the effective integration of the region into a commercial world-wide exchange system, though they won't be considered here.

I should perhaps clarify at once that when I use the term water I don't mean precipitation alone. We are all familiar with the fact that climate is a critical factor in the economic stability or instability of the plains to the west of the Glacial Lake Agassiz Region. In the glacial Lake Agassiz area climate, and in particular precipitation, has great significance too, but one can focus more particularly on the problem of water on the land, its availability or unavailability, and on the drainage of excess water.

In European times the settlers faced the task of maintaining themselves and their families in a commercial society on a specific place. If one assumes the quality of the soil to be good (that is, that the farmer chose his land well), then water is the critical physical variable which must be carefully considered in analyzing man's occupance of the land in the Glacial Lake Agassiz Region.

European man has had many ways, and many technological and
institutional aids at his disposal, to cope with water in the
Glacial Lake Agassiz Region. He has needed them. Let us examine
some of these adaptations.

The earliest settlers overcame any problems involving water
by using discretion in choosing their lots. They avoided the wet
lands and selected dry sites for their farms, as is possible at
the beginning of any colonization when there are few settlers and
there is a wide choice of land.

The riverine settlement established by Lord Selkirk after 1812
along the Red River is an excellent example of selecting a relatively
dry site amidst wet lands. Accessibility by water was a great factor
in choosing the site for the colony, and seems to have outweighed
the danger of the occasional spring flooding to which the settlement
was exposed. In later years other riverine settlements were established along the Assiniboine, Seine, Rat and Morris rivers in the
central part of the Glacial Lake Agassiz Region.

Dry-point sites in higher districts or along ridges and at
scarp-foot locations were also favoured early places for settlement,
when farmers started to enter the Glacial Lake Agassiz Region in
significant numbers after 1870. The Portage Plain, and the Stony
Mountain, Birds Hill, Ridgeville, Clearsprings, Pembina and Balmoral
districts are all dry-point sites in direct contrast with adjacent
land which are not only wet and poorly drained but prone to occasional
flooding. The Sainte Anne and Boyne River districts are combinations
of riverine and dry-point sites. When the accessible dry-point sites
on the Glacial Lake Agassiz clay plain had been occupied, most
settlers leap-frogged the wet lands and moved beyond the Glacial Lake
Agassiz basin to the Manitoba plateau and farther westward.

But some settlers did try their luck on the clay plains in the
1870's. The Mennonites, for instance, began to move on to the clay
plain in the Niverville area, beginning in 1874. The settlement
history of this colony is too complex to take up here, but I will
mention that one difficulty they faced was that of obtaining water
for domestic use and livestock, and another problem was general
flooding of the recently settled land during the heavy rains of the
late 1870's. In fact, many of the original settlements were abandoned
because of flooding. The displaced farmers chose to move to the
present Altona-Gretna area where the land is somewhat higher and not
so liable to inundation.

An example of a settlement on the Glacial Lake Agassiz clay
plain which is more appropriate for discussion here, because of the
time available, is that of the ill-fated Lowe Farm, ten miles west
of Morris in the heart of the plain. In 1878 and 1879 John Lowe of
Ottawa, using capital supplied by his brother James in England,
acquired over 10,000 acres of land with the intention of establishing
a large wheat farm similar to those already in existence in Dakota
Territory. The venture turned into a bitter comedy of expensive
errors extending over 20 years, revealing all too clearly the problems that had to be met in settling the clay plains.

The prairie sod on the Lowe Farm was much more difficult to break than had ever been anticipated and ploughing was slow, but an even worse obstacle was excess water on the land in spring, which delayed field operations, and restricted the men to ploughing the higher patches of land. But this was only the start of the troubles. Paradoxically there was a severe seasonal shortage of water in late summer for the stock and for domestic use. Neither shallow nor deep wells proved successful in supplying water fit for use. In dry summers water had to be hauled up to three miles from natural depressions, and in winter the full distance of ten miles from the Red River, until melting snow in pots provided a laborious though adequate solution. In the 1880's the Lowe Farm became something of an experimental farm when William Stephenson became its manager and tried to use a steam traction engine for ploughing. Mechanical problems abounded, and need not delay us here, but strange as it may seem the steam engine could not be used one season, when all else was miraculously in readiness, because there was not enough water available on the farm to keep the boiler in Stephenson's machine supplied with the required amount of water for raising steam. In fact, this scarcity of water on the farm led to an intensive effort by Lowe and Stephenson to devise a condenser for conserving water when the steam engine was operating! Other solutions to the periodic water shortage on the clay plains were also sought by Lowe and Stephenson. Proposals were made as early as 1881 to dig farm ponds to supply the much needed water, and ultimately two ponds were excavated on Lowe Farm, which must rank amongst the earliest in the Western Interior. Finally, in one last grandiose attempt to find a solution, a company called the Manitoba Farming Colonization and Water Company was incorporated in 1894 to pipe water from the Red River to the Lowe Farm. Nothing came of this scheme, but it does drive home just how desperate the search for water had become.

As a result of all these vicissitudes very little land was broken, and no stability was achieved in this very ambitious farm enterprise. Eventually John Lowe disposed of the property to investors and speculators who held it until large scale drainage works were constructed in the Glacial Lake Agassiz Region in the early 1900's making farming possible. At that time the land was sold to farmers in small individual farm units. The problem of obtaining water in dry years still continued, however, and the farmers were often forced to haul water during abnormally dry seasons from supplies in the artificial ponds at the former Lowe Farm, or from any depressions holding water.

The problem of too much or too little water caused a general lag of settlement throughout the Glacial Lake Agassiz Region, as is shown by contemporary real estate maps of the region. Great areas are indicated for sale between the Burnside beach ridges, with large areas in many townships almost devoid of settlement. I must now turn to the actual schemes which were finally devised and implemented in an endeavour to cope with the problem of water on the clay plains as a whole. As settlers continued to pour into the Western Interior, the number of fine free homesteads available for selection steadily declined while the value of land gradually

increased, and under this economic stimulus strong attempts were
made to bring the thousands of acres of inherently fertile but
wet land into production and on to the tax rolls. Comprehensive
drainage works, organized by the Provincial Government, finally
brought some stability to farming on the clay plains.

The need for drainage had been known for a long time. As
early as 1857 H.Y. Hind suggested that some ditching should be
undertaken in the area close to Red River. The Nor'-Wester of
August 1, 1861, in an editorial headed "Public Improvement" makes
a clear plea for drainage which is worth quoting:

> But we must extend our view. Another and a still greater
> portion of the Settlement suffers from want of drainage.
> The immense swamp which skirts the Settlement from the Frog
> Plain down to Netley Creek is a regular slough of Despond.
> There is no cessation here -- assuredly no improvement --
> every year is making it worse and worse. . . . All that is
> wanted is a good system of drainage. In Canada or the States,
> such an immense marsh so near the inhabitants, and so injuri-
> ously affecting them, would not be tolerated for one year.
> Few or none of the many industrious settlers living between
> the Frog Plain and the 'Water-Mill Creek" can extend their
> farms outside the public road. They are compelled to do all
> their farming within a very contracted area. And not only in
> this respect is it an evil -- the cattle of that district,
> being so much limited in their grazing, are generally-speaking
> in a miserable condition -- and hay-making which is a very
> important matter in a purely agricultural district, is all
> but an impossibility. Indeed, we believe that most of the
> people have to go across the river for that purpose. That
> portion of the settlement is thus, in a great measure,
> rendered worthless, and many are migrating from there to
> Portage la Prairie and other parts.

> Is that part of the Settlement then to be abandoned to its
> fate? Decidedly not. We say, again, Drain!

> The first thing to be done should be the cutting of a good
> large drain length-wise through the middle of the swamp from
> 'Tait's Creek' up to 'Flett's Bridge'. Then, or perhaps even
> before that, run a large drain across the swamp opposite
> John Tait's -- through and through it, so that the waters on
> one side will not communicate with the other side, but flow
> down the mill creek. Then drain off at Rowland's Vincent's
> Dahl's and at the Frog Plain -- all these cross drains to
> lead off from the main artery running lengthwise. To meet
> the necessary expense, we would suggest that all the settlers
> in the district contribute according to the land they hold --
> say 2s. or 3s. per chain -- and, whatever the total of such
> contributions, that an equal amount be granted from the public
> funds.

Little effective drainage was accomplished before 1880, though
some individual initiative was shown in a few places. For instance,
the Mennonites did some ditching in the Niverville area in the very

wet years of the late 1870's. The Provincial Government commenced digging offtake drains to the Assiniboine or to the nearest stub coulees in the late 1870's, and some drains were constructed in connection with the grading of the Pembina to St. Boniface railway line, completed in 1878.

The first Manitoba Drainage Act was passed in 1880, and that year drainage plans were made, surveys undertaken, and some ditching commenced. The ditches were shallow and not very wide and thus rather ineffectual. This work was continued for over a decade in widely scattered parts of the Glacial Lake Agassiz Region, but it gradually became apparent that a more vigorous and more comprehensive programme would have to be started if the land was going to be effectively drained and made ready for settlement. In 1895 "The Land Drainage Act" was passed, providing for the organizing of lands into drainage districts, and making provisions for financing drainage works within these districts. The first drainage district was organized in 1896, and by 1929, when the last one was formed, there were 24 districts, which included practically all the wet land in the central part of the Glacial Lake Agassiz basin.

A great deal of effective ditching was accomplished in these districts. By 1935 over six million dollars had been expended in various drainage works. The drains functioned sufficiently well to make it possible to farm practically all the flat land lying between the Burnside beach ridges. After 1900 the lands which had been empty were beginning to be occupied and turned into farms. First-hand knowledge of what drainage could accomplish was significant in bringing some investors and settlers to the newly drained lands. In the early years of the twentieth century, a considerable number of Americans from the American Middle West acquired land in the basin, including parts of the unfortunate Lowe Farm.

The drains have to be constantly maintained, and at times when this has been neglected serious flooding has occurred. Thus, the fight against flooding is a constant battle. Changes in engineering technology have resulted in significant alterations in the design of the drains and in their efficiency. The earliest drains were narrow shallow ditches built with floating dredges and horse scrapers. After 1914 double-dyked channels were constructed in the area west of Red River, and more recently the bulldozer has made it possible to build wide ditches with gently sloping sides which are easy to maintain. Through these various engineering works, the face of the clay plain in Southern Manitoba has been transformed in the past 90 years, both by the many channels themselves and in the form settlement these channels have made possible.

One problem that remained was that of obtaining water for use on the farms on the clay lands west of the Red River where digging wells had proved useless. We have seen that farm ponds were excavated at Lowe Farm in the 1880's. In the early 20th century a few farmers began to dig ponds for their own use, but it was not until the 1930's, when PFRA subsidized the construction of farm ponds (or dugouts as they are known locally), that ponds were constructed in large numbers. In that part of the Glacial Lake Agassiz clay plain west of the Red River and south of the Assiniboine River there is a more extensive tract of land with a larger number of farm ponds per township than anywhere else in Western Interior Canada.

The solution to most of the problems of instability caused by water in the Glacial Lake Agassiz Region had to wait until the 20th century. Gradually a stable farming community developed as the drains and the dugouts went in; that is, a community stable at least in normal years. A disaster such as the flood of 1950 caused great damage, but with modern institutional and technical resources even the flood of 1950 could be taken in stride, and now long term solutions, such as the Red River Floodway, are being sought for selected heavily populated parts of the region subject to flood hazards.

Regionalization

A region is a useful research device, not only because it is a means of dividing a large area into more manageable units for analytical purposes, but because in the very process of working out regional divisions, one must examine the validity of the criteria used in defining the regions. This leads to a closer scrutiny of the area, and even occasionally to new investigations. It is evident from our discussion thus far that different sub-regions can be defined within the Glacial Lake Agassiz Region, on the basis that particular districts present particular problems and opportunities for settlement to man. It is useful to remember that the sub-regions will be dynamic, even on a short term basis, if they are defined in human terms, and that as the patterns of human behaviour change the regions and the regional boundaries will change. Thus the attempt to discover and to understand the underlying dynamic forces which bring about changes in our sub-regional systems or models leads to further fundamental research into the nature of the Glacial Lake Agassiz Region as a whole.

I won't have time to discuss the sub-regions into which the Glacial Lake Agassiz Region could be reasonably and usefully divided for study purposes at selected periods, since human occupation of the area began, but I will name some possible divisions. If I read MacNeish (1958a) correctly, certain economic or human activity regions can be recognized by scholars for pre-European times. Scholars can certainly do this for European times, as well, but, in addition, they can also deduce from contemporary documents a sense of regionalism or regional consciousness amongst the inhabitants in certain parts of the Glacial Lake Agassiz Region at certain periods.

Amongst the sub-regions which were recognized by settlers in the nineteenth century were the Red River Settlement (an obvious isolated core area for many years), the Portage Plain, the Pembina Country, the Big Plain, the Beautiful Plain (near Arden), the Dauphin Country and the Swan River Country. Some of the above regional names have slipped out of popular usage because the regions themselves no longer have the same validity for people living there today that they had in the 19th century, but new regional designations have emerged, such as the Pembina Triangle in the Winkler-Morden area.

The above "popular" regions can be conveniently related to a
more comprehensive set of regions, based partly on the "popular"
regions themselves, but mainly on the proposals of earth scientists
and geographers: the Manitoba Piedmont (the area below the Manitoba
Escarpment), the Red River Plain, the Southern Great Lakes Region,
and Eastern Manitoba. (It is worth noting that most of the "popular"
regions mentioned above are segments of the Manitoba Piedmont, which
is a distinctive habitat for man in Manitoba.)

The main justification for introducing such regional divisions
into an analysis is heuristic. Regions are not ends in themselves
but means for handling material and for stimulating further investigation. I would suggest to archeologists that they do not adopt the
broader regional divisions of the geologist, botanist, or geographer,
as final regional units for organizing their own work, until they
have fully tested the validity and utility of the regions for their
own purposes. If the physical regions don't correlate with the
archeological evidence, that is, if they don't stand up to the
stern test of helping to illuminate the precise functional relationship of man and natural environment, then they are of limited use.
And take heart, the mental stimulation and speculation that result
from finding out why the regions don't provide much assistance will
be ample reward. Perhaps a new, more valid regional model, or system
of generalizations, may result which will throw a greater light on
man's habitat a millenium or two ago in the Glacial Lake Agassiz
area.

Sources of Data

I want to contrast briefly the kinds of evidence that the prehistorian and the historian and the geographer have to work with --
that is, where and how are the facts obtained which can be used to
analyse changing human occupance and regionalization.

For information on pre-European times the scholar has to depend,
as Mayer-Oakes suggests (in this volume) on the results of archeological digs, collections of artifacts, very careful stratigraphic
correlations, etc. and on the information about the natural environment supplied by geologists, botanists, zoologists, climatologists
and geographers. Artifacts, called settlement facilities, can also
be of great assistance for scholars working on the settlement of
Manitoba in the 19th century. In the drier sections of the Glacial
Lake Agassiz Region, where the lands were occupied first, there are
distinctive house and barn styles, layouts of farmsteads, and shelter
belts which can be used for diagnostic purposes. For instance, there
are very sharp changes in houses across the Burnside beach ridges,
with the gothic-style wooden houses of the 1890's and early 1900's
still standing on dry-point sites above the Burnside beach, as at
Ridgeville, Anola, Carman-Elm Creek, Plumas-Glenella, and with farm
buildings of a later era on the adjacent clay plains where settlement was delayed. It is quite possible to map these buildings
(along, I might add, with the roads and cemeteries associated with

the beach ridges) and thus plot the early agricultural occupance
of the Glacial Lake Agassiz Region. Regression in the agricultural
economy is also observable in places. Some districts of sandy
soil were productive when first settled, but under poor land management the soils did not retain this productivity. Thus the big, old,
substantial homes built in an earlier prosperous era linger on in
dilapidated condition in what has become a poorer farming district,
providing tangible evidence of some fundamental changes in the
rural community.

The Manitoban landscape, however, is very dynamic and many old
buildings are being torn down during the present period of significant change in farming technology, as the implications of the
invention and application to farming of the internal combustion
engine are finally being felt in rural areas. Thus much of the
evidence contained in settlement facilities is being irretrievably
lost. This means that we will have to turn to other sources to
study the 19th century occupance of the Glacial Lake Agassiz Region,
and these fortunately are available. Such sources include the land
records kept in Provincial and Municipal Government offices,
including homestead records, assessment and tax rolls, and the
records kept in the Land Titles Offices. These are the essentail
sources, along with the census records, for tracing the exact history
of the occupance of an area. Through these documents, the constant
re-evaluation by man of the land can be followed, in the full geographical context of changing social aims, technology and economic
conditions.

                              Conclusion

In conclusion, I would suggest that a thorough application of
the comparative method, which I have only been using in an offhand
manner in this brief discussion, may assist in throwing light on
the occupance of the Glacial Lake Agassiz Region. Cross comparisons
of the dynamic relationships between man and the land during various
stages of the occupance of a particular place, such as the Glacial
Lake Agassiz Region, over a long period of time, may not provide
immediate illuminating insights, but they should at least provoke
stimulating new questions worth probing. (Another comparative
technique frequently used is comparing two places, but that need
not be discussed further in the present context.)

Quite likely the benefits of the comparative method will not
be obtained from taking particular research techniques which have
proven useful in investigating a certain stage and applying them
to the study of another quite different stage. Certainly, different
techniques are required in studying pre-European and European stages
of occupance. More likely the contributions of the comparative
method will rise out of the experiment of applying conclusions,
and hypotheses or models, derived from the study of one stage of
occupance in a region to another stage in the same region, in order
to bring out similarities and differences and then attempt to explain

them. Also, the comparative method forces a person to question and test the assumptions which he has made during the course of an investigation. This leavening has considerable value because a person's thinking and approach may gradually harden if he stays isolated in his own particular sphere of interests for too long. That is, comparisons should generally stir things up and stimulate thinking -- as this conference has certainly done.

PREHISTORIC HUMAN POPULATION HISTORY OF THE
GLACIAL LAKE AGASSIZ REGION*

William J. Mayer-Oakes

Introduction

In this paper I am attempting to provide a general outline of the pre-European human population history of the glacial Lake Agassiz region. The outline will stress the results of research activity in archeology as well as the history of archeological work here in Manitoba. I emphasize Manitoba rather than the glacial Lake Agassiz region not only because of space limitations, but also because of the fact that we do not yet have much information from the pertinent parts of Saskatchewan, Ontario and other surrounding areas.

History of Archeological Work in Manitoba

During 1963, Walter Hlady prepared a bibliography of published items bearing on Manitoba archeology. An annotated version of this listing (minus references to newspaper clippings) has recently appeared (Hlady 1964c). From a perusal of this list plus the references listed by MacNeish plus discussions with several historians and local amateur archeologists it is clear that relatively limited archeological work has been carried out in Manitoba and even less of this has been published in any satisfactory way.

The specific history of field work and publication in Manitoba archeology is not very different in sequence and general nature from that characteristic of many other areas of North America. It began seriously only after the turn of the century and entered its current systematic and professionally oriented phase within the last fifteen years. Although friend Morgan Tamplin in his splendid paper at the start of this conference (and earlier in this volume) eschewed the use of early, middle and late as important terms, for convenience we may simplify the pattern in typical archeological way -- seeing three grand stages or periods of work -- Early, Middle and Late, with the present stage being the late one. Table 27 below indicates the names of published contributors to the subject by appropriate stage.

---

*This statement is largely drawn from my 1965 summary article now "in press" at the National Museum of Canada.

TABLE 27

HISTORY OF MANITOBA ARCHEOLOGICAL WORK

	Major Contributors	Minor Contributors	
Early (1868-1940)	Bryce Montgomery Nickerson	Gunn Densmore Downes Fewkes	
Middle (1940-1953)	Rand Vickers Hlady		
Present (1953-1967)	Hlady MacNeish	Cameron Capes Chism Elson Fiske Giddings Gryba	Hill Joyes Mayer-Oakes Nash Pettipas Simpson Steimbring Tamplin

We might characterize the three above stages as follows. The Early period was largely the work of outside professional and/or trained workers although this was mostly prior to the establishment in North America of professional archeological field work. It is characterized by its sporadic or unsystematic nature. The Middle period was largely the work of interested local laymen with training and degree of professionalization varying from zero to undergraduate university level background. The work was limited though often systematic in intent and supported institutionally. The Present period may be thought to date from the entry of the National Museum into the field work scene. MacNeish's efforts as a trained professional overlapped, encouraged and augmented the established and on-going work of the Middle period. Entry of the University and the provincial government into the arena (in 1961) as an institution sponsor is another hallmark for the Present period which is perhaps best to be characterized by the utilization of trained specialists under institutional auspices and carrying out systematic programs of work aimed at the solution of specific archeological problems.

Bryce (1887, 1904), Montgomery (1908, 1910), and Nickerson (1914a,b; Capes, 1963) all were major contributors to the work of the Early period and each of them was primarily concerned with description, location and excavation of burial mounds. The areas of Manitoba covered were limited to the Red River near Winnipeg and the Souris River area in southwestern Manitoba. The most detailed, systematic and useful work is that of Nickerson (n.d.) which is now available as edited and annotated by Capes. A recent study of the skeletal material collected by Montgomery (Cameron 1962) adds greatly to the value of his work. A brief statement by Gunn (1868) falls in this period but is chiefly of interest as it may relate to the work carried out in 1963 by Fiske (1964a,b,c,d,e). Francis Densmore (1929) reports ceramic materials from near Lake Winnipegosis while Downes (1938) records pottery in the far northwestern part of the province. In an article now celebrated as a classic, pointing out technological and stylistic similarities between "Woodland" and "Asiatic" pottery, Fewkes (1937) analyzed a small collection from the lower Red River. Clearly, the major work was done early in this period and most effort after 1915 was quite limited and sporadic. While Bryce was a local resident the other workers of this period came from outside the province.

The work of the Middle period is largely due to the efforts of local people interested in the subject, with varying degrees of local support. Vickers (n.d.; 1945; 1946a,b,c; 1947a,b; 1948a,b,c, d,e,f; 1949a,b,c,d,e, f,g; 1950a,b,c; 1951a,b; 1952; 1953) has published most fully on work of this stage and was supported by modest grants from the Historical and Scientific Society of Manitoba. Attention was concentrated in south-central Manitoba, although some work in the Red River valley was done. As with the Early period intensive work, the cultivated grassland areas received almost exclusive attention. Walter Hlady began work in this period (n.d. a,b,c; 1947; 1948; 1949a,b; 1952; 1960; 1964a,b,c,d,e; 1965; 1966a,b) and continues active in both field work and publication. His work was the first to seriously branch out temporally and geographically from the previous interests and the grassland region. He began the search for "Early Man" evidences and instituted systematic work in the coniferous forest area. Not listed by Hlady (1964c) is the mimeographed manuscript by Rand, *et al* (n.d.) detailing work done by a spirited group in the Whiteshell area east of Winnipeg in the Shield country. Because of the extensive documentation I would like to include this piece of work as a major contribution to the period. During this period there are other unpublished contributions, the activities of the Manitoba Museum Association and the Natural History Society being the pertinent organizations fostering interest in archeology.

Our final period, the Present, obviously overlaps with the Middle period, but has a distinctly different character. While it is contemporary as this article is written it seems clearly to be headed in a significantly different direction. MacNeish's work in the early 1950's continued the Red River valley and southwestern grassland emphasis but expanded into the mixed forest area of the Whiteshell, to the east. The interest of the National Museum was also reflected in an unpublished survey made by Wettlaufer (n.d.)

and in the assistance given in 1962 and 1963 to the program carried
out by the University of Manitoba. Contributions by Capes and
Cameron have been mentioned above. Hlady's work has continued and
one culmination ready for publication is a synthesis of studies
made in the boreal forest area of the Grass River drainage (Hlady
1964e).   Other work in the Whiteshell area, particularly at Jessica
Lake has produced valuable new information. Elson (1957), in a
geological study of glacial Lake Agassiz has posed a number of
interesting archeological questions. Giddings (1956) reports a
most unusual site from the tundra portion of the province, which
is also represented in recent work done by Irving (1965) and the
University of Manitoba (Fiske 1964e) near Churchill. The work
initiated in 1961 at Grand Rapids (Mayer-Oakes 1963b) included
survey as well as excavations in an extensive section of the
coniferous forest area and results of this work will be briefly
presented below in a modification of MacNeish's synthesis. Additional work in the tundra or "barren lands" has been carried out
(Nash 1963, 1964, 1966) in both 1965 and 1967 under the program
of provincial, National Museum and University-supported work, while
an intensive re-investigation of early burial mound data has been
carried out by Fiske (1964a).

     To attempt to delineate the character of the work of the
Present period is perhaps premature or presumptive. It is worth
noting, however, that substantial field work has already been
accomplished and is in process of being prepared for publication;
strong institutional support has been applied to archeological
problems by trained personnel; a program of undergraduate and M.A.
level instruction and training in anthropology and archeology has
been developed in the provincial University; an active group of
interested laymen has formed the Manitoba Archeological Society
which is developing with assistance from professionals in the
University. A planned new provincial museum of natural history
will no doubt carry out and foster work in local archeology as it
has in the past. Successful continuation of these activities
should produce substantially greater understanding of the prehistory
of the province and ultimately of the continent.

                    National Museum Field Results

     In 1951 MacNeish began intensive field work in Manitoba. This
was carried out over a three-year period culminating in a publication
entitled "An Introduction to the Archeology of Southeastern Manitoba"
(MacNeish 1958a) In this monograph the details of his excavations
and survey work are presented. Summary and synoptic statements are
also made. In the present paper we want to present but a digest
of the key general results, particularly as they represent a synthesis
of prehistoric knowledge about the area.

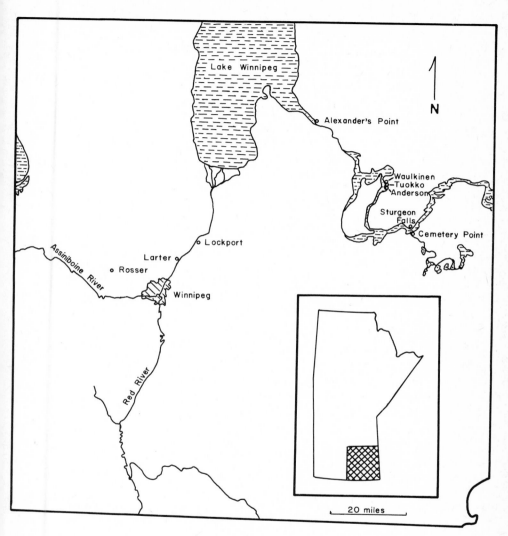

Figure 82. MacNeish's Excavation Sites in Southeastern Manitoba.

The data presented by MacNeish are drawn from excavations at six single component sites (Alexander's Point, Anderson, Larter, Rosser Mound, Sturgeon Falls, and Waulkinen) and three stratified sites (Lockport, Cemetery Point, and Tuokko). Locations of these sites can be seen in Fig. 82. Six of the sites are on the Winnipeg River drainage in Mixed Woodland terrain on the edge of the pre-Cambrian Shield. Three are in the Red River drainage, a sparsely wooded grassland area.

By inter-digitating the single component sites within the sequence of occupations derived by cross-aligning the three stratified sites, MacNeish derives an overall sequence of six foci ranging in age from 3000 B.C. up to the Historic Assiniboine and Cree Indians of A.D. 1750. In Fig. 83 we have rearranged data from MacNeish's Table 1 (adding his dates) in order to make clear these inter-site temporal correlations. The earliest two foci (Whiteshell and Larter) are pre-ceramic. Types of projectile points are used as key indicators of cultural change and relationship at this level. In the four remaining foci ceramics become the primary means for suggesting and interpreting cultural change and relationship -- although projectile points still play an important part in the study. Throughout all foci attention is paid to changing environmental and subsistence conditions. Distinct shifts from grassland to woodland conditions are postulated on the basis of animal bone changes in the food debris associated with cultural remains.

From MacNeish's discussion of ceramics and his Table 7 it is clear that he has used the concept of ware to incorporate the less complex or well-defined bodysherds into his overall scheme. Basically, the bodysherds form the bulk of the specimens undifferentiated as to type. Rimsherds and decorated bodysherds, on the other hand, have been segregated into types. Inspection of his Table 7 confirms the time period allocations he has made but also shows how this technique tends to distort or elongate the temporal dimension. Laurel ware and the Laurel types clearly have their peak frequencies in the two Laurel foci, but persist all through the Manitoba focus time period. Lockport Corded spans Laurel and Manitoba foci. The Manitoba ware is clearly concentrated in the Manitoba focus time period but persists well into Selkirk times. The Manitoba types seem more closely correlated with the Manitoba period. Winnipeg Fabric-Impressed ceramics most clearly are restricted to and characteristic of Selkirk times.

Projectile points seem particularly useful and important in the preceramic foci. Fig. 84 below illustrates the named types. Samples for these types are all limited and also quite variable. "Nutimik Concave" seems to be a distinctive form but it is quite rare. It is typical of and restricted to the Whiteshell focus. "McKean Lanceolat is one of the most distinctive styles known from Manitoba. It occurs in reasonable frequency and is present in both Whiteshell and Larter foci, although it seems most characteristic of the Whiteshell. Both "Sturgeon Triangular" and "Winnipeg Ovoid" are amorphous styles -- the former occurs in Whiteshell, Larter and Anderson foci while the latter seems restricted to Larter. The types "Parkdale Eared",

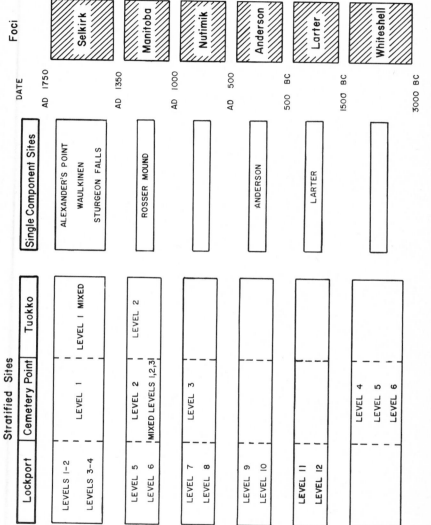

Figure 83. Sites Excavated and Foci Derived For Southeastern Manitoba.

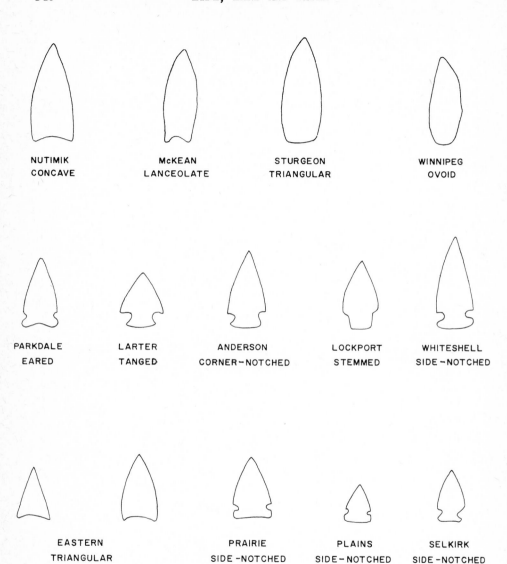

NUTIMIK
CONCAVE

McKEAN
LANCEOLATE

STURGEON
TRIANGULAR

WINNIPEG
OVOID

PARKDALE
EARED

LARTER
TANGED

ANDERSON
CORNER-NOTCHED

LOCKPORT
STEMMED

WHITESHELL
SIDE-NOTCHED

EASTERN
TRIANGULAR

PRAIRIE
SIDE-NOTCHED

PLAINS
SIDE-NOTCHED

SELKIRK
SIDE-NOTCHED

Figure 84.   MacNeish's Projectile Point Types From Southeastern
Manitoba.

and "Larter Tanged" seem quite distinctive and they are restricted
in their occurence to the Larter focus. "Anderson Corner-Notched",
and "Lockport Stemmed", seem to be difficult to distinguish from
other corner-notched and stemmed forms. The stemmed style is
restricted to Anderson focus but the corner-notched style also
occurs in Larter and Nutimik. The "Whiteshell Side-Notched" type
is distinctive in form but seems to have a good deal of size variation.
It is limited in occurrence to the Nutimik focus. Three styles occur
in the Manitoba focus and all three of them also occur in the Selkirk
focus. "Eastern Triangular" has large and small varieties as well
as form variations which may be significant. "Plains Side-Notched"
is most distinctive and is clearly more frequent in Manitoba focus
(80%) but occurs also (20%) in Selkirk. The "Prairie Side-Notched"
style seems less distinctive and it is about equally frequent in
the last two time periods. "Selkirk Side-Notched" is limited to
Selkirk focus; it seems a distinctively crude small form that is
probably derived from "Prairie Side-Notched".

The subsistence, settlement and social organization patterns
known for the area seem to have made significant shifts. During
Whiteshell and Larter foci the predominance of bison bone suggests
emphasis on hunting in a grassland environment. Settlement size
implies the presence of small nomadic bands only. At the Anderson
period more bird and forest animals plus fish remains come in,
implying a broader range of "foraging" activities. With Nutimik
and all later foci the faunal remains suggest presence of an
environment essentially like that of today. Fish bones predominate
in the animal remains from the last three foci. Group size apparently
increases as seasonal food resource concentration brings nomadic bands
together briefly as macro-bands (as known from the historic Cree).
This pattern seems clearly to be related to environmental locale as
some Manitoba focus groups are known to exist on the grassland plains
to the west for bison hunting purposes, while other Manitoba focus
groups are lake and riverside fishers in the woodland country.

Significant ceremonial elaboration of spiritual activities
seem limited to the Manitoba focus where burial mound building is
known. This trait may extend backward in time, but MacNeish presents
no evidence for this from his work.

The Life Zone Concept

The "Economic Atlas of Manitoba" (Weir 1960) is a most useful
source of graphic and statistical data on the various natural
subdivisions of the province. Maps and text outline the facts of
relief and drainage, physiography, topography, geology, surface
deposits and glaciation, soils, climate and temperature, precipitation
and growing season, climatic relationships and natural vegetation.
For our purposes in this summary, the map of natural vegetation seems
most appropriate and a reduced scale (somewhat abridged) version is
shown in our Fig. 80. While the "Arctic Tundra" and "Northern
Transition" areas are shown as originally presented by Weir, we have

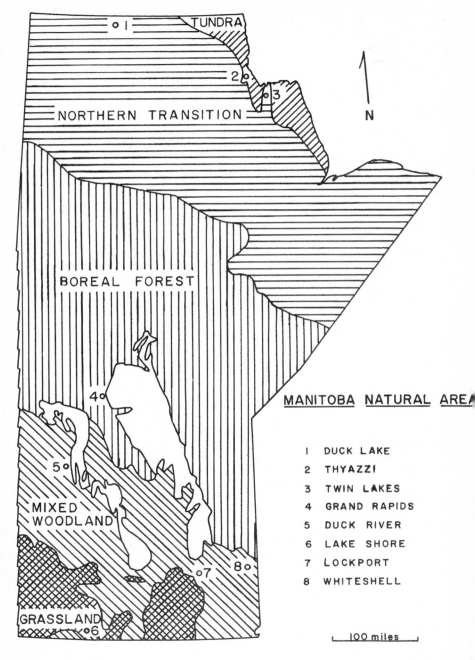

Figure 80. Natural Areas of Manitoba. With list of sites referred to in this paper.

combined "Open Grassland" and "Sparsely Wooded Grassland" to form a
"Grassland" area. We have also combined "Wooded Grassland", "Broadleaf Forest" and "Mixed Woods" into a "Mixed Woodland" area to distinguish these subareas from the boreal forest or "Northern Coniferous
Forest" zone.

In a recent summary of the natural environment of Manitoba, a
biologist (Lukens 1965) makes the following simplifying comments
that are quite appropriate to our interest.

> *The natural vegetation of Manitoba embraces elements of
> three principal plant formations. They are, from north
> to south, the tundra, northern coniferous or boreal
> forest, and grassland. Between the evergreen forest
> and the tundra in the north is an extensive zone of
> transition, the tundra-coniferous forest ecotone or
> subarctic forest. In southern Manitoba the coniferous
> forest-grassland ecotone or aspen parkland is interspersed
> between the evergreen forests and the open grassland.*
>
> *The tundra in Manitoba is confined to a relatively narrow
> strip along the coast of Hudson Bay. The true grasslands
> occupy only a small portion of the south-central and south-
> western corner of the province and are contiguous with those
> of the central plains. The northern coniferous forest, part
> of the North American boreal forest, trends in a broad
> belt northwest-southeast across central Manitoba. These
> three plant formations, broad geographic regions in which
> the life form of the climax vegetation is the same,
> correspond to the biotic communities of the animal ecologist,
> the tundra, coniferous forest and grassland biomes.*

While there is no clear gradation it seems obvious that as one
moves from south to north in Manitoba there is a changing pattern
of climate with the more vigorous winter climate at the extreme northeast part of the province. While temperature isolines tend to parallel
the northwest-southeast trending vegetation boundaries from about 53°
North latitude to the north, the snowfall map (Weir 1960:17) does not.
Rather, it shows a north-south trend so that average annual snowfall
in Churchill is about the same as in Winnipeg.

The tundra, coniferous forest and grassland biomes suggested
above by Lukens are well known general concepts, implying in Manitoba
significant correlation of climatic as well as floral and faunal
distributions. The five areas shown in our Fig. 80 indicate some of
the kind of variation and subdivision necessary to comprehend general
life zones of the province. Weir's maps take this a bit further and
others (see, e.g., Ritchie 1960) specify local variation in a detail
not felt to be necessary for the present overview, but fundamental
to the development of future detailed studies.

As culture historians working with the archeological evidence
of past human occupation in Manitoba and as anthropologists
concerned with man's relationship to his physical environment
we find these generalizing concepts of significant use. For
present purposes, the concept of "life zone" gives us convenient
and potentially significant units for analysis. While much
archeological work in North America has demonstrated the significance of river systems in defining and unifying cultural areas,
the over-riding usefulness of ecological information lies in
recognizing its permissive but still limiting nature with regard
to cultural development. Such ecological boundaries, thus, are
here chosen in preference to artificial or man-made ones, within
our general framework of treating central-northern North America
by the device of provincial (political) units. (A prime limitation to this ecological device is the somewhat unreal static
quality it provides. We are well aware of the significant changes
in natural zonation during the period of human occupation. These
are major problems for current and future research.) It should
be clear that much of our present and future knowledge of Manitoba
archeology has both already established and potentially establish-
able relationships to the knowledge extant in surrounding political
entities.

University of Manitoba and Other Fieldwork, 1961-1967

At the time of the National Museum field work and subsequent
report, there were a number of units of archeological data available
on work done outside the Southeastern part of the province. There
are also now a number of studies that have been produced since
MacNeish's report was prepared. We will summarize both these sets
of data here, in an attempt to look at the province as a whole and
to bring the general outlines of knowledge up to the present state
of that knowledge. Let us examine these by the environmental or
"life zones" described in the first part of the paper. (See Fig.80)

Arctic Tundra

From the tundra or arctic part of the province we know
historically of the use of this terrain by Eskimo groups and its
present day occupation by Eskimo as well as Cree and Chipewyan
Indians. Archeologically we know of one site -- the Thyazzi Site --
published by Giddings (1956). This surface collection of distinctive
small, finely chipped tools was described by Giddings as a "burin,
side-blade" complex similar to the pre-Dorset collection from Sarqaq
in western Greenland. The collection contains distinctive burins,
burin spalls, side-blades, end-blades, and end-scrapers. As a
representative of the "Arctic Small Tool Tradition" this unit is
considered a typical "Arctic" assemblage from the pre-Dorset Eskimo
context. The remains of an Arctic-adapted hunting group, it is
none-the-less still not a distinctive or typical Eskimo cultural
complex. The collection gathered and published by Giddings is now
deposited in the University of Manitoba Laboratory of Anthropology.

Excavations were conducted at this site in 1965 by the University of Manitoba (Nash 1966). Results of this work extend considerably our knowledge of the complex in Manitoba. An Isotopes, Inc. Carbon-14 date of 680 ± 90 B.C. from a hearth at the Thyazzi site is later than both typological and geochronological dates suggest the site to be. If correct, the Carbon-14 date may indicate Thyazzi to be the latest survival and most southern extension of the distinctive small tool tradition. Representative artifacts from the Giddings collection are illustrated in Fig. 85, A-F.

Nash (1966:145) describes the finds at Thyazzi in the following summary.

> *The Thyazzi materials have been provisionally dated at 1500 B.C. and can therefore be compared with most of the previously discussed eastern Arctic Small Tool assemblages which are at least this old. The Thyazzi people were seen to be a predominantly caribou hunting people whose remains are to be found on a beach remnant located near the North Knife River. The extreme southerly position of the site, even below the major tree line indicates that origins and external relationships . . . are to be sought to the north.*

Northern Transition

For this vast region of the northern part of the province we know practically nothing because of its relative inaccessibility. There are, however, two areas that have provided evidence for prehistoric occupation. A distinctive representative of the "Arctic Small Tool Tradition" has been reported by an amateur archeologist with long personal experience in the area. (J. Robertson, personal communication) The Twin Lakes Site he reported had since been visited prior to 1965 by W. Irving (1965) and by Fiske (1964e) and Mayer-Oakes. Although the surface and test excavation collections were of small size, distinctive bifaces, burins and microblades suggested a somewhat different complex of small tools from that present at the nearby Thyazzi Site. Representative artifacts from Twin Lakes surface collections are illustrated in Fig. 85, G-K.

Nash (1966) carried out excavations at the Twin Lakes site in 1965. Results of this work enable him to interpret the Twin Lakes occupation as a seasonal manufacturing and hunting use of an island that was probably within the Arctic Tundra life zone during the period 1000 B.C. to 500 B.C. Typologically, the tool assemblage should be late pre-Dorset and it should date to this time range. Nash (1966:149) summarizes the site briefly for us.

> *The Twin Lakes site just south of Churchill, Manitoba is a late maritime-oriented Arctic Small Tool component located on a former island. The burins, often notched and/or ground form the bulk of the artifacts. The microblade industry is poorly developed and scrapers are crude*

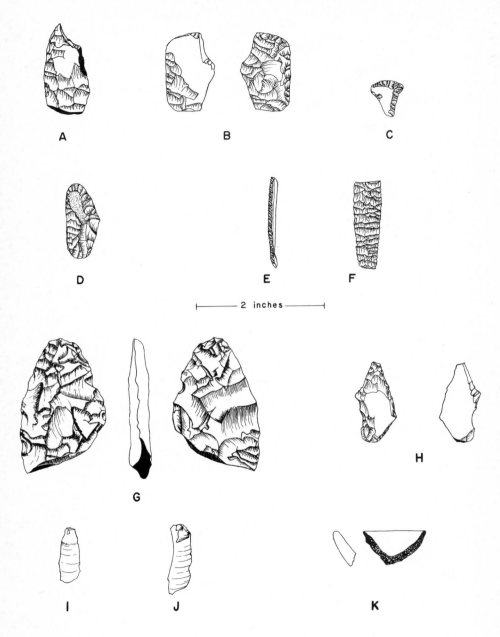

├── 2 inches ──┤

Figure 85.   Artifacts From Thyazzi and Twin Lakes Sites.
Thyazzi Site: A, B, burins; C, end scraper; D, end-and-
side scraper; E, burin spall; F, side blade.
Twin Lakes Site: G, biface; H, burin; I, J, micro-blades;
K, steatite vessel rimsherd.

while end blades are practically non-existent and the
burin spall tool not present at all. Several large bi-
faces are especially notable. While there are some
specific connections to older cultures (e.g., the rect-
angular side blade with Thyazzi and the adze with Baker
Lake pre-Dorset) the impression gained is one of a rela-
tionship to Late Igloolik. The lamp, the grinding and
notching of burins, the adze and possibly the bifaces
tie in with Late Igloolik indicating at least strong
diffusion from that area.

The second area of prehistoric evidence from the "Northern Transition" zone is in the northwestern-most quarter of the province. Here, at a number of sites J. Robertson has collected specimens which apparently represent a wide range of time. Concentrations appear in the Little Duck Lake area of the Wolverine River drainage. A recent brief reconnaissance of this region by Mayer-Oakes is reported by Nash (1963, 1964) who allocates specimen types to Plano, Archaic, and Modern Indian periods. Projectile points are the key comparative artifact used for this purpose and representative specimens are shown in Fig. 86. Irving (in a lecture at the University of Manitoba, March, 1965) has recently suggested that two kinds of Archaic can be discerned in the Keewatin District -- the "Woodland" Archaic preceding the pre-Dorset (Arctic Small Tool Tradition) and the "Late" Archaic following it up to Thule Eskimo. It is possible that some such sequence is characteristic of the Manitoba "barren lands" of the Northern Transition zone. Evidence to date is for an emphasis on big-game, presumably caribou hunting for a long period of time with significant projectile point style variations indicating different cultural groups or stages.

Intensive survey and excavation work was carried out by Nash in the Little Duck Lake area during the summer of 1965 in an attempt to add to our data and eventually, knowledge, about this part of the province. He is currently preparing a report on this work as a Ph.D. dissertation at the University of Calgary. In addition, during the summer of 1967 Nash carried out additional field work in the Egenolf Lake and other areas of the Northern Transition zone. Results of this work will be incorporated into the Ph.D. dissertation.

It is significant to note that at present only non-ceramic sites and data are known from either the Tundra or the Northern Transition regions.

Boreal (Northern Coniferous) Forest

This region has very little data on record but there is actually a good deal of information available. The work of H. Moody in the Flin Flon area as well as other local residents has resulted in sizeable collections of both ceramic and lithic materials (Arima 1959). C. Patterson and J. Robertson have samples from sites in the vicinity of the Pas. W. Hlady began studies in this area in the late 1940's and has recently completed a manuscript (Hlady 1964e) summarizing the data available for this part of the province up to 1961.

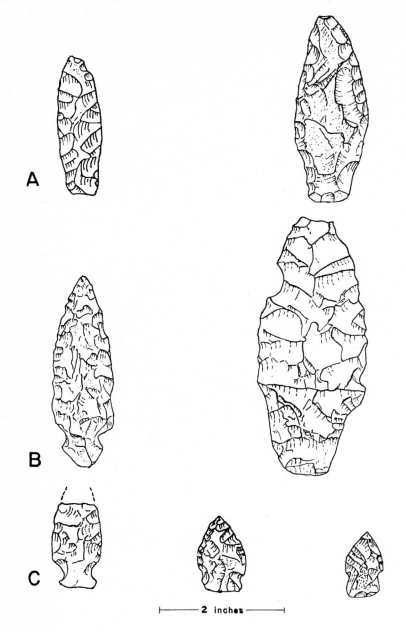

Figure 86.   Projectile Points From the Barren Lands.
             A. Late Paleo-Indian Styles.
             B. Woodland Archaic Styles.
             C. Late Archaic Styles.

Since 1961 intensive studies have been carried out in the Saskatchewan River drainage as part of the Reservoir Salvage Program growing out of the Grand Rapids Hydro-Electric Dam construction project. Mayer-Oakes has reported briefly on this work (1963b,1964) and is preparing a final report on the survey and excavation program carried out over a two-year period.

Hlady's study of the Grass River drainage system (1964e) clearly documents the extension of the distribution of fabric-impressed ceramics to the north and west of the Whiteshell and Winnipeg River loci reported by MacNeish. In addition, by detailed stylistic analysis Hlady defines a new type of the Winnipeg Fabric-Impressed ware (Clear Water Lake Punctate) that seems to be widely distributed throughout the Boreal Forest. In this study, significantly, no Manitoba focus materials were reported. Very little Laurel ware ceramics were recorded. Archaic or pre-ceramic units are only implied by evidence from this area.

Fieldwork done near Flin Flon at the Bakers Narrows and Evans sites (Simpson 1966), however, has produced evidence for a non-ceramic and probably pre-ceramic unit which Hlady has termed the "Athapap Phase".

At the far northern edge of this area, in the Churchill River drainage, Wright (1967) has carried out two seasons of field work on Southern Indian Lake. His finds include both Blackduck and unusual Selkirk ceramics. Radiocarbon dates suggest that the area was not occupied until A.D. 1000. An important contribution of his work is the association of predominantly Selkirk focus archeological materials with an area known to be inhabited by historic Cree people.

The collections gained in the Grand Rapids Reservoir Survey test excavations and major excavations (Mayer-Oakes 1963b) also extend the range of the cultural complexes reported by MacNeish for southeastern Manitoba. Although precise and clear cut stratigraphy is lacking in the sites investigated, typological segregation is possible and this separation is supported by the modest stratigraphic evidence available at the Tailrace Bay Site (GRS-3). Figs. 87, 88, and 89 indicate the range of projectile points found in this key site, suggesting intermittent occupation from approximately 2500 B.C. up to the present.

The "McKean Lanceolate" projectile point style (Fig. 87) which MacNeish cites as a marker for the earliest units in southeastern Manitoba is clearly predominant in the lowest levels at Tailrace Bay. It is not tightly correlated with other parts of an artifact complex although end and side scrapers are associated. The grey (undisturbed) soil zone at the Tailrace Bay site seems to contain an undisturbed ceramic complex -- the earliest at the site -- the Laurel materials of a range of variation which is rare or non-existent in the southeastern Manitoba sites. The type "Laurel Pseudo-Scallop" is in the majority and is well represented. In Fig. 90 the modes from 1 to 9 are all elements of Laurel ware ceramics. Studies of Laurel ware distribution across the Upper

Figure 87.   McKean Lanceolate Projectile Points From Tailrace Bay Site, Grand Rapids.

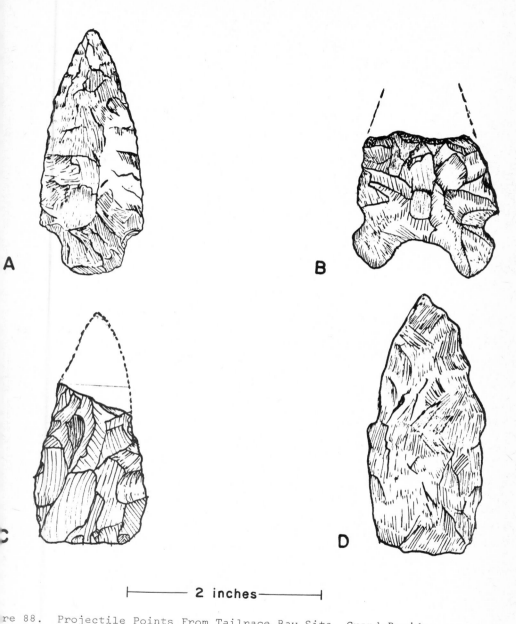

Projectile Points From Tailrace Bay Site, Grand Rapids.
A.   Lockport Stemmed Type.   C.   Nutimik Concave Type.
B.   Parkdale Eared Type.   D.   Sturgeon Triangular Type.

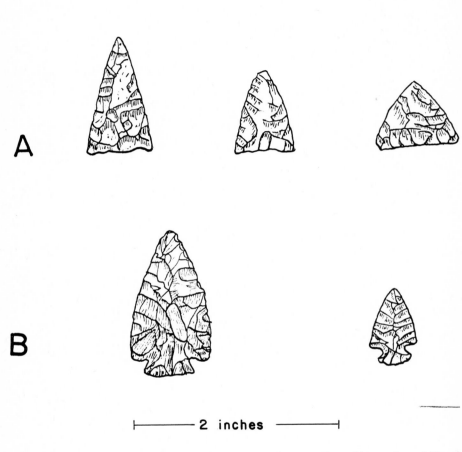

Figure 89. Projectile Points From Tailrace Bay Site, Grand Rapids
            A. Eastern Triangular Type.
            B. Anderson Corner-Notched Type.

Great Lakes area in Canada (Wright 1967) suggest that this pseudo-scallop style rather than the more complex styles represented in Anderson and Nutimik foci is earliest in the Laurel tradition. The types at the Tailrace Bay site correlate best with those recently defined by Stoltman (1962).

Manitoba focus materials are also strongly represented in the Grand Rapids collections, particularly from the Tailrace Bay site. Modes 10 to 12 in Fig. 90 are variations of styles analyzed recently by Evans (1961a,b) in a study of Blackduck ceramics in Minnesota. Here again, as with the Laurel ceramics, the specific details of typology at Grand Rapids seem to relate best to Minnesota complexes, bypassing the intervening Winnipeg River area. Only in the relatively non-distinctive fabric marked class do we seem to be dealing with the same materials as are present in the Winnipeg River, and here our sample from Grand Rapids is very small. Further, the elaboration of this class by Hlady (1964e) for the immediate area seems to better encompass the style variation present at Grand Rapids than does the Winnipeg River typology.

Historic materials present at the Tailrace Bay site span the total range of European contact. Although the present population of the area is Cree Indian, it is possible that this group has intruded into the area during the contact period. Certainly the paucity of Selkirk materials at Tailrace Bay does not support McNeish's association of Historic Cree and this archeological complex.

Animal bone remains from the Tailrace Bay site (Lukens 1964, 1965) support the general evidence for sequential change from large game hunting to fishing which MacNeish has presented. There is little specific evidence for drastic environmental changes here, however.

Mixed Woodland

This area is represented best by the MacNeish study. There are additional data, however. Early projectile point styles (Late Paleo-Indian period) have recently been reported (Fiske 1964b, 1964e) from a surface site near Duck River on the western shores of Lake Winnipegosis. Fig. 91 illustrates styles known to date from 5000 to 8000 B.C. elsewhere. The Angostura and Agate Basin styles seem most common in Manitoba where they are also reported (E. Gryba, personal communication) from the Swan River area and the Whiteshell (W. Kenyon, personal communication; Rand *et al* n.d.).

Steinbring (1963a) has recently described distinctive Old Copper artifacts from this general region of Manitoba. Presumably we have evidence here for "edge-of-the-range" distribution out of the Keewenaw Lake Superior centers of a distinctive Archaic complex. Representative types described by Steinbring are illustrated in Fig. 92. Types listed are in the classification proposed by Wittry (1951).

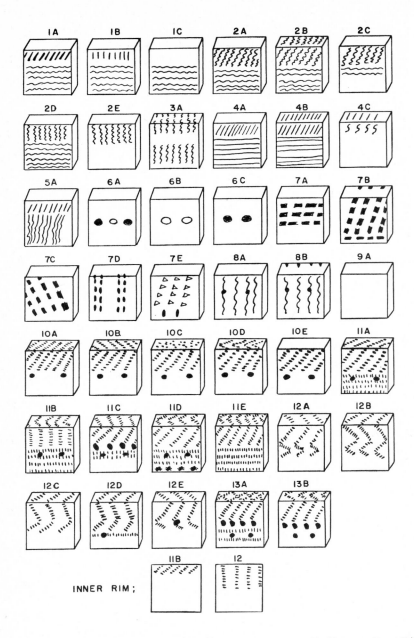

Figure 90. Rimsherd Decoration Modes From Tailrace Bay Site, Grand Rapids.

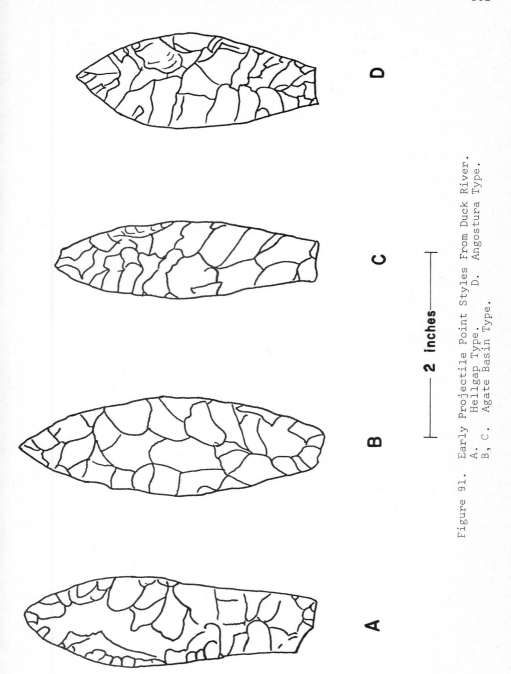

Figure 91. Early Projectile Point Styles From Duck River.
A.   Hellgap Type.   D.   Angostura Type.
B, C. Agate Basin Type.

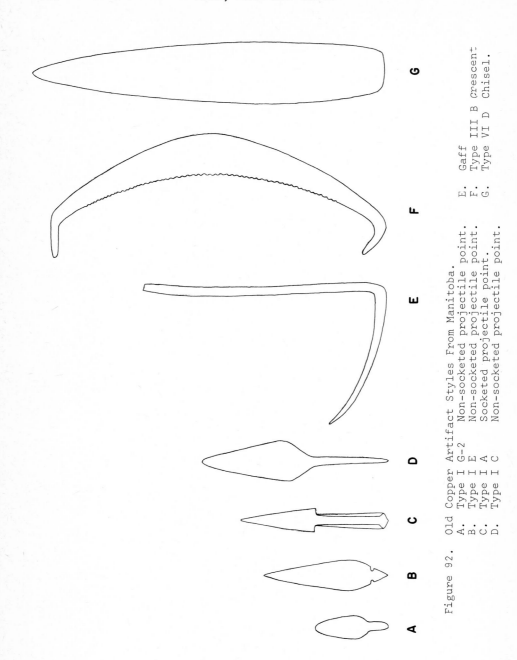

Figure 92. Old Copper Artifact Styles From Manitoba.
A. Type I G-2 Non-socketed projectile point.   E. Gaff
B. Type I E   Non-socketed projectile point.   F. Type III B Crescent.
C. Type II A   Socketed projectile point.   G. Type VI D Chisel.
D. Type I C   Non-socketed projectile point.

Fiske's (1964a,c,d) recent work at the Fidler Mound and Village Site adjacent to MacNeish's Lockport site has suggested that both Anderson and Nutimik (Laurel) materials may be associated with the burial mound construction activity. Possibly the later Manitoba focus is also a part of the mound building and ceremonial complex. The earlier mound studies by Bryce, Montgomery and Nickerson are being re-examined by Fiske in the light of the present status of Manitoba and regional archeology. Sutton (1965) has recently presented a brief statement about the "boulder mosaics", a distinctive but little-known archeological manifestation about which he has collected a large body of data. Examples of these stone alignments are shown in Fig. 93, based on Sutton's drawings.

Since May of 1965, Chism (1966) has been carrying out an intensive excavation program for the University of Manitoba at the historic Hudson Bay Company fur trade center, Lower Fort Garry. Although some prehistoric remains have appeared here, interest is focused on the time period after 1831. Results of this work will be a supplement to the paper on historic settlement given elsewhere in this volume by Warkentin.

Beginning also in June of 1965 a series of summer field seasons devoted to reconnaissance of beaches and other features of Glacial Lake Agassiz has been carried out. Hill (1965) reported on the first season, Tamplin on the second (1966) and is planning a summary of the first three full seasons. In 1965 and 1966 this work traversed both the Mixed Woodland and the Grassland zones; in 1967 Grassland, Mixed Woodland and Boreal zones were investigated. A number of specific problems and projects have already developed from this work, with more coming along. The University of Manitoba Department of Anthropology has taken on this environmental emphasis and approach as one of its major, continuing research programs and has established a base of University, National Museum and National Research Council financial support for this work. A major project now nearly ready for publication is Pettipas' study (1967) of Early Man Projectile point distribution. Other projects are planned for late 1968 and 1969 Publication.

Grassland

In this next to the smallest environmental zone of the province we have apparently the longest and potentially most complex archeological record. The part of the province earliest to be released from both glacial ice and post-glacial meltwater lakes, we should have here the best evidence for Early Man of the fluted point horizon. In fact, the only fluted point reported from the province does apparently come from here (R. W. Sutton, personal communication). Beyond this there are Late Paleo-Indian style points (Hlady 1948) in private collections in the Grassland area (Eden, Plainview, Scottsbluff) but from this level to the next one of substantial data is apparently a big step. Vickers, in a series of reports to the sponsoring organization (Vickers 1946a, 1946b, 1946c, 1948b, 1948d, 1949b, 1950b, 1951a) has outlined his work in this area that has given the sequence presented in Table 28 (Vickers 1950b:

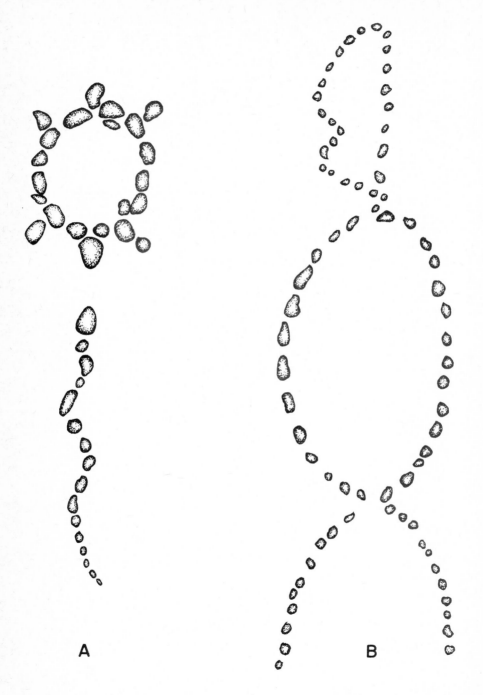

Figure 93.   Boulder Mosaics From the Whiteshell Area.
          A.   Snake and Turtle Effigy.
          B.   Human Effigy.

TABLE 28

SUGGESTED GRASSLAND CHRONOLOGY

Period	Site	Date	Tribe	Focus
Historic 1670-1870 A.D.	East St. Paul grave	circa 1850	Saulteaux ?	
	Snart	1768-1794	Assiniboine ?	Manitoba
	Krieger	circa 1760		Rock Lake
Ceramic 1400-1670 A.D.	Stott	circa 1670	Assiniboine*	Manitoba
	Paddock	circa 1650	?	Rock Lake
	Lowton	circa 1600-1650	?	Pelican Lake
	Montroy	circa 1620	?	Rock Lake
	Avery 1	circa 1600	Assiniboine*	Manitoba
	Avery 2	circa 1500	?	Rock Lake
Preceramic prior to 1400 A.D.	Lake Shore	before 1400	?	?

* Burial Mounds

Table 4). The Lakeshore pre-ceramic unit seems not to exactly fit
the Larter or Anderson foci of the Whiteshell but probably equates
in time. Nor is this unit identical to the nearby Long Creek
(Wettlaufer and Mayer-Oakes, 1960) assemblage. The ceramic units
defined as Rock Lake, Manitoba and Pelican Lake appear to correlate
in sequence with the Nutimik, Manitoba and Selkirk foci of the
Winnipeg River area. Here in the Grassland, however, Vickers
suggests a correlation of Manitoba focus archeological materials
with historically documented Assiniboine.

His extensive collection has now been deposited in the University
of Manitoba's Laboratory of Anthropology and will be re-examined in
detail in the next few years. One collection -- the Avery site --
has already been restudied. The 1966 Lake Agassiz Survey party
carried out excavations at the site, attempting to establish stratigraphic information. Joyes (1967) reports in detail the 1966
findings, as well as making a reanalysis of the earlier collection
made by Vickers. A clear emphasis on use of bison for food resources
can now be documented from this site as well as the presence of
"Besant" and "Avon Lea" type projectile points.

Summary Outline of Population Development

General Remarks

Having now indicated the gross natural areas of Manitoba and
briefly described the nature of the archeological work accomplished
to date, we are in a position to attempt a synthesis of the present
state of knowledge. This must of necessity be brief, first, because
of the limited scope of this paper and second, because of the
imminent completion of other more major studies concerned with
parts of the whole topic. We have thus selected two mechanisms for
the purpose of organizing and outlining a comprehensive statement
of current knowledge. Figure 94, below, lists the major prehistoric
cultural units or phases known from the province within a framework
of time and natural geographic units. This is drawn up on the basis
of the temporal conclusions of others (MacNeish and Vickers, primarily)
as well as the writer's interpretation of all data herein considered.
The cross-cutting lines suggesting withdrawal of ice are based upon
data from Saskatchewan (Christiansen 1965). Lines suggesting release
from Lake Agassiz coverage are based on data supplied by Davies,
et al (1962, especially Figure 35 and text pp. 149-161) and in a
personal communication from John Elson suggesting the very rapid
shrinking of glacial Lake Agassiz II from the Campbell stage to the
present drainage, during the period from 6500 B.C. to 5500 B.C.
We have not attempted to modify this in the light of various new data
and ideas presented elsewhere in this volume. That remains a job for
the immediate future.

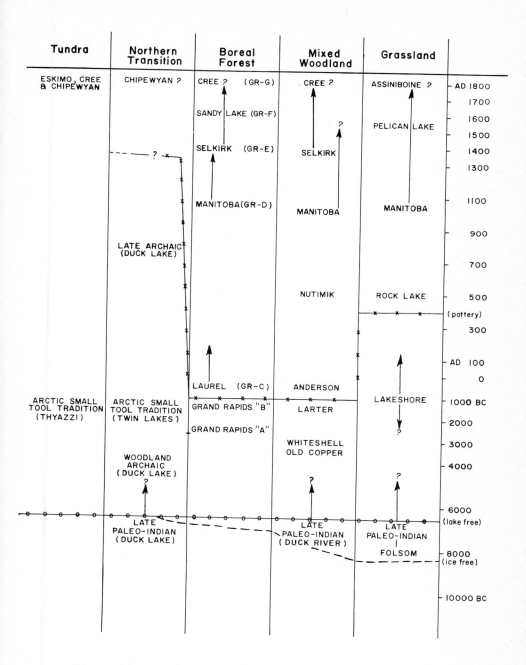

Figure 94. Manitoba Prehistoric Cultural Units.

The second mechanism used here to summarize and synthesize is the concept of "cultural universal". Over the past several years of undergraduate teaching of a course in New World prehistory the author has found this to be a convenient classificatory scheme for presenting an attitude towards interpretation of archeological data. One student (R. Robinson, personal communication) has recently commented on this as follows.

> *The concept of cultural universals is the one which beckons to the archeologist to be an anthropologist. It is here that dull grey pottery and lifeless projectile points take on meaning and become alive. Through cultural universals the archeologist reconstructs the life of the people from artifacts they have left behind. The concept of cultural universals is a crucial one to archeology if the discipline is to be recognized and appreciated by the world at large. The world is interested in the human element and this archeology must give to the world through cultural universals . . . .*

While this may be an over-enthusiastic response to what is basically a kind of check-list reminder of the interpretation and inference possibilities, the device should be useful also for the problem in this paper. The five "cultural universals" or areas of interpretive interest (following Wissler, 1923 and Herskovits, 1948) are as follows:

(1) technology

(2) subsistence

(3) settlement pattern

(4) social organization

(5) spiritual activities

Until rather recently archeologists have tended to emphasize the first of these, naturally enough, since the limitation of data to material items supports this emphasis. With the increasing development of ecological interests in the last twenty years, the subsistence aspects of archeological data have been more frequently utilized. Particularly in the past ten years (since the publication of Willey's 1953 monumental study of Peruvian settlement patterns) the settlement pattern and demographic potentials of archeological data have been widely recognized and utilized. The final two areas of cultural universal are seemingly the farthest removed from empirical data and as yet have not been successfully emphasized or developed from archeological data. There are, of course, some significant developments here. For the North American scene we mention only the programmatic statement by Sears (1961) as an indication of directions and possibilities for archeological research concerned with these aspects of culture.

What we attempt to do below is to recast data and interpretations made by MacNeish (1958) into this framework of cultural universals, adding from the much more diffuse body of data and interpretation presented elsewhere in this paper. Any success for this endeavor is implied by and clearly the result of MacNeish's concern for such inferences. Here it is interesting to observe the development of this kind of concern by comparing his Manitoba work with the current Mexican studies (MacNeish 1962) where there is a more clearly organized and explicit statement of these areas of significant inference.

The following set of statements about Manitoba prehistoric cultural units may be instructive as to details of provincial prehistory. It should also be instructive as to the kinds of details that are absent. Clear also from this review is the changing quality and quantity of data as we move away in time from the historic level.

Our Synopsis

By consulting Fig. 94 the several cultural units (foci, components) can be placed in a time and space framework. Because the Grand Rapids unpublished data and MacNeish's published work constitute the most substantial and detailed corpus of information currently available, we will essentially limit our consideration to the information derived from these two sources. Clearly, there are early hunter manifestations in Manitoba as suggested by the finds interpreted as "Folsom" and "Late Paleo-Indian" (Pettipas 1967). We feel this evidence important enough to warrant detailed statement elsewhere. We herein suggest restating MacNeish's foci as "phases" to use the term defined by Willey and Phillips (1958), and thus include, for present purposes, all the major variations known from Grand Rapids. The following statements, thus, proceed from the latest phase (Selkirk) back to the earliest (Whiteshell) with details on each universal rubric, presented phase by phase.

Selkirk Phase (A.D. 1150 - A.D. 1750)

This latest prehistoric phase is known extensively from the many little units reported by Hlady (1964e) from the Boreal Forest zone, but is defined on the basis of MacNeish's sites particularly Alexander's Point, Waulkinen and Sturgeon Falls. In addition, the Sandy Lake ware pottery from Grand Rapids and the Pelican Lake remains from the grassland area probably relate to similar cultural units. Hunting emphasis in the grassland must, however, be a significant difference.

Technology

Materials used include: chipped stone, ground stone, bone and ceramics. Small round or oblong end scrapers for skin working are distinctive as are "Prairie Side-Notched", "Selkirk Side-Notched", and "Eastern Triangular" projectile points. Size of these points

suggests the use of bow and arrow. Bone was used for the manufacture of awls and needles as well as barbed points. Scapula hoes
or shovels and celts were also made from bone. Ceramics are distinctive. Globular storage and cooking jars covered with fabric
impressions, have simple punctate decoration on the neck area.
Distinctive types are "Sturgeon Punctate", "Sturgeon Falls Fabric-
Impressed", "Alexander Fabric-Impressed". Hlady's type "Clear Water
Lake Punctate" should be included here, too. The overall ceramic
unit containing these types is "Winnipeg Fabric-Impressed Ware".
"Cemetery Point Corded Ware" is also present. Nets and fabrics
made from leather thongs (babiche) are indicated by surface
impressions in the ceramic material. Ground stone work is present
as grooved mauls plus the use of pebbles for hammers and net sinkers.
Birch bark painting and carving in addition to ceramic decoration
indicate artistic activities.

Subsistence

Floral and faunal remains suggest an environment like that
of today. There should be wild rice collecting possibilities.
Food scrap bones are primarily from fish. Harpoon presence suggests
use of the spearing method; babiche fabric impressions on the
ceramics imply the use of knotless nets, probably dip nets. Net
sinkers imply the use of gill nets also. Forest and grassland
animal bones are also present. The use of bow with small arrow
points is presumably primarily for hunting. Foraging activities
are indicated by the presence of clam shells as well as wild fruits
and seeds. Roasting of meat is indicated by hearths, boiling by
carbon-covered potsherds. Food storage in large bell-shaped cache
pits is indicated. These were presumably dug by scapula hoes.
There is probably a seasonal emphasis on fishing.

Settlement Pattern

Large, seasonal camp sites were made by nomadic bands inhabiting
fishing camps. Fireplaces and storage pits are associated with camp
refuse here.

Social Organization

The basic group was probably a nomadic band, possibly seasonally
enlarged to multi- or macro-band size. This was probably the prehistoric pattern for Cree Indians.

Spiritual Activities

Bundle burials indicate scaffold exposure of corpse. Flexed
burial with dog and grave good pottery suggest a belief in the
after life.

Manitoba Phase (A.D. 1000 - A.D. 1350)

Manitoba (or Blackduck as it is called in Minnesota) phase seems to be widespread and consistent, with the major internal difference relating to emphasis on hunting of large mammals (bison) in the grassland version of the phase. Several recent dates suggest the existence of Manitoba phase components up to about A.D. 1600.

Technology

Materials used include chipped stone, ground stone, worked bone and ceramics. "Eastern Triangular" and "Plains Side-Notched" are the distinctive projectile points. Size suggests their use with the bow and arrow. Bone was used for unilaterally barbed harpoon or fish spears; stone flakers; handles for end-scrapers; wedge-shaped fleshers; awls; needles; beaver teeth were used for "crooked knives"; bone also used for whistles. Ground and polished steatite tubes were probably used for smoking pipes. Shell beads from Gulf of Mexico conch shell imply trading contacts with that region. Ceramics are distinctive and numerous. Primarily cooking vessels, globular jars were also used for liquid containers and for storage. "Manitoba Corded" is the major ware consisting of three distinctive types: "Manitoba Horizontal", "Manitoba Herringbone" and "Blackduck Brushed". Two-strand, counter-clockwise, loosely twisted thong or string was probably used in sewing or for lashings.

Subsistence

Floral and faunal remains suggest an environment like that of today. Woodland components of this phase seem to have relied primarily on river or lakeside resources (fish, fowl, clam) with an emphasis on fishing. Grassland components relied primarily on bison hunting, including "stampeding over a jump" technique. Increase in bird bones is correlated with an increase in frequency of small projectile points which suggests the use of bow and arrow for fowl hunting. Pottery with interior carbon incrustations suggests a cooking function. Hammerstones plus smashed longbones imply the extraction of marrow as a food resource.

Settlement Pattern

Large, thin camp sites suggest a seasonal or semi-nomadic pattern of use. Fish camps are seasonally present for woodland components, bison-hunting camps for grassland components.

Social Organization

The settlement type implies a variable band organization with seasonal macro-band groupings. This was probably the prehistoric Assiniboine Indian pattern. Shamanism is suggested by the presence of steatite tubes which were possibly used as sucking or curing tubes.

"Chiefs" for whom burial mounds were built imply social differentiation as do other less important or richly supplied burials.
The work requirements for mound construction suggest a certain
amount of organized work force and thus social leadership and
differentiation activities.

Spiritual Activities

Burial practices imply a concept of "after life". Shamanisn
is perhaps a mechanism related to this as well as to "curing".
Differential burial treatment, use of fire, and offering of grave
goods all imply supra-natural belief systems.

Nutimik Phase (A.D. 500 - A.D. 1000)

Although distinguishable in the work reported by MacNeish,
this phase seems otherwise to be represented only in the Rock Lake
unit from the grassland area.

Technology

Materials used include chipped stone, ground stone and ceramics.
"Anderson Corner-Notched" is a minor projectile point type. "Whiteshell Side-Notched" is the major type. Probably these were darts
or spear points as judged by the size and weight. Bifacially worked
ovate knives as well as lamellar or blade-like flake techniques are
present. The latter blade-like flakes were probably used as side
blades. Both side and end scrapers are common. The beaver-tooth
chisel was a common bone item in use. Ceramics are distinctive,
primarily storage or liquid containers. "Lockport Cord Marked"
ware is represented as a minority by the type "Lockport Cord Wrapped
Stick". "Laurel Plain" is the major ware with "Nutimik Oblique" and
"Cemetry Point Incised" as the major types. "Laurel Dentate",
"Lockport Plain" are the minor types of this ware present. Small
mesh knotted nets were in use. A thick two-strand S-twist string
and single strand thongs were also used. The polished stone adze
and hammerstone are known from this phase.

Subsistence

Floral and faunal remains suggest an environment like that of
today. While fish bones predominate, there are significant quantitie
of bones from woodland mammals as well as clam shells suggesting the
use of these two resources for food. Only a few pots suggest cooking
(that is, boiling) function. Fire-cracked rock hearths suggest
roasting. Conical pits were used for food storage.

Settlement Pattern

Good-sized, thin camp sites along stream or lake margins.

Social Organization

Possibly nomadic bands.

Spiritual Activities

No evidence for activities of this sort.

Anderson Phase (500 B.C. - A.D.500)

This unit is well represented at Grand Rapids in the "C" component, less substantially known from the type site and Lockport in MacNeish's work. A substantial body of data from the "Laurel" sites of Minnesota appear to correlate well with this phase.

Technology

Materials used include chipped stone, bone, and ceramics. "Lockport Stemmed" and "Anderson Corner-Notched" are the most distinctive projectile points. They were probably used as dart or spear tips. There is possibly a greater reliance on snaring and fishing as hunting and gathering mechanisms because of the relative scarcity of projectile points in this phase. Antler flakes and pebble hammerstones were used in the manufacture of chipped stone tools including end and side skin scrapers. Ceramics are quite distinctive and are the earliest known for the Manitoba area. "Laurel Plain" ware is the majority item. Types present at Lockport and Anderson are "Laurel Dentate", "Lockport Linear", "Lockport Cord Wrapped Stick". At Grand Rapids "Laurel Plain" and "Laurel Pseudo-scallop" are majority types with "Laurel Dentate"the most distinctive minor type. String was made presumably for use in dip nets, bags, clothing, and for tying. A bone pottery marker is known and a beaver-tooth chisel was in use for this phase. A variety of types of stone used suggest wide contacts and possibly trade -- Knife River flint from North Dakota and jasper from southern Saskatchewan are present.

Subsistence

Faunal remains suggest a modern type forest environment with subsistence based on hunting woodland animals and fishing as well as the collecting of clams. Because no carbon incrusted pottery has been found there is no direct evidence for cooking, at least not using ceramic containers.

Settlement Pattern

Small, briefly occupied camp sites along waterways.

Social Organization

Small nomadic bands.

Spiritual Activities

No evidence for activities of this sort.

Larter Phase (1500 B.C. - 500 B.C.)

Best known at the type site and at Lockport, sub- or related units are present at Grand Rapids ("B"), in the grassland Lakeshore complex and the distinctive Arctic Small Tool components in the north.

Technology

Chipped stone, pecked stone, and bone were used in this phase. Projectile points account for 25% of all artifacts. Types are "Larter Tanged", "Parkdale Eared", "Winnipeg Ovoid", "Sturgeon Triangular", "McKean Lanceolate". 47% of artifacts are scrapers implying the importance of leather working and associated activities. Choppers and hammerstones are also present.

Subsistence

Predominance of buffalo bone suggests a grassland environment and reliance on the hunting of big game. Some minor fishing was carried out. Meat was roasted and marrow extracted from the long bones.

Settlement Pattern

Small, briefly occupied camp sites are known. Some large and rich sites along waterways imply re-use and/or large community occupancy on a seasonal basis.

Social Organization

Small nomadic bands existed occasionally coalescing to form larger groups.

Spiritual Activities

No evidence for activities of this sort.

Whiteshell Phase (3000 B.C. - 1500 B.C.)

While well-established in the lower three levels of the Cemetery Point site, this phase is even better represented in the earliest Grand Rapids component ("A"). The widespread distribution throughout the southern half of the province of the distinctive "McKean Lanceolate" projectile point implies substantial occupation and movement of a distinctive early hunting group throughout the inhabitable areas available and possibly a much more extensive grassland environment at that time.

Technology

Chipped stone and bone were used in this phase. Projectile points and skin scrapers are distinctive. The projectile point types are "Sturgeon Triangular", "McKean Lanceolate", and "Nutimik Concave". Probably all were used as dart or spear points. The antler multi-barbed point was probably a fish spear used for large fish. Drilled holes in bone suggest the use of a hand rather than the bow drill.

Subsistence

Buffalo bone exclusively present in this phase in the Whiteshell suggests a grassland environment and reliance on big game hunting for primary subsistence support. This is not the case in the Grand Rapids area (see Lukens, this volume). There was also some fish utilization as indicated by the spear.

Settlement Pattern

Small, briefly occupied camp site along waterway.

Social Organization

Small nomadic bands.

Spiritual Activities

No evidence for activities of this sort.

Future Research

Archeological activities in the province are currently underway in a number of areas and concerned with a number of problems. Since June 1, 1965, the University of Manitoba has been carrying out a three year program of historic archeology at Lower Fort Garry. A major continuing program of exploration and survey of the glacial Lake Agassiz shorelines commenced June 1, 1965. The first of a series of planned intensive surveys and excavations in the tundra and northern transition areas also began in June, 1965. Completion of a monograph on the 1961 and 1962 excavations and survey in the Grand Rapids Reservoir is anticipated before the end of 1967. Completion of a monograph on the 1963 and 1964 activities of the Winnipeg Floodway project is expected before the end of 1968.

In addition, during 1968, monographs resulting from the three years of work at Lower Fort Garry and the three years of surveys of glacial Lake Agassiz should be ready for publication.

Plans for archeological development include systematic studies of the Vickers collection with associated field checking and additional excavation. Studies of the early cultures known from the southwestern part of the province will be intensified. This will take serious interest back into the grasslands area. Both the University and probably the Archeological Society will carry out additional work in the boreal forest to extend our meagre knowledge of this vast region. In general, the University plans to develop an emphasis on environmental studies in Manitoba archeology to complement and contrast with the studies carried out by the University in Meso-America, dealing primarily with complex societies.

From the various statements made in this paper and in particular from a glance at Fig. 94 at least two major conclusions about Manitoba prehistory should be made. First, there is only a relatively small amount of work done so far and the big jobs of gathering and observing data yet lie ahead. Second, the present environmental zonation of the province has been a significant factor in producing or at least conditioning cultural variation. In particular, the Arctic and Sub-Arctic zones seem to stand out in contrast to the rest of the province.

In a letter written to me immediately following the November conference recorded in this volume, Dr. J.C. Ritchie made some most interesting and useful comments about where we can improve and strengthen our archeological and paleoecological understanding of the region. Taking the concept of "Site" as used by Warkentin (in this volume), Ritchie suggests that we can map the distribution of "major site regions" of the Glacial Lake Agassiz area, including both vegetation and land form data. This map would then be a regional summary of the landscape regions and might be much more relevant for detailed paleoecological and archeological studies than the simple biotic zone concept and map (Fig. 80) used at the present time. I agree wholeheartedly with Dr. Ritchie's suggestion and expect that studies in the near future will follow up this idea. To the

extent that we can add the dimensions of human perception and
utilization of environment (see Warkentin, this volume) to such
a more refined mapping, our understanding of cultural data from
either prehistory or history should be extended and improved
even further.

From both the conclusions stated above and the suggestions
for improved future work it seems obvious that if field research
activity trends and amounts continue as in the last few years,
this brief and sketchy statement of Manitoba prehistory will soon
be out of date and inadequate. No other development would be more
satisfying to the author.

Acknowledgements

The archeological work of the University of Manitoba referred
to in this paper has been supported by a number of agencies. The
initial work at Grand Rapids was largely financed by the Government
of Manitoba through the Manitoba Hydro and the Department of Mines
and Natural Resources although the University of Manitoba supported
this also in both 1961 and 1962. This work was the first archeological work sponsored by the University of Manitoba. Additional
support for Grand Rapids work came from the National Museum of
Canada. The Winnipeg Floodway project (1963-1964) was supported
by the Government of Manitoba through the Department of Agriculture,
by the University of Manitoba and also by the National Museum of
Canada. Northern Manitoba studies (1965 and 1967) were supported
jointly by the Graduate Research Fund of the University of Manitoba
and the University of Manitoba Northern Studies Committee.

For three years historic archeological work at Lower Fort Garry
has been supported by contracts with the Historic Sites Division of
the Department of Northern Affairs, Ottawa. The Archeological
Survey of Glacial Lake Agassiz has been supported by the University
since its inception and in 1965 and 1966 field work was also
supported by the National Museum of Canada. In 1966 and 1967 field
work has been largely supported by the National Research Council.
Graduate students working with various Manitoba archeological projects
have been supported by the above agencies as well as by assistantships
with the former Department of Anthropology and Sociology.

To all of these supporters and the many people who have assisted,
we are deeply grateful and wish to express our most sincere thanks
for the help without which the work could not have been accomplished.

EPILOGUE

After the Conference had been held at Winnipeg in November, several new papers were contributed. These are the studies by Matsch and Wright, McAndrews, and Winter which are included in this volume. Three of the discussants listed on the program (Bannatyne, Clayton and Klassen) provided brief written statements of their comments. These remarks have not been included in the volume because they were relevant to the oral presentation rather than the written final one which appears here. It is clear to the editor that both the preparation for the Conference and the event itself were important stimuli to the authors represented in this book. Some of them prepared papers before the Conference -- between August and November -- a time when many were completing fieldwork and commencing fall teaching schedules. The rest of the authors prepared papers in final form after the Conference, in some cases within weeks, in others a few months.

The wide span of knowledge necessary to comprehensive and detailed understanding of Glacial-Lake Agassiz is suggested by the range of topics covered in this volume. Current research levels in major areas are indicated by the variety of objectives of the papers presented. It seems clear, for example, that information about human relationships to the Lake is at a much earlier stage of accomplishment than is information from geological and botanical studies. Zoological work in general is only just beginning. Knowledge of the fish population of the Lake, for example, is an obvious area of need.

Six months after the Winnipeg Conference, a field meeting (Midwestern Friends of the Pleistocene) held in North Dakota underscored a problem we face on several fronts in the increasingly complex world of the late Twentieth Century. The field conference was a superb example of careful planning and execution; it dealt with results of important geological studies and presented these to more than 200 participants in a very effective way. But, the size of this group and the consequent requirements to the host institution are so demanding that the continuation of this venerable scholarly group will probably require substantial modification in the nature and scope of its organization. One suggestion has been to have groups concerned with smaller geographic regions. Another, and perhaps for the immediate future a more viable suggestion has been to have topical groups such as the "Great Lakes Conference" or the "Glacial Lake Agassiz Conference".

In whatever ways the problem of increasing numbers and increasing specialization may be handled, the present volume represents a culmination of the attempt by one institution -- the University of Manitoba -- to focus attention on an important phenomenon, while providing the facilities and encouragement for scholars already working on the subject to come together for fruitful exchange of ideas and information. It has been a matter of both pride and pleasure for the editor to have seen this development and to have had an active role in it.

The value and results of the contributions to Glacial Lake Agassiz studies presented in this volume will be determined ultimately by what happens after they appear in print for general use. Already these contributions have had a salutary effect on the scholars directly involved in the Conference. I have no doubt that they will have wider and important consequences for the scholars and others who will read them.

LITERATURE CITED

ANONYMOUS,
    1964 Sediment data for Saskatchewan and Manitoba to 30
          September, 1961. *Water Resources Paper, No. S-1.*
          Queen's Printer, Ottawa.

    1966 Water Networks. *Geotimes.* Vol. 11, No. 3, pp. 24-25.
          Washington.

ANTEVS, ERNST
    1931 Lake Glacial Correlations and Ice Recession in Manitoba.
          Geological Survey of Canada, Memoir 168. Ottawa.

    1951 Glacial Clays in Steep Rock Lake, Ontario, Canada.
          Geological Society of America, Bulletin, Vol. 62,
          Part 2, pp. 1223-1262. New York.

ARIMA, E.Y.
    1959 Archeology in Northeastern Saskatchewan. (Unpublished
          ms. in files of University of Manitoba Laboratory of
          Anthropology.)

ARNOLD, J.R. and W.F. LIBBY
    1951 Radiocarbon Dates. *Science,* Vol. 113, No.   pp.111-120.
          Washington.

AUGUSTADT, WALTER W.
    1965 Drainage in the Red River Valley of the North. *The
          Yearbook of Agriculture,* 1955. Superintendent of
          Documents. Washington.

AYERS, H.B.
    1899 Timber Conditions of the Pine Region of Minnesota.
          U.S. Geological Survey, 21st Annual Report, Report 5,
          pp. 673-689. Washington.

BAERREIS, D.A. and R.A. BRYSON
    1965a Climatic Episodes and the Dating of the Mississippian
          Cultures. *Wisconsin Archaeologist,* Vol. 46, No. 4,
          pp. 203-220. Madison.

    1965b Dating the Panhandle Aspect Cultures. *Oklahoma
          Anthropological Society, Bulletin* Vol. 14, pp. 105-116.
          Norman.

    1967 Climatic Change and the Mill Creek Culture of Iowa.
          Archives of Archaeology,
          Madison. (in press)

BAGDIKIAN, B.H.
    1966 Death in our air. *The Saturday Evening Post,* Oct. 8,
          pp. 31-35; 106-110. Philadelphia.

381

BAKER, C.H., Jr.
    1966a The Milnor Channel, an Ice-marginal Course of the
          Sheyenne River, North Dakota. *U.S. Geological Survey,
          Professional Paper 550B.* Washington.

    1966b Geology and Ground Water Resources of Richland County,
          Part 2. *North Dakota Geological Survey Bulletin 46.*
          Grand Forks.

BAKER, F.C.
    1928a The Fresh Water Mollusca of Wisconsin, part 1, Gastropoda.
          Wisconsin Geological and Natural History Survey Bulletin,
          Vol. 70.

    1928b The Fresh Water Mollusca of Wisconsin, part 2, Pelecypoda.
          Wisconsin Geological and Natural History Survey Bulletin,
          Vol. 70.

BARNES, I.R.
    1966 The Economy of Beauty. *Wildlife Review,* Vol. 4, No. 1,
          pp. 16-17. Victoria.

BARTON. R.H., *et al.,*
    1965 Quaternary. In "Geological History of Western Canada,"
          edited by R.G. McCrossan and R.P. Glaister. *Atlas
          Alberta Society of Petroleum Geologists* , pp 195-200 Calgary.

BASCOM, WILLARD
    1964, *Waves and Beaches.* Anchor Books, Doubleday & Co. Inc.,
          Garden City, N.Y.

BELL,C.N.
    1886a The Mound Builders in Canada. *Proceedings of the Canadian
          Institute,* 3rd Series, Vol. 4 , pp. 131-138.

    1886b Letter to American Antiquarian and Oriental Institute.

    1927 A Prehistoric Copper Hook. *The Historical and Scientific
          Society of Manitoba, Transaction* n.s. Vol. 2. Winnipeg.

BELL, ROBERT
    1879 Report on explorations on the Churchill and Nelson Rivers
          and around God's and Island Lakes, 1879. *Geological Survey
          of Canada, Report on Progress for* 1878-79, part C, 72pp.
          Ottawa.

BENDER, M.M., R.A. BRYSON and D.A. BAERREIS
    1965 University of Wisconsin Radiocarbon Dates I. *Radiocarbon,*
          Vol. 7,   pp. 399-407.   New Haven.

BENTLEY, C.R. *et al.*,
    1964   Physical Characteristics of the Antarctic Ice Sheet.
           *American Geographical Society Antarctic Map Folio
           Series, Folio 2*, 10p., 10 maps. Washington.

BIRD, R.D.
    1947   Report on Investigations at Stott Site 1947. (Manuscript
           Report to the Historic Sites Advisory Board. Winnipeg.)

    1961   Ecology of the Aspen Parkland of Western Canada in
           Relation to Land Use. *Canada Department of Agriculture
           Research Branch, Publication* 1066. Ottawa.

BOYCOTT, A.E.,
    1936   The habitats of fresh-water mollusca in Britain. *Journal
           of Ecology*, Vol. 22, No.   p. 1-38.

BRAY, WILLIAM L.
    1930   The Development of the Vegetation of New York State.
           *New York State College of Forestry Technical Publication
           No.* 29, Vol. 3, No. 2. Oxford.

BRETZ, J.H.
    1951a Causes of the Glacial Lake Stages in Saginaw Basin,
           Michigan. *Journal of Geology*. Vol. 59, No. 3, p. 244-258.
           Chicago.

    1951b The Stages of Lake Chicago, Their Causes and Correlations.
           American Journal of Science. Vol. 249 No. 6, p. 401-429.
           New Haven.

BROECKER, W.S.
    1966   Glacial Rebound and the Deformation of the Shorelines of
           Proglacial Lakes. *Journal Geophysical Research*. Vol. 71,
           No.20, pp. 4777-4783. Washington.

BROOKHART, J.W. and J.E. POWELL
    1961   Reconnaissance of Geology and Ground Water of Selected
           areas in North Dakota. *North Dakota Ground Water
           Studies No. 28*.

BROOKS, C.E.P.
    1949   *Climate Through the Ages*. McGraw-Hill Book Co. New York.

BROPHY, J.A.
    1967   Some Aspects of the Geological Deposits of the Lake Agassiz
           Basin. In "Glacial Geology of the Missouri Coteau", edited
           by Lee Clayton and T.F. Freers, pp. 159-165. *North Dakota
           Geologic Survey Miscellaneous Series No.* 30.   Grand Forks.

BRYAN, M.
    1966   Entire Fish Population of Area Lake Poisoned. *Ottawa
           Journal*, Sept. 26, p. 3. Ottawa.

BRYCE, GEORGE
    1887 The Souris Country: Its Monuments, Mounds, Forts and
          Rivers. *The Historical and Scientific Society of Manitoba
          Transaction* 24. Winnipeg.

    1904 Among the Mound Builders' Remains. *The Historical and
          Scientific Society of Manitoba, Transaction 66.* Winnipeg.

BRYSON, R.A.
    1965 Recent Climatic Episodes in North America. *Proceedings
          of the 21st Southeastern Archaeological Conference
          Bulletin.* No. 3, pp. 78-81. Cambridge.

    1966 Airmasses, Streamlines and the Boreal Forest. *Geographical
          Bulletin.* Vol. 7, No. 2, pp. 228-269. Ottawa.

BRYSON, R.A., W.N.IRVING and J.A. LARSEN
    1965 Radiocarbon and Soil Evidence of Former Forest in the
          Southern Canadian Tundra. *Science*, Vol. 147, No.
          pp. 46-48. Washington.

BRYSON, R.A. and P. JULIAN
    1963 Proceedings of the Conference on the Climate of the
          Eleventh and Sixteenth Centuries, Aspen, Colorado. June
          1962. *National Center for Atmospheric Research, NCAR
          Technical Notes 63-I.*

BRYSON, R.A. and W.P. LOWRY
    1955 Synoptic Climatology of the Arizona Summer precipitation
          Singularity. *Bulletin of the American Meteorological
          Society.*   Vol. 36, No.   pp. 329-399. Boston.

BUTTERS, F.K. and E.C. ABBE
    1953 A Floristic Study of Cook County Northeastern Minnesota.
          Rhodora, Vol. 55, No.650,pp. 21-55, 63-101, 116-154,
          161-201. Cambridge.

BUELL, M.F. and H.F. BUELL
    1959 Aspen Invasion of Prairie. *Bulletin of the Torrey Botanical
          Club.* Vol. 86, No. 4, pp. 264-5. New York.

BUELL, M.F. and J.E. CANTLON
    1961 A study of two Forest stands in Minnesota with an Inter-
          pretation of the Prairie-forest Margin. *Ecology,* Vol. 32,
          No. 2, pp. 294-316. Durham.

BUELL, M.F. and VERA FACEY
    1960 Forest-prairie Transition West of Itasca Park, Minnesota.
          Bulletin Torrey Botanical Club, Vol. 87, No. 1, pp. 46-58.
          New York.

BUELL, M.F. and NIERING
    1957 Fir-Spruce-Birch Forest in Northern Minnesota. *Ecology.*
          Vol. 38, No. 4, pp. 602-610. Durham.

BURGESS, R.L.
      1965   Ninety Years of Vegetational Change in a Township in
             Southeastern North Dakota. *Proceedings of the North
             Dakota Academy of Science*, Vol. 28, No.   pp. 84-94.
             Grand Forks.

CAMERON, NANCY S.
      1962   An Osteological Analysis of an Early Manitoba Population.
             (Unpublished M.A. Thesis, University of Toronto.)

CAPES, KATHERINE
      1963   The W.B. Nickerson Survey and Excavations, 1912-15, of
             the Southern Manitoba Mounds Region. *National Museum
             of Canada, Anthropology Papers*,   No. 4.   Ottawa.

CARSON, R. L.
      1964   *Silent Spring*. Fawcett World Library, New York.

CHAMBERLAIN, T. C.
      1895   In: Upham (1895).

CHARLIER, R.H.
      1966   Probing the Ocean. *Science*, Vol. 153 No.   pp.1421-1423.
             Washington.
CHISM, JAMES V.
      1966   Report on the First Season's Excavations on the Site
             of Lower Fort Garry. Abstract of Paper to 23rd Plains
             Conference, Topeka, Kansas, Nov. 25-27, 1965. In *Plains
             Anthropologist*, Vol. 11, No. 3, p. 238. Lincoln.

CHRISTIANSEN, E. A.
      1965   Ice Frontal Positions in Saskatchewan. *Geology Division,
             Saskatchewan Research Council, Map No. 2*. Saskatoon.

CLAYTON, LEE
      1966   Notes on Pleistocene Stratigraphy of North Dakota.
             North Dakota Geological Survey, Report of Investigation
             No. 44. Grand Forks.

      1967   Stagnant-glacier Features of the Missouri Coteau in North
             Dakota. In "Glacial Geology of the Missouri Coteau,"
             edited by Lee Clayton and T.F. Freers, pp. 25-46. *North
             Dakota Geological Survey, Miscellaneous series 30*.
             Grand Forks.

CLAYTON, LEE, W.M. LAIRD, R.W. KLASSEN, and W.D. KUPSCH
      1965   Intersecting Minor Lineations of Lake Agassiz Plain.
             Journal of Geology, Vol. 73, No. 4, pp. 652-656. Chicago.

COKER, R. E., A.F. SHIRA, H.W. CLARK and A.D. HOWARD
      1919- Natural History and Propagation of Fresh Water Mussels.
      1920   *U.S. Bureau of Fisheries Bulletin*. Vol. 37 No. 893.,
             pp. 75-181.

COLTON, ROGER B.
    1958   Notes on the Intersecting Minor Ridges in the Lake
           Agassiz Basin, North Dakota. *Guidebook, Ninth Annual
           Field Conference, Mid-Western Friends of the Pleistocene.*
           pp. *74-77.* Grand Forks.

COLTON, R.B., R.W. LEMKE, and R.M. LINDVALL
    1963   Preliminary Glacial Map of North Dakota. *U.S. Geological
           Survey Miscellaneous Geological Investigations Map. I-331.*

CONWAY, V.M.
    1949   The Bogs of Central Minnesota. *Ecological Monographs,*
           Vol. 19, No. 2, pp. 173-206. Durham.

COULOMB, JEAN and GEORGES JOBERT
    1963   *The Physical Constitution of the Earth.* Hafner Publishing
           Co.

CRAIG, G.Y.
    1966   Concepts in Paleoecology. *Earth-Science Reviews,* Vol. 2,
           No. 2, pp. 127-155. Chicago.

CURTIS, J.T.
    1959   *The Vegetation of Wisconsin.* University of Wisconsin
           Press, Madison.

CUSHING, E.J.
    1965   Problems in the Quaternary Phytogeography of the Great
           Lakes Region. In "The Quaternary of the United States,"
           edited by H.E. Wright, Jr. and D.G. Frey, pp. 403-416.
           Princeton.

CVANCARA, A.M., and S.S. HARRISON
    1965   Distribution and Ecology of Mussels in the Turtle River,
           North Dakota. *Proceedings of the North Dakota Academy
           of Science.* Vol. 19, No.   pp. 128-146. Grand Forks.

DALY, R.A.
    1926   *Our Mobile Earth.* Scribner. New York.

    1934   [Reprinted 1963], *The Changing World of the Ice Age.*
           Hafner Publishing Co., New York.

DAPPLES, E.C.
    1959   *Basic Geology for Science and Engineering.* Wiley, New York.

DAUBENMEIR, R. F.
    1936   The Big Woods of Minnesota. Its Structure and Relation
           to Climate, Fire and Soils. *Ecological Monographs,* Vol.6,
           No. 2, pp. 233-268. Durham.

DAVIES, J.F., B.B.BANNATYNE, G.S. BARRY and H.R. McCABE
    1962   *Geology and Mineral Resources of Manitoba.* Department of
           Mines and Natural Resources, Province of Manitoba. Winnipeg.

DAWLEY, CHARLOTTE
    1947   Distribution of Aquatic Mollusks in Minnesota. *The American
            Midland Naturalist.* Vol. 38, No.   pp. 671-697. Notre Dame.

DAWSON, G. M.
    1875   Report on the Geology and Resources of the Region in the
            Vicinity of the Forty-ninth Parallel, from the Lake of
            the Woods to the Rocky Mountains.
            Vol.   No.   pp. 248. Montreal.

DAY, P.C.
    1926   Precipitation in the Drainage Area of the Great Lakes,
            1875-1924. *Monthly Weather Review,* Vol. 54, No. 3,
            pp. 85-106, March 1926. Washington.

DEEVEY, E.S. Jr.
    1966   Lake Tahoe. Measured for Pollution. *Science,* Vol. 154,
            No.3745 p.68.   Washington.

DELORME, DENNIS
    1965   Pleistocene and Post-Pleistocene Ostracoda of Saskatchewan.
            (Unpublished Ph.D. thesis, University of Saskatchewan. 245p.)

DENNIS, P.E., P.D. AKIN and   JONES
    1950   Ground Water in the Kindred Area, Cass and Richland
            Counties, North Dakota. *North Dakota Ground Water
            Studies,* No. 14. Grand Forks.

DENNIS, P.E., P.D. AKIN, and G.F. WORTS Jr.
    1949   Geology and Ground-water resources of parts of Cass and
            Clay Counties, North Dakota and Minnesota. *U.S. Geological
            Survey and North Dakota Geological Survey, North Dakota
            Ground Water Studies.*   No. 11. Grand Forks.

DENSMORE, FRANCIS
    1929   Chippewa Customs. *Bureau of American Ethnology, Bulletin*
            86. Washington.

DERRY, D.R. and G.S. MACKENZIE
    1931   Geology of the Ontario-Manitoba Boundary (12th Base Line
            to Latitude 54). *Ontario Department of Mines, Annual
            Report,* Vol. XL

DIEDRICK, R.T.
    1967   Evidence for a Glacial Lake in Western Minnesota.
            (Unpublished Ms.)

DIETZ, R.S.
    1966   Our Deep and Wide Ocean. *Science,* Vol. 153,
            pp. 1423-1428. Washington.

DIMBLEBY,
    1963   In "The Experimental Earthwork on Overton Down,
           Wiltshire, 1960" edited by P.A. Jewell, British
           Association for the Advancement of Science. London.
DIX, T.L. and F.E. SMEINS
    1967   The Prairie, Meadow, and Marsh Vegetation of Nelson County,
           North Dakota. *The Canadian Journal of Botany*, Vol. 45,
           No.   pp. 21-58. Ottawa.

DOWLING, A.B.
    1901   The Physical Geography of the Red River Valley. *The
           Ottawa Naturalist*, Vol. XV, No. 5, pp. 115-120. Ottawa.

DOWNES, P.
    1938   Reindeer Lake Pottery. *American Antiquity*, Vol. 4, No. 1,
           p. 48. Menasha.

EAST, GORDON
    1965   *The Geography Behind History*. London.

ELLIS, J.H.
    1959   *The Soils of Manitoba*. Manitoba Economic Survey Board,
           Winnipeg.

ELSON, JOHN A.
    1955   Surficial Geology of the Tiger Hills Region, Manitoba.
           (Unpublished Ph.D. dissertation, Yale University. 316 pp.)

    1957   Lake Agassiz and the Mankato-Valders Problem. *Science*,
           Vol. 126, No. 3281, pp. 999-1002. Washington.

    1960   Surficial Geology, Brandon West of Principal Meridan,
           Manitoba. Map 1067. *Geological Survey of Canada*, In
           Memoir 300 by E.C. Halstead. Ottawa.

    1961   Soils of Lake Agassiz. In "Soils in Canada", edited by
           R.F. Leggett, pp. 51-79. *Royal Society of Canada, Special
           Publications 3*. Ottawa.

    1962   History of Glacial Lake Agassiz. In "Problems of the
           Pleistocene and Arctic," Vol. 2, No. 2, pp. 1-16. Montreal.

    1965   Western Strandlines of Glacial Lake Agassiz, (abstract)
           *7th Congress, International Association for Quaternary
           Research*. p. 126. Boulder, Colorado.

ERDTMAN, GUNNAR
    1954   An Introduction to Pollen Analysis. *Chronica Botanica*,
           Waltham.

EVANS, G. EDWARD
    1961   A Reappraisal of the Blackduck Focus or Headwaters Lakes
           Aspect. (Unpublished M.A. Thesis, University of Minnesota.)

EVANS, G. EDWARD
    1961 Ceramic Analysis of the Blackduck Ware and its General
          Cultural Relationships. *Proceedings, Minnesota Academy of
          Science*, Vol. 29, pp. 33-35. Minneapolis.

EWING, J.
    1924 Plant Successions of the Brush-Prairie in North-western
          Minnesota. *Journal of Ecology*, Vol. 12, pp. 238-266.
          Oxford.

FALCONER, G., J.D. IVES, O.H. LØKEN and J.T. ANDREWS
    1965 Major end moraines in Eastern and Central Arctic Canada.
          Geographical Bulletin, Vol. 7, No. 2, pp. 137-153.
          Ottawa.

FARB, P.
    1966 *The Land and Wildlife of North America*. Time Inc.,
          New York.

FARRAND, W.R.
    1960 Former Shorelines in Western and Northern Lake Superior
          Basin. (Unpublished Ph.D. dissertation, University of
          Michigan).

FERNALD, M.L.
    1950 *Gray's Manual of Botany*, Eighth Edition. American Book
          Company, New York.

FEWKES, VLADIMIR J.
    1937 Aboriginal Potsherds from Red River, Manitoba. *American
          Antiquity*, Vol. 3, No. 2, pp. 143-155. Menasha.

FISKE, TIMOTHY
    1964a Manuscript on Fidler Mound excavation under Floodway
          Archeological Project. (In files of University of
          Manitoba Laboratory of Anthropology.)

    1964b Manuscript on Archeological Survey and excavations near
          Duck River, Manitoba. (In files of University of Manitoba
          Laboratory of Anthropology.)

    1964c Report of Great Lakes Archeological Conference. *Manitoba
          Archeological Newsletter*, Vol. 1, no. 1, pp. 4-5.
          Winnipeg. (unsigned)

    1964d Research Activities and Preliminary Report. Excavation
          of the Fidler Mounds Lockport, Manitoba. In "Winnipeg
          Floodway Archeological Project Progress Report".
          (Unpublished ms. in files of University of Manitoba
          Laboratory of Anthropology.)

    1964e University of Manitoba Fieldwork. *Manitoba Archeological
          Newsletter*, Vol. 1, No. 4, pp. 3-6. Winnipeg.

    1965 Investigator's Statement. In"Winnipeg Floodway Archeological
          Project Second and Final Progress Report." (Unpublished
          ms. in files of University of Manitoba Laboratory of
          Anthropology.)

FLINT, R.F.
     1957 *Glacial and Pleistocene Geology*. Wiley and Sons, New York.

FORBIS, RICHARD G.
     1961 Review of MacNeish: "An Introduction to the Archeology of
           Southeast Manitoba". *American Antiquity*, Vol. 27, No. 2,
           pp. 252-253. Salt Lake City.

FOWELLS, H.A.
     1965 Silvics of Forest Trees of the U.S. *Agriculture Handbook,
           No. 271, U.S. Department of Agriculture, Forest Service.*
           Washington.

FREY, DAVID G.
     1963 *Limnology in North America*. University of Wisconsin Press,
           Madison.

FRYE, J.C.
     1966 Man and His Environment. *Geotimes*, Vol. 10, No. 9, p. 9.
           Washington.

GIDDINGS, J.L., Jr.
     1956 A Flint in Northernmost Manitoba. *American Antiquity*,
           Vol. 21, No. 3, pp. 255-268. Menasha.

GLEASON, H.A. and A. CRONQUIST
     1964 *The Natural Geography of Plants*. Columbia University
           Press, New York.

GOLDTHWAIT, J.W.
     1910 An Instrumental Survey of the Shorelines of the Extinct
           Lakes Algonquin and Nipissing in Southwestern Ontario.
           *Canada, Department of Mines, Geological Survey Branch,
           Memoir 10.* Ottawa.

GRIFFIN, JAMES B.
     1961 Copper Artifacts from Manitoba. In "Lake Superior and
           the Indians: Miscellaneous Studies of Great Lakes Pre-
           history". *Museum of Anthropology, University of Michigan,
           Anthropological Papers*, No. 17, pp. 124-126, plates XXVI,
           XXVIII, XXIX. Ann Arbor.

GRIPP, R.H. and K. RYUGO
     1966 DDT Soil Residues in Mature Pear Orchards. *California
           Agriculture*, Vol. 20, No. 6, pp. 10-11.

GRYBA, EUGENE M.
     1966 A Possible Midland Point from the Swan Valley of
           Manitoba. *Plains Anthropologist*, Vol. 11, No. 3,
           p. 238. Lincoln.

GUILDAY, J.E., P.S. MARTIN and A.D. McCRADY
    1964   New Paris No. 4, a Pleistocence Cave Deposit in Bedford
           County, Pennsylvania. *Bulletin National Speleological
           Society*. Vol. 26, No. 4, pp. 121-194.

GULIOV, PAUL
    1963   Paleoecology of Invertebrate Fauna from Postglacial
           Sediments near Earl Gray, Saskatchewan.(Unpublished
           M.A. thesis, University of Saskatchewan.)

GUNN, DONALD
    1868   Indian Remains Near Red River Settlement, Hudson's Bay
           Territory. *Annual Report of the Smithsonian Institution
           for the Year 1867*,   *pp. 399-400*.Washington.

GUTENBERG, BENO
    1941   Changes in Sea Level, Postglacial Uplift, and Mobility
           of the Earth's Interior. *Geological Society of America,
           Bulletin*. Vol. 52, Part 1, pp. 721-772. New York.

GUTENBERG, B. and C.F. RICHTER
    1949   *Seismicity of the Earth and Associated Phenomena*.
           Princeton University Press, Princeton.

HAMILTON, R. A.
    1958   *Venture to the Arctic*. Penguin Books Inc., Baltimore.

HARE, F. K.
    1953   Some Climatological Problems of the Arctic and Sub-Arctic.
           In "Compendium of Meteorology", edited by T.F. Malone,
           American Meteorological Society. Vol.   No.   pp.
           Boston.

HEINSELMAN, N.L.
    1963   Forest Sites, Bog Processes, and Peatland Types in the
           Glacial Lake Agassiz Region, Minnesota. *Ecological
           Monographs*, Vol. 33, pp. 327-374. Durham.

HERSKOVITS, MELVILLE J.
    1948   *Man and His Works*. Alfred A. Knopf. New York.

HEUSSER, C.J.
    1959   Radiocarbon Dates of Peats from Pacific North America.
           Radiocarbon, Vol. 1, pp·29-34. New Haven.

HEWES, GORDON W.
    1948   Early Tribal Migrations in the Northern Great Plains.
           Plains Archeological Conference Newsletter, Vol. 1, No.4.
           Lincoln.

HIBBARD, C.W. and D.W. TAYLOR
    1960   Two Late Pleistocence Faunas from Southwestern Kansas.
           *Contributions from the Museum of Paleontology, University
           of Michigan*. Vol. 16, No. 1, pp.1-233. Ann Arbor.

HILL, MATTHEW
    1965   An Archeological Survey in the Glacial Lake Agassiz
           Basin in Manitoba. Laboratory of Anthropology,
           University of Manitoba, Winnipeg. Mimeographed, 25pp.

HIND, H.Y.
    1859   *Report on the Assiniboine and Saskatchewan Exploring
           Expedition.* John Lovell, Toronto.

    1860   *Narrative of the Canadian Red River Exploring Expedition
           of 1857 and of the Assiniboine and Saskatchewan Exploring
           Expedition of 1858.*   London.

HLADY, WALTER M.
    n.d.a An Archeological Survey of the West Bank of the Red River
           in Old Kildonan and West St. Paul Municipalities in
           Manitoba, Canada. (Unpublished ms. in Author's Library.)

    n.d.b The Ceramic Sequence at the Lockport Site and its Bearing
           on North American Archeology. (Unpublished ms. in Author's
           Library.)

    n.d.c The Archeology of the Red River of the North. (Unpublished
           ms. in Author's Library.)

    n.d.d An Introduction to the Archeology of the Woodland Area
           of Manitoba north of the 54th Parallel of Latitude.
           (Unpublished ms. in Files of University of Manitoba
           Laboratory of Anthropology.)

    1947   Report on 1947 Fieldwork. *Plains Archeological Conference
           Newsletter*, Vol. 1, No. 1, p.8. Lincoln.

    1948   The Plainview Culture. *Spade and Screen, Saskatchewan
           Archeological Society.* Saskatoon.

    1949a The Archeology of the Red River of the North and the
           Whiteshell River Areas. *Report of the Fifth Plains
           Archeological Conference, 1947.*   *pp.93-95.*
           Lincoln.

    1949b Report on Manitoba in Notes and News. *American Antiquity,*
           Vol. 14, No. 3, pp. 248-249. Menasha.

    1952   Manitoba Archeology. *The Manitoba Arts Review*, Vol. 8,
           No. 1, pp 24-33. Winnipeg.

    1960   The Occurrence of Plainview Type Projectile Points in
           West Central Canada.

    1964a Fieldwork in Manitoba 1962, 1963. *Manitoba Archeological
           Newsletter*, Vol.1, No. 1, pp. 5-6. Winnipeg.

HLADY, WALTER M.
    1964b Indian Migrations in Manitoba and the West. *Transactions*
        of the Historical and Scientific Society of Manitoba,
        Series 3, No. 17, pp. 23-53. Winnipeg.

    1964c Bibliography of Manitoba Archeology. *Manitoba Archeological*
        Newsletter, Vol. 1, No. 3, pp. 3-20. Winnipeg.

    1964d Fieldwork by the Manitoba Archeological Society - 1964.
        Manitoba Archeological Newsletter, Vol. 1, No. 4, pp. 6-8.
        Winnipeg.

    1965 A Manitoba Source of "Knife River Flint". *Manitoba*
        Archeological Newsletter, Vol. II, No. 2, pp. 3-7.
        Winnipeg.

HLADY, WALTER M. and ALLAN A. SIMPSON
    1965 Additions to the Bibliography of Manitoba Archeology.
        Manitoba Archeological Newsletter, Vol. II, No. 3,
        pp. 7-12. Winnipeg.

    1966a The Robins Mound (C3-SP-2), West St. Paul. *Manitoba*
        Archeological Newsletter, Vol. III, No. 2, pp. 5-6.
        Winnipeg.

    1966b Further Additions to the Bibliography of Manitoba
        Archeology. *Manitoba Archeological Newsletter*, Vol. III,
        No. 3, pp. 3-6, Winnipeg.

HOLMES, ARTHUR
    1965 *Principles of Physical Geology*. Thomas Nelson, London.

HORBERG, LELAND
    1951 Intersecting Minor Ridges and Periglacial Features in
        the Lake Agassiz Basin, North Dakota. *Journal of Geology*.
        Vol. 59, No. 1, pp. 1-18. Chicago.

HOWELL, J.V. *et al.*,
    1960 *Glossary of Geology and Related Sciences*. American
        Geological Institute, Washington. (Second Edition).

HURST, M.E.
    1930 Geology of the Area Between Favourable Lake and Sandy
        Lake, District of Kenora (Patricia Portion). *Ontario*
        Department of Mines, Vol. 38, Part II, 1929, p. 67-68.

HURST, M.E.
    1933 Geology of the Sioux Lookout area. *Ontario Department*
        of Mines, Vol. 41, Part VI, pp. 16-18. Ottawa.

HUTCHINSON, G. EVELYN
    1957 *A Treatise on Limnology. Vol. 1. Geography, Physics,*
        and Chemistry. John Wiley and Sons, Inc. New York.

IMBRIE, J.   and N.D. NEWELL
      1964   The Viewpoint of Paleoecology. In "Approaches to Paleo-
             ecology," edited by Imbrie and Newell. John Wiley and
             Sons, Inc., New York.

INNES, J.S. and A.A. WESTON
      1966   Crustal Uplift of the Canadian Shield and its Relation
             to the Gravity Field. *Annales Academiae Scientiarum Fennicae.*
             Vol. No. A. 111 90, pp. 169-176.

IRVING, WILLIAM N.
      1965 (Unpublished ms. on Artifacts Collected from Twin Lakes
            Site Near Churchill. In Files of University of Manitoba
            Laboratory of Anthropology.)

JANSSEN, C.R.
      1966   Recent Pollen Spectra from the Deciduous and Coniferous-
             Deciduous Forests of Northeastern Minnesota. *Ecology*,
             Vol. 47, No. 5, pp. 804-825. Durham.

JELGERSMA, S.
      1961   A Late-Glacial Pollen Daigram from Madelia, South-central
             Minnesota. *American Journal of Science*, Vol, 260. pp. 522-
             29. New Haven.

JENNY, HANS
      1941   *Factors of Soil Formation.* New York.

JOHNSTON, W.A.
      1915   Rainy River District, Ontario. Surficial Geology and
             Soils. *Geological Survey of Canada, Memoir* No. 82.
             Ottawa.
      1916   The Genesis of Lake Agassiz; a Confirmation. *Journal of
             Geology*, Vol. 24, No. 7, pp. 625-638. Chicago.

      1921   Winnipegosis and Upper Whitemount River Areas, Manitoba,
             Pleistocene and Recent Deposits. *Geological Survey of
             Canada, Memoir 128.* Ottawa.

      1934   Surface Deposits and Groundwater Supply of Winnipeg Map-
             area, Manitoba. *Geological Survey of Canada, Memoir 174.*
             Ottawa.

      1946   Glacial Lake Agassiz, with Special Reference to the Mode
             of Deformation of the Beaches. *Geological Survey of
             Canada, Bulletin 7.* Ottawa.

JOYES, DENNIS
      1967   The Avery Site at Rock Lake, Manitoba. (Unpublished
             M.A. thesis, University of Manitoba.)

KAZMANN, RAPHAEL G.
    1965   *Modern Hydrology.*   Harper & Row, New York.

KEATING, W.H.
    1825   Narrative of an Expedition to the Source of St. Peters
           River, Lake Winnipeg, Lake of the Woods, etc. performed
           in the Year 1823.   Vol. 2, No.
           p. 3. London.

KEHOE, ALICE B.
    1959   Ceramic Affiliations in the Northwestern Plains.
           American Antiquity, Vol. 25, No. 2, pp. 237-246.   Salt
           Lake City.

KENYON, WALTER
    1961   The Swan Lake Site.   *Art and Archeology Division, Royal
           Ontario Museum, Occasional Paper* No.3, pp. 1-37. Toronto.

KING, P.B.
    1965   Tectonics of Quaternary Time in Middle North America.
           In "The Quaternary of the United States," edited by H.E.
           Wright Jr. and D.G. Frey, pp. 831-870. Princeton .

KUCHLER, A.W.
    1964   Potential Natural Vegetation -- United States. *American
           Geographical Society, Special Publication No. 36.*
           New York.

KUMARAPELI, P.S. and V.A. SAULL
    1966   The St. Lawrence Valley System. A North American
           equivalent of the East African Rift Valley System.
           Canadian Journal of Earth Sciences, Vol. 3 No.
           pp. 639-658. Ottawa.

LAIRD, WILSON M.
    1964   The Problem of Lake Agassiz. *Proceedings of the North
           Dakota Academy of Science,* Vol. XVIII, No.
           pp. 114-134. Grand Forks.

LAMB, H.H.
    1963   On the Nature of Certain Climatic Epochs which Differed
           from the Modern (1900-39) Normal. *Proceedings of the
           WMO/UNESCO, Rome 1961 Symposium on Changes of Climate.*
           (Arid Zone Research XX) Paris.

    1966   Climate in the 1960's. *Geographical Journal*, Vol.132. pp.183.
           Ottawa.
LANSING, LIVINGSTON
    1965   Air Mass Modification by Lake Ontario During the April-
           November Period. In "Proceedings, Eighth Conference on
           Great Lakes Research," edited by M.N. Everett, pp. 257-
           261. Ann Arbor.

LA ROCQUE, AURELE
    1952 Molluscan Faunas of the Orleton Farms Mastodon Site,
          Madison County, Ohio. *Ohio Journal of Science*, Vol.52
          No.   pp. 10-27. Bowling Queen.

    1960 Quantitative Methods in the Study of Non-marine Pleistocene
          Mollusca. *21st International Geological Conference,
          Copenhagen*, 1960, Report part 4, p. 134-141.

LARSEN, J.A.
    1966 Relationships of Central Canadian Boreal Plant Communities.
          Studies in Sub-arctic and Arctic Bioclimatology, II.
          Task NR 387-022, ONR Contract No. 1202(07). *Technical
          Report No. 26, Department of Meteorology, University of
          Wisconsin.* Madison.

    1967 Geographical Position of the Central Canadian Northern
          Forest Border. Ms. in preparation, University of Wisconsin.

LEECHMAN, DOUGLAS
    1949 Turtle Mosaic. *Canadian Geographical Journal*, Vol. 39,
          No.   pp. 274-275. Ottawa.

    1950a Notes and News. *American Antiquity*, Vol. 15, No. 3
          p. 265. Menasha.

    1950b An Implement of Elephant Bone from Manitoba. *American
          Antiquity*, Vol. 16, No. 2, pp. 157-160. Salt Lake City.

LEHMER, D.J.
    1966 The Fire Heart Creek Site. *Smithsonian Institution, River
          Basin Surveys, Publication in Salvage Archeology No. 1.*
          Lincoln.
LEIGHTON, M.M.
    1933 The Naming of the Subdivision of the Wisconsin Glacial
          Age. *Science*, Vol. 77, No. 1989, p. 168. Washington.

    1957 Radiocarbon dates of Mankato drift in Minnesota. *Science*.
          Vol. 125, No. 3256, pp. 1037-1039. Washington.

    1958 Important elements in the classification of the Wisconsin
          Glacial Age. *Journal of Geology*, Vol. 66, No. 3,
          pp. 288-309. Chicago.

    1960 The Classification of the Wisconsin Glacial stage of the
          North Central United States. *Journal of Geology*, Vol. 68,
          No. 5,   pp. 529-552. Chicago.

LEONHARDY, F.C. (Editor)
    1966 Domebo. A Paleo-Indian Mammoth Kill in the Prairie-Plains.
          Contribution of the Museum of the Great Plains, No. 1.
          Lawton.

LEVERETT, F.
    1912   Glacial Investigations in Minnesota in 1911. *The
            Geological Society of America Bulletin*, Vol. 23,
            pp. 732-735.

    1932   Quaternary Geology of Minnesota and Parts of Adjacent
            States. *U.S. Geological Survey Professional Paper 161*.
            Washington.

    1936   , In "Pleistocene Man In
            Minnesota," edited by A.E. Jenks, University of Minnesota
            Press, Minneapolis.

LEWIS, T.H.
    1886   Mounds on the Red River of the North. *American Antiquity
            and Oriental Journal*, Vol. 8, No. 6, pp. 369-371.

LIBBY, W.F.
    1955   *Radiocarbon Dating*. Second Edition. University of Chicago
            Press, Chicago.

LISK, D.J.
    1966   Detection and Measurement of Pesticide Residues. *Science*,
            Vol. 154, pp 93-98. Washington.

LLOYD, T.
    1966   A Water Resource Policy for Canada. *Canadian Geographic
            Journal*. Vol. 73, No. 1, pp. 2-17.   Ottawa.

LÖVE, DORIS
    1959   The Post-glacial Development of the Flora of Manitoba --
            A Discussion. *Canadian Journal of Botany*, Vol. 57,
            pp. 547-585. Ottawa.

LUKENS, PAUL W., Jr.
    1964   Progress Report, Tailrace Bay Fauna. (Unpublished ms. in
            files of University of Manitoba Laboratory of Anthropology.)

LUKENS, P.W., Jr.
    1966   The Vertebrate Fauna From the Tailrace Bay Site, Grand
            Rapids, Manitoba. (Unpublished ms. Department of
            Anthropology, University of Manitoba, Winnipeg.)

MACCURDY, GEORGE C.
    1909   Anthropology at the Winnipeg Meeting of the British
            Association. *American Anthropologist*, n.s. Vol. 11,
            No.   pp. 456-477.

MACKAY, G.H.
    1965   A brief Summary of the Hydrology of Lakes Winnipegosis
            and Manitoba. Manitoba Water Control and Conservation
            Branch. Winnipeg.

MACKENZIE, G.L.
    1953 Report on Investigations into Measures for the Reduction
          of the Flood Hazard in the Greater Winnipeg Area. Water
          Resources Division. Ottawa.

MACLAY, R.W. and G.R. SCHINER,
    1962 Aquifers in Buried Shore and Glaciofluvial Deposits
          along the Gladstone Beach of Glacial Lake Agassiz near
          Stephen, Minnesota. *U.S. Geological Survey Professional
          Paper 450-D.*

MACLAY, R.W., T.C. WINTER and G.M.PIKE
    1965 Water Resources of the Middle River Watershed, North-
          western Minnesota. *U.S. Geological Survey Hydrologic
          Investigation Atlas*, HA-201.

MACMILLAN, CONWAY
    1896 Observations on the Distribution of Plants Along Shore
          at Lake of the Woods. *Minnesota Geological and Natural
          History Survey Bulletin No. 9*, Part 2, pp. 949-1043.
          Minneapolis.

MACNEISH, RICHARD S.
    1954a Report in Notes and News. *American Antiquity*, Vol. 19,
          No. 3, pp. 306-307. Salt Lake City.

    1954b The Stott Mound and Village Near Brandon, Manitoba. *Annual
          Report of the National Museum of Canada, 1952-53, Bulletin
          132, pp. 20-65.* Ottawa.

    1956 Summary of Archeological Investigation in Southeastern
          Manitoba. *Annual Report of the National Museum of Canada,
          1954-55, Bulletin* 142, pp. 24-25. Ottawa.

    1958a An Introduction to the Archeology of Southeast Manitoba.
          National Museum of Canada, Bulletin 157. Ottawa.

    1958b Preliminary Archeological Investigations in the
          Sierra de Tamaulipas, Mexico. *Transactions American
          Philosophical Society*, n.s., Vol. 48, Part 6.
          Philadelphia.

    1962 Second Annual Report of the Tehuacan Archeological-
          Botanical Project. *Robert S. Peabody Foundation for
          Archeology*. Andover.

MACNEISH, RICHARD S. and KATHERINE CAPES
    1958 The United Church Site on Rock Lake, Manitoba.
          Anthropologica, No. 6, pp. 119-155, Ottawa.

MANLEY, G.
    1951 The Range of Variation of the British Climate.
          Geographical Journal. Vol.117, No.   p. 43. Norman.

MANSON, PHILIP W.
    1957   *Water and Agricultural Land*. University of Minnesota,
          Agricultural Experiment Station.

MARSCHNER, F.J.
    1930   The Original Forests of Minnesota. U.S. Department
          of Agriculture Map on File at Lakes States Forest
          Experiment Station. St. Paul.

MAYCOCK, P.F.
    1961   The Spruce-Fir Forests of the Keweenaw Peninsula,
          Northern Michigan. *Ecology*, Vol. 42, No. 2, pp. 357-365.
          Durham.

MAYER-OAKES, WILLIAM J.
    1962   Manitoba Preceramic Cultures. Dittoed paper presented
          at 1962 Plains Anthropological Conference. Lincoln.

    1963   Manitoba's Earliest Settlers. *Image* (Manitoba Hydro Magazine),
          Christmas Issue, pp. 6-10. Winnipeg.

    1964   Archeological Investigations in the Grand Rapids, Manitoba
          Reservoir. (Unpublished ms. in files of University of
          Manitoba Laboratory of Anthropology.)

    1965   Manitoba Prehistory - 1965. (ms. accepted for publication
          by National Museum of Canada.)

McANDREWS, J. H.
    1966   Postglacial History of Prairie, Savanna, and Forest in
          Northwestern Minnesota. *Memoirs Torrey Botanical Club*,
          Vol. 22, pp. 1-72. Durham.

McANDREWS, J.H., R.E. STEWART, Jr. and R.C. BRIGHT
    1967   Paleoecology of a Prairie Pothole: A Preliminary Report.
          In "Glacial Geology of the Missouri Coteau," edited by
          Lee Clayton, and T.F. Freers, pp. 101-113. *North Dakota
          Geological Survey Miscellaneous Series 30*. Grand Forks.

McCHARLES, A.
    1887   The Mound Builders of Manitoba. *American Journal of
          Archeology*, Vol. 3, Nos. 1 and 2, pp. 70-74. Baltimore.

McVEHIL, G.E. and R.L. PEACE, Jr.
    1965   Some Studies of Lake Effect Snowfall from Lake Erie.
          In "Proceedings, Eighth Conference on Great Lakes Research,"
          edited by M.N. Everett, pp. 262-272. Ann Arbor.

MEYBOOM, PETER
    1966   Groundwater Studies in the Assiniboine River Drainage
          basin. Part 1: The Evaluation of a flow system in
          south-central Saskatchewan. Queen's Printer, Ottawa.

MOFFITT, F.H.
    1959   *Photogrammetry*. International Textbook Co., Scranton, Pa.

MONTGOMERY, HENRY
        1908   Prehistoric Man in Manitoba and Saskatchewan. *American Anthropologist*, Vol. 10, No. 1, pp. 33-40. Menasha.

        1910   The Calf Mountain Mound in Manitoba. *American Anthropologist*, Vol. 12, No. 1, pp. 49-57. Menasha.

MOORE, J.W.
        1958   *A Provincial List of the Flowering Plants, Ferns, and Fern Allies of Clay County, Minnesota*. Department of Botany, University of Minnesota. Minneapolis.

MORRISON, J.P.E.
        1932   A Report on the Mollusca of the Northeastern Wisconsin Lake District. *Wisconsin Academy of Science, Arts and Letters, Transactions*. Vol. 27, No.   p. 357-396. Madison.

MORTON, WILLIAM L.
        1951   The Significance of Site in the Settlement of the American and Canadian Wests. *Agricultural History*, Vol. 25, No. 3, pp. 97-104. Baltimore.

        1957   *History of Manitoba*. University of Toronto Press. Toronto.

MOYER, L.A.
        1910   The Prairie Flora of Southwestern Minnesota. *Minnesota Academy of Science Bulletin*, Vol. 4, No.   pp. 357-378. Minneapolis.

MUNRO, DAVID A.
        1963   Ducks and the Great Plains Wetlands. *Canadian Audubon*, Sept. - Oct. Vol. 25, No. 4, pp. 105-111. Toronto.

        1965   Waterfowl Management in Canada. *30th Transactions, North American Wildlife Conference*. Vol.   No. pp. 212-222.

NASH, RONALD J.
        1963   Northern Manitoba Preceramic Assemblages. (Unpublished ms. in files of University of Manitoba Laboratory of Anthropology.)

        1966   The Arctic Small Tool Tradition in Manitoba. (Unpublished M.A. thesis, University of Calgary.)

NELSON, S.J. and R.D. JOHNSON
        1966   Geology of Hudson Bay Basin. *Canadian Petroleum Geologists, Bulletin*. Vol. 14, No.   pp. 520-578. Calgary.

NEWCOMB, EDGAR A.
        n.d.   Manuscript Reports and Maps on Archeology in the Bagot, Brookdale and Arden Areas. (In files of University of Manitoba Laboratory of Anthropology.)

NICHOLS, H.
    1967   Central Canadian Palynology and its Relevance to the
           Late Quaternary Climatic History of North-West Europe.
           *Proceedings of the Second International Palynological
           Conference, Utrecht, 1966.*

NICKERSON, W.B.
    n.d.   Archeological Evidences as Applied to Southwestern
           Manitoba.   (Manuscript in National Museum of Canada.)

    1914a On an Archeological Reconnaissance of Manitoba, 1913.
           *Summary Report of the Geological Survey for the Calendar
           Year 1913, Department of Mines,*Vol. 22, No. 26, pp. 387-388.
           Ottawa.

NIKIFOROFF, C.C. *et al,*
    1939   Soil Survey (reconnaisance).   The Red River Valley Area
           Minnesota. *U.S. Department of Agriculture, Bureau of
           Chemistry and Soils, Series 1933, No. 25.* Washington.

NIKOFOROFF, C.C.
    1947   The Life History of Lake Agassiz; alternative interpretation.
           American Journal of Science,   Vol. 245, April   pp. 205-239.
           New Haven.

NORMAN, G.W.H.
    1963   Last Pleistocene Ice-front in Chibougamau District,
           Quebec. *Royal Society of Canada, Transactions.* Series 3,
           Vol. 32, Section 4, pp. 69-86.   Ottawa.

NUTTING, C.C.
    1893   Report on Zoological Explorations on the Lower Saskatchewan
           River. *Bulletin of the Laboratory of Natural History,
           State University of Iowa.* Vol. 2, No. 3, pp. 235-293.
           Iowa City.

OGDEN, J.G. III
    1966   Forest History of Ohio. I.   Radiocarbon Dates and Pollen
           Stratigraphy of Silver Lake, Logan County, Ohio. *Ohio
           Journal of Science,* Vol. 66, No. 1, pp. 387-400.
           Bowling Green.

OWEN, D.D.
    1852   Report of a Geological Survey of Wisconsin, Iowa and
           Minnesota.   , Vol.   No.
           p. 178.   Philadelphia.

PACKARD, V.
    1957   *The Hidden Persuaders.*   David McKay Co., Inc.

PALLISER,
    1863   Journals, detailed Reports, etc. presented to Parliament,
           19th May 1863.   , Vol.   No.   P. 41.

PAULSON, Q.F.
     1953   Ground Water in the Fairmont Ava Richland County,
            North Dakota and adjacent area in Minnesota. *North
            Dakota Ground Water Studies*, No. 22. Grand Forks.

PETTERSSEN, S. and P.A. CALABRESE
     1959   On Some Weather Influences Due to Warming of the Air by
            the Great Lakes in Winter. *Journal of Meteorology*, Vol.16,
            No.   pp. 646-652. Boston.

PETTIPAS, LEO F.
     1966   The Lake Agassiz Field Survey 1965. *Manitoba Archeological
            Newsletter*, Vol. III, No. 2, pp. 3-5. Winnipeg.

     1967   The Paleo-Indian in Manitoba. (Unpublished M.A. thesis,
            University of Manitoba.)

POTTER, L.D. and D.R. MOIR
     1961   Phytosociological Study of Burned Dediacuous Woods,
            Turtle Mountains, North Dakota. *Ecology*, Vol. 42,
            No. 3, pp. 468-480. Durham.

POTZGER, J.E.
     1946   Phytosociology of the Primeval Forest in Central-Northern
            Wisconsin and Upper Michigan, and a Brief Post-Glacial
            History of the Lake-Forest Formation. *Ecological Monographs*,
            Vol. 16, No. 3, pp. 211-250. Durham.

PREST, V.K.
     1963   Red Lake-Lansdowne House Area, Northwestern Ontario.
            Surficial Geology. *Geological Survey of Canada, Paper
            63-6*. Ottawa.

PRUD'HOMME, L.A.
     1937   Les Premiers Aborigenes de Manitoba et les Mandans.
            Memoires de Societe Royale du Canada, Series 3, No. 31,
            pp. 165-174.

RAND, W.H.
     n.d.   Indian Cultures of Manitoba. Neolithic Pottery of Manitoba.
            The Pense and Swanston Middens. (Unpublished ms. in files
            of University of Manitoba Laboratory of Anthropology.)

RAND, W.H.
     1941   The Rosser Mound. *Manitoba Calling*, Vol. 5, No. 9,
            pp. Winnipeg.   .

     1945   The Morden Mound on the Wiebe Farm. *Spade and Screen,
            Saskatchewan Archeological Society*, Vol. 2, No. 1,
            pp. 3-4. Regina.

RAND, W.H.,W. DOWNES, P.W. GRANT, R.K. HELGAR, Mr. and Mrs. P.H. STOKES
    n.d.   Archeological Report, Lamprey Falls, Manitoba, 1951-1952.
           (Mimeographed ms. in Files of University of Manitoba
           Laboratory of Anthropology.)

REID, GEORGE K.
    1961   *Ecology of Inland Waters and Estuaries*. Reinhold, New
           York.

RICHMOND, G.M.
    1965   Glaciation of the Rocky Mountains. In "The Quaternary of
           the United States," edited by H.E. Wright, Jr. and
           D.G. Frey. Princeton.

RITCHIE, J.C.
    1956   The Vegetation of Northern Manitoba. I. The Southern
           Spruce Forest Zone. *Canadian Journal of Botany*,
           Vol. 34, No. 4, pp. 523-561. Ottawa.

    1960   The Vegetation of Northern Manitoba. VI. The Lower Hayes
           River Region. *Canadian Journal of Botany*, Vol. 38, No. 5,
           pp. 769-788. Ottawa.

    1962   A Geobotanical Survey of Northern Manitoba. *Arctic
           Institute of North America. Technical Paper*,
           No. 9. Montreal.

    1964   Contributions to the Holocene Paleo-ecology of Westcentral
           Canada. I. The Riding Mountain Area. *Canadian Journal of
           Botany*. Vol. 42, No.   pp. 181-196. Ottawa.

    1966   Aspects of the Late-Pleistocene History of the Canadian
           Flora. In "The Evolution of Canada's Flora," edited by
           R.L. Taylor and R.A. Ludwig, pp. 68-80. University of
           Toronto Press. Toronto.

RITCHIE, J.C. and B. deVRIES
    1964   Contributions to the Holocene Paleoecology of West Central
           Canada, A Late-Glacial Deposit from the Missouri Coteau.
           Canadian Journal of Botany, Vol. 42, No. 6, pp. 677-692.
           Ottawa.

RITCHIE, J.C. and S.LICHTI-FEDEROVICH
    1967   Pollen Dispersal Phenomena in Arctic-subarctic Canada.
           Review of Paleobotany and Palynology. Vol. 1, No. 3,
           pp.   (in press).

RITTENHOUSE, G.
    1934   A Laboratory Study of an Unusual Series of Varved
           Clays From Northern Ontario. *American Journal of
           Science*, Vol. 27, No. 157, pp. 110-120. New Haven.

ROBIN, G. deQ.
    1962   The Ice of the Antarctic. *Scientific American.*
           Vol. 207, No. 3, pp. 132-146. New York.

ROMINGER, J.F. and P.C. RUTLEDGE
    1952   Use of Soil Mechanics Data in Correlations and
           Interpretation of Lake Agassiz Sediments. *Journal of
           Geology,* Vol. 60, No. 2, pp. 160-180. Chicago.

ROSENDAHL, C.O.
    1948   A Contribution to the Knowledge of the Pleistocene Flora
           of Minnesota. *Ecology,* Vol. 29, No. 3, pp. 284-315.
           Durham.

ROWE, J.S.
    1959   Forest Regions of Canada. *Canada Department of Northern
           Affairs and National Resources, Forestry Branch,
           Bulletin 123.* Ottawa.

RUBIN,M. and CORRINNE ALEXANDER
    1958   U.S. Geological Survey Radiocarbon Dates IV. *Science,*
           Vol. 127, No. 3313, pp. 1476-1487. Washington.

RUDD, V.E.
    1951   Geographical Affinities of the Flora of North Dakota.
           The American Midland Naturalist, Vol. 45, No. 3,
           pp. 722-39. Notre Dame.

SATTERLY, JACK
    1937   Glacial Lakes Ponask and Sachigo, District of Kenora,
           (Patricia Portion) Ontario. *Journal of Geology.* Vol. 45,
           No. 7, pp. 790-796. Chicago.

SCHINER, G.R.
    1963   Ground-water Exploration and Test Pumping in the Halma-
           Lake Bronson Area, Kittson and Parts of Marshall and
           Roseau Counties, Minnesota. *Minnesota Division of Water,
           Bulletin 19.* Minneapolis.

SCHWARTZ, M.L.
    1967   The Bruun Theory of Sea-level Rise as a Cause of Shore
           Erosion, *Journal of Geology,* Vol.75, No.   pp. 76-92.
           Chicago.

SCOTT, G.H.
    1963   Uniformitarianism, the Uniformity of Nature, and Paleo-
           ecology. *New Zealand Journal of Geology and Geophysics,*
           Vol. 75, No.   pp. 510-527.

SEARS, WILLIAM H.
    1961   The Study of Social and Religious Systems in North
           American Archeology. *Current Anthropology,* Vol. 2,
           No. 3, pp. 223-247. Chicago.

SELLARDS, E.H.
    1952   *Early Man in America; A Study in Prehistory.* University
           of Texas Press.

SHAY, C.T.
    1965   Postglacial Vegetation Development in Northwestern
           Minnesota, and its Implications for Prehistoric Man.
           (Unpublished M.S. thesis at University of Minnesota.)

    1967a Field Notes Handout, 1967. Paleoecology at Itasca
           Biological Station, University of Minnesota.

    1967b Vegetation History and Human Ecology in the Southern
           Lake Agassiz Basin During the Past 12,000 years.
           Minnesota Museum of Natural History. Occasional Papers.
           Minneapolis.
    n.d.   (Unpublished Ph.D. dissertation, University of Minnesota,
           in preparation).

SIM, V.M.
    1961   A Note on High-level Marine Shells on Fosheim Peninsula,
           Ellesmere Island, N.W.T. *Geographical Bulletin,* No. 16,
           pp. 120-122. Ottawa.

SIMPSON, ALLAN A.
    1965   Fieldwork in the Province of Manitoba - 1965. *Manitoba
           Archeological Newsletter,* Vol. II, No. 4, pp. 4-7.
           Winnipeg.

    1966   Manitoba Fieldwork in 1966. *Manitoba Archeological
           Newsletter.* Vol. III, No. 4, pp. 6-9. Winnipeg.

SKINNER, ALANSON
    1923   Observations on Sapir's "A Note on Sarcee Pottery".
           American Anthropologist, n.s. Vol. 25, No.
           pp. 428-429. Menasha.

SMITH, HARLAN T.
    1923   An Album of Prehistoric Canadian Art. *National Museum
           of Canada, Bulletin 37,* (Plate XLIV, Fig. 6). Ottawa.

STANTON, M.S.
    1947   Pictographs from Trampling Lake, Manitoba. *American
           Antiquity,* Vol. 13, No. 2, pp. 180-181. Menasha.

STEINBRING, JACK
      1964a The Manufacture and Use of Bone Defleshing Tools.
             (Unpublished ms. in Files of University of Manitoba
             Laboratory of Anthropology.)

      1964b Recent Studies Among the Northern Ojibwa. *Manitoba
             Archeological Newsletter*, Vol. 1, No. 4, pp. 9-12.
             Winnipeg.

      1966a A Scottsbluff Projectile Point From Manitoba. *The
             Wisconsin Archaeologist*, Vol. 47, No. 1, New Series,
             pp. 1-7. Madison.

      1966b Old Copper Culture Artifacts in Manitoba. *American
             Antiquity*, Vol. 31, No. 4, pp. 567-574. Salt Lake City.

STEVENS, O.A.
      1950 *Handbook of North Dakota Plants*. North Dakota State
             University, Fargo.

STEWART, R.E. and H.A. KANTRUD
      1967 Proposed Classification of Potholes in the Glaciated
             Region. *Transactions, Wetlands Seminar, Canadian Wildlife
             Service*. Saskatoon.

STOLTMAN, JAMES B.
      n.d. A proposed Method for Systematizing the Modal Analysis of
             Pottery and its Application to the Laurel Focus.
             (Unpublished 1962 M.A. Thesis, University of Minnesota.)

SUTTON, RICHARD W.
      1965 The Whiteshell Boulder Mosaics. *Manitoba Archeological
             Newsletter*, Vol. 2, No. 1, pp. 4-10. Winnipeg.

TAMPLIN, MORGAN J.
      1966 The Glacial Lake Agassiz Survey, 1966, A Preliminary
             Report. (Unpublished ms. in files of Laboratory of
             Anthropology, University of Manitoba.)

TANNER, JOHN
      1956 (A Narrative of his Life with Indians.)
             Ross and Haines. Minneapolis.

TAYLOR, D.W.
      1965 The Study of Pleistocene Non-marine Mollusks in North
             America. In "The Quaternary of the United States,"
             edited by H.E. Wright and D.G. Frey, pp. 597-611.
             Princeton.

THOMAS, HAROLD E.
      1955 Underground Sources of our Water. *The Yearbook of
             Agriculture*, 1955, Superintendent of Documents, Wash.

      1956 Changes in Quantities and Qualities of Ground and
             Surface Waters. In "Man's Role in Changing the Face of
             the Earth," edited by Wm. L. Thomas, Jr., University of
             Chicago Press. Chicago.

THOMAS, WILLIAM L. Jr. (Editor)
    1956   Man's Role in Changing the Face of the Earth.
           University of Chicago Press. Chicago.

TISDALE, E.W., M.A. FOSBERG, and C.E. POULTON
    1966   Vegetation and Soil Development on a Recently Glaciated
           Area Near Mount Robson, British Columbia. *Ecology,*
           Vol. 47, No. 4, pp. 517-523. Durham.

TROUTMAN, M.A. and E.H. WILLIS
    1966   Isotopes, Inc. Radiocarbon Measurements V. *Radiocarbon,*
           Vol. 8, pp. 161-203. New Haven.

TUTHILL, S.J.
    1962   A Checklist of North Dakota Pleistocene and Recent
           Mollusca. *Sterkiana,* Vol. 8, No. pp. 12-18. Columbus.

    1963a Corrections and Additions to the Checklist of North
           Dakota Pleistocene and Recent Mollusca. *Sterkiana,*
           Vol. 10, No.   pp. 29-30. Columbus.

    1963b Molluscan Fossils from Upper Glacial Lake Agassiz
           Sediments in Red Lake County, Minnesota; *North Dakota
           Geological Survey, Miscellaneous Series. n.20
           Proceedings of the North Dakota Academy of Science,*
           V. 17, No.   pp. 96-101. Grand Forks.

    1964   Unusually well-preserved *Lampsilis luteolus* and
           molluscan fauna in post-Hypsithermal sediments.
           Compass, V. 41, No. pp. 149-155.

    1966   Paleoecologic Implications of Recent Superglacial and
           Proglacial Molluscan Habitats (abstract). Program,
           79th annual Meeting. *Geological Society of America,*
           San Francisco, 14-16 Nov. 1966,   pp.223-225.

TUTHILL, S.J., and W.M. LAIRD
    1963   Molluscan Fauna of Some Alkaline Lakes and Sloughs in
           Southern Central North Dakota. *The Nautilus,* Vol. 33,
           No. pp. 47-55; 61-90. Havertown.

TUTHILL, S.J., W.M. LAIRD, and LEE CLAYTON
    1964   A Comparison of a Fossil Pleistocene Molluscan Fauna
           From North Dakota with a Recent Molluscan Fauna From
           Minnesota. *American Midland Naturalist,* Vol. 71,
           pp. 344-362. Notre Dame.

TUTHILL, S.J., W.M. LAIRD, and R.J. KRESL
    1964   Fossiliferous Marl Beneath Lower Campbell (Glacial Lake
           Agassiz) Beach Sediments. *Proceedings of the North
           Dakota Academy of Science,* Vol. 18, No.   pp. 135-140.
           Grand Forks.

TYRREL, J.B.
     1889   Notes to Accompany a Preliminary Map of the Duck and
            Riding Mountains in North-western Manitoba.
            *Annual Report of the Geological and Natural History
            Survey of Canada for 1887-88,* No. III, Part I,
            pp. 1-16. Ottawa.

     1892   Report on North-western Manitoba with Portions of the
            Adjacent Districts of Assiniboine and Saskatchewan.
            Annual Report of the Geological Survey of Canada,
            No. 5, Section E. pp.   Ottawa.

     1893   North-western Manitoba with Portions of the Districts
            of Assiniboia and Saskatchewan. *Geological and Natural
            History Survey of Canada, Report of Progress.* 1890-91,
            Vol. 5, Part E.

     1896   Is the Land Around Hudson Bay at Present Rising?
            American Journal of Science, 4th series, Vol. 2
            pp. 200-205. New Haven.

     1896   The Genesis of Lake Agassiz. *Journal of Geology,* Vol. 4,
            No. pp. 811-815. Chicago.

UNITED STATES DEPARTMENT OF AGRICULTURE
     1941   *Climate and Man.* United States Department of Agriculture
            Yearbook. Washington.

UPHAM, WARREN
     1880   Preliminary Report on the Geology of Central and Western
            Minnesota. *Eighth Annual Report for the Year 1879 of
            the Geological and Natural History Survey of Minnesota,*
            Vol.   pp. 70-125. St. Peter, Minnesota.

     1890   Report on Exploration of the Glacial Lake Agassiz in
            Manitoba. *Annual Report for 1888-1889 of the Geological
            Survey of Canada,* Vol. IV, Section E. pp. 156, Ottawa.

     1892   Geographic Limits of Species of Plants in the Basin of
            the Red River of the North. *Boston Society of Natural
            History,* Vol. 25, No.   pp. 140-178.   Boston.

     1895   The Glacial Lake Agassiz. *United States Geological Survey*
            Monograph No. 25. Washington.

     1917   Letter in Reply to Johnston, 1916. *Bulletin of the
            Geological Society of America,* Vo. 28, No.   p. 146,
            New York.

VAN DER SCHALIE, HENRY
    1962   Mussel Distribution in Relation to Former Stream
          Confluence in Northern Michigan, U.S.A. *Malacologia*,
          Vol. 1, No. 2, pp. 227-236. Ann Arbor.

    1965   Agricultural Chemical Safety. *California State Polytechnic*
          College, San Luis Obispo.

VICKERS, CHRIS
    n.d.   Check list of Manitoba Mounds. (Unpublished ms. in files
          of University of Manitoba Laboratory of Anthropology.)

    1945   Archeology in the Rock and Pelican Lake Area of South-
          Central Manitoba. *American Antiquity*, Vol. 11, No.2,
          pp. 88-94. Menasha.

    1946a Archeology in the Rock and Pelican Lake Area of Southern
          Manitoba. *Papers Read Before the Historical and Scientific*
          Society of Manitoba, Season 1945-46, pp. 3-9. Winnipeg.

    1946b Aboriginal Backgrounds in Southern Manitoba. *Papers Read*
          Before the Historical and Scientific Society of Manitoba.
          Season 1945-46, pp. 3-9. Winnipeg.

    1946c Notes and News. *American Antiquity*, Vol. 12, No. I,
          pp. 68-69. Menasha

    1947a Burial Traits of the Headwaters Lakes Aspect in Manitoba.
          American Antiquity, Vol. 13, No. 2, pp. 109-114. Menasha.

    1947b Indian Hunting. *Game and Fish*, December Issue, p. 17,
          Winnipeg.

    1948a Unique Artifact from Manitoba. *American Antiquity*,
          Vol. 14, No. 2, pp. 126-127. Menasha.

    1948b Archeological Report, 1945 *Projects of the Historical and*
          Scientific Society of Manitoba. Winnipeg.

    1948c Archeological Report, 1946 *Projects of the Historical and*
          Scientific Society of Manitoba. Winnipeg.

    1948d The Historical Approach and the Headwaters Lakes Aspect.
          Plains Archeological Conference Newsletter, Vol.
          No. 3, pp. 8-11. Lincoln.

    1948e Archeological Report, 1947. *Projects of the Historical*
          and Scientific Society of Manitoba. Winnipeg.

    1948f Cultural Affinity in the Minnesota-Manitoba Region.
          Minnesota Archeologist, Vol. 14, No. 2, pp. 38-41,
          Minneapolis.

    1949a A Page From the Past, In "Southwestern Manitoba". Travel
          and Publicity Bureau. Winnipeg.

VICKERS, CHRIS
    1949b Archeological Report, 1948. *Projects of the Historical and Scientific Society of Manitoba*. Winnipeg.

    1949c The Pine Fort on the Assiniboine River. *The Canadian Historical Review*, March issue, Vol.   No.   pp. 66-68. Ottawa.

    1949d How the Indian Solved His Housing Problem. *Outdoor Canada*, November issue, Vol.   No.   pp. 12-14. Dryden.

    1949e Over-Hunting. Past and Present. *Game and Fish*, Vol. No. 4, pp. 12-13. Winnipeg.

    1949f Report for Manitoba. Laboratory of Anthropology, University of Nebraska, *Proceedings of the Fifth Plains Conference for Archeology, Note Book* No. 1, pp. 32-34. Lincoln.

    1949g Manitoba Pottery Types. Laboratory of Anthropology, University of Nebraska, *Proceedings of the Fifth Plains Conference for Archeology, Note Book* Vol.   No. 1, p. 85. Lincoln.

    1950a Shell Object from Manitoba. *American Antiquity*, Vol. 16, No. 2, p. 164. Salt Lake City.

    1950b Archeological Report, 1949. *Projects of the Historical and Scientific Society of Manitoba*. Winnipeg.

    1950c Report in Notes and News. *American Antiquity*, Vol. 16, No. 2, p. 184. Salt Lake City.

    1951a Archeological Report, 1950. *Projects of the Historical and Scientific Society of Manitoba*. Winnipeg.

    1951b Primitive Fishing Gear in the Fur Trade Days. *Northern Sportsman*, May, Vol. No.   pp. 12-13. Winnipeg.

    1952 Canada had History too. *Onward*, March issue, p. 187, United Church Publishing House. Toronto.

    1953 The Assiniboine of Manitoba. *Papers Read Before the Historical and Scientific Society of Manitoba*, Series 3, No. 8, pp. 40-46. Winnipeg.

VICKERS, CHRIS and R.D. BIRD
    1949 A Copper Trade Object From the Headwaters Lakes Aspect in Manitoba. *American Antiquity*, Vol. 15, No. 2, pp. 157-160. Menasha.

WALKER, J.M.
    1959   Vegetation Studies in the Delta Marsh, Delta, Manitoba.
           (Unpublished Manuscript, University of Manitoba.)

    1965   Vegetational Changes in Falling Water Levels in the
           Delta Marsh, Manitoba. (Unpublished Manuscript, University
           of Manitoba.)

WANEK, W.J., and R.L. BURGESS
    1965   Floristic Composition of the Sand Prairies of Southeastern
           North Dakota. *Proceedings of the North Dakota Academy of
           Science*, Vol. 19, No.   pp. 26-40. Grand Forks.

WARKENTIN, JOHN
    1964   *The Western Interior of Canada*. McClelland and Stewart
           Limited. Toronto.

WARREN, G.K.
    1868   On Certain Physical Features of the Upper Mississippi
           River. *American Naturalist*, Vol. II, No.   pp. 497-502.
           Lancaster.

WATTS, W.A., and R.C. BRIGHT
    1967   Pollen, Seed and Mollusk Analysis of a Sediment Core
           From Pickerel Lake, Northeastern North Dakota. (In press)

WATTS, W.A., and T.C. WINTER
    1966   Plant Macrofossils from Kirchner Marsh, Minnesota.
           A Paleoecological Study. *Geological Society of America
           Bulletin*, Vol. 77, Part 2, pp. 1339-60. Burlington.

WATTS, W.A. and H.E. WRIGHT Jr.
    1966   Late-Wisconsin Pollen and Seed Analysis from the Nebraska
           Sandhills. *Ecology*, Vol. 47, No. 2, pp. 202-10. Durham.

WEAVER, J.E.
    1954   *North American Prairie*. Johnsen Publishing Co.,
           Lincoln.

    1960   Flood Plain Vegetation of the Central Missouri Valley and
           Contacts of Woodland with Prairie. *Ecological Monographs*,
           Vol. 30, No. 1, pp. 37-64. Durham.

WEST, R.G.
    1961   Late-and Postglacial Vegetational History in Wisconsin,
           Particularly Changes Associated with the Valders Advance.
           American Journal of Science. Vol. 259, No.10, pp. 766-783.
           New Haven.

WETTLAUFER, BOYD
    n.d.   Archeological Survey of Manitoba. (Unpublished ms. in
           files of National Museum of Canada.)

WETTLAUFER, BOYD (compiler) and WILLIAM J. MAYER-OAKES (editor)
    1960   The Long Creek Site. *Saskatchewan Museum of Natural
           History, Anthropological Series*, No. 2.   Regina.

WHITEHEAD, D.R.
    1965   Palynology and Pleistocene Phytogeography of Unglaciated
           Eastern North America. In "The Quaternary of the United
           States", edited by H.E. Wright, Jr. and D.G. Frey.
           Princeton.

WHITMANN, N.H. *et al.*
    1941   Grass. *North Dakota Agricultural College Experiment
           Station Bulletin 300*. Fargo.

WEIR, THOMAS R.
    1960   Economic Atlas of Manitoba.   *Manitoba Department of
           Industry and Commerce.*

WILLETT, H.C.
    1949   Long Period Fluctuations of the General Circulation of
           the Atmosphere. *Journal of Meteorology*. Vol. 6, No. 1,
           pp. 34-50, Boston.

WILLEY, GORDON R.
    1953   Prehistoric Settlement Patterns in the Viru Valley, Peru.
           Bureau of American Ethnology, Bulletin 155. Washington.

WILLEY, GORDON R. and PHILIP PHILLIPS
    1958   *Method and Theory in American Archeology.*   University of
           Chicago Press.   Chicago.

WINCHELL, N.H.
    1880   *Eighth Annual
           Report for the Year 1879 of the Geological and Natural
           History Survey of Minnesota*, Vol.   No.   pp.
           St. Peter, Minnesota.

WINTEMBERG, W.J.
    1942   The Geographical Distribution of Aboriginal Pottery in
           Canada. *American Antiquity*, Vol. 8, No. 2, pp. 129-141.
           Menasha.

WISSLER, CLARK
    1923   *Man and Culture.* T.Y. Crowell.   New York.

WITTRY, W.
    1951   A preliminary Study of the Old Copper Complex. *The
           Wisconsin Archeologist*, n.s. Vol. 32, No. 1, pp. 1-18.
           Milwaukee.

WOODBURY, R.B.
    1961 Climatic Changes and Prehistoric Agriculture in the
          Southwestern United States. *Annals of the New York
          Academy of Science*, Vol. 95 No.   pp.235-250.
          New York.

WRIGHT, JAMES V.
    1967a The Laurel Tradition and the Middle Woodland Period.
          National Museum of Canada Bulletin 217. Ottawa.

    1967b Cree Culture History in the Southern Indian Lake Region.
          (in press).

WRIGHT, H.E., Jr.
    1949 Trees. *The Yearbook of Agriculture*. United States
          Department of Agriculture. Washington.

    1960 Soils of the North Central Region of the United States,
          North Central Regional Publication No. 76, *University
          of Wisconsin Agriculture Experimental Station Bulletin
          544.*

    1963 Two Pollen Diagrams from southeastern Minnesota. Problems
          in the regional late and post-glacial Vegetational History.
          The Geological Society of America Bulletin, Vol. 74, Part 2,
          pp. 1371-1396. New York.

    1964 Aspects of the Early Postglacial Forest Succession in
          the Great Lakes Region. *Ecology*, Vol. 45, No. 3, p.439.
          Durham.
    1964 The Classification of the Wisconsin Glaciation. *Journal
          of Geology*, Vol. 72, No. 5, pp. 628-637. Chicago.

    1965 Glacial History of Western Minnesota and Adjacent South
          Dakota; p. 32-38 in C.B. Schultz and H.T.U. Smith, eds.
          *Guidebook for Field Conference C, Upper Mississippi
          Valley, International Association for Quaternary Research*,
          Aug. 13-29, 1965, Nebraska Academy of Science, Lincoln.

WRIGHT, H.E.,Jr. and D. G. FREY (Editors)
    1965 *The Quaternary of the United States*. Princeton University
          Press. Princeton.

WRIGHT, H.E., Jr and R.V. RUHE
    1965 Glaciation of Minnesota and Iowa. In "The Quaternary of
          the United States", edited by H.E. Wright Jr. and D.G. Frey,
          pp. 29-41. Princeton.

ZEUNER, F.E.
    1963 *A History of Domesticated Animals*.
          Hutchinson, London.

ZIMMERMAN, ERICH W.
     1964   *Introduction to World Resources*.   Harper and Row,
            New York.

ZOLTAI, S.C.
     1961   Glacial History of Part of Northwestern Ontario.
            Proceedings, Geological Association of Canada,
            Vol. 13, No.   pp. 61-83. Toronto.

     1963   Glacial Features of the Canadian Lakehead Area. *Canadian
            Geographer,* Vol. 7, No. 3, pp. 101-115. Montreal.

     1965a Kenora-Rainy River, Surficial Geology.   *Ontario Department
            Lands and Forests*. Map S165.

     1965b Thunder Bay, Surficial Geology, *Ontario Department Lands
            and Forests,* Map S265.

     1965   Glacial Features of the Quetico-Nipigon Area, Ontario.
            Canadian Journal of Earth Sciences. (in press). Ottawa.

ZUMBERGE, J.H.
     1952   The Lakes of Minnesota -- Their Origin and Classification.
            Minnesota Geological Survey Bulletin 35. Minneapolis.

     1958   *Elements of Geology*. Wiley, New York.

CORRIGENDA*

P. xv, Fig. 61   : for "Russel" substitute "Russell".
P. 17, Para. 5, L. 6: delete comma after "perhaps".
P. 19,   "   3, "   4: add "s" to "term".
P. 22,   "   3, " 11: for "timer" substitute "timber".
P. 29,   "   4, "   7: insert comma after "criticisms".
P. 29,   "   5, "   6: for "vacant" substitute "recent".
P. 30,   "   6, "   6: for "early" substitute "late".
P. 33,   "   3, " 10: for "column" substitute "code".
P. 33,   "   6, "   2: delete comma after "level".
P. 34,   "   2, "   2: for "two" substitute "three".
P. 34,   "   2, " 10: add the sentence, "The University of
                         Saskatchewan has also embarked on a
                         similar program (supported by NRC) with
                         similar results."
P. 34,   "   3, " 13: insert comma after "essentially".
P. 97,   "   1, "   9: for "fill" substitute "till".
P. 97,   "   1, " 11: for this line substitute --
                         "ings in Fargo. Lake Agassiz Deposits
                         (from the surface downward):".
P. 97,   "   (2), "   3: delete final "s" from "insects".
P. 98, Caption, "   2: for "Dotted" substitute "Heavy solid".
P. 99, Para. 1, "   1: for the first sentence substitute "A
                         subaerial Agassiz I-II interval in the
                         southern basin is indicated also by (1)
                         a desiccation zone in the upper part of
                         Unit 4, (2) a local disconformity between
                         Unit 4 and overlying beds, and (3) linear
                         sand bodies (interpreted as fluvial de-
                         posits) intercalated between units 1
                         and 4."
P. 99,   "   1, " 10: place entire line in brackets.
P. 99,   "   (1), "   8: place the complete sentence in brackets.
P.101,   "   5, "   6: insert ",P" after "Fig. 15".
P.109, Caption, "   3: for "bluffs" substitute "terraces".
P.112,   "   "   2: for "Bluffs" substitute "Terraces".
P.125, Para. 4, "   1: delete comma after "(1967)".
P.141,   "   7, "   4: for "B" substitute "D".
P.160,   "   2, " 10: for "sailors on" substitute "sailors in".
P.160,   "   2, " 23: period should follow reference in
                         parentheses.
P.163,   "   2, " 14: insert "of" after "mechanics".

* This series of corrections to the original edition was compiled by the editor in February, 1969, based on responses from
fourteen of the authors to his request for such corrections.
Although included with the second printing of the book, these
corrections do not include any substantial additions or modifications to the contents of the 1967 printing. In the entries
listed above, both complete and partial paragraphs have been
counted to derive the location statement for each correction.

CORRIGENDA (continued)

P.163, Para. 3, L. 5: insert "not" after "may".
P.169,   "   2, " 12: last word should be ", as".
P.169,   "   2, " 13: insert comma before "follows".
P.169,   "   4, " 6: period should follow reference in
                        parentheses.
P.176,   "   3, " 22: for "inklingking" substitute "inklinking".
P.178,   "   3, " 6: add "n" to "America".
P.178,   "   3, " 11: period should follow reference in
                        parentheses.
P.179,   "   5, " 7: period should follow reference in
                        parentheses.
P.179,   "   6, " 2-3: period should follow reference in
                        parentheses.
P.179,   "   6, " 8: period should follow reference in
                        parentheses.
P.182,   "   1, " 5: period should follow reference in
                        parentheses.
P.183,   "   1, " 6: period should follow reference in
                        parentheses.
P.190,   "   2, " 1: insert *"quadrula"* after *"Quadrula"*.
P.195,   "   3, " 12: for "on" substitute "one".
P.195,   "   5, " 3: insert "high" after "possibly".
P.253,   "   1, " 5: delete "e" from "Rose-".
P.255,   "   3, " 2: insert "mm." after "0.5".
P.257, Table 19,"   4: for "B. pumula" substitute "B. pumila".
P.258,   "   19,"   4: for "Artemisia" substitute "A. ludo-
                        viciana".
P.260,   "   20,Col.3: read "F. pennsylvanica".
P.261, Caption, L. 4: insert parentheses around "1948".
P.267, Para. 1, " 2: for "seim-aquatic" substitute "semi-
                        aquatic".
P.267,   "   3, " 10: insert "was formed but" after "peat".
P.267,   "   5, " 2: for "line" substitute "pine".
P.268,   "   3, " 3-4: delete the words "and type".
P.268,   "   3, " 13: delete "for".
P.269,   "   1, " 4: insert "Cornell College," after "State
                        College,".
P.342,   "   3, " 4: insert a period after "(MacNeish 1958a)".
P.366,   "   2, " 10: for "Avon Lea" substitute "Avonlea".
P.382, Bell,C.N."   2: for *"Institude"* substitute *"Institute"*.
       1886a
P.394, Joyes   "   2: insert "in preparation" after "Manitoba".
P.402, Pettipas "   1: Revised title should read, "Paleo-Indian
       1967   Manifestations in Manitoba: their spatial
                     and temporal relationships with the
                     Campbell strandline."
P.405, Stanton "   1: for "Trampling" substitute "Tramping".
P.408, Tyrrel   "   4: insert "240" before "pp.".
       1892

Comparative vertebrate endocrinology

*For Hans Heller and Harry Waring
who introduced me to
comparative endocrinology*

Comparative
vertebrate endocrinology

P. J. BENTLEY

Mount Sinai School of Medicine of
The City University of
New York

CAMBRIDGE UNIVERSITY PRESS

CAMBRIDGE
LONDON · NEW YORK · MELBOURNE

Published by the Syndics of the Cambridge University Press
The Pitt Building, Trumpington Street, Cambridge CB2 IRP
Bentley House, 200 Euston Road, London NW1 2DB
American Branch: 32 East 57th Street, New York, N.Y. 10022
296 Beaconsfield Parade, Middle Park, Melbourne 3206, Australia

© Cambridge University Press 1976

Library of Congress catalogue card number: 75–10235

   hard covers ISBN: 0521 20726 6
   paperback ISBN: 0521 09935 8

First published 1976

Composed in Great Britain by
William Clowes & Sons Limited, London, Colchester and Beccles
Printed in the United States of America by Vail-Ballou Press, Inc.,
Binghamton, New York

Contents

[v]

Preface

This book has been written primarily for use as a textbook by undergraduate, as well as graduate, students. It is hoped that it may serve as a basis for course work in Comparative Endocrinology and also as an auxiliary text to aid the teaching of Comparative Animal Physiology. In order to gain most from this book, the reader should have a basic knowledge of zoology and animal physiology. I have, nevertheless, attempted to put the endocrinology that is described into a broader biological framework by relating it to the animal's physiology, ecology and evolutionary background. This is one of the reasons why I have departed from the more usual format of previous textbooks in this area which generally deal with each endocrine gland in succession, chapter by chapter. Instead, I have attempted to describe certain broad and basic biological processes the functioning of which is often coordinated by the secretion from several endocrine glands.

No attempt has been made to describe invertebrate endocrinology as the rapid growth of this area really justifies a separate textbook. The book by K. G. Highnam and L. Hill (*Comparative Endocrinology of the Invertebrates*, Elsevier: Amsterdam, 1970) deals admirably with this subject.

It has not been possible in a book of this nature to give a complete list of original references. There are far too many of these and many of the earlier observations are already a part of the 'classical literature'. Instead, I have attempted to refer the reader to more recent papers and reviews that contain references to the material described and can act as useful 'starting points' for those students who wish to study the subject further. In order to keep abreast of developments in the various subject areas described, the current literature should be consulted. The principal journals where papers on these subjects are published are: *General and Comparative Endocrinology*, *Journal of Endocrinology*, *Endocrinology* and *Comparative Biochemistry and Physiology*. There are, in addition, many papers that appear in the standard physiological journals, especially *Journal of Physiology* and *American Journal of Physiology*.

P.J.B.

Mount Sinai School of Medicine of
The City University of New York
September 1974

[ix]

Some commonly used abbreviations in endocrinology

ACTH   adrenocorticotrophic hormone
ADH   antidiuretic hormone
AMP   adenosine 3',5'-monophosphate
AVP   arginine-vasopressin
CBG   cortisol-binding globulin
COMT   catechol-O-methyl-transferase
CRH   corticotrophin-releasing hormone (= CRF)
CT   calcitonin
FSH   follicle-stimulating hormone
GH   growth hormone
Gn-RH   gonadotrophin-releasing hormone (= LH/FSH-RH)
HCG   human chorionic gonadotrophin
HCS   human chorionic somatomammotrophin (= HPL)
HIOMT   hydroxyindole-O-methyl-transferase
HPL   human placental lactogen
HTF   heterothyrotrophic factor
ICSH   interstitial cell-stimulating hormone (= LH)
-IF   – inhibiting-factor
-IH   – inhibiting-hormone
LH   luteinizing hormone (= ICSH)
LTH   luteotrophic hormone (= prolactin)
LVP   lysine-vasopressin
MAO   monoamine oxidase
MI   melanophore index
MSH   melanocyte- (or melanophore-) stimulating hormone
MRH   melanocyte-stimulating hormone-releasing hormone
PNMT   phenylethanolamine-N-methyl-transferase
P-   prolactin (prefix as in P-RH)
PTH   parathormone
-RF   – releasing factor
-RH   – releasing hormone
-R-IH   – release-inhibiting hormone
SHBG   sex hormone-binding globulin
T_3 tri-iodothyronine

T_4	tetra-iodothyronine (= thyroxine)
TBG	thyroid hormone-binding globulin
TRH	thyrotrophin-releasing hormone
TSH	thyroid-stimulating hormone (= thyrotrophin)

1.   Introduction

This book describes a method of transferring information within vertebrates. Such communication is necessary in order to coordinate physiological processes with each other and to the happenings in the external environment. Even unicellular organisms synchronize their various internal life processes. In such small creatures, however, local accumulations of metabolites may exert a direct control on biochemical reactions, while external stimuli have relatively widespread effects so that specialized pathways for communication may not be as necessary. Thus when the distances involved are short, physical processes such as conduction, convection and diffusion may be adequate for the integration of the physiological processes. Nevertheless, even unicellular organisms possess specific coordinating systems such as that seen in the protozoan *Tetrahymena* (Blum, 1967) which possesses adrenaline. This hormone has similar metabolic actions in this protozoan to those which it has in vertebrates.

The problems of communication and coordination are greater in multi-cellular than in unicellular organisms. There are several reasons for this, especially their larger size. As the linear distances between the different parts of an animal increase, simple physical communications become relatively slower and less precise, and so not as effective. In multicellular organisms, the cells are usually specialized and perform different functions which, in combination, are essential for the animal's life. Thus some tissues may be concerned with the formation of reproductive germ cells, several others with the preparation of suitable nutritive materials and yet others with building morphological structures. The ultimate successful completion of these processes will be determined by the effectiveness of the communication between the tissues themselves and the external environment.

The transfer of information in animals

There are three principal ways by which cells in multicellular organisms can communicate with each other. Firstly, when they are in close juxtaposition, and are only separated by narrow fluid-filled spaces, direct electrical and chemical interactions can occur. Cells also maintain some

[1]

structural connections with each other across which they may also communicate. Secondly, contact between more remote cells can be maintained along tracts of nerve cells which are merely tissues that are specialized for such exchanges of information. Thirdly, chemicals may be released, for example from the endocrine glands, into the blood which carries them to special sites that are physicochemically programmed to react and respond to them.

The endocrine glands are tissues that, unlike exocrine glands, have no ducts but release their secretions, called 'hormones', directly into the blood passing through them. It is with the diversity of such hormonally controlled processes that we are going to be principally concerned in this book. It should, however, always be recalled that the endocrine gland represents only a single facet of the animal's communication network, and that nerves are also important. Endocrinologists and neurophysiologists have often only concentrated on their own special fields of study to the relative exclusion of the rest of the animal's physiology. This is unfortunate as the complete animal is an academically and esthetically pleasing thing to see and contemplate, and any single facet taken from the whole becomes less interesting and is physiologically nonsensical. The relations of nerves and endocrines, however, can also be considered from a more direct standpoint as it is apparent that the functions of each are related to each other. They are often mutually interdependent and may even act together to control a single process. Nerve cells thus can respond to hormones in a manner that influences behavior and endocrine glands often receive information and directions from the brain. Both hormones and nerves can act together to control the melanophores in certain fishes. Some hormones, including adrenaline, vasopressin and oxytocin, are even made by nerve cells.

Neural versus humoral coordination

It is uncertain which came first; nerves or hormones. Why do animals have both? It may help us to understand hormones if we compare their respective properties and roles in the body.

The neural transfer of information occurs along distinct morphological pathways made up of chains of nerve cells with their long axons. Transmission along these avenues is fast (up to about 100 m/sec) and is directed precisely to specific sites in the body. Neural transmission involves a series of electrical events interrupted at intervals by a local release of chemicals (transmitters), and is concluded by the release of these, principally acetylcholine or a catecholamine (such as noradrenaline) close to the effector tissue. Such a transmitter is then rapidly destroyed near its site of action. Further stimulation will be dependent on subsequent neural transmission.

The effect is thus rapid in onset, short in duration and can be localized with considerable accuracy.

The hormones, on the other hand, are released into the blood which carries them towards their effector site(s). In most instances this is outside the cardiovascular system so that the hormone must also cross capillaries and diffuse through the intercellular spaces to the site of its action. Not surprisingly, hormonal responses are slower than those mediated by nerves. Hormones are dispersed very widely in the body and so come into contact with a great variety of cells with which an interaction, in most instances, would not be fruitful. The problem of ensuring that hormones only act at specific sites is largely solved by the multiplicity in their chemical structures. (There are over 40 different known hormones in a mammal.) Complementing such variations are parallel differences in the chemical structures of the sites where they interact ('receptors') with their target (or 'effector') cells.

A hormone can exert widespread effects by interacting with different effector tissues (for instance estrogens act on the uterus, mammary glands, liver, brain, etc.). The characteristics of the receptors in each may differ just as the response will vary. A hormone thus may act very specifically at each of several sites in the body and yet, at the same time, exert many different actions.

Perhaps the most physiologically significant difference between neural and humoral communication is in the duration of the actions of the transmitters involved. Because their transmitters are rapidly destroyed, nerves must be repetitively stimulated if their effects are to be prolonged. While hormones also have a finite period of survival, the duration of their effects varies from less than a minute to several days. Some hormones, once released into the circulation, survive in it for many hours. When some reach their receptor sites, the initiated response may be of a persistent nature that is not readily terminated. Thus if an endocrine gland is removed, it may be several days before physiological signs of its absence became apparent. Hormones are thus sometimes described as exerting their effects slowly but persistently, in contrast to the more rapid and transient actions of nerves. There are, however, exceptions to such a generalization.

What is comparative endocrinology?

Comparative endocrinology concerns the study of the endocrine glands in different species of animals, both vertebrates and invertebrates. Its aims are analogous to the older and more classical disciplines of comparative anatomy and comparative physiology. The prime academic objective is to reconstruct evolutionary pathways by the study of extant species. Fig. 1.1 shows the phylogenetic relationships of the vertebrates and this emphasizes

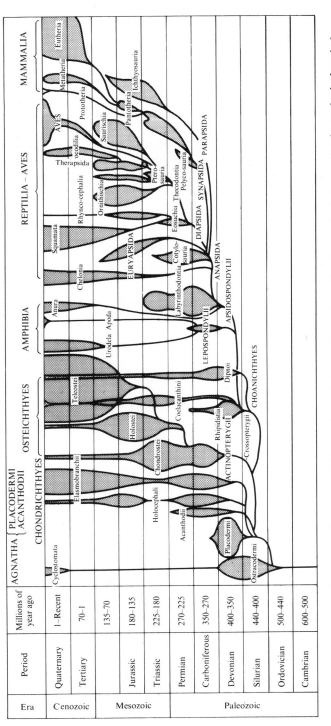

Fig. 1.1. A classification of vertebrates in relation to their phylogenetic origins and a time scale, in terms of paleontological periods. (From Torey, 1971.)

the extant groups which may be particularly interesting in such studies. The mere examination of the endocrine system of some bizarre and exotic vertebrate does not alone constitute 'Comparative Endocrinology' (it may be 'Animal Endocrinology') unless the data can be considered in relation to that in other, phyletically related species. Such information can be used to help confirm, complete and even extend our knowledge of the phylogenetic relationships between vertebrates and to follow the evolution of endocrine mechanisms. The lungfishes (Dipnoi) may afford us an example. These fishes have long been considered, on the basis of morphological information, to be close to the original line of evolution connecting the bony fishes (Osteichthyes) and the Amphibia. As we shall see later, homologous vertebrate hormones often exhibit considerable differences in their chemical structure. Many such differences are apparent between the hormones in fishes and tetrapods. The structure of several hormones present in lungfishes, however, show a greater similarity to those in tetrapods than those in other fishes. For instance, a neurohypophysial hormone called mesotocin is present in amphibians, reptiles and birds but in bony fishes the homologous hormone is isotocin (which differs from mesotocin by a single amino acid substitution) with the exception of the lungfishes, which have mesotocin. It has also been found that the growth hormone and prolactin present in lungfishes are more like those in tetrapods than in other fishes.

Apart from contributing to the over-all phyletic study of vertebrates, the comparative endocrinologist aspires to reconstruct the lines of evolution within the endocrine system itself. This can be done by examining and comparing in different species, the morphology of the endocrine tissues, the structures and activities, both immunological and pharmacological, of their secreted hormones and their different physiological roles.

The uses of comparative endocrinology

The classic, or academic aims, of comparative endocrinology have been described above. The provision of such intellectual satisfaction is not, however, sufficient justification for all! There are, indeed, a number of other contributions that such studies can make to biology, and some examples of these are given below.

The process of reproduction in vertebrates is dependent on the endocrine secretions and an understanding of this relationship can provide information that may be usefully applied when, for esthetic or economic reasons, we may wish to increase, or decrease, the fecundity of a species. This type of study thus constitutes a contribution to the field of 'biological control' (Bern, 1972).

Knowledge of the endocrine system in man has largely been made possible by experiments on other animals. This has principally involved mammals like rats, rabbits, and monkeys but also some more exotic and bizarre creatures. Quantitative measurements of gonadotrophins and melanocyte-stimulating hormone (MSH) were originally made (and sometimes are still) using the responses of the clawed toad (*Xenopus laevis*), while prolactin levels can be measured by its effects on the pigeon's crop-sac or on the behavior of a newt. Oxytocin is assayed by utilizing its ability to decrease the blood pressure of chickens, and the rate of water movement across the toad's urinary bladder can be used to distinguish between two, chemically different, mammalian antidiuretic hormones (ADHs).

The responsiveness of a toad's urinary bladder to ADH and aldosterone is used to study the 'mechanism of action' of these hormones on membrane permeability. Such preparations provide useful 'models' of hormonal effects on the mammalian kidney.

The relationship of the structure of a molecule, to its biological activity, is a field of considerable interest to biologists. The diversity, or polymorphism, in the structure of vertebrate hormones, together with their disparate effects on different tissues and in various species, offers a natural 'laboratory' for such studies. Nature has had a long time and wide opportunities to experiment with the effects of changes in molecular structures on the activities of such excitants. At present, this is most clearly seen among the neurohypophysial hormones of which there are at least nine known chemical variants among the vertebrates. These hormones are peptides containing eight amino acids and often only differ from one another by a substitution at a single chemical locus. They are very reactive molecules and can exert actions at many different sites ranging from the uterus and mammary gland to blood vessels, the kidney, and the amphibian skin and urinary bladder. Analogous effector tissues in different phyletic groups exhibit different abilities to respond to each such hormone, be it a natural one or a variant made in the chemist's laboratory. There are available, and in use, more than 20 different effector-preparations that can be used to study the effects of changes in chemical structure among these hormones on its biological effectiveness. Natural variants of hormones, in which the biological activity has been altered in some way, may be of potential use to man. For instance, calcitonin (a hormone concerned with the regulation of calcium in the body) from the salmon ultimobranchial bodies is far more potent in man than the natural hormone he possesses.

The diversity of vertebrates as a background for endocrine variation

There are some 42 000 extant species of vertebrate animals. The vertebrates originated some 400 million years ago as creatures who apparently lived in the sea or, possibly, in fresh water. They subsequently evolved and occupied almost every conceivable habitat in the oceans, in fresh-water rivers and lakes, and on the land. Their abodes range from the cold polar regions to hot equatorial ones, from deserts to swamps, from high mountains to the ocean deeps. The considerable morphological and physiological diversity of vertebrates mirrors their success in this multitude of environmental conditions. It is thus not surprising to find that the endocrine system exhibits inter-specific differences that reflect adaptations to such different environments. Nevertheless, it is also somewhat unexpected to find that considerable similarities are still apparent in the endocrine systems of species as distantly related as the hagfish (Cyclostomata) and man.

The endocrine glands of vertebrates have special roles to play in the regulation of many types of physiological processes which include reproduction, osmoregulation, intermediary and mineral metabolism, and growth and development (Table 1.1). The nature of the responses to hormones differ considerably but can be classified into several major groups including their actions on membrane permeability, muscular contraction, the transformation of substrates involved in intermediary metabolism and growth, and a controlling (or trophic) action on other endocrine glands (Fig. 1.2).

Many, though not all, of the endocrine glands are essential for life and the reproduction and survival of the species. In other instances, however, their immediate importance for survival is not clear. Animals cannot reproduce if the endocrine function of their gonads is compromised and death soon follows complete destruction of the adrenal cortex. Life may be shortened if the Islets of Langerhans fail to produce sufficient insulin and normal growth, development and maturation of the young will not occur if the secretion of pituitary growth hormone or thyroid hormone is inadequate. On the other hand, antidiuretic hormone from the neuro-hypophysis, is not essential for life though in its absence very large volumes of urine are secreted by the kidney. In man this is an annoying condition as prolonged sleep is not possible and even during the waking hours it can lead to social difficulties but it is not fatal. If drinking water were in limited supply, however, dehydration could be a potential problem and absence of this hormone may then affect survival. It should also be remembered that while too little of a hormone can constitute a problem, too much may also result in physiological difficulties. Hormone imbalances can result from genetic abnormalities, the presence of tumors, and accidental disruption of the events controlling secretion of the hormone. A few examples of such endocrine dysfunction and their effects are summarized in Table 1.2.

Endocrine glands, or tissues, have been identified among all of the vertebrates. Those common to the major groups (from the Cyclostomata to the Mammalia) are the pituitary, thyroid, endocrine pancreas, adrenal

TABLE I.I. *The secretions of the endocrine glands*

Gland	Hormones	Target tissues
Pituitary		
Adenohypophysis		
Pars distalis	Follicle stimulating hormone, FSH	Ovary and testis
	Luteinizing hormone, LH (also called interstitial-cell stimulating hormone, ICSH)	Ovary and testis
	Thyrotrophic hormone, TSH	Thyroid
	Corticotrophic hormone, ACTH (adrenocorticotrophic hormone)	Adrenocortical tissue
	Growth hormone, GH (somatotrophic hormone)	Liver forms somatomedins which alter tissue metabolism (liver, muscle, adipose tissue)
	Prolactin (luteotrophic hormone, LTH)	Mammary glands, fish gills, tadpole metamorphosis, corpus luteum, kidney, skin, etc.
	Lipotrophin	Adipose tissue
Pars intermedia	Melanocyte stimulating hormone, MSH	Melanocytes, pigmentation and color change
Neurohypophysis		
Pars nervosa	Vasopressin, ADH, vasotocin	Kidney, amphibian skin and urinary bladder
	Oxytocin	Mammary gland, uterus
Hypothalamus	Pituitrophins; FSH/LH-RH, P-IH, MSH-R-IH, CRH, TSH-RH, GH-RH, etc.[1]	Release of hormones by the adenohypophysis

Thyroid gland	Thyroxine (T$_4$) Tri-iodothyronine (T$_3$)	Tissue metabolism and differentiation; calorigenic (mammals), morphogenetic (amphibians)
Parathyroid glands	Parathormone, PTH	Bone, kidney and (?) gut
Ultimobranchial bodies ('C' cells in mammalian thyroid)	Calcitonin, CT (also called thyrocalcitonin)	Bone and (?) kidney
Adrenal glands		
Cortex (interrenals in sharks and rays)	Cortisol, corticosterone, cortisone, 1α-hydroxycorticosterone	Tissue metabolism (liver, muscle), proteins to amino acids, gluconeogenesis. Intestine (teleosts)
	Aldosterone	Na and K in kidney, sweat and salivary glands, gut, amphibian skin and bladder, fish gills
Medulla (chromaffin tissue)	Noradrenaline (norepinephrine) Adrenaline (epinephrine)	Tissue metabolism (liver, muscle, adipose tissue), glycogenolysis, mobilization fatty acids, calorigenic, constriction and relaxation of smooth muscle
Islets of Langerhans		
Alpha-cells	Glucagon	Liver (glycogenolysis), adipose tissue (fatty acid release)
Beta-cells	Insulin	Liver, muscle and adipose tissue (amino acids to protein, glucose to fat and glycogen)
Gonads		
Ovary		
Graafian follicle	Estrogens (estradiol)	Female sex organs and characters, mammary glands, brain
Corpus luteum and interstitial tissue	Progestins (progesterone)	Uterus and mammary glands

TABLE 1.1 – *continued*

Gland	Hormones	Target tissues
Testis		
Interstitial tissue (Leydig cells)	Androgens (testosterone)	Male sex organs and characters, sperm maturation, brain
Sertoli cells (?)	Androgens	Sperm maturation
Placenta (pregnant eutherian mammals)	Estrogen (estriol), progesterone	Uterus, mammary glands, fetus
	Chorionic gonadotrophin, HCG	Corpus luteum
	Placental lactogen, HPL (somatomammotrophin, HCS)	Mammary glands
Gut		
Stomach (pyloric mucosa)	Gastrin	Stimulates secretion of gastric juice
Intestine (mucosa)	Enterogastrone	Inhibits secretion of gastric juices
	Secretin	Stimulates secretion of pancreatic juices from exocrine pancreas and hormones from endocrine pancreas
	Cholecystokinin–pancreozymin	Enzyme secretion from pancreas and hormones from endocrine pancreas
	Enteroglucagon	As for glucagon
Kidney		
Tubular cells	1,25-dihydroxycholecalciferol (1,25-(OH)$_2$-vitamin D$_3$)	Intestine, bone
Juxtaglomerular cells	Renin	Plasma α2-globulin-angiotensinogen→ angiotensin (targets: adrenal cortex, vascular smooth muscle)
Putative endocrine glands		
Pineal gland	Melatonin	Hypothalamus (inhibits release MSH and gonadotrophins), melanocytes (larval anurans, cyclostomes ?)

Corpuscles of Stannius (some bony fishes)	'Hypocalcin'	Calcium metabolism, osmoregulation
Urophysis (some fishes)		Osmoregulation, smooth muscle contractions (?)
Thymus	Thymic hormone(s)	Immunological maturation via induction of immunological competence of lymphocytes, etc.

[1] For explanation see list of abbreviations.

TABLE 1.2 *Some effects of endocrine dysfunction in man*

Gland	Secretory activity	Abnormality	Principal effects
Pituitary			
Adenohypophysis (growth hormone)	↑	Giantism, acromegaly	Excessive growth
	↓	Dwarfism	Retarded growth
Neurohypophysis	↓	Diabetes insipidus ADH	Excessive loss of water in urine
	↑	Schwartz–Bartter syndrome ADH	Low plasma Na
Thyroid gland	↑	Graves disease	High metabolic rate and nerve cell activity
	↓	Myxedema	Low metabolic rate
	↓	Cretinism	Inadequate development and growth
Parathyroids	↑	Hyperparathyroidism	Hypercalcemia, polyuria, reduced bone calcium
	↓	Hypoparathyroidism	Muscle tetany
Islets of Langerhans			
Beta-cells	↓	Diabetes mellitus	Hypoglycemia, muscle wasting
Adrenal cortex	↓	Addisons disease	Renal Na loss and K retention (low plasma Na, high plasma K), low blood pressure, muscle weakness
	↑	Cushings syndrome	High blood pressure, obesity, retarded growth
Adrenal medulla	↑	Phaeochromocytoma	Hyperglycemia, high blood pressure
Ovaries			Sterility, failure to develop or maintain secondary sex characters
Testis	↓		As above

↑ Increased activity.
↓ Decreased activity.

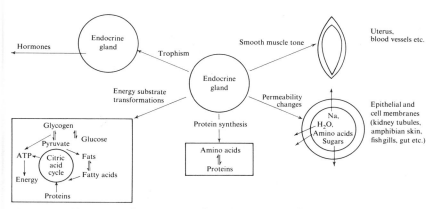

Fig. 1.2. A diagrammatic summary of the basic types of actions of hormones in vertebrates.

chromaffin and cortical tissues, and gonads. The parathyroid glands have been found in the tetrapods but not in the fishes. The ultimobranchial bodies or their homologues, the thyroid 'C' cells, have been identified in all groups except the cyclostomes. Such tissues secrete more than 40 different hormones in a mammal. If we include all the naturally occurring analogues of these hormones that occur among the vertebrates, we can account for at least twice this number of hormones and there are undoubtedly many more.

Apart from these glands, other tissues that may have an endocrine function (putative endocrine glands) have also been identified in a number of vertebrates. A tissue is considered to have an endocrine function if it releases a product into the circulation that has an excitatory or inhibitory effect on some distant effector gland organ or tissue. The precise status of the pineal body as an endocrine gland is still equivocal though many consider that it has such a function especially as one of its products, melatonin, has been identified in the blood. Two other tissues, that are present in some fishes, the urophysis and corpuscles of Stannius also have a putative endocrine status.

It is conceivable, indeed likely, that other endocrine glands exist among the vertebrates. Even within the last 10 years a new endocrine tissue, the ultimobranchial bodies (the thyroid 'C' cells in mammals), has been identified. This tissue is concerned with the regulation of calcium levels in some vertebrates. Despite the busy, even frantic, activity of endocrinologists the hormonal role of this gland had previously not been confirmed.

Despite their anatomical and embryological homologies the endocrine glands of vertebrates display considerable diversity in their morphological arrangements, the chemical nature of their secretions and even their physiological role in the body. It is principally about these differences that we will be concerned in the succeeding chapters.

Conclusions

Physiological processes are coordinated with the aid of both nerves and hormones. Each of these mechanisms has special characteristics that may be suited to the needs of the particular process involved and they often both operate together. During the course of geological time vertebrates have evolved and acquired morphological features and physiological processes that have permitted them to adapt to changing environments and to occupy a variety of ecological habitats. Such biologically important changes are accompanied by the neural and humoral processes necessary for their coordination. Contemporary species of vertebrates exhibit considerable structural and functional diversity that can be related to the nature of the life that they lead and to their ancestry. They are classified into systematic groups that are also thought to reflect their evolution. Thus a comparison of the endocrine function of contemporary species of vertebrates is not only of importance in fully understanding how they live today, in a particular environmental situation, but also may tell us how such hormonally mediated processes evolved.

2. Comparative morphology of the endocrine tissues

Endocrine glands and tissues display a diversity in their gross morphological and histological patterns. This is particularly apparent when comparing species from phyletically distant groups. In some instances the physiological significance of these differences has been recognized but in most this is not so and may be related to the initial pattern of embryonic growth. If, however, one intuitively suspects a close relationship between structure and function, then the lack of a known correlation may merely reflect our ignorance.

The endocrines may display several different types of morphological variation. Their position in the body may not be the same. This variation can be of a minor nature, such as is seen with the ultimobranchial bodies which can be situated near the heart or the thyroid gland. In some fish, however, thyroid tissue may vary in position from the branchial region to the kidney. Endocrine cells may show varying degrees of association and be scattered in small segments, or 'islets', or be closely associated as a compact gland enclosed in a capsule. Such aggregation of an endocrine tissue is commonly seen as one ascends the evolutionary (or the phyletic) scale. In addition, different endocrine tissues may display diverse associations with each other, as for instance the conglomeration of chromaffin and interrenal (or adrenocortical) tissue in the adrenal gland. Their relationship to the neural and vascular tissues can be very important. Pituitary tissues thus cannot function properly if they are transplanted to other parts of the body (ectopic transplant) or if the small blood vessels between the gland and the brain are cut. The major blood vessels not only carry hormones away from endocrine tissues but also supply them with nutrients and controlling stimuli. The pattern of the vasculature within the gland can also be important for its correct functioning.

The types of cells that make up an endocrine gland are, not surprisingly, similar in homologous glands among the vertebrates. Such similarities as reflected by their microscopic anatomy (size, shape, the presence of inclusions, granules, etc.) and their reactions with dyes (tinctorial relationships) serve to aid in their identification. More recently, antibodies to specific hormones have been used to identify the cells where they are formed. These antibodies may be labelled with radioactive materials or fluorescent dyes so that the precise locus where they react can be seen. The histological appearance of endocrine cells may change somewhat at different times depending on their secretory state. This characteristic can be used to predict their activity and physiological role. Inactive thyroid cells thus have a flattened, instead of columnar appearance which is typical of their active state, while neurohypophysial tissue that is depleted of its hormone has little stainable (with Gomori chrome–alum hematoxylin) neurosecretory material.

The pituitary gland (see Fig. 2.1)

The pituitary is a conglomerate of tissues and cells that reflect the ten major hormones it secretes. These hormones help regulate the activities of the thyroid, adrenal cortex and gonads, and contribute to the control of various other physiological activities including water and salt metabolism, growth, lactation, parturition and the pigmentation of the skin. A comparative account of the anatomy of this gland has recently been provided by Holmes and Ball (1974). Embryologically, the pituitary arises as a result of a downgrowth of tissue (the infundibulum) from the brain and an upgrowth (the hypophysis) from the roof of the mouth. Enclosed within these tissues is a piece of mesoderm that forms a net of blood vessels sometimes called the 'mantle plexus'. The pituitary lies in close apposition to the hypothalamus at the base of the brain. In mammals it is usually enclosed in a small, bony chamber, the sella turcica, from which it is connected by a stalk of nervous tissue to the brain, just behind the optic chiasma. The hypophysis partly differentiates into the adenohypophysis that secretes seven or eight hormones which, so the histologists tell us, are formed by a similar number of distinctive types of cells. These are most descriptively labelled by the name of the hormone they secrete followed by the suffix *troph*. We thus have thyrotrophs, gonadotrophs, somatotrophs and so on. An alternative terminology utilizes the Greek alphabet: α-cells = somatotrophs, β-cells = gonadotrophs and so on. The adenohypophysis can be divided on a gross morphological basis into three or four sections: the pars tuberalis, the pars distalis (sometimes with a rostral and caudal section) and the pars intermedia. The latter gives rise to the melanocyte-stimulating hormone (MSH) while the rest of the hormones come from the pars distalis. The pars tuberalis lies between the pars distalis and the brain (in the region of the median eminence) and is associated with the blood vessels that connect the two.

The neural, or infundibular, tissue forms the neurohypophysis which basically lies caudally to the adenohypophysis; hence the terms anterior and posterior lobes of the pituitary. The neurohypophysis is connected to

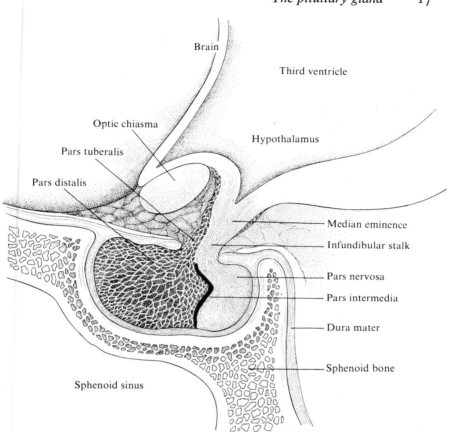

Fig. 2.1. The pituitary gland of man. It lies in a bony chamber at the base of the brain to which it is connected by a stalk. The pars intermedia is quite small in man but may be much larger in other species. (From R. Guillemin and R. Burgus, *The Hormones of the Hypothalamus*. Copyright © 1972 by Scientific American, Inc. All rights reserved.)

the brain by the infundibular stalk. The two hormones (ADH and oxytocin in mammals) it secretes are formed in nerve cells (by a process called neurosecretion) which originate in the supraoptic and paraventricular nuclei in the brain of amniotes or the preoptic nucleus of amphibians and fishes. The axonal tract running from the bodies of these nerve cells, in the nuclei, to the periphery, where they are stored and released, is called the supraopticohypophysial tract. The neurohypophysis thus consists of the distal parts of nerve cells interspersed with glial cells and pituicytes. The function of the latter is unknown.

'Primitive type' as in some reptiles

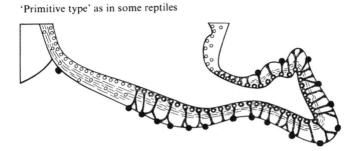

Birds and reptiles

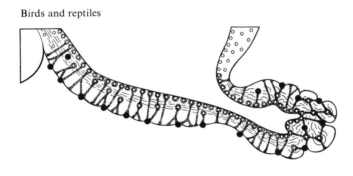

Mammals

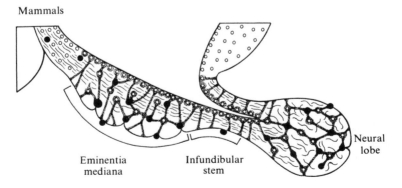

Eminentia   Infundibular   Neural
mediana   stem   lobe

Fig. 2.2. Histological differentiation of the amniote neurohypophysis.
The 'primitive form' is seen in reptiles such as the Rhynchocephalia, Chelonia
and some Lacertilia. Solid black lines are the blood vessels, nerve fibers are
thinner lines. (From Wingstrand, 1951.)

Three regions of the neurohypophysis can be distinguished. The rostral *median eminence* is part of the wall of the hypothalamus and lies in close conjunction with the adenohypophysis to which it is usually connected by a system of portal blood vessels which originate from the mantle plexus. The median eminence is contiguous with the *infundibular stalk* which connects it to the most prominent part of the neurohypophysis, the *pars nervosa* (or *neural lobe*). The latter is much more highly developed in terrestrial tetrapods than in the fishes. The phyletic development of the amniote neurohypophysis is shown in Fig. 2.2.

Comparative morphology of the pituitary

The diverse morphology of the vertebrate pituitary provides us with some information (albeit equivocal) about the nature of the evolutionary changes that may have taken place in this gland. Attempts have been made to choose or construct, the pituitary that is considered most typical of each major phyletic group. Considerable differences from a 'median gland' may nevertheless exist among various species within each systematic group.

The structure of the pituitaries of fishes, from the Cyclostomata to the Dipnoi are shown in Fig. 2.3. The cyclostomes have a simple type of pituitary in which the different regions are only loosely associated with each other. The parts of the adenohypophysis in these phyletic prototypes are often termed the pro-, meso- and meta-adenohypophysis. They are thought to correspond respectively to the cephalic part of the pars distalis (or possibly the pars tuberalis), the caudal pars distalis and the pars intermedia of other vertebrates. The close proximity of the adenohypophysis to the brain may not be functionally essential in these lowly fishes. Considerable intraspecific variation occurs and ectopic transplants of the adenohypophysis to others parts of the body do not appear to compromise its function, at least in hagfishes (Myxinoidea) (Fernholm, 1972).

The actinopterygian fishes possess a pituitary in which there is a close association between the various component tissues. The homologies of these tissues to those in tetrapods have on occasion been difficult to recognize but they undoubtedly exist. The neurohypophysis is not a very discrete tissue in fishes (there is no distinct neural lobe) and shows considerable admixture with the pars intermedia into which it sends finger-like projections and shares a common blood supply (see Fig. 2.3). Portal blood vessels connecting the median eminence and adenohypophysis have been described in all groups of actinopterygians except the teleosts. Considerable variation has been observed among the latter in which the blood supply to the adenohypophysis passes initially through the neurohypophysis. No clear portal system, as seen in other actinopterygians, is apparent in

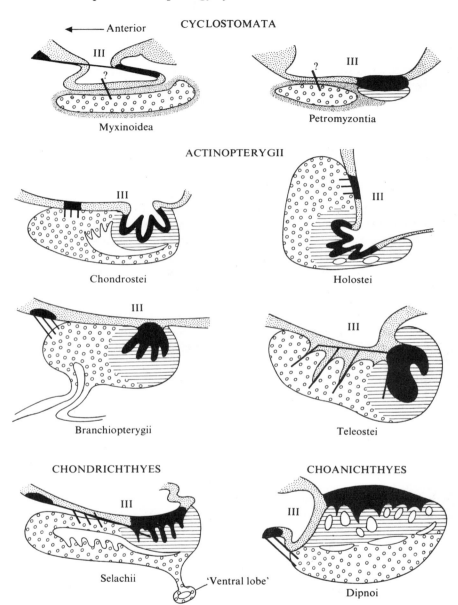

Fig. 2.3. The pituitary glands of fishes. Diagrammatic representation from midsagittal section.

Small dots = nervous tissue; black = neurohypophysial tissue; large open dots = pars distalis; horizontal lines = pars intermedia.

teleosts. At least five distinct types of cells have been identified in the fish pituitary as shown in Fig. 2.4 which is that of a teleost, the eel *Anguilla anguilla*. These cells are present in separate zones in contrast to the tetrapods and lungfishes (Dipnoi) where they are intermingled with each other.

The chondrichthyean fish (sharks and rays) have a pituitary which on superficial examination looks rather different from that of other fishes. It displays, however, a similar basic structure, though gross differences, such as a rather large pars intermedia, are often apparent. A characteristic and distinct lobe of the adenohypophysis lies below the pars distalis, this is called the '*ventral lobe*', which has been shown to be the site of formation of a gonadotrophin. Like most actinopterygians, chondrichthyeans have a distinct portal blood system connecting the hypothalamus and adenohypophysis but this special blood supply does not extend to the ventral lobe.

The pituitary of lungfishes shows more similarities to that of tetrapods than to those of other fishes. This is especially interesting in view of the special phyletic relationship that is usually considered to exist between

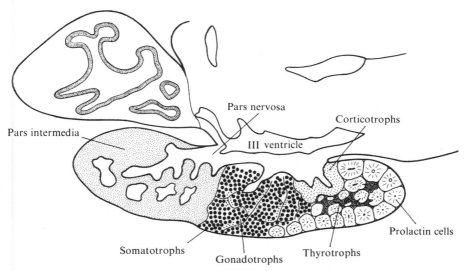

Fig. 2.4. Diagram from midsagittal section of the pituitary of a teleost fish (the eel *Anguilla anguilla*).

The cells (trophs) that produce the hormones in the pars distalis can be seen to lie generally in distinct zones. (From Olivereau, 1967.)

Thick black lines = blood vessels which carry neurosecretory products to the adenohypophysis, or in Myxinoidea to the neurohypophysis.

III = third ventricle. (From Ball and Baker, 1969, modified slightly according to Holmes and Ball, 1974.)

lungfishes and tetrapods. The gross similarities between the amphibian and lungfish pituitaries can be seen in Fig. 2.5. The different types of cells in the adenohypophysis are intermingled in lungfishes (not separated as in other fishes), just as in the tetrapods. The neurohypophysis of the lungfishes also displays the beginnings of the differentiation of a neural lobe.

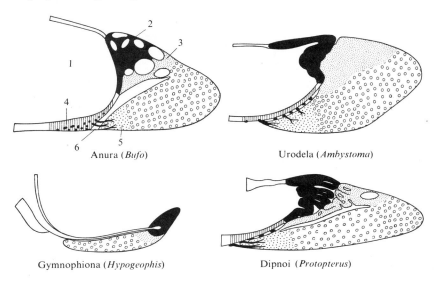

Anura (*Bufo*)   Urodela (*Ambystoma*)

Gymnophiona (*Hypogeophis*)   Dipnoi (*Protopterus*)

Fig. 2.5. The pituitaries of the three main groups of the Amphibia compared to that of a dipnoan (lungfish).
1 = Saccus infundibuli; 2 = neural lobe; 3 = pars intermedia; 4 = median eminence; 5 = 'zona tuberalis'; 6 = portal blood vessels. (From Wingstrand, 1966. Originally published by the University of California Press; reprinted by permission of The Regents of the University of California.)

The neural lobe, which is a characteristic of the tetrapods, is formed by the enlargement, in a posterior direction, of the neurohypophysis. Wingstrand (1966) has suggested that this change may be related to a terrestrial manner of life in which the secreted hormones had a special significance. This theory is consistent with measurements showing a much greater amount of stored hormonal material in the neurohypophysis of tetrapods than in that of fishes (Follett, 1963).

The basic morphological pattern of the tetrapod pituitary is well exemplified in the reptiles (Fig. 2.6). It can, however, be seen that even here differences between the major systematic groups occur. Such variations usually reflect the relative degree of development of the neurohypophysis and the presence, reduction or absence of the pars tuberalis. The reptilian adenohypophysis has distinct cephalic and caudal zones.

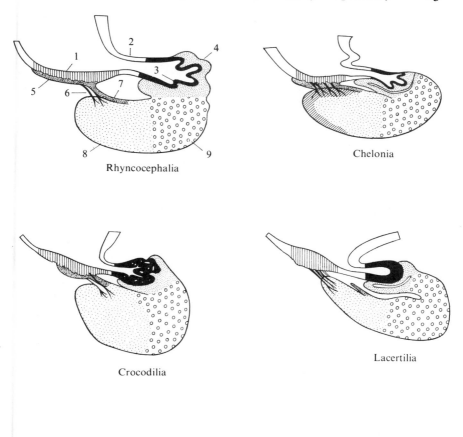

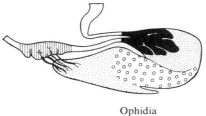

Fig. 2.6. The pituitaries of the five main groups of the Reptilia.
1 = Median eminence; 2 = infundibular stem; 3 = neural lobe (pars nervosa); 4 = pars intermedia; 5 = pars tuberalis; 6 = portal blood vessels; 7 = pars tuberalis interna; 8 = cephalic lobe of pars distalis; 9 = caudal lobe of pars distalis. (From Wingstrand, 1966. Originally published by the University of California Press; reprinted by permission of The Regents of the University of California.)

The pituitaries from more than 100 species of birds have been examined and, as in the reptiles, the pars distalis has two distinct regions. It is interesting that a pars intermedia has not been identified among the birds. The hormone typically secreted by this tissue, MSH, has nevertheless been identified in the pituitary of the domestic chicken (Shapiro *et al.*, 1972). This absence of a pars intermedia is not unique to birds; it is not present in elephants or whales either.

Among the mammals, considerable morphological differences exist in the intimate arrangement of the tissues within the pituitary (see Hanstrom, 1966). The detailed embryonic development of the pars distalis differs from that of other amniotes. The mammalian pars distalis arises mainly from the aboral lobe of Rathkes pouch, which in birds and reptiles forms the caudal section of the pars distalis. The oral lobe, which forms the cephalic part of the pars distalis in the last two groups, fails to develop in mammals (Wingstrand, 1966). In addition to being absent in whales and elephants, the pars intermedia is very much reduced in adult primates, including man. The simplest type of pituitary is seen in the echidna, *Tachyglossus aculeatus* (an egg-laying monotreme) and some rodents and insectivores. It is interesting that the echidna shows a pattern that is considered to be like a 'primitive' mammal. The echidna's pituitary is, however, typically mammalian in its embryonic origins. It has nevertheless some features, including a prominent porto-tuberal tract between the median eminence and pars distalis, which are seen more often in birds and some reptiles.

The endocrine glands of the pharynx: thyroid, parathyroids and ultimobranchial bodies

Apart from the adenohypophysis, which has its origins in the roof of the mouth, three (or four if one includes the thymus) other endocrine glands arise from the pharyngeal tissues: the thyroid gland from the floor of the pharynx, the parathyroids from the II, III and IV gill pouches and the ultimobranchial bodies from the last, VI, pair of these.

The thyroid

Thyroid tissue is present in all vertebrates though its gross morphological arrangement varies somewhat. Its hormones have ubiquitous effects on tissue metabolism, differentiation and maturation. The 'thyroid-unit' is a follicle in which a group of epithelial cells surround a central cavity which is filled with a glycoprotein secretion called thyroglobulin (Fig. 2.7). The encompassing cells have a columnar appearance when they are most active and a flattened one when they are least active. Thyroid follicles have a

(a)

(b)

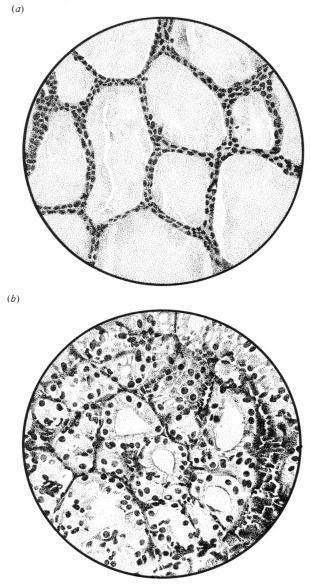

Fig. 2.7. The thyroid gland of the laboratory rat showing the follicles surrounded by epithelial cells.

(a) The inactive condition where the cells are flattened and the follicles are distended with 'colloid' which contains the thyroglobulin. (b) The active condition where the epithelial cells are columnar and little colloid is present.

remarkable ability to trap inorganic iodide which can be stored and transposed into hormones which are, in turn, stored in the follicle cavity. It is probably the only endocrine gland that stores its products outside of the cells.

In man, the thyroid gland is situated in the region of the neck and it has a generally comparable position in other vertebrates. In cyclostomes and most teleost fishes the thyroid follicles lie scattered along the blood vessels under the pharynx. Occasionally they may be found further afield, even in the kidneys. In chondrichthyean fish (sharks and rays) and some teleosts, like the Bermuda parrot fish and tuna, the follicles are aggregated into a distinct glandular mass. This pattern persists in higher vertebrates; there are two such aggregates in amphibians, birds and many reptiles. In lizards these two lobes are joined, a situation that is also usually characteristic of mammals.

TABLE 2.1. *The thyroid in the phylum chordata.* (From Rall, Robbins and Lewallen, 1964)

Subphylum	Class	Species[1]	Thyroid gland	Thyroid-like[2] activity
Hemichordata[3]		*Glossobalanus minutus*	−	−
Protochordata				
Urochordata	Ascideacea	*Ciona intestinalis*	−	+
(Tunicate)	(sea-squirt)	*Clavelina lepadiformis*	−	+
	Larvacea		−	+
	Thaliacea	*Salpa maxima*	−	+
Cephalochordata	Amphioxi	*Branchiostoma lanceolatum* (amphioxus)	−	+
Vertebrata	Agnatha	(Lamprey)		
	(cyclostoma)	ammocoete larva	−	+
		adult	+	+
		(Hagfish)	+	+
	Chondrichthyes (elasmobranch)	(Shark)	+	+
		(Skate)	+	+
	Osteichthyes		+	+
	(teleost)		+	+
	Amphibia		+	+
	Reptilia		+	+
	Aves		+	+
	Mammalia		+	+

[1] Not a complete list. Common names are given in parentheses.
[2] That is, synthesis of iodothyronines.
[3] Not usually classified as Chordata at present time, but included for reference in the light of earlier discussions.

The thyroid appears to have the longest phylogenetic history of any endocrine gland (see Table 2.1). It is not only present in vertebrates; tissues that may be homologous, though not having the characteristic follicular units, have been identified in protochordates, including *Amphioxus* (Cephalochordata) and various ascidians (sea-squirts, Urochordata). The development of the thyroid in lampreys can be followed during the metamorphosis of its ammocoete larva. This beast collects small particles of food by filtering water that passes, with the help of ciliary action, through its pharynx. This process is aided by a ventral outgrowth from the floor of the mouth called the endostyle or subpharyngeal gland. An analogous tissue also exists in *Amphioxus* and ascidians. It secretes a sticky mucus that traps the food particles before they can pass out across the gills. This action has been likened to that of a 'moving flypaper'. Embryologically, the endostyle of the lamprey ammocoete larva differentiates to form the adult thyroid. This has given rise to speculation as to whether or not the endostyle in the ammocoete and in protochordates has some thyroid function.

The endostyle does not contain thyroid-like follicles. It has, however, been shown (see Barrington, 1962), like the thyroid, to be able to accumulate selectively and concentrate radioactive iodide. This has not only been demonstrated in the lamprey ammocoete but also in *Amphioxus* and several ascidians. The iodine is bound in organic form with tyrosine and organo-iodine compounds (*iodothyronines*), including, possibly, small amounts of thyroxine (for a summary see Table 2.1).

Iodine readily reacts with proteins containing the amino acid tyrosine. Indeed, in one extensive investigation when cows were being fed experimental diets containing thyroid compounds to improve their milk yields, these were made by incubating proteins, such as casein, with iodine at an appropriate pH and temperature. Thus, the spontaneous formation of organo-iodine compounds in nature would not be surprising. Indeed among the ascidians, the outer tunic or coat contains scleroproteins that combine with iodine; possibly even more readily than the tissues associated with the endostyle. Iodinated tyrosines have also been isolated in many other non-vertebrates, including coelenterates. Barrington (1962) has conjectured about the possibility that the spontaneous occurrence and availability of such compounds in nature may have led to their use as hormones. Subsequently their formation may have become more localized in special tissues.

Parathyroid glands and ultimobranchial bodies

These glands secrete hormones that contribute to the control of calcium in the body fluids. Embryologically, there are initially three pairs of parathyroids in tetrapods but those from the II pair of branchial pouches usually disappear; two or sometimes only one pair persist. When one pair persist they are usually derived from the III gill pouch. Two pairs of parathyroids are usually present in amphibians. Among reptiles this number varies. One pair is present in the Crocodilia, two pairs in the Chelonia and Ophidia, and one to three pairs in the Lacertilia. Birds and mammals have one or two pairs. The number found does not seem to follow any phyletic pattern.

A pair of ultimobranchial bodies is present in all the vertebrates from the birds to the chondrichthyean fish. They are apparently absent in cyclostomes. In mammals this tissue is embedded in the thyroid gland, where it makes up the parafollicular or 'C' cells.

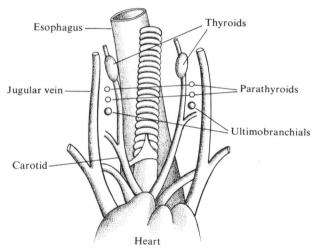

Fig. 2.8. The position of the thyroid gland, the parathyroids and the ultimobranchial bodies in the domestic fowl, *Gallus domesticus*. (From Copp, Cockcroft and Keuk, 1967*b*. Reproduced by permission of the National Research Council of Canada.)

The association of the thyroid, parathyroids and ultimobranchial tissues may be somewhat complex. The last two tissues are histologically different from the thyroid and they lack the typical follicular structure of that gland. Their positions in the domestic fowl are shown in Fig. 2.8. The morphological distribution of these three glands has often made it difficult to dissociate the effects of the latter two, which both elaborate secretions having opposite effects on blood calcium concentrations. The parathyroids, especially in mammals, are usually closely associated with the thyroid though not to the same extent as the ultimobranchial tissues. Removal of the mammalian thyroid, including that in man, is often associated with low blood calcium levels and an associated muscle tetany. This is the result of removal of or damage to the parathyroid gland; an observation that furnished an important clue as to its possible endocrine significance. The concomitant absence of the 'C' cells was not initially apparent and only became so after examination of the effects of thyroid extracts on plasma calcium levels.

In order to elucidate the respective roles of the 'C' cells and the parathyroids in mammals, morphological variations between species have been usefully exploited. In dogs, which are common experimental animals, there are two pairs of parathyroids, one embedded deeply in the thyroid. Rats, however, only have a single pair of parathyroids which are at the surface of the thyroid and so can be destroyed with a cautery. In neither species is it possible to isolate the blood supply of the parathyroids from that of the thyroid, which contains the 'C' cells, so that many crucial endocrine experiments cannot be performed on them. Sheep and goats have two pairs of parathyroids and one of these is situated near the thymus, where it has a separate blood supply from that of the thyroid. These animals have played an important role in elucidating the respective roles of the endocrines in calcium metabolism (Hirsch and Munson, 1969). In addition, the pig has also proved to be useful and in this species the thyroid has no attached parathyroid tissue so that one can deal with the 'C' cells in relative isolation from the former.

In non-mammals the ultimobranchial bodies are usually separated from the thyroid. Nevertheless in birds, for example the domestic fowl, they may contain parathyroid tissue (Copp, 1972). In pigeons, calcitonin is not only found in the ultimobranchials but also in the parathyroids and thyroid.

The admixture of these three distinct endocrines may have some fundamental significance but this is unknown. It has been suggested that the differentiation of the 'C' cells is aided by their association with the thyroid tissue. It is also possible that, as has been observed in the adrenals (see later), some functional symbiosis may occur. Much of the variation, however, would appear to be the result of embryological complications. Although this has certainly helped to hide their effective roles from the endocrinologist, it has nevertheless provided him with some fascinating intellectual exercises during which he has utilized for his own purposes much of the interspecific variation that initially served to deceive him.

The adrenals

The adrenal glands are so named from their position adjacent to the kidneys. In mammals, they are a composite gland made up of two distinct tissues arranged in two zones, an outer cortex surrounding an inner medulla. The cortex is mesodermal in its origins and secretes several steroid hormones involved in the regulation of intermediary and mineral metabolism. It is called the interrenal or adrenocortical tissue. The medulla, on the other hand, is neural tissue homologous to that of the sympathetic ganglia.

(a)   *(b)*

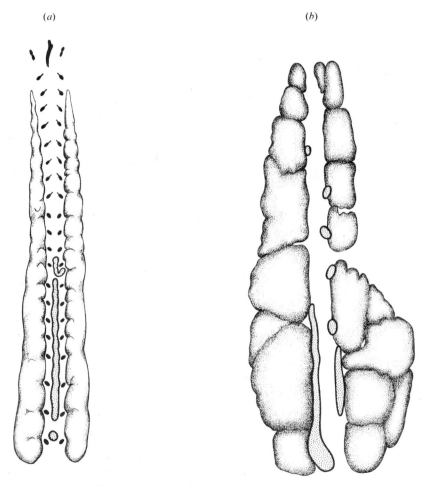

Fig. 2.9. Adrenal tissues in the Chondrichthyes.
(*a*) The smooth dogfish (*Mustelus canis*). Double row of black dots = chromaffin tissue lying between the two kidneys. Interrenal (adrenocortical) tissue = stippled. This lies in several pieces between the kidneys. (*b*) The skate (*Raja laevis*). The broken U-shaped interrenal is shown lying between the kidneys. (From Hartman and Brownell, 1949.)

Because it stains dark brown with chromic acid it is called chromaffin tissue. It secretes the catecholamine hormones adrenaline and noradrenaline (also called epinephrine and norepinephrine). These have several roles, including the mobilization of fats and carbohydrates as well as influencing the tone of many blood vessels. While these two endocrine tissues are closely associated in mammals, they are separated in many fishes. In the cyclostome fishes the chromaffin tissues are widely dispersed in small islets along certain blood vessels. Putative adrenocortical tissues have been identified embedded in the posterior cardinal veins. This tissue has, however, not been conclusively shown to secrete steroid hormones (Weisbart and Idler, 1970). In teleost fishes adrenocortical tissues lie along the posterior cardinal veins in the anterior part of the kidney (the head-kidney) where they may or may not be associated with the chromaffin tissue. In sharks and rays (Chondrichthyes) the adrenocortical tissue forms a more compact glandular mass lying between the kidneys; hence the name interrenals. In the dogfish (Fig. 2.9a) islets of chromaffin tissue lie along the inner borders of the kidneys while the interrenal forms a fairly complete mass between them. The adrenocortical tissue of the skate, on the other hand, forms several lobules (Fig. 2.9b).

In the Amphibia, chromaffin and adrenocortical tissues are usually associated with each other, lying in islets on the ventral surface of the kidney (Fig. 2.10). Considerable differences can be seen between various species. In urodeles, they are in scattered groups; in *Siren* (Fig. 2.10a) they lie in rows between the kidney, while in *Necturus* and *Amphiuma* (Fig. 2.10b, c) they are on its surface. Anurans, like the leopard frog (*Rana pipiens*), have contiguous strips of adrenal tissue (Fig. 2.10d). It is interesting that in the African lungfish (*Protopterus*), adrenocortical tissues lie in islets along the post-cardinal veins and on the ventral surface of the kidney, a pattern similar to that seen in urodeles (Janssens *et al.*, 1965).

In anamniotes, the adrenocortical tissues and the mesonephric kidney have a common embryological origin so that their close association is not unexpected. Amniotes, however, have a metanephric kidney (the mesonephros is not seen in adults) so that the kidneys and adrenals are less intimately connected. The adrenals, more predictably, form separate compact masses of tissue lying near the kidneys. Considerable variations nevertheless still exist as seen among the different major groups of the reptiles (Fig. 2.11). The chromaffin tissues of reptiles are more closely intermingled with the adrenocortical tissues than they are in amphibians. This admixture of the two tissues is even more apparent in birds (Fig. 2.12) where the adrenals may be fused to form a single gland. Mammals have paired adrenal glands (Fig. 2.13) with a distinct cortex and medulla. It is interesting that this is not as well defined in the echidna *Tachyglossus*

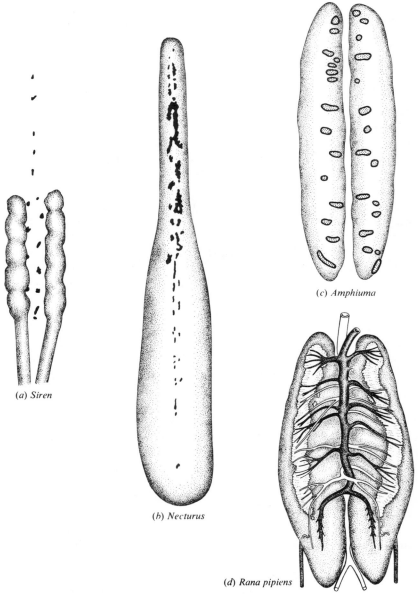

(a) *Siren*

(b) *Necturus*

(c) *Amphiuma*

(d) *Rana pipiens*

Fig. 2.10. Adrenal tissues in the Amphibia.
Urodela: (a) *Siren*; (b) *Necturus*; (c) *Amphiuma*. The adrenal tissue is shown as
the dark area lying on the ventral surface or between the kidneys.
Anura: (d) *Rana pipiens*. The adrenal tissues lie in two strips (light color) along
the outer ventral border of each kidney.
(From Hartman and Brownell, 1949.)

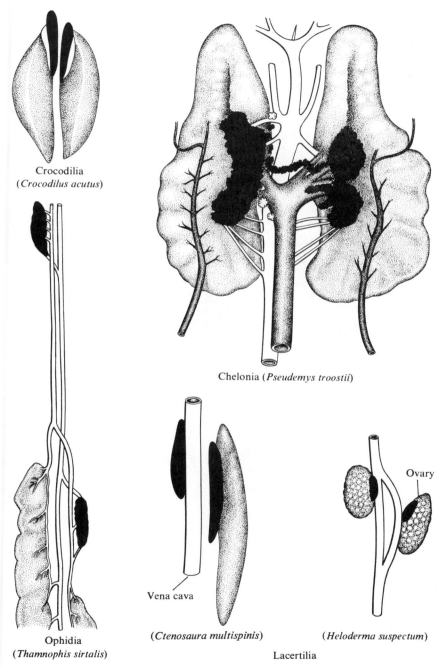

Crocodilia
(*Crocodilus acutus*)

Chelonia (*Pseudemys troostii*)

Ovary

Vena cava

Ophidia
(*Thamnophis sirtalis*)

(*Ctenosaura multispinis*)

(*Heloderma suspectum*)

Lacertilia

Fig. 2.11. The adrenal tissues in the Reptilia.
The adrenals are shown in black in relationship to the kidney(s) (shaded).
(From Hartman and Brownell, 1949.)

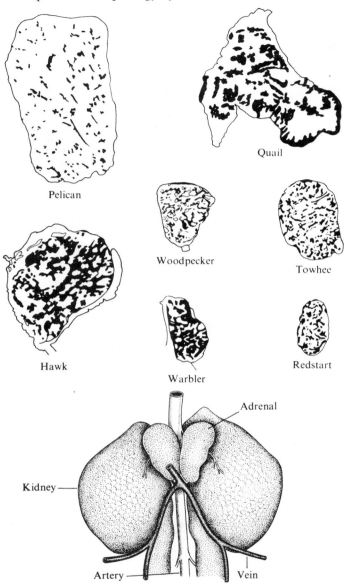

Fig. 2.12. The adrenals in birds.
Top. Cross-section of the adrenal glands from various species showing the distribution of the chromaffin tissue (black) and the adrenocortical tissue (white).
Bottom. The adrenals of the herring gull (*Larus argentatus*).
(From Hartman and Brownell, 1949.)

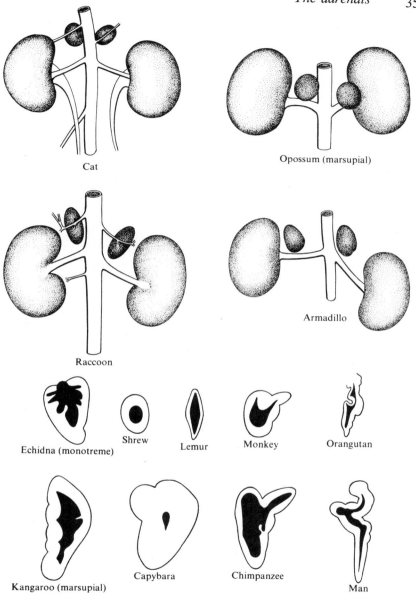

Fig. 2.13. The adrenals in mammals.
Top. The position of the adrenals in relation to the kidneys in a variety of species.
Bottom. Cross-section of the adrenals from various species showing the chromaffin tissue (black) and adrenocortical tissue (white).
(From Hartman and Brownell, 1949.)

aculeatus (an egg-laying monotreme), whose adrenals are considered to be similar to those of reptiles (Wright, Chester Jones and Phillips, 1957).

The relative amounts of adrenocortical and chromaffin tissues vary in different species. As shown in Table 2.2, there are similar amounts of both

TABLE 2.2. *Weights of the adrenal medulla and cortex in various species.* (From Hartman and Brownell, 1949)

Animal	Weight	Medullae (g)	Cortices (g)	Proportion
Fowl	2000	0.1	0.1	1:1
Dog	15000	0.25	1.25	1:5
Cat	3000	0.02	0.35	1:17.5
Rat	200	0.002	0.04	1:20
Rabbit	3000	0.01	0.4	1:40
Guinea-pig	500	0.008	0.5	1:62.5

in the domestic fowl; in the dog, adrenocortical tissue is five times more predominant, while in the guinea-pig there is more than 60 times as much adrenocortical as chromaffin tissue. Adrenocortical tissues may also show considerable variability depending on the season, diet and physiological condition of the animal. It is well known that in many reptiles and amphibians the adrenocortical tissue regresses in winter and proliferates in summer. This can also be related to breeding and has been observed in teleost fish (see for instance Robertson and Wexler, 1959; Chan and Phillips, 1971; Lofts, Phillips and Tam, 1971). Birds from marine habitats, where a lot of salt is present in the diet, have larger adrenals than those species where fresh water is freely available. Glaucous-winged gulls (*Larus glaucescens*) reared with only salt solutions to drink have much larger adrenals than those given fresh water (Holmes, Butler and Phillips, 1961).

The mammalian adrenal cortex is histologically composed of three types of cells situated in three layers or zones. These are the outer *zona glomerulosa* (round cells, rich in mitochondria and poor in lipids), an intermediate *zona fasciculata* (columnar cells, rich in lipids) and a smaller inner *zona reticularis* (flattened cells poor in lipids) (see Fig. 2.14). The zona glomerulosa is not apparent in all mammals; such as some mice, lemurs and monkeys. It appears that the three zones are each principally (though possibly not exclusively) involved in the formation of different hormones; the zona glomerulosa forms aldosterone, the zona fasciculata cortisol and corticosterone, while the zona reticularis can secrete androgenic steroids. This last zone hypertrophies in certain conditions associated with an excess production of these hormones in man. Aldosterone assists regulation of

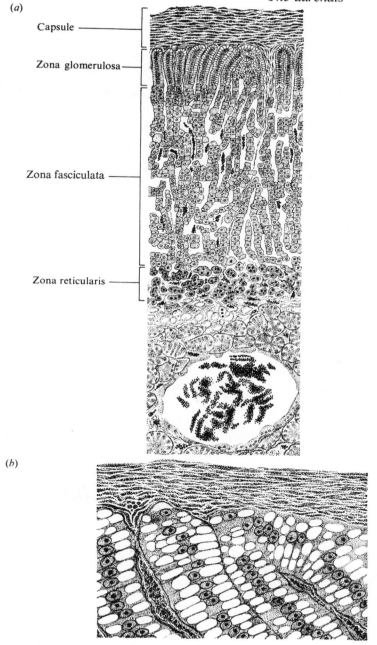

(a)

Capsule

Zona glomerulosa

Zona fasciculata

Zona reticularis

(b)

Fig. 2.14. (a) Histological section of the adrenal of a mammal, the racoon, showing the zonation of the adrenal cortex. (b) Enlargement of the capsular glomerular zone. (From Hartman and Brownell, 1949.)

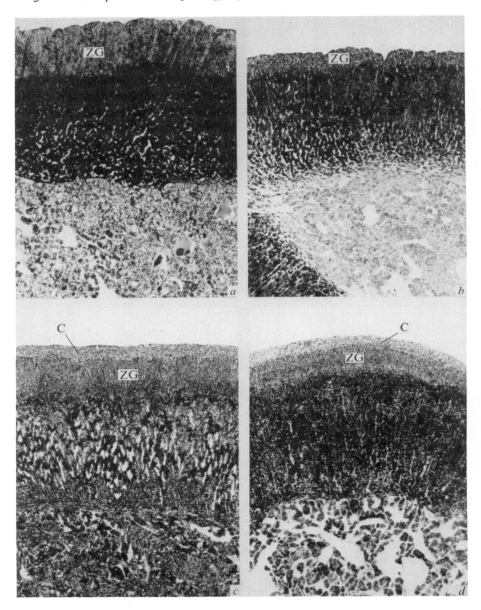

Fig. 2.15. The adrenal glands, in section, from two marsupials from sodium-deficient and sodium-replete areas.
   Macropus giganteus (kangaroo): (*a*) Sodium-deficient; (*b*) sodium-replete.
   Vombatus hirsutus (wombat): (*c*) Sodium-deficient; (*d*) sodium-replete.

sodium metabolism in mammals. It is therefore not unexpected to find that the zona glomerulosa can undergo considerable hypertrophy in mammals, such as rabbits and kangaroos, that live in areas where the salt content of the diet is low (Fig. 2.15) (Blair-West *et al.*, 1968).

Intraspecific differences in the size of the adrenals, the volumes of the cortex and medulla, and the cells of the cortex may be determined genetically. Shire (1970) has observed such differences in several strains of mice. In one strain, 'CBA', both the cortex and medulla are larger than in another, 'strain A'. The volume of the medulla in CBA mice is 0.35 mm^3 per 25 g body weight, while it is only 0.18 mm^3 in strain A. Similarly the cortex has a volume of 1.5 mm^3 in the CBA strain and 0.82 in the other mice. The differences have been shown to reflect genetic variation at one or two gene loci for the cortex and at at least two such loci in the case of the medulla. The CBA mice have a well-developed zona glomerulosa but attempts to correlate this with more production of aldosterone (as compared to a less well-endowed strain) have not been successful (Stewart *et al.*, 1972).

Among the vertebrates, there appears to be an evolutionary trend towards a more intimate association of the adrenocortical and the chromaffin tissue. This tendency may partially reflect their embryogenesis; such as the tissue aggregation that follows the loss of the mesonephros. One is tempted to ask if the relationship of the two endocrine tissues has any functional significance. The adrenocortical tissue can certainly function in the absence of the chromaffin tissue as seen *in vitro* in the laboratory. There is, however, some question as to the chromaffin cell's ability to produce optimal amounts of catecholamines. The mammalian adrenal medulla contains an enzyme, phenylethanolamine-N-methyl-transferase or PNMT, that, by methylating noradrenaline, converts it to adrenaline. The formation of this enzyme is induced by steroid hormones from the adrenal cortex (Pohorecky and Wurtman, 1971). The concentrations of the steroids must be high; far higher than normally present in the systemic circulation. This is achieved by the direct transfer of the steroids to the medulla through a local portal blood system. PNMT activity has also been identified in frogs but the enzyme is different from that in mammals and cannot be induced by corticosteroid hormones. It seems likely that such a physiological relationship between the adrenal cortex and the medulla may have arisen following their morphological juxtaposition.

Note that the zona glomerulosa is wider in sodium-deficient animals. In the wombat a thicker capsule lies at the outer border of this cell layer. C = capsule, ZG = zona glomerulosa. (From Blair-West *et al.*, 1968, and J. R. Blair-West, personal communication.)

The endocrine hormones of the gut

Several hormones are formed, and released from the posterior part of the foregut and its derivative glands. The most notable of these are insulin and glucagon from the pancreas; gastrin from the stomach; and secretin, cholecystokinin–pancreozymin, entero-glucagon and enterogastrone from the duodenum and upper parts of the jejunum. These hormones integrate and control the processes that result from feeding; which include the secretion of digestive enzymes and the concentrations of the absorbed nutrients in the blood.

Gastrin is present in the pyloric gland area of the stomach where, with the aid of immunofluorescent antibodies, it has been identified in special endocrine cells that are called *G-cells* situated in the deeper regions of the pyloric glands. Secretin has been identified, using similar techniques, in numerous epithelial cells, the *S-cells*, lining the crypts and villi of the duodenum and jejunum. At the time of writing, the site of formation of cholecystokinin–pancreozymin has not, apparently, been identified but it is considered to be only a matter of time before this is done. The other intestinal hormones; entero-glucagon and entero-gastrone, have not been specifically isolated and chemically purified, and although they are thought, on physiological grounds, to be formed in the upper regions of the intestine their precise sites of formation are uncertain. Indeed, although immuno-logical evidence for the existence of entero-glucagon has been obtained, entero-gastrone has remained a rather elusive 'hormone'.

Insulin and glucagon, as well as small amounts of gastrin, are found in special tissues situated in the pancreas called (after their discoverer) *Islets of Langerhans* (see Falkmer and Patent, 1972). Several types of cells have been identified in these tissues. The hormone-secreting cells contain granules and are distinguished from each other by their different appear-ances following exposure to histological fixatives and dyes. They are named in several ways: *A-cells* (also called α- or α_2-) which form glucagon, *B-cells* (β-) forming insulin and *D-cells* (δ or α_1-) which probably contain gastrin. B-cells are present in all vertebrates while A-cells are absent in cyclostome fishes and some urodele amphibians. The status of the D-cells is not clear and they may represent a stage in the development of the A-cells. As insulin-like hormones have also been identified in a number of inverte-brates the presence of comparable types of cells has also been sought in them but with equivocal results.

The morphological disposition of hormone-secreting cells of the pancreas differs considerably among vertebrates (for summary see Table 2.3). They are most often associated with the exocrine pancreas. This gland is formed from one or more diverticula of the gut and contains exocrine acinar cells

TABLE 2.3. *Evolution of the endocrine pancreas in vertebrates.* (From Pictet and Rutter, 1972)

Pisces	Agnatha	Myxinoidea (Hagfish):	Endocrine pancreas is a separate organ derived from the biliary duct; exocrine pancreas partially incorporated into the liver.
		Petromyzontia (Lamprey):	Endocrine pancreas is a separate organ derived from the duodenum.
	Chondrichthyes	Elasmobranchii (Shark, Torpedo):	Endocrine pancreas is formed of cells located around the medium- and small-sized pancreatic ducts; exocrine pancreas completely separated from the liver.
		Holocephali (Chimaera):	Endocrine cells are integrated in the exocrine tissue; they are accumulated in clusters, which are not vascularized.
	Osteichthyes	Crossopterygii Coelocanthini (*Latimeria*):	Endocrine cells located around the ducts as in Elasmobranchii. First evidence of islet formation: some B-cells are organized around the capillaries between the acini; exocrine pancreas separated from the liver.
		Teleostei: (95% of the living fishes, the most evolved fishes):	Endocrine pancreas either forms a separate organ (principal islets or Brockmann bodies) (goosefish, toadfish, etc.) or is integrated to exocrine pancreas.
		Dipnoi:	Forms a separate organ, 'principal islets', as in teleosts.
Amphibia	Urodela		Endocrine cells scattered in the exocrine tissue or gathered in islets. Some species have no A-cells.
	Anura		Endocrine cells originate from the pancreatic ductule during larval stage and accumulate in islets, which persist during and after metamorphosis.
Reptilia			Endocrine cells form islets. Sometimes they accumulate around duct as an external coat (in some snakes).
Aves Mammalia			Endocrine pancreas mostly found as vascularized islets free of exocrine tissue.

and their ducts. The endocrine secretory cells are formed from the ducts and in several fishes they lie around them. The cyclostome fishes lack such a discrete pancreas and the B-cells are found in the submucosal part of the anterior region of the intestine or around the bile duct.

In mammals the endocrine cells lie in small groups (or islets) that are about 100 to 200 μm in diameter. They are quite distinct from the exocrine tissue. A man has about 2 million of these while the guinea-pig has 15 to 40 thousand. These islets may be an admixture of the three types (A-, B- and D-) of cells or principally composed of a single type; as seen in rabbits and rats. B-cells are about five times more common than A-cells in mammals. Cyclostome fishes only have B-type cells. In the hagfishes (Myxinoidea), they are situated in a distinct gland, around the bile duct near its entrance to the intestine (Fig. 2.16*a*). Lampreys (Petromyzontia) also have a well-defined region of B-cells that extends along the submucosa of the duodenum. The B-cells form follicles (*Follicles of Langerhans*, Barrington, 1942) enclosing a cavity containing material which may represent the storage site for the insulin.

The Chondrichthyes also have different distribution patterns of A- and B-cells. In the Selachii (sharks and rays), the cells are usually situated near or around the ducts of the exocrine pancreatic tissue. In the Holocephali (chimaeroid fishes), this tissue extends more amongst the exocrine cells though it retains its association with the ducts. (see Fig. 2.16*b*).

There is also considerable diversity in the arrangement of the A- and B-cells among bony fishes (Osteichthyes). Some teleosts (toadfish and goosefish) show an aggregation of these cells into two pea-sized glands called '*principal islets*' or *Brockmann bodies* (Fig. 2.16*c*). Others, such as the eel (Fig. 2.16*c*), have islets of tissue scattered among the exocrine tissue as in mammals. In lungfishes (Dipnoi), the tissue is congregated into teleostean-like principal islets, while the Coelacanth (Crossopterygii) has a Selachii-type arrangement where the tissue is associated with the ducts of the acinar cells.

Some of the urodele Amphibia lack A-cells but in a few species, like the axolotl, the tissue forms distinct islets. The anurans, on the other hand, have assumed the tetrapod-like pattern which persists in the reptiles and birds. The latter, however, exhibit some distinctive characteristics not found in other vertebrates. There is a much higher proportion of A-cells which probably accounts for the large amount of glucagon that can be extracted from their pancreas. Three types of islets are present: dark islets containing mainly A-cells, light islets with B-cells and mixed islets with both types.

What is the significance of all this morphological variation in the distribution of A- and B-cells? 'Why are the Islets of Langerhans?' (Henderson,

(*a*)   CYCLOSTOME (*Myxine*)

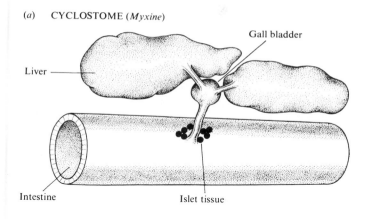

Gall bladder

Liver

Intestine

Islet tissue

(*b*)   CHONDRICHTHYES

Islet tissue

Exocrine pancreas

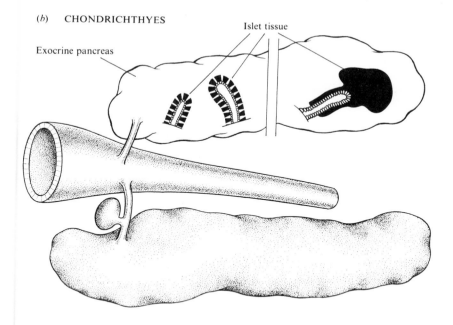

Fig. 2.16. The various types of pancreas in fishes.
(*a*) Cyclostome-type (*Myxine*): ring-like arrangement around the bile duct.
(*b*) Chondrichthyean-types. Left = many elasmobranchs; right = Holocephali.

(c)   ACTINOPTERYGII (Type i)

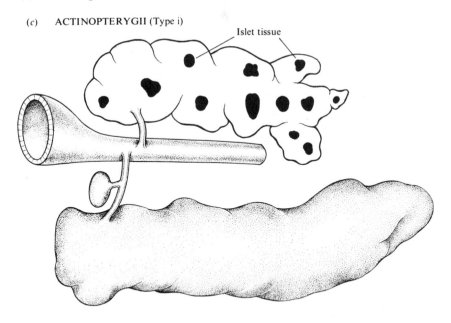

ACTINOPTERYGII (Type ii)

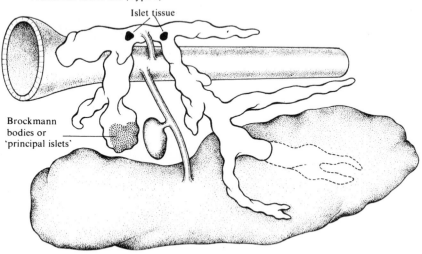

(c) Actinopterygian-types. (i) *Anguilla*; this is present in a few teleosts and is similar to that in tetrapods. (ii) The more general teleost with Brockmann bodies or 'principal islets'. (From Epple, 1969.)

1969). Why, in so many different vertebrates, is the endocrine tissue dispersed so widely amongst the exocrine tissue? While in some fishes the endocrine tissues may tend to retain the site of their embryonic origins from the acinar duct epithelium, there seems to be an evolutionary tendency towards aggregation of the cells. This aggregation sometimes results in relatively large pieces of tissue, the 'principal islets' of the teleosts and dipnoans. Among tetrapods, the small islet arrangement is universal. Henderson (1969) has conjectured that this may reflect a dependence of the exocrine acinar cells on the endocrine tissues that secrete insulin, glucagon and gastrin. The small islets increase the surface area of the endocrine tissues and promote their contact with the exocrine tissue so that high local levels of hormones can be maintained. It has indeed been noticed that, in diabetes mellitus (a lack of insulin) in man, the exocrine pancreas tends to atrophy and become invaded with excess fat and fibrous tissue. The admixture of the A-cells and the B-cells also may have functional significance and there is evidence to suggest that glucagon may have an insulinogenic effect on the A-cells.

The gonads

While the ovaries and testes are not essential for the survival of the individual, they are for the propagation of the species. They have a dual but related function; the production of ova and sperm as well as several hormones that are concerned with the development of the germ cells and the fertilized egg.

The gonads are formed from the dorsal coelomic epithelium. The adrenocortical (or interrenal) tissue has a similar origin and both secrete related steroid hormones. The primordial gonadal tissue consists of a cortex and a medulla. The latter differentiates into the testis, the former the ovary. The steroidogenic cells that are present in the gonads (as well as the adrenals) have a distinctive structure. They contain a very well developed endoplasmic reticulum, mitochondria that have tubular cristae, and usually lipids that histochemically behave like cholesterol. A notable characteristic that helps histological identification of steroidogenic cells in the gonads is the presence of the enzyme 3β-HSDH (Δ^5-3β-hydroxysteroid dehydrogenase). It is responsible for the conversion of certain precursors of the steroid hormones into progesterone and androstenedione which may subsequently be converted to other hormones.

The gonads are usually paired structures lying in the body cavity near the kidneys. The testes of most mammals (except a few such as whales, the elephant and guinea-pig), however, are suspended outside the abdominal cavity in the scrotal sac. Some species have only a single gonad which usually reflects the degeneration of the other or possibly their fusion. The cyclostome fishes only have a single testis and ovary in the median line, while in nearly all birds only the left ovary reaches full development. A single ovary is also sometimes present in teleost and chondrichthyean fishes.

Considerable diversity exists in the relationship of the gonads to their excretory ducts. These are lacking altogether in cyclostomes where the eggs and sperm are released into the body cavity and thence through pores to the exterior. Some fishes, especially teleosts, have gonaducts that are merely extensions of the ovaries. In most vertebrates including many bony fishes, sharks and rays, and tetrapods, the germ cells pass through a homologous series of ducts derived from the Wolffian duct in the male and the Mullerian duct in the female.

Testis

The testis shows a considerable degree of uniformity among the vertebrates (see Dodd, 1960; Lofts, 1968; Lofts and Bern, 1972). The formation of sperm occurs in two principal ways. In amniotes, it differentiates from the germinal epithelium situated in the wall of the seminiferous tubules. Anamniotes, on the other hand, do not have such continuous tubules but those which they have may be branched and divided into lobules. The sperm in these instances is differentiated into groups contained within small envelopes called 'cysts' (cystic spermatogenesis). Two principal types of cells are concerned with the secretion of the male sex hormones. (1) in tetrapods (except for urodele amphibians) groups of cells lying between the seminiferous tubules and called *interstitial* or *Leydig cells* (Fig. 2.17a) are the site of formation of testosterone. In urodele amphibians and fishes, the walls of the testicular lobules contain cells called '*boundary cells*' that apparently have a similar role (Fig. 2.17b). Embryologically, the interstitial and boundary cells are thought to be homologous. Some fishes, including lampreys, possess tetrapod-like interstitial cells. (2) Associated with the basement membrane of the seminiferous tubules are the *Sertoli cells*. Their function has for a long time been controversial and it was suggested that they were concerned with the nourishment of the sperm (hence they are also called 'sustentacular cells'). It now seems clear that they are the site of production of sex hormones that are probably involved in the growth and maturation of the sperm. These cells have been identified in nearly all vertebrates that have been examined. In those species that have a cystic spermatogenesis, they lie juxtaposed to the heads of the sperm in the spermatic cysts.

The testes undergo considerable structural changes associated with the periodic, or cyclical, breeding behavior. These changes are reflected in the size and lipid content of the interstitial and Sertoli cells.

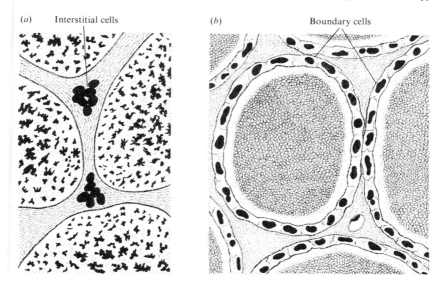

Fig. 2.17. The testis.

(*a*) Sections from a reptile, the viper, showing the lipid-filled interstitial (Leydig) cells. (*b*) A teleost fish; the pike, showing the boundary cells in the wall of the testicular lobule. These are the homologues of the interstitial cells which are absent in most of the fishes. (From Gorbman and Bern, 1962, based on data from B. Lofts and A. J. Marshall.)

The ovaries

The ovaries contain several distinct types of cells and tissues (see Lofts and Bern, 1972; Dodd, 1960) (Fig. 2.18). (1) The *germinal epithelium* that envelops the ovaries and from which the developing eggs and their surrounding sheet of granulosa cells are formed. (2) The latter is called the *theca interna* which, in turn, is surrounded by a fibrous *theca externa*. The complete structure, ovum and its surrounding membranes, is called the *Graafian follicle*. (3) Following the maturation and expulsion of the ova the granulosa cells may form the *lutein cells* that compose the *corpus luteum*. Also present in the ovary are structures formed as the result of the degeneration (atresia) of unovulated follicles, the *corpora atretica*. (4) Lying in between all these structures is the *interstitial tissue* which anatomically, and probably functionally, is analogous to the tissue of the same name in the testis.

Estrogenic hormones are formed by the cells of the theca interna and possibly the granulosa cells of the developing follicles. Progesterone arises from the lutein cells of the corpus luteum and, at least in the rat, the interstitial tissue. The latter also produces androgenic hormones.

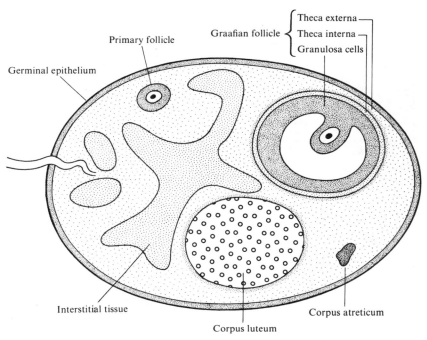

Fig. 2.18. The ovary. Diagrammatic representation of the various tissues present. (From Lofts and Bern, 1972.)

The basic structure and endocrine role of the ovaries persists throughout the vertebrates. There are some points worthy of comment. The corpus luteum is not present in all species, especially oviparous ones. It is absent in birds which nevertheless have progesterone in their ovaries and blood. Corpora lutea appear sporadically among other vertebrate groups. They are present in ovoviviparous and viviparous amphibians, chondrichthyeans and some teleosts. A corpus luteum also appears following ovulation in *Myxine* (hagfish) while all reptiles (including oviparous ones) develop a corpus luteum after ovulating. Indirect, histological, and more direct chemical evidence indicates that it produces progesterone in all groups. It is possible that the corpora atretica also produce hormones but many consider this to be doubtful.

Putative endocrine glands

The pineal body

Some argue that, at least in mammals and probably also in birds, the pineal body deserves the title of gland and should not be classified as a putative endocrine. It forms melatonin which exerts an antigonadotrophic action in some vertebrates and pales the skin in larval amphibians and cyclostomes.

The pineal (see Ariëns Kappers, 1965, 1970; Oksche, 1965; Wurtman, Axelrod and Kelly, 1968) originates as a sac-like evagination from the dorsal part of the brain (the diencephalon) (Fig. 2.19*a, b*). It lies beneath the cranium in the mid-line position and is also called, especially in mammals, the *epiphysis cerebri*. Embryologically, its hollow stem maintains contact with the III ventricle and this pattern persists in many non-mammals.

The pineal body is present in most vertebrates. It is, however, absent in hagfish (myxinoid cyclostomes), crocodiles, at least two species of chondrichthyeans (*Torpedo ocellata* and *T. marmorata*) and several mammals, including whales. The pineal is very small in the elephant and rhinoceros.

In man, the pineal is a relatively simple knob of tissue but in other vertebrates it is more complex. It appears to have undergone considerable changes in its structure (and no doubt function) during its evolution. Noteworthy is the differentiation of an associated tissue that comes to lie nearer to the roof of the skull. This is variously called the *parapineal* (in fishes), *frontal-* (in amphibians) and *parietal-* (in reptiles) *organ*. In many species, especially lizards, it penetrates through the brain case and lies just beneath the skin. The parapineal is connected to the roof of the brain, or the pineal body proper by nerve cells. In fishes, amphibians and certain reptiles (not the snakes), the parapineal and even the pineal body contain photoreceptor cells. In lizards and the tuatara (Rhyncocephalia), the pineal takes the form of a well-differentiated 'third eye' that even contains struc-

(*a*)

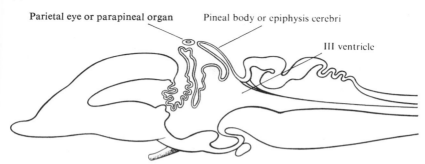

Fig. 2.19. (*a*) The pineal body in relation to the brain (in section) of a lower vertebrate. (From Bargmann, 1943.)

(b)

LAMPREY

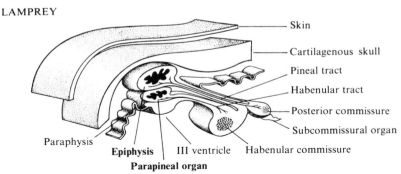

- Skin
- Cartilagenous skull
- Pineal tract
- Habenular tract
- Posterior commissure
- Subcommissural organ

Paraphysis

Epiphysis | III ventricle   Habenular commissure

Parapineal organ

TELEOST FISH

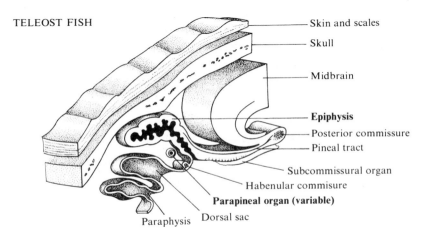

- Skin and scales
- Skull
- Midbrain
- **Epiphysis**
- Posterior commissure
- Pineal tract
- Subcommissural organ

Habenular commisure

Parapineal organ (variable)

Paraphysis   Dorsal sac

ALBINO RAT

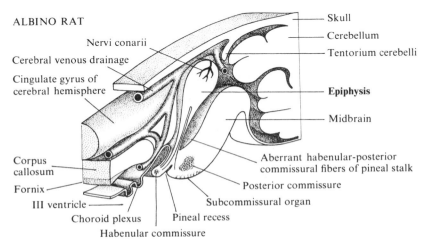

Nervi conarii

Cerebral venous drainage

Cingulate gyrus of
cerebral hemisphere

- Skull
- Cerebellum
- Tentorium cerebelli
- **Epiphysis**
- Midbrain

Corpus
callosum

Fornix

III ventricle

Choroid plexus | Pineal recess

Habenular commissure

- Aberrant habenular-posterior
  commissural fibers of pineal stalk
- Posterior commissure

Subcommissural organ

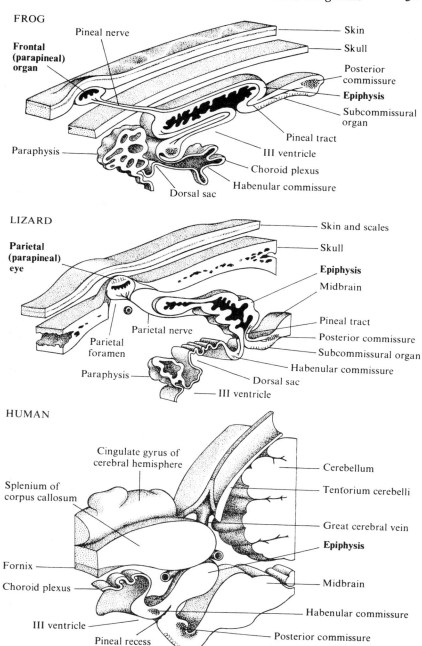

FROG

Pineal nerve — Skin

Frontal (parapineal) organ — Skull

Posterior commissure

Epiphysis

Subcommissural organ

Pineal tract

III ventricle

Choroid plexus

Paraphysis — Habenular commissure

Dorsal sac

LIZARD

Skin and scales — Skull

Parietal (parapineal) eye

Epiphysis

Midbrain

Parietal nerve

Pineal tract

Parietal foramen

Posterior commissure

Subcommissural organ

Paraphysis

Habenular commissure

Dorsal sac

III ventricle

HUMAN

Cingulate gyrus of cerebral hemisphere

Cerebellum

Tentorium cerebelli

Splenium of corpus callosum

Great cerebral vein

Epiphysis

Fornix

Midbrain

Choroid plexus

Habenular commissure

III ventricle

Posterior commissure

Pineal recess

Subcommissural organ

(*b*) The pineal of various vertebrates in relation to the dorsal diencephalic roof region. (From Wurtman *et al.*, 1968.)

tures analogous to the cornea and lens of lateral eyes. In such vertebrates the pineal has a sensory function.

The pineal of mammals lacks functioning photosensory cells but these have been modified to form secretory cells (*pinealocytes*) that seem to have an endocrine function. The presence of photosensory cells in the bird pineal is equivocal but pinealocytes are present. Whether or not the pineal of other vertebrates secretes hormone-like products is uncertain. In the simplest interpretation of pineal evolution, it may be viewed as evolving from a sensory structure in fish to an endocrine gland in birds and mammals.

Embryologically, the pineal body is a hollow sac-like structure and this persists in most vertebrates. In mammals, it is filled with parenchymous cells (the pinealocytes) which are derived from the photoreceptor cells seen in lower vertebrates. Some birds (many Passeriformes) exhibit the primitive

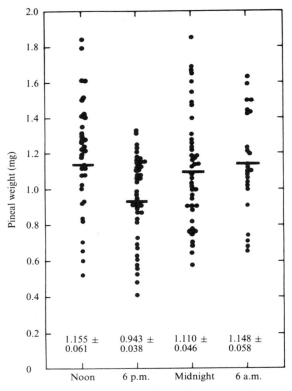

Fig. 2.20. Rhythmical changes in the weight of the rat's pineal throughout the day. These changes are associated with changes in various biochemical products that are present in the gland. (From Axelrod, Wurtman and Snyder, 1965.)

hollow condition while others, like the domestic fowl, have a solid pineal containing pinealocytes. In mammals and birds, the pineal organ has an autonomic sympathetic innervation arising from the superior cervical ganglion, the destruction of which (in rats anyway) has profound effects. In other vertebrates, the pineal seems to maintain direct neural contact with the brain but an autonomic innervation is also evident in fish, amphibians and reptiles. The pineal has been shown to form several substances that have potent biological effects. These include noradrenaline (in nerve cells) and serotonin and melatonin (in the pinealocytes). Melatonin has been identified in the circulation and may represent the pineal's endocrine product. Melatonin and serotonin have also been identified in the bird and amphibian pineal. One of the enzymes responsible for its formation, HIOMT (hydroxyindole-*O*-methyl-transferase), has been found in the pineal of fish and all the tetrapod groups as well as in the lateral eyes of fish, amphibians, reptiles and birds (but not in mammals).

The pineal of rats undergoes a number of changes associated with the exposure of the animals to light. It increases in weight in rats kept in the dark and decreases on exposure to light. Weight changes can be seen to follow a circadian rhythm over a normal 24-hour period (Fig. 2.20). As we shall see later, this change in weight may reflect its role (?) as a 'neuro-endocrine transducer' in the control of reproductive cycles.

The pineal body has often been described as a 'vestigial' organ. Despite the implied slight about its usefulness, it has shown considerable phylogenetic persistence during which it appears to have evolved from a mainly sensory organ to an endocrine one.

Corpuscles of Stannius and the renal juxtaglomerular cells

These cells are both associated with the kidneys and may possibly produce some secretions that are similar to each other. Hence for convenience they will be dealt with together.

The corpuscles of Stannius

These tissues are so named after their discoverer (Stannius, 1839). They appear to form a hormone that decreases blood calcium levels and may also have osmotic effects in fishes. They are distinct well-vascularized masses of tissue that are present near the kidney of some, but not all, fishes. Their number varies considerably, 40 to 50 are present in the bowfin, *Amia calva* (Holostei), while in the Teleostei the number varies from two to six. They are absent in some teleosts, including the Salmonidae, as well as the Chondrostei (sturgeons) (Krishnamurthy and Bern, 1969). In the corpuscles, one, or sometimes two, types of cells can be distinguished that are usually arranged in rows to form lobules around a central core. These cells contain granules, the number and appearance of which can be seen to vary conspicuously with changes in the breeding cycle, the life cycle and the osmotic environment. This has led to the suggestion that they may have an endocrine role. Indeed, as will be related later, extracts of these tissues have been shown to contain materials that in some instances may alter sodium and calcium metabolism as well as exhibit a vasopressor effect similar to that of a kidney hormone called renin.

The corpuscles of Stannius are usually derived from the pronephric duct (in some instances they are formed from the mesonephric duct). The presence of the renin-like material in the tissue extracts may be a reflection of this origin.

The Holostei have the largest number of corpuscles of Stannius and it has been suggested that the reduction among the Teleostei, culminating in their absence in the Salmonidae, may reflect an evolutionary trend. In one study (Krishnamurthy and Bern, 1969) 28 species of teleosts from 16

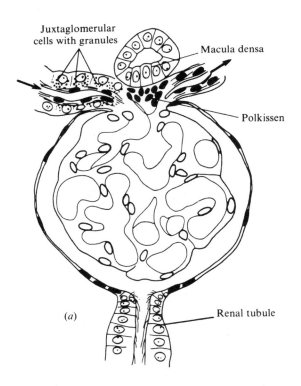

(a)

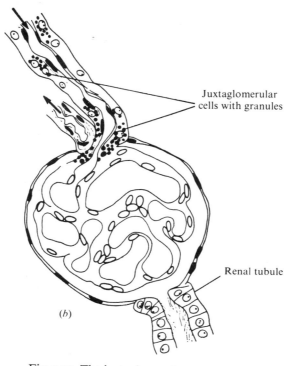

Juxtaglomerular cells with granules

Renal tubule

(b)

Fig. 2.21. The juxtaglomerular apparatus.
(a) The laboratory rat. (b) The bullfrog (*Rana catesbeiana*) showing the absence of a macula densa and polkissen. (From Sokabe *et al.* (1969). *Texas Reports Biol. Med.* **27**, 3.)

different families were examined but no conclusions as to any evolutionary relationships in their morphology could be drawn.

The juxtaglomerular apparatus

The kidney is the site of formation of a protein called *renin*, considered by some to be an enzyme and by others a hormone, which can be released into the circulation. This secretion initiates the formation of a peptide, called *angiotensin*, in the plasma, which contributes to the regulation of sodium retention in the body and possibly also increases blood pressure. Renin is widely considered to be formed by cells situated near the renal glomerulus at a site called the juxtaglomerular apparatus. In mammals it consists of *juxtaglomerular cells* (on the afferent glomerular arteriole) and the *macula densa*, which is a thickening of the distal renal tubule in the region where it abuts onto a glomerular area called the *polkissen* (or extraglomerular mesangium) (Fig. 2.21*a*). In non-mammals the situation is less complex (Fig. 2.21*b*) as the macula densa and polkissen are absent (the former may be present in birds). Many species, however, still have the juxtaglomerular cells (see Fig. 2.22). They contain 'granules' that can be stained histo-

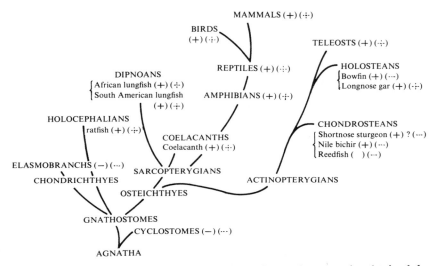

Fig. 2.22. Phylogenetic distribution of juxtaglomerular granules (stained by Bowie's method) and renin activity in the kidneys of vertebrates: (+) or (−), presence or absence of renin; (·∹·) or (···), presence or absence of granules. It can be seen that while the two are always associated with each other in tetrapods and most fishes this is not so in all holosteans or chondrosteans. (From Nishimura, Ogawa and Sawyer, 1973, modified by H. Nishimura.)

logically in a distinctive way (Bowies method). Such juxtaglomerular granules occur in arterioles often distant from glomeruli in teleost, dipnoan and coleacanth fishes and even in aglomerular fishes but in most vertebrates they occur in the afferent glomerular arteriole. The latter type of cells are present in birds, reptiles, amphibians and teleost fishes but neither these cells nor Bowie's granules have been identified in the elasmobranchs or cyclostomes (see Ogawa *et al.*, 1972). These observations parallel the identification of renin in the kidneys of these groups. An inconsistency exists in that juxtaglomerular cells with granules stainable by the Bowie method have not been found in many of the Chondrostei or Holostei even though there is evidence to suggest the presence of renin in such fish. Renin has also been tentatively identified in the corpuscles of Stannius in teleost fishes (Chester Jones *et al.*, 1966; Sokabe *et al.*, 1970) but it is not clear if Bowie's granules are also present in these tissues (compare for instance Sokabe *et al.*, 1970; Krishnamurthy and Bern, 1969).

The macula densa may be concerned with the regulation of the release of renin in mammals (and birds?). Renin and angiotensin contribute to the regulation of sodium levels in the bodies of mammals. It has been suggested that local changes in the sodium permeability of the macula densa may regulate the release of renin from the juxtaglomerular cells (Vander, 1967). Sodium-depletion increases the release of renin and this response has been shown to be dependent on a renal 'vascular receptor' (Gotshall *et al.*, 1973). In this respect it is noteworthy that a reduction in renal blood flow, such as results from hemorrhage or stimulation of the renal nerves, also promotes renin release in mammals but this response can be blocked by a β-adrenergic blocking drug (propranolol) that acts distally to the renal vascular muscle (Coote *et al.*, 1972). Thus several steps appear to be involved in the release of renin but more precise evidence as to the role (if any) of the macula densa is lacking. It is interesting that non-mammals may also utilize the renin–angiotensin system to aid sodium-regulation in the body and as these animals lack a macula densa it presumably does not have an essential role in this process in all vertebrates. It remains possible, however, that it could mediate some effect on the release of renin that is special to the mammals.

The urophysis

Tucked away beneath the vertebrae in the tail of teleost fishes is a lump of tissue that has been called the urophysis and which may influence their osmoregulation and assist smooth muscle contraction in the urinogenital tract. This 'gland' was first described in 1813 and has since been identified in some 400 different species of teleost fishes. Despite its widespread distribution and systematic persistence, its physiological role is still not understood but has captured considerable attention from several endocrinologists (see Fridberg and Bern, 1968).

The urophysis, like the neurohypophysis, is composed of neural tissue, whose cell bodies are situated in the posterior part of the spinal cord. Axons of these cells pass outside the spinal column ventrally where they make contact with blood vessels (that lead through the kidneys) to form a neuro-hemal junction. Such an arrangement is admirably suited to the discharge of endocrine secretions into the circulation. Whether this occurs or not is, however, equivocal. These nerve cells contain granules and appear to be typical neurosecretory cells such as those seen in the neurohypophysis, though their tinctorial characteristics differ. Extracts of this tissue show several biological activities; they can alter the permeability of some membranes to water and sodium, contract certain smooth muscle preparations, increase the blood pressure of eels and lower the blood pressure of rats.

A distinct neurohemal urophysis has only been identified in teleost fish. The chondrichthyeans, however, also possess neurosecretory-type cells in the caudal part of the vertebral column. These cells are giant neurons, about 20 times the size of an ordinary motor neuron and, in *Raja batis*, extend along the last 55 vertebrae. They are called *Dahlgren cells* after their discoverer and send their axons out of the ventral part of the spinal

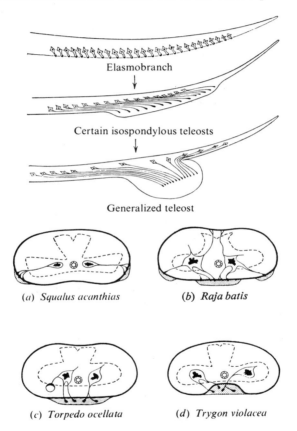

Fig. 2.23. The urophysis.

Top. Proposed evolution of the teleost urophysis from elasmobranchs which have neurosecretory Dahlgren cells. Longitudinal section through the tail.

Bottom. (*a*) to (*d*). Different configurations of the Dahlgren cells among the elasmobranchs.

Transverse sections through the spinal cord. The vascular beds are shaded and the menix is represented by a heavy line. (From Fridberg and Bern, 1968.)

cord to make contact with blood vessels there. The tissue is thus more widespread along the spinal cord. Comparable tissues appear to be present in holostean fishes but not in cyclostomes.

The types of such structures present in chondrichthyeans and teleosts are shown in Fig. 2.23. The diffuse distribution of tissue seen in the sharks and rays may represent a primitive pattern which has subsequently evolved among teleosts to form a discrete aggregation. The widespread distribution and systematic persistence make one suspect that the urophysis serves a physiological role. Its histological and cytological appearance, similarity to the neurohypophysis and its neural and vascular connections suggest an endocrine gland. Conclusive evidence is, however, not yet available.

The thymus

The thymus, like the parathyroids and ultimobranchial bodies, is derived, embryologically, from the gill pouches and so is situated in the region of the neck or upper thorax. In fishes all the gill pouches may be involved but in amniotes usually only numbers III and IV. The thymus is present in all groups of vertebrates, from cyclostomes to mammals, but is more prominent in young and larval forms than adults where, in some species, it may even disappear. The thymus tissue may exist in varying degrees of agglomeration, from a single bilobed organ, as in mammals, to paired structures, as in frogs, or in several dispersed nodes, as in the domestic fowl. The ultimobranchial bodies and even parathyroids may on occasions be associated with the thymus.

The endocrine function of the thymus is not an established one. A number of biologically active materials have, however, been extracted from it and these (several proteins and a steroid) have been called 'thymic hormones' (see Luckey, 1973). During early life the thymus produces lymphocytes that are involved in the development of immunity. It has been proposed that the so-called thymic hormone(s) may initiate development of immune competence (ability of cells to react to the presence of foreign substances or antigens) in the lymphocytes and bone marrow. Such 'hormones' thus could be considered to be involved in embryonic differentiation.

One of these 'hormones' (see Bach *et al.*, 1972; Goldstein *et al.*, 1974) has been isolated from the thymus and is a polypeptide with a molecular weight of about 1000. It has been called thymosin and has been identified in the blood of the mouse and man. The circulating concentrations decline with age and after thymectomy. In man the thymosin concentration in the blood starts to decrease at 30 to 40 years of age and it disappears after about 50 years. There is considerable medical interest in these discoveries as the blood levels have also been shown to be low in diseases where immune responses are deficient and it fails to decline with age in people suffering from myasthenia gravis. The latter disease (a failure of skeletal muscles to be able to contract adequately) can often be ameliorated by thymectomy. Another intriguing possibility is that the decline in the activity of the thymus contributes to the process of aging and an increased susceptibility to infectious diseases. It seems likely that this interesting tissue will gain the status of a true endocrine gland.

Conclusions

It can be seen that while the endocrine glands display considerable inter-specific differences in their morphology many of these variations can be placed into categories that correspond to major systematic groups of vertebrates. It would thus appear that the endocrines have evolved in a relatively orderly manner that may be influenced by broad structural considerations, such as the animal's shape, size and pattern of embryonic differentiation, as well as its particular hormonal requirements. Such evolutionary changes are not, however, confined to the glands' morphology for, as we shall see in the next chapter, considerable variation also occurs in the chemical structures of the hormones themselves.

3. The chemical structure and polymorphism, and evolution of hormones

In a mammal the endocrine glands secrete more than 40 distinct hormones. In addition, different species may form many hormones that, while being structurally analogous, nevertheless display chemical differences. Such natural variants are usually characteristic of a single species and represent a polymorphism of the excitant's molecular structure. This change has a genetic basis. For example, it may only be the substitution of a single amino acid in the molecule of a peptide hormone or it may be much more extensive. The biological effects of such differences can be considerable or negligible.

Vertebrate hormones belong to two principal classes of chemical compounds. Some are made from cholesterol. These are the steroid hormones from the adrenal cortex and the gonads. The others are made up of amino acids and range in complexity from those, like adrenaline, that are derived from a single tyrosine molecule, to others like the pituitary growth hormone that contain about 190 such units. The molecular weights can vary from about 200 to 30 000.

What properties do these molecules have that make them suitable to be hormones? What characteristics may be important for their utilization as such? Armed with considerable hindsight about endocrine physiology some answers can be offered. The basic requirements will not be the same for all hormones but will depend on what they do. The steroid hormones are poorly soluble in water but readily soluble in lipids. This will facilitate their penetration into the cell and fixation at intracellular sites. Such lipid solubility will also be important if a hormone is to penetrate the blood–brain barrier. Transport in the blood is essential for a hormone to fulfil its physiological role so that, if they are hydrophobic molecules, they must either be effective at very low concentrations or be attachable to protein components which carry them to their sites of action. This binding is especially prominent among the steroid and thyroid hormones. An ability to interact with other biological molecules is also important for 'triggering' the excitant effects of hormones. They must be capable of interacting with a receptor molecule in, or on, the effector tissue. Such an interaction must not be of a strong covalent nature but must involve chemical forces whereby an equilibrium of a reversible nature occurs. Above all, a hormone must have a high degree of specificity towards its target receptor site. Necessarily this is a property

[61]

of both structures. The manner by which it is accomplished is still largely conjectural. Hormones have complex three-dimensional structures which contain various components that may be electrically charged, hydrophilic or hydrophobic, acidic or basic, and so on. Such properties together may constitute a 'key' to which the receptor acts as a complementary 'lock'. Obviously, large hormone molecules offer the possibilities of more complex 'keys' and greater specificity. They are also more liable to genetically mediated structural changes. The latter are very common events in nature. The contribution of size to specificity of effect is, however, not at all clear. Indeed, it is difficult to comprehend why such gigantic molecules as the pituitary adenohypophysial hormones are necessary to mediate their effects. There is no evidence to indicate that evolution towards smaller, more compact hormone molecules has occurred, such as would perhaps be expected if they initially contained much superfluous material. Indeed some hormone molecules, for instance parathormone, contain sections that are not needed for their biological activity.

In order to function optimally, a hormone molecule needs to possess some other properties consonant with its physiological role. For adequate control, hormonal responses often need to be rapidly terminated. The excitant can either be readily excretable in the urine or bile, or, by virtue of the presence of chemical groups that can be changed by metabolic processes, be converted to an inactive form. The synthesis of hormones is not always rapid enough to meet the immediate demands for their release, so that their accumulation and storage in glandular tissues may be necessary. In this instance the molecule should possess a considerable measure of innate stability and be able to interact with cellular (or even extracellular; as for thyroxine) binding proteins that facilitate this storage. Related to such a process is an ability to undergo rapid mobilization from such storage sites so that the hormone can be released into the blood.

Clearly, hormones are highly specialized molecular structures incorporating (or programmed for) several important interrelated properties. They are not just 'keys' that fit various 'locks'. In order to function as a hormone a molecule must also exhibit a variety of other physical and chemical properties consistent with the hormone's synthesis, storage, release, transport, and removal from the body.

Structural differences between hormones are tentatively assumed on the basis of differences in their biological actions. They are confirmed by the demonstration of variations in their chemical behavior and ultimately by the determination of their molecular structure. It is usually a comparatively simple procedure to show that two hormones differ from each other. Tests for biological activity; for instance changes in blood glucose levels, an ability to alter blood pressure, decrease urine flow and so on, are reasonably straightforward laboratory procedures. Broad chemical differences in even very impure preparations can often be seen when, for instance, one compares their stabilities at different temperatures and pH's, solubilities in different solvents, relative rates of destruction when incubated with various enzymes and so on. Such biological and chemical characterization can be used to identify and measure the relative quantities of the hormonal material present in an extract. Determination of chemical composition and structure is a more complex procedure and, before this can be done, highly purified preparations must be made.

Differences in the composition of related homologous hormones in distinct (or even on occasion the same) species are more difficult to detect. The molecules may only exhibit quite small quantitative, in contrast to qualitative, differences in a common biological activity.

Several procedures are available to help us make such distinctions.

(1) Biological activities can be compared. A simple cross-test between two or more species can be informative. For instance, a comparison between the action of extracts of the neurohypophyses of frogs with those from mammals indicated the presence of different but analogous hormones. Heller (in 1941) found that extracts from the neurohypophyses of European frogs (*Rana temporaria*) were about 20 times as active in eliciting water retention in frogs than a comparable amount of a hormone extract from the mammalian pituitary. The two extracts (frog and mammal) were each standarized by their ability to contract the guinea-pig uterus and to increase the blood pressure of cats. Equal amounts of activity, as measured in these ways, showed that the homologous frog hormone was much more active in frogs than the mammalian one. As we shall see, this change reflects a single amino acid substitution in the octapeptide molecule of mammalian antidiuretic hormone. Similar comparisons have been made between many species and usually the more distantly related they are the greater their effects differ. Even two closely related species may show distinct differences; thus pituitary growth hormone from animals, including other primates, is completely ineffective in man even though that from man is active in many other species. Hormones often exhibit a variety of biological actions and, by comparing them in several assay systems, a pharmacological profile or 'fingerprint' can be made. This can be used to characterize some hormones with a considerable degree of accuracy.

(2) The chemical behavior of hormones can be shown to differ. In closely related molecules this may be difficult to detect. It may depend on differences in electrophoretic or chromatographic mobilities in different solvent systems. A correlation (isopolarity), however, does not necessarily confirm the chemical identity of two molecules. Steroid molecules are often

chemically altered, for instance by methylation, and their chromatographic behavior is again compared. If it still corresponds, the evidence of identity is much stronger. The absorption spectra of extracts can also be compared. This measurement may involve the use of ultraviolet and infrared light when the hormones are dissolved in different solvents. Mass spectrometry and nuclear magnetic resonance spectrometry are effective but expensive methods for identifying many hormonal materials. Using such procedures a chemical 'fingerprint' can be obtained for comparison with standard preparations of known structure. Such chemical methods are particularly useful in aiding the identification of steroid hormones (see Brooks *et al.*, 1970; Sandor and Idler, 1972).

(3) Immunological responses are used to predict the differences in the structure of protein hormones. Antibodies (or antisera) to purified hormones can be made following their injection into another species, often a rabbit. The degree of interaction of protein hormones with such antisera can be followed in a precipitin test or by comparing their abilities to displace known radio-iodinated hormones from binding with the antibodies. Apart from indicating similarities and differences between hormones, such immunological procedures are now widely used to measure the quantities of hormones by radioimmunoassay. This procedure is not confined to protein hormones, as antibodies to other hormones including steroids and thyroid hormones, can be made by conjugating them to a protein molecule and using this to elicit formation of antibodies.

(4) The chemical structure of a hormone may be determined. This is ultimately desirable and allows one to relate the structure of the molecule to its biological actions and even predict the genetic basis of its formation and possible evolution. As some hormones are very complex structures containing as many as 200 amino acids, knowledge of their precise chemical structure has been somewhat slow in coming. A special relationship with immunological procedures also exists, as these can be used to confirm the chemical proposals. Initial chemical analyses of human growth hormone and prolactin indicated that they had identical chemical structures but this was not confirmed immunologically. Presumably small, as yet undetected, differences exist in man, as has been shown between these hormones in other species.

While the chemical structure of many hormones is known, this knowledge is mainly confined to the mammals, especially with respect to the larger protein hormones. In addition, although the disposition of chemical groups and the sequence of amino acids may be known, little information is available as to their three-dimensional (tertiary) arrangement. Such data will ultimately be required if we are to understand properly how the hormones work.

Steroid hormones

Steroids are chemical compounds derived from cholesterol. They consist of a series of carbon rings, the basic unit being the cycloperhydrophen-

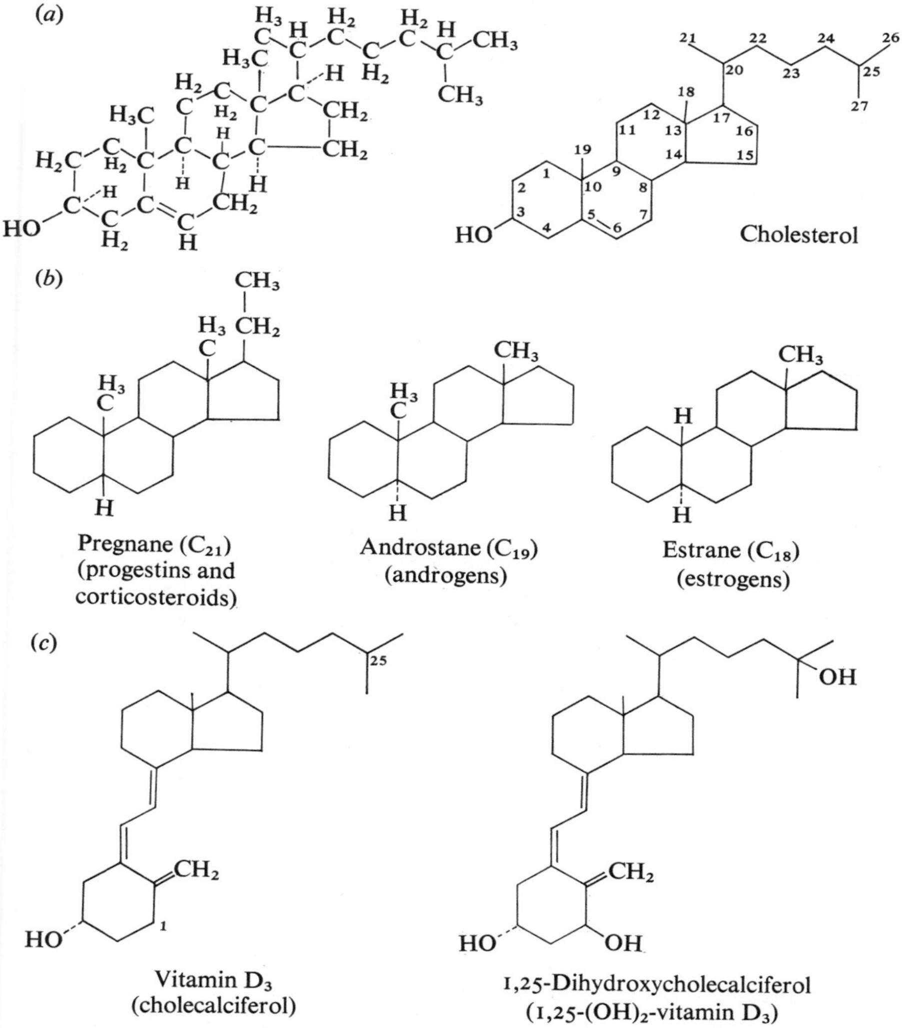

(a)

Cholesterol

(b)

Pregnane (C_{21})
(progestins and
corticosteroids)

Androstane (C_{19})
(androgens)

Estrane (C_{18})
(estrogens)

(c)

Vitamin D_3
(cholecalciferol)

1,25-Dihydroxycholecalciferol
(1,25-$(OH)_2$-vitamin D_3)

Fig. 3.1. (a) The chemical structure of cholesterol and the conventional manner of numbering the carbon atoms.

(b) The parent steroid compounds for the progestins and corticosteroids (C_{21}), androgens (C_{19}), and estrogens (C_{18}).

(c) Vitamin D_3 and its active metabolite 1,25-dihydroxycholcalciferol.

anthrene nucleus. Such compounds occur widely in nature and are not confined to the animal kingdom. Plants contain many steroids and some of these may even exhibit activities reminiscent of those of the mammalian hormones: for example, catkins of the pussywillow plant contain steroids that have the effects of female sex hormones (estrogenic activity). Steroids obtained from plants are indeed often used as starting materials for the preparation of vertebrate-like hormones in the laboratory.

Several different types of steroids function as hormones in vertebrates. These and the parent cholesterol molecule are shown in Fig. 3.1*a*, *b*. They are often classified in the following manner: (1) Those based on pregnane and containing 21 carbon atoms (C_{21}). These include the adrenocortical steroids and progesterone which, apart from being a metabolic intermediate in the formation of most steroid hormones, also acts as a sex hormone, especially during pregnancy. (2) Androstane compounds with 19 carbons (C_{19}) and which include the androgens that have the actions of male sex hormones. (3) Estrane (C_{18}) compounds that have actions of female sex hormones (estrogenic). (4) Vitamin D (Fig. 3.1*c*), a group of sterols the precursors of which are commonly obtained in the diet and which can be converted (see Chapter 6) into hormones that influence calcium metabolism.

The hormones from the gonads and adrenal cortex are all derived from cholesterol compounds. In the instance of C_{18}, C_{19}, and C_{21} steroids, various metabolic pathways, usually involving several hydrolase enzymes, lead to the formation of the ultimate hormone product (Fig. 3.2). These include the female sex hormones, called *estrogens* (C_{18}) – estradiol-17β, estrone and estriol; the *androgens* (C_{19}) mainly testosterone but also its metabolic precursor androstenedione; *progestins* (C_{21}), progesterone and the *adrenocorticosteroids* (C_{21}) cortisol, corticosterone, aldosterone and 1α-hydroxycorticosterone. Some other adrenocorticosteroids, such as cortisone, are also sometimes found in the blood.

Many other steroids are found in the steroidogenic tissues where they constitute intermediates of the hormones, while others may represent products of steroid catabolism. The chemical structures of these hormones are shown in Fig. 3.2.

The C_{18}, C_{19} and C_{21} steroids have been identified in tissues and also often in the blood of all the main groups of vertebrates. The compounds present are, however, not identical in all of these while the evidence of their precise identity in some (for instance cyclostomes) has been noted as 'tentative' or 'only suggestive' (see Idler, 1972). Steroids of a hormonal nature, nevertheless, undoubtedly have a wide phyletic distribution among vertebrates.

The sex hormones show a remarkable uniformity; testosterone, progesterone and estradiol-17β are common throughout the vertebrates. This possibly reflects the 'conservative' nature of the sexual process and the early evolution of a mechanism of such efficiency that little subsequent endocrine modification of the hormonal excitants could be advantageous. It can be seen in Fig. 3.2 that, when the structures of the steroid hormones are compared, the chemical differences appear surprisingly minor. Nevertheless each molecule exerts distinct effects. A high degree of specificity based on such simple structural differences probably allows little room for subsequent successful evolutionary 'experiments'.

Among the adrenocorticosteroids different molecules have emerged and these often have a distinct systematic distribution (Fig. 3.3). There is some doubt as to whether such corticosteroid hormones exist in the cyclostome fishes (see Weisbart and Idler, 1970). The steroid 1α-hydroxycorticosterone is widespread in the adrenal tissues and blood of the Chondrichthyes. This hormone is, however, only present in the Selachii (sharks and rays) and not the Holocephali (chimaeroids) which instead have cortisol (see Idler and Truscott, 1972). Among the Actinopterygii (including the Holostei, Chondrostei and Teleostei) cortisol is the predominant corticosteroid in the blood. Cortisone, aldosterone and corticosterone have also been identified in teleosts but the quantities appear to be small. The criteria for such identifications are, however, sometimes in doubt. The Dipnoi (lung-fishes) possess cortisol, like other bony fishes, and recently a fascinating discovery has been the additional identification of aldosterone in the South American lungfish *Lepidosiren paradoxa* (Idler, Sangalang and Truscott, 1972). Aldosterone has been identified in the blood of representatives of all the tetrapod groups so that its presence in the Dipnoi, but not apparently in most other fish (though it has been found in the Atlantic herring) is consistent with their suggested phylogenetic relationships to tetrapods. A second major corticosteroid, corticosterone, is also present in amphibians, reptiles and birds. This hormone is also the major corticosteroid in some mammals while in others cortisol is predominant.

The ratio of cortisol to corticosterone varies among the mammals. Rats, rabbits and mice secrete little or no cortisol from their adrenal cortices; corticosterone (aldosterone is also present) predominates. Other mammals secrete a mixture of cortisol and corticosterone, usually with the former predominant. It was at one time suggested that the ratio cortisol: corticosterone may be a characteristic of a species and therefore be determined genetically. It has, however, been subsequently found that this ratio can vary considerably, even in a single animal, depending on the physiological conditions. Nevertheless, the inability of the rat to form cortisol reflects the absence of an enzyme, 17α-hydroxylase, and it seems likely that this, at least, is genetic. Most mammals, including placentals and marsupials, secrete more cortisol than corticosterone. An interesting exception is the

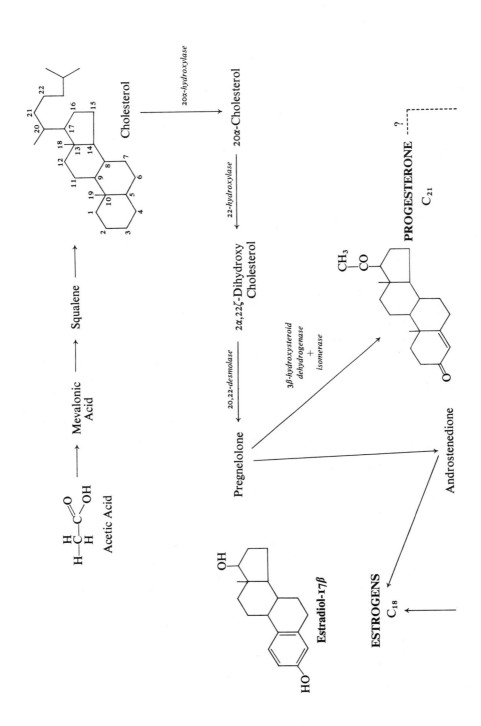

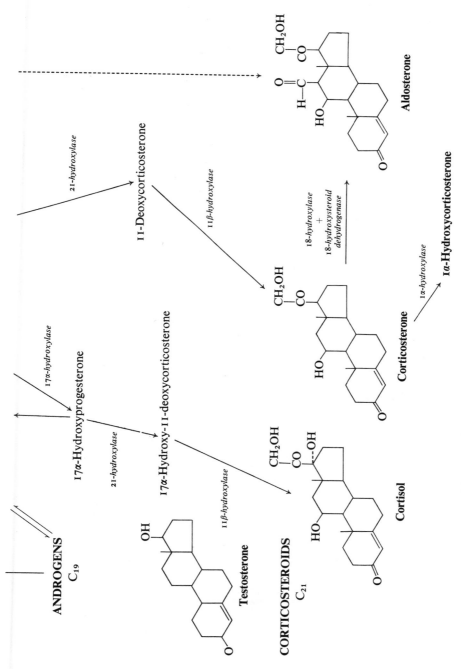

Fig. 3.2. Interrelationships and formation of the steroid hormones.

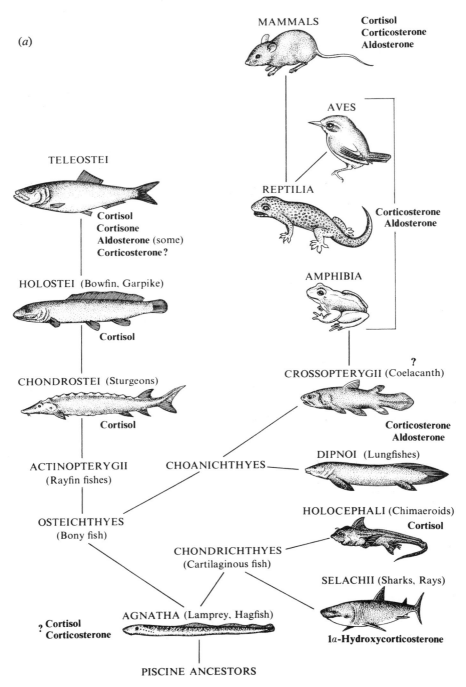

Fig. 3.3. (a) Phyletic distribution of the adrenocorticosteroids in the vertebrates.

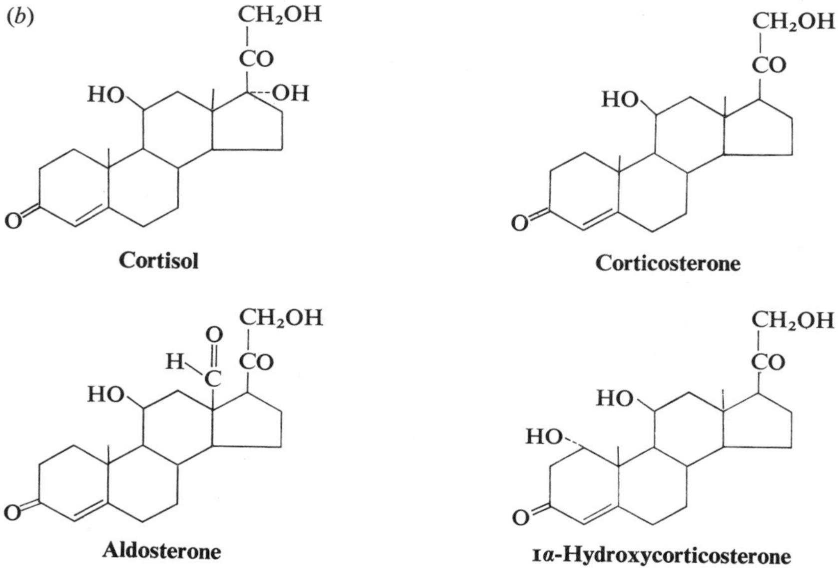
(b)
CH₂OH
CO
HO
OH
O
Cortisol
CH₂OH
CO
HO
O
Corticosterone
CH₂OH
O
H
C
CO
HO
O
Aldosterone
CH₂OH
CO
HO
HO
O
1α-Hydroxycorticosterone

(*b*) The principal structures of the corticosteroid hormones.

echidna *Tachyglossus aculeatus*, a monotreme in which corticosterone predominates (Weiss and McDonald, 1965). This pattern is more like that in reptiles and birds than that in most other mammals.

The corticosteroids, in contrast to the sex steroids, display different chemical structures that probably reflect evolutionary changes. Sex is a relatively uniform process but the roles of corticosteroids show some variation. This may be reflected in the different structures of these steroids. The role of 1α-hydroxycorticosterone in the Selachii is unknown. In other vertebrates, cortisol and corticosterone influence intermediary metabolism, which is a basic function in all vertebrates. Aldosterone, and to a lesser extent corticosterone, exert a prominent effect on sodium and potassium metabolism in tetrapods. These animals have special osmotic problems not faced by their piscine ancestors, so that it is conceivable that the solutions to them were not only accompanied by the evolution of special effector mechanisms but also hormones to fit them.

Hormones made from tyrosine

Catecholamines

The adrenal medulla and other chromaffin tissues secrete two hormones, adrenaline and noradrenaline (Fig. 3.4). These are amine derivatives of

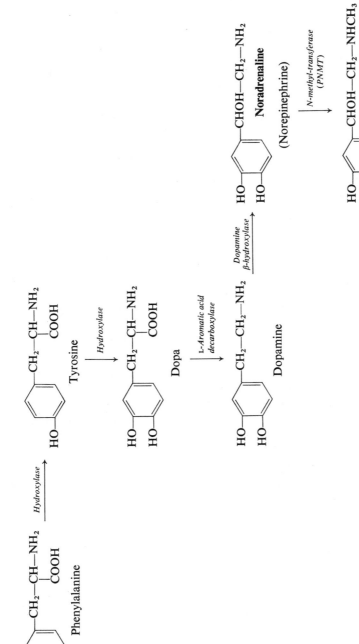

(b)

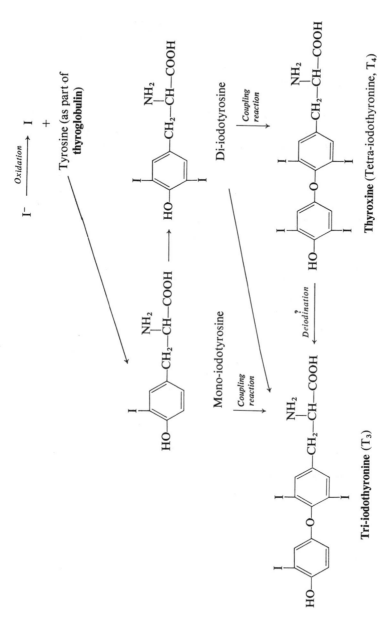

Fig. 3.4. Chemical structure and biological synthesis of (a) the catecholamine hormones; (b) the thyroid hormones.

catechol; hence their name catecholamines. Such compounds are found in all vertebrates where they also act as neurotransmitters in the sympathetic nervous system. They are also present in many invertebrates and even in the ciliated protozoan *Tetrahymena* where they influence metabolism in a manner reminiscent of that in more sophisticated metazoan animals (Blum, 1967).

Using phenylalanine, then tyrosine, as substrates, noradrenaline (or norepinephrine) is formed in chromaffin tissue. This may, under the influence of a methyl transferase enzyme PNMT (phenylethanolamine-*N*-methyl-transferase) have a methyl group added to become adrenaline (or epinephrine). These two hormones have differing actions though a cross-over of their effects occurs. Their actions are separately classified as α-adrenergic and β-adrenergic that can each separately be prevented by specific drugs. β-Adrenergic actions include stimulation of the heart, relaxation of the bronchi, dilatation of certain blood vessels and increase in blood glucose levels. These are principally seen in response to adrenaline rather than noradrenaline which does, however, affect the heart. The constriction of peripheral blood vessels and the sphincter muscles in the gut and bladder are α-adrenergic effects. Both noradrenaline and adrenaline are effective at such sites but adrenaline is more versatile and also has β-adrenergic effects.

The ratio of adrenaline to noradrenaline in the adrenal chromaffin tissue varies considerably among vertebrates. This is illustrated in Table 3.1

TABLE 3.1. *Noradrenaline as per cent of total catecholamines in the adrenals of various species of vertebrates.* (Based on West, 1955)

	Noradrenaline as % total catecholamines
Whale	83
Domestic fowl	80
Dogfish	68
Turtle	60
Pigeon	55
Frog	55
Toad	55
Pig	49
Sheep	33
Ox	26
Man	17
Rat	9
Rabbit	2
Guinea-pig	2

where it can be seen that noradrenaline makes up about 80% of the total catecholamines in whales and the domestic fowl (an ill-assorted phyletic pair) and as little as 2% in rabbits and guinea-pigs. No phyletic pattern in the distribution can be seen. Young and fetal animals possess a predominance of noradrenaline because of the relative lack of the methylating enzyme (see West, 1955).

Thyroid hormones

These are unique hormones as they contain, as part of their structure, the halogen iodine. The formation of thyroxine (tetra-iodothyronine or T_4) and tri-iodothyronine (T_3) is shown in Fig. 3.4. The thyroid gland also contains, probably mainly as metabolic intermediates, mono- and di-iodotyrosine. Thyroxine and tri-iodothyronine differ quantitatively in their effects; those of the former are much slower in onset but longer in duration than those of the latter. It has been suggested that in order to act, T_4 must be converted to T_3 but this is uncertain. T_4 can be bound more strongly to plasma proteins in a complex which may contribute to the difference in the time course of its effects from T_3. In mammals, T_4 is probably secreted at about five times the rate of T_3.

Biologically-active iodothyronine compounds occur throughout the vertebrates and have also been identified in a number of protochordates. Claims as to their presence in non-chordates have not been substantiated though iodotyrosines undoubtedly exist. Iodine readily combines with proteins containing tyrosine (*in vitro*) so that the natural occurrence of such compounds, especially in iodine-rich solutions like sea-water, is perhaps not surprising. Their transformation to iodothyronine compounds, however, seems to depend on specialized metabolic pathways and conditions such as those that occur in the thyroid gland, which has a unique ability to trap and oxidize iodide. Nevertheless, this process can be imitated *in vitro* providing the appropriate amounts of iodine and tyrosine-containing proteins are incubated together.

The spontaneous occurrence of thyroxine compounds in nature, even before the origin of the thyroid gland, is not inconceivable. Whether such compounds did arise and acquire a usefulness as hormonal excitants is sheer conjecture. If this did occur, subsequent specializations may have led to the hormones' more efficient formation in the thyroid gland.

Finally, we may consider the question of why iodine is present in the thyroid hormone molecules. It has been suggested that it plays a vital part in the initiation of the hormonal effect, the hormone acting as a 'carrier' moving iodine into the cell. Thyroxine-like molecules that contain no iodine have been made, however (Taylor, Tu and Barker, 1967). These contain bromine and *iso*propyl groups instead of iodine and yet they still exhibit considerable biological activity. Iodine thus does not appear to have a unique role in the action of thyroid hormones. Presumably, however, it was available in the environment and this, along with its ready chemical reactivity with ty. osine, resulted in its utilization.

The thyroid and catecholamine hormones are clearly very 'conservative' with respect to evolutionary changes of their chemical structure. This would seem to be, at least partly, because of their small size which limits the possibility for change in their molecules, and the fact that they are made from simple precursors that are abundant in nature. The catecholamines and thyroid hormones (and to a slightly lesser extent the steroid hormones) provide us with an illustration of the dictum that 'it is not the hormones that have evolved but the uses to which they have been put'. As will become particularly apparent in the succeeding sections, this is not always true.

The peptide hormones of the neurohypophysis

Two chemically related hormones are usually secreted by the neurohypophysis. These are peptides containing eight amino acids. They are arranged in a 5-membered ring, joined by a disulfide bridge (contributed by two half-cystine residues) and a side chain with three amino acids (Fig. 3.5

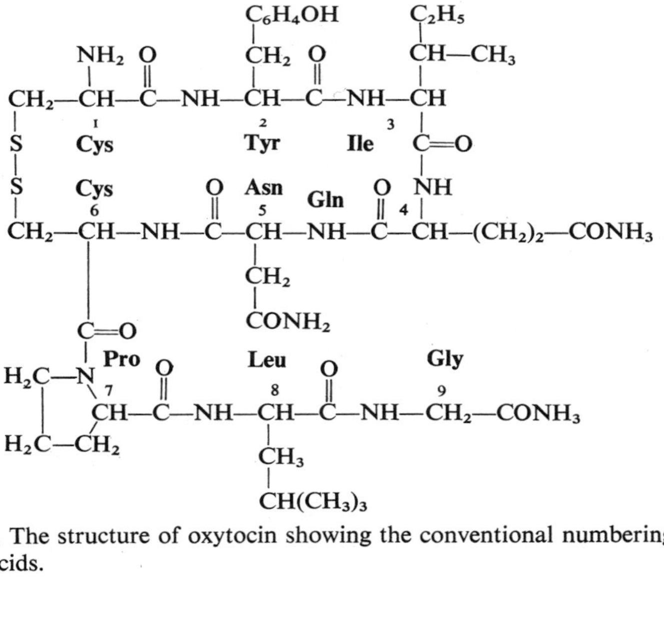

Fig. 3.5. The structure of oxytocin showing the conventional numbering of the amino acids.

TABLE 3.2. *Amino acid sequences of known neurohypophysial hormones.* (Heller, 1974)

Common structure (Variations in positions 3, 4, and 8 indicated by (X))	1 Cys	2 Tyr	3 (X)	4 (X)	5 Asn	6 Cys	7 Pro	8 (X)	9 Gly(NH$_2$)
Basic peptides			Amino acids in position						
			3	4				8	
Arginine vasopressin (AVP)			Phe	Gln				Arg	
Lysine vasopressin (LVP)			Phe	Gln				Lys	
Arginine vasotocin (AVT)			Ile	Gln				Arg	
Neutral (=Oxytocin-like) peptides									
Oxytocin			Ile	Gln				Leu	
Mesotocin			Ile	Gln				Ile	
Isotocin (= ichthyotocin)			Ile	Ser				Ile	
Glumitocin			Ile	Ser				Gln	
Valitocin			Ile	Gln				Val	
Aspartocin			Ile	Asn				Leu	

and Table 3.2). In most mammals the two hormones are arginine-vaso-pressin (AVP, also called antidiuretic hormone or ADH) and oxytocin. These differ by two amino acid substitutions; vasopressin has phenyl-alanine and arginine at positions 3 and 8 in the molecule, where oxytocin has *iso*leucine and leucine. This change confers considerable differences in biological activity; vasopressin enhances water reabsorption across the renal tubule, and so reduces urine flow, while oxytocin can contract the uterus and initiate 'milk let-down' from the mammary glands. There is little cross-over in their actions.

Homologous hormones have been identified in the neurohypophyses of representatives of all the systematic groups of vertebrates. Considerable differences in chemical structure however exist so that, so far, nine such peptides have been identified in nature. Amino acid substitutions occur at the 3, 4 and 8 positions in the molecule (Table 3.2). The occurrence of these natural analogues has a well-defined systematic distribution (Fig. 3.6). For example, arginine-vasopressin is confined to mammals while arginine-vasotocin (a combination of the ring of oxytocin and the side chain of vasopressin) is present in all other vertebrates. The second, oxytocin-like (or neutral) peptide in non-mammals exists in five variant forms; mesotocin (*iso*leucine instead of leucine at position 8) is present in birds, reptiles, amphibians and lungfishes; isotocin (*iso*leucine at 8, serine instead of glutamine at 4) is found in all the myriad of bony fishes except lungfishes.

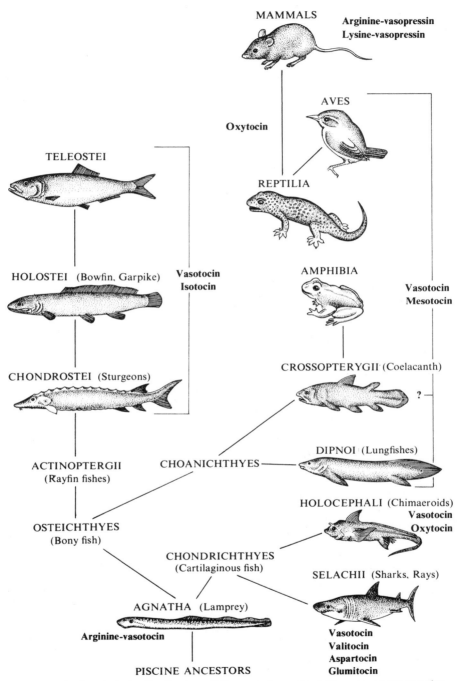

Fig. 3.6. The phyletic distribution of the neurohypophysial hormones among the vertebrates.

The chondrichthyeans exhibit more variability; vasotocin and oxytocin being present in the Holocephali, and vasotocin as well as glumitocin, valitocin and aspartocin are distributed among the Selachii (see Fig. 3.7). While the physiological roles of vasopressin and oxytocin in mammals, and vasotocin in tetrapods, are reasonably well understood, the functions of the other peptides remain unknown, particularly in fish. They are nevertheless present and, from our knowledge of extant species, apparently have persisted for about 500 million years since the first cyclostomes evolved (see Fig. 3.7).

Such polymorphism of the hormones is genetically determined. It can be examined more closely among mammals where a variant of arginine-

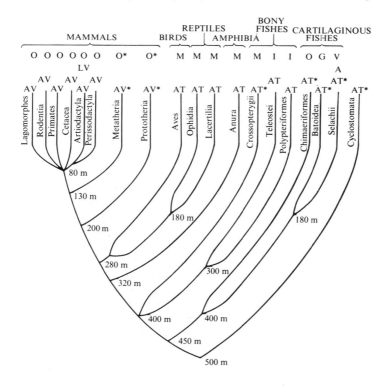

Fig. 3.7. Evolution of the neurohypophysial hormones.
Letters represent hormones that have been identified in extant species from each group. O, oxytocin; AV, arginine–vasopressin; LV, lysine–vasopressin; A, aspartocin; V, valitocin; G, glumitocin; AT, arginine–vasotocin; M, mesotocin.
500 m indicates 500 million years since divergence, and so on.
*, Identification is pharmacological, not chemical. (From Acher, Chauvet and Chauvet, 1972.)

vasopressin occurs. Many pig-like mammals (Suiformes; including the true pigs, Suidae, the peccaries, Tayassuidae and the hippopotamus, Hippopotamidae) possess a vasopressin with lysine instead of arginine present in the 8 position. This probably arose as a result of a single-step mutation from arginine-vasopressin. Its present distribution suggests that this transformation occurred in an ancestor of the Suiformes before the Hippopotami broke away from the pig–peccary stock (Ferguson and Heller, 1965). The change occurred in the Eocene, about 60 million years ago. The neurohypophyses of domestic pigs only contain lysine-vasopressin (and oxytocin) but among other Suiformes, such as peccaries, warthogs and hippopotami, both arginine- and lysine-vasopressin may be present in the same individual. The homozygotes contain one such peptide, the heterozygotes both. The evolutionary persistence of lysine-vasopressin seems to reflect the fact that its biological potency is only a little less than that of its arginine-containing relative so that it is not appreciably disadvantageous. In addition, an adaptive increase in sensitivity of the kidney to lysine-vasopressin may occur (Stewart, 1973). It is, of course, possible that the presence of this hormone also confers adaptive advantages which we do not know about.

Mutations that result in such changes in the amino acid composition of the neurohypophysial peptides may occur periodically. A strain of mice descended from some wild Peruvian specimens has been shown to contain lysine-vasopressin which is not usual in this species (Stewart, 1968). Also, a strain of laboratory rats (Brattleboro) has been found to lack vasopressin altogether and so cannot regulate its urine flow normally (Valtin, Sawyer and Sokol, 1965). When these rats are bred with normal rats the pituitary glands of the heterozygotes contain reduced amounts of vasopressin. Such genetic changes may reflect the complete absence of such a peptide or a mutational 'mutilation' of the molecule so that it has no biological action. The physiological result to the animal would be the same.

A number of biologists have played genetic games with the neurohypophysial peptides. Forearmed with the structures of the natural analogues and the genetic code it is possible to construct feasible lines for their evolution. These are usually calculated on the basis of the minimum number of mutations needed to produce a change from one amino acid at a certain position in a molecule, to another. Four such schemes (that do not include the diverse chondrichthyean hormones) are shown in Fig. 3.8. Most consider vasotocin to be the 'parent' or original, ancestral molecule.

The chemists have made more than 600 analogues of the neurohypophysial hormones that have not been identified in nature (see Berde and Boissonnas, 1968). By looking at the biological activity of these we can speculate about why the nine identified natural analogues have arisen.

Mutations have been perpetuated at only three positions, 3, 4 and 8, in these molecules. With regard to the 8 position, basic amino acids like arginine and lysine endow it with the most activity on the mammalian kidney and non-mammalian effectors such as the frog and toad skin and urinary bladder (osmotic water transfer across these preparations is increased by such peptides). Less-basic amino acids such as ornithine and histidine are much less effective. Similarly leucine at the 8 position in oxytocin results in a hormone that is most potent in its ability to contract the mammalian uterus and stimulate milk let-down from the mammary gland. Substituents at positions other than 3, 4 or 8 usually result in drastic reductions in biological activity. It seems that of all the thousands of possibilities available, nature has, in the course of time, provided the hormones with a structure optimal to that of the receptors. There is, however, an interesting exception. If threonine is substituted for glutamine in the 4 position of oxytocin a peptide is formed that is about four times as effective on the mammalian uterus as oxytocin itself (Manning and Sawyer, 1970). Why then is this not found in nature? The transition to this molecule from oxytocin would require two successive mutations, the first being the substitution of lysine or proline in the 4 position. Such analogues have a very low activity and so may not survive in nature. The succeeding mutation to threonine may thus not have been possible.

The quantities of the hormones stored in the neurohypophysis as well as the ratios of their concentrations are also determined genetically. Storage of these peptides in the neurohypophysis of fishes is more than ten times less than that normally seen in tetrapods. Five inbred strains of mice have been shown to exhibit a two-fold range of variation in the stores of vasopressin and oxytocin in their neurohypophyses (Stewart, 1972). The molecular ratio of vasopressin to oxytocin (V/O ratio) however remained a steady 1.5. As seen in Table 3.3 systematic variations in this V/O ratio occurs among the mammals. The marsupials have a much higher V/O ratio than most other mammals. It is also interesting that two geographically-separated members of the Tylopoda, the camel (from Asia) and the llama (from South America) both have a V/O ratio of about 3, which is higher than that observed in other placentals. The nature of such hereditarily determined differences could be in the ratio of neurosecretory fibers, if one type made oxytocin and another vasopressin. Alternatively if the two hormones are made together, in the same neuron, this synthesis may be regulated by a control system of genes.

The neurohypophysial peptides are stored in granules in the secretory neurons and are associated with proteins (with molecular weights about 10 000) called neurophysins. Two (or possibly even more) such neurophysins (I and II) occur in mammals and it is possible that one of these is

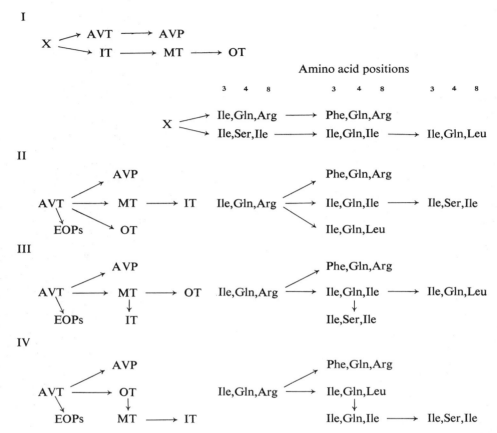

Fig. 3.8. Schemes that have been suggested to represent the successive steps in the molecular evolution of the neurohypophysial peptide hormones (from Geschwind, 1969).

Each transition has been represented as a single amino acid replacement and in some instances it can be seen that two successive changes must be proposed to account for a hormones evolution from the 'parent' molecule; usually considered to be 8-arginine-vasotocin.

Such changes in amino acid composition can be described according to codon base changes in the genetic code. These transformations are often consistent with a single base change (one-step mutation) but in other instances, two base replacements would be needed; such as the transition from isotocin to mesotocin. In this instance the intermediate could be 4-proline, 8-isoleucine-oxytocin but this peptide has not been identified in nature. At the time that the proposed schemes were advanced the structures of the chondrichthyean neurohypophysial peptides (EOPs; glumitocin, aspartocin and valitocin, see Fig. 3.5) were unknown but it was suggested that they also arose from vasotocin. This is still thought to be likely but the transitions may involve more than a single unknown intermediate

TABLE 3.3. *Examples of the distribution of mole ratios of neurohypophysial hormones in mammalian taxonomic groups. The ratio of arginine-vasopressin to oxytocin is shown.* (From Heller, 1966)

Order or suborder	Species	V/O
Order: Marsupialia	American opossum	2.9
	Australian opossum	6.2
	Wallaby	3.8
	Red kangaroo	4.8
Order: Perissodactyla	Horse	0.93
	Zebra	0.44
	Tapir	0.72
	Black rhinoceros	0.77
Order: Artiodactyla		
Suborder: Ruminantia	African buffalo	0.9
	Kongoni	1.5
	Topi	1.4
	Blue wildebeeste	1.3
	Kob	1.4
	Bushbuck	1.4
Suborder: Tylopoda	Llama	3.1
	Camel	3.6

associated with the storage and synthesis of oxytocin and the other with vasopressin. Domestic pigs and warthogs that have lysine-vasopressin have been shown to possess a neurophysin (II) that shows chemical and immuno-logical differences from that in other mammals (Uttenthal and Hope, 1972). The mutational changes in the hormone's structure thus appear to be accompanied by changes in its binding neurophysin. This association may reflect a common synthetic pathway for both the hormone and neurophysin.

Arginine-vasotocin is present in the neurohypophyses of non-mammals but not in those of adult mammals; it was fascinating to find that vasotocin occurs in the fetuses of sheep and seals (Vizsolyi and Perks, 1969).

The neurohypophysial peptide hormones are apparently not confined to the neurohypophysis, as vasotocin has also been identified in the pineal

---

'hormone'. 8-Lysine-vasopressin (present in the Suina) probably evolved from arginine-vasopressin by a single base replacement.

AVT = arginine-vasotocin, AVP = arginine-vasopressin, IT = isotocin, MT = mesotocin, OT = oxytocin, EOPs = the chondrichthyean neurohypophysial hormones and X = a 'parent' molecule of unknown composition.

gland (see Pavel *et al.*, 1973) and probably the teleostean urophysis (see Chapter 8). Vasopressin has also been identified in some cells from human tumors from non-endocrine tissues.

The neurohormones of the median eminence

The median eminence, at the base of the brain, is the site of release of several hormones that pass into the portal blood vessels of the adenohypophysis (see Schally, Arimura and Kastin, 1973). There is reasonable evidence to indicate that at least nine such hormones (Table 3.4) exist which stimulate or inhibit the release of the adenohypophysial hormones.

TABLE 3.4. *Hypothalamic hormones believed to control the release of pituitary hormones.* (Based on Schally, *et al.*, 1973. Copyright © 1973 by the American Association for the Advancement of Science)

Hypothalamic hormone (or factor)	Abbreviation
Corticotrophin (ACTH)-releasing hormone	CRH or CRF
Thyrotrophin (TSH)-releasing* hormone	TSH-RH or TRH or TRF
Luteinizing hormone (LH)-releasing* hormone	LH-RH or LH-RF
Follicle-stimulating hormone (FSH)-releasing* hormone	FSH-RH or FSH-RF
Growth hormone (GH)-releasing* hormone	GH-RH or GH-RF
Growth hormone (GH) release-inhibiting hormone–somatostatin	GH-R-IH or GIF
Prolactin release-inhibiting hormone	P-R-IH or PIF**
Prolactin-releasing hormone	PRH or PRF***
Melanocyte-stimulating hormone (MSH) release-inhibiting hormone	MSH-R-IH or MRIH or MIF
Melanocyte-stimulating hormone (MSH)-releasing hormone	MRH or MRF

* Or regulating hormone.   ** ? Dopamine.   *** ? TRH.
The evidence for the presence of some of these hormones is still equivocal.

These are, like the neurohypophysial hormones, thought to be secretory products of neurons present in the hypothalamus. Similarly, they are, chemically, usually thought to be peptides (it is possible that prolactin-R-IH is dopamine, MacLeod and Lehmeyer, 1974) and are called releasing- or inhibiting-hormones (-RH or -IH). For instance, the one that releases corticotrophin is called corticotrophin-releasing hormone or CRH, and that which inhibits the release of melanocyte-stimulating hormone (MSH),

Thyrotrophic-stimulating hormone-releasing hormone, TRH or TSH-RH

(Pyro) (Glu)(His)(Pro)—(NH₂)

Luteinizing hormone/follicle-stimulating hormone-releasing hormone,
LH/FSH-RH, Gn-RH

(Pyro)(Glu)(His)(Trp)(Ser)(Tyr)(Gly)(Leu)(Arg)(Pro)(Gly)—NH₂

Growth hormone-releasing hormone, GRH or GHRH

H—(Val)(His)(Leu)(Ser)(Ala)(Glu)(Glu)(Lys)(Glu)(Ala)—OH

Growth hormone-release-inhibiting hormone (somatostatin)

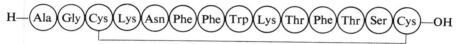

H—(Ala)(Gly)(Cys)(Lys)(Asn)(Phe)(Phe)(Trp)(Lys)(Thr)(Phe)(Thr)(Ser)(Cys)—OH

Melanocyte-stimulating hormone-releasing -inhibiting hormone,
MSH-R-IH or MRIH

(Pro)(Leu)(Gly)—NH₂

Melanocyte-stimulating hormone-releasing hormone, MRH

H—(Cys)(Tyr)(Ile)(Gln)(Asn)—OH

Fig. 3.9. The amino acid sequences of some of the hormones from the median eminence that influence the release of adenohypophysial hormones. The structures of GH-RH and MSH-RH are tentative, they exhibit such activity but have not been positively identified in the median eminence. Some doubt has even been expressed about MSH-R-IH.

melanocyte-stimulating hormone-release-inhibiting hormone or, much more conveniently, MSH-R-IH.

The amino acid sequence in some of these hormones has been elucidated. Thyrotrophin-releasing hormone, TRH, is a tripeptide containing glutamine, histidine and proline; luteinizing hormone-RH and follicle stimulating hormone-RH (LH/FSH-RH) is a decapeptide (see Fig. 3.9). This RH stimulates release of both the gonadotrophins and so is also called gonadotrophin-releasing hormone or Gn-RH. It is uncertain whether the structures proposed for growth hormone-RH (GH-RH) and MSH-RH are the same as those that exist in the median eminence and the identity of MSH-R-IH has also been questioned.

Little is known about the presence or chemical identities of such hormones in the median eminence of non-mammals but sporadic evidence suggests that they are present. Mammalian LH/FSH-RH promotes ovulation in the domestic fowl and a hormone that also has this effect has been found in the fowl's median eminence (van Tienhoven and Schally, 1972; Smith and Follett, 1972). Using an immunoassay, TRH has been identified in the hypothalamus of a variety of non-mammals, including the domestic fowl, a reptile, an amphibian, a teleost fish and even from the brain of a larval cyclostome and the head region of a protochordate *Amphioxus* (Jackson and Reichlin, 1974). It is also interesting that TRH has been identified in other parts of the brain, apart from the hypothalamus, in both mammals and non-mammals, suggesting that it may have a more widespread role as a neurotransmitter.

Polymorphism among these hormones has not been documented. Porcine and ovine TRH are identical. As this hormone is a tripeptide there is little opportunity for change and substituted synthetic analogues have little activity. It is, however, noteworthy that while mammalian TSH can stimulate the thyroid gland in the African lungfish, mammalian TRH is ineffective in these fish (Gorbman and Hyder, 1973). This observation suggests that, as in frogs, a different mechanism or molecular variant of TRH may be present in non-mammals. LH/FSH-RH is similar in pigs and sheep. The biological activity of this molecule is usually decreased when amino acid substitutions are made in it but when the terminal glycinamide (see Fig. 3.9) is replaced by structures lacking an electrical charge, a much more potent substance results (Rippel *et al.*, 1973). It would thus appear that the chemist in his laboratory can improve somewhat on nature's hormone. MSH-R-IH is an interesting tripeptide as its composition seems to be identical to that of the side chain of oxytocin (Celis, Taleisnik and Walter, 1971; Celis, Hase and Walter, 1972). It can be formed from this neurohypophysial hormone as a result of the action of an enzyme present in the median eminence. Tripeptides with the side chain of lysine- and arginine-vasopressin also have MSH-R-IH activity, though somewhat less than that of the side chain of oxytocin. Another remnant of the oxytocin molecule, a 5-membered pentapeptide, has been found to increase the release of MSH (MSH-RH?) but this molecule has not been positively identified in the median eminence. The activity of those peptides formed from oxytocin, which thus acts as a pro-hormone, suggests that comparable median eminence hormones in other vertebrates may have structures which reflect that of the particular neurohypophysial peptide they possess.

It is even possible that other fragments of these molecules may influence the release of other adenohypophysial hormones.

The neurohypophysial hormones themselves have also been identified in the median eminence and the injection of vasopressin has been shown to stimulate the release of corticotrophin and growth hormone. It is thus possible that these peptide hormones may also influence the normal release of the adenohypophysial hormones and indeed vasopressin has recently been identified, in high concentration, in the blood of the hypophysial portal vessels of monkeys (Zimmerman *et al.*, 1973).

The renin–angiotensin system

It has been known since the turn of the century that saline extracts of the mammalian kidney, when injected into mammals, produce a large increase in the blood pressure. This effect is due to the interaction of an enzyme present in the kidney called renin which, as described in the last chapter, is formed by the juxtaglomerular cells. Renin interacts with an α-2 globulin in the blood plasma to form angiotensin I which is converted by a 'converting' enzyme, to angiotensin II which is the hormone that actively constricts the peripheral blood vessels. Angiotensinogen is the substrate.

Renin has a wide phyletic distribution in bony fishes and tetrapods. It is, however, absent in cyclostomes and chondrichthyean fishes (Nishimura *et al.*, 1970). Renin has also been tentatively identified in the corpuscles of Stannius of some bony fishes. It thus appears to have made a slightly later entry into the vertebrates than most other hormones.

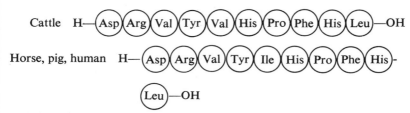

Fig. 3.10. The amino acid sequence of angiotensin I derived from the ox and horse, and pig and man. The active octapeptide, angiotensin II, is formed by removal of the histidine and leucine residues by a 'converting enzyme'.

Angiotensin I is a decapeptide (Fig. 3.10) which is activated by conversion to an octapeptide on the removal of histidine and leucine from one end of the molecule. Species differences in structure exist as can be seen in Fig. 3.10. There is also evidence indicating that marsupial angiotensinogen (from kangaroos) differs from a placental (sheep) substrate (Simpson and

Renins

	Fish	Amphibian	Reptile	Aves	Mammal
Mammal	—	—	—	—	+
Aves	—	—	—	+	—
Reptile	—	−/+	+	+	—
Amphibian	—	+	+	+	—
Fish	+	+	+	+	—

Angiotensinogens

Fig. 3.11. The interactions of renin and angiotensinogen, from different vertebrates, to form angiotensin. On the ordinate are the renins from the different
vertebrates and on the abscissa, the angiotensinogens. +, Angiotensin (or
angiotensin-like) formed; −, no interaction. (From Nolly and Fasciola, 1973.
Reprinted with permission of Pergamon Press.)

Blair-West, 1972). The structures of angiotensin have not been determined
in non-mammals but differences in their chemical and pharmacological
behavior indicate that structural variation is widespread (Sokabe and
Nakajima, 1972).

Considerable differences have also been observed in the interactions
between renins and angiotensinogens from the various major phyletic
groups (Fig. 3.11). Fish (teleost) renin interacts with angiotensinogens (to
form angiotensin) from all the tetrapods except mammals. Mammalian
renin will not interact with the plasma substrate from non-mammals. Bird
renin is also very specific while that of other vertebrates is less so. Amphibian
renin interacts with the angiotensinogens from birds and reptiles and
reptilian renin reacts with those of birds and amphibians.

Parathormone and calcitonin

Parathormone and calcitonin are, respectively, the peptide hormones
originating in the parathyroids and ultimobranchial bodies (or in mammals

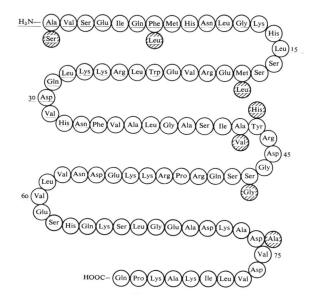

Fig. 3.12. Amino acid sequences of parathyroid hormone from the ox (main structure) and the substitutions that occur in that from the pig (shaded residues). (From Aurbach *et al.*, 1972.)

the thyroid 'C' cells). Parathormone increases calcium levels in the plasma and calcitonin decreases them. Parathormone contains 84 amino acids and is present in all tetrapods but not fishes. Variations in its structure undoubtedly exist but have not been chemically elucidated in non-mammals. The porcine and bovine hormones differ from each other by seven amino acid substitutions (Fig. 3.12) which can each be accounted for genetically by a single base change. When tested in the rat (*in vivo*, blood calcium levels) these two parathyroid hormones do not exhibit different biological activities, though human parathormone is only about $\frac{1}{3}$ as active. When bovine and porcine parathormone are compared *in vitro* (by their ability to activate renal adenyl cyclase) the porcine hormone is less effective. This observation reflects differences in their rates of inactivation by the kidney tissue *in vitro* (Aurbach *et al.*, 1972). It is likely that the active hormone at the effector site only represents a portion of the whole polypeptide molecule and that the hormone, once released, is converted at some peripheral site into an active fragment. The complete molecule is not essential for the exertion of a biological effect as it has been shown that a portion, the amino acids 1 to 34 at the amino-terminal of the bovine hormone, has a similar activity to the complete molecule with its 84 amino acids (Tregear *et al.*,

TABLE 3.5. *Calcitonin concentration in glands from various vertebrates.* (From Copp, 1969)

| | Units (MRC)/g fresh gland wt | | | |
| | | | | |
Class and species	Thyroid	Ultimo-branchial	Internal parathyroid	Unit/kg body wt
Mammalia				
Man, *Homo sapiens*				
Normal thyroid	0.4	–	0.1–0.5	0.16
Medullary cell carcinoma of thyroid	17	–	–	–
Rat, *Rattus rattus*	5–15	–	–	0.2–0.6
Hog, *Sus scrofa*	2–5	–	–	0.4–0.8
Dog, *Canis familiaris*	1–4	–	1.5–3.3	0.25–0.50
Rabbit, *Oryctolagus cuniculus*				
Lower pole	1.5–2	–	2.1–2.5	–
Upper pole	a	–	–	–
Aves				
Domestic fowl, *Gallus domesticus*	a	30–120	–	0.5–0.8
Turkey, *Meleagris gallopavo*	a	60–100	–	0.5–0.9
Reptilia				
Turtle, *Pseudemys concinna suwaniensis*	a	3–9	–	0.002–0.006
Amphibia				
Bullfrog, *Rana catesbeiana*	–	0.5–0.8	–	0.001–0.002
Teleosti				
Chum salmon, *Oncorhynchus keta*	–	25–40	–	0.4–0.6
Gray cod, *Gadus macrocephalus*	–	10–20	–	0.2–0.4
Elasmobranchii				
Dogfish shark, *Squalus suckleyi*	a	25–35	–	0.25–0.40

a, No detectable hypocalcemic activity.

1973). This observation suggests that considerable polymorphism of the parathormone molecule is possible.

Calcitonin activity has been measured in all vertebrates except the cyclostomes (Table 3.5). The hormones contain 32 amino acids. Chemical analysis indicates that considerable differences in their sequence occur that result in quantitative differences of biological activity. The amino acid sequence of the calcitonins in four mammals and a teleost fish (salmon) are

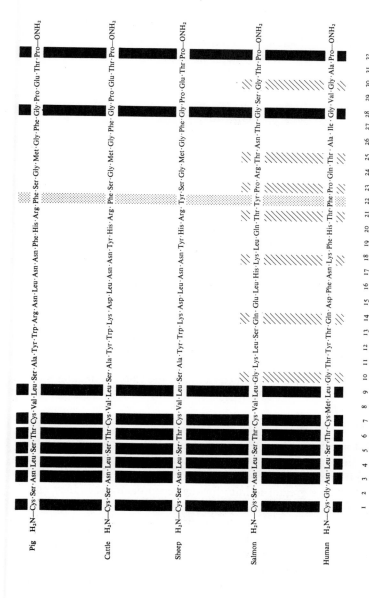

Fig. 3.13. A comparison of the amino acid sequence of calcitonin in four mammals and the salmon. The solid bars indicate the amino acids are homologous in all species. It can be seen that extensive differences exist, especially in the central parts of the molecules. Cross-hatched bars indicate homologies between salmon and human; stippled bar indicates comparable hydrophobic residues. (From Potts *et al.*, 1972.)

Pig   H₂N—Cys·Ser·Asn·Leu·Ser·Thr·Cys·Val·Leu·Ser·Ala·Tyr·Trp·Arg·Asn·Leu·Asn·Asn·Phe·His·Arg·Phe·Ser·Gly·Met·Gly·Phe·Gly·Pro·Glu·Thr·Pro—ONH₂

Cattle H₂N—Cys·Ser·Asn·Leu·Ser·Thr·Cys·Val·Leu·Ser·Ala·Tyr·Trp·Lys·Asp·Leu·Asn·Asn·Tyr·His·Arg·Phe·Ser·Gly·Met·Gly·Phe·Gly·Pro·Glu·Thr·Pro—ONH₂

Sheep   H₂N—Cys·Ser·Asn·Leu·Ser·Thr·Cys·Val·Leu·Ser·Ala·Tyr·Trp·Lys·Asp·Leu·Asn·Asn·Tyr·His·Arg·Tyr·Ser·Gly·Met·Gly·Phe·Gly·Pro·Glu·Thr·Pro—ONH₂

Salmon H₂N—Cys·Ser·Asn·Leu·Ser·Thr·Cys·Val·Leu·Gly·Lys·Leu·Ser·Gln·Glu·Leu·His·Lys·Leu·Gln·Thr·Tyr·Pro·Arg·Thr·Asn·Thr·Gly·Ser·Gly·Thr·Pro—ONH₂

Human   H₂N—Cys·Gly·Asn·Leu·Ser·Thr·Cys·Met·Leu·Gly·Thr·Tyr·Thr·Gln·Asp·Phe·Asn·Lys·Phe·His·Thr·Phe·Pro·Gln·Thr·Ala·Ile·Gly·Val·Gly·Ala·Pro—ONH₂

1 2 3 4 5 6 7 8 9 10 11 12 13 14 15 16 17 18 19 20 21 22 23 24 25 26 27 28 29 30 31 32

shown in Fig. 3.13. Only nine amino acid positions are commonly shared by all five species. The differences, however, can nearly all be accounted for by single-base changes in the genetic code (Potts *et al.*, 1972).

The salmon calcitonins are of special interest. Three variants have been identified among four different species of salmon with amino acid substitutions at four or five positions (Fig. 3.14). All species have a common hormone, calcitonin I, but others, calcitonin II or III, may also be present.

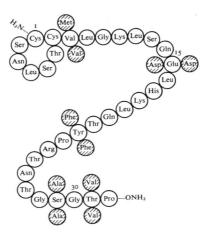

Fig. 3.14. The three variant forms of salmon calcitonin. The main amino acid sequence is that of calcitonin I. Calcitonin II differs by only four residues; valine is still present at position 8. Calcitonin III has 5 substitutions. Among the four species of salmon examined all form calcitonin I, the Chum, Pink and Sockeye salmon also form calcitonin II while the Coho salmon has calcitonin III. (From Potts *et al.*, 1972.)

Salmon calcitonin is much more active when tested in mammals (20–100-fold) than is the natural (homologous) hormone. This is probably a unique situation and is due to two factors: a slow rate of destruction of the piscine hormone as well as a greater affinity for the receptor in the kidney and in bone (Marx, Woodward and Aurbach, 1972). This is a very interesting situation theoretically and shows that a species need not necessarily have evolved a hormone with a structure that has the maximal possible biological activity. It is nevertheless conceivable that other factors may be involved in the 'choice' of such a molecule and sheer persistency in the circulation may even be a disadvantage. Calcitonin could even have other roles in mammals that are not reflected in its ability to increase calcium concentrations in the bioassay system.

The hormones of the Islets of Langerhans and the gastrointestinal tract

Insulin

This hormone has an important role in controlling several processes in intermediary metabolism that involve levels of glucose, fatty acids and proteins. It has been identified in all vertebrate groups and, in addition, in extracts of the gut, and its associated tissues, of many invertebrates. Some coelenterates, crustaceans, molluscs and protochordates have been shown to possess insulin-like substances. This activity has been demonstrated in biological assays in mammals and also by the interaction with antibodies to ox insulin (see Falkmer and Patent, 1972). The chemical nature of the pre-vertebrate 'insulin' is uncertain and it may be a large molecule, a pro-insulin, that can react with vertebrate antibodies and from which bio-logically active fragments may be split off. It has been suggested (Steiner *et al.*, 1972) that insulin may have originated from a large proteolytic digestive enzyme, a proto-pro-insulin, in such a manner that when it was absorbed into the blood it became associated with certain metabolic processes in the body.

Several of the vertebrate insulins have been described chemically. The molecule consists of two main parts, an A-chain with 21 amino acids and a B-chain with 31. These are joined by two disulfide bridges contributed by four cysteine residues (Table 3.6). Among the 20 species so far examined amino acid substitutions have been recorded at 29 of the 51 positions in the insulin molecules. The A-chain is identical in the insulin present in man, pigs, rabbits, dogs and sperm whales while the B-chain is the same in pig, horse, ox, dog, sheep, goat, sperm whale and sei whale. The intact insulin in the pig, dog, sperm whale and fin whale are identical. Most of the differences that occur in mammals are localized at three positions (8, 9, 10) in the A-chain and in one position (30) in the B-chain. In the guinea-pig, however, changes have occurred, compared to the pig, at 17 positions in the molecule.

Fish (teleost) insulins show a number of distinct differences from those of mammals (Fig. 3.15). Amino acid substitutions occur at more than 15 loci. The B-chain also has an additional amino acid at its *N*-terminal end while the mammalian *C*-terminal amino acid is missing.

The laboratory rat and mouse and some fishes each have two insulins (see Smith, 1966 and Fig. 3.15). The two rodents have insulins which differ by two amino acids (in the B-chain) and both hormones are present in the same individuals. This is thought to be a homozygous condition which nevertheless could be the result of a gene duplication so that two genes are present, each controlling the form of one insulin. It is unknown whether the intraspecific polymorphism among the fish insulins is similar to that in the rodents or whether each hormone is present in separate, individual, fish.

Despite the chemical differences in the structure of the vertebrate insulins there is surprisingly little demonstrable variation in their specific biological activities when they are tested on mammalian preparations.

TABLE 3.6. *Amino acid sequence in vertebrate insulins.* (From Humbel, Bosshard and Zahn, 1972)

The italicized amino acids indicate the principle differences
(a) Amino acid sequences of insulin A chains

Type of insulin	1	2	3	4	5	6	7	8	9	10
Human*	Gly	Ile	Val	Glu	Gln	Cys	Cys	Thr	Ser	Ile
Sei whale	Gly	Ile	Val	Glu	Gln	Cys	Cys	*Ala*	Ser	*Thr*
Horse	Gly	Ile	Val	Glu	Gln	Cys	Cys	Thr	*Gly*	Ile
Beef	Gly	Ile	Val	Glu	Gln	Cys	Cys	*Ala*	Ser	*Val*
Sheep, goat	Gly	Ile	Val	Glu	Gln	Cys	Cys	*Ala*	*Gly*	*Val*
Elephant	Gly	Ile	Val	Glu	Gln	Cys	Cys	Thr	*Gly*	*Val*
Rat, mouse (I and II)	Gly	Ile	Val	*Asp*	Gln	Cys	Cys	Thr	Ser	Ile
Guinea-pig	Gly	Ile	Val	*Asp*	Gln	Cys	Cys	Thr	*Gly*	*Thr*
Chicken, turkey	Gly	Ile	Val	Glu	Gln	Cys	Cys	*His*	*Asn*	*Thr*
Cod	Gly	Ile	Val	*Asp*	Gln	Cys	Cys	*His*	*Arg*	*Pro*
Tuna (II)	Gly	Ile	Val	Glu	Gln	Cys	Cys	*His*	*Lys*	*Pro*
Angler fish	Gly	Ile	Val	Glu	Gln	Cys	Cys	*His*	*Arg*	*Pro*
Toadfish (I)	Gly	Ile	Val	Glu	Gln	Cys	Cys	*His*	*Arg*	*Pro*
Toadfish (II)	Gly	Ile	Val	Glu	Gln	Cys	Cys	*His*	*Arg*	*Pro*

11	12	13	14	15	16	17	18	19	20	21
Cys	Ser	Leu	Tyr	Gln	Leu	Glu	Asn	Tyr	Cys	Asn
Cys	Ser	Leu	Tyr	Gln	Leu	Glu	Asn	Tyr	Cys	Asn
Cys	Ser	Leu	Tyr	Gln	Leu	Glu	Asn	Tyr	Cys	Asn
Cys	Ser	Leu	Tyr	Gln	Leu	Glu	Asn	Tyr	Cys	Asn
Cys	Ser	Leu	Tyr	Gln	Leu	Glu	Asn	Tyr	Cys	Asn
Cys	Ser	Leu	Tyr	Gln	Leu	Glu	Asn	Tyr	Cys	Asn
Cys	Ser	Leu	Tyr	Gln	Leu	Glu	Asn	Tyr	Cys	Asn
Cys	*Thr*	*Arg*	*His*	Gln	Leu	Glu	*Ser*	Tyr	Cys	Asn
Cys	Ser	Leu	Tyr	Gln	Leu	Glu	Asn	Tyr	Cys	Asn
Cys	*Asp*	*Ile*	*Phe*	*Asp*	Leu	*Gln*	Asn	Tyr	Cys	Asn
Cys	*Asn*	*Ile*	*Phe*	*Asp*	Leu	*Gln*	Asn	Tyr	Cys	Asn
Cys	*Asn*	*Ile*	*Phe*	*Asp*	Leu	*Gln*	Asn	Tyr	Cys	Asn
Cys	*Asp*	*Ile*	*Phe*	*Asp*	Leu	*Gln*	*Ser*	Tyr	Cys	Asn
Cys	*Asp*	*Lys*	*Phe*	*Asp*	Leu	*Gln*	*Ser*	Tyr	Cys	Asn

(b) *Amino acid sequences of insulin B chains*

Type of insulin	−1	1	2	3	4	5	6	7	8	9	10	11	12	13	14	15	16	17	18	19	20	21	22	23	24	25	26	27	28	29	30
Pig**		Phe	Val	Asn	Gln	His	Leu	Cys	Gly	Ser	His	Leu	Val	Glu	Ala	Leu	Tyr	Leu	Val	Cys	Gly	Glu	Arg	Gly	Phe	Phe	Tyr	Thr	Pro	Lys	Ala
Man, elephant		Phe	Val	Asn	Gln	His	Leu	Cys	Gly	Ser	His	Leu	Val	Glu	Ala	Leu	Tyr	Leu	Val	Cys	Gly	Glu	Arg	Gly	Phe	Phe	Tyr	Thr	Pro	Lys	*Thr*
Rabbit		Phe	Val	Asn	Gln	His	Leu	Cys	Gly	Ser	His	Leu	Val	Glu	Ala	Leu	Tyr	Leu	Val	Cys	Gly	Glu	Arg	Gly	Phe	Phe	Tyr	Thr	Pro	Lys	*Ser*
Rat, mouse (I)		Phe	Val	*Lys*	Gln	His	Leu	Cys	Gly	*Pro*	His	Leu	Val	Glu	Ala	Leu	Tyr	Leu	Val	Cys	Gly	Glu	Arg	Gly	Phe	Phe	Tyr	Thr	Pro	Lys	*Ser*
Rat, mouse (II)		Phe	Val	*Lys*	Gln	His	Leu	Cys	Gly	Ser	His	Leu	Val	Glu	Ala	Leu	Tyr	Leu	Val	Cys	Gly	Glu	Arg	Gly	Phe	Phe	Tyr	Thr	Pro	*Met*	*Ser*
Guinea-pig		Phe	Val	*Ser*	*Arg*	His	Leu	Cys	Gly	Ser	*Asn*	Leu	Val	Glu	*Thr*	Leu	Tyr	*Ser*	Val	Cys	*(Gln*	*Asp*	*Asp)*	Gly	Phe	Phe	Tyr	*Ile*	Pro	Lys	*Asp*
Chicken		*Ala*	*Ala*	Asn	Gln	His	Leu	Cys	Gly	Ser	His	Leu	Val	Glu	Ala	Leu	Tyr	Leu	Val	Cys	Gly	Glu	Arg	Gly	Phe	Phe	Tyr	*Ser*	Pro	Lys	Ala
Cod	Met	*Ala*	*Pro*	*Pro*	Gln	His	Leu	Cys	Gly	Ser	His	Leu	Val	*Asp*	Ala	Leu	Tyr	Leu	Val	Cys	Gly	*Asp*	Arg	Gly	Phe	Phe	Tyr	*Asn*	Pro	Lys	
Tuna (II)	*Val*	*Ala*	*Pro*	*Pro*	Gln	His	Leu	Cys	Gly	Ser	His	Leu	Val	*Asp*	Ala	Leu	Tyr	Leu	Val	Cys	Gly	*Asp*	Arg	Gly	Phe	Phe	Tyr	*Asn*	Pro	Lys	
Angler fish	*Val*	*Ala*	*Pro*	*Ala*	Gln	His	Leu	Cys	Gly	Ser	His	Leu	Val	*Asp*	Ala	Leu	Tyr	Leu	Val	Cys	Gly	*Asp*	Arg	Gly	Phe	Phe	Tyr	*Asn*	Pro	Lys	
Toadfish (I)	Met	*Ala*	*Pro*	*Pro*	Gln	His	Leu	Cys	Gly	Ser	His	Leu	Val	*Asp*	Ala	Leu	Tyr	Leu	Val	Cys	Gly	*Asp*	Arg	Gly	Phe	Phe	Tyr	*Asn*	Pro	Lys	
Toadfish (II)	Met	*Ala*	*Pro*	*Pro*	Gln	His	Leu	Cys	Gly	Ser	His	Leu	Val	*Asp*	Ala	Leu	Tyr	Leu	Val	Cys	Gly	*Asp*	Arg	Gly	Phe	Phe	Tyr	*Asn*	Ser		

* Sequence is identical in man, rabbit, dog, pig and sperm whale.
** Sequence is identical in pig, horse, ox, dog, sheep, sperm whale and sei whale.

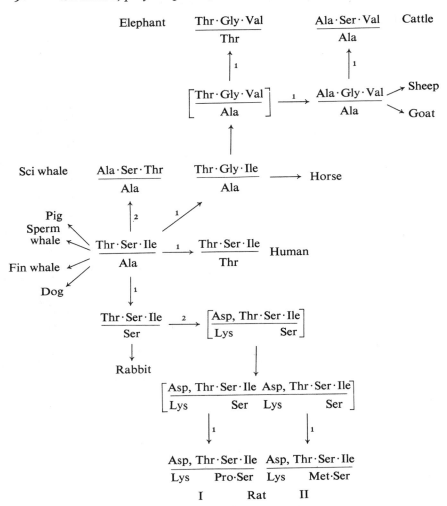

Fig. 3.15. A scheme for the evolution of the mammalian insulins. The sequences of the A-chain are given above the line and the B-chain below it. Numbers alongside the arrows are the minimum number of base changes (mutations) required for the amino acid substitution. The sequences given in brackets are postulated intermediates that have not been identified in nature. The amino acids in the A-chain are those at positions 8, 9 and 10 or in the rat 4, 8, 9, 10.

In the B-chain they refer to the 30 position or in the rat 3, 29 and 30. The rat produces two insulins (I and II), a process that may be due to a gene duplication and a mutation that occurred subsequently in one of the gene-pairs. (From L. F. Smith, 1966 and personal communication.)

Attempts to relate the similarities and differences in the amino acid composition of the insulins to the closeness of the relationship and systematic position of the species have not been very successful. Guinea-pig insulin differs from that in man by 17 amino acid substitutions (16 in a close relative, the elephant). That of the chicken and man (and the elephant) have only six such disparities. Nevertheless an attempt has been made to trace the evolution of the mammalian insulin. The 'parent', or prototype, may be the most common form; which is found in the pig and others. The successive mutations that would be required to produce the hormones present in other mammals can then be traced (Fig. 3.15). As with the neurohypophysial hormones this must be considered a 'game' which is fun and may even be partly correct.

Glucagon

This hormone is a smaller molecule than insulin, consisting of a single chain of 29 amino acids. It has been identified in teleost fishes and all the main tetrapod groups. Glucagon has not been identified in the Chondrichthyes or Cyclostomata though immunological evidence suggests its possible presence in invertebrates including some molluscs and protochordates (see Falkmer and Patent, 1972). The teleost's 'glucagon', while biologically effective (it has a hyperglycemic action) in fish, has no effect in the rabbit. This fact suggests structural differences from the homologous mammalian hormone(s). Failure to detect glucagon in other fishes could reflect even greater structural disparities.

Glucagon-like activity has also been identified in various segments of the mammalian gut (stomach, duodenum, jejunem and colon). Immunological behavior indicates that these excitants from the gut differ structurally from pancreatic glucagon (Samols *et al.*, 1966; Heding, 1971) and are called entero-glucagon.

Secretin

Glucagon and another gut hormone, secretin (which stimulates the exocrine pancreatic secretions), have a remarkable number of similarities in their structure (Weinstein, 1968, Fig. 3.16). Porcine secretin has two less amino acids than porcine glucagon but shares 15 amino acids at identical positions in the molecule. This strongly suggests a common origin. The number of genetic base-changes necessary for the difference involve one or two mutations in each of the disparate amino acid positions. From information about spontaneous mutation rates it has been calculated that gene duplication (of the parent molecule) would have occurred 200 million years ago,

Glucagon

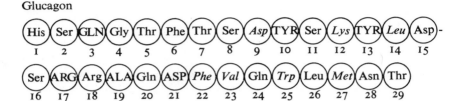

Secretin

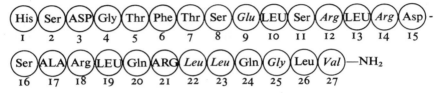

Base changes: glucagon versus secretin

| 0 | 0 | 2 | 0 | 0 | 0 | 0 | 0 | I | 2 | 0 | I | 2 | I | 0 | - |
| 0 | 2 | 0 | 2 | 0 | 2 | I | I | 0 | I | 0 | I | | | | |

Fig. 3.16. The amino acid sequence of pig glucagon and secretin. They are aligned for direct correspondence between the amino acid positions. When no substitutions have occurred ordinary letters are used, with 'conservative' substitutions capitals are used, and 'radical' changes are italicized. (From Weinstein, 1968.)

early in the Mesozoic period. If glucagon really exists in teleost fish, this genetic event may have occurred somewhat earlier. The 'parent' molecule could, however, possess some glucagon-like activity. Weinstein considers it most unlikely that glucagon could have arisen from an insulin-like molecule as has been suggested by some.

Gastrin

This hormone (which stimulates gastric acid secretion) has been found in the D-cells of the pancreatic islets and in the pyloric region of the stomach. Its distribution in non-mammals has not yet been systematically explored. Early reports have indeed failed to confirm its presence. Several gastrins have been identified in mammals. The structures are shown in Fig. 3.17. Amino acid substitutions (accounted for by single mutations) occur at three positions in the molecule and result in considerable variation in their biological activities. When tested by their ability to alter gastric juice secretion (in cats) the ratio of activities in ovine:porcine:human:canine gastrins were 1.8:1.0:0.5:0.3 (see Bromer, 1972).

(a)   GASTRIN I   1   2   3   4   5   6   7   8   9   10   11   12   13   14   15   16   17

Human   Pyr-Gly-Pro-Trp-Leu-Glu-Glu-Glu-Glu-Ala-Tyr-Gly-Trp-Met-Asp-Phe—NH₂

Pig   Pyr-Gly-Pro-Trp-*Met*-Glu-Glu-Glu-Glu-Ala-Tyr-Gly-Trp-Met-Asp-Phe—NH₂

Cat   Pyr-Gly-Pro-Trp-Leu-Glu-Glu-Glu-Glu-*Ala*-Ala-Tyr-Gly-Trp-Met- Asp-Phe—NH₂

Dog   Pyr-Gly-Pro-Trp-*Met*-Glu-Glu-Glu-*Ala*-Glu-Ala-Tyr-Gly-Trp- Met-Asp-Phe—NH₂

Cattle, sheep Pyr-Gly-Pro-Trp-*Val*-Glu-Glu-Glu-Glu-*Ala*-Ala-Tyr-Gly-Trp-Met-Asp-Phe—NH₂

(b)   Cholecystokinin–Pancreozymin

Lys · (Ala₁, Gly₁, Pro₁, Ser₁) · Arg · Val · (Ileu₁, Met₁, Ser₁) · Lys ·

Asn · (Asx₁, Glx₁, His₁, Leu₂, Pro₁, Ser₂) · Arg · Ileu (Asp₁, Ser₁) ·

$$\overset{\displaystyle SO_3H}{\mid}$$

Arg · Asp · Tyr · Met · Gly · Trp · Met · Asp · Phe · NH₂

Terminal Octapeptide

$$\overset{\displaystyle SO_3H}{\mid}$$

Asp · Tyr · Met · Gly · Trp · Met · Asp · Phe · NH₂

Fig. 3.17. (a) Amino acid sequences of some mammalian gastrins. Residues in italics indicate differences from the hormone present in man. (From Bromer, 1972.)

(b) Tentative amino acid sequence of porcine cholecystokinin–pancreozymin. The active C-terminal octapeptide is also shown. It can be seen that the last five amino acids in the gastrin and cholecystokinin–pancreozymin molecules are identical. (From Rubin et al., 1969.)

Gastrin has not been identified in birds but a polypeptide, which stimulates acid secretion from the avian proventriculus, and so has a 'gastrin-like' action, has been found in the pancreas (Hazelwood *et al.*, 1973). This has been identified in 10 species of birds and in the circulation of the chicken so that it could have an hormonal role. It may thus be a third pancreatic hormone in birds (in addition to insulin and glucagon) and has been dubbed 'APP', which stands for avian pancreatic polypeptide. The chemical structure of APP is quite unlike that of mammalian gastrin as it consists of 36 amino acids (molecular weight, 4200) and contains glycine at its *N*-terminus and tyrosine-amide at its *C*-terminus. It is interesting, however, that the pancreas of several mammals has been shown to contain a similar peptide which shares a common sequence of 16 amino acids with APP. Such a polypeptide has not been identified in amphibians or snakes and it does not act like gastrin in mammals. The structural similarities between the avian and mammalian pancreatic polypeptides, however, suggest that they may have a common ancestry and that, in the birds, the molecule has been used as a hormone (like gastrin) that stimulates the secretion of acid in the gut.

Enterogastrone

On physiological grounds a hormone called enterogastrone, that inhibits the secretion of acid by the stomach, is thought to be released from the upper part of the intestine. This 'hormone' has, however, defied attempts to isolate it chemically so that its existence as a distinct hormone remains in doubt.

Cholecystokinin–pancreozymin

Cholecystokinin is a gastrointestinal hormone that is released from the mucosal cells in the upper regions of the intestine. Pancreozymin was originally thought to be a separate hormone but the two are now known to be identical (Jorpes and Mutt, 1966) and the hormone is called cholecystokinin–pancreozymin. Materials that behave in a similar biological and chemical manner have also been isolated from the intestines of cyclostomes (lampreys, *Lampetra fluviatilis* and *Petromyzon marinus*), a teleost (the eel, *Anguilla anguilla*), and a chondrichthyean (the holocephalian fish *Chimaera monstrosa* (Barrington and Dockray, 1970, 1972; Nilsson, 1970). This hormone thus appears to have a long phylogenetic history. It is a single chain polypeptide containing 33 amino acids, the tentative sequence of which is given in Fig. 3.17. The *C*-terminal octapeptide part of the molecule possesses all of the biological actions of the intact molecule (Rubin *et al.*, 1969). The *C*-terminal pentapeptide (= pentagastrin) is identical to the *C*-terminal sequence in gastrin and this fragment of the molecule exerts all the important actions of gastrin (Tracy and Gregory, 1964). These similarities in the structures of the active sections of these gastrointestinal hormones contribute to the cross-over that is often observed in their actions and suggests that they may have had common ancestral origins.

Adrenocorticotrophin (ACTH), melanocyte-stimulating hormone (MSH) and β-lipotrophin

These pituitary hormones are polypeptides that share a number of common features. They all possess a common core of seven amino acids while the ones adjoining it are also often similar (Table 3.7). They possess, with a few variations, common sequences of up to 20 amino acids. This is reflected in a cross-over in their biological activities; all, for instance, exhibit an ability to stimulate amphibian melanophores.

MSH (Table 3.7) exists in many polymorphic forms though the chemical structures of only a few are known. α-MSH has the same structure in many species (13 amino acids in a chain) but the associated β-MSH (usually 18 amino acids but 22 in man) shows considerable variation. They all, however share the same 'core'. Dogfish MSH has more recently been described chemically and is similar to α-MSH but contains two less amino acids (Lowry and Chadwick, 1970). Comparison of the chromatographic, immunological and biological behavior indicates that many variants of MSH exist among the vertebrates. The differences are seen in such diverse species as the codfish, *Gadus morhua*, the frogs, *Rana catesbeiana* and *R. pipiens*, the lizard, *Anolis carolinensis*, and the domestic fowl, *Gallus domesticus*, to name but a few (see Burgers, 1963; Shapiro *et al.*, 1972). The polymorphism exhibited by MSH is not only an interspecific one. In the sheep, for instance, three chemically distinct MSHs have been found within a single pituitary gland. Apart from indicating considerable genetic variation the reasons for their perpetuation are not apparent, especially as the role of such peptides in mammals is unknown.

ACTH, which stimulates the adrenal cortex to secrete certain steroid hormones consists of a chain of 39 amino acids in mammals. While variations in configuration undoubtedly occur, the chemical structure of ACTH of a non-mammal has not yet been described. The ability to stimulate adrenocortical tissue resides in the first 19 to 23 amino acids at the amino-terminus. Synthetic peptides with such structures have been made and exhibit a similar biological potency to the intact hormone. Differences between the amino acid sequences of ACTH have been described in man,

TABLE 3.7. *Amino acid sequences of meloncyte-stimulating hormones (MSH), adrenocorticotrophin (ACTH) and lipotrophin. The relative MSH activity (as tested on amphibian color change) of some of the materials is shown in the last column*

Hormone	Structure	Relative MSH potency *in vitro*
α-MSH: Pig, cattle, horse, man, monkey	Acetyl-Ser-Tyr-Ser-Met-Glu-His-Phe-Arg-Trp-Gly-Lys-Pro-Val-NH₂ 1 4 10 13	1.00
MSH : Dogfish	Ser-Met-Glu-His-Phe-Arg-Tyr-Gly-Lys-Pro-Met-NH₂ 2 8 11	–
β-MSH: Man	Ala-Glu-Lys-Lys-Asp-Glu-Gly-Pro-Tyr-Arg– 1 Met-Glu-His-Phe-Arg-Trp-Gly-Ser-Pro-Pro-Lys-Asp 11 17 22	0.23
Monkey	Asp-Glu-Gly-Pro-Tyr-Arg-Met-Glu-His-Phe-Arg-Try-Gly-Ser-Pro-Pro– 1 7 13 Lys-Asp 18	–
Pig, sheep	Asp-Glu-Gly-Pro-Tyr-Lys-Met-Glu-His-Phe-Arg-Trp-Gly– 1 7 13 Ser-Pro-Pro-Lys-Asp 18	0.26

Cattle, sheep	Asp–Ser–Gly–Pro–Tyr–Lys–Met–Glu–His–Phe–Arg–Trp–Gly– 1 7 13 Ser–Pro–Lys–Asp 18	0.66
Horse	Asp–Glu–Gly–Pro–Tyr–Lys–Met–Glu–His–Phe–Arg–Trp–Gly– 1 7 13 Ser–Pro–Arg–Lys–Asp	–
ACTH:	Ser–Tyr–Ser–Met–Glu–His–Phe–Arg–Trp–Gly–Lys–Pro–Val–Gly– 1 10 Lys······Phe 4 15 39	0.01
Lipotrophin	Ala–Glu–Lys–Lys–Asp–Asp–Ser–Gly–Pro–Tyr–Lys–Met–Glu–His–Phe–Arg–Trp– 37 47 Gly–Ser–Pro–Pro–Lys–Asp······Gln 53 58 90	–

Italicized amino acids indicate different from human MSH.

ox, sheep and pig. The substitutions occur in the less important part of the hormone between positions 25 and 33. The last six amino acids are identical in these mammals.

A large polypeptide, which has an ability to mobilize lipids in the body, called β-lipotrophin, is present in the adenohypophysis of sheep, cattle, pigs and possibly man (Li *et al.*, 1965; Desranleau, Gilardeau and Chrétien, 1972). In the sheep, it contains 90 amino acids. Immunological comparisons indicate that this polypeptide is structurally similar in sheep, cattle and pigs but that in man it is different. The structure of this molecule is of special interest in relation to that of MSH and ACTH. As can be seen in Table 3.7, it shares a common sequence with them, at positions 47 to 53. In addition, with two exceptions, positions 37 to 58 are identical to that of β-MSH in man. These molecules, MSH, ACTH and β-lipotrophin thus share many common chemical features. It has been suggested that they could arise in the pituitary from a single parent protein though this is difficult to reconcile with the dispersion of the morphological sites where they are found within the gland. It remains likely, nevertheless, that such chemical similarities reflect their evolution from a common ancestral molecule.

The pituitary glycoprotein hormones: luteinizing hormone (LH), follicle-stimulating hormone (FSH) and thyrotrophic hormone (TSH)

The gonadotrophins, LH and FSH, and TSH originate in the adeno-hypophysis. They exert trophic actions on the gonads and thyroid gland, stimulating their development and growth as well as the formation and secretion of their hormones.

These three hormones are large molecules (with a molecular weight of about 30 000) composed of amino acids and certain carbohydrate moieties (14 to 18 % of their weight). The precise chemical structure of bovine and ovine LH and TSH is now known, while considerable information is also available about FSH. They are each composed of two subunits termed α- and β- (or sometimes CI and CII) (see Papkoff, 1972). The subunits TSH-α and LH-α (or ICSH-α) each contain 96 amino acids and are virtually identical (Fig. 3.18). The differences in the molecules, and hence their biological specificity, reside in the structure of their β-subunits. LH-β contains 120 amino acids while TSH-β has 113. These alone have little or no action in mammals. If THS-α is joined to LH-β the LH activity is restored and in the same way if LH-α and TSH-β are combined the molecule has the usual TSH activity.

The precise chemical constitution of these adenohypophysial molecules is only known in mammals. Extracts of the pituitaries of other vertebrates have similar biological actions on the gonads and thyroid which are seen when homologous extracts are injected into a species or even when such preparations are tested on other vertebrates. Some gonadotrophins and TSH in non-mammals have been chemically identified as glycoproteins. An amino acid analysis has been made on a highly purified preparation of a teleost gonadotrophin (the carp) and this shows considerable differences from that of mammalian LH and FSH (Burzawa-Gerard and Fontaine, 1972). Chemical behavior (principally the ability to separate the biological activities chromatographically or electrophoretically) of extracts from non-mammals suggests that the gonadotrophic activities may reside in a single molecule which incorporates both FSH- and LH-like activities. A distinct LH and a FSH have been isolated in mammals, in birds and a chelonian but in other reptiles, amphibians and fishes a single gonadotrophin seems to be present which can react with more than one type of effector and so fulfill the dual functions of FSH and LH.

The principal evidence that vertebrate gonadotrophin(s) and TSH exist in various polymorphic forms comes from comparative measurements of their activities using bioassay preparations derived from different species. The ratio of the biological activity of two glandular extracts can be initially compared in one type of assay system and then repeated in other, different, types of preparations. If the ratio differs in the two or more systems used for the measurements it suggests that the activities result from hormones that differ somewhat in their chemical structures. For the measurement of gonadotrophic activity such assay preparations include stimulation of the uptake of radioactive phosphorus (^{32}P) by the testes of day-old chicks or eels, spermiation in amphibians and teleosts, maintenance and development of the gonads and secondary sex characters in lizards and ovulation in amphibians and mammals. Comparison of TSH activity depends on measurements of ^{131}I uptake by the thyroid gland, the release of thyroxine and the histological appearance and size of the cells in the thyroid. Phyletically diverse species have been used for these comparative assays ranging from mammals to teleosts and chondrichthyean fishes.

'There are no clear cut, well documented cases of species specificity of gonadotrophic hormones' (Nalbandov, 1969). Different species invariably show *some* response to heterologous gonadotrophins. There are, however, considerable variations in the biological potency of such hormones indicating that polymorphic variations exist. Mammalian gonadotrophins exhibit some activity in all vertebrates. In teleost fish, mammalian LH (and human chorionic gonadotrophin, HCG) are sometimes effective but FSH is inactive (Burzawa-Gerard and Fontaine, 1972). Teleost gonadotrophin, on the other hand, while being very active in teleosts, has little effect in mammals. Amphibians, reptiles and birds show considerable responsiveness

(a) H—(Phe)(Pro)(Asp)(Gly)(Glu)(Phe)(Thr)(Met)(Gln)(Gly)(Cys)(Pro)(Glu)(Cys)-
                                                    10

(Lys)(Leu)(Lys)(Glu)(Asn)(Lys)(Tyr)(Phe)(Ser)(Lys)(Pro)(Asp)(Ala)(Pro)-
                                    20

(Ile)(Tyr)(Gln)(Cys)(Met)(Gly)(Cys)(Cys)(Phe)(Ser)(Arg)(Ala)(Tyr)(Pro)-
            30   40

CHO
|
(Thr)(Pro)(Ala)(Arg)(Ser)(Lys)(Lys)(Thr)(Met)(Leu)(Val)(Pro)(Lys)(Asn)-
                            50

(Ile)(Thr)(Ser)(Glu)(Ala)(Thr)(Cys)(Cys)(Val)(Ala)(Lys)(Ala)(Phe)(Thr)-
            60   70

CHO
|
(Lys)(Ala)(Thr)(Val)(Met)(Gly)(Asn)(Val)(Arg)(Val)(Glx)(Asn)(His)(Thr)-
                            80

TSH-α: (Cys)(Ser)
(Glu)(Cys)(His)(Ser)(Cys)(Thr)(Cys)(Tyr)(Tyr)(His)(Lys)(Ser)—OH
                            90

CHO
|
(b) H—(Ser)(Arg)(Gly)(Pro)(Leu)(Arg)(Pro)(Leu)(Cys)(Glu)(Pro)(Ile)(Asn)(Ala)-
                                                    10

(Thr)(Leu)(Ala)(Ala)(Glu)(Lys)(Glu)(Ala)(Cys)(Pro)(Val)(Cys)(Ile)(Thr)-
                            20

(Phe)(Thr)(Thr)(Ser)(Ile)(Gly)(Ala)(Tyr)(Cys)(Cys)(Pro)(Ser)(Met)(Lys)-
            30   40

(Arg)(Val)(Leu)(Pro)(Val)(Pro)(Pro)(Leu)(Ile)(Pro)(Met)(Pro)(Gln)(Arg)-
                            50

(Val)(Cys)(Thr)(Tyr)(His)(Gln)(Leu)(Arg)(Phe)(Ala)(Ser)(Val)(Arg)(Leu)-
            60   70

(Pro)(Gly)(Pro)(Cys)(Pro)(Val)(Asp)(Pro)(Gly)(Met)(Val)(Ser)(Phe)(Pro)-
                            80

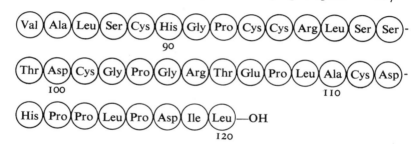

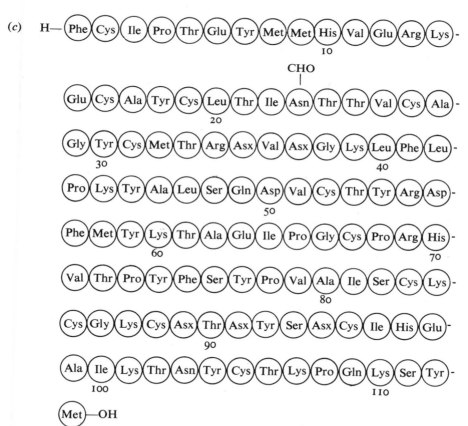

Fig. 3.18. Amino acid sequences the α- and β- chains of mammalian thyrotrophic hormone (TSH) and luteinizing hormone (LH, *or* ICSH).

(*a*) Ovine ICSH-α and bovine TSH-α; (*b*) ovine ICSH-β; (*c*) bovine TSH-β. (From Papkoff, 1972.)

to gonadotrophins from teleost, chondrichthyean and dipnoan fishes as well as those from mammals. The avian hormones are more effective in lizards than in mammals (Burzawa-Gerard and Fontaine, 1972; Donaldson *et al.*, 1972; Licht and Stockell Hartree, 1971; Scanes, Dobson, Follett and Dodd, 1972). While a reptilian gonadotrophin preparation, from the snapping turtle, is ineffective *in vivo* on mammalian test-preparations it stimulates the ovarian granulosa cells of a monkey *in vitro* and is also active in birds, amphibians and other reptiles (Channing *et al.*, 1974; Licht and Papkoff, 1974*a*). No gonadotrophin preparations thus would appear to be completely species specific but they exhibit considerable differences in their activity when tested on preparations from other phyletic groups. Such differences are assumed to reflect variations in their molecular structures.

Immunological cross-reactions are also indicative of chemical relationships between hormones. Antibodies to highly purified preparations of LH from the domestic fowl have been tested on a variety of vertebrates (Scanes, Follett and Goos, 1972). Such antiserum reacted with pituitary gland extracts and plasma from 10 other species of birds as well as three species of reptiles and a dogfish. Non-parallel dose–response reactions were observed with preparations from three amphibians, a lungfish and one teleost (the goldfish) while no reaction could be seen in another teleost (the carp). One cannot trace the phylogenetic history of hormones in this way but it emphasizes the variations between them. It should be emphasized that similarities and differences in biological and immunological responses of hormones need not parallel each other, as the associated changes in the molecules may have evolved independently for each type of activity.

In 1940 Gorbman found that the goldfish thyroid tissue was stimulated by pituitary extracts from a teleost fish, two amphibians, a bird and a mammal. This suggested that TSH had a wide phyletic distribution. Subsequent measurements using a greater variety of species to compare the activity of such glandular extracts (in addition to the goldfish, a salamander, lizard and guinea-pig were used) indicated the hormones present in the various species were not identical, though they exerted the same general biological effects. While mammalian TSH preparations are active in teleosts, teleost TSH has little activity in mammals (Fontaine, 1969*a*, *b*). As the phyletic scale is ascended it is found that TSH preparations from a lungfish (*Protopterus*), amphibians, reptiles and birds can exert well-defined effects on the thyroid of both mammal (mouse) and teleost fish (trout). The thyroid of chondrichthyean fish (the stingray, *Dasyatis sabina*) while responding to its own, homologous TSH shows no response to the mammalian or even teleost hormones (Jackson and Sage, 1973). Chondrichthyean TSH, on the other hand, stimulates the mammalian thyroid

(Dodd and Dodd, 1969). Mammalian TSH increases thyroidal activity in the Pacific hagfish, *Eptatretus stouti* (Cyclostomata), though TSH-activity (when tested in mammals) has not been demonstrated in the pituitary of the Atlantic hagfish, *Myxine glutinosa* (Kerkof, Boschwitz and Gorbman, 1973; Dodd and Dodd, 1969). One obviously cannot construct an ordered story from these observations but they serve to show that TSH, like other hormones, has suffered, during evolution, changes in its structure.

The mammalian gonadotrophins have a thyrotrophic effect when they are injected into teleost fishes, an action that was initially attributed to the presence of a distinct heterothyrotrophic factor, or HTF, in the mammalian pituitary (Fontaine, 1969a). This cross-over in the actions of gonadotrophins and TSH presumably reflects similarities in the chemical structure of teleost TSH, and mammalian FSH and LH. It has been proposed (Fontaine, 1969a) that the gonadotrophins and TSH in extant species evolved from a common ancestral molecule, probably by a process of gene duplication and subsequent genetic change. It is interesting that there is no clear evidence for the presence of a distinct TSH in cyclostome fish where hypophysectomy (in the lamprey) has no effect on thyroidal activity (see Sage, 1973). It has also been observed that reproductive rhythms in fish are associated with parallel changes in the activity of the thyroid tissue. It has thus been suggested that the ancestral, or parent, molecule had a gonadotrophic role which was extended to a thyrotrophic one when the thyroid gland assumed a role in reproduction in fishes.

Growth hormone, prolactin and human chorionic somatomammotrophin

These three hormones are proteins containing about 190 amino acids and they show many structural and functional homologies to one another. Growth hormone and prolactin are formed in the adenohypophysis, the former being concerned with the regulation of growth and the latter with diverse processes ranging from lactation in mammals to osmoregulation in some fish. Human chorionic somatomammotrophin (or human placental lactogen) has been isolated from the placenta of man, and some other primates, and exerts some of the effects of both its adenohypophysial analogues.

The amino acid sequence of the hormones has been described. That of human growth hormone is shown in Fig. 3.19. Human chorionic somatomammotrophin and ovine prolactin have similar structures to this hormone. Human prolactin has not been isolated but sensitive bioassay and immunological techniques indicate that it exists as a distinct entity, apart from growth hormone, although this was once in doubt. The amino acid sequence of the three hormones has been compared (Fig. 3.20) and considerable

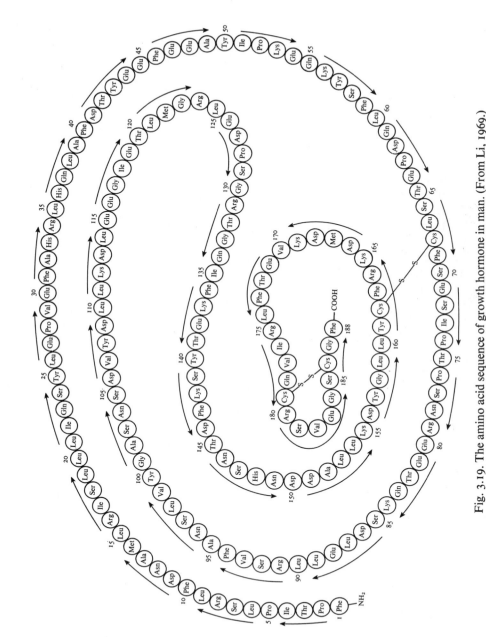

Fig. 3.19. The amino acid sequence of growth hormone in man. (From Li, 1969.)

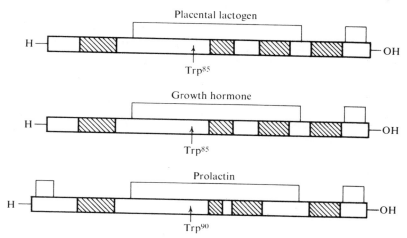

Fig. 3.20. Diagrammatic representation of the structures of placental lactogen (chorionic somatomammotrophin) and growth hormone from man, and pro- lactin from sheep. The cross-hatched areas represent regions of internal homology in the sequence of the amino acids. Other similarities can be seen in the presence of disulfide bridges (narrow lines) and the tryptophan residues at position 85 in placental lactogen and growth hormone and 90 in prolactin. (From Niall *et al.*, 1971.)

homologies exist. There are thus 160 (out of 190) identical residues in human growth hormone and chorionic somatomammotrophin while, of the remainder, only seven positions are occupied by what are considered 'non-homologous' amino acids (Li, 1972). Such similarities have led to the suggestion (Bewley and Li, 1970; Niall *et al.*, 1971) that the three hormones may have arisen from a common ancestral molecule. Various segments of each hormone molecule also bear considerable similarities to each other (internal homologies). The ancestral molecule may have been a smaller peptide of 25 to 50 amino acids that, by a process of genetic reduplication in a 'tandem' manner, led to an increase in the chain length of the hormones.

The chemical similarities in the molecules are reflected in their biological activities. Apart from the dual effects of chorionic somatomammotrophin on growth and lactation, prolactin exhibits considerable growth hormone- like activity while growth hormone has (though more limited) prolactin- like actions.

Growth hormone and prolactin are present throughout the vertebrates (with the possible exception of the cyclostomes).

Growth hormone can be measured by its ability to increase growth of the tibia of young, hypophysectomized rats. Pituitary extracts from all the groups of tetrapods exhibit this effect but it is not manifested by those of teleost or chondrichthyean fish (see Geschwind, 1967). Extracts from teleosts, however, have a comparable effect on growth when injected into another teleost, the killifish, *Fundulus kansae*. Pituitary extracts from the lungfish (Dipnoi), the bowfin and garpike (Holostei) and sturgeon and paddlefish (Chondrostei), all stimulate growth of the rat's tibia (Hayashida and Lagios, 1969; Hayashida, 1971). It would thus seem that the teleost growth hormone has a greater degree of structural dissimilarity from the homologous rat hormone than do growth hormones from other bony fishes. Other bioassay test systems are responsive to a phyletic range of growth hormone preparations. Such tests include the incorporation of sulfate into the cartilage of embryonic chicks as well as growth in toads (Meier and Solursh, 1972; Zipser, Licht and Bern, 1959), lizards (Licht and Hoyer, 1968) and turtles (Nichols, 1973). These tests also show that not only the hormone, but a similar biological response to it, occurs in many vertebrates.

Growth hormones from all species do not always exhibit an effect when injected into an heterologous species. This is seen very clearly in man who is unresponsive to all animal growth hormones, including those from other primates. As indicated earlier, this is an observation of some practical significance as the supply of growth hormone for administration to man has to be obtained from human cadavers and is thus limited.

Immunological evidence also emphasizes the differences, and similarities, among growth hormones from different vertebrates. Growth hormones show varying activities as antigens, depending on the species of the donor and the recipient. Rat growth hormone is not antigenic in rabbits but is very effective when injected into monkeys. Primate growth hormone is, however, antigenic in rabbits. Rabbit antiserum to human growth hormone has been shown to react (as measured by complement-fixation) with hormone preparations from other primates and in nine such species (Fig. 3.21) the degree of these interactions was closely correlated with their phyletic relationships.

A wider survey has shown that pituitary growth hormone extracts from most vertebrates can react with monkey antiserum that is formed in response to injected rat growth hormone (Hayashida and Lagios, 1969; Hayashida, 1970, 1971, 1973). Measurements of the relative ability of such pituitary extracts to antagonize the interaction of rat growth hormone with its antisera, in radioimmunoassays, has shown that the wider the phyletic distance between the species the less effective this antagonism (or ability to react with the antisera) becomes (Fig. 3.22a). No significant interaction was seen in glandular extracts from teleost fishes (which also lacks activity in the rat-tibia bioassay test). Hormones from other vertebrates, including the lungfish, have an interaction in this system which

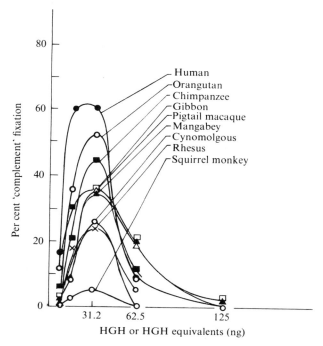

Fig. 3.21. The interactions between rabbit antiserum to human growth hormone and growth hormone from 9 different species of primates. The values given are for complement-fixation curves. The equivalence points of all the curves have been aligned with the antigen-concentration of human growth hormone which gave the maximum value. The degree of the immunological relationship is directly proportional to the amount of complement fixed at equivalence by that of the human and animal growth hormones. (From Tashjian, Levine and Wilhelmi, 1965.)

increases as the phyletic scale is ascended. It is also notable (Fig. 3.22*b*, *c*) that pituitary extracts of chondrichthyean, holostean and chondrosten fishes show abilities to antagonize the reaction of rat growth hormone with its antiserum. These reactions parallel their abilities to stimulate growth in the rat-tibia test.

Prolactin increases milk secretion in mammals and this response can be used to measure the hormone's activity even in the low concentrations that appear in the plasma (Frantz, Kleinberg and Noel, 1972). Pituitary extracts from birds, reptiles and amphibians all promote this response but not those from fishes. Pigeons secrete a milk-like paste (pigeons' milk) from their crop-sac, with which they feed their young. This response is stimulated by prolactin from tetrapods *and* lungfishes but that from other fishes is

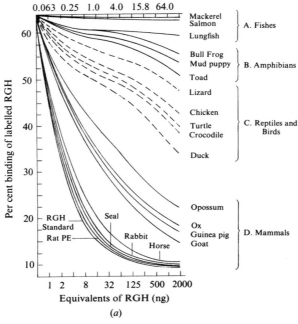

Pituitary tissue (μg)

0.063 0.25 1.0 4.0 15.8 64.0

Mackerel
Salmon   } A. Fishes
Lungfish

Bull Frog
Mud puppy   } B. Amphibians
Toad

Lizard
Chicken
Turtle   } C. Reptiles and
Crocodile   Birds
Duck

Opossum
Ox
Guinea pig } D. Mammals
Goat

RGH
Standard
Rat PE

Seal

Rabbit

Horse

Per cent binding of labelled RGH

1   2   8   32 125 500 2000

Equivalents of RGH (ng)

(a)

Pituitary tissue (μg)

0.063 0.25 1.0 4.0 15.8 64.0

Skate

Gar

Bowfin

Turtle

RGH
Standard

Per cent binding of labelled RGH

1   2   4   8   32 128 500 2000

RGH standard (ng)

(b)

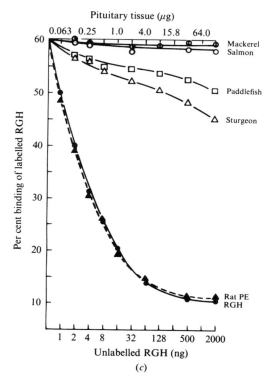

Fig. 3.22. Diagrams showing the immunochemical relationships of different vertebrate growth hormones.

The curves represent the relative abilities of these preparations to reduce the binding of ^{131}I-labelled rat growth hormone to monkey antiserum (to rat growth hormone). Thus rat growth hormone (RGH) nearly completely displaced the labelled rat growth hormone, while that from the mackerel, salmon and skate was completely ineffective. Growth hormone from other sources fell between these extremes. (*a* and *b* from Hayashida, 1970, 1971; *c*, Hayashida and Lagios, 1969.)

ineffective. Prolactin, when injected into certain newts (*Notophthalmus* (*Diemictylus*) *viridescens*) at a particular stage in their life cycle, causes them to seek water preparatory to breeding. This is called the 'eft (or newt) water-drive response' and can be initiated by prolactin from all the principal groups of vertebrates [except the cyclostomes which seem to lack a prolactin hormone (see Bern and Nicoll, 1968)]. This response cannot be mimicked by any other pituitary hormone and has been used to demonstrate the presence of an analogous prolactin-like secretion throughout the vertebrates. Further evidence of the occurrence of this hormone in fishes has followed the recent discovery that certain teleost fishes, when in fresh water, usually die following removal of the pituitary gland, and this is due to excessive losses of sodium. When injected with mammalian prolactin they retain sodium and survive. Teleosts's pituitaries contain a 'hormone' that also has the latter effect and which, as a reflection of its difference from mammalian prolactin, has been called 'paralactin'. The phyletic distribution of all these effects follows a precise pattern which is shown in Fig. 3.23.

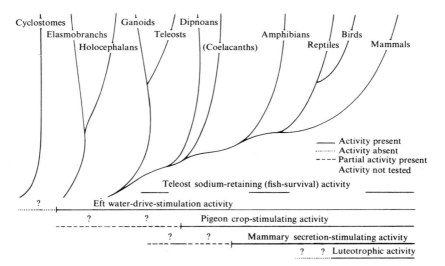

Fig. 3.23. Distribution of some of the biological activities that can be initiated by mammalian prolactin and prolactin-like hormones from other vertebrates. (From H. A. Bern, personal communication in Bentley, 1971.)

The observations described above suggest two things: first, that the prolactin hormone is not identical in all vertebrates and has been subject to evolutionary change and second, it seems likely that it has assumed diverse biological roles.

The precise chemical structure of prolactins from non-mammals has not yet been described. The similarities and differences in their biological effects (see Table 3.8) nevertheless indicate that, while they are basically analogous, differences exist in their structure. The 'ancestral' molecule may have been relatively less specific in its action than, for instance, that present in contemporary mammals. This may be reflected in the one-way specificity of mammalian prolactin which acts in fish while fish prolactin fails to have an effect in mammals. With the origin of the tetrapods, changes occurred in the molecule which are illustrated by its ability to stimulate the pigeon

TABLE 3.8. *Distribution of several prolactin activities in vertebrate pituitaries. (Group in which pituitary has been examined for prolactin activity; from Bern and Nicoll, 1969)*

Prolactin activity	Cyclostomes	Chondrichthyes	Teleosts	Lungfish	Amphibians	Reptiles	Birds	Mammals
Osmoregulatory (in teleosts)			+/–					+
Water-drive-inducing (in efts)	–?	+	+		+	+	+	+
Growth-stimulating (?) (in tadpoles)			–		+	+	+	+
Crop-sac-stimulating (in pigeons)	–	–*	–*	+	+	+	+	+
Mammotrophic (in mice)		**	–**	–	+	+	+	+
Luteotrophic (in mice)						–?	+?	+

* Partial activity has been reported from these groups; this is considered to be minimal and not fully crop-sac-stimulating in the manner seen with lungfish and amphibians.

** Partial activity has been reported from these groups, which is distinguished from the 'fully effective' response seen with tetrapods.

crop-sac and mammary gland. This evidence is, of course, derived from extant species and, if it indeed did occur in that long-past time, the particular effects were not then of contemporary biological significance. The pigeon crop-sac and mammary gland were not to appear for many millions of years. It seems quite likely that prolactin had other roles at that time.

As described above, human chorionic somatomammotrophin has both prolactin- and growth hormone-like action in mammals. When tested in non-mammals, however, this hormone behaves differently to the mammalian pituitary hormones as it exhibits no 'eft water-drive' activity, does not increase growth in tadpoles and fails to promote sodium retention in a teleost fish, *Tilapia mossambica* (Gona and Gona, 1973; Clarke *et al.*, 1973). Thus, while human chorionic somatomammatrophin shares some actions with mammalian prolactin and growth hormone, these do not necessarily extend to the effects of the last two in non-mammals.

Tetrapod prolactins have been shown to exhibit differing chemical behavior. The electrophoretic mobilities (R_f), reflecting size and electrical charge, show considerable differences (Fig. 3.24) from each other and cross an almost five-fold range. No phyletic order is apparent; the ox, duck and frog all have a similar R_f, while the rat, quail, turtle and toad are all much higher. Interspecific differences, nevertheless, can be seen to exist. Growth hormones can also be separated in this way and, while they also exhibit differences in electrophoretic mobility, they are quite distinct from the prolactins (Fig. 3.24). The two hormones may still exhibit immunochemical similarities as seen in amphibians where the electrophoretically separated

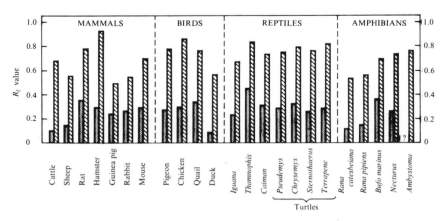

Fig. 3.24. A comparison of the electrophoretic mobilities (R_f) of prolactins and growth hormones from different species of tetrapod vertebrates, stippled bars, growth hormone; cross-hatched bars, prolactin. (From Nicoll and Licht, 1971.)

hormones both compete with rat growth hormone for binding to rat growth hormone antiserum (Hayashida, Licht and Nicoll, 1973).

The prolactins exhibit a multitude of different biological effects. These (Bern and Nicoll, 1968) have been classified into several categories including actions related to reproduction and parental care, osmoregulation, growth, metabolism and the integument. In all, over 60 different effects have been described. It is unlikely that these all reflect physiological roles but they do illustrate the considerable biological reactivity of the prolactin molecule. This may provide it with an adaptability, and propensity, to be utilized in a great diversity of physiological roles, only some of which have already been identified, or even applied. Prolactin would seem to be a hormone whose structure, as well as physiological role, have both evolved. Its diverse biological actions suggest that it is the most versatile vertebrate hormone.

Evolution of hormones: general comment

While it is difficult to make any generalizations about the directions and effects of the evolution of the structure of hormones, a certain amount of speculation on this subject has been made. It has been observed that, while the homologous hormones of 'higher' vertebrates may interact with receptors, and elicit a response, in 'lower' vertebrates the reverse is seen less often. There are, however, many exceptions and one must be cautious about accepting such occurrences as a 'rule'. The one-way phenomenon is, nevertheless, often apparent though it does not always follow phyletic lines strictly. For example: the growth hormone of the teleostean fishes does not elicit effects in mammals, but that from the phyletically less-advanced holostean and chondrosteans is effective. Also, chondrichthyean thyro-trophic hormone is effective in mammals but that from mammals, or teleosts, has no action in chondrichthyeans. With such exceptions to the one-way rule in mind, we may nevertheless consider what the structural basis for the differing interspecific effects of hormones may be and what effects such changes may have on the actions of the hormones themselves.

As indicated earlier, in order to elicit a response, hormones interact with a specific chemical entity which has been called the receptor. The precise nature of such receptors is still largely unknown but they are thought of as being a group of chemical properties arranged in such a manner as to be able to combine, or interact, with molecules of a certain specific form. Several types of interactions may occur and not all of these will necessarily initiate a response or even equal responses. A 'successful' combination (that results in a biological effect) in some manner, not well understood, triggers a reaction(s) that initiates an effect. This process could be the activation of an enzyme, the supplying of an essential substrate or cofactor, or a structural change in the cell membrane such as may alter its permeability.

Properties that may determine the ability of a hormone to interact with such a receptor site include its size, shape, electrical charge, disposition of hydrophobic and hydrophilic groups, the presence of acidic or basic moieties, its ability to form hydrogen bonds, ionic bonds and so on. The hormone and its receptors thus must exhibit a complex affinity for each other that is complementary.

Changes in the structure of a hormone, if it is to remain effective, need to be accompanied by changes in the receptor. The evolution of both must therefore occur in some sort of harmony. By utilizing such parallel changes, the specificity of the hormones can be maintained, or altered in such a direction as may be advantageous (or possibly disadvantageous) to the animal.

Changes in the structure of a hormone, especially a large polypeptide, can influence, in either of two ways, its ability to combine with a receptor (see for instance Fontaine, Y-A., 1964):

(1) Each group of phyletically related hormones may possess a 'common-core' in which the attachment sites for the receptor reside. These structural features are primarily essential for the hormone's interaction with its receptor. Modifications that survive in nature may involve other, less essential, parts of the molecules that 'mask' the 'common-core' in such a way that it cannot interact with its receptor unless aligned in a special way. Alternatively, it may be necessary to 'activate' the molecule by removing part of it as the result of the action of an enzyme. The receptor necessarily must possess a complementary arrangement to insure that such effects are possible. This hypothesis tends to gain support from observations of common amino acid sequences in phyletically diverse molecules and the retention of biological activity by fragments of these.

(2) The activity of a hormone molecule may be intrinsically related to its over-all structure. The entire configuration of the molecule could contribute to its interaction with the receptor.

A parent, or ancestral, hormone is sometimes thought of as being more 'simple' in structure than its evolutionary descendants. As a result of mutational changes, it may be altered in several ways. Single-base changes at individual gene loci may occur that result in amino acid substitutions. Depending on the nature of the substituent amino acid this may influence its reaction at the receptor; it could facilitate it, make little difference, decrease or even make such an interaction impossible. If the change were not too disadvantageous it is possible that compensatory changes in the receptor may also arise subsequently, or that the molecule may even be able to act at hitherto inaccessible sites. Complex changes of the hormones' structure may result from genetic reduplication, like those of the 'tandem' type proposed for prolactin and growth hormone and which result in an increase in the size of the molecule. Evidence for this type of change among extant species is equivocal as there is little indication of dramatic differences in the size of analogous hormones in different species.

Changes in a hormone's structure may, providing receptors can adapt to it, make possible a greater specificity of its action in the body which could be advantageous. There is much evidence available from the examination of cross-reactivity in extant species to suggest that such changes in hormones and their receptors has occurred during the course of evolution. This may also contribute to an explanation of 'one-way specificity' in the effects of hormones. Thus the hormones and their receptors that are present in some phyletic groups may be less fastidious as compared to those in others. A mammalian hormone, such as a gonadotrophin or thyrotrophin, may be able to interact (though possibly not as readily) with a less discriminating receptor in, for instance, a teleost fish. On the other hand, a more specific receptor (such as may have evolved in conjunction with the homologous hormones in a mammal) can no longer react with the teleost hormones. This theory is still, however, highly speculative and, as we have seen, one cannot make generalizations from the evidence obtained from extant species.

Conclusions

An examination of the chemical, biological and immunological behavior, as well as the chemical structure, of homologous hormones from different species suggests that many of these may have been subject to an orderly evolutionary change. This possibility is also indicated by the similarities that persist between each hormone from closely, in contrast to distantly, related species and within the principal systematic groups of the vertebrates. In some instances, a genetic background for such changes has been described. It is nevertheless noteworthy that some hormones display little or no difference in their structure even when they are present in such distantly related species as a lamprey and a man. On some occasions it even appears that a completely 'new' hormone that lacked a genetic homologue in its ancestors has evolved.

While the evolution of 'new' hormones has potential importance in novel processes of coordination in the body, the functional significance of alterations in the structure of 'old' hormones is less clear. Such changes may take place at chemical sites on the hormone molecule that are not essential for its action and so have little or no effect on its functioning.

However, if more important sites are involved the hormone's activity may be altered and this could have important results in the animal. These changes may include a virtual absence of its effect, differences in the quantities of the hormone required to mediate the response or an alteration in its relative ability to influence different processes within the same animal (specificity). As we shall see in the succeeding chapters, the roles of hormones in the body have often changed completely during the course of evolution. Such a modification of a hormone function is not necessarily accompanied by an alteration in its chemical structure, but it often is; though we are uncertain as to how important this change may be in the transition.

4. The life history of hormones

The use of hormones for the purpose of coordination involves a complex series of physiological events. Such a life history begins with the formation of the excitant by the endocrine glands and concludes with the response of a target, or effector tissue, and the hormone's ultimate destruction or its excretion from the body. The events that determine the action of a hormone are shown in Fig. 4.1. This basic pattern persists throughout the vertebrates, though, as will be described, certain differences exist.

The formation of hormones

While the formation of all hormones is determined at the genetic level it can be either a relatively direct translational procedure or, alternatively, occur as a result of the prior formation of enzymes that mediate synthesis.

Translational formation of hormones

It seems likely that the sequences of amino acids in the polypeptide and protein hormones directly reflect genetic translation via messenger RNA. Some of the small peptides, however, like thyrotrophin-releasing hormone (TRH), which is a tripeptide, may be assembled separately, in this instance as a result of the action of a TRH synthetase enzyme present in the hypothalamus (Mitnick and Reichlin, 1972). Even when a direct translation of genetic material into the amino acid sequence of a hormone is made, the active hormone product does not always result. Many peptide hormones, including glucagon, corticotrophin, MSH, the neurohypophysial peptides and calcitonin, contain relatively few amino acids and may be formed as a result of a process of disassembly from larger protein molecules. In addition, some polypeptide hormones are not simple strings of amino acids but consist of subunits as seen in insulin, the gonadotrophins and TSH. The assemblage of these subunits into a hormone must occur subsequent to the formation of the individual parts. The formation of polypeptide hormones thus often involves the initial formation of a parent molecule called a *pro-hormone*. As a result of post-translational changes, such as cleavage by enzymes, the pro-hormone is broken up to form the hormone itself. There

[123]

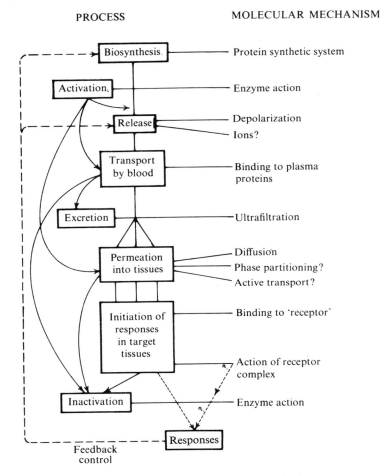

PROCESS   MOLECULAR MECHANISM

Fig. 4.1. Diagrammatic summary of the life history of a hormone commencing with its biosynthesis and concluding with the response and its inactivation. (From Rudinger, 1968. Reprinted by permission of the Royal Society.)

is good evidence to indicate that this occurs in the formation of parathormone, the neurohypophysial peptides, and insulin, and probably other examples occur.

Such a process of hormone formation is well illustrated in the production of insulin (Steiner *et al.*, 1972). Tumors with B-cells of the Islets of Langerhans contain a molecule that exhibits insulin-like activity, both biologically and immunologically, but which is about 1.5 times larger than insulin itself. A small quantity of this material has been found in normal

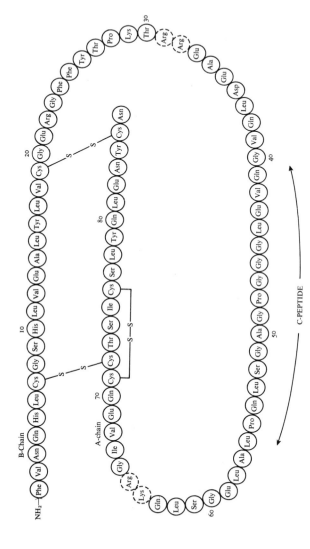

Fig. 4.2. The proposed amino acid sequence in proinsulin from man. The basic residues indicated by the broken circles have been assigned as they are known to occur in bovine and porcine proinsulin. (From Oyer *et al.*, 1971.)

B-cell extracts as well as in the 'principal islets' tissue of a teleost fish (the cod). When this pro-hormone molecule is treated with a proteolytic enzyme, trypsin, a product is formed that behaves similarly to true insulin. It thus appears that the latter is formed post-translationally from a large parent molecule. The chemical structure of human pro-insulin is shown in Fig. 4.2. It incorporates the B-chain of insulin at the amino-terminus which is followed by the A-chain. Interposed between these sections is a segment of amino acids called the 'C' peptide. The transposition to insulin takes place in the B-cells, as a result of the action of two enzymes; one like trypsin and the other like carboxypeptidase B. The final products of the actions of these enzymes are shown in Fig. 4.3. The folding arrangement of the pro-

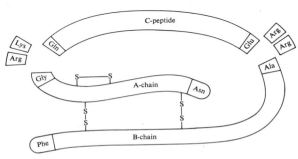

Fig. 4.3. Products formed as a result of the conversion of proinsulin to insulin in the pancreatic B-cells. (From Steiner *et al.*, 1972.)

hormone is an important feature that ensures the correct alignment of the cysteine residues to form the disulfide bridges that are present in the hormone proper. The amino acid sequence of the 'C' peptide can be seen to differ in various species (Fig. 4.4).

Many polypeptide hormones are stored in granules present in the endocrine cells. These organelles are bounded by membranes and are 0.1 to 0.4 μm in diameter. They appear to originate in the Golgi apparatus of the cell. The precursor, or pro-hormone, becomes associated with the granules and it seems likely that conversion to the hormone takes place in these. The granules can travel to the peripheral regions of the cell, and, in response to releasing-stimuli, combine with the plasma membrane and discharge their contents into the region of blood vessels. A summary of this process as it is thought to occur for insulin is shown in Fig. 4.5.

Such granules apparently furnish sites for the formation and storage of many hormones. If released into the cytoplasm of the cell the hormones may be destroyed as has been observed for the catecholamines when they are exposed to the mitochondrial enzyme monoamine oxidase (MAO). In

	1	2	3	4	5	6	7	8	9	10	11	12	13	14	15	16
Human	Glu	Ala	Glu	Asp	Leu	Gln	Val	Gly	Gln	Val	Glu	Leu	Gly	Gly	Gly	Pro
Monkey	Glu	Ala	Glu	Asp	Pro	Gln	Val	Gly	Glx	Val	Glu	Leu	Gly	Gly	Gly	Pro
Pig	Glu	Ala	Glu	Asn	Pro	Gln	Ala	Gly	Ala	Val	Glu	Leu	Gly	Gly	Gly	Leu
Cattle	Glu	Val	Glu	Gly	Pro	Gln	Val	Gly	Ala	Leu	Glu	Leu	Ala	Gly	Gly	Pro

	17	18	19	20	21	22	23	24	25	26	27	28	29	30	31
Human	Gly	Ala	Gly	Ser	Leu	Gln	Pro	Leu	Ala	Leu	Glu	Gly	Ser	Leu	Gln
Monkey	Gly	Ala	Gly	Ser	Leu	Gln	Pro	Leu	Ala	Leu	Glu	Gly	Ser	Leu	Gln
Pig	Gly	—	Gly	—	Leu	Gln	Ala	Leu	Ala	Leu	Glu	Gly	Pro	Pro	Gln
Cattle	Gly	Ala	Gly	—	—	—	—	—	Gly	Leu	Glu	Gly	Pro	Pro	Gln

Fig. 4.4. A comparison of the amino acid sequences of the human, monkey, porcine and bovine C-peptides. The solid bars indicate residues that are identical in all species. (From Steiner et al., 1972.)

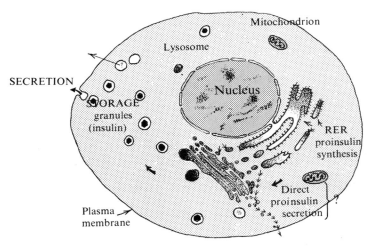

Fig. 4.5. Subcellular organization of the processes involved in the biosynthesis of insulin in the cell. The proinsulin is formed in the ribosomes of the rough endoplasmic reticulum (RER). This polypeptide rapidly folds and assumes its normal conformation during its transfer to the Golgi region. The storage granules are formed in this part of the cell from the Golgi apparatus and these travel to the peripheral regions of the cells. The contents of these granules may be secreted following fusion of the granule to the plasma membrane. (From Steiner *et al.*, 1972.)

addition, storage granules may afford convenient vehicles in which hormones can be transported for considerable distances along nerve cells.

Some neurons form hormones by a process called *neurosecretion*. These are like ordinary nerve cells and consist of a cell body with an extended axon and they can also be depolarized and so convey electrical information. The axon instead of terminating at another neuron or an effector tissue, like a gland or muscle, lies near to a capillary into which it can discharge certain of its products (Fig. 4.6). These products may be hormones, the formation of which is initiated some distance away in the cell body. The hormones, parceled up in their granules, travel along the nerves to the peripheral sites in the axon where they can be released into the blood.

Hormones that are formed as a result of neurosecretion are those of the neurohypophysis and median eminence including vasopressin, oxytocin and the various releasing-hormones that control the adenohypophysis. In mammals, vasopressin and oxytocin are formed in the supraoptic and paraventricular nuclei which are situated at the base of the brain. These hormonal products pass down the axons in granules to the neural lobe. Inside the granules they are attached to protein molecules of neurophysin,

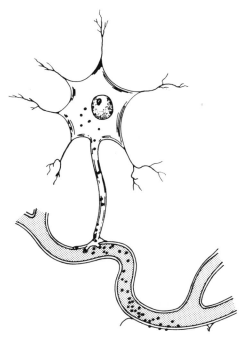

Fig. 4.6. A neurosecretory cell. The hormonal products are transported from the cell body down to the axon from which they can be released into capillaries. In contrast, ordinary nerve cells have axons that abut onto other neurones (instead of capillaries). (From R. Guillemin and R. Burgus, *The Hormones of the Hypothalamus*. Copyright © 1972 by Scientific American, Inc. All rights reserved.)

the synthesis of which seems to be closely associated to that of the hormone. What relationship neurophysin has to a pro-hormone is, however, as yet unknown. Amphibians and fishes have a single preoptic nucleus where the neurohypophysial hormones originate. The putative hormones of the urophysis in fishes (see Chapter 2) are also apparently formed by a process of neurosecretion.

The formation of hormones by enzymically controlled synthesis

Thyroid hormones

The endocrine secretions of the thyroid, the adrenal medulla, the gonads and the adrenal cortex, are the result of biosynthetic processes controlled by enzymes. While the enzymes themselves are the result of genetic translational processes, the hormones are assembled as a result of chemical reactions controlled by the enzymes. This synthesis may involve many reactions, some of which have been summarized in Fig. 3.2 (for steroid hormones) and Fig. 3.4 (for thyroid and catecholamine hormones).

Thyroid hormones contain iodine and the thyroid gland has a special ability to concentrate inorganic iodide from the blood. This ability to transport iodide actively against an electrochemical gradient is shared by some other tissues, including the intestine and salivary glands. This ability may be controlled by a single gene: in man a congenital inability to accumulate iodide in the thyroid is accompanied by a parallel deficiency at the other iodide transport sites. The accumulated iodide is oxidized to iodine, which combines with tyrosine to form the precursor of thyroxine and tri-iodothyronine. The latter reaction occurs with the tyrosine residue that is part of a large protein, thyroglobulin (molecular weight 670 000), that is stored extracellularly in the thyroid follicles. Each molecule of thyroglobulin binds two of thyroxine and on the average, less than one tri-iodothyronine. Thyroglobulin itself does not appear to be a particularly remarkable protein; it contains about 30 molecules of tyrosine (or about 3 % by weight), and about 0.5 % iodine. It nevertheless provides a site for the synthesis and storage of the thyroid hormones. The biosynthetic process for the thyroid hormones appears to be common to all vertebrates and was apparently attained early in their evolution. Nevertheless most of our information has been derived from studies of mammals.

Thyroglobulins have been identified in thyroid tissues of species from most groups of vertebrates, even including larval cyclostomes (lampreys) where it is present in the subpharyngeal gland or endostyle (Suzuki and Kondo, 1973). These proteins exhibit many similarities with respect to their molecular size (though a few differences have been observed), as determined by centrifugation in sucrose gradients, but their amino acid constitutions may differ. Thyroglobulins also exhibit different immunological behavior. Antibodies to specific thyroglobulins have been prepared and these react, *in vitro*, with the homologous protein, which can be radioactively labelled. Thyroglobulins from different species may compete with this labelled protein for binding to its antibodies. The relative ability to do this suggests the degree of immunological similarity to the homologous thyroglobulin. Considerable interspecific differences have been observed in such radioimmunoassays (Torresani *et al.*, 1973). Sheep thyroglobulin readily displaces its labelled form from anti-sheep thyroglobulin antibodies but thyroglobulins from other mammals, such as pigs and rabbits, are much less effective. Thyroglobulin from a python and a crocodile also compete with the homologous labelled protein for such binding but this is also much less so than that for the sheep protein. Bird thyroglobulin, from ducks, had no ability to bind with the sheep antibodies. While it is tempting to construct phylogenetic trees with such information the paucity of species examined makes such predictions of doubtful significance but the measurements nevertheless illustrate the diversity that can occur among thyroglobulins from different species.

Catecholamines

Adrenaline and noradrenaline are formed in chromaffin tissues. These hormones are present not only in the adrenal gland but also are associated with nervous tissue in other parts of the body. Noradrenaline is also formed in certain nerve endings in the sympathetic nervous tissue and the brain. The original precursor of these catecholamines is tyrosine which by a series of enzymically controlled reactions is converted to 3,4-dihydroxy-phenylalanine, or dopa, and thence to dopamine. These reactions occur in the cell's cytoplasm. The dopamine is accumulated by storage granules in which it is converted, under the influence of dopamine β-hydroxylase to noradrenaline. Noradrenaline can be N-methylated to adrenaline under the influence of the enzyme phenylethanolamine-N-methyl-transferase (PNMT) which, in mammals (see Chapter 3), can be induced in the presence of high concentrations of corticosteroids. There is evidence to suggest that nor-adrenaline and adrenaline are stored in different granules and even different cells in the adrenal medulla. This could be determined by regional differences in the access of corticosteroids to the medullary tissue thus influencing the local levels of PNMT (Pohorecky and Wurtman, 1971).

Steroid hormones

The formation of the steroid hormones also appears to be basically the same in all vertebrates (Sandor, 1969). All of these are formed from cholesterol which is present in high concentrations in the steroidogenic endocrine glands. This parent molecule may be formed *in situ* from acetate (Fig. 3.2) or be accumulated from the plasma. It has been suggested that the synthesis of some steroid hormones may not involve cholesterol as a precursor but this is difficult to prove. The enzymic conversion of chol-esterol to pregnelolone and progesterone is common to all of the steroid-ogenic endocrine glands. Sandor (1969) has suggested that the use of steroids as hormones may have been determined by a primeval mutation which invented the enzyme systems that determine this transformation of cholesterol. The conversion of progesterone to the androgen, estrogen and adrenocorticosteroid hormones involves the successive actions of diverse enzymes that hydroxylate, oxidize and reduce the steroid at some of the

21 carbon positions present. The ability of a species to synthesize steroid hormones with differing structures depends on the presence or absence of the enzymes that mediate these changes. The chondrichthyean fishes that secrete 1α-hydroxycorticosterone possess an enzyme, 1α-hydroxylase (that converts corticosterone to the hormone), that has not been found in other vertebrates. The formation of aldosterone in tetrapods is determined by the presence of 18-hydroxylase (it converts corticosterone to aldosterone). Rats and mice cannot form cortisol and lack 17α-hydroxylase (that converts progesterone to 17α-hydroxyprogesterone) in their adrenal cortex. Mutations may also arise that influence the ability of a species to form certain hormones. In man, a congenital condition known as the adrenogenital syndrome is due to the complete or partial block of the 21-hydroxylating

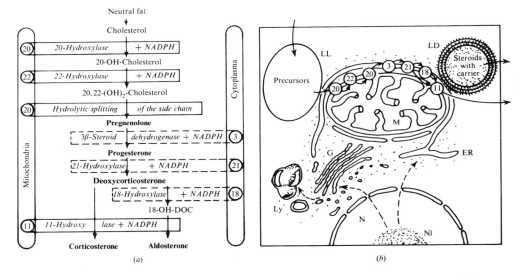

Fig. 4.7. The biosynthesis of corticosteroid hormones (*a*) in the adrenocortical tissue of a frog. This is illustrated with reference to the cell organelles (*b*). Corticosterone can also act as a precursor for aldosterone. In some species, 18-hydroxylase may be a mitochondrial rather than a microsomal enzyme. In vertebrates that form cortisol another microsomal enzyme, 17α-hydroxylase, active on progesterone and leading to 17α-OH-progesterone, deoxycortisol and cortisol, is present.

ER, endoplasmic reticulum; G, Golgi apparatus; N, nucleus; LD, electron dense lipid droplet; LL, electron lucid lipid droplet; Ly, lysosomes; M, mitochondrion; Nl, nucleolus.

Solid arrows are pathways of steroid synthesis from precursors to steroid bound to a carrier; broken arrows indicate cellular responses activated by ACTH. (From Lofts and Bern, 1972.)

system (the conversion of progesterone to deoxycorticosterone and 17α-hydroxyprogesterone to 17α-hydroxy-11-deoxycorticosterone). Such enzymic differences determine the presence or absence of the various steroid hormones and furnish the raw materials of evolutionary change.

The steroidogenic enzymes are associated in the cytoplasm of the cell and the mitochondria. The pathways and sites of the enzymes determining the formation of adrenocorticosteroids in the frog's interrenal are shown in Fig. 4.7.

The release of hormones from endocrine glands

Nature of the stimuli

The role of the endocrine glands in the regulation of bodily functions is dependent on the release of their secretions on appropriate occasions. Secretion is initiated upon the receipt, by the gland, of a suitable stimulus which may increase or decrease, the discharge of its hormone. The message may arrive either by way of a nerve or be carried in the blood that perfuses the tissue. The primary event that initiates this stimulus may arise either from the external environment, exteroceptive stimulus, or inside the body, interoceptive stimulus.

Exteroceptive stimuli that may affect the endocrine glands include the receipt of light, a change in temperature or of the osmotic concentration (of an aqueous environment) and the acquisition of food, water and salts. Social situations such as the proximity of prey, a predator, a mate or the young may evoke psychogenically-mediated responses in the endocrine glands. Climatic events such as rain, temperature and even, possibly, humidity and atmospheric pressure can also influence a hormone's release. The receipt of and endocrine response to such external stimuli helps the animal to maintain an equitable relationship with the events that happen around it. Exteroceptive stimuli are especially useful in providing cues that are involved in reproduction.

Interoceptive stimuli are those that result from changes in the physico-chemical conditions within the body. Ultimately they may reflect the external conditions: for instance a lack of drinking water and a hot, dehydrating environment will lead to an increase in the osmotic concentration of the body fluids. Internal stimuli include: changes in the concentration of salts, such as sodium, potassium and calcium, in the body fluids, alteration of the hydrostatic pressure of the blood vascular system, oscillations in the levels of nutrients, like glucose, amino acids and fatty acids, as well as changes in the body temperature. The physiological factors influencing release of hormones are summarized in Table 4.1.

TABLE 4.1. *Principal stimuli influencing the release of hormones*

Hormone	Releasing stimuli
Adrenaline	Neural stimuli (mediated by acetylcholine)
Aldosterone	Low plasma Na concentration, angiotensin
Angiotensin	Renin
Calcitonin	Hypercalcemia
Cortisol and corticosterone	Corticotrophin
Enterogastrone	Fats and oils in intestine
Entero-glucagon	Feeding
Estrogens	FSH
FSH	External stimuli, such as light, low estrogen levels
Gastrin	Feeding (vagal reflex; local reflex from food in stomach)
Glucagon	Hypoglycemia, gastrin, pancreozymin, high amino acids and low fatty acids in plasma, exercise
Growth hormone	Sleep, exercise, apprehension, hypoglycemia
Insulin	Hyperglycemia and amino acids in plasma, glucagon, growth hormone, in ruminants high levels of propionic and butyric acid, vagal stimulation, pancreozymin and secretin. Inhibition by adrenaline
LH or ICSH	External stimuli, sexual excitement (male), estrogen 'surge' (female), low progesterone or testosterone levels
MSH	Light on retina, low plasma corticosteroids levels, inhibition by neural stimuli and MSH-R-IH
Melatonin	Darkness (adrenergic neural stimulation)
Oxytocin	Suckling, parturition
Pancreozymin–cholecystokinin	Digestive products in the upper intestine
Parathormone	Hypocalcemia
Pituitrophins: CRH, TRH, etc.	Hypothalamic neuronal stimuli (dopamine and monoamine transmitters), inhibited by negative-feedback mechanisms carried by hormones and metabolites
Progesterone	LH, chorionic gonadotrophin, prolactin
Prolactin	Diurnal rhythm (sleep), suckling, parturition, plasma osmotic concentrations (low in fish, high in mammals?), estrogens
Renin	Low Na in plasma, hemorrhage, reduced renal blood flow, nerve stimulation (β-adrenergic), increased osmotic concentration in renal blood supply
Secretin	Acid in upper intestine
Testosterone	LH or ICSH
Thyroid hormones	TSH
TSH	Low thyroxine, temperature reduction
Vasopressin	Increased osmotic concentration of plasma
1,25-$(OH)_2$-vitamin D_3	Low Ca and phosphate levels in plasma; parathormone

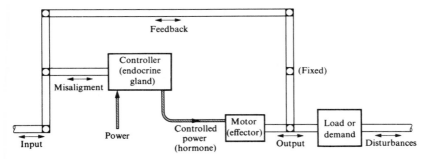

Fig. 4.8. Schematic diagram of a servo-system showing the analogies of the classic engineering control mechanism of physiological coordination by the endocrines. The double arrows indicate that the links can move to and fro. Stimuli (both input and feedback) are fed into the controller (endocrine gland in the physiological analogy) through a misalignment detector which is sensitive to changes from a certain set-point. It is conceivable that the latter may be reset in certain physiological conditions (such as hibernation). In response the controller varies its power output (or hormone secretion) to the motor or effector. The latter adjusts the physiological needs and tends to restore equilibrium (of metabolites, salts, water, other hormones, temperature, etc.) the degree of which is transmitted back to the controller via the feedback arc. (From Bentley, 1971.)

Hormones can exert trophic effects on other endocrine glands and the terminal secretions, once released, may travel back to the region where the trophic hormone originated and inhibit its further release. This last effect completes the cycle of events that closes the loop of a *negative-feedback system* that plays a vital role in regulating the endocrine system. Such a control-system is well known to engineers and its action is illustrated in Fig. 4.8. The release of hormones from the median eminence, that in turn controls the formation and discharge of the trophic hormones of the adenohypophysis, is regulated in this manner. The hormones that exert the inhibitory effects in the median eminence may alter the thresholds for stimulation of the neurosecretory cells. In addition, such a negative-feedback can also act directly on the adenohypophysis as seen with the action of thyroid hormones which inhibit the release of thyrotrophic hormone in this way. The interrelations of the hormones of the hypothalamus, adenohypophysis and more peripheral endocrine glands are shown in Fig. 4.9.

The feedback mechanisms involving the action of the peripheral endocrine secretions on the hypothalamus is called a *long-loop feedback*. There is also evidence suggesting that the adenohypophysial secretions may exert a similar action on the hypothalamus by what is termed a *short-loop feedback*. It should be noted that peripheral hormones do not necessarily initiate a

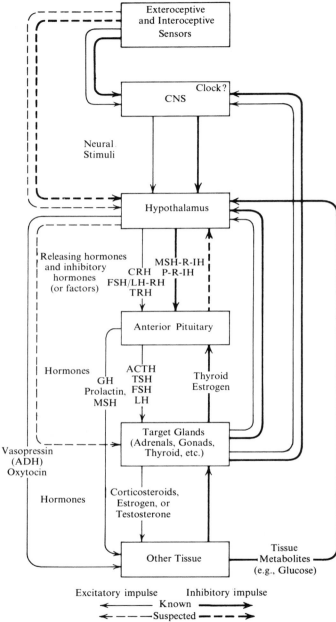

Fig. 4.9. Factors controlling the release of hormones from the anterior pituitary (Adenohypophysis). This illustrates the use of negative-feedback inhibition of secreted hormones and tissue metabolites in influencing further hormonal release.

negative-feedback inhibition on the hypothalamus. High estrogen levels can stimulate the release of LH/FSH-RH which initiates the events that result in ovulation. Such a positive-feedback has also been shown in the hypothalamus of the goldfish where thyroxine stimulates the release of a thyrotrophin-inhibiting hormone (Peter, 1971). The sporadic information available from experiments on non-mammals suggests that feedback control working through the hypothalamus, and, in the instance of thyrotrophin, the adenohypophysis, is widespread. More information is needed and there is some doubt as to the importance of such effects in cyclostomes (Larsen and Rosenkilde, 1971; Fernholm, 1972).

A negative-feedback inhibition of hormone secretion also results from changes in the concentrations of the products of the hormone's actions. The retention of water or sodium, as a result, respectively, of the actions of antidiuretic hormone and aldosterone, reduces the further release of these hormones. Comparable mechanisms exist involving glucose levels and the regulation of insulin, glucagon and growth hormone, as well as calcium and parathormone, and calcitonin.

The endocrines, apart from influencing each other's release through trophic and feedback mechanisms, may also interact with each other and so modify their secretory activity. Adrenaline can inhibit the release of antidiuretic hormone from the neurohypophysis and that of insulin from the Islets of Langerhans. This inhibition is an α-adrenergic effect which contrasts with the β-adrenergic effect which increases the release of insulin. Glucagon promotes the release of insulin and growth hormone directly; such effects do not depend on changes in blood glucose levels. Excesses of growth hormone are diabetogenic and inhibit the formation of insulin, though smaller amounts apparently stimulate its release.

Many less-precise and less-specific stimuli than those described above can initiate the discharge of hormones from endocrine glands. Such stimuli may contribute to the homeostatic process though they may also confuse it. No endocrine gland can exist and be uninfluenced by events outside what we may like to think of as its homeostatic area of influence. Non-specific stimuli, especially if strong enough, can elicit a discharge of many hormones. This is sometimes referred to as 'stress' and is particularly likely to occur in experimental situations that contribute to the confusion of the perpetrating scientists.

The trophic effects of hormones on the secretion of other endocrine glands can contribute to the processes of biological amplification in the

As can be seen, the hypothalamus (and its associated median eminence) plays a central role in this process. Stimulatory effects are shown by thin lines and inhibitory processes by thick lines. (From Krieger, 1971.)

body. An initial stimulus may only produce a change that involves a very small amount of energy while the energetic demands of the response may be relatively immense. The quantities of the excitants necessary to initiate an effect and the amount of the products formed (on a weight for weight basis) are illustrated in Fig. 4.10. We have no information as to the quantity

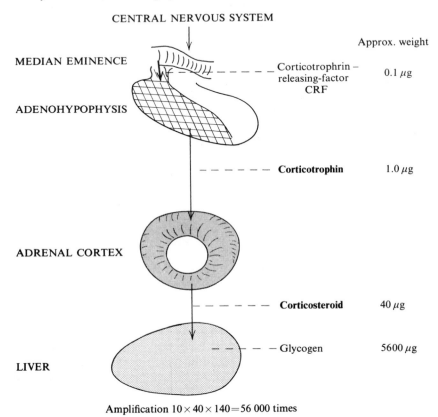

CENTRAL NERVOUS SYSTEM

Approx. weight

MEDIAN EMINENCE

Corticotrophin –
releasing-factor
CRF

0.1 μg

ADENOHYPOPHYSIS

Corticotrophin   1.0 μg

ADRENAL CORTEX

Corticosteroid   40 μg

Glycogen   5600 μg

LIVER

Amplification 10 × 40 × 140 = 56 000 times

Fig. 4.10. An illustration of biological amplification as shown in the endocrine system. Corticotrophin-releasing hormone initiates the release of corticotrophin (ACTH) which leads to the deposition of glycogen in the liver.

of neural transmitters necessary to trigger a release of corticotrophin-releasing hormone from the median eminence but quantitative changes have been estimated for the subsequent physiological events. The final release of cortisol promotes the formation of 5600 μg of glycogen. The initial amount of CRH required to do this is about 0.1 μg so that the final response represents an amplification of 56 000 times.

Cyclical release of hormones

Many hormones are released periodically: at certain well-defined hours of the day (diurnal or circadian rhythms), during the reproductive cycle, or at certain seasons and times of the year (circannual rhythms). Such timing may be especially important in coordinating the events of the reproductive cycle and insuring that this occurs during the times of the year most appropriate to the survival of the young. A predictably functioning release mechanism also insures that adequate hormone levels, necessary for the animal's optimal daily activities, are available. Such release of hormones is usually controlled by centers in the brain (sometimes called 'biological clocks') which are programmed by stimuli that include the length of the daily period of light, the external temperature, changes in the seasons, as well as certain interoceptive stimuli.

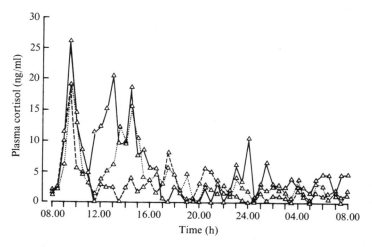

Fig. 4.11. Diurnal variation in the levels of plasma cortisol in three sheep. It can be seen that the highest concentrations were recorded during the early hours of daylight. The concentrations of cortisol in the plasma were not uniform but showed continual oscillations suggesting that it is released in sudden 'spurts'. (From McNatty, Cashmore and Young, 1972.)

The levels of corticosteroids in the blood vary in a distinct pattern during the course of the day. In mammals, this is well known in primates including man, and dogs, rats and mice. Release is related to the incidence of light and the corticosteroids are lowest in concentration during the night and reach a distinct peak after various periods of daylight. In man and sheep (Fig. 4.11), this is seen in the morning hours, soon after dawn, though in laboratory rats, which are nocturnal, it is delayed until the early evening hours (Fig. 4.12). Comparable changes in the plasma corticosteroid concentrations have been observed in some teleost fishes [the channel catfish, *Ictalurus punctatus* (Boehlke *et al.*, 1966), and the gulf killifish, *Fundulus grandis* (Srivastava and Meier, 1972)] where peak concentrations occur about eight hours after the onset of light. In another teleost (the eel *Anguilla rostrata*), diurnal variation of plasma cortisol levels does not seem to occur (Forrest *et al.*, 1973*a*). Prolactin and growth hormone in man are released in greatest amounts during the period of sleep (Fig. 4.13) and does not appear to be directly dependent on light.

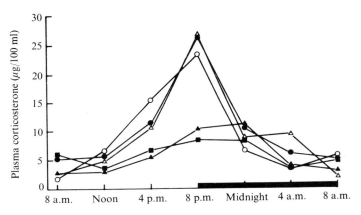

Fig. 4.12. The circadian pattern in the concentration of corticosteroids in the plasma of rats. The effects of the administration of exogenous corticosteroids to young, developing rats on the subsequent circadian periodicity in the endogenous corticosteroid levels. It can be seen that the administration of dexamethasone or hydrocortisone (cortisol) on days 2 to 4 after birth suppressed the rhythmical release. However, when dexamethasone was given on days 12 to 14 after birth no effect was seen: ●, control; ○, saline, 0.1 ml, day 2–4; ■, hydrocortisone acetate, 500μg, day 3; ▲, dexamethasone PO₄, 1 μg, day 2–4; △, dexamethasone PO₄, 1 μg, day 12–14. (From Krieger, 1972. Copyright © 1972 by the American Association for the Advancement of Science.)

The release of gonadotrophins from the adenohypophysis may also occur at precise times of the day. In the Japanese quail (*Coturnix coturnix japonica*), the pituitary is depleted of gonadotrophin over a period of four hours commencing about 16 hours after dawn (Follett and Sharp, 1969). This release is seen in birds kept on a long-day cycle of light, 20 hours light/4 hours of dark. When they are exposed to a short-day of 6 hours light/18 hours dark such oscillation is not observed. This long-day photoperiodic pattern is similar to that which quail experience in nature where

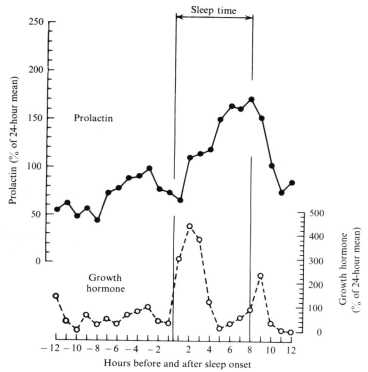

Fig. 4.13. The diurnal pattern in the release of prolactin and growth hormone in man. It can be seen that the release of both these hormones was accentuated during sleep. (From Sassin *et al.*, 1972. Copyright © 1972 by the American Association for the Advancement of Science.)

it is associated with the onset of breeding. Comparable precise patterns in the daily release of pituitary gonadotrophins have been observed in brook trout (*Salvelinus fontinalis*) and rainbow trout (*Salmo gairdneri*) as well as in leopard frogs (*Rana pipiens*) (O'Connor, 1972).

The pineal gland of the rat shows an interesting cyclical pattern in activity during the day which may be related to reproduction. As described in Chapter 2, the weight of this gland is lowest at the end of the daylight hours and rises during the hours of darkness. The enzyme, hydroxy-indole-*O*-methyl transferase (HIOMT) is essential for the synthesis of melatonin (which is secreted by the pineal) and its activity also increases at night (Fig. 4.14). Noradrenaline is present in the pineal and it attains higher levels in rats during darkness. Blinding the rats, cutting the sympathetic nerve supply to the pineal or placing them in continuous light prevents this

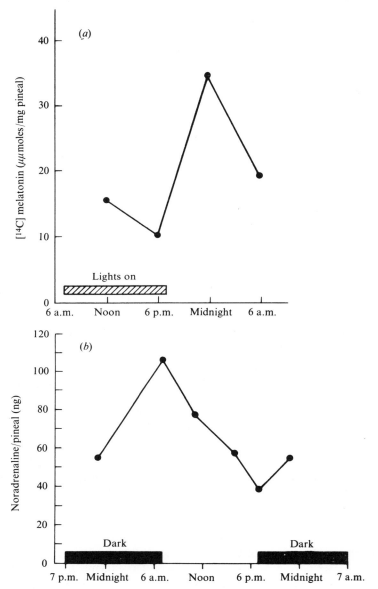

Fig. 4.14. Diurnal changes in the activity of the rat pineal gland.

(*a*) Increases in the levels of the enzyme HIOMT during the hours of darkness. (From Axelrod *et al.*, 1965.)

(*b*) The rise in the glandular content of noradrenaline during the night and the decline in the daytime. (From Wurtman and Axelrod, 1966.)

circadian rhythm of activity. The precise events involved in this cycle in the pineal appear to be as follows (Axelrod, 1974). During the hours of darkness there is an increase in the release of the neurotransmitter nor-adrenaline and a rise in the sensitivity of its pineal receptor. These changes result in the synthesis of the enzyme serotonin-*N*-acetyltransferase. This response is a *β*-adrenergic one involving cyclic AMP. The *N*-acetyl-serotonin that is formed from serotonin is then converted to melatonin under the influence of HIOMT. This rhythm in pineal activity is thought to be controlled by a biological clock that is situated in the hypothalamus, near the suprachiasmatic nucleus, which can be inhibited as a result of the receipt of light by the retina. In some birds and baby rats, blinding does not affect the rhythm as light can apparently impinge through their thin skulls onto photoreceptors in the brain.

In many vertebrates, melatonin inhibits growth of the gonads and this can be correlated with the inhibitory effects of darkness on this process. It is unknown how widespread this nocturnal rhythm in the activity of the pineal is. Periods of prolonged darkness or light, however, have been shown to change the activity of the pineal in other vertebrates. In mammals this activity, and the melatonin levels, are enhanced by darkness but depressed by light, but at this time the observations appear to be confined to rats. In the domestic fowl, however, melatonin levels still rise at night, just like in rats and this increase (a 10-fold one) is related to elevated levels of *N*-acetyltransferase though HIOMT declines (Binkley *et al.*, 1973). Changes in HIOMT concentration do not appear to be essential for forma-tion of melatonin. In another bird, the Japanese quail, and an amphibian, the frog *Rana pipiens*, no change in the synthesis of melatonin could be pro-duced by altering the lighting conditions (see Wurtman, Axelrod and Kelly, 1968). It has been suggested that the pineal, by responding to a biological clock, functions like the median eminence as a neuroendocrine-transducer that modifies the actions of other endocrine glands. It thus may provide an important pathway whereby light provides cues to the endocrine system.

The activity of the endocrine glands and the release of their hormones often shows profound changes that are associated with the season of the year. The diurnal patterns of release just described may be initiated at such times or be superimposed on these gross changes in activity. Such changes have most often been observed in relation to the breeding season which, especially in animals from non-equatorial regions, usually only occurs at certain times of the year. Reproduction may be dictated by predictably favorable seasons or in less-favored areas, like deserts, by the sudden appearance of rain. Apart from pituitary and gonadal sex hormones, cyclical changes in the activity of the thyroid gland and the adrenal cortex and medulla have been observed. The thyroid of the Japanese quail follows a pattern of activity that parallels that of the gonads (Follett and Riley, 1967). Thyroid activity (Leloup and Fontaine, 1960) is increased in fishes undergoing seasonal migrations. In the African lungfish (*Protopterus annectens*), thyroid activity is lowest during estivation at the time of seasonal drought. In toads and frogs, adrenaline attains its highest concentration in the plasma during autumn and winter (Donoso and Segura, 1965; Harris, 1972). Stores of growth hormone are highest in the pituitary of the perch (*Perca fluviatilis*) in June, a few weeks prior to the summer rapid-growth period (Swift and Pickford, 1965).

The cyclical and episodic release of hormones is usually controlled through the brain. This is especially apparent when light provides the cues for these changes. External temperature may also be involved in controlling reproductive and possibly other cycles, especially in poikilotherms (see Licht, 1972). It is likely that such heat stimuli act through the central nervous system but they could also exert more direct effects on the pituitary and gonads and even influence the rates of a hormone's metabolism. The principal photoreceptors are the eyes but there is evidence that in some vertebrates others may exist, such as those of the pineal gland. Temperature impinges on receptors present in the skin but may also directly influence the brain.

The diurnal rhythm of activity of glands such as the pineal and the adrenal cortex is not present at birth. In rats, the rhythmical release of corticosteroids from the latter usually arises about 21 days after birth while in man it takes two to eight years to appear. The adequate development of a biological clock is thought to require the presence of optimal levels of hormones. If newborn rats are injected with cortisol two to four days after they are born, the subsequent normal pattern of diurnal release of the corticosteroids is suppressed (Fig. 4.12). Similarly, the normal pattern in the cyclical activity of the gonads is prevented when newborn female rats are injected with androgens. If newborn male rats are castrated soon after birth the hypothalamus develops along the female pattern. When ovaries and a vagina are grafted into these animals they undergo cyclical changes typical of the female. Such endocrine manipulation can also contribute to behavioral abnormalities.

Systematic differences in releasing stimuli

There are many instances among the vertebrates in which the physiological roles of analogous hormones exhibit systematic differences. Such a change in the use of a hormone necessarily results in an altered responsiveness to excitatory stimuli that prompt the endocrine gland to discharge its secretion. When certain teleost fish move from fresh water to sea-water they lose water and accumulate salt so that the concentration of sodium in their body fluids rises. This initiates a release of corticosteroids. Tetrapods, on the other hand, usually release such analogous hormones in response to declines in the sodium concentration of the body fluids. Prolactin and oxytocin are released during suckling in mammals. Other vertebrates lack mammary glands so that this represents a unique and phyletically novel stimulus. On the other hand, in certain teleost fish a prolactin-type hormone is released when the fish migrate from the sea into fresh water. In homeotherms, thyroid hormones are discharged following a decline in the temperature of the blood flowing through certain areas in the hypothalamus but there is no indication that this happens in poikilotherms. Indeed thyroid secretion usually increases in cold-blooded vertebrates exposed to elevated temperatures. Changes in glucose concentrations usually determine insulin release, but in ruminants (sheep and cattle) fatty acids are more important. In fishes, amino acids may be the major stimulant for secretion of insulin. Such phyletic differences in the propensity of endocrine glands to respond to certain stimuli are necessary for the evolution of a hormone's physiological role.

Conduction of stimuli to the endocrines

The conveyance of a stimulus to an endocrine gland may involve a complex series of events that take place along rather circuitous pathways. These are consistent with, and indeed are dictated by, the particular physiological requirements of the animal. The initial stimulus is usually translated into another form that may be a chemical compound or an electrical event or both. It travels to the endocrine gland, in such a modified form, by routes of varying complexity and may suffer further translation on the way. During this voyage, the stimulus may be modulated and interpolated with other information that is already available, and other stimuli that also impinge on that particular communication pathway. This may take place in the brain and endocrine glands that are temporally proximal to the gland that is destined to receive, eventually, the final message. Such intermediary substations may involve neural areas in the brain, interconnecting endocrine glands, like the median eminence and the pineal, as well as the pituitary gland.

These events can be illustrated by summarily following the effects of light on reproduction. The stimulus is received by the eye where it is translated by the retinal receptors to electrical impulses that travel along nerves within the brain. These messages, after further translation to other transmitter substances (such as acetylcholine, noradrenaline and dopamine) eventually reach the median eminence and, probably also, in some species, pass through the pineal gland which may release melatonin. The median eminence modulates its release of LH/FSH-RH that crosses, in the short,

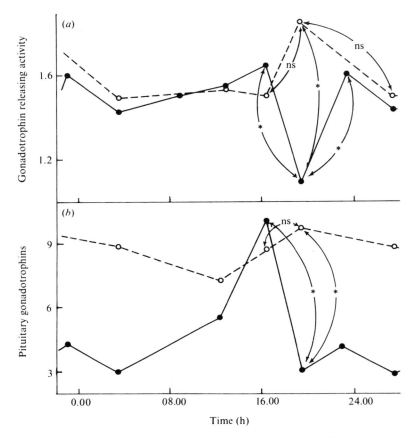

Fig. 4.15. The effects of different daily photoperiods (day-length) on the levels of hypothalamic gonadotrophin-releasing activity (*a*) and pituitary gonadotrophins (*b*) in the quail (*Coturnix coturnix*). The length of the day was either 20 hours light/4 hours dark (●——●) for ten days, or 6 hours light/20 hours dark also for 10 days (○----○).

The values are expressed as gonadotrophic-releasing activity, μg equivalents NIH standard/mg/pituitary tissue/hour; gonadotrophin, μg equivalents NIH standard/gland; ns, not significantly different; *, difference statistically significant.

It will be noted that no significant changes occurred in the birds on the 'short day' but in those on long day there was a periodic (and corresponding) release of both hormones in the late afternoon. (From Follett and Sharp, 1969.)

portal blood vessels to the adenohypophysis. The receipt of this information will be further interpreted (in a process which possibly involves the formation of cyclic AMP) in terms of an appropriate release of FSH and/or LH which are carried in the blood to the ovaries or testes. Such an effect is illustrated by the levels of gonadotrophin-releasing hormones and the gonadotrophins in the hypothalamus and pituitary of the Japanese quail. As can be seen in Fig. 4.15, there is a drop in the concentration of gonadotrophin-releasing hormone which corresponds to the release of adenohypophysial gonadotrophins. The gonadotrophins may influence such events as ovulation and the formation and release of estrogens and progesterone as well as testosterone. These latter steroids, in turn, are carried back to the brain (in the vicinity of the median eminence) where they provide information about the current hormone levels that will be used to modify stimuli that subsequently pass through this tissue. The process is, in detail, undoubtedly even more complex than that which has been described.

In other instances, the mechanism of the hormone's release may be simpler. The discharge of vasopressin (or antidiuretic hormone) from the neurohypophysis can occur in response to small increases in the osmotic concentration of plasma. This is thought to induce changes in osmoreceptors in the region of the supraoptic nucleus, possibly by releasing small amounts of acetylcholine, which initiates a wave of depolarization along the axons of the supraopticohypophysial tract. This results in the release of ADH from the storage granules at the terminus of the nerve. Neurohypophysial hormones may also be released in other circumstances. This release may involve non-specific stimuli, often termed 'stress', that pass through higher centers in the brain to the nerve cells of the gland. Oxytocin is discharged in response to suckling in mammals, the initial receptor is in the nipple of the mammary gland from which it is transmitted along nerves to the paraventricular nucleus which contains the cell bodies of the oxytocinergic neurons of the neurohypophysis.

Even simpler processes, not involving nerve pathways, may exist and determine the release of hormones in the body. The release of insulin can be demonstrated in isolated, perfused, pieces of pancreatic tissues containing the Islets of Langerhans. Elevated glucose and certain amino acid concentrations in the perfusate initiate a release of insulin. In a similar way, glucagon is discharged when the blood glucose concentration is depressed. Although it is difficult to be completely certain (as these preparations of Islets' tissue are not pure B-cells) it is considered that glucose reacts with a 'glucoreceptor' associated with the B-cells. This event, which results in the formation of a metabolite, then initiates the release of the hormone. Even at this level the process may be quite complex and involve several intermediate metabolites, ionic changes (especially that of calcium), and possibly cyclic AMP. Glucagon potentiates the release of insulin and the α-adrenergic effects of catecholamines can inhibit it. The events that occur near or in the endocrine cell itself are summarized in Fig. 4.16*a* and in the next section.

The mechanism of release of the hormones

Upon receiving a stimulus an endocrine gland may release its hormones from their storage sites. Many hormones, such as catecholamines, neurohypophysial peptides and insulin are spewed from their storage granules, steroid hormones are released from lipid droplets and thyroid hormones are detached from thyroglobulins. In some instances, this is preceded by the formation of cyclic AMP as in the thyroid gland, the adrenal cortex, the ovary and possibly the adenohypophysis and pancreatic B-cells.

The release of hormones from intracellular storage granules has been studied in detail in the instances of the secretion of catecholamines from the adrenal medulla and vasopressin and oxytocin from the neurohypophysis (Douglas, 1968; Kirshner and Viveros, 1972). Hormones that are stored in granules exist there as a non-diffusible complex with proteins and adenine nucleotides. Their release from the cell involves the process of emiocytosis (exocytosis or reverse pinocytosis) across the cell membranes. The nature of the events that result in such a release of hormones can be studied *in vitro* and is as follows:

(i) As a result of nerve stimulation the cell membrane is depolarized and ions enter the cells. *In vitro*, this can be performed by exposing the tissue to high concentrations of potassium or by stimulating it electrically.

(ii) An increase in the concentration of intracellular Ca^{2+} occurs, as a result of its uptake across the cell membrane and probably also its dissociation from binding within the cell. No release of hormone occurs *in vitro* following depolarization if the external media contains no Ca^{2+} which thus appears to be vital for excitation–release coupling.

(iii) Excitation–release coupling involves a migration of the hormone storage granules towards the cell membrane; a process that may involve the cell microtubular system.

(iv) When contact between the cell membrane and the granules is made they fuse and Ca^{2+} may be important in the structural links. The entire contents of the granule, hormones, proteins and adenine nucleotides are then extruded and pass into the capillaries. The empty granule may then be reconstituted and return to the cell cytoplasm.

Modifications of this process may occur in different endocrine glands. Insulin is released as a result of nerve stimulation but glucose and amino acids have direct effects and these apparently also result in the admission

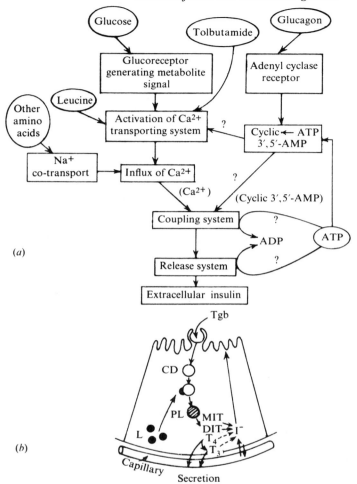

Fig. 4.16. (*a*) A diagrammatic representation of the events that result in the release of insulin from the B-cells of the Islets of Langerhans.

Changes in calcium concentration in the cell have a central role and 'couple' the primary stimuli (glucose, amino acids, etc.) to the secretion of insulin from its storage granules. β-Adrenergic stimulation, which results in increased concentrations of cyclic AMP, can also mediate a release, probably via such a calcium mechanism, while α-adrenergic excitation opposes this effect and reduces hormone secretion. (From Randle and Hales, 1972.)

(*b*) The secretion of thyroid hormones. Thyroglobulin (Tgb) is transported by endocytosis from the follicles into the thyroid cells where it appears as the colloid droplets (CD) that fuse with lysosomes (L) to form phagolysosomes (PL) in which proteolytic digestion of the thyroglobulin occurs. The iodothyronines (MIT, DIT, T_4 and T_3) are released and the active hormones pass out of the cell. Iodine (I^-) is reaccumulated. (From Greer and Haibach, 1974.)

of Ca^{2+} into the cell which results in hormone release (Fig. 4.16a). The activation of the enzyme adenyl cyclase and the formation of cyclic AMP (see p. 158) also appear to be involved in the release of insulin (as well as several other hormones, see below) where it may promote the accumulation of Ca^{2+} or act more directly in the excitation–release coupling process.

Thyroid hormones are stored extracellularly, combined with thyroglobulin in the colloid of the thyroid gland follicles. Stimulation by TSH results in an activation of adenyl cyclase in the thyroid cells and the formation of cyclic AMP. In a manner that is not yet understood, this nucleotide is thought to stimulate pinocytosis during which fragments of follicular colloid are broken off and taken up by the thyroid cells; this process is thus called endocytosis. Lysosomes in the cell cytoplasm (Fig. 4.16b), that contain digestive protease enzymes, combine with these ingested pieces of colloid to form phagolysosomes which move towards the basal regions of the cell. During this migration, the colloid is digested and its components are separated so that thyroxine and tri-iodothyronine are freed to pass out of the cell. The iodotyrosines present are deiodinated and the iodine is either retained by the cell or, if also extruded, is subsequently reaccumulated.

The precise mechanism by which steroid hormones are released from the cell is not clear. The amounts stored in lipid droplets within the cell are relatively small compared to the large amounts of those hormones that are accumulated in granules. The synthesis and release of steroid hormones is promoted by various substances, including trophic hormones. Corticotrophin and LH activate adenyl cyclase so that cyclic AMP is formed which plays a vital part in the initiation of the hormone synthesis and release: these two processes have not, however, been satisfactorily separated. It is possible that an increased hormone synthesis inevitably leads to its release by a type of 'overflow mechanism' but this is usually considered to be an unsatisfactory explanation.

The concentration of hormones in the blood

Hormones are normally present in the peripheral plasma at concentrations as low as 10^{-12} M and in-vitro observations suggest that these levels may, in some instances, be similar to those necessary to stimulate the effector. However, for several reasons it is difficult to predict with certainty what the latter concentration will be. As we have seen, endocrines discharge their secretions in response to a great variety of stimuli; in some instances they may be sudden, or acute, occurrences while at other times they are of a more sustained, or chronic, nature. In the first case the hormones may appear as a single 'spurt' of activity in the blood, such as seems to occur with the release of oxytocin in response to suckling. Thus high concentrations of hormones may exist locally, which briefly stimulate the effector and which are subsequently dissipated so that the remaining concentrations in the peripheral blood are not effective ones. It is difficult to obtain precise information about the temporal pattern of a hormone's release but undoubtedly many hormones, like those from the thyroid and gonads, are released in such a manner that fairly uniform levels appear and persist in the circulation. This may occur continually as a series of small spurts such as seen with corticosteroids (Fig. 4.11). A sustained release of a hormone may be necessitated by a continual demand by many tissues in the body.

Differences in the patterns of release combined with seasonal and diurnal rhythms make it difficult to generalize as to the concentrations of hormones that are normally present in the blood. The antidiuretic hormone is normally present in the peripheral plasma of mammals at concentrations of 10^{-12} to 10^{-11} M. It is higher in small animals, like the mouse, 2×10^{-11} M, than large ones such as man, where it is 4×10^{-12} M (see Table 4.2). In the

TABLE 4.2. *The concentrations of vasopressin or vasotocin in the plasma of vertebrates. The animals were normally hydrated except where indicated.* (From Heller, 1966: Heller and Štulc, 1960; Robinson and MacFarlane, 1957; Bentley, 1969)

	Hormone concentration (moles/l)
Mammals	*Vasopressin*
Mouse	2×10^{-11}
Rat (i) normal hydration	1×10^{-11}
(ii) dehydrated	2.5×10^{-10}
Guinea-pig	8×10^{-12}
Cat	2×10^{-12}
Rabbit	1.6×10^{-12}
Dog	2×10^{-12}
Man	4×10^{-12}
Bandicoot, wallaby and possum (Marsupials) dehydrated	1.8×10^{-10}
Amphibians	*Vasotocin*
(Anura) dehydrated	4 to 8×10^{-10}

laboratory rat, ADH concentration increases about 25-fold during dehydration: from 10^{-11} M to 2.5×10^{-10} M. Some dehydrated amphibians (frogs and toads) have similar circulating levels of vasotocin: about 6×10^{-10} M (Bentley, 1969). In others such as the mudpuppy and a teleost fish, the eel *Anguilla rostrata*, the hormone is not detectable (less than 10^{-11} M) under such conditions. Other polypeptide hormones like glucagon and insulin are normally present in the blood of mammals at a concentration of about 10^{-9} M.

The steroid hormones (see Idler, 1972) attain much higher concentrations in the blood than the polypeptides, thus plasma cortisol and corticosterone levels in teleostean fish are about 10^{-7} M though in the holostean and chondrostean fishes it is 10 times less than this. In chondrichthyeans 1α-hydroxycorticosterone usually has a concentration of 10^{-8} M in plasma. Aldosterone, compared to other corticosteroids, is present at much lower concentrations, about 10^{-10} M in mammals and 10^{-9} M in birds, though it is 10^{-8} M in amphibians. The steroid sex hormones are, due to the cyclical nature of their release, present in widely differing concentrations in the peripheral plasma: 10^{-7} M to 10^{-10} M.

Hormones act when present in extremely dilute solution. The levels vary somewhat with different species. The reasons for variation appear to be related to the animal's size, metabolic rate and the hormone-binding capacity of the plasma. It seems likely that differences in concentration may also be influenced by the body temperatures at which the animals usually function, because they affect the rate of the hormones' reactions with the effectors. Differences in the potencies of homologous hormones, as reflected in their chemical structure, may also contribute to variations in plasma levels. A mutation that initiates the formation of a less active hormone analogue could be compensated for physiologically by its release in greater quantity. An example of such an adaptation may be seen in mammals (Suiformes) that have lysine- instead of arginine-vasopressin.

Transport of hormones in the blood

Following their release from storage sites in the endocrine glands the hormones are carried, in the blood, to their various effector sites. This may be for very short distances, such as from the median eminence to the adenohypophysis, or involve much longer journeys, like from the neurohypophysis to the kidney. Some hormones have a relatively long life in the circulation and may recirculate many times before they are finally destroyed or excreted.

The blood plasma is an aqueous solution that contains high concentrations of proteins made up of several distinct components, or fractions. The hormone molecules may be dissolved in this solution or a substantial proportion can be bound to some of the proteins that are present. The binding of hormones in the blood is particularly important in the instances of the thyroid and steroid hormones.

The chemical nature of the binding of such hormones to plasma proteins is such that an equilibrium exists between the molecules that are bound and those that remain in solution. In other words, the binding is a reversible phenomenon and thus involves relatively weak chemical forces such as hydrogen and ionic bonds and Van der Waal's forces. The relative strength of these bonds, however, may vary considerably (high and low affinity) depending on the particular hormone and the nature of the binding protein. As we shall see, in some instances special proteins are present that appear to be able specifically to bind certain hormones.

There are several consequences of a hormone's binding to a protein in the plasma.

(1) Hormones are usually assumed to be unable to initiate their effects when so bound. The receptor is envisaged as interacting with hormone molecules present in the aqueous phase. Their removal from solution shifts the equilibrium and may thus result in a dissociation into solution of some of the hormone that is bound to the proteins. It is implicit that the receptor has an even stronger ability than the plasma proteins to bind the hormone and it is even possible that more direct exchanges may occur between binding proteins and the receptors.

(2) The process of the hormone's inactivation, such as can occur in the liver, and its excretion, mainly in the urine and bile, is delayed while it is in the bound form.

(3) The bound hormone may constitute a circulating pool of the excitant that can extend or moderate the hormone's action. For instance, in pregnant women and guinea-pigs, a plasma protein is formed that can bind testosterone and so may protect the mother from the effects of this steroid.

(4) The distribution of the hormone within the body can be influenced by its binding to plasma proteins (Keller, Richardson and Yates, 1969). A hormone–protein complex may have a special propensity to pass through the capillaries in certain vascular beds. It may thus help specifically to determine where the hormone is going.

(5) Protein-binding may contribute to the specificity of a hormone's action in the cell (Funder, Feldman and Edelman, 1973). In the instance of the corticosteroids, two types of response can occur, mineralocorticoid and glucocorticoid (referring to their effects on electrolytes and intermediary metabolism), for which there are two types of receptors in the cell. Although the aldosterone receptors have a higher affinity for aldosterone than corticosterone, the normal excess of the latter hormone (in the plasma of rats) would be sufficient to negate this difference so that corticosterone would be expected, inappropriately, to occupy the aldosterone receptors. Most of the corticosterone in the plasma, unlike aldosterone, is bound to proteins in such a way that it does not obscure the effect of the aldosterone.

High proportions of hormones often exist in a bound form in the plasma. In the instance of testosterone, it is usually greater than 90% of the total present though it is less in other cases. Cortisol binding in the plasma of teleost fishes varies from 30 to 55% of the total (Idler and Truscott, 1972). Thyroxine and tri-iodothyronine also are substantially associated with plasma proteins; thus, in the plasma of kangaroos, more than 95% of the thyroxine and 90% of the tri-iodothyronine is so bound (Davis, Gregerman and Poole, 1969).

The hormones may be bound to different protein components present in the blood plasma. In some instances, specialized proteins are present that have a high affinity (they are strongly bound) for the hormones. These include a globulin that binds cortisol, cortisol-binding globulin or *CBG*, which is also called *transcortin*. This protein is present in all vertebrates though quantitative differences in cortisol-binding capacities of the plasma exist, indicating that interspecific variations occur (Seal and Doe, 1963). Cortisol binding is much less in the plasma of fishes than in most mammals (Idler and Truscott, 1972) and it is unlikely that the proteins are identical in the different species. Transcortin also binds corticosterone and progesterone (but not aldosterone) and in mammals its levels increase during pregnancy as a result of the action of estrogen which promotes its formation in the liver. Another plasma globulin that binds sex hormones, *sex hormone-binding globulin* or *SHBG*, is found in women (where its level also increases in pregnancy) and various other vertebrates including chondrichthyean and teleostean fishes and amphibians (Ozon, 1972). It is unlikely that this protein is chemically identical in all these groups. Many mammals possess an α-globulin that preferentially binds thyroxine, *thyroxine-binding globulin* or *TBG*, but which is absent in non-mammals (Farer *et al.*, 1962; Tanabe, Ishii and Tamaki, 1969). It also binds tri-iodothyronine but only about one-third as strongly as it does thyroxine. Although such plasma proteins strongly bind hormones, they are present in relatively small quantities so that the total amount of hormone that they can associate with is limited (low binding capacity). The plasma albumins on the other hand, have a high binding capacity though their affinity is low. In species that lack such specialized hormone-binding proteins, or if the amount of hormone present exceeds their binding capacity, large amounts are bound to plasma albumin. In primates, and even their phyletically distant relatives, the marsupials, thyroxine is principally bound to a pre-albumin (thyroxine-binding pre-albumin, *TBPA*) while tri-iodothyronine combines with albumin. In some birds, reptiles and fishes, thyroxine is bound principally to albumin while in others it is associated with both pre-albumin and albumin (Tanabe *et al.*, 1969).

Differences in binding proteins exist between species. In some Australian marsupials (kangaroos), 75 % of the thyroxine is bound to the pre-albumin while only about 10 % is associated with the post-albumin. On the other hand, in an American marsupial, the opossum, about 60 % of the thyroxine is bound to the post-albumin (Davis and Jurgelski, 1973). Even among these opossums differences were observed: the post-albumin exists in two different polymorphic forms PtA_1 and PtA_2. Six, out of 177 sera examined, possessed PtA_2, which has different physicochemical properties to PtA_1; for example, PtA_1 binds tri-iodothyronine but PtA_2 does not.

Peripheral activation of hormones

Some hormones are chemically altered, at sites peripheral to the endocrine gland from where they originated, in a manner that enhances their biological activity. This process is sometimes referred to as 'activation' and may occur in the plasma or at tissue sites.

Angiotensin I is thus converted to its active octa-peptide form, angiotensin II, by the action of converting enzymes. Not all the tri-iodothyronine present in the circulation is directly released from the thyroid gland. Some is formed from thyroxine in the liver and kidneys (Sterling, Brenner and Saldanha, 1973). An integral step in the action of testosterone involves its conversion at its target site by 5α-reductase, to 5α-dihydroxytestosterone. Cortisone can also be converted peripherally to the more active steroid cortisol. Cholecalciferol (vitamin D_3) undergoes several transformations before it can exert its effects. These changes involve the formation of 25-hydroxycholecalciferol in the liver and a further hydroxylation to 1,25-dihydroxycholecalciferol in the kidney (Lawson *et al.*, 1971). The latter has twice the biological activity of its immediate parent compound. It is also possible that some of the large protein hormones are fragmented peripherally into smaller pieces prior to their action. There is evidence that this may occur in the instance of parathormone while large amounts of pro-insulin are normally present in the plasma which, possibly, may also be converted into the active hormone.

Termination of the actions of hormones

The durations of action of hormones vary: they may persist for many hours and even days, or only have a short-lived, transitory, effect. This is usually in keeping with the nature of the homeostatic processes that they mediate. Even a prolonged effect, however, will necessitate the renewed release of hormones because of the metabolic and excretory processes that inevitably result in their inactivation and elimination from the body.

Hormones persist in the circulation for different periods of time. The half-life of human vasopressin is about 15 minutes, that of cortisol is about one hour, while that of thyroxine is nearly a week. This reflects the speed of their degradation in the body, the rate that they may be eliminated in the urine and bile and the protection afforded them as a result of binding to proteins. The effects of the latter are well illustrated by comparing the rates of removal (clearance) of corticosteroid hormones from the blood. In man, about 1600 liters of plasma are normally completely cleared of aldosterone each day. In the instance of cortisol, however, only about 180 liters are so purged in this time. The difference principally reflects the strong binding of cortisol to cortisol-binding globulin (transcortin) in the plasma. Considerable interspecific differences are apparent in the half-lives of hormones: arginine-vasopressin (ADH) has a half-life of about one minute in laboratory rats, compared to 15 to 20 minutes in man. This probably reflects the effects of size: small animals destroy and eliminate hormones more rapidly than large ones. The precise chemical structure of the hormone may also be important; lysine-vasopressin has a half-life that is nearly twice as long in the rat as arginine-vasopressin (Ginsburg, 1968). The considerable differences that have been observed in the potency of human, porcine and salmon calcitonin substantially reflect the differences in their degradation rates (Habener *et al.*, 1971; DeLuise *et al.*, 1972). In rats, porcine calcitonin is destroyed by the liver while that from man and the salmon are degraded by the kidney. Salmon calcitonin is much more resistant to inactivation (in rats, dogs and man) than the mammalian hormones. Body temperature will also be expected to have an effect on the rate of inactivation of hormones so that, in cold-blooded vertebrates, the inactivation and excretion process will be modified accordingly. In the toad *Bufo marinus*, at 26 °C arginine-vasotocin has a half-life of 33 minutes while in the domestic fowl (at 43 °C) it is only 18 minutes (Hasan and Heller, 1968). The effects of differences in size, species and temperature on hormone metabolism have not yet, however, been thoroughly evaluated.

The action of a hormone may be terminated in several ways.

(1) In order to act it must attain a certain critical concentration in the neighborhood of its receptor site. If a hormone is released in a short burst as, for instance, usually occurs with oxytocin, the receptor will respond to a local high concentration that is sequestered like a small packet in the plasma. The response will then be terminated simply as a result of the subsequent dilution and redistribution of the hormone in the body fluids. A hormone may also be removed if it is bound or has accumulated at tissue sites. Adrenaline is readily taken up by the adrenergic nerve terminals. Less-specific binding to tissues, such as that of neurohypophysial peptides to skeletal muscle, may also contribute to the removal of hormones from the circulation.

(2) Small amounts of hormones may be eliminated unchanged in the urine and bile but this usually amounts to less than 5 % of the total released. The activity of hormones is generally reduced or destroyed as a result of their metabolism by enzymes in the tissues, particularly in the liver and kidneys. They are transformed in various ways and the by-products are usually then excreted in the urine and bile. The hormone's chemical structure may be altered in several ways. The catecholamines can be methylated by catechol-*O*-methyl transferase (COMT) or, to a lesser extent, they may be deaminated as a result of the action of monoamine oxidase (MAO). The action of the thyroid hormones is largely destroyed by the removal of iodine from the molecule by a deiodinase enzyme. Protein hormones are broken up by proteolytic enzymes. Steroid hormones (and to some extent thyroxine) are combined chemically with glucuronic and sulfuric acids, in a process called conjugation that results in increased solubility which enhances their chances for excretion in the urine and bile. Prior to such a conjugation considerable changes may be wrought in the chemical architecture of the steroids. Despite such chemical alterations, some hormones may still retain some of their biological activity. This is especially apparent in the gonadotrophins that appear in large quantities in the urine of mammals during pregnancy. The activity of such urine in promoting ovulation and spermiation in various animals is used as a basis for pregnancy tests. Despite the retention of such biological effects, the products in the urine exhibit a different chemical behavior to that of the gonadotrophins present in the pituitary gland. Urinary FSH and LH apparently undergo some changes prior to their excretion, possibly involving a fragmentation of their molecules.

Mechanisms of hormone action

Hormones exert actions on every major group of tissues in the body. The nature of their effects are numerous and include changes in the intermediary metabolism of fats, proteins and carbohydrates, growth and development of the tissues, changes in the permeability of membranes and the contraction or relaxation of muscles. The precise manner in which they effect such processes is only incompletely understood.

It is generally considered that a hormone, in order to act, must eventually influence an enzyme activity. It may do this by a process of activation, promoting enzyme formation (induction) or possibly acting as, or providing, a cofactor in the chemical reaction that it promotes. As described earlier, this process is thought to be initiated as a consequence of the hormone's combination with a precise chemical moiety in the cell which is called its receptor. The exact role of this hormone–receptor unit in triggering the response is uncertain. It may provide a carrier for the hormone and so facilitate its transfer to a vital site in the cell or, conversely, the hormone may facilitate transfer of the hormone receptor to an essential site. It is also possible that the receptor–hormone complex itself could act as an enzyme activator (or inhibitor) or cofactor. The receptor could exist as a part of an enzyme so that an activating effect of a hormone could be direct, but this is uncertain.

Hormonally mediated responses to hormones may take place in successive steps involving numerous enzymes. Conceivably, by acting at a single rate-limiting stage in such a process and altering the supply of an essential metabolite, a hormone could influence a complex series of metabolic events in the cell. It is also possible that a hormone may directly influence more than a single process in such a chain of events.

Hormones often initiate responses in several different tissues in the body. In such instances, the basic effects may be similar or even differ from one another. For instance, aldosterone initiates a change in membrane permeability to sodium in the kidney, salivary glands, sweat glands and, in amphibians, the skin and urinary bladder. Alternatively, adrenaline mobilizes fatty acids from fat cells but glucose from muscle cells. Despite the diverse tissue sites and the nature of the processes involved, the underlying initiating mechanism is generally the same. For instance, the effects of adrenaline on fat and muscle cells are both mediated by the action of cyclic AMP (see later).

At the present time the mechanisms of action of hormones are thought to be affected through either of two major groups of processes in the cell (others may also exist). The nucleotide adenosine-3′,5′-monophosphate, or cyclic AMP, is a vital link in many endocrine responses and its formation is promoted, or inhibited, by numerous hormones. Other hormones, by regulating genetic transcription in the cell nucleus, can control the formation of proteins and enzymes that are essential for a response. Not all the actions of all the hormones are even partially understood. It is likely that some which have multiple actions may utilize several different mechanisms. Some hormones, notably insulin, do not easily fit into either of the above classifications.

The role of adenosine-3′,5′-monophosphate (cyclic AMP)

Our knowledge of the part played by adenosine-3′,5′-monophosphate, or cyclic AMP, in the action of many hormones is primarily due to the work of Earl Sutherland (see Robison, Butcher and Sutherland, 1971; Sutherland, 1972). This adenine nucleotide is chemically related to ATP from which it is formed. Its chemical structure is shown in Fig. 4.17.

The discovery of the endocrine role of cyclic AMP was made during an investigation of the mechanism of action by which adrenaline and glucagon convert glycogen to glucose in the liver. This reaction is dependent on several enzymes but the presence of a phosphorylase is rate limiting. This enzyme exists in two forms, a relatively inactive phosphorylase *b*, which on the incorporation of phosphate is converted to the much more active form, phosphorylase *a*. This activation takes place not only in intact cells but also in broken-cell preparations upon the addition of adrenaline or glucagon to them. The phosphorylase is a soluble enzyme which can be separated in

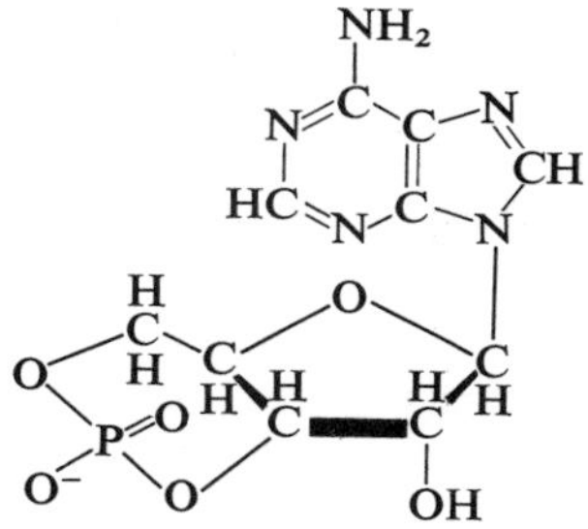

Fig. 4.17. The structural formula of adenosine-3′,5′-monophosate (cyclic AMP).

the supernatant fraction of the broken cells. This enzyme, however, cannot be activated by the hormones when alone in this solution; the presence of the particulate cell material is a necessary condition. When the latter fraction is exposed to adrenaline or glucagon a substance can subsequently be washed from the cell particles which, when added to the supernatant, activates the phosphorylase. This activating chemical was found to be cyclic AMP and it is formed from ATP as a result of the action of an enzyme, *adenyl cyclase* (more correctly adenylate cyclase), that is part of the cell membrane. In the liver, this enzyme is activated by adrenaline or glucagon and in skeletal muscle preparations only by adrenaline.

Adenyl cyclase has been found in many animals: mammals, birds, amphibians and fishes, as well as many invertebrates. This enzyme is also present in bacteria, though apparently not in higher plants. Most tissues in the body contain adenyl cyclase. Apart from liver, they include muscle, kidney, heart, brain, adipose tissue, bone and many endocrine glands (Table 4.3).

The role of adenyl cyclase and cyclic AMP in mediating the effect of hormones was first described for the actions of glucagon or adrenaline on glycolysis in the liver or skeletal muscle. A description of this process can thus be used as a prototype for its role. It should, however, be remembered that although the initiating reactions may be similar for many tissues and various hormones, the responses of the final effector (or responding system) will often differ. As summarized in Fig. 4.18, the initiating event is the interaction of the hormone and its receptor, in the cell membrane, which results in the activation of (or sometimes the inhibition) adenyl cyclase. The nature of the relationship between the receptor and the enzyme is uncertain; it could involve a series of chemical reactions or the two components may constitute part of a single structural complex. The simplest interpretation is that the receptor and enzyme are considered to constitute two subunits, an outward-facing receptor portion and an inner enzyme part which has access to the cellular ATP. The activated adenyl cyclase reacts with the latter to form the cyclic AMP. This does not directly

TABLE 4.3. *Distribution and hormonal sensitivity of mammalian adenyl cyclase.* (From Robison *et al.*, 1971)

Tissue	Hormone
Liver	Glucagon and adrenaline
Skeletal muscle	Adrenaline
Cardiac muscle	Catecholamines
	Glucagon
	Tri-iodothyronine
Kidney	Vasopressin
	Parathyroid
Bone	Parathyroid
	Calcitonin
Brain	Catecholamines
Adrenal	ACTH
Corpus luteum	LH and prostaglandins
Ovary	LH
Testes	LH and FSH
Thyroid	TSH
	Prostaglandins
Parotid	Catecholamines
Pineal	Catecholamines
Lung	Adrenaline
Spleen	Adrenaline
Adipose	Adrenaline
Brown adipose	Catecholamines
Platelets	Prostaglandins
Leucocytes	Catecholamines and prostaglandins
Erythrocytes	None demonstrated
Uterus	Catecholamines
Pancreas	None demonstrated
Anterior pituitary	Several
Vascular smooth muscle	None demonstrated

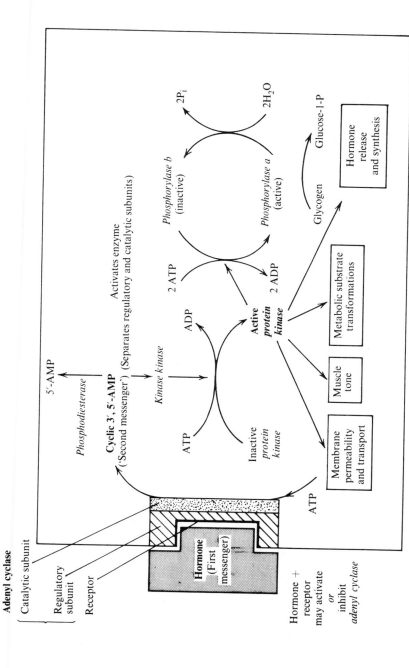

Fig. 4.18. A diagrammatic representation of the role of cyclic AMP as a 'second messenger' in the mechanism of a hormones action.

A variety of protein kinases are thought to be present in different cells which, when activated by cyclic AMP, can mediate the phosphorylation or dephosphorylation of certain proteins. This may result in diverse responses.

activate the phosphorylase *b* enzyme but initiates a sequence of chemical events that has this effect. Initially, the cyclic AMP activates a protein kinase kinase (also called kinase II or phosphorylase *b* kinase kinase) enzyme in the cell. The inactive form of the enzyme is thought to exist as a combination of a regulatory and a catalytic subunit. The nucleotide combines with the former upon which the subunit separates so that the catalytic part can exert its action. This kinase kinase activity, with the aid of ATP, activates phosphorylase *b* kinase which, in turn, converts phosphorylase *b* to phosphorylase *a*. The latter enzyme initiates the breakdown of glucose to glucose-1-phosphate.

Cyclic AMP can mimic the actions of many hormones on a variety of tissues. The formation of this nucleotide, as a result of hormonal activation of adenyl cyclase, appears to mediate the actions of such hormones as (apart from adrenaline and glucagon) melanocyte-stimulating hormone, vasopressin, corticotrophin, thyrotrophic hormone, luteinizing hormone and parathormone (see Table 4.4). The ultimate responses are very diverse and

TABLE 4.4. *Relations between the metabolic actions of some hormones and cyclic AMP*

Hormone	Actions shared by cyclic AMP
Adrenaline	Glycolysis (liver and muscle), lipolysis (fat cell)
	Heart muscle contraction
ACTH	Steroid synthesis in adrenal cortex
LH	Steroid synthesis by corpus luteum
TSH	Production and release of thyroid hormones
Growth hormone	Lipolysis (?)
Vasopressin	Increased water movement in renal tubule
MSH	Melanophore, dispersion of melanin
Glucagon	Glycolysis (liver), lipolysis (fat cell)
Parathormone	Mobilization of bone calcium

include glycolysis, lipolysis, changes in the permeability of membranes to water, sodium and calcium, the dispersion of melanin in the melanophores and the formation and release of many other hormones including thyroxine, corticosteroids and sex steroids.

The nature of the effector response to hormones differs widely. It has, however, been suggested that in those processes that involve the action of cyclic AMP as a 'second messenger', this is always the result of the phosphorylation, or dephosphorylation, of a protein and involves a protein kinase. In the instance of the glycolytic and lipolytic effects of adrenaline and glucagon, this results from enzyme activation. The formation of

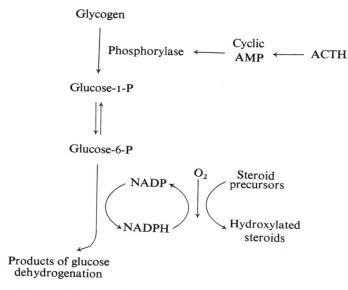

Fig. 4.19. The mechanisms of action of corticotrophin (ACTH) and cyclic AMP in stimulating the synthesis of corticosteroids by the adrenal cortex. This is the Haynes hypothesis.

steroids in the adrenal cortex and gonads may proceed as a result of an increased supply of NADPH from glucose-6-phosphate that also results from the activation of a phosphorylase and glycolysis (Fig. 4.19). In addition, an increased supply of cholesterol due to an increased activity of cholesterol esterase may also contribute to steroid synthesis. The mechanism by which membrane permeability is changed in response to neurohypophysial hormones is poorly understood but it may involve conformational alteration of constituent proteins as a result of their dephosphorylation by a protein phosphatase. The responses are stopped as a result of the replacement of phosphate at its effector sites by a phosphorylase enzyme.

Apart from initiating increases in levels of cyclic AMP in cells it is possible that some hormones may act by bringing about a decrease in the nucleotide's concentration. As described earlier, the catecholamine hormones exhibit two types of actions called α-adrenergic and β-adrenergic effects. The latter are associated with activation of adenyl cyclase and increases in cyclic AMP. On the other hand, α-adrenergic responses involve reduced levels of the nucleotide; possibly mediated by an inhibition of adenyl cyclase. Such inhibitory effects of catecholamines have been described in processes involving the release of insulin from B-cells, increase of the osmotic permeability of membranes by neurohypophysial peptides and the dispersion of melanin in melanophores by MSH. It has been suggested that some hormone receptors may contain a moiety which, when combined with α-adrenergic agents, initiates this inhibition. The anti-lipolytic effects of insulin in fat cells are accompanied by a decline in cyclic AMP levels. Prostaglandins are a group of excitants which have been found in extracts from many tissues and which have diverse effects. These substances, which possibly function as locally acting hormones, can also decrease (though sometimes they increase) cyclic AMP levels in tissues and this could mediate some of their effects. Processes may thus exist in cells which alter the concentrations of cyclic AMP in either direction and so determine the nature of the ultimate response.

The inactivation of cyclic 3',5'-AMP to 5'-AMP in cells is normally due to the action of the enzyme *phosphodiesterase*. This enzyme could provide a potential site for the action of hormones but such effects have not been described. Phosphodiesterase can be inhibited by certain drugs, notably the methylxanthines which include caffeine.

The activation of adenyl cyclase can be accomplished by several hormones, in various tissues, and can result in diverse responses. The actions of hormones are, however, relatively specific, so how, when several utilize cyclic AMP, can a separation of their roles and effects be accomplished? In some instances more than one hormone is thought to act on a single adenyl cyclase. This seems to be so in the effects of adrenaline, glucagon, ACTH and TSH on fat cells *in vitro*. The effects of the two latter hormones may not be physiological but reflect the relative non-specific reactivity of the receptors, and the adenyl cyclase, that are present. The adenyl cyclase that mediates the effects of ADH on the kidney is much more specific in its reaction with hormones. This selectivity is probably dictated by the nature of the hormone receptors. In some instances, a tissue exhibits more than one adenyl cyclase-mediated response to a single hormone. Neurohypophysial hormones increase both water and sodium transfer across amphibian skin and urinary bladder and these effects are mediated by different receptors and effectors. In the amphibian membranes, it seems likely that two adenyl cyclases and/or two 'pools' of cyclic AMP exist in the tissue, each mediating a distinct response.

Differences in the ability of various hormones to activate adenyl cyclase from different tissues or species could reflect a polymorphism in the enzyme's structure. If the receptor is considered to be an integral part of the enzyme, then this polymorphism undoubtedly occurs, but it is not known if such an association is present. Cell-free preparations of adenyl cyclase exhibit different quantitative responses to hormone analogues. Adenyl cyclase preparations from rat, mouse, rabbit and ox kidney are more readily activated by arginine-vasopressin than by lysine-vasopressin (and much less by oxytocin). On the other hand, the enzyme prepared from the kidneys of pigs is most responsive to lysine-vasopressin (Dousa *et al.*, 1971). This relative sensitivity corresponds to that of the homologous hormones present in each species, while oxytocin does not normally act on the kidney anyway. These differences, however, as discussed above, may only reflect the response of a receptor that need not necessarily be a part of the enzyme itself. The properties of renal adenyl cyclase from a number of vertebrates has been compared (see Table 4.5). Mammal, bird, reptile and amphibian enzymes were all strongly activated in the presence of fluoride. The mammalian enzymes were also activated by neurohypophysial

TABLE 4.5. *Stimulation of renal adenyl cyclase in various vertebrate species.* (From Dousa *et al.*, 1972)

Species	Neurohypophysial hormones	Parathyroid hormone	Fluoride
Rat	++++	++++	++++
Mouse	++++	++++	++++
Pigeon	o	+++	++++
Alligator	o	++	++++
Toad	±	o	++++
Bullfrog	+	o	++++

+ Indicates strength of response; o, no response; ±, rudimentary response. Homologous neurohypophysial hormones were tested.

hormones but this response was much less prominent, or even undetectable, in the non-mammals. This lack of response could, however, merely reflect the presence of only small amounts of the appropriate enzyme in the kidneys of the non-mammals or its lack of importance in mediating the renal responses in those species. It is notable that adenyl cyclase obtained from amphibian urinary bladder is strongly stimulated by neurohypophysial hormones. The renal adenyl cyclase that is activated by parathormone (a distinct entity from that responding to the neurohypophysial hormones) was stimulated in enzyme preparations made from the kidneys of mammals, birds and reptiles but not in those made from amphibian kidneys. This may reflect an absence of a renal effect for parathormone in the Amphibia. Except in bacteria, adenyl cylase has not been prepared as a soluble enzyme so that the precise studies that may confirm its polymorphism are not feasible. This limitation and the uncertainties as to its relationship to the hormone's receptor limit speculation as to the possible evolution of this enzyme.

Hormonal effects mediated by changes in the transcription of DNA in the cell nucleus

The synthesis of proteins is primarily controlled by the cell nucleus through the coding DNA that is contained in the chromosomes. Our knowledge of the manner by which this genetic material is utilized to regulate the synthesis of specific proteins in the cell is largely the result of the work of Jacques Monod and his collaborators (Monod, 1966).

For an understanding of how hormones may act at this level it is necessary to recapitulate, briefly, the nuclear processes thought to control protein synthesis. It should be noted however, that these have been principally worked out using bacteria. The basic unit carrying the genetic code for the synthesis of proteins is the *structural gene* whose actions are regulated in a complex manner. Adjacent to the structural gene is a special genetic segment called the *operator*.[1] The structural gene and the operator together form a unit called the *operon*. The operator is, in turn, controlled negatively by a *regulatory gene* that can produce a molecule, a *repressor*, that may specifically combine with, and so inhibit, the operator (Fig. 4.20). This regulatory compound has an ability to bind with other materials that can either result in its activation, which will result in decreased protein synthesis or its inactivation that will produce an increase. There are thus several possible places where an external controlling substance, such as a hormone, can act. The position of the site of action is still largely open to speculation but it could involve a repression of the regulatory gene, the inactivation of the repressor, or the masking of the operon from repressor action.

The effects of the steroid hormones, as well as the thyroid hormones and growth hormone, are most obviously manifested as increases in growth, development and differentiation of tissues. These changes are especially clear when one observes the effects of estradiol-17β on the uterus. Such growth is associated with a marked increase in the rate of protein synthesis. More subtle changes may accompany other responses to such hormones. For instance, aldosterone, which increases the rate of sodium transfer across some membranes, may induce the formation of a permease, or some other enzyme, that increases active sodium transport. It is not always possible to identify the specific proteins formed, but progesterone is known to increase the formation of avidin in the chick oviduct, while cortisol

---

[1] In the *lac* operon a 'promoter' is present which is a binding site for RNA polymerase. This enzyme is released when the repressor is absent from its site on the operator.

enhances the production of Na–K activated ATPase in several tissues including the kidney and, in some fish, the gills and intestine.

The evidence about the effects of hormones on the synthesis of proteins can be derived from direct measurements of their concentrations or from changes in the rate of their incorporation of radioactively labelled amino acids. Protein synthesis is a cytoplasmic process taking place in association with the ribosomes which follow the translation pattern provided by the messenger RNA which is derived from the chromosomal DNA.

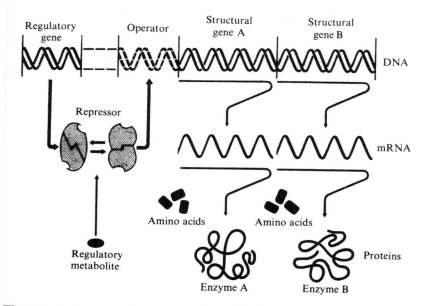

Fig. 4.20. A diagrammatic representation of the function and regulation of the operon. (From Monod, 1966.)

While it is possible that hormones exert some direct effects on the ribosomal protein formation this does not usually appear to be so. One of the earliest distinguishable effects of the action of hormones that influence protein synthesis is the formation of RNA by the nucleus and the incorporation of tritiated uridine into it. This process is accompanied by an induction or release of RNA polymerase, that catalyzes the separation of the messenger-RNA from DNA and which can be inhibited by actinomycin D. The effects of steroid hormones can be prevented by this antibiotic. The protein synthesis by the ribosomes can also be blocked by puromycin, which acts on the cytoplasmic translational process but does

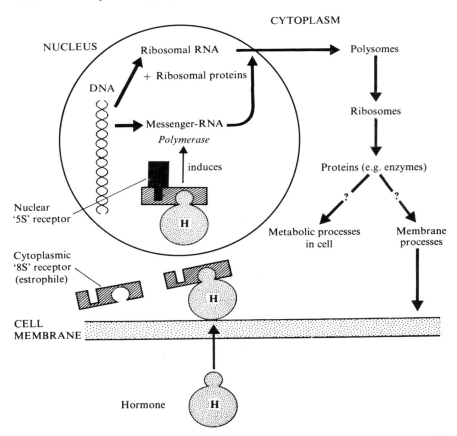

Fig. 4.21. A diagrammatic representation of the mechanism of action of a steroid hormone that is acting by influencing genetic transcription. This scheme is not completely understood and will undoubtedly be modified as new information becomes available.

not stop the early formation of the messenger-RNA. A further indication as to the nuclear site of action of hormones is their autoradiographic identification in the chromatin.

The processes by which hormones act to initiate protein synthesis, via increases in nuclear transcription of the genome, have been most completely described for the action of estradiol-17β on the uterus (see Jensen and DeSombre, 1972, 1973; O'Malley and Means, 1974) and have been summarized in Fig. 4.21. Comparable mechanisms also appear to exist for progesterone, the androgens, cortisol, aldosterone and also probably thyroid hormone and growth hormone.

The estrogenic hormone molecule, upon crossing the plasma membrane and entering the cell's cytoplasm, is bound to a protein which has been called its cytoplasmic receptor. These proteinaceous units are also called *estrophiles*. The hormone–receptor combinations can be isolated *in vitro*. They pass intact through a gel filtration column and can be separated from other cell constituents by ultracentrifugation in a sucrose gradient where they have a sedimentation coefficient of about 8 S. In the presence of salt solutions this changes to 4 S, indicating that the receptor–hormone unit can be broken into subunits, and it is possible that these may have functional significance in mediating the subsequent effects. There are about 100 000 estrophiles in each uterine cell, which is a much higher number than is present in non-target tissues. The binding for a particular hormone is relatively specific and can be prevented by substances that block their effects *in vivo*.

At a temperature of 2 °C, 75% of the hormone is present in the 8 S complex in the cytoplasm, but if the tissue is warmed to 37 °C most of it moves across into the nucleus. The estrophilic complex may be acting as a carrier for the hormone or the hormone may facilitate the transfer of one of the subunits of 8 S that could initiate the formation of messenger-RNA. The estradiol-17β in the nucleus is bound in another proteinaceous form that can be separated in KCl solution and which has a sedimentation coefficient of 5 S. This complex is clearly distinguishable from the 8 S one in the cytoplasm. The 5 S nuclear complex can be freed from the chromatin by the action of DNAase, indicating that it is closely associated with DNA. Other evidence suggests an interaction with acidic proteins in the chromatin. The 5 S nuclear receptor has not been found in the nucleus prior to its exposure to the 8 S complex, suggesting that the latter may first be converted to 5 S which has an acceptor site in the nucleus. The free hormone does not readily bind to the chromatin. The precise site of the combination with the chromatin is not known nor is it clear how a hormone–nuclear receptor complex influences the metabolism of messenger-RNA. It could for instance promote its synthesis on the chromatin by combining with a repressor gene, or prevent the activation of a repressor substance, or by association with the operon be masking it from the latter's action. Alternatively, an activation of RNA polymerase would also have such an effect. Other mechanisms, however, could be involved, such as a reduced rate of destruction of RNA and an increase in the rate of its transfer from the nucleus to the cytoplasm.

At the present time not all the actions of hormones can be accounted for by the two preceding types of mechanism. Hormones have multiple effects and not all the effects of a single hormone can always be accounted for by a single mechanism. Thyroxine, growth hormone and prolactin can stimulate protein synthesis in the cell and, while these actions can be prevented by inhibition of RNA polymerase (with actinomycin D), just how primary, or universal, this effect is in these hormones' actions is not clear. Insulin influences protein synthesis not by direct involvement of genetic translation but by post-translational events. Insulin has profound effects in facilitating uptake of glucose and amino acids across the cell membrane and many of its effects can be accounted for by this transport process which involves a mechanism which is at present unknown. Other effects of insulin, however, such as the formation of glycogen in the liver and muscle, cannot be accounted for completely by this transport mechanism. Changes in the activity of glycogen synthetase are involved but just how this is brought about is not clear. Growth hormone also increases protein synthesis and it is possible that it also acts on the cell membrane.

Some speculations on the evolution of the actions of hormones in cells

The two basic control mechanisms involving cyclic AMP and the regulation of genetic transcription exist in all animals as well as many micro-organisms. We may thus suspect that these basic mechanisms, upon which hormones can impinge their actions, have always been present in animals, even in unicellular ones.

Cyclic AMP exists in bacteria, where it also appears to have a role in regulating cellular activities. Adenyl cyclase in bacteria is an intracellular enzyme and it has been suggested that this represents the primitive condition, though it may be more true to say that it is the situation in unicellular organisms. This internal site would appear to be most suitable for an enzyme that has to respond to changes in the intracellular nutrients and metabolites. In metazoan animals, adenyl cyclase appears to be confined to the cell membrane, a position that may be more apt for its interaction with metabolites and chemicals coming from other cells. These include the hormones. Such a membrane site for adenyl cyclase may thus be more opportune for intercellular cooperation and especially for interactions with molecules like the polypeptide hormones that cross cell membranes with some difficulty. The lack of information about the nature of the relationship of the hormone receptor and adenyl cyclase has already been discussed. It is unnecessary to postulate evolutionary changes in the structure of adenyl cyclase, only in the receptor which may be a subunit of it. The specificity of the receptor for a particular hormone has also been described earlier. The simultaneous evolution of the complementary nature of both the hormone and its receptor is difficult to envisage. One wonders, when considering all the possible differences in structure, how they ever got together and how, at the same time, they acquired their complementary relationships.

The transcription of genetic material plays a basic role in the life of cells. In unicellular organisms, this need only be controlled by internal accumulations of nutrients and metabolites. These may act by combining with structural units, analogous to the subunits of the 8 S cytosol receptors. With the onset of need for intercellular communication these controlling subunits may have contracted an ability to combine with materials originating outside the cell. In other words, they may have acquired, or been transformed so as to incorporate, a hormonal receptor. Steroid hormones are non-polar materials that readily gain access to cells and so would appear to be well suited to such an intracellular reaction. They would, however, because of their water-insoluble, non-ionic, non-polar nature be unsuitable as agents that act allosterically on enzymes. The required mobility of the 8 S-type regulatory units would, in such a simple system, preclude fixed receptor sites on the membrane.

It is not difficult to envisage, using the Monod model, how hormones with a nuclear site of action may have acquired different functions. Genetic rearrangement of the chromosomal material could, for instance (see Monod, 1966), move the control of a structural gene from one operator segment to another. If a hormone were acting through such an operator this would be accompanied by the transfer of its endocrine control to another structural gene. Such a mechanism could be completely inappropriate, but in some instances could provide a basis for the change, and evolution, of the role of a hormone.

Conclusions

In the following chapters we will be examining the roles of hormones in coordinating different physiological processes in the body. In the present chapter we have looked at the manner by which the endocrine system itself works. Although information about non-mammals is rather sparse it appears that the underlying mechanisms of a hormone's synthesis, release, transport, mechanism of action and its destruction are rather similar in all vertebrates. Even when different hormones are involved, the general underlying processes involved are often similar; but major differences are often apparent between the general types of hormones, especially those made from cholesterol (steroids), and those derived from amino acids. There are a number of interspecific differences in the 'life history' of particular hormones in the body and these can be related to the animal's manner of life. The natures of the stimuli that initiate a particular hormone's release are especially variable among the vertebrates and are dictated by the different physiological roles that a hormone may have assumed. In addition, quantitative differences may arise with respect to a hormone's rates of synthesis, destruction, the quantities that are stored in the gland and the concentrations that appear in the blood. Such differences can arise at distinct stages of the life cycle of an animal but they are also observed between various species where they can be related to such characteristics as size, rates of metabolism, and environmental factors like temperature and the availability of different nutrients, salts, and water.

5. Hormones and nutrition

Animals require a continual supply of food in order to sustain life. Such nutrients, in the first instance, are obtained from the external environment. These materials are used as an energy supply, as building blocks for growth and reproduction, and also as a source of certain essential chemicals necessary to the adequate functioning of the metabolic machinery in the body. The processes involved are thus basic to life and are regulated to a considerable extent by hormones.

Animal cells, including tissues isolated from metazoan species, can survive *in vitro*, in the absence of hormones, for extended periods of time. Except, however, for cancer cells, their life and continual perpetuation cannot go on indefinitely. Even the more limited survival of normal tissues *in vitro* depends on an adequate supply of special nutrients that are chosen for their ability to be utilized by that particular tissue. One cannot run a gasoline engine on diesel fuel and in the same way cells can only metabolize certain forms of nutrients.

The foods that animals obtain from the environments where they live are usually chemically far more complex than can be used by their cells. The original nutrients are transformed in the body into compounds that may sometimes be immediately metabolized by the cells, or may be converted into substances that can be stored for subsequent transformation into such compounds.

Hormones play an important role in regulating the interconversions of nutrients to metabolic substrates and their stored forms. The endocrine secretions may help to regulate the levels of nutrients by contributing to the control of their absorption from the gut, their levels in the blood, the nature and rate of their storage, their release from tissues, and their assembly into the structural elements of the body.

Animals lead diverse lives in a plethora of environmental conditions. The definitive metabolic processes are basically similar in all animals and lead to the utilization of ATP, for the supply of energy, and the building of cells. Nevertheless the physiological processes leading to these accomplishments may differ considerably. Such processes are dictated by numerous circumstances and events.

The chemical nature of the foodstuffs that animals obtain from their environments may differ greatly. In their feeding habits, animals may be carnivorous, herbivorous or omnivorous. Even within these categories considerable differences exist in the types of food animals eat. Some animals may feed principally on invertebrates such as insects, molluscs and worms that live in terrestrial, freshwater or marine environments. Other animals feed on vertebrates. Plants from equally diverse situations are also used for food. The possibilities for gastronomic experiments thus appear to be endless but only a limited number can furnish a particular species with its needs.

Animals have different patterns of feeding. Some eat almost continually, such as cattle and sheep that nibble plants for hour after hour. Large predatory carnivores, like lions, snakes and crocodiles, may only feed intermittently with days or even weeks separating their meal-times. Circumstances, such as an unexpected drought, may inadvertently result in enforced fasting or even starvation. A dependence on body stores of nutrients for prolonged periods of time may be a fairly predictable part of an animal's life cycle, such as dictated by hibernation during winter, estivation during hot, dry summers and migrations to more equitable regions for food and in order to breed.

The nutritive requirements of animals may differ considerably. The normal rate of metabolism of different species can differ by more than 100-fold. Warm-blooded homeothermic animals usually have a higher metabolic rate than cold-blooded poikilotherms. Even among homeotherms the basal metabolic rate differs considerably; for instance it is about 35 times greater in the shrew than in the elephant. Factors such as size, patterns of activity and the environmental temperatures experienced, contribute to the differences in metabolic requirements of animals. Young, growing animals have special nutrient requirements, while breeding and care of the young alter the needs of adults.

Dominating all these differences, and dictating many of them, is the phylogeny of the species. The genetic constitution of a species determines the pattern of its nutrition and the mechanisms involved in the regulation of it. These physiological processes are presumably the result of a prolonged evolution and adaptation to environmental conditions. This is reflected in the diversity of the endocrine mechanisms that control the metabolism of animals.

Endocrines and digestion

Apart from catching or collecting and then eating food, the first physiological event in the nutritional process is digestion. Food is usually broken down to simpler chemical compounds prior to its absorption from the gut. This process involves the actions of acids, alkalis and enzymes secreted

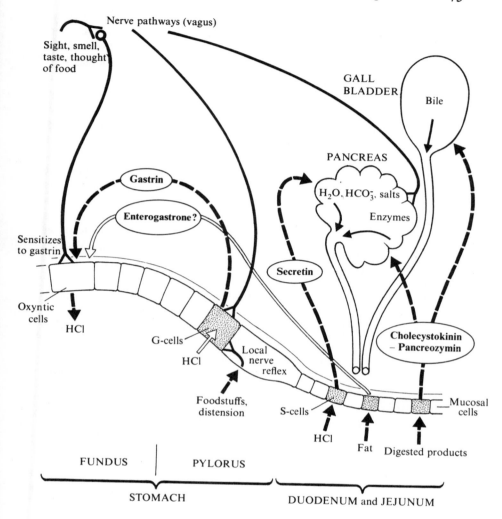

Fig. 5.1. The role of hormones in controlling gastric acid secretion, pancreatic secretion of salts and enzymes, and the contraction of the gall bladder. *Gastrin*, from the pylorus, initiates secretion of hydrochloric acid by the oxyntic cells in the fundus.

The duodenal–jejunal hormones, *secretin* and *cholecystokinin–pancreozymin*, initiate the secretion of, respectively, pancreatic juice and enzymes. *Entero-gastrone*, from the duodenum–jejunum, inhibits gastric acid secretion (the existence of enterogastrone is in doubt). The double open arrows indicate an inhibitory effect; the dashed ones a stimulation.

It should be noted that neural pathways can initiate and modify these effects.

by glands in the wall of the stomach and intestines as well as the exocrine, or acinar, cells of the pancreas. The orderly flow of these juices is controlled by hormones as well as by nerves (see Fig. 5.1). Indeed the discovery of the role of *secretin* in stimulating the secretion of the exocrine pancreas into the intestine, was the first unequivocal demonstration of the role of a hormone in the body and it was in connection with this discovery that the term 'hormone' was initially used. Bayliss and Starling performed the crucial experiment in 1902. A loop of the jejunum of an anesthetized dog was tied at both ends and was denervated. When acid (0.4% HCl) was introduced into this sac (or the duodenum) secretion of pancreatic juice was stimulated. An extract of the jejunal mucosa was made by rubbing it with sand in the presence of the HCl solution. When (after filtering) this was injected into the jugular vein of the dog, pancreatic secretion was also stimulated. Starling remarked 'then it must be a chemical reflex'. This experiment was performed at University College, London on the afternoon of 16 January, 1902 and has been summarized thus (Sir Charles Martin, see Gregory, 1962): 'it was a great afternoon'.

Secretin that is released as a result of the action of acid on the duodenal and jejunal mucosa stimulates the formation of a voluminous pancreatic juice, rich in bicarbonate and salt but poor in enzymes. The secretion of proteolytic, amylolytic and lipolytic enzymes (but not water and salt) can be stimulated by the vagus nerve as a result of feeding. Another hormone, however, also assists this process. This is *cholecystokinin–pancreozymin*, the role of which was not established until 40 years after that of secretin (Harper and Raper, 1943). This endocrine secretion is also formed in the upper parts of the intestine from which it is released in response to the presence of the digestive products.

Gastric secretion is also controlled by nerves and hormones. Stimulation by the vagus initiates the formation of acid by the oxyntic cells and enzymes from the chief cells. The action of the vagus on acid secretion is mediated by the release of *gastrin*, a hormone formed in the pyloric region of the stomach, which stimulates the oxyntic cells to secrete acid. The vagus also sensitizes the oxyntic cells to the action of gastrin. The complete reflex arc, which is initiated by feeding, initially involves nerve stimulation along cholinergic nerves to the pyloric cells that release gastrin. This hormone then closes the reflex arc and acts on the oxyntic cells. Secretion of gastrin also results from the initiation of a local nerve reflex due to the presence of food in the stomach. Gastric acid secretion can be inhibited when fat or oils pass into the upper parts of the intestine. This stimulus apparently initiates the release of another hormone, *enterogastrone*, which inhibits secretion from the oxyntic cells. As described previously, the distinct hormonal characteristics of this material remain in some doubt.

The presence of fats in the intestine initiates the release of bile from the gall bladder, and this also involves an endocrine reflex due to the release of *cholecystokinin–pancreozymin* that contracts the gall bladder and relaxes the sphincter of Oddi (Ivy and Oldberg, 1928). This hormone has several roles in the body and, apart from its actions on the gall bladder and the endocrine and exocrine pancreas, can elicit a sensation of satiety. Injected cholecystokinin–pancreozymin thus reduces feeding in rats (Gibbs, Young and Smith, 1973).

Secretin, gastrin and cholecystokinin–pancreozymin can also initiate the release of insulin or glucagon. The physiological significance of this stimulation is uncertain but it has been suggested that such effects may contribute to the homeostasis during feeding. Such signals could mobilize insulin and glucagon in anticipation of the absorption of digested nutrients.

The presence of these humoral reflex arcs influencing digestion have been shown in several mammals but direct evidence as to their presence in other vertebrates is lacking. It seems likely that, from the sporadic evidence available, they exist. Indeed, further experiments by Bayliss and Starling in 1903 indicated that this is so with respect to the effect of secretin on the pancreas. They performed experiments on a variety of mammals, including monkey, dog, cat, rabbit, and a bird (a goose, 'in the process of fattening for Christmas') and confirmed the wider phyletic distribution of this humoral reflex. Secretin-like activity was also shown to be present in the duodenum of man, ox, sheep, pig, squirrel, pigeon, domestic fowl, tortoise frog, salmon, dogfish and skate. This interesting paper by Bayliss and Starling (1903) is entitled 'On the uniformity of the pancreatic mechanism in vertebrates' and must be one of the earliest contributions to comparative endocrinology.

The transformation of metabolic substrates: the role of hormones

The diversity of intermediary metabolism in vertebrates

Nutrients that are utilized for the production of energy can be classified into three major groups: carbohydrates, fats and proteins. These compounds, especially the latter, are also incorporated into the cell structure and so are essential for growth and reproduction.

The nature of the nutrients upon which the animal's metabolism is based depends, in the first instance, on its diet. In carnivores, this consists mainly of protein and fat. The carbohydrates obtained by herbivores may consist of materials such as starches and sugars that can be broken down into simpler sugars by the digestive enzymes. The major organic constituent of most plants is cellulose which is fermented by micro-organisms present

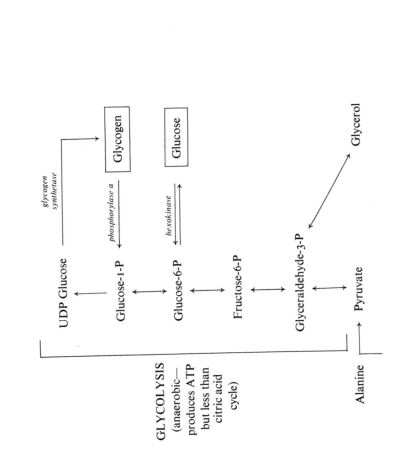

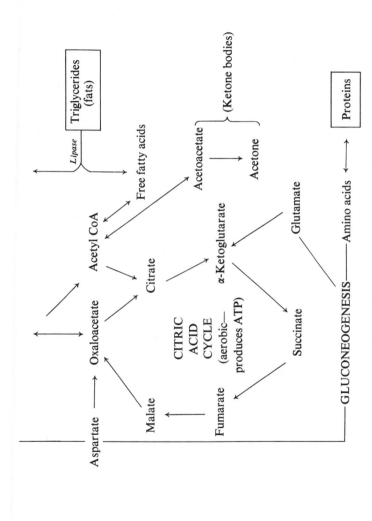

Fig. 5.2. A diagrammatic summary of the processes, enzymes and major compounds involved in the metabolic transformations of glucose, triglycerides and proteins.

Hormones may either increase or decrease certain of these reactions, as indicated in the text and subsequent Figures.

in various compartments of the gut (the cecum, the colon, or the rumen) and which produces short-chain fatty acids. These are mainly propionate, butyrate, and acetate. Such fermentation by symbiotic micro-organisms is widespread in herbivorous mammals, especially in the sacculated rumen of ruminants (cattle and sheep) as well as the colon of horses and the cecum of lagomorphs, like rabbits, as well as the sacculated stomach of some marsupials. In non-mammals the situation is less clear but micro-organisms undoubtedly aid digestion in these animals also.

Different species of animals thus show differing dietary dependencies on proteins, fats and carbohydrates. Proteins can be broken down to their constituent amino acids, fats to fatty acids and glycerol, and carbohydrates to simple sugars, like glucose, or, with the aid of micro-organisms, can give rise to fatty acids. The resulting basic subunits can be utilized directly for the production of energy or they may undergo transformations (see Fig. 5.2) into forms that can be stored and provide a readily accessible reserve. Apart from their reassembly into more complex units, interconversions of one such type of chemical compound into another may also take place in the body. Glucose can thus be readily converted in liver, adipose tissue and the mammary glands into triglycerides (fats). Some amino acids are transformed by the process of gluconeogenesis, in the liver, to glucose while others are changed into fatty acids. The transformation of fatty acids to sugars is not as common, though in ruminants propionate, which is formed in large amounts, is converted to glucose. Glycerol can also be transformed into glucose.

The reserves of protein that are maintained in the body are small and in any case it is not a very suitable substrate for the storage of energy. During starvation, protein may, nevertheless, make an important contribution to an animal's energy requirements. Substantial amounts of glucose are stored as glycogen in the liver and muscles but these reserves are inadequate to maintain an animal for prolonged periods of time. Triglycerides provide the most economic and convenient storage-form for energy. One gram of fat furnishes 9500 calories while the same amount of carbohydrate and protein, respectively, only supply 4200 and 4300 calories.

Stored fat may be dispersed widely among the tissues in the body but it usually predominates at certain sites. Adipose tissues thus exist at subcutaneous, mesenteric, perirenal and periepididymal sites in mammals. The large fat-bodies near the gonads in the abdominal cavity of Amphibia are familiar to student dissectors. The tail of urodeles and lacertilians is also a common site for fat storage. Large quantities of fats may also be stored in the liver of poikilotherms and this is especially important in chondrichthyean fishes, though it is also seen in other vertebrates. In many fishes, fats are stored in close proximity to the muscle fibers which directly utilize their fatty acids. A characteristic type of adipose tissue called *brown fat* is present in embryonic mammals and also some adults such as rats and hibernating species like hedgehogs, moles, bats and squirrels. Brown fat is capable of undergoing very rapid metabolism, with considerable production of heat, particularly during arousal of hibernating animals.

The transformation, storage and utilization of fats, proteins and carbohydrates is regulated to a considerable extent by hormones. The relative differences in the availability and importance of such substrates in different species, not surprisingly, may be reflected in the animal's particular response to hormones. Quantitative, or even qualitative, differences may be observed. Some such variations in the responsiveness of different species of reptiles and amphibians to injections of insulin and glucagon, as well as pancreatectomy, are shown in Fig. 5.3. It can be seen that changes in the blood glucose levels following these treatments show considerable interspecific variability in the speed of onset, and the magnitude and the duration of the responses.

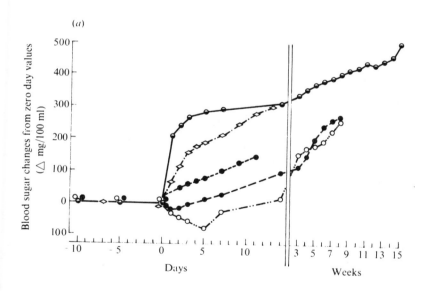

Fig. 5.3. Effects of various experimental treatments on blood glucose concentrations in amphibians and reptiles.

(*a*) Changes in the blood glucose concentrations following pancreatectomy in various reptiles and amphibians. It can be seen that the elevation in the glucose occurred relatively promptly in the alligators and toads but was considerably delayed in the lizards and snakes.

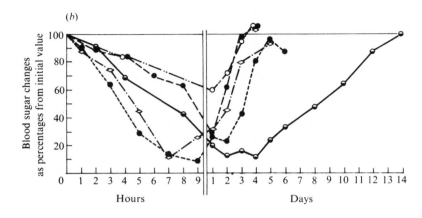

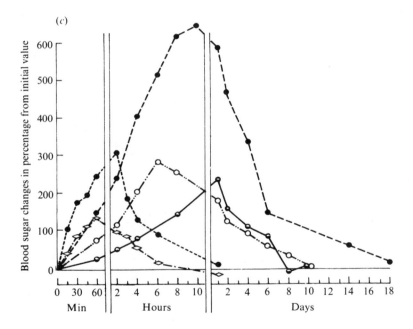

(*b*) Effects of injected insulin (1 unit/100 g body weight). The amphibians responded more rapidly than the reptiles but the response was usually more prolonged in the latter.

(*c*) Effects of injected glucagon (10 μg/100 g body weight). The reptiles responded more slowly than the amphibians but the response in the former lasted for a longer time. ⊖—⊖, Alligators; ◇—·—◇, toads; ●---●, snakes; o—··—o, lizards; ●---●, frogs. (From Penhos and Ramey, 1973.)

Hormones that influence intermediary metabolism

When considering hormones that influence the transformation, deposition, mobilization and utilization of fats, carbohydrates and proteins in the body, we should be careful to distinguish between those that function physiologically and those actions that probably do not normally occur in the animals (pharmacological effects). For instance, lipolytic activity can be exhibited by at least seven pituitary hormones and also several secretions from other endocrine glands. It is possible, however, that a pharmacological action of a hormone in one species, or tissue preparation, may reflect a physiological role in some phyletically distant species.

Insulin plays a central role in intermediary metabolism and this may be associated, especially during fasting, with the actions of the *corticosteroids*. *Glucagon* and *adrenaline* also contribute to the control-system. *Growth hormone* and *thyroid hormones* modulate the processes involved in many

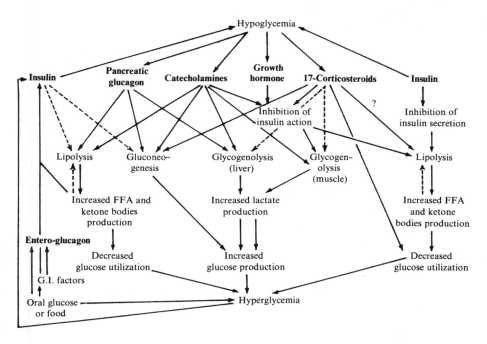

Fig. 5.4. A summary of the role of hormones in stimulating, or inhibiting, metabolic processes and transformations that control the glucose concentrations in the blood. Solid line, stimulation or increase; dotted line, inhibition or decrease. (Modified from Foà, 1972.)

chemical pathways. *Prolactin* (Bern and Nicoll, 1969) stimulates the formation of milk proteins in the mammary glands and in the pigeon crop-sac. Prolactin also, when injected, may have a hyperglycemic action and promote the deposition of fat in teleost fish, amphibians, reptiles and birds. Several hormones usually interact with each other in such metabolic processes, none can function normally in complete isolation from all the others (Fig. 5.4). As so well stated by Tepperman and Tepperman (1970), 'It is virtually impossible to separate out one set of signals which control lipogenesis, another which controls gluconeogenesis and a third which controls ketogenesis. All these processes share so much of the metabolic machinery . . .'. With this reservation in mind we can consider the effects of various hormones on the processes of intermediary metabolism.

Insulin

This hormone decreases plasma glucose concentrations and, in mammals at least, also reduces free fatty acid levels. In the absence of insulin, muscle wasting occurs due to the excessive mobilization of proteins. These effects are the result of several actions, at various sites; principally the liver, muscle and adipose tissue. *The processes mediated by insulin* are basically (see Fritz, 1972) as follows:

(i) Increase in the rate of uptake of glucose across the cell membranes of skeletal and cardiac muscle, adipose tissue, and mammary gland. Organs like liver, kidney or brain do not respond in this way to insulin.

(ii) Insulin facilitates glycogen formation from glucose. This is partly the result of the more rapid accumulation of glucose but is also due to an increased activity of glycogen synthetase in liver, muscle and possibly even adipose tissue.

(iii) An inhibition of the mobilization of glycogen to form glucose.

(iv) Inhibition of gluconeogenesis from amino acids.

(v) Insulin increases the accumulation of fatty acids across the cell membranes of adipose cells.

(vi) An inhibition of lipolysis of triglycerides to form fatty acids.

(vii) Insulin increases lipogenesis, from glucose, in adipose tissue.

(viii) There is an increased uptake of amino acids by muscle and liver cells.

(ix) An inhibition, by insulin, of the mobilization of amino acids from protein [related to (iv)].

The effects of insulin can thus be broadly divided into its actions on the accumulation of nutrients across cell membranes and its facilitation, or inhibition, of metabolic synthesis in cells.

Variations in the responsiveness to insulin among vertebrates

The actions of insulin on intermediary metabolism have been principally studied (*in vitro* and *in vivo*) in mammals, usually in laboratory rats. The hypoglycemic action of insulin nevertheless appears to be widespread in vertebrates (see Bentley and Follett, 1965; Falkmer and Patent, 1972); it occurs among animals ranging from cyclostomes to mammals. Differences in sensitivity nevertheless are apparent, reptiles and especially birds being relatively insensitive to injected mammalian insulin. The pancreas of birds contains little insulin and this is only released 'sluggishly' in response to hyperglycemia (Hazelwood, 1973) so that this hormone may not play such an important role in these as in other groups of vertebrates. Some urodeles fail to respond to injected insulin; yet others do respond (McMillian and Wilkinson, 1972). Among mammals, ruminants are less sensitive than carnivores. Such variations appear to depend on the source of the exogenous insulin, the metabolic rate and condition of the animals, and the presence of compensatory mechanisms, such as release of glucagon and adrenaline, as well as the normal diet of the animals. The hypoglycemic effect of insulin appears to be a universal one among vertebrates. Differences have been observed, however, in its ability to promote deposition of glycogen in liver or muscle or both. For instance, in lamprey liver, but not muscle, glycogen is increased by insulin injections. Muscle glycogen is increased in the skate (Chondrichthyes) and scorpion fish (Teleostei) (Leibson and Plisetskaya, 1968) where the effects on the liver are less pronounced. Insulin has unpredictable effects on plasma fatty acids; it decreases them in mammals but may have no effect or even increase their concentration in birds.

The sensitivity of different species to insulin may be related to their dietary habits. It has been noted that herbivorous mammals withstand an absence of insulin far more readily than carnivorous ones (Gorbman and Bern, 1962; Fritz, 1972). Carnivores only eat periodically so that they may have a sudden large intake of nutrients which must be stored for utilization during the fast between meals. Herbivores, on the other hand, graze for long periods of the day and are continually absorbing the products, mainly fatty acids, from the large stores of digesting food in their guts. Coordination of the storage and mobilization of nutrients in the body are thus expected to be more important for periodic eaters like carnivores, than herbivores (which have aptly been called 'nibblers').

Catecholamines

Adrenaline can increase the concentration of both glucose and fatty acids in the plasma. These effects are mediated in the liver and muscles, as a result of activation of phosphorylase, and in adipose tissue by activation of lipase. Both effects are due to the formation of cyclic AMP. The hyperglycemic effect of adrenaline is seen in species from all the main groups of vertebrates though the site of its action may differ. For instance, in lampreys, adrenaline mobilizes glycogen in liver but not muscle, while in the Chondrichthyes, glycogen from both sites is depleted, as in mammals (Bentley and Follett, 1965; DeRoos and DeRoos, 1972). The hyperlipidemic response to adrenaline has not been studied on such a broad phyletic scale and even mammalian adipose tissue from all species studied is not uniformly responsive. Thus mobilization of fatty acids in response to adrenaline has been shown in the rat, dog, goose and owl but not the duck, chicken, rabbit or pig (Prigge and Grande, 1971; Table 5.1). Adrenaline increases plasma fatty acids in the eel *Anguilla anguilla* (Larsson, 1973) but this is not seen in all fish (Minick and Chavin, 1973) and may reflect an indirect effect by inhibiting release of insulin.

There is some doubt, at least in mammals, as to the efficacy of the circulating concentrations of adrenaline in stimulating glycogenolysis. The concentration usually observed in the plasma appears to be too low to act physiologically on the liver. Adrenergic effects on mobilization of glucose in the liver may thus be mediated by stimulation of the sympathetic nerves. Whether this applies to all tissues, and other species, is unknown.

Glucagon

This pancreatic hormone exerts a hyperglycemic action in mammals as a result of the mobilization of liver glycogen following activation of phosphorylase. It does not have this action on skeletal muscle. Gluconeogenesis is increased. Plasma fatty acid levels are elevated by glucagon in birds and mammals but at somewhat higher concentrations than affect glucose. Lipolysis is promoted in adipose tissue from rat, rabbit, goose, duck and fowl, but not in the dog (Prigge and Grande, 1971). Glucagon has widespread hyperglycemic effects in mammals, birds and reptiles but is relatively ineffective on cyclostomes, chondrichthyeans and some teleosts though it is very effective in the eel (Patent, 1970; Larsson and Lewander, 1972). In contrast to mammals and birds, eel plasma fatty acids are unaffected by glucagon (Larsson and Lewander, 1972).

Other peptide hormones

Other hormones can also influence glucose and fatty acid metabolism. The neurohypophysial peptides (when injected), vasopressin, oxytocin and vasotocin, exhibit hyperglycemic effects that can be demonstrated in

TABLE 5.1. *Species sensitivity to hormonal stimulation of free fatty acid release from adipose tissue.* (Based on Shafrir and Wertheimer, 1965)

	Rat	Mouse	Rabbit	Hamster	Guinea-pig	Cat	Dog	Pig	Chicken	Man
Adrenaline or noradrenaline	++	++	o	++	o	+	++	o	o	+
Corticotrophin	++	++	++	++	+	+	o	o	+	++
Cortisol	+				++				o	++
Glucagon	+		+	+	+					
Thyrotrophin	+ or ++		o	o	++	o	+	+	+	
MSH (α or β)	o		++	o	+		+	o		
Vasopressin	o		++	o	++		o	o		

++, Strong response; +, moderate or weak response; o, no response.

cyclostome fishes, amphibians, birds and mammals (see Bentley, 1966) and have also been more recently described in reptiles (LaPointe and Jacobson, 1974).

Vasotocin also increases plasma fatty acid levels in birds (John and George, 1973). The pituitary hormones MSH, ACTH, TSH and growth hormone may all, depending on the species and the adipose tissue preparation used, facilitate mobilization of fatty acids from mammalian adipose tissue (Table 5.2; Mirsky, 1965). These actions are probably not normal physiological ones and it is unknown whether they are widespread in non-mammals.

TABLE 5.2. *Hormonal effects on fat mobilization.* (Based on Fritz and Lee, 1972)

	Fat mobilization from adipose tissue	
Hormones	*In vitro*	*In vivo* (FFA) plasma
Glucagon	↑	↑
Adrenaline	↑	↑
Noradrenaline	↑	↑
ACTH	↑	↑
TSH	↑	
Growth hormone	↑	↑
Insulin	↓	↓
Cyclic 3′,5′,-AMP	↑	

ACTH: adrenocorticotrophic hormone; TSH: thyroid-stimulating hormone; ↑: increase; ↓: decrease, in rate of metabolic process indicated in column by hormone designated in row; (FFA) plasma: plasma concentration of free fatty acids.

Adrenocorticosteroids

The steroid hormones have profound effects on intermediary metabolism (especially in fasting animals), reproductive processes, growth and lactation. The corticosteroids increased blood glucose concentrations and promote gluconeogenesis and the deposition of glycogen in the liver. In excess, corticosteroids promote muscle wasting and a negative nitrogen balance, while in young animals they inhibit growth. These two effects reflect their action on protein catabolism. *The actions of corticosteroids on intermediary metabolism* can be summarized thus:

(i) Increase in gluconeogenesis in the liver following a mobilization of proteins from skeletal muscle and the deamination of the amino acids that are released. This action is most important, especially during fasting.

(ii) Glycogen is deposited in the liver because of an increase of the glycogen synthetase reaction.

(iii) Corticosteroids inhibit glycogenolysis.

(iv) There is a reduction in peripheral oxidation and utilization of glucose.

(v) Corticosteroids inhibit the conversion of amino acids to proteins, and fatty acids to triglycerides.

Such effects appear to be widespread in the vertebrates although the information available in non-mammals is sporadic (see Chester Jones *et al.*, 1972). Hyperglycemia in response to the injection of corticosteroids has been shown in vertebrates that range phyletically from cyclostomes to mammals. This response is associated with gluconeogenesis and elevation of tissue glycogen levels. The facilitation of gluconeogenesis is associated with increased levels of liver transaminase enzymes of teleost fishes, amphibians, birds and mammals (though it had once been thought that this increase only occurred in the latter two groups of vertebrates) (see Janssens, 1967; Freeman and Idler, 1973). An inhibition of growth or loss in body weight has been shown in the domestic fowl and the amphibian *Xenopus laevis*, as well as two species of teleosts, *Salmo gairdneri* and *Salvelinus fontinalis* (Bellamy and Leonard, 1965; Freeman and Idler, 1973; Janssens, 1967), as well as in mammals. The actions of corticosteroids on growth and metabolism appear to be basically the same in all vertebrates.

Steroid sex hormones

Estrogens and androgens have widespread metabolic effects on the growth and differentiation of tissues, especially the reproductive organs. They may, however, also influence other tissues in the body, principally by promoting the formation of proteins. Androgens when administered have anabolic effects on skeletal muscle (myotrophic action), promoting the formation of proteins. The magnitude of this effect depends on the species, age and the hormonal status of the animal. It is greatest in young male animals with deficient circulating androgens; it is also apparent in females but has little effect in older animals. Estrogens increase plasma lipid levels in mammals and also have an anabolic effect but this is principally confined to the mammary glands and reproductive organs. In oviparous species, estrogens promote the formation of lipoproteins in the liver which are incorporated into the yolk of the egg. Progesterone increases the formation of avidin by the oviduct of the chicken and this is also incorporated into the egg.

Thyroid hormones, growth hormone and prolactin

These hormones also contribute to metabolic regulation. The consumption of oxygen by homeotherms is depressed in the absence of thyroid hormones and they are also necessary for adequate growth and differentiation. The actions of several other hormones are not as pronounced in the absence of the thyroid secretion. Such reduced responses are seen for the catecholamines and corticosteroids. The thyroid gland seems to modulate the levels and activity of metabolic enzymes in cells; in the instance of adrenaline this action may involve an increase in adenyl cyclase (Krishna, Hynie and Brodie, 1968). Growth hormone promotes growth and stimulates the formation of protein in cells. At least some of its actions are mediated by *somatomedin* (see later), a protein whose formation it promotes (or into which it is transformed) in the liver. Growth hormone facilitates uptake of amino acids by liver and muscle cells but inhibits the action of insulin on glucose uptake and thus may have a diabetogenic effect. It has a lipolytic action on adipose tissue. Growth hormone has been shown to influence growth in mammals, birds, reptiles, amphibians and teleost fish (see Chapter 3) so that its actions have a wide phyletic distribution. Somatomedin has been identified in several mammals where its action appears to be less specific to any one single species than growth hormone itself (see Tanner, 1972). Prolactin influences the intermediary metabolism of the mammary glands (present in mammals) and the crop-sac of pigeons. As we shall see, prolactin may also promote fat deposition in a number of vertebrates.

Conclusions

Hormones can thus be seen to exhibit widespread actions on intermediary metabolism. In some instances, several secretions can exert similar effects though, in the animal, these may not all be physiologically equivalent. In other cases, hormones may exert opposing effects, either by acting on different processes or by a more direct inhibition. Hormones can also (see Chapter 4) directly influence one another's release and so mimic or oppose the actions of other hormones. Intermediary metabolism, while being extremely complex and involving several tissues, many chemical reactions and numerous metabolites, is a well-integrated process. This is largely the result of the actions of hormones at different types of sites (some of which are summarized in Fig. 5.5), both within the same cell and in different kinds of cells, as well as their ability to act in harmony with each other.

The underlying roles and actions of hormones in regulating intermediary metabolism appear to be basically similar in all vertebrates. The relative

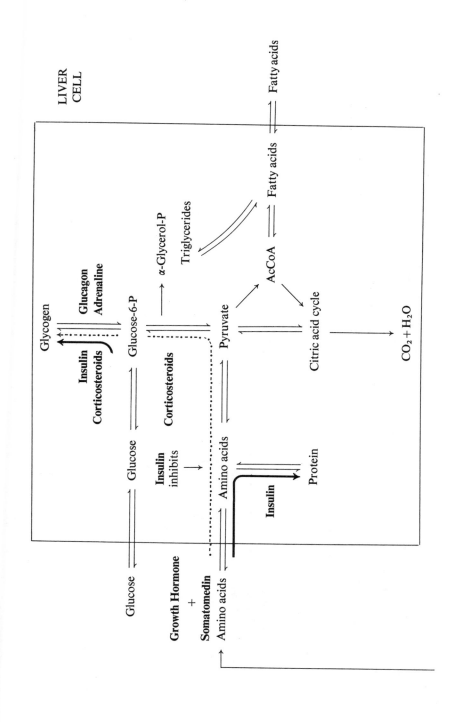

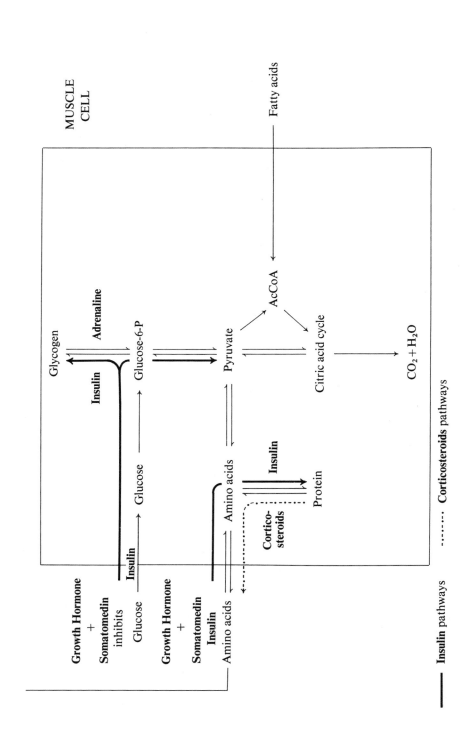

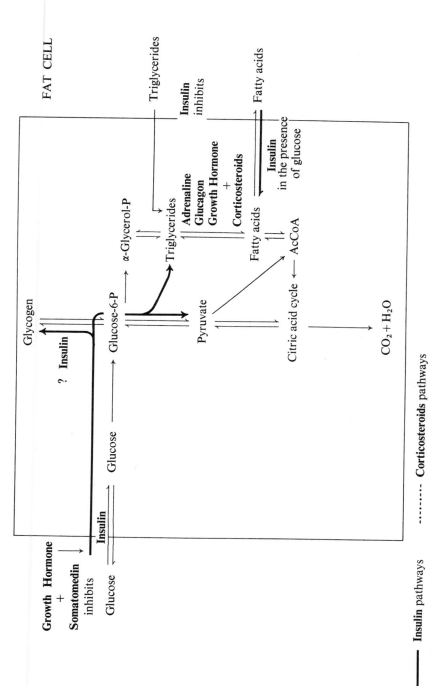

Fig. 5.5. A diagrammatic summary of the effects of hormones on the transfer of metabolites across the cell membranes and the metabolic transformation within liver cells, muscle cells and fat cells.

The principal metabolic transformations that are influenced by insulin are indicated by the heavy solid lines and those by corticosteroids by the broken lines.

—— **Insulin** pathways   ········ **Corticosteroids** pathways importance of each action of the hormone may, however, differ, depending on the animal's usual life-style and the particular stage of its life cycle. Events like fasting, associated with hibernation, estivation and migration, and reproduction (including the formation of eggs, pregnancy, lactation and the growth, maturation and metamorphosis of the young) are all associated with special metabolic needs and hormonally mediated effects. Some of these will be described in more detail.

Hormones and calorigenesis

The production of heat in the body

The chemical reactions that are continually taking place in cells are associated with the production of heat. This can be quantitatively expressed in terms of calories; hence the term calorigenesis. This heat represents:

(i) A by-product resulting from the energy requirements of the body. This heat may result from mechanical activity of muscle contractions or from the more ubiquitous metabolic transformations of chemical substrates.

(ii) In homeotherms, the production of heat energy *per se* may be necessary to maintain the body temperature of the animal.

All the tissues of the body contribute to the release of heat in the body and this predominates in skeletal muscle and liver. In some species, the brown fat may also be an important site of calorigenesis, especially in newborn animals and in hibernators during awakening or arousal. In the cold-adapted laboratory rat, the skeletal muscles are thought to contribute about 50% of the heat produced, the liver 25% and brown fat only 10% (this value is greater for newborns). During arousal from hibernation, brown fat may contribute as much as 40% of the body heat of hamsters, and 60% in ground squirrels (Janský, 1973).

In adult homeotherms, added heat requirements for maintaining the body temperature in cold environments are largely met by a skeletal muscle activity called shivering. The rest of the heat is produced from other metabolic activities that are continually proceeding in the body. The amount of heat produced can also be increased, in response to homeothermic need, in a manner that is independent of shivering. This is called non-shivering thermogenesis (or NST) and is greater in young animals and small species than in adult or large animals. A hamster can increase its metabolism four-fold in this manner, while in man the change is negligible (see Janský, 1973).

Thyroid hormones

Thyroxine and tri-iodothyronine have an important role in maintaining the production of heat (and the associated oxygen consumption) in mammals and birds. In the absence of the thyroid gland, the oxygen consumption of mammals declines by as much as 50% while an increase in the rate of thyroid secretion can stimulate metabolism by a similar amount. Thyroxine administration can nearly double the basal rate of metabolism in the golden hamster (Janský, 1973). The thyroid is thought to play a permissive role in cell metabolism rather than contribute to acute changes in metabolism. Thyroid hormones act slowly, thyroxine taking several days to exert its maximal effect. They are usually considered to contribute to thermogenesis by maintaining the metabolic machinery in a manner that allows it to function optimally. Nevertheless, in mammals, increased thyroid activity is associated with exposure to low temperatures (thyroidectomized rats have a limited survival in the cold) and it decreases with high temperatures. These changes are mediated by the response of the hypothalamic centers to alteration in the temperature of the blood that perfuses them (Collins and Weiner, 1968).

There are some reports that thyroid hormones increase calorigenesis in poikilotherms though it is not always possible to demonstrate this effect (indeed a decrease has sometimes been observed). The evidence is considered to be equivocal. The injection of thyroxine into the lizard *Eumeces fasciatus* results in a 30% increase in oxygen consumption at 30 °C but there is no effect at 20 °C (Maher, 1965). A similar increase in oxygen consumption has been seen in the leopard frog *Rana pipiens* (McNabb, 1969) at different temperatures. Thyroid activity also varies with the body temperature of poikilotherms; it is greater at higher temperatures, which is the reverse of what happens in homeotherms. The latter's response, however, presumably reflects a homeostatic role of the thyroid in calorigenesis which would not appear to be present in cold-blooded vertebrates.

Catecholamines

Adrenaline and noradrenaline may play an important role in regulating the production of heat in the body. In homeotherms, a sudden exposure to cold conditions results in an increased production of heat. If mice are transferred from a temperature of 25 °C to 0 °C they normally adjust their metabolism and nearly all of them survive. When, however, they are pretreated with drugs that inhibit the β-adrenergic effects of catecholamines (for example propranolol) they all die within three hours (Estler and Ammon, 1969) because of an inability to increase heat production. Normally under these conditions, this thermal response is mediated, in mice, by catecholamines, principally noradrenaline which is released from the nerve endings of the sympathetic nervous system. Adrenaline, which is secreted by the adrenal medulla, is not usually effective (though it is so in rats) but a suggestion has been made that it also may have such an effect in some circumstances and constitutes a second line of defense.

Such an adaptational effect of catecholamines in calorigenesis can be seen in the adjustment of hypothyroid rats to a cold environment (Sellers, Flattery and Steiner, 1974). When rats are exposed to a temperature of 4 °C their urinary excretion of catecholamines increases, which probably reflects their role in increasing heat production. If such rats are thyroid-ectomized, they cannot then increase their production of heat but the injection of small amounts of thyroxine allows this increase to occur so that they survive. In the hypothyroid rats, the urinary excretion of catechol-amines increases even more than in the normal rats exposed to cold. It has been suggested that an increased activity of the sympathetic nervous system, including the adrenal medulla, facilitates the survival of these hypothyroid rats. It should be emphasized, however, that some thyroid hormones are essential as in the absence of the excitants (see p. 198) rats do not exhibit a calorigenesis in response to catecholamines. The two types of hormones, however, appear to act in conjunction with one another in adapting the rats to cold.

Apart from laboratory rodents such as rats and mice there is little information about the role of the thyroid and catecholamines in cold-adaptation of other mammals.

It is notable that adrenaline may, in addition to being calorigenic, help promote heat loss in some mammals. Sweating during exercise in monkeys is dependent on circulating adrenaline and is considerably reduced following denervation of the adrenal medulla (Robertshaw, Taylor and Mazzia, 1973). This poses an interesting conflict of interest in the physiological role of adrenaline, its potential calorigenic effect presumably being minimal in circumstances where it also contributes to the dissipation of heat. The role of adrenaline in temperature regulation is even more diverse when one recalls that adrenergic nerves, by a peripheral vasoconstrictor action, can also promote heat conservation. This affords another interesting example of the evolution of a hormone's role.

There is little information about the effects of catecholamines on calori-genesis and oxygen consumption in non-mammals (see Harri and Hedenstam, 1972). This effect apparently cannot be demonstrated in birds (pigeon, titmouse and gull) nor in fishes. There seem to be no reports about such an action in reptiles either. In European frogs, *Rana temporaria*, injections of noradrenaline and adrenaline increase oxygen consumption by 25 to 35 %. The response depended somewhat on the particular frogs used; it was seen in cold- and warm-adapted summer frogs but not warm-adapted winter frogs. The physiological role of catecholamines in calorigenesis of non-mammals remains in doubt.

Mechanisms of actions of hormones on calorigenesis

Calorigenesis is stimulated in tissues as a result of their mechanical activity, as in muscles, and also accompanies more general metabolic transformations. It is on the latter ubiquitous processes that the catecholamines and thyroid hormones act to stimulate thermogenesis. Their precise sites of action in the cells are uncertain. Heat may be produced as a result of an increased turnover of ATP or by an accelerated rate of mitochondrial respiration mediated by an increase in protein synthesis which, it has been suggested, may be influenced by thyroid hormones. The formation of cyclic AMP, from ATP, as a result of the action of hormones probably

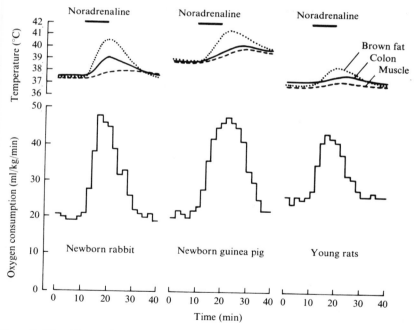

Fig. 5.6. The effects of noradrenaline (intravenous infusion) on the subcutaneous temperatures over *brown fat, colon* and *muscle* and the oxygen consumption of newborn rabbits, newborn guinea-pigs and young rats.

The calorigenic effects of noradrenaline are especially prominent in the brown fat while the basal rate of oxygen consumption in each species increased more than two-fold. (From Cockburn, Hull and Walton, 1968.)

results in substantial heat production (Robison *et al.*, 1972). Hormones involved in this process, or released by it, increase the supply of available glucose and fatty acids that can function as substrates for the production of energy in cells. The effects of noradrenaline on oxygen consumption and the associated subcutaneous temperature of brown fat in rabbit, rat and guinea-pig is shown in Fig. 5.6. The calorigenic effects of catecholamines on brown fat can be seen dramatically *in vitro* where oxygen consumption can be increased four-fold (Table 5.3). This is the result of

TABLE 5.3. *Stimulation of oxygen consumption of slices of rat brown adipose tissue by hormones added* in vitro. (Based on Joel, 1965)

Hormone	Hormone concentration (μg/ml)	Oxygen consumption (μmoles/100 mg fresh tissue per 2 h incubation)	
		Control	Plus hormone
Noradrenaline	0.46	14.9	53.8
Adrenaline	0.50	13.9	64.7
Glucagon	1.0	13.7	35.3
ACTH	10	14.3	28.9
TSH	30	17.7	23.4

mobilization of fatty acids following the activation of lipase by cyclic AMP. It can be seen (Table 5.3) that several other hormones, glucagon, ACTH and TSH mimic the effects of the catecholamines on brown fat but it is unknown whether or not they contribute physiologically to the dramatic increases in metabolism that are observed in this tissue.

The effects of catecholamines on calorigenesis are facilitated (at least in the rat) by the action of thyroid hormones (Lutherer, Fregly and Anton, 1969) at several sites including adipose tissue. In thyroidectomized rats, catecholamines have little effect on oxygen consumption but if thyroxine is injected their effects are increased. This can be related to an increase in the amounts of adenyl cyclase present in the fat cells (Krishna *et al.*, 1968).

Conclusions

The calorigenic actions of hormones are most important in homeothermic vertebrates where they assist in the process of temperature regulation. The production of heat by the cells in such animals is a basic underlying characteristic, the levels of which may, within limits, be modified. Nutrients, especially proteins, obtained from the diet have apparently a direct effect on these processes, termed the 'specific dynamic action of foods'. The hormones act in concert with this effect. Other physiological effects mediated by nerves and hormones indirectly influence thermoregulation by facilitating or diminishing losses of heat from the body. This involves evaporation which occurs from the respiratory tract and the skin where the control of sweat gland activity (referred to above) is important. The blood supply to the peripheral parts of the body, which is controlled by sympathetic nerves that release catecholamines and promote piloerection, influences heat exchanges that occur by conduction. It is unlikely that circulating adrenaline significantly alters peripheral blood flow in such circumstances. Hormones thus do not predominate but do contribute to the regulation of body temperature in mammals and birds. This effect represents an evolution of a physiological role which is not apparent in their phyletic forbears.

The storage of nutrients and their utilization during fasting

The diversity of feeding–fasting patterns in vertebrates

As described earlier, sufficient food may only be available to animals at irregular intervals of time separated by several hours, many months or even years. In some instances, when climatic conditions are unfavorable, animals may sequester themselves in protected havens where metabolic activity is minimal. Hibernation during the winter months is well known in many small mammals (especially among the Insectivora, Rodentia and Chiroptera) that seek refuge in burrows and allow their body temperatures to decline to levels similar to the ambient one. Other animals become inactive during hot, dry periods of drought which result in a limited food supply and a shortage of water that may produce severe osmotic problems. In the latter instance, called 'estivation', the body temperature is also similar to the ambient one, but as this is usually relatively high, metabolism would be expected to be greater than in those animals that are hibernating. Animals may survive for many months or possibly even years under these conditions. A recent report from Russia (*Nature*, **242**, 1973) described a live newt that was found in a piece of ice in Siberia which, according to carbon-dating, had been entombed for nearly 100 years. African lungfish can survive for two to three years in a state of estivation, though more usually it is for four to six months between seasonal rains. Such periods of estivation are also common among amphibians that live in hot, dry deserts.

While hibernation and estivation are associated with minimal activity and metabolic needs, other situations associated with fasting require a high expenditure of energy. Such an occasion is most dramatically seen during seasonal and breeding migrations. Birds may fly many hundreds, or even thousands, of miles from temperate regions, at the beginning of winter, to warmer tropical climes and then return again in the spring. Fishes, such as lampreys and salmon, when they become mature, migrate from the rivers, where they grew up, into the sea from which they later return in order to breed. Eels make the opposite migration from breeding grounds in the sea to rivers and then later the young return to the sea to breed. Other sea-going creatures, such as turtles and whales, also make long journeys. On many of these occasions, the animals do not feed or only do so infrequently. Reserves of nutrients are amassed in the body in preparation for the migrations during which they are expended. The endocrine glands undoubtedly have a role to play in such storage and the subsequent utilization of nutrients but the available information is only fragmentary. Further clues can be obtained from the voluminous studies of endocrine function during normal feeding and fasting.

Endocrines and feeding

The release of hormones

Feeding, like so many other physiological processes, is a process that involves the secretion of several hormones. This begins with the release of hormones that are associated with digestion: gastrin, secretin and cholecystokinin–pancreozymin. These excitants, as well as entero-glucagon from the intestinal tract, promote the early release of insulin and glucagon from the Islets of Langerhans. The absorbed nutrients also influence the secretion of these hormones; glucose increases insulin release, while amino acids initiate the discharge of both hormones. Nerve stimulation, via the vagus, can also stimulate insulin release. The endocrine response differs somewhat with the diet, depending on the relative amounts of protein and carbohydrate present (Table 5.4). A high carbohydrate diet is associated with high insulin and low glucagon levels while a predominance of protein elevates the concentrations of both of these hormones. In ruminants, the fatty acids that are absorbed from the rumen may also stimulate the release of insulin (Manns, Boda and Willes, 1967).

The disposal of absorbed nutrients

The nutrients that are absorbed from the digestive tract can be disposed of in the body in several ways. They may be used immediately as a source of energy. This process may be relatively direct, such as the oxidation of

TABLE 5.4. *Interrelationship of metabolism with the nutritional state of mammals.* (From Cahill, Aoki and Marliss, 1972)

Nutritional states	Hormonal states		Liver				Muscle			Adipose		
	Insulin	Glucagon	Glycolysis	Lipo-genesis	Gluconeo-genesis	Keto-genesis	Glucose uptake	Protein synthesis	Proteo-lysis	Glucose uptake	Lipo-genesis	Lipolysis
Carbohydrate-fed	+++	±	++	++	0	0	++	±	0	++	++	0
Protein-fed	++	+++	0	+	++	0	+	++	0	+	+	0
Carbohydrate- and protein-fed	++++	±	+	+++	0	0	++	++	0	+++	0	0
Fasting (low insulin)	+	++	0	0	++	++	0	0	+	0	0	++
Diabetes (absent insulin)	0	++++	0	0	++++	++++	0	0	++	0	0	++++

+ to 0, either concentration of the hormone or rate of function described.

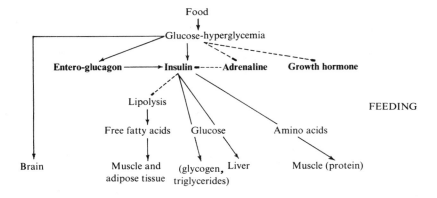

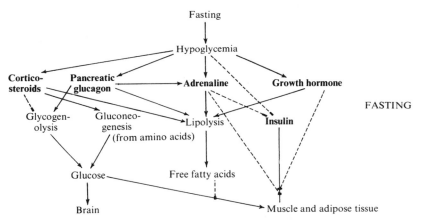

Fig. 5.7. The role of hormones in intermediary metabolism during *feeding* and *fasting*.

Solid line, stimulation or increase; dashed line, inhibition or decrease. (Modified from Foà, 1972.)

glucose and fatty acids. Amino acids can be transformed to glucose in the liver. The large amounts of propionate absorbed by ruminants can also be converted to glucose. Certain amino acids can also be changed into fatty acids. These products can be more readily transformed into energy. Gluconeogenesis is stimulated by glucagon and corticosteroids. This process is especially important in ruminants that must dispose of large amounts of fatty acids. As we shall see, gluconeogenesis is also fundamental for homeostasis during fasting in other species. The over-all processes of oxidation of nutrients are, at least in mammals, chronically influenced by thyroid hormones but more acutely by the levels of the energy substrates themselves, as well as certain other hormones (see section on calorigenesis).

Nutrients that are not required for the immediate production of energy by the animal are stored (usually following their metabolic transformation) and can be subsequently utilized during fasting. Elevated insulin levels play a central role in this process (Fig. 5.7; see also Table 5.4). Insulin facilitates the conversion of glucose to glycogen and triglycerides, of amino acids to protein, and of fatty acids to triglycerides. Simultaneously, insulin inhibits further gluconeogenesis and lipolysis. Other hormones may impinge their influence on these processes but usually in a negative manner. For instance, a decreased secretion of glucagon and adrenaline are favorable to lipogenesis. Growth hormone favors incorporation of amino acids into proteins. Prolactin may (see later), on certain occasions, facilitate the deposition of fat in some species.

The principal energy store utilized by animals during periods of prolonged fasting is fat, though proteins can also undoubtedly be used. Obese animals fare better and survive longer. The immense fat reserves of migrating birds, fish and whales are well known. The continual food collecting and feeding activities of small mammals prior to winter hibernation is almost legendary. The total fat content of the body is normally controlled (by processes that are not understood) within limits that can be considered modest, both physiologically and esthetically. In man, it has recently been suggested that obesity is associated with a decreased secretion of glucagon (Wise, Hendler and Felig, 1972) but this is, almost certainly, only one facet of the endocrine involvement in this process.

Preparations for migration

Animals periodically show dramatic departures from their normal limits of fat content which may be associated with their potential requirements during a period of fasting. The maximum accumulations of fat in several species of migratory birds may be equivalent to about 50% of the total body weight (Table 5.5). The normal fat levels in such birds are 3 to 10% of their body weight. This fat is contained in various parts of the body but especially in cutaneous and subcutaneous sites and can be deposited very rapidly in one to two weeks. The timing of this activity appears to be the result of changes in the length of the day and so is under photoperiodic control. Depending on the season the stimulus may be an increase (as in spring) or a decrease (as in autumn) in the hours of daylight (King and Farner, 1965). Such changes in day-length are associated, in birds, with a nocturnal restlessness and activity (*Zugunruhe*), frantic feeding, development of the gonads and changes in the pituitary gland. It is thus reasonably

TABLE 5.5. *Maximum lipid deposition as indicated by fattest individual so far extracted in samples of 20 or more birds of each of seven species of seven families that undertake long overseas migratory flights in autumn.* (From Odum, 1965)

Species and family	Sex	Total wet wt (g)	Total extracted lipids (g)	Fat-free wet wt (g)	Non-fat dry wt (g)	Fat index (g fat/g non-fat dry wt)
Ruby-throated hummingbird (Trochilidae)	Female	5.65	2.59	3.06	0.74	3.50
Blackpoll warbler (Parulidae)	Male	24.08	12.29	11.79	3.59	3.42
Red-eyed virco (Virconidae)	Male	25.37	11.02	14.35	4.36	2.53
Summer tanager (Thraupidae)	Female	37.82	21.77	16.05	7.08	3.07
Swainson thrush (Turdidae)	Male	53.11	25.94	27.17	9.02	2.88
Bobolink (Ictridae)	Male	50.26	24.67	25.59	9.04	2.73
Yellow-billed cuckoo (Cuculidae)	Female	93.50	46.54	46.96	15.48	3.01

suspected that the deposition of fat in these circumstances is associated
with endocrine signals but the evidence is difficult to interpret. The problem
is probably largely the result of trying to define the role of single hormones

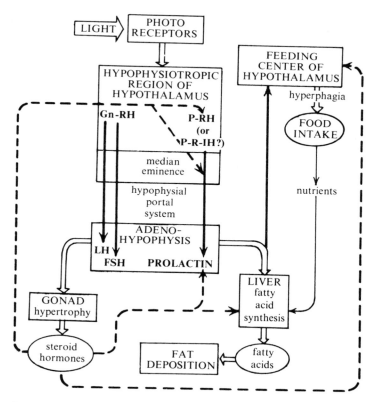

Fig. 5.8. A proposed scheme whereby nerves and hormones may mediate the
changes in avian gonadal growth and deposition of fat that occur seasonally in
response to photoperiodic stimulation. This scheme is based on observations in
white-crowned sparrows (*Zonotrichia l. gambelii*).
  The dashed lines represent possible actions of the gonadal steroid hormones
and the heavy solid lines neurotransmitter roles of the hormones (that of prolactin
on the feeding-center is uncertain). (Modified from Stetson and Erickson, 1972.)

when the interactions of several are involved. The effects of photoperiodic
stimulation are (possibly apart from those in the pineal gland) conveyed
to the endocrine system through the pituitary gland, which is suspected of
playing an early role in the preparations for migration.
  Prolactin, when injected, can accelerate deposition of fat in birds (white-

crowned sparrows, *Zonotrichia leucophrys gambelii*) whether they have been subjected to photostimulation or not (Meier and Farner, 1964). Such injections must be given at certain times of the day and they act optimally at times related to the cyclical release of thyroxine and corticosteroids (Meier, 1970; Meier *et al.*, 1971). Such an effect of prolactin has also been observed in teleost fishes, amphibians and reptiles. The temporal relationship of gonadal development and fat deposition in birds led to the early proposal that these may be related (Rowan gonadal hypothesis) and this (despite earlier contradictions) has recently been, at least partly, confirmed (Stetson and Erikson, 1972). When white-crowned sparrows are castrated *prior* to photostimulation the hyperphagia and fat deposition do not occur. A proposed scheme that relates some of these endocrine events is shown in Fig. 5.8. It has also been suggested that reduced levels of glucagon may promote fat deposition in migratory birds (Goodridge, 1964), an observation that is consistent with the more recent suggestions as to the causes of obesity in man.

Knowledge of the endocrine processes controlling deposition of fat is, despite a widespread applicability in animal and human nutrition, not well understood. It seems to involve several hormones but these, and the pattern of their effects may differ depending on the species, the diet and the physiological occasion.

Endocrines and fasting

Hormones and the utilization of stored nutrients

During fasting, the animal is dependent on its endogenous stores of nutrients for energy. These must be converted to substrates that can be metabolized, principally glucose, fatty acids and ketone bodies, the levels of which are increased by a low insulin and a high glucagon level in the plasma (Table 5.4).

During periods of fasting that last only a few hours, or in times of sudden acute need, such as for violent action, mobilization of glycogen stores in the liver and muscles may be sufficient. This transformation is increased by the action of glucagon (on the liver) and, on occasions, also catecholamines (Fig. 5.7).

During longer periods of time, when no food is available, the liver and muscle stores of glycogen are usually maintained. Fatty acids are mobilized from triglycerides in adipose tissue and are used to provide energy. This may be a direct process involving β-oxidation or result in the formation of ketone bodies. These latter substances, acetoacetate, β-hydroxybutyrate and acetone, are produced mainly in the liver but in ruminants they are also formed by the rumen epithelium and the mammary glands. Fatty acid mobilization is favored (see Table 5.4 and Fig. 5.7) by low insulin levels, resulting from hypoglycemia as well as elevated glucagon concentrations. Catecholamines and growth hormone can also promote lipolysis. The common denominator mediating this lipid mobilization may be increased levels of the tissue's cyclic AMP. Glucose is also necessary for adequate utilization of ketone bodies in the citric acid cycle while certain tissues, especially brain, have a specific requirement for glucose. This substrate is obtained during starvation, as a result of gluconeogenesis, from certain amino acids as well as from propionate and glycerol. Gluconeogenesis is stimulated by glucagon and corticosteroids. As a prerequisite, amino acids must be mobilized and proteolysis is favored by low insulin levels and is promoted by corticosteroids.

While fat is the main source of energy during prolonged fasting in vertebrates, considerable protein catabolism also occurs and indeed, in the more terminal stages of starvation, may be inevitable. This protein utilization may be more important in poikilotherms. During estivation in amphibians and lungfishes, very high concentrations of urea accumulate in the body fluids (McClanahan, 1967; Smith, 1930) indicating substantial protein catabolism (Janssens, 1964). These animals tolerate high urea concentrations (as much as 600 mM) in their body fluids; levels that would be fatal to a mammal. Aquatic species that form ammonia instead of urea would be more readily able to excrete the toxic by-products of protein catabolism during fasting. In addition, mammals that hibernate and birds that migrate are subjected to circumstances that are often associated with limited supplies of water and may (apart from the associated muscle wasting) find excessive protein catabolism an added disadvantage, because of the problem of extra nitrogen excretion.

Stored nutrients may be mobilized and oxidized, to produce energy at greatly contrasting speeds. A bird during a non-stop migratory flight of up to 2400 km may use up almost its entire fat reserves in 40 to 60 hours (Odum, 1965). Hibernating and estivating animals, on the other hand, have relatively small energy requirements so that the rate of utilization of stored nutrients is much slower than usual. No definitive information is available about the catabolic role of the endocrines in these circumstances.

Migration of fishes

High levels of corticosteroids are present in the plasma of migrating and spawning salmon and rainbow trout (Robertson *et al.*, 1961) and it seems likely that they facilitate gluconeogenesis. These steroids are also released in response to exercise in the trout, *Salmo gairdneri* (Hill and Fromm, 1968) and stress in the sockeye salmon (Fagerlund, 1967). Such stimuli could be occurring during migration. As described earlier, injected glucagon fails to increase free fatty acid levels in the blood of eels, while catecholamines are ineffective in the goldfish. It is nevertheless possible that they may be effective in migrating fishes. An increase in the activity of the thyroid gland occurs in migrating Atlantic salmon (*Salmo salar*) (Leloup and Fontaine, 1960) and may facilitate fasting metabolism.

Lampreys, *Lampetra fluviatilis* (on histological evidence), appear to have an active thyroid gland at the beginning of their breeding migration from the sea into rivers (Pickering, 1972), although this activity declines as sexual maturity is approached. Normally the digestive tract degenerates during the migration but this can be prevented if the lampreys are gonadectomized (Larsen, 1969). It thus appears that gonadal hormones, either by direct action, or possibly due to a change via a negative-feedback mechanism in the pituitary or hypothalamus can influence tissue catabolism in migrating lampreys. Unlike in salmon, corticosteroids cannot be detected in the plasma of the migrating sea lamprey, *Petromyzon marinus* (Weisbart and Idler, 1970), so that their gluconeogenic role in migrating cyclostomes is doubted.

Bird migration

We can only speculate about the effects of hormones in the metabolism of birds during migratory flights. Glucagon has a potent effect in increasing free fatty acid levels in the plasma of birds so that this hormone, which is present in substantial quantities in the avian Islets of Langerhans, may be important on these occasions. The potent effects of injected vasotocin in elevating free fatty acid concentrations in the plasma of pigeons are also interesting. This hormone can be released in response to dehydration and stress, which are situations that may be expected to occur in migrating birds, so that (as suggested by John and George, 1973) its lipolytic action could be useful during migratory flight.

Hibernation in mammals

It has been suggested that there is decline in the activity of the endocrine glands during hibernation (Hoffman, 1964) but there is little information about the direct role of hormones during this period of dormancy or in its 'onset' and 'awakening'. Hibernation is prevented by an active reproductive system and thyroid gland but the adrenal may play a more active role.

It is suspected that both the catecholamine hormones and the corticosteroids may contribute to the events of hibernation but this is largely hypothetical and based on the known effects that such hormones have on intermediary metabolism and calorigenesis. In a hibernating rodent, the woodchuck *Marmota monax*, the rates of urinary excretion of catecholamines have been shown to be lowest in January, just prior to the onset of hibernation, and they may reach their highest values just before awakening in April (Wenberg and Holland, 1973). Metabolites of steroid hormones are excreted at very low levels early in hibernation but these rise steadily towards the time of arousal in spring. Indeed, it has been found that the injection of a corticosteroid hormone, cortisol, into a monotreme, the echidna *Tachyglossus aculeatus*, can delay or prevent the onset of the hibernation (referred to as 'torpor') that these animals may assume when they are exposed to low environmental temperatures during fasting (Augee and McDonald, 1973). It has, in addition, been observed that echidnas pass into torpor far more readily following adrenalectomy (an operation which they are well able to survive!). The rate of metabolism, blood glucose concentration and body temperature all decline in hibernating echidnas and it appears the gluconeogenic actions of corticosteroids may oppose this. It seems likely, however, that such a process must continue during hibernation or after adrenalectomy, albeit at reduced levels, in order to mobilize nutrients that are necessary to sustain the life of the animal.

Estivation in African lungfish

Estivation may last two to three years in African lungfish. During this phase of its life cycle *Protopterus annectens* only secretes thyroid hormone at about 1/75 of the rate that it does in its normal free-swimming state (Leloup and Fontaine, 1960). The TSH content of the pituitary is similar in both conditions so that the release of TSH may be inhibited by estivation. Godet (1961) has suggested that an inhibition of the adenohypophysis precedes estivation in these lungfish. It was found that when the pituitary was removed after estivation had commenced there was no effect on the subsequent torpor. An intact pituitary gland was, however, indispensable for the fishes' survival on emergence from estivation. Many amphibians also estivate during periods of drought, but their endocrinology does not appear to have been investigated on these occasions.

Hormones and lactation

Lactation, or the secretion of nutrients by the mammary glands, in order to feed the young, is an activity confined to the mammals. Somewhat analogous processes, such as the formation of pigeons' milk by the crop-sac of some birds, can occur in other vertebrates.

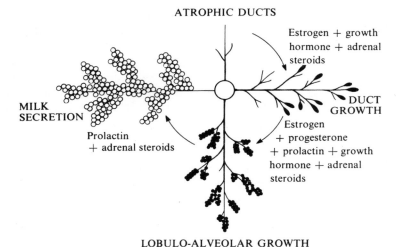

ATROPHIC DUCTS

Estrogen + growth
hormone + adrenal
steroids

MILK
SECRETION

DUCT
GROWTH

Prolactin
+ adrenal steroids

Estrogen
+ progesterone
+ prolactin + growth
hormone + adrenal
steroids

LOBULO-ALVEOLAR GROWTH

Fig. 5.9. The role of hormones in the growth of the mammary gland and the secretion of milk. In this instance the example is the *laboratory rat*, but in other species different combinations of hormones (called the 'lactogenic complex') may be required (see text). (Based on Lyons, 1958, from Cowie, 1972.)

Milk is a nutrient solution, the composition of which differs depending on the species and the duration of the lactation. (For a complete account see Cowie and Tindal, 1971.) It contains fats, carbohydrates and proteins as well as minerals and other essential dietary items. The fat content of milk varies from 0.3 % in the rhinoceros to 49 % in porpoises; the lactose from 0.3 % in whales to 7 % in man and the protein from 1.2 % in man to 13 % in whales. The contained energy is equivalent to 500 kcalories/kg milk in the rhinoceros to 2773 kcalories/kg in the reindeer (Kleiber, 1961). The nutritional requirements of the mother may thus be considerable.

The mammary glands, like adipose tissue, can make triglycerides and also lactose. The proteins present are largely synthesized by the mammary tissue though some, such as serum albumin and immunoglobulins, are transferred directly from the plasma. In order to deliver these nutrients efficiently to the young, the mammary tissue differentiates into a complex system of alveoli and ducts. These processes, morphological differentiation and the secretion of nutrients, are regulated by several hormones so that the mammary glands afford an example of the multiple actions that hormones may have on a tissue.

A diagram of the arrangement of the mammary gland tissues and a summary of the activities of hormones on them is given in Fig. 5.9. The milk is secreted into the alveoli and passes down the duct prior to release from the teat or nipple. Experiments on animals with an intact pituitary, but with the ovaries removed, indicate that development of the alveoli is influenced largely by estrogens and progesterone while the duct system responds principally to estrogens. The neurohypophysial hormone, oxytocin, is released (see Chapter 4) as a result of a suckling-stimulus on the nipple. It contracts the myoepithelial cells that surround the alveoli, and results in milk let-down (the *galactobolic effect*). Initiation of the secretion of milk (*lactogenesis*) by the alveoli is dependent on prolactin which is released during parturition and as a result of suckling. While these hormones are directly essential for the activities mentioned, adequate circulating levels of other hormones, including thyroid hormones, corticosteroids and growth hormone, are also necessary. The experiments that demonstrate this are complex ones and involve restoration of the growth and function of the mammary glands in animals from which the pituitary and the ovaries have been removed. No single hormone appears to be effective on one function but combinations involving ACTH or corticosteroids, prolactin, growth hormone, thyroid hormones, estrogens and progesterone are necessary. The metabolic effects of the absence of certain of these hormones appear to inhibit or limit the actions of other hormones that act more directly.

Species differences are common. In the hypophysectomized rabbit, lactogenesis can be initiated by a single hormone, prolactin. In hypophysectomized goats, prolactin plus growth hormone plus corticosteroid plus tri-iodothyronine are required, while in rats and mice corticotrophin plus prolactin are needed. Some strains of mice also require growth hormone. When a group of hormones is needed for normal lactation (the more usual situation) this is referred to as a '*lactogenic complex*'.

The maintenance of lactation is called *galactopoiesis* and the hormonal requirements of this are often difficult to distinguish from lactogenesis. Species differences again exist. Generally, the following occurs: removal of the ovaries once lactation has been established does not influence lactation; indeed estrogens, and estrogens plus progesterone, are often used to terminate, or dry-up, the secretion of milk. Removal of either the thyroid, adrenals, parathyroids or the endocrine pancreas depresses lactation. The administration of thyroid hormones has a well-established effect in increasing milk production in dairy cows. At one time this treatment was seriously considered as a method to increase the yield of milk. The role of such hormones in maintaining lactation probably reflects their roles in maintaining the metabolic transformations of energy substrates in cells generally. It is not unexpected that such metabolic processes are necessary, directly and indirectly, for the adequate secretion of milk by the mammary tissue.

At the cellular level three important stages in the process of lactation have been distinguished (Baldwin, 1969; Turkington, 1972). These events (usually based on *in vitro* observations in rats and mice) are as follows:

(i) Mammary cell proliferation. The increase in the rate of division of the mammary tissue cells has been shown *in vitro* to depend on the presence of insulin and is enhanced by estradiol-17β. This cell division is manifested as an increase in DNA synthesis. Progesterone also assists this process and may direct, or organize, it in such a manner as to allow the orderly development of the duct system.

(ii) Differentiation of the mammary cells, which includes the acquisition of the enzymes necessary for the formation of the constituents of the milk. This requires (*in vitro*) the presence of insulin, cortisol and prolactin (placental somatomammotrophin is also effective). Prolactin initiates transcriptional processes and the formation of messenger RNA which appears to mediate the formation of milk proteins and the enzyme lipoprotein lipase (Zinder *et al.*, 1974). The latter regulates the uptake of triglycerides by the mammary tissue.

(iii) The utilization (or expression) of the alveolar cells' capacity to produce milk protein, triglycerides and lactose. Little is known about this process but in order to function optimally an adequate and continuing complement of hormones is necessary.

The mammalian lactational process is a phylogenetically novel one that has arisen in the later stages of vertebrate evolution. Its complexities, not surprisingly, necessitate coordination by the endocrines. The hormones involved probably existed prior to the mammary gland itself so that an evolution of their role in the body has occurred in this case. Certain processes occur in vertebrates which are analogous to mammalian lactation. The formation of pigeon's milk, by the crop-sac of pigeons and doves, with which they feed their young, is an example. This process, which involves the proliferation of the crop-sac epithelium, can be induced by prolactin. In certain teleost fishes, mucous secretion from the skin can be stimulated by prolactin (see Bern and Nicoll, 1968). In one such fish (*Symphysodon*), the newly hatched young have been observed to feed off the surface of the parental fish, suggesting another possible 'lactational' role for prolactin.

Storage of nutrients in the egg

The early development of the young is supported by nutrients stored in the egg. These materials may be sufficient for the complete embryonic development of the young (megalecithal eggs) or only support more limited differentiation (alecithal) that leads to the emergence of a free-swimming larva. An even more limited growth may precede viviparous development in the uterus. Alecithal eggs are usually confined to species that develop in a watery environment. Megalecithal eggs are common in terrestrial species as well as certain fishes including the Agnatha and Chondrichthyes (see Fig. 5.10).

Estrogens and progesterone may play important roles in the growth and maturation of the egg which are summarized in Fig. 9.17.

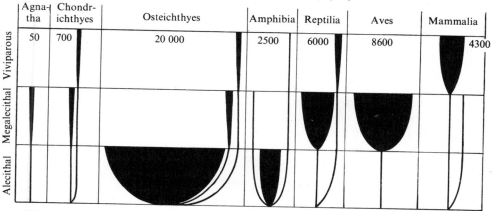

Fig. 5.10. A diagrammatic representation of the relative frequency of the occurrence in the vertebrates of megalecithal eggs (with large amounts of stored yolk) and alecithal eggs. Alecithal eggs are confined to aquatic species; the production of eggs with small amounts of yolk in terrestrial vertebrates necessitates the viviparous habit which is also included. It should, however, be noted that megalecithal eggs and viviparity also occur among the aquatic fishes and amphibians. Numbers = no. of species. (From Browning, 1969, based on a drawing by H. A. Bern.)

The 'white' of the megalecithal eggs contains water, salts and proteins, including avidin, which, as we have seen, can be formed by glands in the chicken oviduct as a result of stimulation by progesterone. Progestins may also stimulate the secretion of the jelly from the oviductal glands that surrounds alecithal eggs, as in amphibians.

The yolk of eggs contains most of the nutrients required for the predicted development of the young. In the domestic fowl, about 50% of this is composed of fats and proteins. The number of eggs produced successively in one period of time (the clutch) varies considerably in different species but 20 to 30 are not uncommon in birds and reptiles. Under domestic conditions, a chicken may produce 200 to 300 eggs in a year. Even species that produce alecithal eggs must contribute considerable amounts of nutrients to the eggs, especially as such species often produce many hundreds of such eggs.

The deposition of the yolk is called *vitellogenesis*. Estrogens can promote the appearance in the blood of elevated concentrations of calcium and phosphorus, and certain proteins and lipids. These usually exist as a single calcium-binding phospholipoprotein, though in birds two components, phosphovitin and lipovitellin, can be distinguished. These phospholipoproteins (also called vitellogenin) are formed in the liver in response to stimulation by estrogen. They are then carried in the blood to the ovaries for transfer to, and deposition in, the eggs. This effect of estrogens is very specific (it is not seen when other steroid hormones are injected) and is prominent in oviparous species (Urist and Scheide, 1961; Urist, 1963; Urist *et al.*, 1972). The vitellogenic effect of estrogens is absent in mammals, cyclostomes and chondrichthyeans but is seen in teleosts, lungfishes, amphibians, reptiles and birds. The situation in the Monotremata (oviparous mammals) does not seem to have been explored. Apart from their vitellogenic effects estrogens exert remarkably similar actions in all vertebrates but hormones may acquire special roles of which this effect is a good example for the estrogens.

Hormones and growth and development

The process of growth may place considerable nutritional demands on an animal. The development of the young is associated with rapid increases in the mass of the body and thus has special nutritional requirements. The development of the young *in utero* also contributes indirectly to the mother's nutritional requirements. In addition, growth processes also occur continually in the bodies of adult animals and involve cyclical changes in the reproductive organs as well as the replacement of cells, due to age and general wear and tear. These growth processes principally involve the formation of proteins (and thus a positive nitrogen balance) and phospholipids. The contribution of minerals, especially calcium and phosphorus, should not be forgotten.

Like lactation, successful growth requires the harmonious regulatory activities of several hormones. Those more directly involved in development and maturation of the young are growth hormone and the thyroid hormones. Androgens and estrogens also contribute to the control of the maturation of the reproductive system and, in adults, help maintain it and regulate the cyclical changes in these tissues. Androgens, as we have seen, may also exert anabolic effects and promote protein formation in muscle. A hormonal background of adequate insulin, that promotes conversion of amino acids to protein, and a not over-adequate supply of corticosteroids, that facilitate proteolysis, is also important.

The process of growth consists of (*a*) an increase in the number of cells;

(*b*) an enlargement in their size; (*c*) increases in their complexity and differentiation; (*d*) replacement of cells as a result of loss due to age, wear and tear, injury or as part of morphogenetic differentiation as in (*c*).

Growth hormone produces a striking increase in cell DNA, indicating an increase in cell number. Cell size is also increased. This effect is manifested in all tissues, including cartilage, and leads to the building of bone. Growth hormone promotes the accumulation of amino acids across the cell membrane and enhances the formation of messenger-RNA which determines the formation of specific proteins, which presumably contribute to the structural elements as well as cell growth and reproduction. Growth hormone also promotes the incorporation of sulfate into cartilage. This observation led to the discovery that growth hormone was not necessarily acting directly on the tissues (see Daughaday, 1971). The incorporation of sulfate into cartilage was found to be due to a protein present in the plasma which was initially called 'sulfation factor'. In addition, this factor also promotes the incorporation of uridine into RNA and thymidine into DNA in the tissue. The formation of this intermediary is promoted in the liver by growth hormone and it has been renamed *somatomedin* (Daughaday *et al.*, 1972). It seems likely that somatomedin also mediates other effects of growth hormone. Somatomedin persists for a longer time in the plasma than growth hormone which thus need not be released continually in order to exert its effects. It is also interesting that somatomedin has a stronger effect in tissues from weanling rats than from fetal and old rats. The last two are known to be unresponsive *in vivo* to such effects of growth hormone (Heins, Garland and Daughaday, 1970). The widespread actions of growth hormone in mammals, birds, reptiles, amphibians and teleost fish have already been described (Chapter 3).

As indicated earlier (Chapter 3) prolactin and growth hormone share a number of activities, a property that may reflect their structural similarities. It is therefore not surprising to find that in some species injected prolactin may influence growth. This effect of injected mammalian prolactin has been observed in the pigeon, the lizard, *Lacerta s. sicula*, and tadpoles of the frogs *Rana temporaria* and *R. pipiens* (Bates, Miller and Garrison, 1962; Licht and Hoyer, 1968; Frye, Brown and Snyder, 1972). Metamorphosis in the larval amphibians is prevented by injected prolactin. It is uncertain if such effects reflect another physiological role of prolactin or are merely due to similarities between its structure and activity to that of the homologous growth hormones.

Apart from their calorigenic effects in homeotherms, thyroid hormones play an important role in the body, contributing to an optimal and orderly growth and development. This is most apparent in mammals that lack sufficient thyroid hormone during postnatal development. The thyroid hormones are especially necessary for adequate development of the brain, skeletal system and reproductive organs. The disease of cretinism that results from insufficient thyroid hormones in man during infancy has been observed in other domestic animals. In newborn rats deprived of thyroid hormone, it has been shown that development of the brain is slowed but the same number of cells (DNA content) appear to develop though they remain smaller (higher concentration of DNA) than in the normal rat. The rate of multiplication of the cells is reduced in thyroid deficiency. The smaller size of the cells is reflected in neural tissue by a reduction in the development of the nerve-endings while the incorporation of amino acids into proteins is diminished (Balazs *et al.*, 1971). When tadpoles are deprived of thyroid hormone, they continue to grow but fail to metamorphose. On the other hand, if tadpoles are fed thyroid hormone they undergo an earlier metamorphosis. This latter transformation is associated with the acquisition of many adult characteristics along with the induction of certain enzymes that mediate reabsorption of the tail. The thyroid is also necessary for the maturation of the gonads in some teleost fish (Sage, 1973).

The morphological effects of thyroid hormones in mammals are also not strictly analogous to their morphogenetic effects in amphibians. Myant (1971) suggests that amphibian metamorphosis may have arisen as a special adaptation in which differentiation is suppressed during a period of rapid growth, and is then stimulated under the influence of thyroxine (see Chapter 9). The morphogenetic effect of thyroid hormones in amphibians has no true analogy in other vertebrates and appears to be a specialization. Thyroid hormones, however, appear to have a basic ability to stimulate protein synthesis in cells of homeotherms and possibly some poikilotherms like tadpoles. Such a basic effect, if exerted at strategic sites in the cell, could support multiple, different actions of the hormones on cells. The thyroid hormones thus may potentially be able to assume various functions and be especially suited to their proposed 'permissive' role in cellular processes; at least in homeotherms and amphibian tadpoles.

Conclusions

The processes of nutrition, whether involving the digestion of food materials or their transformation, storage and utilization, following absorption, or the feeding and growth of the young are very dependent on the actions of hormones. It is especially notable that several hormones are usually involved in such processes ('multihormonal' effects) probably more often than elsewhere, and these excitants have widespread effects both with respect to the types of tissues that they act upon and the nature of the underlying biochemical events that they influence. Such ubiquitous endocrine effects are well integrated with each other by a series of feedback controls that involve the levels of metabolites and the hormones themselves. The latter indeed often directly influence each others' release. The hormonal pathways that function, or predominate, in the control of nutrition of a particular species seem to depend more on its feeding habits and the stage of its life cycle, than on its phylogenetic origins. This probably reflects the common biochemical pathways underlying nutritional processes in all vertebrates. The principal species' differences in responsiveness to hormones are quantitative ones, though when novel processes have evolved, such as lactation in mammals, this has been accompanied by adaptations of the roles of hormones to integrate the new systematic features.

6. Hormones and calcium metabolism

Calcium is vital for animal life. In vertebrates, this divalent ion is present at various sites, including the body fluids, structural parts of the cell (especially the endoplasmic reticulum), and in most species it is also a major component of the endoskeleton. The outer shell of the eggs of birds and many reptiles also consists principally of calcium. The physiological role of calcium appears to be the result of a rather unique set of physicochemical properties. In aqueous solution, calcium can exist in a soluble form, which is important for its mobility in the body, and yet, equally essential to its role, many of its salts, including phosphates and carbonates, have a low solubility so that a physicochemical equilibrium may exist between its solid and aqueous forms. The quantity of calcium free in solution is thus restricted in the presence of certain anions. In addition, such relatively insoluble salts in certain of their crystalline forms, principally calcium phosphate and calcium carbonate, can contribute to the mechanical support and stability of biological structures. Calcium also has a ready propensity to associate with, and combine to, proteins. Such combinations are seen in the body fluids, where a considerable portion of the calcium is bound to serum proteins, and in cells, where it contributes to their structural stability by helping maintain essential ionic bridges at vital points in protein molecules; thus, when tissues are placed in calcium-free solutions they tend to disintegrate and the cells swell and fall apart.

Calcium plays an essential role in coordinating many events in the body that may reflect those general properties described above. Calcium stabilizes membranes and this effect can be seen in the hyperactivity of nerve fibers placed in solutions with low calcium concentrations. Such instability and the repetitive electrical depolarization of the nerve cell membrane result in tetanic contractions of the muscles they supply. Muscle contraction requires the presence of calcium; when released from the sarcoplasmic reticulum within the cell, calcium couples the initiating electrical depolarization of the cell membrane to those processes that initiate changes in the contractile proteins. In a comparable manner, calcium is necessary for the ultimate initiation of many endocrine events such as the release of hormones (see Chapter 4, p. 148) and the responses of their definitive effectors.

The availability of calcium to animals varies considerably, depending on the environment and their diet. The physiological need for calcium may also vary a great deal. Young, growing animals, especially those that are forming large amounts of bony tissue, have much greater requirements than adults. The latter, however, periodically need more calcium for reproductive processes, as during pregnancy and lactation in mammals, and in birds and reptiles, the production of large cleidoic eggs that are covered with a shell of calcium carbonate. Even fishes and amphibians that do not have cleidoic eggs, require substantial amounts of calcium for the production of their eggs. The availability of calcium in the environment varies a great deal. The concentration in sea-water is even higher than that in the body fluids of vertebrates but in fresh water, little calcium is usually present (Table 6.1); thus vertebrates living in the sea or fresh water may be expected to experience very different problems with respect to the availability of this ion. Terrestrial animals obtain most of their calcium from their diet which may include appreciable amounts obtained from

TABLE 6.1. *Calcium and phosphate in serum and in the environment.* (From Copp, 1969)

Environment and representative species	Total Ca (mmole/liter)	Ionic Ca²⁺ (mmole/liter)	Total P (mmole/liter)
Environment			
Pacific Ocean	10.0 ± 0.1	10.0	0.00
Brackish water	2–5	–	–
Lake Huron	0.9 ± 0.1	0.9 ± 0.1	0.003
Marine invertebrate			
Nephrops	11.95	–	–
Cyclostomes			
Hagfish, *Eptatretus stoutii*	5.4 ± 0.1	3.0 ± 0.4	1.5 ± 0.2
Lamprey, *Petromyzon marinus* (from fresh water)	2.60 ± 0.1	1.74 ± 0.2	1.3 ± 0.1
Chimaeroid			
Ratfish, *Hydrolagus colliei*	4.8 ± 0.3	–	2.2 ± 0.4
Elasmobranchs			
Marine shark, *Carcharhinus leucas*	4.50 ± 0.9	3.10 ± 0.4	2.0 ± 0.6
Freshwater shark, *C. leucas nicaraquensis*	3.0 ± 0.2	1.7 ± 0.1	1.6 ± 1.7
Teleost			
Marine, *Paralabrax clathratus*	3.2 ± 0.8	2.0 ± 0.9	2.0 ± 0.2
Freshwater, *Megalops atlanticus*	2.5 ± 0.2	1.8 ± 0.2	1.2 ± 0.4
Mammal			
Man, *Homo sapiens*	2.32 ± 0.08	1.15	–

certain drinking waters. In times of extra need for calcium, vertebrates, especially birds during egg-laying, may consume inorganic calcium-containing minerals, such as the so-called 'grit' fed to domestic fowl. The ultimate acquisition of calcium, whether from the external bathing solutions, drinking water or food, takes place principally from the gut. Absorption across the intestine is regulated in relation to the animal's needs.

The calcium that is not absorbed from the intestine, either due to a lack of physiological need for it, or, if it is present in chemical combination that makes this process impossible, is excreted in the feces. Additional amounts of calcium are also excreted by the kidney in the urine. Urinary losses of calcium should not only be viewed as an excretory mechanism for ridding the body of an excess of this ion but also as part of an unavoidable loss that results from the formation of urine. The calcium that is not bound to plasma proteins is filtered across the renal glomerulus but most of this ion is subsequently reabsorbed by the renal tubules. This conservation is less effective in the presence of a high plasma calcium concentration so that extra amounts of this ion are excreted in the urine. Conversely a hypocalcemia results in an increased renal reabsorption of calcium which is accompanied by an increased phosphate excretion. The excretion of calcium and phosphate in the urine is thus subject to physiological control.

The bony skeleton possessed by most vertebrates plays a central role in calcium metabolism. Calcium phosphate salts are an integral part of this structure and make the principal contribution to skeletal rigidity. Not all vertebrates, however, have a bony calcareous skeleton; it is absent in the cyclostome and chondrichthyean fishes that have a more elastic cartilaginous skeleton in which little calcium is deposited. In the bony vertebrates, the skeleton is the predominant quantitative site of calcium in the body though this should not be taken to reflect its relative importance, as its presence is equally vital to the soft tissues. The calcium in the bones and that in the body fluids and soft tissues exists in equilibria with each other. Two processes are involved in this: first, there is a relatively static *physicochemical* equilibrium that reflects the solubility (and insolubility) of the calcium salts in the body and which only results in small exchanges of calcium; second, the major exchanges of calcium between the bones and body fluids are due to a *dynamic*, physiologically mediated equilibrium that results from the activities of cells in the bone; the *osteoblasts, osteocytes* and *osteoclasts*.

Bone, despite its mineral-like appearance, is a living tissue. Some fishes, however, possess acellular bone which, once formed, is much less labile than the cellular-type of bone that is characteristic of the tetrapods. Cellular bone has a microscopic honeycomb-like appearance due to the presence of numerous small chambers, or lacunae, each of which contains an osteocyte bone cell. Numerous fine channels (canaliculi) radiate from the lacunae to the surrounding mineralized tissue and these provide a pathway through which the bone fluids and the dendritic-like extensions of the osteocytes maintain contact with the tissue. The osteocytes act as sentinels controlling local mineral exchanges. Bone also has an extensive network of blood vessels through which the supply of blood can be regulated according to its metabolic needs. Exchanges of bone minerals take place at any of the bone's free surfaces; the canaliculi, at the inner and outer borders of the limb bones (periosteum and endosteum), the channels through which the blood vessels pass and special tunnels, called 'cutting cones', which are excavated in the tissue. Minerals are principally mobilized from the cortical regions of the shafts of the long bones but a labile store also occurs in the medullary regions of the bones of birds where it is an especially important store during the egg-laying cycle.

Bone is formed by the osteoblast bone cells. These cells extrude collagen which is laid down as a matrix into which calcium, phosphate and some carbonate are subsequently deposited (called 'accretion'). It is possible that the osteoblasts also play some direct role in the process of deposition but this is not essential. Minerals are deposited as two phases, initially as an amorphous form of calcium phosphate which is subsequently changed to a structurally stronger, crystallized form resembling the mineral apatite. The osteoblast, after surrounding itself with such tissue, then is transformed into an osteocyte. The mineralized bone is not necessarily a permanent structure but can be modified and remodelled and the calcium and phosphate may be returned to the tissue fluids. This process of 'resorption' occurs more readily from the amorphous than the crystallized phase but the latter can also be broken down. Resorption of minerals from bone is associated with an increase in the activity of the osteoclasts, and the osteocytes are also involved. The process of resorption involves the secretion of enzymes by the bone cells and these facilitate the dissolution of the minerals. This process can be regulated.

Physiological control of calcium levels in vertebrates can thus be affected at three major sites: the intestine, by the control of absorption; the kidney, by the regulation of reabsorption from the glomerular filtrate, and the bones which act as a storage site for calcium phosphate. The very important role of bone in calcium homeostasis cannot be overemphasized but it should be recalled that this tissue is not present in all vertebrates. The coordination of the exchanges of calcium at these three sites is under the control of hormones. These are parathormone, from the parathyroids (which are absent in fishes), and calcitonin from the thyroid 'C' cells and the ultimobranchial bodies. To these hormones can be added another (or others) that are derived from vitamin D_3. These are 25-hydroxycholecalciferol and 1,25-dihydroxycholecalciferol. It is of further interest that removal of the corpuscles of Stannius that are present in certain bony fishes (see Chapter 2) results in an elevation of plasma calcium levels, suggesting that these tissues may also secrete a hormone that regulates calcium metabolism in such fish. Estrogens aid mobilization of medullary bone in birds during egg-laying.

A historical note about the discovery of parathormone and calcitonin

The discovery of the roles of the parathyroids, the mammalian thyroid 'C' cells, and the ultimobranchial bodies in the regulation of calcium metabolism is an interesting endocrine tale. It is not an example of a triumph of 'goal-oriented' research but rather that of serendipity and the persistent following up of a series of unexpected observations. Species differences in the endocrine tissues have played an important part in establishing the role of these glands.

As we have seen (Chapter 2), two types of endocrine tissues are now known to be concerned with regulating calcium metabolism. These tissues are present in close morphological association with the thyroid gland. Early efforts to remove thyroid tissue surgically in man were sometimes seen to result in tetanic muscular contractions such as are associated with low plasma calcium concentrations. Closer examination revealed that in these instances the parathyroid tissues had been removed. Subsequently other experiments in animals confirmed the importance of the parathyroids in maintaining optimal calcium levels in the blood and extracts of these glands were shown to exhibit a hypercalcemic action. Such experiments, to demonstrate the role of the parathyroids, are relatively simple in the rat, where there are two distinct bodies of parathyroid tissue present on the surface of the thyroid gland. In another favored experimental animal, the dog, substantial amounts of parathyroid tissue (as well as 'C' cells) are present, embedded deeply in the thyroid gland, so that this species is not an ideal one for such experiments and has, in the past, contributed to some misinterpretations.

As related by Hirsch and Munson (1969), the rat is an ideal species, and favorite subject, for parathyroidectomy and following this operation provides an excellent preparation for the bioassay of injected parathormone. Two methods have been used to remove the rat parathyroids. A simple surgical removal of the two glands can be performed or they can be destroyed with an electrocautery. In the 1950s, the latter procedure was more popular. When, however, a comparison, partly retrospective, of blood calcium levels following each type of operation was made, the resulting hypocalcemia was observed to be much greater following electrocautery than following surgical excision. This observation probably did not initially gain the serious attention it deserved. In retrospect it has, especially when it was observed that stimulation of the thyroid gland by the electrocautery at sites removed from the parathyroid tissue also produces a drop in blood calcium concentration. The possibility was then considered that this stimulation resulted in a release of a substance from the thyroid that exhibited a hypocalcemic action. A couple of years prior to the latter observation, D. H. Copp (see Copp *et al.*, 1962) proposed the presence of a hypocalcemic hormone in mammals that he called calcitonin, which at the time he considered to be formed by the parathyroid glands. The proposal of the presence of a new hormone was based on experimental observations involving perfusion of the thyroid–parathyroid complex in dogs. Blood containing abnormally high or low concentrations of calcium was perfused through the arteries supplying these tissues and the resulting venous outflow was then passed back into the dog and the effects on the general, systemic, plasma calcium levels were observed. It was found that, when the perfusing blood had a low calcium concentration, the outflowing blood, when passed into the dogs' general circulation, produced a hypercalcemia such as could be accounted for by the presence of parathormone. In the opposite type of experiment, in which the thyroid–parathyroid complex was perfused with blood having a high calcium concentration, the parathormone level would be expected to decline; as indeed it does. The basic question that was asked was this: Is such a decline in parathormone sufficient to bring about a decline in the calcium concentrations from hypercalcemic to normal calcium levels? In other words, while parathormone exerts a positive effect in elevating blood calcium concentration, is the mere absence of this hormone all that is needed to adjust the calcium level in a downward direction? Copp found that this was not so. While the venous perfusate from the thyroid–parathyroid complex that was exposed to high calcium concentrations produced a drop in calcium levels, when infused systemically, this hypocalcemia was much greater than could be produced after removing the glandular complex (Fig. 6.1). The implication was drawn that the response is a positive one involving the action of a hormone that has a hypocalcemic action, which Copp called calcitonin.

It was thought at first that calcitonin came from the parathyroids and, as commented upon above, in view of the intermixture of tissues that occurs in the thyroid region in dogs such an error was not surprising. Hirsch and Munson, on the basis of their experiments on rats, proposed the presence of a hypocalcemic hormone in the thyroid gland itself, which, in order to distinguish it from Copp's hormone, they called thyrocalcitonin. These two hormones are in fact identical and in mammals this hormone originates from the thyroid gland. By the choice of an appropriate species,

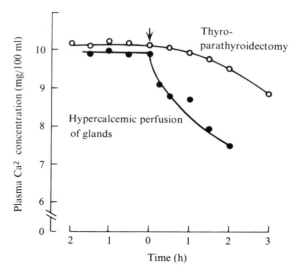

Fig. 6.1. The hypocalcemic response of dogs following perfusion of the thyroid–parathyroid gland complex with hypercalcemic solutions. In intact animals, the decline in plasma calcium concentration (at time zero) occurs promptly, but if the glandular complex is removed, the resulting hypocalcemic response is much slower. This suggests the action of a hypocalcemic hormone in the intact dogs. (From Hirsch and Munson, 1969; from data of Copp *et al.*, 1962.)

this time the pig, in which the thyroid contains no parathyroid tissue, appropriate perfusion experiments of the thyroid alone, similar to those described above, demonstrated the presence of calcitonin in the venous effluent blood.

The question then arose as to what is the site of origin of calcitonin in the thyroid tissue. Is it also produced by the same tissue that forms thyroxine? The answer is no. Calcitonin is formed by the parafollicular or 'C' cells that are present in the mammalian thyroid and this tissue is quite distinct from that which secretes thyroxine. The presence of these secretory cells was first described by E. C. Baber in 1876 but their function was unknown until recently. Radioimmunofluorescent studies, using fluorescent antibodies to calcitonin, show quite clearly that the 'C' cells form this hormone.

The 'C' cells are present in the mammalian thyroid but not that of non-mammals. Embryologically they are derived from the ultimobranchial bodies that are present in all non-mammals except the cyclostomes. An early clue to the function of this tissue was described by Rasquin and Rosenbloom in 1954, several years before the discovery of calcitonin. It was found that Mexican cave fish *Astyanax mexicanus*, when kept for prolonged periods of time in complete darkness, suffered skeletal deformities associated with an hyperplasia of the ultimobranchial bodies. Rasquin and Rosenbloom suggested that the ultimobranchials contained a parathyroid-like hormone. Extracts of the ultimobranchial bodies obtained from chickens and subsequently from many other species, including even dogfish, showed that, when injected into rats, they exhibited a hypocalcemic effect caused by the presence of a calcitonin-like hormone which was not present in the thyroid glands of these species (Copp, Cockcroft and Keuk, 1967a).

Vitamin D and 1,25-dihydroxycholecalciferol

Vitamin D has been classified as a vitamin as it is principally acquired in the diet. It exists in two forms, a synthetic one, ergocalciferol (D_2), and the natural material, cholecalciferol (D_3), which is a precursor or pro-hormone (see Fig. 3.1). Cholecalciferol is converted in the liver into 25-hydroxycholecalciferol (25-OHD_3). This steroid is further hydroxylated in the kidney into the active hormonal substance 1,25-dihydroxycholecalciferol or $1,25\text{-}(OH)_2D_3$. Production of this latter hormone, in common to other endocrine secretions, is subject to feedback control. The production of $1,25(OH)_2D_3$ by the kidney is reduced during hypercalcemia and is promoted by hypocalcemia or hypophosphatemia (see Tanaka, Frank and DeLuca, 1973). An increased production of $1,25\text{-}(OH)_2D_3$ can be stimulated by parathormone, which is secreted in response to hypocalcemia, probably by decreasing the inorganic phosphorus levels in the renal cells. Low inorganic phosphorus concentrations, however, can stimulate formation of $1,25\text{-}(OH)_2D_3$ even in conditions when there is a hypercalcemia and parathyroid secretion is, presumably, depressed. Such an effect is seen in rats on low phosphorus diets and suggests that phosphorus levels in the renal cells are of basic importance in controlling the formation of $1,25\text{-}(OH)_2D_3$.

Mechanisms and interactions of parathormone, calcitonin and vitamin D on calcium metabolism

Regulation of the calcium levels in the body depends on the interactions of three effectors: bone, intestine and kidney. These respond to various combinations of parathormone, calcitonin and hormonal metabolites of vitamin D.

The initial accumulation of calcium in the body depends on its absorption across the wall of the intestine and this process is controlled by vitamin D_3. The metabolites of this steroid stimulate the active transport of calcium from the intestinal lumen to the blood. It is notable that the effect of vitamin D_3 on the intestinal calcium transport is not prompt but is delayed for several hours following its administration (see DeLuca, 1971). This delay is due to several important events that concern the vitamin's mechanism of action. Vitamin D_3, as described above, must first be converted to 1,25-dihydroxycholecalciferol, which is the active hormone. Following this activation of vitamin D_3 there is a further delay in the response that reflects a process involving the formation of RNA and protein synthesis. Actinomycin D, which prevents the formation of RNA, inhibits the effect of vitamin D_3 on the intestine. The events that occur in the intestinal mucosal cells in response to vitamin D_3 are summarized in Fig. 6.2. 1,25-Dihydroxycholecalciferol may act at a genetic locus in the cell nucleus to stimulate the

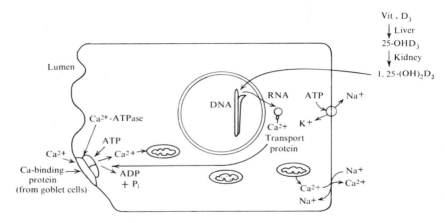

Fig. 6.2. Diagrammatic representation of the action of vitamin D in increasing calcium absorption from the intestine. 25-OHD_3 = 25-hydroxycholecalciferol; $1,25$-$(OH)_2D_3$ = 1,25-dihydroxycholcalciferol.
    The calcium is actively absorbed with the aid of a Ca-activated ATPase at the mucosal (luminal) side of the intestine, carried across the cell in the mitochondria and is then extruded from the serosal side of the cell in a process that is Na-dependent. (Modified from DeLuca, 1971.)

formation of a calcium-transport protein. This protein may be the calcium-binding protein in the microvilli or calcium-dependent ATPase that is present at the luminal boundary of the cell. This enzyme mediates the accumulation of calcium (phosphate follows this ion) which is then taken up by the mitochondria from which it is subsequently released and extruded, with the aid of a Na–K ATPase, across the opposite, serosal, side of the cell. It is considered unlikely that parathormone or calcitonin influence calcium transport across the intestine but there is some evidence to suggest that they might.[1] 1,25-Dihydroxycholecalciferol, however, certainly exerts a prominent action on calcium transport at this site and parathormone is probably acting indirectly by increasing the formation of this steroid (Garabedian *et al.*, 1974). The calcium that is absorbed into the blood may be either deposited in the bones or excreted by the kidney.

Regulation of the urinary excretion of calcium appears to be principally due to the action of parathormone. This hormone promotes phosphate excretion by inhibiting its reabsorption from the proximal renal tubule and it also reduces urinary calcium loss by promoting its reabsorption from the distal tubule (Agus *et al.*, 1973). These processes are the result of an activation of adenyl cyclase and the formation of cyclic AMP in the kidney cortex. Calcitonin and vitamin D do not appear to have direct effects on the renal control of calcium or phosphate excretion but this possibility has not been completely excluded.

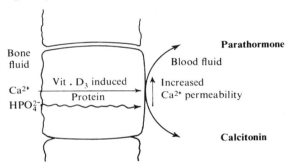

Fig. 6.3. A model for the endocrine control of calcium exchange in bone. The process of calcium resorption from bone is dependent on the presence of vitamin D_3 which apparently induces the formation of a protein that acts as a 'Ca-carrier' that transfers calcium from the bone fluids to the vicinity of the blood plasma. The final 'jump' across the cell membrane depends on its permeability to calcium and this is increased by parathormone and reduced by calcitonin. (Modified from DeLuca, Morii and Melancon, 1968.)

The bones are the sites where vitamin D_3, parathormone and calcitonin interact with each other to promote, or inhibit the resorption, into the blood, of calcium and phosphate. Parathormone stimulates resorption from the bone by an action on both the osteocytes and, principally, the osteoclasts. In vitamin D-deficient animals this effect is, however, considerably reduced or even absent. Vitamin D_3 appears to stimulate the formation of a substrate that functions as a carrier for the transfer of

---

[1] Swaminathan, Ker and Care (1974) have found that the prolonged administration of calcitonin to sheep and parathyroidectomized pigs decreases the absorption of calcium from the intestine.

calcium from the bone fluids into the osteoclasts. This accumulated calcium may then be released from the opposite side of these cells and pass into the blood. Parathormone increases the permeability of the outer membrane to calcium, an effect which, like in the kidney, is mediated by the formation of cyclic AMP. Calcitonin opposes the resorption process in bone, and is thought to oppose directly the action of parathormone on the outer cell membrane. These events are summarized in Fig. 6.3, and the over-all integrated process in bone, intestine and kidney is shown in Fig. 6.4.

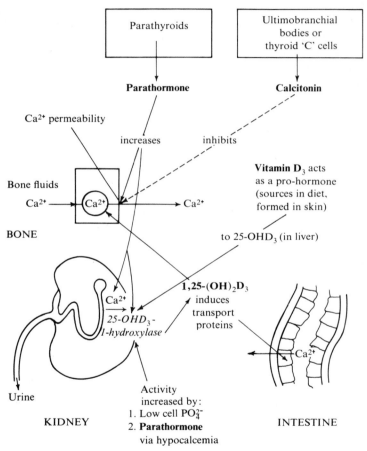

Fig. 6.4. Summary of the effects of parathormone, calcitonin and vitamin D_3 on calcium metabolism in mammals. There are three main sites of action; the kidneys, intestine and bone. The possibility that calcitonin acts on the kidney and para-thormone and/or calcitonin changes absorption of calcium across the intestine has not been completely excluded.

The hormonal regulation of calcium metabolism outlined above is based principally on experiments using mammals and, in a few instances, birds. Calcium metabolism in non-mammalian vertebrates, however, may exhibit some interesting differences. Such variations are to be expected on quantitative grounds, as in the hen during its egg-laying when relatively vast amounts of calcium are rapidly utilized. Qualitatively predictable differences arise as the parathyroids are absent in fishes while the cyclostomes appear to have neither these glands nor ultimobranchial bodies. The absence of a calcified bony skeleton in the chondrichthyeans and cyclostomes may also be expected to be a matter of some physiological consequence in calcium metabolism.

Phyletic differences in the role of hormones in calcium metabolism

Mammals

Mammalian calcium metabolism has been described in some detail in the preceding section along with some of the anatomical variations in the distribution of the parathyroid tissues. A variety of mammals including man, dog, rat, pig, sheep and goat have been examined, and the regulation of calcium levels in the blood is related to the activities of the parathyroids and the thyroid 'C' cells. The former have a vital role to play, as mammals deprived of these tissues suffer tetanic seizures because of a hypocalcemia. The rachitic effects of vitamin D-deficiency on bone are also well known. It is, however, not clear how physiologically essential the thyroid 'C' cells normally are in mammals. During calcium stress, when large increases in blood calcium levels occur, calcitonin undoubtedly facilitates the homeostatic adjustment of the concentration of this ion; however, the role of calcitonin in the regulation of the smaller and more usual changes in calcium concentration is uncertain.

This question of what is the normal physiological role of calcitonin in mammals, has been examined in young pigs (Swaminathan, Bates and Care, 1972). Removal of the thyroid results in a rapid rise (in one to two hours) of the plasma calcium concentration. This hypercalcemia is presumed to be the result of a lack of calcitonin, as it can be corrected by infusing small amounts of this hormone into the animal (Fig. 6.5). It is notable, however, that when these thyroidectomized pigs were allowed to recover, without injections of calcitonin, blood calcium levels returned to normal after 24 to 48 hours. This recovery is probably the result of an adjustment in the rate of secretion of parathormone. It has also been found that calcitonin aids, but is not essential, in regulating calcium metabolism in young, growing rats. In adult rats on a normal diet, the evidence to

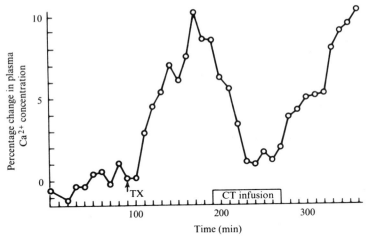

Fig. 6.5. The observed increase in plasma calcium concentration in young pigs following removal (TX) of the thyroid (and its contained calcitonin-secreting 'C' cells). Infusion of calcitonin (CT infusion) restored the calcium concentration to normal, but as soon as this ceased the levels climbed again. After about a day, the calcium levels returned to normal, probably as a result of other physiological adjustments including a decline in secretion of parathormone. (From Swaminathan *et al.*, 1972.)

indicate that calcitonin has a physiological role is contradictory (Kumar and Sturtridge, 1973; Harper and Toverud, 1973).

Thus, while calcitonin seems to contribute to the regulation of calcium levels in mammals, its role may only be vital when there is a large increase in blood calcium. In this respect, it is difficult to see how it could be essential to life, but then neither are some other hormones, including those from the neurohypophysis.

Birds

Birds, especially during their egg-laying cycle, have a very high rate of calcium turnover (Copp, 1972). A domestic hen may then utilize an amount of calcium equivalent to 10% of that in its body each day. Most of this calcium is derived directly from the food. When compared on a unit body-weight basis the domestic hen during egg-laying absorbs calcium across its intestine 100 times more rapidly than a man. Vitamin D, as in mammals, increases the rate of calcium absorption from the intestine of the domestic fowl (Fig. 6.6). At other times, such as during the nocturnal fast, calcium is also mobilized from the bones, principally from medullary bone rather than cortical bone. This distinction is of some endocrine importance as

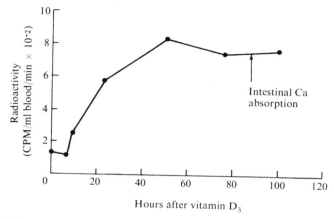

Fig. 6.6. The effect, in young chicks, of an oral dose of vitamin D$_3$ on calcium absorption from the intestine. The chicks were on a low-calcium diet. (Modified from Harmeyer and DeLuca, 1969.)

estrogens can influence the turnover of calcium in medullary bone while parathormone only acts on cortical bone.

As described in Chapter 5, estrogens facilitate the formation of a particular phospholipoprotein (vitellin) in the liver of female birds that appears in the blood and is incorporated into the yolk of the developing egg. This plasma protein binds calcium and so its presence is associated with elevated blood calcium concentrations. This interesting hypercalcemic effect of estrogens is prominent in birds as well as other oviparous 'bony' vertebrates, but is absent in mammals which may be related to their viviparity. Such a response is especially appropriate to the needs of vertebrates that produce large megalecithal eggs that contain a lot of calcium.

Both the parathyroids and the ultimobranchial bodies hypertrophy in egg-laying hens, suggesting that they are involved in regulating the calcium turnover in such birds. However, the precise contribution of each of these glands to avian calcium metabolism is still not clear.

Removal of the parathyroids results in hypocalcemia in birds and this is particularly dramatic in young, growing chicks. Injections of parathormone elevate blood calcium concentrations through an effect on cortical bone and, possibly, also by increasing intestinal absorption of this ion. The latter effect is suggested (Copp, 1972) as the response to parathormone is much less in domestic fowl on a low than on a higher calcium diet (see for instance Fig. 6.7). Injected parathormone has an extremely rapid hypercalcemic action in the laying hen (Fig. 6.7); it acts six to eight times more rapidly than in the dog (Mueller *et al.*, 1973). This rapid initial phase of the

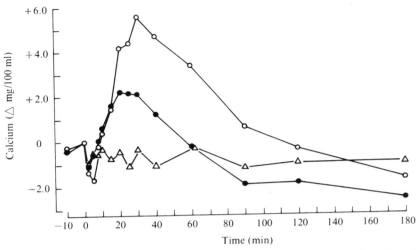

Fig. 6.7. The hypercalcemic effects of parathormone injections into female domestic fowl. The response was enhanced in those birds receiving a higher supplement of dietary calcium, suggesting that this hormone may be increasing intestinal calcium-absorption or the diet decreases basal PTH levels: o, 31 units PTH/kg, 5.00% dietary calcium; •, 31 units PTH/kg, 2.26% dietary calcium; △, control. (From Mueller *et al.*, 1973.)

response in these birds cannot readily be related to an increased activity of the osteoclasts, suggesting that a dual mechanism of action of parathormone may exist. Parathormone preparations when injected have been shown to increase the blood supply to bone and this effect could be important for the rapid and massive mobilization of calcium that occurs during egg-laying in birds. Alternatively an inhibition of the rate of accretion of calcium into bone may be involved (Kenny and Dacke, 1974).

Calcitonin has been identified in the blood of several species of birds including: pigeon, goose, duck, domestic fowl and Japanese quail (Kenny, 1971; Boelkins and Kenny, 1973). The plasma concentrations of calcitonin are much higher in these birds than normally observed in mammals and they can be increased by injecting calcium solutions (Fig. 6.8). In immature Japanese quail, the increase can be as great as 15-fold. It is, therefore, rather surprising that it has not been possible to demonstrate a physiological role of the ultimobranchial bodies in normal calcium metabolism in birds. Injections of calcitonin usually fail to elicit a hypocalcemia but it is possible that this reflects a high basal rate of calcium turnover and a rapid compensatory release of the endogenous parathormone. It thus seems possible that calcitonin could be especially important during egg-laying when it could reduce excessive oscillations in blood calcium levels and

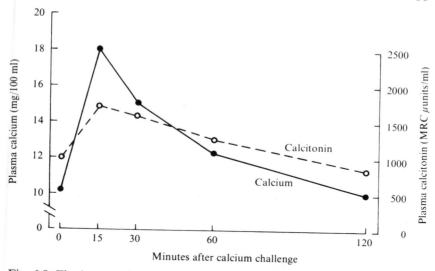

Fig. 6.8. The increase in calcitonin level in the plasma of Japanese quail given intraperitoneal injections of calcium (50 mg/kg). (Modified from Boelkins and Kenny, 1973.)

possibly even influence calcium deposition in the egg. The blood calcitonin levels, however, do not change during the egg-laying cycle of the domestic hen, nor does ultimobranchialectomy significantly influence calcium metabolism in these birds (Speers, Perey and Brown, 1970). In addition, this operation does not significantly influence the development of the skeleton in growing chickens; thus, although some people believe that the ultimobranchial bodies may have a role in regulating calcium metabolism in birds this has not been established. Possibly calcitonin has some other physiological role.

Reptiles

Parathyroidectomy (see Clark, 1972) results in a hypocalcemia and tetanic muscular contractions in several species of snakes and lizards. Such effects are, however, difficult to demonstrate in turtles though a small decline in plasma calcium concentration has been demonstrated following removal of the parathyroids of the Japanese turtle *Geoclemys reevesii* (Oguro and Tomisawa, 1972). It has also been shown, histologically, that in three species of young growing turtles parathormone increases osteocytic calcium mobilization from bones and this effect is inhibited by calcitonin (Bélanger, Dimond and Copp, 1973). It thus seems unlikely that basic differences of a phyletic origin exist between this response in saurian and chelonian reptiles. Rather the variation in the response may reflect the relative ease with which calcium can be normally mobilized and it has been suggested that the bony carapace of turtles provides a calcium store that may facilitate adjustments of the calcium in the blood.

The sites of action of parathormone in reptiles are uncertain. While bone seems to respond, the kidney may not do so. Parathormone stimulates phosphate excretion in the urine of snakes (genus *Natrix*) but neither the injection of this hormone nor parathyroidectomy could be shown to alter urinary calcium loss (Clark and Dantzler, 1972). The latter observation is in contrast to the effect of parathormone in mammals but the experiments should be extended to other reptilian groups before any generalizations as to broad phyletic differences are made.

Despite repeated attempts (on lizards, turtles and snakes), injections of calcitonin have not been shown to exhibit a hypocalcemic effect in reptiles. Although these observations are somewhat unexpected they conform with those in birds which, we are told, are descended from reptiles. Reptiles, like birds, exhibit a hypercalcemic response to injected estrogens (see Clark, 1967).

Reptiles have common phyletic affinities to mammals as well as birds so that their endocrine function is of rather special interest. The reptiles share with birds the problems associated with the production of large cleidoic eggs that in many species are covered with a calcareous shell. It should thus not be surprising to observe similarities in their calcium metabolisms. Reptiles are, however, poikilotherms and this may influence the relative importance of processes that are involved in the metabolic coordination of calcium levels as the speed of the adjustments need not be as great.

Amphibians

The amphibians have a special position with regard to our understanding of vertebrate calcium metabolism, as it is in this group that the parathyroid glands first appear on the phyletic scale. On the other hand, the ultimobranchial bodies have persisted from their piscine ancestors. The information that is available is relatively sparse and is not consistent with the special interest that these animals deserve.

Parathyroidectomy reduces plasma calcium levels in anuran amphibians and this effect seems to be the result of a decreased rate of calcium resorption from bone (see Cortelyou, 1967). Injections of parathormone have a hypercalcemic action. The effects of parathormone on renal calcium excretion are not clear as parathormone, as well as parathyroidectomy, increase urinary calcium loss. It has been suggested that the response to parathormone could be complicated because of the presence of different thresholds in the sensitivity of the kidney and bone, but further observations seem to be needed to clarify this paradox.

Parathyroidectomy has inconsistent effects in urodele amphibians (Oguro, 1973). Hypocalcemia, accompanied by tetanic convulsions, has been observed following removal of these glands in the newt, *Cyanops pyrrhogaster*. The Japanese giant salamander, *Megalobatrachus davidianus*, is, however, unresponsive to parathyroidectomy and this is reminiscent of early observations in three other species of urodeles in which this operation failed to induce tetany. The giant salamander appears to have parathormone present in its parathyroids, as extracts of these tissues have a hypercalcemic effect when injected into parathyroidectomized *C. pyrrhogaster*. It has thus been suggested that this salamander lacks a target-organ system for parathormone and this may also be so in some other urodeles.

Anuran amphibians (*Rana pipiens* has been principally studied) possess 'lime-sacs' that are novel sites for the storage of calcium in the body (see Robertson, 1969*a*, *b*), These organs are extensions of the lymph sacs and they extend caudally along the vertebral canal and emerge between the vertebrae. They contain calcium carbonate, instead of calcium phosphate as in bone, and this exhibits a mobility that includes an added storage following the administration of calcium chloride or vitamin D. Such treatment, that produces a hypercalcemia, also results in the hypertrophy of the ultimobranchial bodies (Robertson, 1968).

Removal of the ultimobranchial bodies in *Rana pipiens* results in an initial elevation in plasma calcium concentration. After about six weeks, however, a hypocalcemia occurs (Robertson, 1969*a*, *b*). It is thought that these responses are the result of an excessive mobilization of calcium from the lime sacs (as well as the bones) which subsequently become depleted. Calcitonin may promote the laying down of calcium at these two sites and it may also reduce the excretion of this ion in the urine.

The lime-sacs are also present in tadpoles where they may contribute to the release of calcium in answer to the needs of metamorphosis. Ultimo-branchialectomy in young tadpoles limits their ability to accumulate calcium in the lime sacs whether they are kept in a solution with either a high or a low calcium concentration (Table 6.2). At metamorphosis, the tadpoles in the high-calcium medium can accumulate calcium in their lime-sacs despite the absence of the ultimobranchial bodies. Ultimo-branchialectomized tadpoles in the low-calcium medium, however, fail to do this and as a result the bones of the adults are poorly ossified.

Although the number of species studied is limited the Amphibia appear to utilize parathormone, calcitonin and vitamin D_3 for the regulation of calcium metabolism. The sites of their effects, however, are not always clear but in the Anura include an interesting and novel effector, the para-vertebral lime-sacs.

TABLE 6.2. *Subjective analysis of amount of calcium carbonate in the paravertebral lime sacs of tadpoles* (Rana pipiens) *tabulated as estimated from X-rays.** (From Robertson, 1971)

Tadpole development stage	Tap water		High calcium	
	Normal	UBX	Normal	UBX
I–V	+	±	+	±
VI–X	++	±	++	±
XI–XVII	++	±	++	±
XVII–XXV	++	±	++	+++

* Concentration of calcium in tap water was 3 meq/l. High-calcium water was 15 meq/l with treatment extended for 6 weeks in all groups except in limb bud stages (I–V), which was for 2 weeks. UBX, ultimobranchialectomized; +, degree of response.

The fishes

A considerable diversity in the mechanisms for the regulation of calcium metabolism is not unexpected in the fishes. This may result from their great phyletic diversity, their ability to live in aqueous environments containing high (sea-water) or low (most freshwater) levels of calcium, the possession of either a bony or a cartilaginous skeleton and the presence or absence of the ultimobranchial bodies and the corpuscles of Stannius.

Paleontological evidence suggests that the ostracoderms, which were the jawless ancestors of modern fishes, had a bony dermal exoskeleton and, sometimes, also a bony endoskeleton that had the appearance of a tissue that functions as a store for calcium (see Copp, 1969). These fishes lived in fresh water where the calcium concentration was, presumably, low so that calcium storage in the bones may have been physiologically important. When such ancestral fishes returned to the sea, where there was an unlimited quantity of calcium, they lost their bony skeleton, and this situation persists in present day cyclostomes and chondrichthyeans. We can extend this speculation (and that is all it is!) and consider whether or not such vertebrates possessed an endocrine system for controlling calcium concentration in the body. In extant species of cyclostomes and chondrichthyeans, there is as yet no evidence for such a control mechanism. In the ancestral freshwater ostracoderms such a control could have been more important and may possibly have occurred. It is even possible that the chondrichthyean ultimobranchial bodies represent a survival from those times. The ancestral freshwater ostracoderms need not, however, have possessed such a system for controlling calcium metabolism as there is, for instance, no evidence for the endocrine control of such processes in some contemporary freshwater fishes like lampreys and the lungfishes (Urist, 1963; Urist *et al.*, 1972).

Many cyclostome fishes live in the sea but others spend their entire life in fresh water. Lampreys migrate from the sea into fresh water where they survive for several months without feeding and produce large numbers of eggs. Cyclostomes are considered to regulate calcium levels by utilizing a so-called 'open system' whereby calcium transfer takes place across the membranes of the body; such as the intestine, gills and kidney. The absence of the endocrine tissues known to influence calcium metabolism in other vertebrates, however, should not be taken to indicate a lack of such control mechanisms. Further investigation of calcium metabolism of these very interesting fish is clearly to be desired.

While vitamin D_3 has been shown to have a role in regulating calcium metabolism in many tetrapods, there is little information to indicate that it also has such a function in fishes. Vitamin D_3 is stored in the liver of teleosts (usually more in marine than freshwater fish) but little or none of this steroid has been identified in the livers of chondrichthyeans or cyclostomes (Urist, 1963). Neither administration of vitamin D_3 to sharks and rays nor vitamin D_3 and 25-hydroxycholecalciferol to the South American lungfish had any effect on their blood calcium levels (Urist, 1962; Urist *et al.*, 1972). There is thus, at present, little to indicate that vitamin D_3 has an endocrine role in regulating calcium levels in fishes, but we should await more extensive experiments before drawing any phyletic conclusions as to the possible evolution of its role as a hormone.

The chondrichthyeans possess ultimobranchial bodies that contain a calcitonin that has a hypocalcemic action, when injected, in mammals. It is unknown what effects, if any, injected calcitonin has in chondrichthyeans but as they lack a bony skeleton, which is this hormone's principal effector in other vertebrates, a response, if present, would be expected to be somewhat different. Possibly calcitonin exerts other actions in chondrichthyeans that may even be unrelated to calcium metabolism. The injection of estrogens also fails to elicit a hypercalcemia in sharks (*Triakis semifasciata* and *Heterodontus francisci*) though a very small (11 %) increase in calcium concentration has been observed in the dogfish *Scyliorhinus caniculus* (Urist and Scheide, 1961; Woodhead, 1969). A hypercalcemic response to the estrogens is also absent in cyclostomes and may not have developed until the emergence of the bony fishes where they produce a 15-fold increase in protein-bound calcium in the plasma in teleosts and lungfishes (Urist *et al.*, 1972).

The bony fishes are a very diverse group and information about the regulation of calcium metabolism is almost entirely limited to teleosts. Within this group few species have been studied but considerable variability seems to exist. One of the reasons for these differences is that although all teleosteans possess a calcified endoskeleton, in some of these fishes, especially marine species, the bone is acellular so that the calcium deposits are relatively immobile. In other teleosts, notably those that can live in fresh water, the bone is cellular and can participate in calcium regulation. Teleosts like the eel also have large stores of calcium present in their muscles; these may be five times as great as those in tetrapods and could provide an additional site for the regulation of calcium exchange.

The injection of calcitonin into teleost fishes may or may not have a hypocalcemic action (see Chan, 1972). In the killifish *Fundulus heteroclitus*, which has acellular bone, calcitonin has no effect on plasma calcium concentration. In the eels *Anguilla anguilla* and *A. japonica*, and the freshwater catfish *Ictalurus melas*, calcitonin has been reported to decrease the blood calcium concentration but the results are equivocal (see Pang, 1973) (Fig. 6.9). These calcitonin-responsive teleosts possess cellular bone that displays osteocytic and osteoclastic activity and these cells probably are the principal site of calcitonin's action.

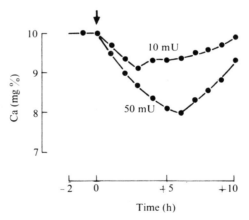

Fig. 6.9. The hypocalcemic effects of injections of two doses (10 and 50 milliunits, mU) of porcine calcitonin in a teleost fish, the eel *Anguilla anguilla*. (From Copp, 1969.)

The classical observations of Rasquin and Rosenbloom in 1954, showing a hypertrophy of the ultimobranchial bodies in Mexican cavefish subjected to continuous darkness, has been described earlier. This change in the activity of the ultimobranchial bodies was associated with osteoporotic degeneration of the bones in these fish.

The corpuscles of Stannius that are present in most bony fishes (see Chapter 2) also may influence calcium metabolism and an interaction between these tissues and the ultimobranchial bodies seems to occur. M. Fontaine, in 1964, found that removal of the corpuscles of Stannius in the European eel *Anguilla anguilla*, results in a marked increase (1.4-fold) in the plasma calcium concentration. This effect of Stanniectomy has been confirmed in other teleosts such as the goldfish *Carassius auratus* and the Asiatic and North American eels *A. japonica* and *A. rostrata* (see Chan, 1972). These hypercalcemic effects are accompanied by a reduced calcium excretion in the urine, and an increased osteoclastic activity which mobilizes calcium from the bone. The hypercalcemic effect of Stanniectomy can be prevented by the transplantation, or the injection of extracts, of the corpuscles of Stannius into the deficient fishes. The hormone has been called 'hypocalcin' which reflects its hypocalcemic action (Pang, Pang and Sawyer, 1974).

The activity (from histological observations) of the corpuscles of Stannius of the killifish *Fundulus heteroclitus*, appears to be greater in normal sea-water than in an artificial sea-water where the calcium concentration is low (see Pang *et al.*, 1973). Stanniectomy in these fish only results in hypercalcemia when they are bathed by solutions with a high calcium concentration; if they are in artificial calcium-poor sea-water or calcium-poor fresh water, blood calcium concentrations are unaffected; thus, the corpuscles of Stannius may play a physiological role in teleosts that live in solutions with a high calcium concentration, such as sea-water, where their secretions exert a hypocalcemic action.

What are the respective roles of the ultimobranchial bodies and the corpuscles of Stannius in teleost fish? Both appear to mediate a hypocalcemic effect! Calcitonin fails to elicit hypocalcemia in eels following Stanniectomy. The absence of its usual effect may reflect a high endogenous release of calcitonin in these fish, in response to the elevated plasma calcium levels, that may mask the action of additional injected calticonin. This possibility is consistent with an observed hypertrophy of the eel's ultimobranchial bodies following Stanniectomy. It is also interesting that ultimobranchialectomy results in an atrophy of the corpuscles of Stannius but it is difficult to interpret this observation which could reflect a direct trophic action on the corpuscles of Stannius, a decrease in their rate of secretion or a release and subsequent exhaustion of this tissue. It is nevertheless noteworthy that an interaction between the ultimobranchial bodies and the corpuscles of Stannius occurs and this is consistent with the possibility that they both interact in the regulation of calcium metabolism in teleosts.

When *Fundulus heteroclitus*, kept in artificial sea-water with a low-calcium concentration, are hypophysectomized they undergo tetanic muscular contractions associated with a considerable decline in the plasma calcium levels (Pang, 1973). This response is not seen if the fish are kept in ordinary sea-water with high concentrations of calcium. The effects in the low-calcium solution can be prevented by injecting the hypophysectomized fish with extracts of the pituitary or by transplanting this gland under the skin. The precise nature of the hypercalcemic 'hormone(s)' that may be involved is uncertain but they may be prolactin and corticotrophin. These pituitary hormones may have a hypercalcemic effect in teleosts that live in environments with a low-calcium concentration, like fresh water, while the corpuscles of Stannius may mediate the opposite, hypocalcemic, response in fish living in solutions with a high-calcium level, like sea-water.

The plasma calcium levels in the female plains killifish, *Fundulus kansae*, increase three-fold in the summer compared to the winter (Fleming, Stanley and Meier, 1964). This change in plasma calcium is not seen in the male killifish. In the female, it can, however, be imitated in winter by injecting them with estradiol, which suggests that it is a response associated with breeding. Even the male fish increase their rate of calcium uptake from the external solutions in the summer and in some circumstances this process may be stimulated by injected calcitonin (Fleming, Brehe and Hanson, 1973). The mechanism for the increased accumulation of calcium is not understood.

While knowledge about the regulation of calcium metabolism in fishes is incomplete, several intrinsically interesting facts are known. We have seen that endocrine control of this process may be related to the corpuscles of Stannius which are only present among the Osteichthyes. The secretion of the ultimobranchial bodies, calcitonin, has been shown to exert a hypocalcemic action which is, however, dependent on the presence of cellular bone and this is similar to its effect in other vertebrates. While chondrichthyeans possess calcitonin its physiological role is unknown. The estrogens can exert a marked hypercalcemic action, associated with the formation of the egg, and this emerges in the teleosts and is also seen in lungfishes and non-mammallian tetrapods. Almost nothing is known about the regulation of calcium metabolism in sharks and rays while lampreys and hagfishes may be dependent on an 'open system' which does not involve the action of hormones. The regulation of calcium metabolism in cyclostomes and chondrichthyeans undoubtedly will provide a very interesting area in which to pursue this subject further.

Conclusions

Calcium is essential for the life of vertebrates but their requirements for this mineral, and its availability in the environment, vary considerably. This need can be related to vertebrate phylogeny because of the systematic presence or absence of a bony calcareous skeleton and the characteristic life of some groups in the sea which is rich in calcium. It is, therefore, not surprising to observe that the role of hormones in the regulation of calcium metabolism appears to have changed considerably during the course of evolution. In marine fishes that lack a bony skeleton, hormonal regulation of calcium does not seem to occur. When such an endocrine control system is present, as in marine bony fishes, it is concerned with limiting concentration of calcium and lowering its levels in the blood (hypocalcemic effects) and the bone itself is an important effector site. This response possibly involves calcitonin, which is present in all vertebrates except cyclostomes, and, probably in teleosts, a secretion, hypocalcin, from the corpuscles of Stannius. Teleost fishes in fresh water, where the calcium levels are low, may utilize a pituitary hormone, possibly prolactin or corticotrophin, to help maintain adequate concentrations of calcium in their body fluids. Tetrapods, on the other hand, have acquired a 'new' hormone, parathormone, whose role is to mediate a hypercalcemia, and again bone is the major site of its action. A physiological role for calcitonin is doubtful in many species of tetrapods where it may not be as important as it was in ancestral marine fishes. Two other hormones contribute to the regulation of calcium metabolism but apparently in distinct groups of vertebrates, vitamin D has an hormonal function in tetrapods where it facilitates the accumulation of calcium in the body but it is uncertain whether it has such a role in fishes. Estrogens have assumed a 'special' endocrine role in many 'bony' vertebrates where they assist the deposition of calcium in the developing egg; apart from chondrichthyeans and cyclostomes this effect is also absent in mammals.

7. Hormones and the integument

The skin and gills of vertebrates constitute the major external interface between the animal and its environment. This integument is physiologically and anatomically a very important tissue which exhibits considerable diversity reflecting the differences which exist in the physicochemical gradients between the vertebrates and their environments. The integument may thus play a role in the animal's osmoregulation, thermoregulation and respiration. In addition, the integument provides signs and signals that can promote social and sexual contact and can help the animal to blend in with its surroundings and so protect it from predators, or help it catch its food. Of primary importance is the skin's role as an integumental skeleton by which it contains the animal in a condition that facilitates its locomotion. The relative importance of these various roles of the integument varies in different species and the structure varies accordingly also.

In fishes and larval amphibians, the gills, which function as organs of respiration, make up a large part of the animal's external surface. Exchanges of oxygen and carbon dioxide readily occur across these highly vascularized tissues which are also the sites of considerable movements of water and salts. Many fishes contain special cells in their gills called 'chloride-secreting cells' (or 'ionophores') that are the site for active extrusion of salts. The endocrine control mechanisms influencing the permeability of the gills are described in Chapter 8.

The skin is the major non-branchial interface between the animal and its environment. In its simplest form, the skin consists of two major layers of tissues, an outer epidermis which has several strata of cells, and an inner dermis. However, such a simple arrangement does not exist in nature, as various other structures are also included in the skin that modify its properties. These structures include scales, hair, feathers, pigment cells, secretory glands and certain sense organs. Such accessories contribute to the particular physiological properties exhibited by the integument of each species.

The skin is thus a complex tissue that has different physiological needs that depend on the species, the environment and the stage of the animal's life cycle. The constitution of the skin is not static but undergoes continual change commensurate with the normal needs of growth and repair. In addition, rapid changes in the physiological properties of the skin also can occur, such as involve an increased blood supply and the secretion of sweat in response to the need to dissipate heat in the mammals, and an increased osmotic permeability to water, as a result of dehydration, in anuran amphibians. Many cold-blooded vertebrates can rapidly alter the distribution of pigment in the skin so that they blend more closely with the shades and hues of their surroundings. Seasonal changes commonly occur in the integument, such as the changes in pigmentation that may be associated with breeding and alteration of the color, length and density of fur and feathers in summer and winter. Such changes in the fur and feathers may alter the insulative properties of the integument and contribute to the animal's camouflage.

While the skin has a considerable innate ability to regulate its functions it is also dependent on the nervous and endocrine systems with whose aid it can coordinate its activities with the rest of the body. The skin has a plentiful nerve supply that mediates its sensory functions and regulates its blood supply. The secretions of cutaneous glands are also predominantly under neural control, though circulating catecholamines exert some effects on them. Rapid changes in the distribution of pigment may be controlled by nerves but hormones are also very important. The endocrines help in the maintenance of the nutritional and anatomical integrity of the skin as well as such processes as molting, pigmentation and the function of certain cutaneous glands. Hormones that influence cutaneous function include several from the pituitary such as prolactin, MSH, vasotocin, ACTH, LH and TSH, and also thyroxine, the catecholamines, corticosteroids, gonadal steroids and melatonin. Some of the actions of these hormones are confined to relatively few species while the effects of a hormone on the skin may be quite different in one species as compared with another. The variation that is observed in the cutaneous effects of particular hormones suggest that considerable evolution has occurred in their special roles. It is also often difficult to decide whether the actions following an excess or deficiency of a hormone are the result of its direct action on a specific cutaneous effector or are due to merely a more diffuse, indirect effect such as may result from general changes in the animal's physiological and nutritional status.

Hormones and molting

The epidermis is regularly renewed as its outer layers drop off and are replaced by new cells that are formed from the underlying epithelium. This may be a more or less continuous process, such as is common in mammals, or it may take place suddenly at regular intervals varying from a few days, as in many amphibians, to several months in certain lizards and snakes. The hair of mammals and feathers of birds are also subject to such periodic renewal and this may also occur at precise times of the year such as at the onset of winter or spring or just before, or after, the breeding season (pre- and post-nuptial molts). In reptiles the shedding of the epidermis is often called *sloughing* while the shedding of the pelage in mammals, the plumage of birds and the epidermis in amphibians is called *molting*.

It is generally considered that the regular cyclical molting that occurs in fish, reptiles and amphibians reflects an autonomous rhythm in the skin upon which the actions of hormones can impinge in a permissive manner (Ling, 1972). The seasonal molts that occur commonly in birds and mammals are more closely allied to the external stimuli, principally the photoperiod, but they are also modified by the external temperature and the nutritional condition of the animal.

The pituitary and the thyroid glands are the principal endocrines that influence molting in vertebrates.

Removal of the pituitary usually prevents, or considerably prolongs, the length of the reptilian and amphibian molting cycles and blocks the seasonal molts observed in many birds and mammals. This effect of hypophysectomy is the result of the absence of several hormones, a lack of TSH, with its trophic effect on the thyroid, is very important but the lack of prolactin and corticotrophin may also contribute to the debility. In lacertilian reptiles, urodele amphibians, birds and mammals the thyroid hormones accelerate the molting process; thyroidectomy has an inhibitory effect. It is interesting that in ophidian reptiles (snakes) removal of the thyroid results in a decrease in the length of the sloughing cycle which is in direct contrast to what is observed in their lacertilian relatives (Chiu and Lynn, 1972; Maderson, Chiu and Phillips, 1970). Differences in the effects of hormones on molting also occur within the Amphibia, for while this process is facilitated by the thyroid gland in *Ambystoma mexicanum* (Urodela) this is not so in *Bufo bufo* (Anura) (Jorgenson, Larsen and Rosenkilde, 1965). In the latter toads, however, corticotrophin and the corticosteroids (corticosterone is most active) are necessary for successful molting. To further complicate any attempts to define a phyletic uniformity, it has been found that corticotrophin completely *inhibits* sloughing in the lizard *Gekko gecko* (Chiu and Phillips, 1971a).

Prolactin has diverse actions in vertebrates and it is especially notable that many of its effects are on the integument or derivatives of it, most notably the mammary glands (which are merely modified sweat glands). It has been shown that the injection of prolactin decreases the length of the sloughing cycle in the lizard *Anolis carolinensis* (Maderson and Licht, 1967). As thyroxine has a similar effect and prolactin has been shown to exhibit a thyrotrophic action, it seemed possible that the action of prolactin was not direct, but was mediated by its release of thyroxine. However, it has been shown that prolactin can reduce the length of the sloughing cycle in thyroidectomized lizards, *Gekko gecko* (Chiu and Phillips, 1971*b*) so that it may have a direct effect on the skin. Prolactin has been found to facilitate the growth and increase the appetite of lizards so that its effect could also reflect their nutritional condition. In this respect, it should also be remembered that hypophysectomized lizards usually do not eat and are not in perfect health. Prolactin injections have also been shown to accelerate molting in a urodele amphibian, the red eft, *Notophthalmus viridescens* (Chadwick and Jackson, 1948), though such an action has not been demonstrated in other amphibians. It is interesting that, in this newt, prolactin promotes the transition (or metamorphosis) from the terrestrial form into the aquatic breeding stage when it returns to water ('water-drive effect' of prolactin) and this is associated with cutaneous changes. Whether the effect on the skin is a primary one is uncertain, as the prolactin could be stimulating some non-cutaneous process concerned more generally with the metamorphic change.

The seasonal changes that occur in the pelage of mammals and the plumage of birds appear to be principally under photoperiodic control. Changes in the hours of light are transmitted via the eyes and hypothalamus to the pituitary. Such photoperiodic changes also control the gonadal cycles so that it may be difficult to separate the two events. Removal of the pituitary prevents the short-tailed weasel (*Mustela erminea*) from growing a brown spring coat (they stay white), even when they are exposed to a photoperiod that induces this growth in intact weasels (Rust and Meyer, 1969). The effects of photoperiod on the pelage and plumage appear to be mediated through the action of the gonadal steroids, corticosteroids and thyroxine which are in turn controlled by the hypothalamus and pituitary (Ebling and Hale, 1970).

The precise manner in which hormones influence molting is not understood. Cyclical changes in molting in poikilotherms are usually characterized by brief periods of cellular activity and rapid cell division interspersed by periods when little activity occurs, which are referred to as the 'resting-phases'. It is thought that, when they are acting, thyroxine and prolactin shorten the resting-phase (except in snakes!) during which the skin's activity is reduced by lower levels of these hormones. In newts, however, prolactin has been shown to promote active cell division in the epithelium and this is reminiscent of its action on the crop-sac epithelium in pigeons. In toads, the absence of the pituitary does not prevent the formation of new layers of epidermis (or sloughs) but prevents the shedding, or casting off, of these cells. This shedding is promoted in toads by corticotrophin and corticosteroids. It is interesting that some frogs which estivate during periods of drought are protected from excessive dehydration by a cocoon which is composed of accumulated layers of epithelial cells (Lee and Mercer, 1967) and it seems possible that this may reflect a decline in their pituitary and adrenal function.

While not strictly an example of molting, balding (loss of the hair on the scalp) in man is known to be dependent on the activity of androgenic hormones. The sex hormones also control the development at puberty of the typical patterns in distribution of hair in men and women. A rather interesting observation (Fig. 7.1) is that the growth of the facial hair in man shows a rapid increase when female company is restored following a period of abstinence. This change probably reflects a surge in the release of LH and the secretion of testosterone.

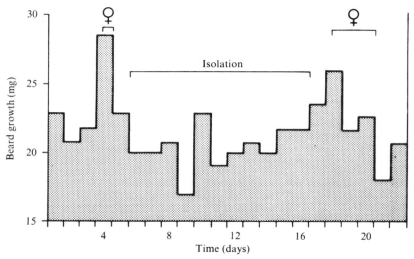

Fig. 7.1. Beard growth in man is less during periods of isolation from women. Restoration of female company results in a sudden 'spurt' in the growth of the facial hair and it has been suggested that this is the result of the release of male sex hormones, probably pituitary LH. (From Anon., 1970.)

Hormones and skin glands

Vertebrates possess several types of secretory glands in their skin which serve a variety of functions (Quay, 1972). These glands can be classified into two major groups: the mucous glands and the proteinaceous glands.

The proteinaceous-type glands have undergone considerable evolutionary modification and include (to name only a few) a variety of venom glands in fishes and amphibians, the uropygial (or preening) gland that is present in many birds and the sebaceous glands, sweat glands and mammary glands of mammals. The sweat glands play an important role in temperature regulation in mammals. The sebaceous glands are associated with hair follicles and the fatty sebum that they secrete serves to protect the hair from wetting. The sebaceous glands and the sweat glands sometimes secrete special odoriferous substances that may play an important role in territorial behavior (by defining territorial limits) and also act as sexual attractants. Such scent glands may become enlarged and congregate in distinct areas of the body. Examples of this include the 'side glands' on the heads of shrews, the 'anal glands' and submandibular 'chin glands' in rabbits and the 'ventral gland' in gerbils.

The maturation and function of the sweat glands and sebaceous glands in mammals are influenced by hormones (Strauss and Ebling, 1970). The odoriferous scent glands are commonly observed to be larger in the male than the female while maturation of sebaceous and sweat glands occurs during puberty in man. It thus seems likely that they are influenced by sex hormones, and androgenic steroids are undoubtedly involved. Natural

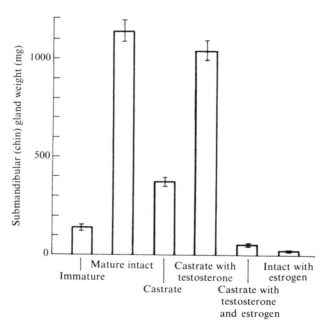

Fig. 7.2. The effects of gonadal hormones on the weight of the submandibular (chin) glands in male rabbits. It can be seen that these glands exhibit considerable increases in weight after sexual maturity, an effect that is prevented by castration. Testosterone injections overcome this effect of castration while injected estrogens bring about an involution of the glands. (From Strauss and Ebling, 1970.)

and experimental differences in the development of the submandibular chin glands in rabbits are shown in Fig. 7.2. These glands are much larger in sexually mature than immature rabbits and they decrease in size when the testes are removed. Injections of testosterone promote the development of the chin glands while estrogens inhibit it. Progesterone also increases their weight but this may be due to the inherent androgenic activity of this steroid hormone. Comparable effects of the gonadal steroids are seen on the sebaceous and apocrine sweat glands of other mammals. Apart from promoting the development of sebaceous glands, androgens also increase the production of sebum.

In primates, especially man, the watery-secretion of the eccrine sweat glands play an important role in providing water that can be evaporated from the body surface and so aid in the dissipation of heat (see Chapter 8). Sweat contains dissolved salts, including sodium and potassium, the concentration of which is influenced by aldosterone; the sodium/potassium ratio declines under its influence. In addition, while the secretion of sweat is primarily under neural control in primates it is also increased, during exercise, by circulating adrenaline.

Mucous glands are present in the integument of fishes and amphibians. Their role is contentious but seems to be related to an aquatic life where it has been suggested that the mucous secretion may have a protective action on the skin as well as serving certain special functions such as the formation of a cocoon in estivating African lungfish and providing food for the young of a cichlid teleost. In the latter fish, this mucous secretion is promoted by the injection of prolactin (Egami and Ishii, 1962). It has also been suggested that prolactin may limit the permeability of teleost fish and urodele amphibians to water and sodium (see Chapter 8) by an action on the mucous glands but the evidence for this is equivocal.

Knowledge about the role of hormones in regulating growth, development and secretion of the integumental glands is incomplete. Clearly, however, some such glands do respond to hormones though the primary importance of neural secretory stimuli should not be forgotten. The functions of such glands vary considerably in different vertebrates and it is interesting that many have attained a responsiveness to certain hormones. The nature of these effects appears to be related to the other basic functions of the hormones in the body; thus gonadal steroids influence skin glands that are involved in sexual activities and aldosterone acts in a manner commensurate with its role as a hormone that conserves sodium in the body.

Information about hormone effects on skin glands in non-mammals is sparse. Adrenaline stimulates chloride secretion from the skin glands of European frogs and this may reflect a direct action of such hormones in the body or a mimicking of a stimulation of the sympathetic nerves.

Adrenaline, as well as vasotocin, has also been shown to stimulate the secretion of a sticky, milky-white material from the proteinaceous skin glands of the South African clawed toad, *Xenopus laevis* (Ireland, 1973). The effect of the catecholamine, but not vasotocin, can be prevented by an α-adrenergic blocking drug.

The control of epidermal skin proliferation – a note on chalones

The control of cell proliferation in the skin has elicited much interest, especially among dermatologists. Apart from the control of the normal replacement of the epithelium, the rapid but controlled processes of repair that accompany wound healing are rather remarkable. These processes, like other changes in the skin, are thought principally to involve an internal control mechanism upon which hormones may impinge their influence.

Chalones are substances that have been isolated from a number of tissues including the mammalian epidermis (see Bullough, 1971). They inhibit the mitoses of epidermal cells including melanocytes and keratinocytes. The chalones are glycoproteins that act both *in vitro* or *in vivo* and show a considerable degree of tissue specificity. It is thought that chalones form an active complex with adrenaline. As cortisol also inhibits mitosis of epidermal cells it may also contribute to this complex. Alternatively, it has been suggested (see Quevedo, 1972) that the effect of adrenaline, in inhibiting cell mitosis, may involve the formation of cyclic AMP and that chalones may be part of the cyclic AMP–adenyl cyclase system. The promotion of rapid epidermal cell growth, such as following a wound, appears to be stimulated as a result of the inactivation of the chalone but it is unknown how this is done. It has been suggested that a local release of prostaglandins may overcome the inhibitory effects of the chalone complex.

Hormones and pigmentation

The integument of most vertebrates contains pigment that makes a major contribution to what is often a very colorful appearance. Pigment may be present within the epidermis or dermis itself or color the integumental appendages, such as scales, hair and feathers. Apart from contributing to man's esthetic delight in contemplating nature, it seems likely that an animal's coloration may be useful to its physiology (Hadley, 1972). Appropriate pigmentation may contribute to the animal's camouflage, protect the internal organs from solar radiation, promote the absorption or reflection of heat and light and so aid in photoreception and contribute to the synthesis of vitamin D in the skin. Integumental colors also provide signs that are important for appropriate dimorphic sexual behavior and reproduction.

Pigments of different colors are usually present in the skin in cells called chromatophores. These cells commonly contain a black or brown pigment called melanin and are called melanocytes or, if the intracellular distribution of pigment can be changed, melanophores. The yellow and red pigments (xanthines and carotenes) that also occur in the skin of vertebrates are contained in, respectively, xanthophores and erythrophores. Some chromatophores also contain pteridine platelets which reflect light, giving an iridiscent appearance, and are thus called iridophores. The complex and beautiful colors of many vertebrates are the result of blending the colors reflected by the various chromatophores.

Many vertebrates can alter their coloration in response to environmental and behavioral needs. Such changes may take place in a relatively slow manner, as when the total amount of pigment in the epidermis, or its appendages, changes. The result is a relatively static coloration that is attained over a period of days or weeks. This process is called *morphological color change* (which may involve melanocytes or melanophores) and is seen when we tan in the sun or when an animal changes the color of its pelage or plumage with the onset of summer or winter or in preparation for the breeding season. In addition, many cold-blooded vertebrates can rapidly change their color, a process that only takes a few minutes or at the most several hours. This relatively rapid response is called *physiological color change*. Both morphological and physiological color change are influenced by the actions of hormones, especially the pituitary melanocyte-stimulating hormone.

The melanophores are cells with long dendritic-like extensions that radiate from a central core. In shape they resemble nerve cells from which they are derived. The melanin is contained within cellular organelles called melanosomes. Darkening and lightening of the skin, as occurs in physiological color change, reflects a migration of the melanosomes in dermal melanophores so that they are widely distributed in the cell (dark color, the melanin is said to be dispersed) or they aggregate in small globs in the center of the cell (light color, the melanophore is said to have a punctate appearance) (Fig. 7.3). The more gross effects of these changes on the color of frog skin is shown in Fig. 7.4. The dispersal of the melanin in the melanophores may depend on a microtubular system in the cell, as certain drugs, for example cytochalasin B, that break such tubules also prevent dispersion of the pigment. The other chromatophores have a rather similar structure to the melanophores but contain different pigments. Iridophores that respond to MSH do so in the opposite manner to that of the melanophores; the platelets of reflecting materials aggregate so that the cell has a punctate appearance. Not all chromatophores exhibit a physiological color change response to MSH and indeed this is not usually seen in the xanthophores and erythrophores (Bagnara, 1969; Taylor and Bagnara, 1972). In epidermal melanocytes (unlike the dermal melanophores), the pigment is relatively fixed in its position so that differences that occur usually reflect

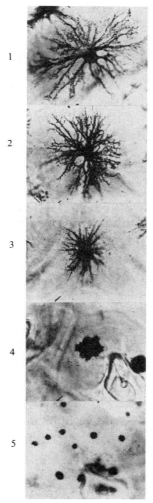

Fig. 7.3. The microscopic appearance of the dermal melanophores of the dogfish *Scyliorhinus canicula*. When the fish is maximally dark, as in 5, the melanosomes are dispersed throughout the cell which can then be seen in outline, while when pale they are aggregated in the central regions (as in 1) so that definition of the cell outline is obscured. The numbers, 1 to 5, correspond to the 'melanophore index'. (From Wilson and Dodd, 1973a.)

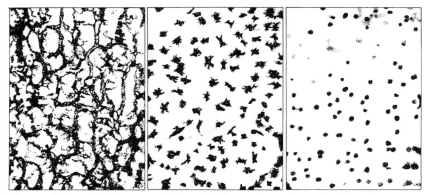

Fig. 7.4. The gross appearance of amphibian melanophores (under a low power microscope) when the animal is (left to right): dark, intermediate and pale in color. (From *The Pigmentary Effector System* by L. Hogben (1924). With permission of the publishers Oliver & Boyd, Edinburgh.)

the total quantities of pigment that are present (morphological color change).

The different types of chromatophores present in colorful animals, including many frogs and lizards, are arranged in layers and changes in the distribution of pigment within these zones alters the transmission of light and the color that is perceived. The innermost layer consists of melanophores and these are overlain by the reflecting iridophores. The xanthophores form a layer closer to the surface of the skin. Changes in the density of the melanophores, that absorb light, and the iridophores that can reflect it, thus can alter the color of a frog from a light to a dark color and influence the display of the colorful pigments in the superficially placed xanthophores. The melanophores, iridophores and xanthophores together make up what is called a 'dermal chromatophore unit'.

The mechanism of release of melanocyte-stimulating hormone

As we shall see in the succeeding sections, the release of MSH plays a most important role in both physiological and morphological color change in vertebrates. The principal stimulus, especially in cold-blooded species, is the receipt of light usually by the lateral eyes but the pineal may also function as a photoreceptor in some species. In addition to directly influencing MSH release, in acute situations, light may also contribute to a cyclical, photoperiodic, release of this hormone in some mammals that seasonally change the color of their pelage. Other stimuli that result in a release of MSH include a deficiency of adrenocorticosteroids and suckling and copulation in mammals, and increases in the osmotic concentration of the plasma in a variety of species. The latter effects may not have any physiological significance but this remains to be further explored. The intimate mechanisms that control the release of MSH from the pars intermedia are only partly understood and appear to be quite complex (see Howe, 1973).

When the pars intermedia is transplanted ectopically, to another part of the body away from the hypothalamus, or if its connections to this part of the brain are severed, MSH is secreted in an apparently uncontrolled manner. The regulation of hormone release thus appears to be under an inhibitory control originating in the hypothalamus.

The pars intermedia has a nerve supply that comes from the base of the brain which contains three types of neurons; aminergic ones that secrete catecholamines, neurosecretory fibers that release peptide hormones and (possibly less important) cholinergic nerves. The vascular supply to the tissue shows considerable species variability but portal vessels coming from the hypothalamus and neural lobe have been described. The controlling stimuli appear to involve the nerves but also possibly portal blood vessels, as in the pars distalis.

Neural stimuli are undoubtedly important in controlling the release of MSH and appear to involve α-adrenergic-type receptors which inhibit the release of MSH. In-vitro studies on rodent and frog pituitaries also indicate that a β-adrenergic-type stimulation can oppose this and prompt MSH release (Bower and Hadley, 1973; Bower, Hadley and Hruby, 1974). As we have seen earlier (Chapter 3), an MSH-release-inhibiting hormone, MSH-R-IH, has been identified in the hypothalamus and this seems to contribute to the control of the hormone's release. MSH-R-IH is a peptide, such as formed by neurosecretory cells, but it is unknown whether it is released directly from such nerve endings in the pars intermedia or is formed in the hypothalamus and carried in portal vessels to the gland. In addition, an MSH-releasing hormone (MRH) may also be present in the hypothalamus, and this could be opposing the action of MSH-R-IH and/or inhibitory neural stimuli. The interactions and possible linkages (for instance do α-adrenergic stimuli act alone or through MSH-R-IH release) between these neural and humoral processes are not yet fully understood. To complicate matters even further, it has been proposed (see p. 268) that melatonin, from the pineal gland, may mediate photoperiodic release of MSH by an action on the hypothalamus. Melatonin injections have been shown to increase release of MSH and a physiological rise in the levels of the former, such as occurs during darkness, could result in the latter's release under normal conditions. Finally, it should be noted that there is evidence to indicate that MSH can exert a negative-feedback inhibition via the hypothalamus which restricts its further release.

Physiological color change

Physiological color changes occur in many cold-blooded vertebrates, from the cyclostomes to reptiles. These changes in the distribution of the pigment in the skin occur in response to a variety of conditions and stimuli. Many vertebrates exhibit a diurnal rhythm in the degree of aggregation and dispersion of melanin in the melanophores. They turn pale at night and dark during the day. This change may reflect the perception of light and be mediated by receptors in the eyes and the pineal, and sometimes can result from a direct stimulation of the melanophores by light. In other instances such as in the lizard *Anolis carolinensis*, a diurnal rhythm can even be seen when the animals are kept in complete darkness. As it is not seen in these lizards after they are hypophysectomized, it probably reflects an inherent diurnal rhythm in the activity of the pituitary gland. Superimposed on such rhythmical changes in skin color are direct, and adaptive, responses to external stimuli. These stimuli include the perception of certain light patterns due to the color and shade of the substrate on which the animal is placed (*background-response*), and to a lesser extent the external temperature and 'excitement'. The latter two effects, which have been observed more commonly in lizards, may override the background-response.

The first recorded observations of physiological color change are more than 2000 years old but our understanding of the mechanism involved is quite recent. An appreciation of the role of hormones in these responses principally resulted from the pioneering studies of Hogben and Winton in the 1920s. An excellent account of the work of the Hogben school in England and that of many others, including Parker in the United States, has been given by Waring (1963). Waring joined the Hogben school in the 1930s and his account of the processes involved in regulating color change is an ideal example of the stringent analytical approach and the application of formal logic that we should all aspire to in scientific investigations. Although physiological color change does not occur in mammals or birds the elucidation of its mechanism has contributed a great deal to our understanding of the role of hormones in physiological coordination. The following account is largely based on Waring's but one should also consult the book by Bagnara and Hadley (1972).

Types of melanophores responses

Non-visual

(*a*) Coordinated; these responses may be abolished by denervation of the skin or the removal of the pituitary or the adrenals.

(*b*) Uncoordinated; where the melanophore (or possibly a skin-receptor close to it) directly responds to a stimulus. This type of response can be seen rather clearly in the horned toad, *Phrynosoma blainvilli*. If these lizards are blinded, hypophysectomized, and the pineal eye is covered, and they are then placed in a black box with no light, they become a pale color. When, however, a thin beam of light is focused on a piece of denervated skin in these lizards this darkens in comparison to the rest of the integument. A localized response to temperature can also be demonstrated in *Phrynosoma*, for when an area of the skin of a maximally dark lizard is exposed to water at 37 °C it pales in that region. Similarly, maximally pale skin will darken locally at a temperature of 1 °C. Chameleons also exhibit dramatic localized changes in skin color; the skin of blinded animals turns dark in light but if a certain area is shaded by an object a lighter colored 'print' or outline of this object can be seen. Such responses do not involve hormones or the ordinary nerve supply and appear to reflect a direct response of the melanophore; however, a local nerve reflex initiated from a nearby cutaneous receptor or a release of a local hormone could be involved.

The visual response

This response is the result of the reception of light by the lateral eyes or in certain species, including some larval amphibians and cyclostomes, and possibly even some lizards, the pineal. The responses may be a generalized lightening (in the dark) or darkening (in the light) of the skin or be influenced by the color of the background: the background-response. When the animal is on a white substrate with overhead illumination, it may turn a pale color and if on a black background (also with overhead illumination) it may turn a dark color. These changes are called the white (or tertiary) and black (or secondary) ocular-background responses. The different effects of light in these two sets of circumstances appear to be due to the stimulation of different parts of the retina; thus, the retina of a frog in a black tank of water (Fig. 7.5) receives light only on the more basal parts of the retina, the 'B' (for black) area, but in a white tank, where the light is reflected into the eye from all sides, the entire retina, including a 'W' (for white) area, is stimulated. Such special receptor areas for light in the retina have also been found in teleost fishes and lizards.

Quantitation of the melanophore response

Early observations of vertebrate color change have been described in general subjective terms such as 'pale', and 'a tint rather dark than pale' that lack adequate precision for a proper scientific analysis and make

(*a*)

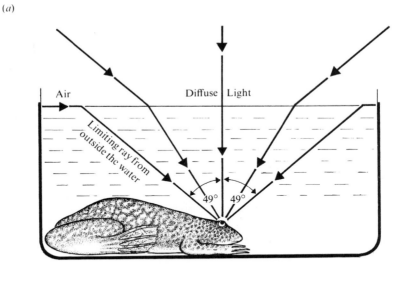

(*b*)   (i)   (ii)

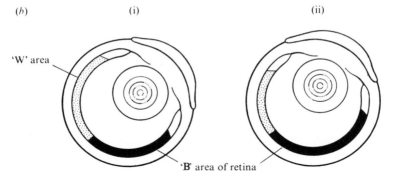

Axis of symmetry 35° to horizontal   Axis of symmetry 65° to horizontal

Fig. 7.5. (*a*) The manner by which the reception of light initiates the dispersion of melanin in the melanophores of a frog (in this instance *Xenopus*) sitting in a tank of water with a black background and overhead illumination.

As the tank has black sides all light will enter the water from above and enter the lens at an angle which is the critical angle for air and water (49°). (From Waring, 1963.) Using this data, as well as the dimensions of the eye and the refractive index of the lens (*Xenopus* has its eyes on the top of its head), Hogben provided a diagram (*b*, i, ii) that shows the area of the retina which receives such light rays. As these conditions result in a darkening of the skin, this has been called the B-area (for black) as opposed to the W-area (for white) which initiates skin lightening in frogs on a white background when light reaches wider areas of the retina. (From Hogben, 1942. Reproduced by permission of the Royal Society.)

comparisons of results from different laboratories almost impossible. Hogben introduced a more stringent quantitative description called the melanophore index (or MI) (Figs. 7.3 and 7.6) which has a gradation of 1, for maximally pale, with the melanin fully aggregated to 5 when the animal is dark and the melanin is fully dispersed. In lizards, this can be translated, as in chameleons, to 1 = yellow, 3 = medium-green and 5 = black. This simple standard of measurement allowed considerable advances to be made in the analysis of the mechanism of color change. Today, electrophoto-receptive devices are also used to quantify the melanophore responses.

Color change in amphibians

The earliest observations on the role of hormones in vertebrate color change were made on European frogs, *Rana temporaria*, and subsequently the

	Appearance of melanophores	Melanophore Index (MI)
Intact Anurans		
In complete darkness		2.5 to 3.0
Light overhead:		
White background		1.5
Dark background		4.5 to 5.0
'Complete' hypophysectomy;		
(light or dark background)		1.0
Denervation of pars intermedia		
(light or dark background)		4.5
Eyeless (light or dark background)		2.5 to 3.0

Chart of Melanophore Index for amphibians:

1   2   3   4   5

Fig. 7.6. The melanophore responses, mediated through the eyes, of anurans in relation to the receipt of light when on a white or a dark background. The effects of surgical changes of the pituitary on these responses have been summarized. The melanophore index (MI) in relation to the degree of dispersion, or aggregation, of melanin in the melanophores is given in the lower section. For a description and explanation of these responses the text should be consulted. (Based on Bradshaw and Waring, 1969.)

South African clawed toad, *Xenopus laevis*. With overhead illumination (see Fig. 7.6), on a white background these amphibians are pale (melanophore index about 1.5) and on a black background they are dark (MI about 4.5). When placed in complete darkness, or if they are blinded, they have an intermediate shade (MI = 2.5). In *Xenopus*, this change in melanin distribution in the melanophores is seen as a white or a black coloration but in frogs, which have overlying layers of yellow-green pigment, this appears as a pale green or yellow to a black color. When amphibians are 'completely' hypophysectomized so that no pituitary tissue remains (such remnants commonly *do* remain, as in *Xenopus*) the animals become maximally pale, the MI is 1 and they cannot respond to changes in the background color. If the pars distalis is removed carefully so that the pars intermedia and pars tuberalis remain intact, the background responses are retained. This operation is relatively simple to perform in *Rana* but it is more difficult in *Xenopus* where the pars tuberalis is usually removed together with the pars distalis. This results in an inability of *Xenopus* to display a background response and it becomes permanently dark (MI = 5). The pars intermedia has a nerve supply coming down from the hypothalamus and when this is cut the anurans also have an MI of 5. Removal of the pars tuberalis appears to be associated with an interference of the hypothalamic connections to the pars intermedia and, as these are of an inhibitory nature a sustained release of its secretion, MSH, occurs.

Melanocyte-stimulating hormone (MSH) when released from the pars intermedia is carried in the blood to the melanophores where it promotes a dispersion of melanin so that the animal darkens.

The sequence of events resulting in the black-background response is summarized in the following section (Fig. 7.7). Light from an overhead source, in frogs on a dark background, falls on the 'B' area of the retina where it stimulates receptors that transmit messages along the optic nerve. These messages, travelling along pathways that are as yet unknown, inhibit the normal inhibitory effects of the nerves supplying the pars intermedia and this results in a release of MSH. Whether or not this involves just neural stimuli, a release of MSH-RH and/or an inhibition of release of MSH-R-IH is not clear. When the frogs are on a white background, light also falls on the retina but on the receptors in the 'W' area and this reduces the release of MSH. Normally anurans kept in the dark, as well as blinded animals, have an MI of about 3 which appears to reflect a sustained, but submaximal, release of MSH. Stimulation of the 'W' retinal receptors in some way inhibits this release even further, possibly by increasing the inhibitory nerve impulses or stimulating the release of MSH-R-IH or both.

Pallor of the skin is thus usually thought to result from a decline in the levels of MSH in the blood. In the amphibia, in contrast to some teleosts

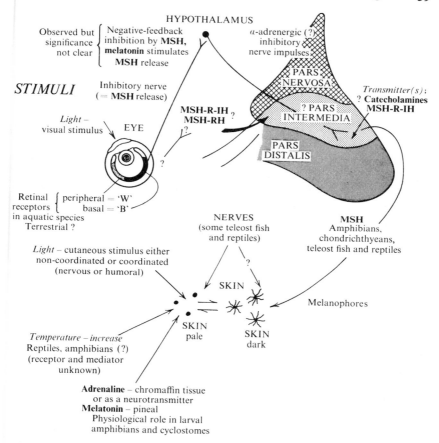

Fig. 7.7. A composite diagram summarizing the humoral and neural control of color change in vertebrates.

and reptiles, nerves are not involved in the aggregation of melanin in the melanophores. The possibility that a melanin-aggregating hormone or MAH may be present in the amphibian pituitary has been considered. This concept was partly based on the observation that an intact pars tuberalis was necessary for the occurrence of a white-background in *Xenopus*. It is now, however, agreed that removal of this tissue results in the severance of the inhibitory hypothalamic connections to the pars intermedia that are necessary for maximum color change to occur (see Bradshaw and Waring, 1969).

The injection of adrenaline into *Rana* produces a skin lightening and an aggregation of melanin in the melanophores which is an α-adrenergic response. On the other hand, in *Xenopus laevis* and in the spade foot toad, *Scaphiopus couchi, in vitro,* catecholamines disperse melanin which is due to an increased formation of cyclic AMP following β-adrenergic stimulation (Goldman and Hadley, 1969; Abe *et al.,* 1969). The normal physiological importance of such actions *in vivo* is unknown.

When dried bovine pineal glands are fed to anuran tadpoles, the melanin in the melanophores on the body, but not the tail, aggregates and the animal's body pales (see Bagnara and Hadley, 1970). Under these conditions, the tadpole's internal organs can be seen clearly. This effect is due to the action of melatonin that is formed in the pineal gland. Normally, tadpoles, such as those of *Xenopus laevis,* pale at night and darken during the day and this can be prevented if the pineal, but not the lateral eyes, are removed. Formation and release of melatonin occurs in darkness and this appears to mediate the diurnal rhythm of color change in these tadpoles. The effect of melatonin on the melanophores is a direct one and is not mediated through the pituitary as has sometimes been suggested, as the effect of melatonin is not prevented by hypophysectomy. This physiological effect of melatonin is confined to tadpoles and does not contribute to skin lightening in adult amphibians.

Color change in the chondrichthyes

Many sharks and rays exhibit dramatic changes in color depending on the shade of the background; with overhead illumination they become dark on a black background and pale on a white one. Two dogfish (*Scyliorhinus canicula*) in their dark and pale phases are shown in Fig. 7.8. Waring, in 1936, found that when he transplanted a dogfish pituitary into another dogfish, that was pale in color, it turned dark due to a dispersion of melanin in the melanophores. The release of the MSH is due to the absence of the hypothalamic neural inhibitory control mechanism which is present in these fish (Wilson and Dodd, 1973a). An analysis of the color change in these fish, *Squalus, Scyliorhinus* and *Raja,* shows that they exhibit white- and black-background responses that are mediated humorally by MSH, just as in amphibians. Direct neural control of the melanophores does not appear to occur in the Chondrichthyes.

The background response is not seen in blinded dogfish though the fish show a slight paling in darkness which suggests the presence of a non-visual response (Wilson and Dodd, 1973a). When kept in total darkness, the pallor exhibited by these dogfish is not seen if the pineal is removed and they become darker. The pineal may thus contribute to non-visual color change as observed in tadpoles and cyclostomes (see later).

Fig. 7.8. Two dogfish, *Scyliorhinus canicula*, in their dark and pale color phases (×0.33). (J. F. Wilson, personal communication.)

Color change in teleosts

While the chondrichthyean fishes and amphibians that have been examined all have humoral control of their color change the teleosts, which lie phyletically between these two groups, may also possess a neural coordinating mechanism. The teleosts, as has become apparent in the comparison of their other biological systems, exhibit considerable inter-specific differences in the control of color change that presumably reflect the systematic diversity within this large group of fishes.

Stimulation of nerves controlling melanophores usually results in an aggregation of the melanin and a paling of the skin color in teleosts. A dispersion of melanin, in response to neural stimuli, however, may also occur in some species but the evidence for this is equivocal. I have been unable to ascertain with certainty whether the autonomic nerve fibers involved in such color changes are cholinergic or adrenergic, though the aggregating effects of injected adrenaline would tend to favor the latter; however, species differences may exist and it has been suggested that in the eel *Anguilla anguilla*, melanin dispersion is an adrenergic response while the aggregation is a cholinergic one. Alternatively, melanin aggregation may be an α-adrenergic response and dispersion a β-adrenergic one.

Responses of melanophores to neural stimuli are very rapid and may take place within several minutes. The humoral effects of MSH are, in contrast, slow and usually take one to two hours for their completion. This tardiness reflects the gradual build up or removal of MSH from the circulation rather than any lethargy on the part of the melanophores themselves.

One can readily foresee the prospective biological advantages of an ability to change color rapidly as this may help protect the animal from a predator or assist it to catch food. Rapid color change may be especially important in animals that live in places where the background colors are variegated and across which the animals constantly travel in their search for food and sexual companionship. Many teleost fishes that roam about gaily colored reefs may find such rapid color change an especial advantage.

In the Teleostei, color change can be mediated by three types of mechanisms: (*a*) a humoral one, (*b*) a neural one or (*c*) a combination of both neural and humoral processes.

Anguilla (*the eel*)

Eels exhibit black- and white-background responses but only change their color slowly, like amphibians. Hypophysectomy abolishes the full expression of these responses and as the pituitary contains a material that, when injected, disperses melanin in the melanophores, the response is considered to be predominantly a humorally mediated one.

Following hypophysectomy, the eel is not maximally pale but has a melanophore index of 1 to 2 and this has contributed to speculation that a melanocyte-aggregating hormone is also present in the pituitary, as, if only MSH were involved, one would expect a MI of about 1. It has been suggested that, alternatively, melanophore-dispersing nerve fibers are present.

In contrast to amphibians, hypophysectomized eels continue to exhibit a small background response; the MI is 3.5 on a black background and 1.8 on a white one. This response is abolished by the severance of cutaneous nerves that are known to innervate the melanophores; thus, although the predominant mechanism mediating color change in eels is humoral there is an underlying neural control that only becomes apparent after the pituitary is removed.

Adrenaline, when injected, readily produces an aggregation of melanin in the melanophores of eels. This hormone is produced by widely distributed chromaffin cells in teleosts but it is unknown if it has a normal role in mediating their color changes.

Fundulus heteroclitus (*the killifish*)

Killifish exhibit the usual black- and white-background responses but these are *not* abolished following hypophysectomy. *Complete* darkening, or dispersal of melanin, does not occur following this operation, indicating that pituitary MSH may be necessary for the full expression of the black-background response.

The overriding control is, nevertheless, a neural one. Injection of MSH into pale fish does not disperse melanin and electrical stimulation of cutaneous nerves in dark fish evokes pallor. The injection of MSH into pale fish that have had parts of their skin denervated results in a melanin dispersion in these localized areas. Extracts of *Fundulus* pituitaries can evoke such dispersion of melanin.

In *Fundulus*, color change thus occurs in response to neural stimuli to the melanophores; there are melanin-aggregating nerve fibers, and possibly even 'dispersing fibers'. Underlying this mechanism, but generally overridden by it, is an ability to respond to MSH and this hormone is necessary for a maximal darkening of the fish.

Phoxinus phoxinus (*the European minnow*)

In minnows, there is little evidence for a role of endogenous hormones in the dispersion of melanin. Black and white-background responses are not prevented by hypophysectomy, though it has been observed that such fish cannot sustain a black coloration as readily as intact fish. Denervation of the skin abolishes the background-responses and the melanin fully disperses. Nerve stimulation evokes an aggregation of melanin and aggregating nerve fibers undoubtedly exist. There is also some evidence that suggests the presence of melanin-dispersing fibers.

The injection of extracts of the pituitaries from *Phoxinus* does not disperse melanin in either the intact or denervated skin of these fish. MSH from anurans will, however, darken the denervated skin of *Phoxinus*. There is no evidence for a melanin-dispersing hormone in *Phoxinus* and indeed pituitary extracts have an opposite, aggregating, effect.

Color change, thus, in the teleost fish may be influenced by three types of mechanisms:

1. A predominantly humoral one that overrides a neural mechanism, as in *Anguilla*.

2. Predominantly neural coordination that overrides a humoral process but which is still important, such as in *Fundulus*.

3. A neural coordinating mechanism with no evidence for an effect of endogenous MSH, as in *Phoxinus*.

Color change in reptiles

The reptiles have either humoral or neural mechanisms coordinating their color changes but as yet no transitional arrangements, which involve both, have been described. Most observations, certainly the most detailed ones, have been made on lacertilians that often display very dramatic changes in color as epitomized by the chameleons.

Snakes and crocodilians also possess chromatophores, and a chelonian, *Chelodina longicolis*, has also been shown to exhibit background-responses that are mediated by MSH (Woolley, 1957).

The lizard, *Anolis carolinensis*, exhibits both visual and non-visual background-responses that are abolished following hypophysectomy. The non-visual response, which can be overridden by the visual one, may be the result of photostimulation of the pineal.

Excitement, such as results from electrical stimulation of the mouth or cloaca, results in a mottling of the skin color patterns in *A. carolinensis* because of a dispersion of melanin in some melanophores and an aggregation in others. This effect can be mimicked by the injection of adrenaline which may normally mediate the response. The melanophores are not innervated and cutting the general nerve supply to the skin does not influence color change.

Chameleons, *Chamaeleo pumila*, and *Lophosaura pumila*, exhibit rapid and dramatic changes in color that are either visual responses or are due to photoreceptors that are apparently present in the skin. The observations that have been made on these responses suggest that there is a neural control of the melanophores; nerve stimulation results in an aggregation of melanin. It is also possible that melanin dispersing nerve fibers are present. It thus seems that the control of color change in chameleons is a neurally coordinated process though, as no experiments seem to have been done on hypophysectomized animals, a subsidiary role of MSH cannot be completely excluded.

Color change in cyclostomes

The control of color change in the lampreys (Petromyzontoidea) and hagfishes (Myxinoidea) is intrinsically very interesting because of their lowly phyletic position on the vertebrate scale.

A background-color response, pale on a white substrate, dark on a black one, has been described in the hagfish, *Myxine glutinosa*, but the coordinating mechanism for this change is unknown.

Lampreys appear to lack a background-response but exhibit a diurnal rhythm in color, dark in the day and pale at night, that in some species is mediated by the pineal gland. Young, in 1935, found that removal of the pituitary abolishes this rhythmical color change in adults and ammocoete larvae of *Lampetra planeri* and the lamprey then becomes permanently pale in color. In the ammocoetes, pinealectomy also abolished this diurnal rhythm but, in contrast to hypophysectomy, the animals were permanently dark. These observations have recently been extended (Eddy and Strahan, 1968) to two species of Australian lampreys. These antipodeal cyclostomes also exhibit a diurnal rhythm in color which stops following hypophysectomy. In larval *Geotria australis*, pinealectomy also abolishes the rhythm but in metamorphosing larval *Mordacia mordax*, the lateral eyes must be removed to see this effect.

As described earlier, the pineal is the site (especially in the dark) of formation of melatonin which in anuran tadpoles is a very potent stimulant of melanin aggregation and so pales the skin. It has been found that the injection of melatonin into larval *Geotria* also results in skin pallor but this effect is absent in *Mordacia*. In addition, if the pineal is transplanted under the skin of *Geotria* a local paling is observed. Melatonin may thus be involved in regulating the rhythmical changes in color seen in the ammocoetes of *Geotria* both by the production and release of melatonin and by acting as a photoreceptor organ. Following pinealectomy, the ammocoetes are permanently dark, which may reflect either the lack of an inhibitory effect of melatonin on the release of MSH or, more likely, a direct antagonism to the action of MSH on the melanophores. It also seems likely, in retrospect, that the same mechanism(s) regulates color change in the ammocoetes of *Lampetra planeri*.

The involvement of melatonin in color change in some larval cyclostomes, some amphibians and a chondrichthyean, is most interesting. Melatonin does not seem to have this role in many vertebrates but nevertheless it is present in representatives of all the vertebrate groups. The propensity of

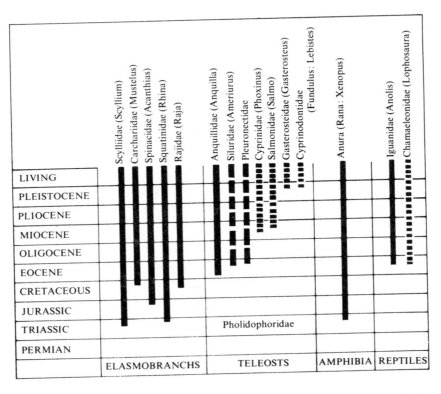

Fig. 7.9. The geological age of the different vertebrate groups in relation to the types of mechanisms (humoral, neural, or both) that they utilize to coordinate their melanophore background color responses.

The solid bars represent the possession of predominant humoral mechanisms; the broken bars, mixed, humoral and neural mechanisms; the small squares, predominantly neural control.

To this diagram could be added the Chelonia (*Chelodina oblonga*) and the Ophidia (*Crotalus*) both of which have a humoral control mechanism and which are identifiable from the Triassic.

It can be seen that humoral mechanisms appear to be the oldest and suggests that neural control is a later acquisition. (From Waring, 1942.)

the pineal to respond to diurnal changes in light makes it a potentially valuable gland for mediating endocrine rhythms which are dictated by changes in the seasons. As we shall see in Chapter 9, the pineal may in this manner contribute to the control of reproductive cycles in some vertebrates.

Evolutional color change mechanisms in vertebrates

From the preceding observations on the mechanisms controlling color change, we may make some guesses about the evolution of this process in vertebrates. Information of a comparative nature about extant species from diverse phyletic groups can be interpreted in a manner that may help us to reconstruct the past. Waring has summarized the available information about vertebrate color change in Fig. 7.9 but states that he has been sternly warned 'about pressing this kind of thing too far'.

The original underlying mechanism coordinating color change in vertebrates would appear to have been a humoral one as this has been observed exclusively in the Chondrichthyes (elasmobranchs) and has persisted in the Anura and Chelonia, all of which can be traced back to the Triassic. Superimposed, and probably subsequent to this, has been the evolution of a neural control of the melanophores which is seen in some teleosts and reptiles. In the teleosts, there is evidence of transitional changes as some species appear to utilize both neural and humoral mechanisms. The eels (Anguillidae) are specially interesting in this respect as they are normally completely dependent on humoral control, but there is also clear evidence for the presence of a neural mechanism that normally does not appear to contribute to color change. We can only speculate as to whether the eel represents a stage in the evolution towards a neural control of color change or is an evolutionary regression from this development. At the bottom of the vertebrate phyletic tree are the cyclostomes that possess an MSH that helps mediate a diurnal rhythm in color change but there is little evidence to suggest that these lowly fishes have an adaptive background color response. We can speculate even less as to whether or not the role of melatonin in controlling color changes in larval cyclostomes, reflects a primeval effect of this hormone, though it might!

Morphological color change

Several hormones influence morphological changes in the color of the integument. They include MSH and sex hormones, and corticotrophin and melatonin may also be involved. Such humoral effects on pigmentation are less well characterized than those of MSH on physiological color changes. Considerable interspecific differences in humoral effects on morphological pigmentation occur that make it impossible to give any generalized definition of their respective roles.

Melanin is formed from tyrosine by a complex chain of reactions which initially involves a copper-containing enzyme called tyrosinase. This enzyme may be in a soluble form in the cytoplasm of the melanocyte but when active it is attached to the melanosomes. A genetic absence of tyrosinase results in albinism though other factors, including ultraviolet light and several drugs, can also contribute quantitatively to changes in pigmentation. Increased levels of integumental melanin are associated with increased tyrosinase activity which can be influenced by hormones.

The morphological pigmentation of the skin, as well as fur and feathers, is in the first instance the result of the formation of melanin in the epidermal melanocytes, where it is attached to the melanosomes. In the skin, each melanocyte is associated with several keratinocytes to which the melanosomes, with their attached pigment, can be transferred. This functional association is called the 'epidermal-melanin unit' (Quevedo, 1972). In birds and mammals, the melanin is passed from the melanocytes associated with the feather tracks or hair follicles to the developing feathers or fur.

Dramatic changes in pigmentation associated with endocrine function have been noted in mammals that show seasonal differences in coat color, in birds that display sexual dimorphism in plumage color and in mammals suffering from endocrine imbalances. Many monkeys display prominent changes in color of parts of their skin associated with the sexual cycle and the areas are called the sex skin. At ovulation the buttocks enlarge and become red in color because of an engorgement of blood in the large venous sinuses. There is also an accumulation of mucopolysaccharides in the skin. This development of the sex skin is under the control of estrogens. These are only a few examples of the pigmentary changes that may occur in vertebrates and which are influenced by the action of hormones.

Hormones and seasonal changes in fur color

As described earlier, short-tailed weasels (*Mustela erminea*) change their coat color from brown to white with the onset of winter (Rust and Meyer, 1968). This change is a photoperiodic response due to changes of the length of the daylight hours and can be prevented by hypophysectomy. The latter operation results in a permanent white coat but the growth of new brown fur can be promoted when the weasels are injected with MSH or corticotrophin. In addition, if the pituitary is transplanted to the kidney, where MSH release is increased due to a lack of hypothalamic inhibition, brown fur also grows on previously white animals.

If melatonin, in a 'slow-release vehicle' of beeswax, is implanted under the skin, weasels that are undergoing a normal spring molt from a white to brown pelage, regrow white, instead of brown, fur. Rust and Meyer (1969) suggest that this is the result of a stimulation by melatonin of the release of MSH-R-IH from the hypothalamus so that the MSH levels drop. This experimental treatment of weasels also prevents the development of the gonads and the onset of normal spring reproductive cycles, so that it is possible that an interference with the normal levels of other hormones, apart from MSH, is also contributing to the effect. Precise experiments of this kind, to determine the role of hormones in seasonal changes of coat color in mammals, have been rare but, as described below, there are several other examples of pigmentary changes in coat color that can be induced by a deficiency or excess of MSH.

Hormones and morphological color change in cold-blooded vertebrates

Cold-blooded vertebrates that undergo physiological color changes have also been shown to increase the levels of melanin in their skin in response to a continual environmental 'black background' stimulation of MSH secretion. Such a change has been observed in amphibians, teleosts and chondrichthyeans. In the goldfish, *Carassius auratus*, corticotrophin increases the cutaneous levels of melanin and the activity of tyrosinase (Chavin, Kim and Tchen, 1963); an effect that cannot be mimicked by mammalian MSH. In contrast, MSH, but not corticotrophin, increased cutaneous melanin synthesis in the killifish, *Fundulus heteroclitus* (Pickford and Kosto, 1957) and one must, therefore, be careful not to draw any general systematic conclusions about the role of such hormones in melanin synthesis in the Teleostei. As the hormone preparations used in the fishes were of mammalian origin the differences in the responses could reflect the degree of similarity of these exogenous hormones to the particular endogenous MSH present in each species of fish.

The effects of changes in the level of endogenous MSH on melanin levels in the melanophores has been observed in the dogfish *Scyliorhinus canicula* (Wilson and Dodd, 1973b). Removal of the neurointermediate lobe of the pituitary in this chondrichthyean resulted in an almost complete loss of melanin from the skin. In the converse experiment, when increased circulating levels of MSH were promoted by severing the inhibitory hypothalamic connections to the intermediate lobe, there was an increased concentration of melanin in the skin.

Cold-blooded vertebrates may also exhibit morphological changes in skin color and pattern that are of a rather colorful nature. Some female lizards develop colored, orange and orange-red, spots on various parts of their bodies during the period of the development of their eggs in the body; they are thus called 'pregnancy spots' (Cooper and Ferguson, 1972; Ferguson and Chen, 1973; Medica, Turner and Smith, 1973). Such changes in color have a hormonal basis which has been examined in the collared lizard, *Crotaphytus collaris* and the leopard lizard *C. wislizenii*. The injection of progesterone induces such pigmentation in ovariectomized lizards and estrogen increases the response though it is ineffective alone. The natural levels of these hormones change during the growth of the eggs and their circulating concentrations have been measured in such lizards and can be correlated with the development of the pregnancy spots. The injection of FSH also induces the formation of such pigmented areas in leopard lizards. It would thus appear under natural conditions that a release of this pituitary hormone stimulates the development of the ovarian follicle together with a release of gonadal steroids (see Chapter 9), and these directly mediate the response. The role of pregnancy spots in these lizards is uncertain but it has been suggested that they may deter the males from inappropriate amorous advances.

Hormones and sexual dimorphism in avian plumage color

The mechanisms of the effects of hormones in mediating the seasonal sexual dimorphism in the color of plumage in weaver birds, *Steganura paradisaea*, and the non-seasonal differences in domestic brown leghorn fowl have been studied by Hall (1969).

The male weaver bird grows prominent black feathers just before (pre-nuptial) the breeding season. When areas of white feathers are plucked from the these birds the injection of pituitary ICSH (or LH) results in the appearance of melanin granules in the feather tracts of these areas and a related growth of black feathers. The formation of melanin is associated with an increased activity of tyrosinase in the feather tracts. The effect of ICSH is direct and is not mediated through any action on the gonads as it is still seen in castrated birds.

The male house finch, *Carpodacus mexicanus*, has red or orange feathers on its crown, throat and belly, which is in contrast to the female in which this plumage is brown. When the colored feathers are plucked from cas-trated males the new, regrown feathers are of the female, brown type which contrasts with the renewal of the colored plumes in intact birds (Tewary and Farner, 1973). It thus appears that, like in the male weaver bird, the more gaily colored plumage of the male is determined by the presence of male sex hormones. It seems, however, that these hormones are from the gonads of the finches, though an indirect action that could involve the pituitary is also possible.

The male domestic brown leghorn fowl has black feathers on its neck and breast while those in the female are a pinkish-brown. In this instance, the coloration of the male plumage is not hormone dependent but that of the female is due to the action of estrogens. The injection of estradiol increases melanin formation and the activity of tyrosinase. The estrogens act directly on the feather tracts as their action is a local one at the site of the injection (Greenwood and Blyth, 1935).

Hormones and pigmentation during endocrine imbalance

Changes in endocrine function associated with the adrenal cortex and pituitary have often been observed in man and experimental animals. Addison's Disease, which results in a deficiency of corticosteroids, is associated with the deposition of excessive pigment in the skin of man and a rise in the blood MSH levels (Thody and Plummer, 1973). Cortico-steroids, by a feedback mechanism, normally prevent an excessive secretion of MSH and this latter hormone promotes the formation of melanin in the skin. Direct injections of MSH have been shown to deepen the skin color of African negroids (Lerner and McGuire, 1961). Pregnancy in women is also often associated with an increased pigmentation in certain areas of the skin and this change is also thought to reflect an extra release of MSH. Adrenalectomy in the prairie deer mouse (*Peromyscus m. bairdii*) results in a darkening of the coat color which is associated with an increase in circulating MSH concentration. This change in release of MSH, in response to adrenalectomy, does not, however, occur in laboratory mice so that a broad generalization cannot be made about this effect (Geschwind, Huseby and Nishioka, 1972). Certain genetic strains in mice respond to injections of MSH, or the implantation of pituitary tumors containing MSH, by developing a dark color in newly grown fur (such as that formed following plucking) (Geschwind *et al.*, 1972). This melanotrophic effect of MSH thus appears to be fairly common but its significance in normal regulation of melanin synthesis still eludes us.

Mechanisms of hormone-mediated changes in integumental melanin distribution

Physiological color change is an alteration in the dispersion of melanin in the melanophores, such as that mediated by MSH and adrenaline, and this is related to the level of cellular cyclic AMP. This nucleotide is formed in the presence of MSH as a result of the activation of adenyl cyclase which is presumably associated with the melanophores. Cyclic AMP stimulates a dispersion of the melanosomes. This response requires the presence of calcium and may involve a microtubular system in the cell but the details of this are unknown (Novales, 1972). Adrenaline, on the other hand, may inhibit adenyl cyclase and decrease the formation of cyclic AMP (α-adrenergic effect) or in some instances, as in the spade foot toad, *Scaphiopus couchi*, and the lizard *Anolis carolinensis*, it also activates the enzyme (β-adrenergic effect) and so mimics the effect of MSH (Abe *et al.*, 1969; Goldman and Hadley, 1969). The neural responses of the melanophores also appear to be mediated by changes in the levels of cyclic AMP (Novales, 1973). The aggregating nerve fibers may exert an α-adrenergic effect and dispersing fibers a β-adrenergic one. The latter effect is observed *in vitro* but its significance *in vivo* is unknown.

The increase in melanin synthesis that occurs in morphological color change appears to be due to an increase in the activity of tyrosinase. As we have seen, this enzyme is associated with the action of MSH in mammals and also ICSH and estrogens in birds. The precise mechanisms by which this change occurs may, however, differ for each hormone. Lee, Lee and Lu (1972) have studied the effect of MSH on a mouse skin tumor that contains a high concentration of melanocytes (a melanoma). The increase in tyrosinase activity in response to MSH in this tumor does not appear to be the result of formation of new enzymes but rather the activation of those already present; possibly by the removal of an inhibitor. In the amphibian skin, a different mechanism may operate, and it is thought that a trypsin-like enzyme is released which activates tyrosinase which is present in the cytoplasm. The latter enzyme is then attached to the melanosome where it initiates the conversion of tyrosine to dopa that eventually leads to the formation of melanin. In birds (Hall, 1969), the action of ICSH in increasing cutaneous tyrosinase activity also does not appear to involve the synthesis of a new enzyme, as its effect is not inhibited by puromycin. The effect of estradiol on pigmentation in the brown leghorn fowl, however, *is* inhibited by puromycin so that the action of this hormone may then be due to an induction of tyrosinase. The many effects of hormones on integumental pigmentation thus may be reflected in a diversity in the mechanisms by which they exert their effects. At the present time, however, it would appear that the activity of tyrosinase is central to their morphological actions.

Has there been an evolution of the role of MSH?

While MSH has well-established effects in mediating color change in cold-blooded vertebrates, its normal role in birds and mammals is uncertain. MSH undoubtedly, in some circumstances and in certain species, stimulates the synthesis of melanin in the skin of mammals but whether this is its normal physiological role is not clear. It is possible that MSH may exhibit such a function especially in species like the weasel that seasonally change the color of their coat. Such an effect is, however, limited to a relatively few species and yet mammals, as well as birds, possess MSH and sometimes in several molecular forms (see Chapter 3). Does it then have other physiological effects in these animals? Despite a widespread search no satisfactory answer to this has emerged. Several other effects of MSH have been noted, such as an ability to promote the regeneration of visual purple in the retina (Hanaoka, 1953) and an antagonism to the hyperglycemic effect of adrenaline (Munday, 1957). Is it possible then that the MSH is merely a vestigial hormone in most birds and mammals? Its tenacious phyletic persistence in the pituitary makes this intuitively difficult for some to believe!

There is also an unanswered question as to whether or not the effects of MSH on melanin dispersion in the melanophore and melanin synthesis in the melanocyte reflect the same basic effect. In other words, does the effect on synthesis represent a distinct and separate evolution of the hormone's role and is the fact that melanin is involved in both merely fortuitous? If these effects are quite distinct it is possible that they have both existed, side by side, for a long time. Birds and mammals may have only lost the melanin-dispersing action together with the responding melanophores. The MSH's, corticotrophin and lipotrophin exhibit many structural similarities to each other and it has even been suggested that they could have arisen from a single 'parent' molecule. A loss of MSH may thus not be genetically simple, even in a species where the hormone may have no present use.

Conclusions

The integument is a very complex tissue that may be involved in several physiological phenomena including osmoregulation, color change, temperature regulation and reproduction. There are many characteristic processes involved in such mechanisms that have a definite systematic distribution (for example, sweat glands, mammary glands and branchial chloride-secreting cells) so that when hormones are involved, as they often are, their effects follow phyletic suite. Such responses must have also arisen at distinct times during vertebrate evolution. It is interesting to observe that there is often a definite relationship between the nature of the particular hormone and the general physiological process involved; sex hormones influence sexual processes in the skin, as well as elsewhere, and adrenocorticosteroids regulate (see Chapter 8) electrolyte movements in sweat glands and across the amphibian skin, as well as in the kidney. Some hormones have a special propensity to mediate processes in the integument. MSH thus influences pigmentation in nearly all groups of vertebrates commencing phyletically with the cyclostomes and on occasions it may even promote formation of melanin in mammalian skin. Its action, however, appears to be rather 'conservative' as it has no other established effect on any other types of process in the body nor for that matter in the integument either. In contrast, prolactin is 'versatile' as, apart from effects at non-ectodermal sites, it influences many integumental processes including molting cycles, the secretions from the mucous and mammary glands, proliferation of the crop-sac and development of the brood-patch in birds, and the control of water and salt movements across the gills of fishes. Some of these effects will be described in the next chapters.

8. Hormones and osmoregulation

About 70% of the body weight of animals is water in which are dissolved a variety of solutes, the presence of many of which is vital for life. Within the body, the solutions inside the cells differ from those that bathe the outside and the composition of each of these solutions must be maintained so as to provide an environment with an electrolyte content and osmotic concentration suitable for life. These intra- and extracellular fluids provide the framework in which life exists.

The physicochemical properties of the body fluids in animals usually differ greatly from those of their external environment. Animals continually suffer exposure to the whims of the exoteric conditions and this will tend to change the composition of their body fluids. In addition, although the intra- and extracellular fluids have identical osmotic concentrations, there are qualitative differences in the solutes they contain, and equilibration, due to diffusion, will tend to occur. Such animals, however, maintain the gradients between their body fluids and the environment; an equilibrium that is maintained as a result of a complex pattern of physiological events. These processes involve the cells, and special tissues and organs that are concerned with osmoregulation. The integration of the functions of these homeostatic tissues relies largely on hormones. The nervous system makes little direct contribution to such regulatory processes though at the cellular level itself considerable autoregulation, independent of hormones, exists. Hormones do ultimately influence some cellular processes of course, but they generally appear to do this in effector tissues like the kidney, gills and gut, which are especially concerned with the overall osmoregulation of the animal. For a more complete account of the role of hormones in osmoregulation the book by Bentley (1971) could be consulted.

Animals occupy diverse osmotic environments; the major ones are the sea, fresh water like rivers and lakes, and dry land. Differences exist between the availability of water and salts within these environments and this is particularly apparent to animals that lead a terrestrial life. Water may be relatively freely available to some terrestrial species that live in areas where rainfall is high, and lakes, ponds and rivers exist in close proximity to where they live. Other animals, however, live in dry, desert regions where water may only be available sporadically and in limited quantities. Salts are freely available to marine animals but in fresh water the supplies are more restricted, and some terrestrial animals may occupy regions where a low salt content in the soil may be reflected in a salt-deficient diet. It is thus not surprising to find that the processes for controlling the water and solute content of the body, called osmoregulation, can differ considerably between species that habitually occupy diverse ecological situations. These differences may be manifested as a tolerance to osmotic changes but are principally seen as differences in the functions of the tissues and organs concerned in maintaining the composition of the body fluids. Not unexpectedly, the evolution of the tissues and organs concerned with osmoregulation has been accompanied by changes in the role of the endocrine glands that help integrate their functioning.

Homeostatic events that contribute to osmoregulation may involve changes in either the rates of loss of water and solutes or in the processes of their accumulation.

Osmoregulation in terrestrial environments (see Fig. 8.1)

Terrestrial vertebrates may lose water as a result of evaporation from the skin and respiratory tract. This loss is greatest in hot, dry air in which little water vapor is present. In homeotherms, evaporation from the respiratory tract and the skin may be increased. In the latter this may be due to the activity of the sweat glands, as a result of the need to dissipate heat. While evaporation will be the predominant route for water loss in animals living in hot, dry conditions, additional quantities pass out of the kidneys in the urine, and out of the gut in the feces. Reproductive processes, such as egg-laying and lactation, will also result in increased water losses. Water is gained in the food, from which substantial quantities may be absorbed across the intestines, and as a result of drinking. In addition, amphibians, like frogs and toads, can absorb water across their permeable skin, from damp surfaces and pools of fresh water. Any excessive water that may be gained in such ways is excreted by the kidneys.

Salt losses in land-living vertebrates occur in the urine and feces and, in mammals, in the sweat gland secretions. Some birds and reptiles possess special glands in their heads called nasal salt glands which have an ability to secrete concentrated solutions of salts. Some regulation of the losses from the sweat glands and gut occurs, and the secretion of the kidneys undergoes a rigorous process of conservation so that salts that are deficient in the body may be conserved. Additional conservation of urinary salts can occur from urine during its storage in the urinary bladder of amphibians and some reptiles. Birds and many reptiles lack a urinary bladder but in such animals the urine passes into the cloaca and up into the large intestine

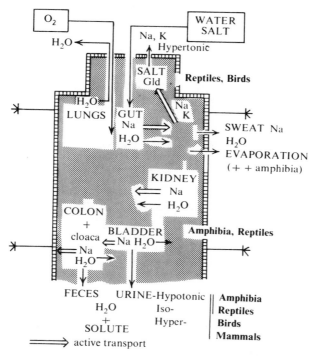

Fig. 8.1. A diagrammatic summary of the pathways of water and salt losses and gains in vertebrates living on dry land. (From Bentley, 1972.)

where some of its contained salts and fluid can be transported back into the blood. Salts are mainly gained in the diet of terrestrial animals and the drinking of brackish water may also result in salt accumulation. The latter process, however, only occurs rarely in nature. Excesses of accumulated salts can be excreted by the kidneys and in many birds and reptiles by the nasal salt glands.

Osmoregulation in fresh water (see Fig. 8.2)

Many species of vertebrates live in fresh water, a solution that is hypo-osmotic to the body fluids and which only contains small amounts of dissolved solutes. Water will thus tend to be gained by osmosis across the integument of such animals. Amphibians have a relatively permeable skin and can take up large amounts of water in this way. Fishes respire with the aid of gills which, apart from allowing the exchange of oxygen and carbon dioxide, are also permeable to water and so are an additional route for the

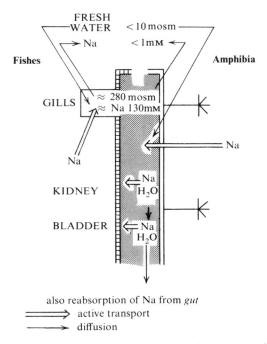

Fig. 8.2. A diagrammatic summary of the pathways for water and salt losses and gains of fishes and amphibians that live in fresh water. (From Bentley, 1972.)

accumulation of water in the body. The skin of reptiles and mammals that frequent fresh water is usually quite impermeable so that little water is accumulated through this channel and, as they breathe with the aid of lungs, they do not suffer the osmotic problems associated with the presence of gills.

Vertebrates living in fresh water may be prone to a greater salt loss than their terrestrial or marine relatives. When the integument is permeable, such as the skin in the Amphibia and the gills of fish, salt loss may be expected to occur as a result of diffusion. Such potential losses, however, are rather limited and are much smaller than may be expected on a simple physicochemical basis. In addition, salt losses may continually occur in the urine because of the necessity for the excretion of water that has accumulated by osmosis.

The solute excretion in the urine is reduced by its reabsorption from the renal tubules. In aquatic amphibians and reptiles, like turtles, and some fishes, sodium is also reabsorbed from the urine that is stored in the urinary bladder.

Salts are principally obtained from the food of aquatic vertebrates. However, additional gains of sodium chloride may be made as a result of their active transport, against electrochemical gradients, across the skin of amphibians and the gills of fish. It has also been suggested that some turtles may actively accumulate sodium across their pharyngeal and cloacal membranes during their irrigation by the external freshwater solution.

Osmoregulation in the sea (see Fig. 8.3)

Most species of fishes as well as a number of reptiles and at least one frog (the crab-eating frog, *Rana cancrivora*) live in the sea. This solution is strongly hyperosmotic to the body fluids of most vertebrates. The exceptions are the hagfishes (Agnatha), the sharks and rays (Chondrichthyes)

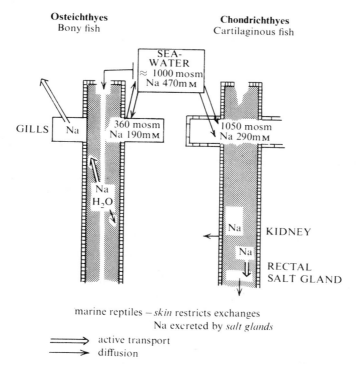

Fig. 8.3. A diagrammatic summary of the pathways for water and salt losses and gains in osteichthyean and chondrichthyean fishes that live in the sea. (From Bentley, 1972.)

and the coelacanth which are isoosmotic, or slightly hyperosmotic, to sea-water. The crab-eating frog is also slightly hyperosmotic to the sea-water in which it lives.

Most of the bony fishes (Osteichthyes) thus tend to lose water by osmosis, especially across their gill membranes. The Chondrichthyes and myxinoid Agnatha, on the other hand, may gain small amounts of fluid in this way. The sodium chloride concentration in the sea-water is much higher than that in the blood of osteichthyean, or even chondrichthyean fishes so that an accumulation of salt will tend to occur.

The mechanisms utilized to maintain osmotic balance in sea-water are varied. Marine teleost fish drink sea-water and much of the salt that is present is absorbed across the gut wall and water follows this solute by osmosis. The salt is excreted by special cells called 'chloride-secreting cells', or 'ionophores', present in the gills. Divalent ions are either excreted in the feces or urine. The gain of salts by marine chondrichthyeans is small compared to that of teleosts, and this is excreted in the urine and as a concentrated solution from a tissue unique among the vertebrates, the rectal salt gland. This salt-secreting organ is situated in the nether regions of the gut. Marine reptiles appear to have a relatively impermeable integument that restricts the gain of salt but excesses, such as may be gained in the food, can be excreted by the cephalic salt glands that are often modified tear, or orbital, glands.

It can be seen that the osmotic problems of vertebrates differ considerably and depend on the environment where they live as well as the anatomical and physiological wherewithal that is conferred by their phylogeny. The maintenance of osmotic homeostatis is dependent on a variety of tissues and glands, some of which, like the kidney, are present in all the major phyletic groups of vertebrates, and others, like cephalic salt glands and the rectal gland, which have a more restricted distribution. The activity of many of the organs and tissues involved in osmoregulation are controlled by hormones. A summary of these is given in Table 8.1.

Osmoregulation in vertebrates is dependent on the active participation of such tissues as the kidneys, gills, skin, urinary bladder, gut and certain salt-secreting glands. These tissues contribute to the excretion and conservation of water and salts, and their roles and physiological significance are not the same in all species.

The hormones that influence osmoregulation most directly are the neurohypophysial hormones, principally vasotocin and vasopressin (ADH), the adrenocorticosteroids, the catecholamines and prolactin. Corticotrophin and angiotensin are indirectly involved because of their roles in controlling the release of adrenocorticosteroids. Angiotensin may also have a more direct effect on some membranes while the urophysis and corpuscles of Stannius, which have putative endocrine functions, may also be involved.

Active transport and secretion of ions, especially sodium, potassium, bicarbonate and chloride, across, or from the epithelial membranes that make up the tissues that effect osmoregulation, are basic to their physiological function. Such membranes are osmotically permeable to water, which can pass across them with an ease that may vary, depending on the membrane and the physiological conditions. The adequate functioning of these osmoregulatory tissues is ultimately dependent on their blood supply. Hormones may thus influence the activity of osmoregulatory tissues by actions at several sites:

(1) Hormones may alter the processes of active sodium and chloride transport and the secretion of hydrogen ions, bicarbonate and potassium. Cortisol and aldosterone can alter sodium and potassium movements across many epithelial membranes. Vasotocin and ADH may also promote such transmural sodium transport. Catecholamines can increase transport and secretion of chloride ions in several tissues and also can inhibit the effects of ADH. All these hormones act directly on the cells involved.

(2) Osmotic and diffusional movements of water and sodium across epithelial membranes can be changed by hormones. Vasotocin and ADH may increase the permeability to water of the renal tubule (in some species) as well as amphibian skin and urinary bladder. Prolactin can reduce the permeability of the gills of certain teleost fishes to sodium, thus limiting diffusional losses of this ion in fresh water.

(3) The catecholamines and neurohypophysial peptides can alter the diameter of blood vessels and so may influence the functioning of osmoregulatory tissues by virtue of their vasoactive actions. The urine flow, especially in non-mammals, may be influenced by changes in the rate of filtration of plasma across the glomerulus and this process can be altered by these hormones. Alterations in secretion and absorption of ions across the gills of fishes may also be changed by such hormonally mediated variations in the regional blood flow.

While this chapter is principally concerned with hormones, the role of nerves in osmoregulation should also be mentioned. Neural integration is not common, though it does occur. The nasal salt-secreting glands in birds and reptiles are stimulated to secrete as a result of the stimulation of autonomic cholinergic nerves. Corticosteroids may contribute to the well-being of the underlying processes but do not directly stimulate secretion. The sweat glands of mammals secrete in response to the need to dissipate heat and this usually occurs following stimulation of autonomic cholinergic or adrenergic nerves (as described earlier, Chapter 5). However, sweat gland

TABLE 8.1. *Target organs for osmoregulatory-type responses to hormones in vertebrates*
The responses in *italics* appear to be physiological ones while others are either only pharmacological or the evidence for their normal, in-vivo role is as yet equivocal. The responses are not necessarily present in all members of the orders of vertebrates that are indicated.

Target organ	Phyletic distribution of target organ	Stimulatory hormone	Nature of response	Phyletic distribution of responsiveness
Kidney	All vertebrates	Vasotocin	*Decreased glomerular filtration rate (GFR) and increased renal tubular water reabsorption = decreased urine flow (antidiuresis)*	Amphibians, reptiles and birds
			Decreased GFR = antidiuresis	Teleost (eels)
			Increased GFR = diuresis	Some teleosts and lungfishes
		Vasopressin	*Increased renal tubular water reabsorption = antidiuresis*	Mammals
		Prolactin	Decreased renal Na excretion	Mammals (rat, man)
			Increased urine flow (increased GFR, decreased renal tubular water reabsorption)	Some teleosts
Urinary bladder	Most vertebrates (except birds, some reptiles and many fishes)	Vasotocin	*Increased water and Na reabsorption*	Amphibians (mostly anurans)
		Aldosterone	Increased Na reabsorption	Amphibians and reptiles
		Prolactin	Reduced water permeability, increased Na reabsorption	Teleost (Starry flounder)

Site	Group	Hormone	Effect	Occurs in
Gills	Fishes and larval amphibians	Cortisol	*Increased outward Na secretion*	Marine teleosts
			Increased inward Na absorption	Freshwater teleosts
		Vasotocin	Increased inward or outward movements of Na	Freshwater (inward) or marine (outward) teleosts
		Aldosterone	Uptake across larval amphibian gills?	
		Adrenaline	Decreased secretion by Cl-secreting cells	Marine teleosts
		Prolactin	*Decreased Na diffusion outwards and water accumulation (inwards)*	Freshwater teleosts
			Decreased Na extrusion	Marine teleosts
Skin	All vertebrates	Vasotocin	*Increased water and Na absorption*	Some amphibians
		Aldosterone	*Increased Na absorption*	
		Angiotensin	As above	
		Prolactin	Decreased permeability to water and Na	Urodele amphibians (?)
Sweat glands	Mammals	Aldosterone	*Reduced Na loss in sweat*	
		Adrenaline	*Increased secretion during exercise*	
Salt glands	Some birds and reptiles (nasal and orbital glands) and chondrichthyeans (rectal glands)	Cortisol	Facilitates secretion	Birds and reptiles
		Cortisol	Reduces secretion	Chondrichthyeans
		Aldosterone	Reduces Na secretion	Lizard
		Prolactin	Increases secretion	Bird
		Vasotocin	Increases secretion	Bird

TABLE 8.1 – *continued*

Target organ	Phyletic distribution of target organ	Stimulatory hormone	Nature of response	Phyletic distribution of responsiveness
Salivary glands	Mammals	Aldosterone	*Decreases Na and increases K loss*	
		Adrenaline	*Dries up secretion*	
Intestine	All vertebrates	Cortisol	*Increased NaCl absorption*	Teleosts
		Aldosterone	Increased NaCl absorption in colon	Mammals, amphibians
		Angiotensin	As above	Mammal (rat)
		Prolactin	Decreased salt and water absorption	Teleosts
			Increased fluid absorption	Mammal (rat)

secretion during exercise may depend on circulating adrenaline. The vasoconstrictor tone of blood vessels is primarily dependent on the activity of adrenergic nerves which can thus, indirectly, alter the functioning of tissues. This effect is sometimes observed in the kidney of animals but is probably not a usual physiological mechanism.

The role of hormones in osmoregulation

Mammals

These vertebrates have a complement of hormones, similar to other vertebrates, that can influence osmoregulation, though the roles of such secretions may differ somewhat from those in non-mammals.

Vasopressin is unique to the mammals. It reduces urinary water losses (antidiuresis) as a result of an increased osmotic reabsorption of water from the kidney tubules. Vasopressin's phyletic forebear, vasotocin, as we have seen, has a slightly different chemical structure that confers on it a pronounced ability to contract smooth muscle such as in the oviduct and uterus and also, when injected, to promote contractions of the myo-epithelial cells in the mammary glands. Injected vasotocin also has an antidiuretic action in mammals and it could thus conceivably function in such a physiological role. Vasopressin, however, lacks the prominent effects that vasotocin has on non-vascular smooth muscle contraction and so exerts a more specific action in the body. Its evolutionary perpetuation in mammals is therefore not surprising. Vasopressin does not appear to have any other physiological role, on other organs, in mammals. It can, however, exert other effects, such as increasing the blood pressure, contracting the uterus and raising blood sugar levels, when it is injected in large amounts.

Adrenocorticosteroids play an important role in controlling sodium and potassium metabolism in mammals. The absence of the adrenal cortex in mammals quickly results in death, resulting mainly from losses of sodium and an accumulation of potassium. Aldosterone is the most effective of the adrenocortical hormones that exhibit actions on sodium and potassium metabolism in mammals, though the others, especially corticosterone, can also exert such effects. Sodium excretion from the kidney, sweat glands and salivary glands is reduced while potassium loss is increased; there is a drop in the ratio of sodium/potassium in the secreted fluids. It also seems likely that aldosterone can promote sodium reabsorption from the large intestine (this has been demonstrated *in vitro*) and the mammary gland ducts (Yagil, Etzion and Berlyne, 1973). The osmoregulatory effects of the cortico-steroids in mammals are thus all directed to the same general purpose:

sodium conservation and potassium excretion, and seem to involve at least five different target tissues.

Adrenaline has a less prominent role in osmoregulation. Its action in stimulating sweat gland secretion has already been mentioned. In addition, adrenaline can antagonize the release, and the effects, of ADH on the kidney. Such inhibition is an α-adrenergic action that can be demonstrated in experimental animals, though its possible physiological importance is not yet clear.

Angiotensin, apart from initiating the release of aldosterone, has been shown to promote sodium reabsorption from the kidney tubule and the rat colon. Another interesting effect of angiotensin is its ability, when injected, to promote drinking in rats, as well as some other mammals (Fitzsimons, 1972). Drinking is elicited by the sensation of thirst which arises in the brain in a number of circumstances, including a reduction in the volume of the extracellular fluids. This latter response is reduced if the kidneys are removed, suggesting that the renin–angiotensin system may be involved. Indeed, the injection of small amounts of angiotensin II into the region of the 'thirst center' in the anterior diencephalon of the brain promotes drinking. The physiological importance of these effects of angiotensin is not yet clear.

Birds

Birds possess osmoregulatory hormones that are similar to those of other non-mammalian tetrapods.

Vasotocin acts as an antidiuretic hormone comparable in its effect to vasopressin in mammals. Vasotocin increases water reabsorption from the renal tubule of birds and in slightly higher, but still physiological, concentrations also decreases the GFR (Skadhauge, 1969). The hormone thus has two effects on the avian kidney, both of which decrease urinary water loss. Two types of nephrons have been identified in the kidney of the desert quail, *Lophortx gambelii* (Braun and Dantzler, 1972, 1974), a mammalian-type, with a loop of Henle and a reptilian-type that lacks this tubular segment. Glomerular filtration across the reptilian-type nephron is more variable than in the mammalian-type and the former cease functioning when excess sodium chloride is administered. The reptilian-type nephron is the site where vasotocin acts when it decreases the GFR in the desert quail.

It is interesting that vasotocin probably has another physiological role in birds, as it contracts the oviduct and so can assist oviposition. Vasotocin may thus have two physiological, but unrelated, roles and this situation may also occur in reptiles and amphibians. As described earlier (Chapter 5), vasotocin, when injected, also has a hyperglycemic and hyperlipidemic effect in birds, and it can also stimulate secretion from the nasal salt glands. The physiological spectrum of vasotocin's action could thus be even larger than just an involvement with osmoregulation, but the importance of such non-osmoregulatory effects in the body are in doubt.

The *adrenocorticosteroids*, of which birds possess aldosterone and corticosterone, reduce renal sodium loss and facilitate potassium excretion, just as in mammals. Adrenalectomy, in ducks, also reduces the ability of the nasal salt glands to secrete hypertonic salt solutions. Corticosterone, but not aldosterone, can restore this deficiency in adrenalectomized ducks. Corticotrophin and corticosteroids also enhance salt gland secretion when they are injected into intact ducks. These effects, however, are probably indirect and the result of an elevated glucose concentration in the blood (see Peaker, 1971; Phillips and Ensor, 1972).

The immediate stimulus for secretion of the avian salt glands is a neural one that is initiated by a hypertonicity of the plasma. Hormones may, however, impinge their effects on this process. Adrenaline inhibits the salt gland's response to hypertonic saline which probably reflects its vaso-constrictor effect. Hypophysectomy abolishes the secretory response of the salt gland and this deficiency can be partly restored by the injection of corticotrophin or prolactin. Injections of prolactin into normal ducks also stimulates salt gland secretion. This action of prolactin is an interesting one for, as we shall see later, this hormone has an osmoregulatory function in some teleost fishes. It is, however, likely that its action in birds is indirect, due to its role in maintaining an optimal intake of food and water, especially following hypophysectomy (see Ensor, Simons and Phillips, 1973).

The adrenal cortex of birds is influenced by the amount of salt in their diet and this effect can be seen in nature. It has been observed (Holmes, Butler and Phillips, 1961) that birds living in environments near the sea or supplies of brackish water, where their salt intake may be high, have larger adrenal glands than species that habitually have fresh water to drink.

The *prolactin* stores in the pituitary are also influenced by the bird's salt intake. Herring gulls, *Larus argentatus*, given salt solutions to drink suffer a depletion in the stores of prolactin in their pituitaries, which is associated with an elevated osmotic concentration of the plasma (Fig. 8.4). The functional significance, if any, of these observations is unknown; for, as we have seen, we do not know of any clear role for prolactin in avian osmoregulation. It is interesting that prolactin levels in the pituitaries of rats also decline in response to dehydration (Ensor, Edmondson and Phillips, 1972). In some teleost fishes, prolactin is released in response to hypoosmotic conditions (see later) and this hormone serves an important role in their osmoregulation. The depletion of pituitary prolactin in birds could represent a non-specific response (stress) or the activation of a

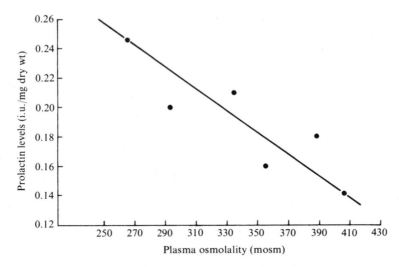

Fig. 8.4. The relationship of plasma osmolality and the storage of prolactin in the pituitary gland of juvenile herring gulls or black-backed gulls (*Larus argentatus* and *L. fuscus*). These birds were given saline-solutions of different concentrations to drink. As the concentration of this drinking water was increased the plasma osmolality rose while the prolactin storage declined. (From Phillips and Ensor, 1972.)

pathway for the hormone's release, that is a phyletic survivor from ancestral forms. However, prolactin could serve a physiological role in osmo-regulation that is, as yet, to be defined.

The possible interrelations of nerves and hormones in influencing the electrolyte metabolism of birds that possess nasal salt glands is sum-marized in Fig. 8.5. The avian adrenal, as in mammals, can be controlled by both the adenohypophysis and a renin–angiotensin system.

The cloaca of birds appears to play a role in their osmoregulation. Urine passes into this segment of the gut, from which it travels up into the large intestine which is the site of fluid reabsorption. It seems likely that this reabsorption may be influenced by hormones. Vasotocin does not seem to be involved but some indirect evidence suggests that corticosteroids may increase salt absorption, as in the mammalian colon. However, the evidence for this is still only fragmentary (Crocker and Holmes, 1971).

Reptiles

Reptiles are poikilothermic, a process that profoundly influences their osmoregulation, and represent a substantial metabolic departure from the

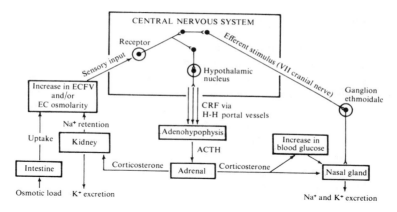

Fig. 8.5. A diagrammatic summary of the physiological and endocrine processes that appear to be involved in controlling sodium and potassium excretion in marine birds. It should be noted that not all species of birds possess a functioning nasal salt gland and that the evidence for the scheme depicted above is largely based on observations on the domestic duck and gulls. (From Holmes, 1972.)

birds and mammals. These animals live in diverse osmotic habitats including the sea, fresh water, and terrestrial situations ranging from deserts to tropical rain forests.

Reptiles possess *vasotocin* and this, when injected, can decrease urine flow by a dual action (as in birds), namely an increase of the renal tubular reabsorption of water and a decrease of the GFR (see LeBrie, 1972).

The role of the *adrenocorticosteroids* in reptilian osmoregulation is not clear. Adrenalectomy has been variously reported to cause no change in plasma electrolytes, result in a potassium accumulation or sodium loss or, as in birds and mammals, to have both of these effects. These diverse observations may be the result of the longer periods of time that poikilo-therms often take to respond to altered physiological and environmental circumstances. Injected aldosterone can increase renal tubular reabsorption of sodium in the snake, *Natrix cyclopion*, but only after it has received additional sodium chloride which, presumably, decreases endogenous levels of the steroid hormone (LeBrie, 1972). On the other hand, the injection of aldosterone into a saline-loaded lizard, *Dipsosaurus dorsalis*, has no effect on renal electrolyte excretion (Bradshaw, Shoemaker and Nagy, 1972). *Dipsosaurus dorsalis*, like many birds and other reptiles, has a functional nasal salt gland, but injected corticosteroids do not initiate secretion from this gland (Shoemaker, Nagy and Bradshaw, 1972). Indeed, the sodium secretion is abolished by aldosterone injections. It has been suggested that in the lizard salt gland, aldosterone may promote sodium reabsorption from the tubules in the glands as it does in the mammalian kidney.

When excesses of sodium chloride are administered to the lizards, *Dipsosaurus dorsalis* and *Amphibolurus ornatus*, corticosteroid levels in the plasma increase (see Bradshaw, 1972). This effect contrasts with what is seen in mammals and amphibians where a sodium deficiency is associated with increased release of corticosteroids. In these species of lizards, the increased level of corticosteroids facilitates urinary sodium losses by decreasing renal sodium reabsorption, a response that is opposite to that seen in mammals where renal sodium reabsorption is increased.

The role of the adrenocorticosteroids in controlling sodium and potassium metabolism in reptiles is not completely understood. Some of the responses are reminiscent of those in other phyletic groups of vertebrates but some are quite different. One cannot, at present, draw any unified picture about the role of adrenocorticosteroids in the Reptilia.

Aldosterone may act at extrarenal sites in some reptiles. The urinary bladders of reptiles are the site of active sodium reabsorption from the urine that is stored there. This salt transport can be increased, *in vitro*, by aldosterone in the tortoise, *Testudo graeca*, and the freshwater turtle, *Pseudemys scripta* (Bentley, 1962; LeFevre, 1973). It is unknown whether this effect of aldosterone exists normally in these chelonians but it could reflect an evolution of this hormone's osmotic role. As we shall see, aldosterone also stimulates sodium transport across the amphibian urinary bladder.

The amphibians

Osmotically, the amphibians are a very interesting group as they bridge the gap between the fishes and the amniotes. Phyletically, they represent the first terrestrial vertebrates yet they are still largely dependent on the ready availability of fresh water and have aquatic larvae. The Amphibia, therefore, are a group of considerable interest both with respect to osmotic regulation and the endocrine mechanisms they utilize for this process.

Vasotocin has an antidiuretic effect in most, but not all, amphibians. Mesotocin, the other amphibian neurohypophysial hormone, has little effect on the kidney. As in the birds and reptiles, vasotocin initiates both the reabsorption of water from the renal tubules and a decrease in the GFR (Sawyer, 1972*a*). The tubular response may, however, be lacking in the urodele amphibians.

The magnitude of the antidiuretic effect of the neurohypophysial hormones also varies in different species. Vasotocin, for instance, does not reduce urine flow in the South African clawed toad, *Xenopus laevis*. This toad is aquatic, a situation where such a response to released vasotocin would be physiologically inappropriate and could even lead to death resulting from hyperhydration. Other aquatic amphibians, like the mud-puppy, *Necturus maculosus*, the mud eel, *Siren lacertina*, and the congo eel, *Amphiuma means*, exhibit antidiuretic effects after injections of vasotocin but the responses are small and the amounts of hormone required are large so that the physiological significance of this effect is doubtful (Bentley, 1973). Young tadpoles do not exhibit water retention (reflecting an anti-diuresis) in response to injected vasotocin, but as bullfrog (*Rana catesbeiana*) tadpoles approach metamorphosis such a response becomes increasingly apparent, though it does not reach its full expression until after meta-morphosis has occurred (Alvarado and Johnson, 1966).

Vasotocin exerts several other interesting effects with respect to the osmoregulation of amphibians. The skin of amphibians is permeable to water, which moves across it by osmosis. In anurans (frogs and toads), water crosses the skin much more readily when the tissue is stimulated by vasotocin. This hormone appears to make the integument less waterproof; an action that is is also seen on the renal tubule. This cutaneous effect of vasotocin is not seen in urodeles (newts and salamanders) nor in some anurans, including tadpoles and *Xenopus laevis*. The ability of vasotocin to increase the skin's osmotic permeability appears to be greater in species that normally occupy dry, rather than relatively wet or damp, habitats. Amphibians do not drink, and an increased rate of water accumulation across the skin may aid rehydration in some species, such as those from desert areas, where water is only available sporadically.

Amphibians usually possess a large urinary bladder in which they can store water equivalent to as much as 50% of their body weight. This water can be reabsorbed in times of need and so constitutes a store that may be very useful to some species. Vasotocin, or dehydration which releases this hormone into the blood, increases the rate of water reabsorption across the urinary bladder of many amphibians. This effect is, however, mainly seen in anurans; the urodeles examined (except for the fire-salamander, *Salamandra maculosus*) lack this response.

The crab-eating frog, *Rana cancrivora*, lives in the sea-water in coastal mangrove swamps in Southeast Asia. As described earlier, this interesting amphibian maintains its blood plasma at a hypertonic concentration with respect to the external solution by retaining additional salts and urea. The skin of these amphibians is not responsive to vasotocin, but this hormone increases the permeability of the urinary bladder to urea (as well as water) and so, by permitting its reabsorption from the urine, apparently con-tributes to the conservation of this solute in the body (see Dicker and Elliott, 1973). A cutaneous response would be a disadvantage to such animals as it would increase the rate of water loss if they entered hypertosmotic solutions.

The tetrapod urinary bladder has no true embryological analogue in the fishes and appears to have first evolved in the Amphibia. It is interesting that some species of this group utilize it for water storage, and possibly urea conservation, with which use it has also acquired a responsiveness to vasotocin. A comparable effect on the bladder has not been demonstrated in any other vertebrate group so that this endocrine adaptation is unique.

When amphibians, in water, are injected with neurohypophysial hormones, they gain weight due to a water retention. This action is known as the 'Brunn effect', or 'water balance effect', and is due to a stimulation by vasotocin at the three distinct sites described above: the kidney, the skin and the urinary bladder. A single hormone thus has multiple effects, all of which are directed to the same physiological purpose, namely the conservation of water.

As in other vertebrates, the neurohypophysial hormones can be shown, when injected *in vivo* or *in vitro*, to have other actions including a hyperglycemic effect and an ability to contract the oviduct. However, the physiological significance of these effects is not clear.

The *catecholamines*, including adrenaline, have ubiquitous effects on tissues. One of these, which has been shown *in vitro*, is an ability to antagonize the osmotic effects of neurohypophysial hormones (Handler, Bensinger and Orloff, 1968). Injected adrenaline has also been shown to increase cutaneous water uptake by the toad, *Bufo melanostictus* (Elliott, 1968). The action of vasotocin on the osmotic permeability of membranes is mediated by the adenyl cyclase–cyclic AMP system. Catecholamines can inhibit the formation of cyclic AMP which is a manifestation of their α-adrenergic effects. In addition, these hormones can increase the levels of cyclic AMP, which is a β-adrenergic effect. These actions of adrenaline and noradrenaline on membrane permeability are therefore not unexpected though their physiological significance is unknown in the Amphibia. Catecholamines could, however, modulate the actions of vasotocin.

The sodium metabolism of amphibians can also be regulated by hormones that can act at several different sites in the body. Vasotocin, *in vitro*, stimulates sodium transport across the skin, from the external media to the blood, and its reabsorption from the urinary bladder. These effects, though prominent, do not seem to persist for a prolonged time and are difficult to reconcile with normal physiological regulation of sodium in the intact animal. *Aldosterone* has more persistent effects in increasing such sodium transport across the skin, the urinary bladder, and the colon, in frogs and toads (Crabbé and De Weer, 1964; Cofré and Crabbé, 1965). It seems likely that aldosterone also acts on the urinary bladder of urodeles but the evidence for this is equivocal. As this corticosteroid is released in response to sodium-depletion in amphibians and is effective at low concentrations, it seems likely that it normally adjusts sodium transport at these sites. As we have seen, aldosterone stimulates sodium reabsorption from the kidney tubules in mammals, birds and possibly reptiles, but despite frequent attempts to demonstrate it, this action appears to be lacking in amphibians. This is an interesting endocrine situation, as aldosterone makes its initial phyletic appearance in the lungfishes and the amphibians, yet the important renal action of this hormone does not appear to have evolved until much later.

The *renin–angiotensin* system is present in the Amphibia and, as in other tetrapods, contributes to the release of aldosterone. The renin concentration in the kidney of salt-depleted frogs increases (Capelli, Wesson and Aponte, 1970). When renin from frog kidney is injected back into frogs, the aldosterone (but not corticosterone) concentration in the plasma rises (Johnston *et al.*, 1967); however, the plasma renin activity has been measured in bullfrogs and shown to *increase* following intravenous infusions of sodium chloride solutions (dehydration decreases it) which is opposite to the response observed in mammals (Sokabe *et al.*, 1972).

The involvement of the renin–angiotensin system in the specific control of aldosterone release may be present in the Amphibia and this effect could be one of its earliest evolutionary manifestations. There appear, however, to be differences from the physiological situation in mammals. It has even been suggested that angiotensin may constrict the efferent glomerular arterioles and so control the GFR in lower vertebrates, including amphibians. The possible role of the renin–angiotensin–aldosterone system in lungfishes, where aldosterone first appears on the phyletic scale, has not been investigated and this would be particularly interesting.

The 'water-drive' effect of injected *prolactin* in newts, *Notophthalmus viridescens* (see Chapters 3 and 7), is associated with changes in the skin, including a 'thickening' and an increased secretion of mucus. It would not be surprising if this second metamorphosis, from life in a terrestrial to an aquatic environment, were associated with osmoregulatory adjustments. The injection of prolactin plus thyroxine into these newts, when they are in their terrestrial phase, has been found to result in a decrease in the the permeability of the skin to water and sodium (Brown and Brown, 1973). This change could facilitate their osmotic adaptation to an aqueous environment and, as we shall see later (p. 302), the decrease in the permeability of the skin to sodium has some similarities to the effects of prolactin on the gills of some teleost fish. A phyletically closer analogy has been observed in another amphibian, the mudpuppy, *Necturus maculosus*, which possesses external gills. When this neotenous urodele is hypophysectomized it loses sodium at increased rates and its serum sodium concentration declines (Pang and Sawyer, 1974). The precise route for such sodium loss has not been described but, as in teleosts, it can be prevented by the injection of prolactin.

The fishes

The fishes are phyletically very diverse and contain several distinct groups that osmoregulate differently. These include the Osteichthyes (bony fishes), the Chondrichthyes (elasmobranchs, cartilaginous fishes) and the Agnatha (cyclostomes or jawless fishes, lampreys and hagfishes). Most of the available information about the role of hormones in osmoregulation applies to a single order of the Osteichthyes, the Teleostei. The role of the gills in osmoregulation in fishes has been thoroughly summarized by Maetz (1971).

Neurohypophysial hormones

The well-known antidiuretic effect of vasotocin, that is seen in tetrapods, does not seem to occur in most fishes. Indeed some fishes, but not all, exhibit a diametrically opposite response; the urine flow is increased. This diuresis is seen in some teleosts, like the goldfish, *Carassius auratus*, and the eel, *Anguilla anguilla*. It is also interesting that such a diuretic response is very prominent in two of the extant lungfishes, the African lungfish, *Protopterus aethiopicus*, and the South American lungfish, *Lepidosiren paradoxa* (Sawyer, 1972*b*). The diuretic effect of vasotocin in fishes reflects its action in increasing the glomerular filtration rate. This effect, as suggested by Sawyer, is not very different, basically, from the mechanism with which vasotocin produces the reduction in GFR that is seen in tetrapods. In the latter, vasotocin constricts the *afferent* glomerular arteriole while, to have a diuretic action, a similar effect, but on the *efferent* arteriole, would result in the observed increase in the GFR. Thus, a vascular effector site may merely have shifted from one branch of the glomerular arteriole to the other. Not all the glomeruli may be responsive to vasotocin as there is plenty of evidence in the fishes that a change in the GFR can reflect an alteration in the number of functioning glomeruli (glomerular recruitment) rather than a change in the hemodynamics in individual nephrons.

To complicate the situation further it has recently been shown that, while large doses of injected vasotocin have a diuretic action in freshwater European eels, relatively small amounts (less than 10^{-10} g/kg body weight) have an antidiuretic action as in tetrapods (Babiker and Rankin, 1973; Henderson and Wales, 1974). This response is the result of a decreased

GFR and presumably reflects changes in the opposite direction from that of glomerular recruitment; tubular water reabsorption is unchanged. It thus appears that the eel afferent glomerular arteriole may also respond to vasotocin and there may be a balance between the hormonal effects at this site and the efferent arteriole; the over-all response depending on the concentration of the peptide hormone. An action at the latter site may be able to override an effect on the former.

It should be emphasized that the diuretic effects of vasotocin do not occur in all fishes or even all teleosts and the antidiuretic effect has only been observed in freshwater European eels. This makes it difficult to envisage whether or not the neurohypophysial peptides really have a physiological action on the kidney or whether, on injection, the exogenous hormones are merely exerting their well-known pharmacological effects on blood vessels. Indeed vasotocin has not even been identified in the blood of fishes. A diuretic effect of vasotocin could, however, be useful to species living in fresh water, as it may facilitate the excretion of water that is accumulated by osmosis, while an antidiuretic effect may be useful when the fishes are bathed in hyperosmotic solutions like sea-water. In lungfishes that undergo a period of estivation, enclosed in a cocoon in the dried mud at the bottoms of lakes and rivers where they live, the initiation of a diuresis could aid excretion of both accumulated solutes and water taken up by the fish during its 'awakening' in fresh water. Indeed, African lungfishes from which the pituitary has been removed cannot survive once they are replaced in water.

Neurohypophysial peptides, when injected, have also been shown to increase the turnover of sodium chloride in some teleosts, such as eels, when they are transferred from fresh water to sea-water. Such hormones may also increase active ion uptake in some freshwater teleosts. It is possible that these hormones have a direct effect on the permeability of the gill epithelium which would be analogous to some of their actions in tetrapods. Alternatively, it has been shown (Maetz and Rankin, 1969) that regional changes in the branchial blood flow occur which could mediate alterations in ion transfer; thus, adrenaline which increases the blood supply to the respiratory areas of the gills, produces a decline in salt excretion from the chloride cells. This change may be the result of a shunting of blood away from the central part of the gill filaments that contain the chloride cells. Neurohypophysial peptides (and acetylcholine) have the opposite action on the blood supply in the gills (see Fig. 8.6) and so could facilitate the functioning of the chloride cells. We can thus conjecture that the vasoactive effects of the neurohypophysial peptides may be phyletically older than their direct actions on the permeability of epithelial membranes (Maetz and Rankin, 1969). Such vascular effects can be seen in *some* fishes where

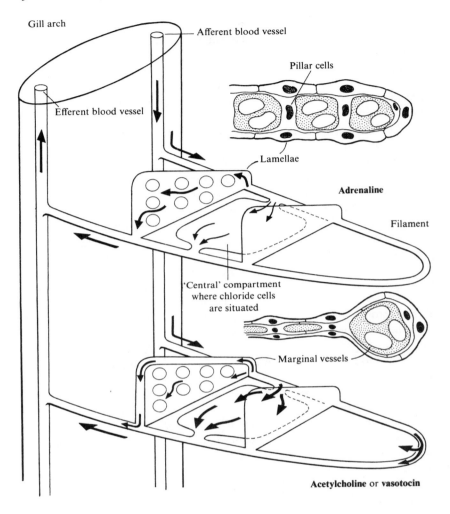

Fig. 8.6. A hypothetical model illustrating how hormones may alter the distribution of the blood flow in the gills of teleost fish and so alter their respiratory and osmoregulatory functions. Adrenaline increases the blood flow to the *lamellae* of the gills, which have a predominant respiratory function, by causing a relaxation of the *pillar cells* (PC). Acetylcholine or neurohypophysial peptides (including vasotocin and isotocin) constrict the lamellae (possibly by contracting the pillar cells) and divert blood to the central compartment. The chloride-secreting cells are situated in the interlamellar region of the central compartment so that their function is facilitated by the presence of the neurohypophysial hormones. (From Rankin and Maetz, 1971.)

they mediate changes in renal and gill functions that influence osmo-regulation.

Vasotocin has no effect on the urine flow in Agnathan fishes (or at least in *Lampetra fluviatilis*). The rate of sodium loss in the urine is, however, increased (Bentley and Follett, 1963) while the branchial losses of sodium are unchanged. The effects of vasotocin on osmoregulation in chondrich-thyean fishes do not appear to have been investigated.

Differing physiological roles of vasotocin in eliciting an antidiuresis in tetrapods and a diuresis, or antidiuresis in some teleost fishes, would necessitate different mechanisms for regulating the release of this hormone;

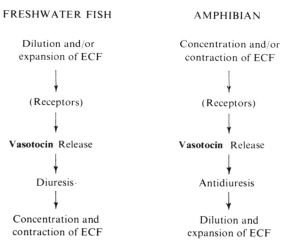

Fig. 8.7. A hypothetical scheme showing the possible stimuli that may effect the release of vasotocin in fishes as compared to the typical tetrapod release reflex (such as exemplified in amphibians). The releasing-stimuli may be diametrically opposite to each other, for while *concentration* (or contraction) of the extra-cellular fluid (ECF) brings about vasotocin release in amphibians, in the fresh-water fishes this would need to occur in response to a *dilution* if vasotocin were to mediate a diuresis physiologically. (From Sawyer, 1972a.)

thus, in freshwater fish, vasotocin may possibly be released in response to a dilution, or expansion, of the body fluids, while in tetrapods (and possibly the sea-water eel), it is secreted following a concentration of the extra-cellular fluids. The possible contrast in these two mechanisms in fish and amphibians is summarized in Fig. 8.7, though it should be noted that the release mechanism in the fish is still hypothetical.

The contrasting roles of vasotocin in altering urine flow via different mechanisms, involving the renal tubule or glomerulus, are shown in Fig. 8.8.

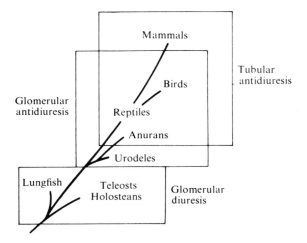

Fig. 8.8. A schematic diagram showing the phyletic distribution of the responses of the kidney to neurohypophysial hormones in vertebrates.

An exception may occur in the European eel (Teleostei) where small amounts of vasotocin may also have an antidiuretic effect (see text). (From Sawyer, 1972*b*.)

Vasotocin can elicit a glomerular antidiuresis in non-mammalian tetrapods and a glomerular diuresis in fishes. To this should be added a glomerular antidiuresis in the eel. In addition, vasotocin can promote water reabsorption from the renal tubules (a tubular antidiuresis) from all tetrapods (possibly with the exception of the urodeles and crocodilians).

Catecholamines

It is uncertain if the catecholamine hormones have a physiological role in the osmoregulation of fishes but adrenaline, when injected, can alter the movements of water, sodium and chloride across the gills (see Pic, Mayer-Gostan and Maetz, 1973). In teleosts in sea-water, injected adrenaline reduces the active extrusion of sodium and chloride from the gills. It increases branchial permeability to water in either fresh water or sea-water. The effects on ion movements can be prevented by α-adrenergic blocking drugs and that on water by β-adrenergic inhibitors. β-Adrenergic receptors mediate the increases of blood flow to the central lamellar regions of the gills (see the last section) and this effect could be contributing to the osmotic change. A more direct effect on the permeability of the gill epithelium to water is, however, considered to be a more likely mechanism. The ionic responses to adrenaline also appear to be due to a direct effect on the tissue resulting from an inhibition of the activity of the chloride-secreting cells.

The over-all effects of injected adrenaline on fluid balance in teleosts are a hypernatremia and hyperosmolarity in sea-water and an accumulation of water in fresh water; these changes are consistent with the observed responses of the gills. Stress, such as associated with laboratory handling or forced swimming, results in elevated levels of catecholamines in the blood of teleosts and also produces disturbances in fluid balance. It thus seems likely that catecholamines may influence osmoregulation in unusual circumstances but it is not clear whether or not they have such a role in more equitable conditions.

Adrenocorticosteroids

The corticosteroids, mainly cortisol, have a far better established effect on osmoregulation in fishes than do the neurohypophysial peptides. Again, this is predominantly seen in teleost fishes and in this group most of the experiments have been carried out on eels from Europe, *Anguilla anguilla*, North America, *Anguilla rostrata*, and Asia, *Anguilla japonica*. Apart from their ready availability and the feasibility of performing surgical procedures on them, eels can osmoregulate in either fresh water or the sea and during their normal lives migrate between these two environments. In sea-water, radioactive ion flux measurements indicate that teleosts, including eels, have a very large turnover of sodium amounting to as much as 50 to 60% of the total present in their body every hour, but in fresh water this is less than 1% per hour. In sea-water, this ion exchange is the result of a rapid transfer of salts across the gills and the drinking of sea-water which is absorbed from the fish's gut. The excess sodium chloride is excreted across the gills by the chloride cells. The kidney plays little part in the excretion of the excess solutes in teleosts as it lacks an ability to form a hypertonic urine. The influx of sodium across the gills in sea-water appears to be a passive process possibly involving exchange diffusion; the sodium that enters being exchanged for sodium leaving the body. The absorption of sea-water across the gut depends largely on active transport of sodium and this is related to the presence of the enzyme Na–K activated ATPase. This enzyme has also been localized in the chloride cells (Kamiya, 1972). The maintenance of adequate levels of Na–K ATPase in the gut, gills and kidneys depends on the action of cortisol which, in turn, is regulated by corticotrophin from the pituitary (Epstein, Cynamon and McKay, 1971; Pickford *et al.*, 1970). When eels enter sea-water there is an increase in the concentration of cortisol in their blood which persists for several days (Hirano, 1969; Ball *et al.*, 1971; Forrest *et al.*, 1973*b*). After this time, however, the steroid level declines so that it is similar to that in eels adapted to fresh water. In teleost fishes, the corticosteroids contribute to osmoregulation, as in other vertebrates. Removal of the adrenals in freshwater eels results in a decline in plasma sodium but in sea-water, there is an accumulation of this ion. This effect can be overcome by injecting cortisol (Chan *et al.*, 1967; Butler *et al.*, 1969; Mayer *et al.*, 1967; Henderson and Chester Jones, 1967). It is interesting, however, that the principal steroid involved is cortisol which, in the tetrapods, mainly influences intermediary metabolism. In teleosts, cortisol may fulfill both physiological roles.

Although the corticosteroids influence osmoregulation in the fishes, as well as the tetrapods, the mechanisms involved differ. The use of the gills is a piscine (and possibly larval amphibian) prerogative and they are thus a site for the steroid's action that is confined to the fishes. In addition, the relative importance of the effects of corticosteroids on the gut of teleosts living in sea-water may be greater than their action at this site in tetrapods or even in freshwater teleosts. The mechanisms by which the hormones

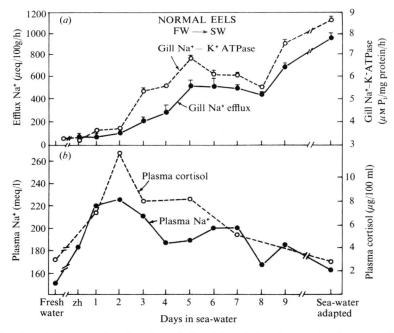

Fig. 8.9. A diagram showing the relationships of the changes in plasma sodium and cortisol concentrations (*b*), the efflux of sodium and the branchial Na–K ATPase in North American eels (*Anguilla rostrata*) following transfer from fresh water to sea-water (*a*). It can be seen that the cortisol concentrations in the plasma initially rise and this is followed by increased Na–K ATPase levels in the gills, which parallels added sodium efflux and the resulting decline in the plasma sodium concentration. (From Forrest *et al.*, 1973*a*, *b*.)

facilitate sodium transport may also differ, for in the tetrapods there is little evidence to suggest that corticosteroids exert their acute effects on sodium transport by increasing the levels (or inducing formation) of Na–K ATPase. Instead it seems more likely that aldosterone increases the activity (or rate of turnover) of the sodium pump (directly or indirectly) rather than by increasing its total capacity, such as would be expected if an increase of Na–K ATPase occurred. In fishes, cortisol may still have an additional, acute, type of effect like that of aldosterone in tetrapods, as there is evidence to suggest that when fish are transferred from fresh water to sea-water corticosteroid-mediated changes occur independently of any alteration in the level of Na–K ATPase (see Forrest *et al.*, 1973*a*). The temporal relationship between plasma cortisol and sodium levels, Na–K ATPase concentration in the gills and the branchial efflux of sodium in eels during adaptation to sea-water is shown in Fig. 8.9.

There is little information about the action of corticosteroids in non-teleost fish. Adrenocorticosteroids appear to have no effect on renal electrolyte losses in freshwater lampreys though they can decrease the rate of sodium loss across the gills (Bentley and Follett, 1963). The possible effects of corticosteroids in electrolyte balance in chondrichthyean fishes has not been very extensively studied, though in the shark, *Hemiscyllium plagiosum*, secretion from the rectal salt gland may be decreased by injected cortisol (Chan, Phillips and Chester Jones, 1967). The control of the rectal salt gland secretion is, however, not understood and it is uncertain how this effect of cortisol (which is not an homologous hormone in elasmobranchs) is related to the over-all regulatory mechanism.

Pituitary hormones; corticotrophin and prolactin

The pituitary has an essential role to play in influencing osmoregulation in fishes. Its effects are principally due to two of its hormones, corticotrophin and prolactin (or paralactin). The importance of the effects of these two hormones, however, differs considerably between species of fish and depends on whether they are living in fresh water or the sea. Hypophysectomy thus may have little osmotic effect on some species though in others dramatic changes may occur, especially if they are living in fresh water.

When freshwater eels are hypophysectomized they can survive for several weeks though there is a slow depletion of their electrolytes (Fontaine, Callamand and Olivereau, 1949; Butler, 1966). When placed in sea-water, these eels cannot osmoregulate properly and they accumulate excess sodium. Hypophysectomy results in a considerable lowering of plasma cortisol levels which can then be elevated by injecting corticotrophin (Hirano, 1969); thus, a pituitary interrenal (or adrenal) control-axis exists in the fishes, the interruption of which can upset osmoregulation (see Maetz, 1969). This is manifested by low levels of Na–K ATPase and reduced fluid and ion movements across the gills and gut which can be substantially corrected by injected cortisol (Epstein, Katz and Pickford, 1967; Butler and Carmichael, 1972). This hormone, however, does not completely restore osmotic balance, suggesting that other factors may be involved.

The osmotic deficiencies resulting from surgical removal of the pituitary are also due, apart from a lack of corticotrophin, to the absence of prolactin. Pickford and Phillips, in 1959, found that when killifish, *Fundulus heteroclitus*, were hypophysectomized they were able to survive in salt water but they soon died when placed in fresh water. If, however, they were injected with mammalian prolactin, their survival in fresh water was considerably prolonged. No other hormones were found to have this effect. Many species of fishes die in fresh water following hypophysectomy though others, like the goldfish, eel and trout, can survive for considerable periods of time. The importance of the pituitary for survival in fresh water varies considerably among the teleost fishes; thus, 18 species of the order Antheriniformes were found to be unable to survive hypophysectomy if kept in fresh water though many of the order Ostariophysi survive (Schreibman and Kallman, 1969).

Death in fresh water following hypophysectomy was found in *Poecilia latipinna* to be accompanied by a considerable loss of sodium which was prevented by the injection of prolactin (Ball and Ensor, 1965, 1967). This observation has been confirmed in other species of fish and is due principally to an excessive loss of sodium across the gills (see Lam, 1972; Ensor and Ball, 1972). The lack of such osmotic sensitivity in some fish, like eels and goldfish, to hypophysectomy seems to be the result of the more restricted permeability of their bodies to sodium, but even in these species prolactin can be shown to decrease branchial sodium loss (efflux). The mechanism of the effect of prolactin on the ionic permeability of the gills is uncertain.

Circulating levels of prolactin are probably low in fish adapted to seawater. The importance of this is emphasized by the observation that when sea-water-adapted *Tilapia mossambica* are injected with this hormone their plasma sodium concentration increases (Dharmamba *et al.*, 1973). This treatment, if continued, would probably kill these fishes. The accumulation of sodium is the result of a reduced rate of sodium chloride secretion from the branchial chloride-secreting cells, possibly as a result of an inhibition of Na–K ATPase. The reduced activity of the chloride cells helps effect the adaptation of these fish to fresh water but in sea-water such an action would be disastrous.

Prolactin also influences the permeability of teleosts to water. The results *in vivo* have been a little contradictory as they usually indicate that the hormone increases branchial osmotic permeability but, depending on the species studied, a decrease may also be observed. In-vitro observations on the gills of goldfish also suggest that prolactin reduces permeability to water (see also Ogawa, Yagasaki and Yamazaki, 1973). In intact fish, it is often difficult to decide which effect and site of action is the primary one; thus, prolactin can increase the urine flow and this could be either a direct action on the kidney or the result of an increased branchial permeability to water. Prolactin is thought to have a direct effect on the kidney in fishes, mediated by an increased GFR or a reduced tubular reabsorption of water, or both. Apart from the kidneys, prolactin can also reduce the transfer of fluid across the fish intestine and urinary bladder (Utida *et al.*, 1972). Prolactin may restrict the osmotic permeability of membranes at three distinct sites: the kidney tubules, the intestine and the urinary bladder, and a similar effect on the gills may also occur but this is controversial. Prolactin may have a physiological action in preventing over-hydration of fish in fresh water by facilitating the excretion of water.

Mammalian prolactin, when injected, is effective in promoting changes in water and salt metabolism in teleost fishes but this does not constitute proof that the endogenous hormone also acts in this way in the fishes. Teleost prolactin (or paralactin) can elicit many of the same osmotic actions as the exogenous mammalian hormone. The amount of prolactin stored in the pituitary of the teleost *Poecilia latipinna* is six times greater in fish living in fresh water than in those in salt water, while the activity of the pituitary *eta* cells indicates that the hormone is being released in the freshwater fish (Ball and Ingleton, 1973). The pituitary glands of *Poecilia*, adapted to one-third sea-water, contain about three times the quantity of prolactin as sea-water-adapted fish (see Fig, 8.10). When the one-third sea-water-adapted fish are transferred to fresh water, the level of stored prolactin initially declines because of its release but the rate of synthesis increases so that after about eight days the amount stored in the pituitary rises to about six times the concentration seen in sea-water-adapted fish. Transfer of *Poecilia* from fresh water to sea-water has little immediate effect on the glandular stores, but these do show a gradual decline, presumably due to a decreased rate of synthesis.

Prolactin appears to have an important role in the migration of stickle-backs, *Gasterosteus aculeatus*, between the sea and rivers (see Lam, 1972). These fish normally spend the autumn and winter in the sea but in the spring migrate into rivers to breed. Sticklebacks caught in winter, in the sea, soon die if they are placed in fresh water but if they are first injected with prolactin they survive for much longer. This increased survival ability is also seen in fish in the autumn if they are kept under conditions of long

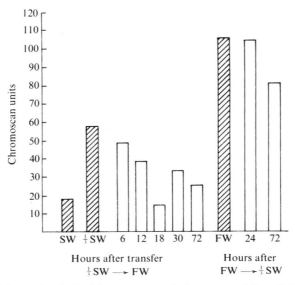

Fig. 8.10. The prolactin (in 'chromoscan units') content of the pituitary glands of the teleost *Poecilia latipinna* following transfer from one-third sea-water (SW) to fresh water (FW), and then to one-third sea-water. After transfer from one-third sea-water to fresh water the prolactin storage initially declines but subsequently increases and after 8 days reaches a level that is about six times greater than in sea-water-adapted fish. Cross-hatched bars show initial control values. (From Ball and Ingleton, 1973.)

day-length. It seems that, due to photoperiodic stimulation (the lengthening of the day) there is an increase in the activity of the prolactin cells which prepares the fish for its future migration into fresh water, during which the hormone is released into the blood.

These interesting observations on the role of prolactin in teleostean osmoregulation have drawn attention to comparable effects in other vertebrates. Among fishes little is known about the role of prolactin in osmoregulation of non-teleosts. In three species of chondrichthyeans, the water uptake across the gills is decreased following hypophysectomy and is restored by injected prolactin (Payan and Maetz, 1971). This effect is similar to that observed in goldfish but is not consistent with the observations on teleostean gills *in vitro*. This effect in chondrichthyeans, as described earlier, could be the result of a primary diuretic action on the kidney rather than the gills. The possible role of prolactin in maintaining optimal hydration in birds and its effects in newts and mudpuppies have already been described and there are even some reports about its osmotic effects in mammals. It has, for instance, been found that prolactin may help maintain hydration in rats during lactation, possibly via an antidiuretic action and by facilitating fluid absorption from the gut (Ensor, Edmondson and Phillips, 1972; Ramsey and Bern, 1972). Urinary sodium retention has also been observed in rats following the injection of crude prolactin preparations (Lockett and Nail, 1965) and the same effect has been shown to occur in man (Horrobin *et al.*, 1971).

The urophysis, corpuscles of Stannius and juxtaglomerular cells

These tissues have a glandular appearance and have a putative endocrine function in some fishes. Their structure and distribution among the fishes has been described earlier (Chapter 2). There are several types of evidence suggesting that these glands may have an osmoregulatory function including:

(i) Changes in their histological appearance in different osmotic circumstances.

(ii) Deficiencies in the fish's capacity to adapt to fresh water or sea-water following surgical removal of the tissues.

(iii) The ability of injected extracts of these glands to alter the fish's balance of water and electrolytes.

At this time no unequivocal conclusions as to the suggested osmotic importance of these tissues is available. This lack of consensus is largely the result of variations in the responses of different species of teleosts to various experimental procedures; nevertheless, the urophysis, corpuscles of Stannius and teleostean juxtaglomerular cells contain biologically active substances and it remains possible that these materials may act as 'hormones' at sites unconnected with osmoregulation.

The cichlid euryhaline fish, *Tilapia mossambica*, and the stickleback, *Gasterosteus aculeatus*, suffer an increased mortality, following transfer from fresh water to saline solutions, if their urophyses are removed (Takasugi and Bern, 1962; Ireland, 1969). This effect has not been demonstrated in all species though it is possible that the rapid regeneration of this tissue may contribute to the observed differences. The histological appearance of the urophyses of *Tilapia mossambica* suggest a depletion of the contained neurosecretory material when these fish are kept in sea-water, as compared with fresh water. The Hawaiian o'io, *Albula vulpes*, also displays such histological variations in urophysial activity (see Fridberg and Bern, 1968). The rate of electrical firing of the urophysial nerve cells has also been shown to be altered in response to osmotic changes. Both a decrease and an increase in spontaneous electrical discharge have been observed in response to hypotonicity and they depend on the particular species examined.

Considerable advances have been made in characterizing the biologically active materials present in the teleostean urophysis (see Zelnik and Lederis, 1973). These substances have been separated into several components with characteristic chemical and pharmacological actions. They are proteins and polypeptides and have been classified in the following way:

(i) Urotensin I, which when injected decreases the blood pressure of rats.

(ii) Urotensin II, which contracts various smooth muscle preparations, including the trout urinary bladder, can increase the blood pressure as well as the urine flow in eels.

(iii) Urotensin III. This promotes sodium uptake across the gills of goldfish, an effect that has not been observed in other species.

(iv) Urotensin IV, which increases water transfer across the toad urinary bladder (*in vitro*) and has other similarities to vasotocin with which it may be identical.

None of these substances has yet been identified in the circulation of fish but urotensin II is discharged from the urophysis under *in-vitro* conditions, which supports the possibility of its hormonal nature (Berlind, 1972*a*). The venous effluent of the urophysis passes into the renal portal blood vessels via the caudal vein, and so any urophysial secretions are in a potentially excellent situation to influence kidney function.

When the euryhaline marine teleost, *Gillichthys mirabilis*, is placed in fresh water the urophysial content of urotensin IV declines but urotensin II is unchanged (Berlind, Lacanilao and Bern, 1972). Two other proteins, that are characteristically present in the urophysis of *Gillichthys*, also show a considerable decline if these fish are kept in fresh water for six days.

Somewhat sporadic evidence thus suggests the possibility that the urophysis may influence osmoregulation in fish. It may, however, have other possible endocrine functions. Urotensin II contracts the smooth muscle of the urinogenital tract, including the sperm duct in *Gillichthys mirabilis* (Berlind, 1972*b*). It has thus also been suggested that the urophysis may have a role in reproduction of fishes, such as in promoting spawning.

The probable role of the corpuscles of Stannius in calcium metabolism in teleost fishes has been described earlier (see Chapter 6). The hypercalcemia that is observed in eels following Stanniectomy is accompanied by a decline in plasma sodium concentration and a rise in potassium (M. Fontaine, 1964). These changes in sodium and potassium in the plasma can be corrected by injecting aldosterone, though this corticosteroid does not appear to be present in fishes. It is, however, likely that other corticosteroids, such as cortisol, which can act as a mineralocorticoid in teleosts, may also have this effect.

Several possible mechanisms have been considered that could be responsible for the effects of Stanniectomy on sodium and potassium metabolism in teleosts:

(i) Because of initial confusion as to distinction of the morphology of the corpuscles of Stannius from the interrenal tissues, it was once proposed that the corpuscular tissues may secrete adrenocorticosteroids. Despite much contradictory evidence, it is now considered that this is not so, though these tissues may metabolize some steroids (but so do many other tissues) (Colombo, Bern and Pieprzyk, 1971). Nevertheless, as we have seen, the profound changes in sodium and potassium balance that accompany Stanniectomy can be compensated for by the injection of corticosteroids, and in the eel this operation is accompanied by a decrease in the plasma cortisol concentration (Fenwick and Forster, 1972). This decline is always accompanied by a hypercalcemia which is consistent with the evidence of Leloup-Hatey (1970) that indicates that the elevated calcium concentrations inhibit the action of corticotrophin and corticosteroidogenesis. The actions of the corpuscles of Stannius on steroid metabolism and osmoregulation thus appear to be indirect effects resulting from an absence of their hypocalcemic-hormone secretion.

(ii) Extracts of the corpuscles of Stannius, when injected, elevate the blood pressure of rats and eels in a manner suggesting that they contain a renin-like substance that can promote the formation of angiotensin (Chester Jones *et al.*, 1966; Sokabe *et al.*, 1970). Removal of the corpuscles of Stannius results in a decrease of the blood pressure of freshwater eels to levels that are normally seen when these fish are adapted to sea-water. As the decline in the GFR observed in sea-water is probably the result of the drop in blood pressure it is possible that the two events may be related. This interesting suggestion, however, does not appear likely as Stanniectomy (in North American eels, *Anguilla rostrata*) is not accompanied by a significant change in the GFR (Butler, 1969). In addition, plasma renin activity has been shown to *increase* in eels placed in sea-water (Sokabe *et al.*, 1973) which, if anything, would be expected to increase, not decrease, the blood pressure.

(iii) It is possible that a renin–angiotensin system exists in the teleosts which controls the formation and release of adrenocortical steroids in a manner comparable to its effects on aldosterone in mammals (Chester Jones *et al.*, 1966). The kidney of teleost fishes contains renin in relatively large amounts compared to the corpuscles of Stannius so that it is considered unlikely (Butler, 1969) that the levels in the latter tissues are of critical importance. Indeed renin-like substances have been identified in a number of other tissues so that their presence in the corpuscles of Stannius may be a 'red herring'. There is no conclusive evidence that renin is involved in the osmoregulation of fishes.

The nature of the processes controlling osmoregulation in fishes is incomplete and much of the information about the role of hormones in this process is still speculative. It is thus still an exciting field of study for the comparative endocrinologist.

Conclusions

The regulation of the water and salt content of vertebrates is primarily mediated by the kidney but several other glands and tissues are also involved. Many of these 'accessory' osmoregulatory organs have a distinct systematic distribution; for instance, gills in fishes, nasal salt glands in birds, and sweat glands in mammals. The osmoregulatory functions of most such organs are controlled by hormones which each tend to contribute to this process in a specific manner. Thus the neurohypophysial hormones increase osmotic permeability whether it be in the tetrapod kidney or the amphibian skin and urinary bladder. Similarly adrenocorticosteroids help regulate sodium metabolism by increasing transmural sodium transport in the renal tubule of mammals, the skin and urinary bladder of amphibians, the sweat, salivary and mammary glands of mammals, and the gills of many fishes. Thus the same type of hormone is often concerned (or is 'utilized') with coordinating the same general physiological process, though in somewhat different ways in various groups of vertebrates. There are, however, exceptions and systematically unique features, like the role of the gills in osmoregulation of fishes, is accompanied by what may be a unique type of action of a particular hormone; in this instance the ability of prolactin to control the permeability of the branchial (and other) epithelial membranes in teleosts. In mammals, this hormone appears to be principally concerned with the regulation of lactation though it is now suspected that it may also be capable of influencing osmoregulation in some tetrapods. The physiological significance of the effects in the latter is at the time of writing still in doubt and could represent a 'vestigial' endocrine response.

9. Hormones and reproduction

The reproductive process is not essential for the life of the individual, though it may make it more interesting, but it is necessary for the perpetuation of the species. In many so-called lower forms of life, reproduction may be an asexual process. A notable disadvantage of this type of reproduction is a diminution in the chances of genetic variability, and the transmission of such inherited changes to other individuals, so that evolutionary adaptation is hampered. The effects of the absence of sexual propagation is more likely to be apparent in vertebrates, that take a relatively long period of time to reproduce. The lapse of time between the generations may thus be large compared, for instance, to that in unicellular organisms. Reproduction is a complex process and this is especially true in species that occupy environments where the conditions are variable and large physicochemical changes occur. The young, developing animal is not usually as adaptable as the adult to such changes in the environment, and so must either be protected from these deviations by the parents or be produced on occasions that are most suitable to its more limited physiological capabilities. In vertebrates both conditions usually prevail; the embryo may develop to a quite advanced stage before becoming independent of the parent and it is usually produced during a season when such conditions as the temperature and food and water supply are favorable.

Reproduction in vertebrates thus involves considerable physiological coordination. The sexual process that requires the union of the sperm and ova necessitates complex physiological, social and morphological arrangements to ensure that these gametes each ripen at a similar time, and that the two sexes then meet and effect their union. The growth and differentiation of the fertilized egg often involves complex parental care, which may occur *in utero*, within the parent itself, or in an egg that is specially produced to meet the potential needs of the embryo. Care of the young often continues for a period of time following such initial development in the egg or *in utero*. The foregoing events may not be possible, or successfully accomplished, except during certain seasons of the year when the conditions are favorable.

In vertebrates, the coordination of all the processes outlined above involves hormones and the degree of complexity of their actions directly reflects the intricacies of the reproductive processes in a particular species.

The endocrine control of reproduction in man is thus more involved than in a jawless fish, like the lamprey. The basic pattern, however, is remarkably uniform and involves the endocrine secretions of the pituitary and the gonads. The influences of the hypothalamus and the median eminence on the pituitary gonadotrophin release is vital in most groups of vertebrates, but this control seems to be lacking in the cyclostomes and chondrichthyeans. The pituitary gonadotrophic hormones in vertebrates are chemically analogous but have undergone evolutionary changes in their structures. The gonadal steroids on the other hand are identical throughout the vertebrate series. One of the most notable endocrine differences among the vertebrates is the ability of the placenta of eutherian mammals to produce hormones that are similar to those secreted by the gonads and the pituitary. Otherwise the evolutionary changes are largely a matter of detail. These adaptations include modifications of the gonadal ducts, such as may assist in the processes of fertilization, the production of different types of eggs and the internal incubation of the embryo. A plethora of secondary sex characters, involving such morphological factors as size, color and scent glands have appeared in the different vertebrate groups and these help to ensure that the sexes meet and mate in the breeding season. Also involved in the mating procedure are a multitude of different patterns of pre-nuptial behavior. The precise manner by which the time of breeding is controlled also varies in different vertebrates and may involve differences in the length of the gonadal cycle and adaptations to the receipt of different environmental signals, such as light, which is predominant in birds, and temperature, that seems to be more important in reptiles. Variation in the functioning of the hypothalamus, pituitary and gonads may reflect such differences in the manner of timing of breeding.

There are several major differences in the patterns of reproduction in vertebrates that have considerable effects on the endocrine control of reproduction. These concern the manner by which fertilization is accomplished and the site where the embryo differentiates and grows.

Life in an aqueous medium, such as the sea, lakes and rivers, provides a relatively stable physicochemical environment for ova, sperm and the fertilized eggs. Many fishes ensure their reproduction by producing vast numbers of ova, often millions at a time that are extruded, before fertilization, into the external solution. The reproductive activities of the male are coordinated to this oviposition so that vast numbers of sperm are released amongst the eggs and *external fertilization* occurs. This process, which also takes place in most amphibians, has the advantage of simplicity but is only possible in aqueous situations. A general physiological corollary of external fertilization is that usually the eggs are small and contain relatively few nutrients for the support of the young. The animal thus, nutritionally, can afford to produce the vast numbers of ova necessary to assure fertilization on a scale that is adequate for the survival of a sufficient number of the young. Primarily terrestrial species, like the reptiles, birds and mammals, must of necessity resort to *internal fertilization*. This process requires the production of fewer eggs but more intimate contact and collaboration between the sexes. Internal fertilization also occurs among fishes including some bony fishes, all of the chondrichthyeans and some amphibians.

There are also considerable differences, again with important endocrine repercussions, between the eggs of different vertebrates and the processes that assist in their successful transposition into viable young. These differences are partly related to the nature of the fertilization process (due to the number of eggs that must be produced) and to life in a terrestrial environment. Eggs that are produced by most fishes and amphibians are highly prone to evaporation and so cannot readily survive on dry land. Some frogs deposit such eggs in damp burrows but this is unusual. Birds, most reptiles and prototherian mammals, such as the platypus, produce eggs that are covered with a protective shell, that limits evaporation, and they contain large amounts of nutrients that are sufficient to sustain the young until it reaches a stage of development when it can fend for itself. Similar eggs with a horny shell and large amounts of nutritive yolk are also produced by the chondrichthyean fishes and hagfishes. The production of eggs from which the young develop in the external environment is a process called *oviparity* and the eggs are termed alecithal and megalecithal eggs depending on the amounts of yolk nutrients that they contain. In many species, including some chondrichthyean and teleost fishes (where the ovum is often fertilized within the follicle in which it develops), amphibians and reptiles, the eggs may be retained for prolonged periods in the oviduct during which time the young develops in a relatively protected and secluded situation. This is called *ovoviviparity*. A more intimate contact between the eggs and the wall of the oviduct or uterus may occur whereby the developing young can exchange respiratory gases and even gain fluids and nutrients. This condition is called *viviparity* and as nutrients may be gained from the parent, the eggs usually contain far less yolk. Viviparity has evolved many times in nature and is present among chondrichthyeans, teleosts (where the young are usually contained within a hollow ovary), amphibians, reptiles and mammals. There are many endocrine variations that result from these different ways of providing for the development of the young including hormonal influences on the maturation and formation of the different types of eggs, the morphological development and physiological behavior of the oviducts and the triggering, at the appropriate time, of the expulsion of the egg (oviposition) or young (parturition).

The eggs and young of many species receive little or no parental care once they are separated from the mother. In some species, however, they are cared for and this may be necessary for their survival. Some teleost fishes are known to deposit their eggs in specially prepared nests which they protect and over which they may circulate water. Others such as the teleosts *Tilapia mossambica* keep a brood of hatched young in the fastnesses of a large mouth from which the young can emerge or retreat to. Several species of frogs (*Pipa pipa, Gastrotheca marsupiata*) and the sea-horse (*Hippocampus*) keep young in a pouch, or marsupium, on their backs while frogs incubate them in modified vocal sacs. Some snakes and most birds personally incubate their eggs and the care with which birds feed and protect the newly hatched young is well known. Birds usually collect food, which they present to their young and often this is predigested. Pigeons and doves produce a special pasty secretion, that contains a high concentration of fat and protein, from their crop-sac, the so-called pigeon's milk. The formation of such a special milk secretion with which to feed the young is a characteristic systematic feature of mammals. Such processes, whether it is 'tender loving parental care', 'broodiness' in birds, or lactation in mammals, are all largely controlled by hormones.

The reproductive apparatus of vertebrates

The gonads of vertebrates have a dual function, as they not only produce the germ cells but also some of the hormones that control the reproductive process; thus the testis in addition to being the site of formation and maturation of the sperm also produces androgens, principally testosterone and androstenedione in the interstitial tissue (or Leydig cells) and, probably, also in the Sertoli cells. The ovary contains vast numbers of germ cells (primordial follicles) some of which, following a period of growth and maturation, ripen into ova. The follicles in which this latter process occurs are also the site of formation of estrogens. Following extrusion of the mature ovum (ovulation) from its follicle, the tissue 'heals' and this may involve an invasion and proliferation of lutein cells so that a corpus luteum is formed. In many species, this structure is the site of formation of progesterone which can also sometimes be produced by the interstitial tissue of the ovary. A more detailed description of the structure of the gonads and the hormones that they produce is given in Chapters 2 and 3.

Associated with the gonads are the duct systems through which the germ cells are delivered to the outside of the animal. Discrete gonadal ducts are absent in the cyclostomes where the eggs and sperm are shed directly into the body cavity from which they escape to the exterior through pores that are formed in the region of the cloaca.

In the teleost fishes, the ovarian ducts represent extensions of the gonadal tissue but in other vertebrates, they are modified Mullerian ducts that differentiate in the embryo under the influence of estrogens to form the oviducts or uterus. The oviducts and uterus are surrounded by a sheath of smooth muscle fibers that, by rhythmical contractions, can propel objects, like eggs, towards the exterior. This musculature may be relatively weak, as in the amphibians, or, as in mammals, be capable of very strong contractions and make up a major portion of the uterine wall. In mammals, this muscle layer is called the *myometrium*. The contractility of such muscle can be influenced by hormones, especially those from the neurohypophysis, that stimulate their contraction. Underlying the muscles of the gonaducts is an inner lining of cells that in mammals is referred to as the *endometrium*. This inner layer of tissue contains numerous glandular cells and may be modified in various ways so that it contributes to the well-being of the egg and, if internal fertilization occurs, the survival of the sperm and its union with the ovum. In oviparous species, segmental differences in function may occur along the length of the oviduct, such as are associated with the formation of albumin and the secretion of a hard outer shell. In amphibians, the jelly-like secretion so characteristic of clumps of frogs' spawn is secreted by glandular cells in the oviduct. In ovoviviparous and viviparous vertebrates, the lining of the oviduct is modified so as to furnish an appropriate environment for maintaining the retained egg or to allow for the implantation and development of the blastocyst and the formation of a placenta. The activity of the surrounding musculature is reduced on such occasions. The female gonaducts (oviduct or uterus and vagina) thus undergo considerable structural change during the reproductive cycle which is mediated by the actions of estrogens and progesterone.

The sperm are conveyed from the testis along the vas deferens, which is also a tube surrounded by an outer layer of smooth muscle, during which time they may be mixed with secretions from certain accessory sex glands that include the prostate or prostate-like glands. The maintenance of the structure and function, and cyclical changes of the male gonaducts, their associated accessory sex glands as well as the external genitalia, such as the penis, are due mainly to the action of testosterone. In the absence of this hormone, structural and physiological degeneration of such tissues take place.

Secondary sex characters in vertebrates

The secondary sex characters are so named because they are not primarily involved in the formation and delivery of the sperm or ova. They nevertheless may play an important part in the prenuptial and nuptial events and contribute to the behavioral and functional synchronization necessary for the fertilization of the ripened ova, the mechanical success of copulation and the survival of the young. The secondary sex characters differ in each sex and contribute to the dimorphism of the male and female. The differences in appearance between the sexes are basically controlled genetically and the expression of them may be influenced by the actions of sex hormones. Broad differences, such as those of size, are usually independent of the continuous action of sex hormones while in other instances only the initial differentiation of a sexual character during early life may depend on hormones. Hormones are, however, not necessarily continuously needed to maintain such organs after their differentiation; thus, the changes in the larynx of boys at puberty, that results in a deeper voice, require the presence of testosterone though subsequent castration does not result in a return to the prepuberal soprano condition. In other instances, however, a continuous supply of hormones may be required to maintain a secondary sex character, as is seen in the instance of the penis in man and the breasts in women. Some secondary sex characters may undergo periods of development and involution that correspond to the changes in the sexual cycle and the differences in the rates of hormone production that occur during these periods. The seasonal development and subsequent shedding of the antlers of deer are well-known examples of this but there are numerous others. Dodd (1960) and Parkes and Marshall (1960) give an excellent account of these structures in cold-blooded vertebrates and birds.

In *cyclostome fish*, the endocrine control of secondary sex characters has been studied in lampreys (see Larsen, 1965, 1969, 1973). One cannot distinguish, from their external appearance, between the male and female lamprey during the early part of their autumnal breeding migration into the rivers. With the approach of spring and the onset of breeding, an anal fin appears in the female while the dorsal fins of the male heighten. Such morphological changes do not occur if the animals are hypophysectomized or gonadectomized. There is also a swelling of the cloacal region in both sexes just before breeding and the urinogenital papilla grows larger in the male. These latter characters do not, however, appear to depend on the presence of steroid sex hormones.

The *chondrichthyean fishes* also display few dimorphic secondary sex characters. In some species, the most notable difference is the presence of a pair of copulatory organs called claspers in the external cloacal region of the male. These rod-like organs develop at puberty and their size can be increased by the administration of testosterone but this effect is not large.

The *osteichthyean fishes* show a considerable range in dimorphic sexual differences. In some species it is difficult to detect such variations, but in others there may be prominent differences in size. The male is sometimes much smaller than the female; variations in color may occur and there may be differences in the size of the fins. Such diversity may only arise, or be accentuated, during the breeding season. The dorsal fins of the bowfin, *Amia calva*, thus become a brilliant green color prior to breeding while the belly turns a pale green. In the female the latter is white. The anal fins sometimes become enlarged in fishes such as *Gambusia affinis* and *Xiphophorus*, where it is called the 'sword' and functions as an organ for copulatory intromission called a gonapodium. The injection of testosterone into the female fish may result in the development of secondary sex characters just like those in the male.

During the breeding season, the male South American *lungfish*, *Lepidosiren paradoxa*, develops long finger-like out-growths from the fore- and hind-limbs. These organs are bright red in color due to a rich blood supply and it has been suggested that they may function as respiratory organs. The eggs of these lungfish are laid in burrows where the oxygen tension of the water is low. It has been surmised that the male, who guards this nest and fans the eggs may secrete oxygen from these organs into the oxygen-poor water of the burrow. The growth of these, so-called, limb-gills can be induced by the injection of testosterone (Urist, 1973) which confirms their nature as that of a secondary sex organ.

Amphibians often display prominent sexual differences during the breeding season. The bright orange coloration and the dorsal crest of the male crested newt, *Triturus cristatus*, can be induced in non-breeding animals following the injection of testosterone. The development of the nuptial thumb-pads in frogs is under hormonal control. Testosterone not only stimulates the development of these tissues but, in *Bufo fowleri*, can also promote the development of the vocal sacs in immature males and prompt them to give their characteristic mating calls or croaks.

It is usually rather difficult to distinguish between the sexes in *reptiles*. The males of many lizards, however, possess appendages about their heads and throats that have a fan-like appearance and can be erected for display. Dorsal crests are also present in some lizards. The tails of male turtles often grow longer than those of the females and aid in copulation. Some reptiles, especially snakes, possess erectile peni that differentiate from their cloacal tissues. The males in many species of snakes and lizards also possess a special secretory segment in the distal part of the renal tubule, called the 'sexual segment' and the development of this is under androgenic control.

The colorful dimorphic differences in the plumage of *birds* is well known, and generally (though not always) appears to be under the control of estrogens in the female; thus, the bright coloration of the male in domestic fowl, quail and pheasants is not dependent on androgenic hormones but the duller, more conservative plumage of the female is under estrogenic control. The injections of estrogen into male birds can stimulate the formation of female plumage. The color of the beaks of birds also is influenced by sex hormones during the breeding season. The beak of the male house sparrow is normally black in the breeding season and this coloration can be induced at other times of the year, or in castrates, by administering androgens and FSH or LH and FSH (Lofts, Murton and Thearle, 1973). The domestic fowl possesses a red fleshy structure, called the comb, on its head and this is much more developed in roosters than in hens but it regresses following castration (caponization). The comb of the domestic fowl is extremely sensitive to the presence of androgens which induce its hypertrophy. This response in capons has been widely used to identify androgenic materials, and indeed provided the first unequivocal evidence for the presence of androgenic hormones in the mammalian testis.

It is unnecessary to recall the secondary sex characters in man. In other *mammals* differences in size and coloration commonly occur. The red 'sex

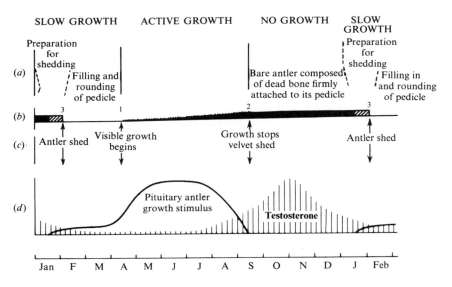

Fig. 9.1. The seasonal cycle in the growth of the antlers of the male Virginia deer (*Odocoileus v. borealis*) in relation to testosterone. This is controlled by light mediating the (hypothetical) release of pituitary hormone(s).

(*a*) The three major phases; growth is slow, fast, and then ceases.

(*b*) The changes in the physical size of the antlers during these periods in (*a*). .

(*c*) The principal events in the cycle.

(*d*) The increases in the pituitary growth stimulus which rises in the spring and subsides in the autumn when it is inhibited by the rising levels of testosterone. The precise nature of the pituitary stimulus is not clear but is probably a gonadotrophin(s). (Modified slightly from Amoroso and Marshall, 1960, taken from Waldo and Wislocki, 1951.)

skin' of the buttocks of some female monkeys during the sex cycle has been referred to in Chapter 7. Scent glands, that are under androgenic control, are also common in many mammals. The wild boar and male members of the cat family secrete odoriferous materials (pheromones) into the urine from special cells in the kidney and these glands are controlled by testosterone. The antlers of deer start to grow in the spring, apparently under the influence of pituitary hormones. In the autumn, when these animals breed, the antlers lose their covering of 'velvet', stop growing and come under the control of the rising testosterone levels in the blood. When the concentrations of this hormone subsequently decline the antlers are shed, usually at about the end of January (Fig. 9.1).

Finally it should be stressed that the behavior of vertebrates during the breeding season is also a secondary sex character (a most important one) that is influenced by androgenic and estrogenic hormones (see Goy and Goldfoot, 1973). The often bizarre (as it may appear to us) behavior of animals during courtship and mating is usually the result of the actions of the sex hormones and can often be initiated by the injection of these.

Periodicity of the breeding season; rhythms in sexual activity

Most vertebrates only breed periodically but, nevertheless, at fairly precise times of the year. In temperate zones, this more usually occurs in the spring but in some species, like deer, sheep, goats, badgers and grey seals, it occurs in the autumn. In equatorial regions where the climate and food supply are relatively similar throughout the year, breeding may often take place at any time. Similarly, some domesticated species, like the laboratory rat, the domestic fowl and man may breed throughout the year; a situation that appears to reflect continuously favorable circumstances.

An ability to reproduce during predictable seasons of the year clearly may be of considerable advantage as the young can then be produced at a time when such factors as the environmental temperature and the food and water supply are adequate. The chances for the survival of the young will thus be enhanced.

How is such precise timing possible? In temperate zones, the environmental conditions that prevail in a certain season are usually fairly predictable; thus, the animals can be expected to take their 'cues' and make their reproductive preparations on a basis of the solar calendar. Changes in the length of the day are a direct reflection of these events so that the length of the periods of light and darkness may furnish an excellent calendar to work by. Indeed, such photoperiodic stimulation is basic for the control of the reproductive cycle in most vertebrates. The first clear indication that light influences vertebrate gonadal function was made in

1925 by a Canadian zoologist called William Rowan. He found that the gonads of the junco finch, which normally enlarge when the days grow longer in the spring, could be stimulated to grow, even in winter when the birds were subjected to artificially prolonged periods of light. Other factors, however, can also impinge on the onset of the reproductive cycle and even override it. These include temperature, the nutritional condition of the animal and the related availability of supplies of food and water. There is also evidence for the presence of an internal inherent rhythm in the sexual activity of some species. It is often difficult to disentangle these various factors and to decide which is predominant.

The effects of light on reproduction have been studied in many species of birds but fewer mammals and cold-blooded vertebrates. Preparations for

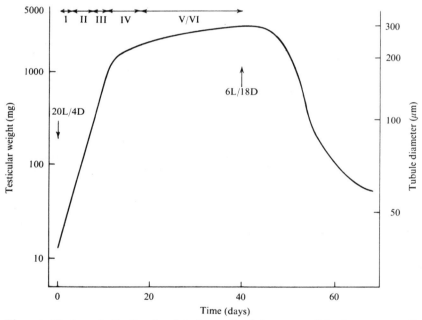

Fig. 9.2. Photoperiodically stimulated growth of the testes of the Japanese quail. For the first 40 days the birds were subjected to long, daily photoperiods of 20 h light and 4 h dark (20L/4D) and after this to short day-length of 6 h light and 18 h darkness. The diameter of the seminiferous tubules (for a given testis weight) is given on the scale on the right.

At the top of the diagram (Roman numerals) the changes in the development of the sperm are given; I = spermatogonia only, II = spermatogonia dividing, a few spermatocytes, III = numerous spermatocytes, IV = spermatocytes and spermatids and V, VI = spermatids and mature sperm. (Modified from Lofts, Follett and Murton, 1970.)

spring breeding often commence about the end of December when the length of the daylight hours starts to increase. As shown by Rowan, these conditions can be copied in the laboratory and dramatic increases in the activity of the gonads can then be shown to occur; thus, in the Japanese quail subjected to long-day photoperiods of 20 hours light and 4 hours darkness, the weight of the testes increases from 8 mg to 3000 mg in about three weeks (Fig. 9.2). The subsequent substitution of a short-day photoperiod, of six hours light and 18 hours darkness results in a decline in the weight of the testes. The gain in testicular weight is due mainly to an increase in the length and diameter of the seminiferous tubules though increases in the activity of the Leydig and Sertoli cells also take place. Comparable increases in development also occur in the ovaries of birds.

Studies in mammals have been made on the laboratory rat which, if kept in continuous light, suffers deficiencies in the development of its reproductive system and eventually becomes infertile. Alternate periods *per se* of light and dark also appear to contribute to gonadal stimulation in animals. The breeding cycle of the ferret has also been shown to be dependent on the length of the daily period of light. Shielding the eyes from light, or cutting the optic nerves, usually abolishes the effect of such photostimulation, receptors for which appear to be present in the eye. Such ocular receptors, however, are not always vital as it has been shown, for instance, that the domestic duck still exhibits its periodic breeding behavior even after it is blinded. It has been suggested that breeding activity is due to direct photostimulation of parts of the brain, a process that may occur through their translucent skull, or it may reflect an endogenous rhythmical cycle that is inherent.

The reproductive cycles of all birds or mammals do not necessarily respond to light. Such photostimulatory effects are absent in rabbits, guinea-pigs, ground-squirrels and guinea fowl. These differences in response to external stimuli may reflect the effects of domestication or, possibly, in the case of guinea-pigs and guinea fowl, their origin from equatorial regions where animals do not experience large changes in day-length. Tropical deer that normally breed all the year round also persist in this habit after many years in Europe even though they experience cold winter conditions. Deer from equatorial regions that normally have a seasonal cycle also persist in their pattern of reproduction when moved to Europe.

Amoroso and Marshall (1960) have classified animals into those that have 'a long day' and 'short day' breeding season. Long-day animals, which breed in spring, include most birds, as well as horses, donkeys, ferrets, cats and racoons. Goats, deer and sheep are short-day species that breed in the autumn when the day-length is declining.

The effects of light in stimulating development of the gonads and the timing of reproduction are not seen in the absence of the adenohypophysis or when the hypothalamic connections to the median eminence are cut. Differences in the length of the daily photoperiods of light and darkness control the release, via the optic nerve, of LH/FSH-RH from the median eminence which, in turn, initiates the release of gonadotrophins from the pituitary. The gonadotrophins, FSH and LH (and sometimes also pro-lactin), exert their various effects on the development of the germ cells and the formation and release of the gonadal steroid hormones. While a distinct FSH and LH exist in mammals and birds it appears that in most other vertebrates there is a single molecule (see Chapter 3) that has sufficient of both activities to control gonadal development.

As mentioned above, the reproductive rhythms of all animals are not responsive to light. The environmental temperature, for instance, may also play an important role. While birds and mammals often will not breed in extremely hot or cold conditions, thermal changes are usually not of great importance in determining breeding in such homeotherms. In poikilotherms, however, such effects may be more significant. Spallanzani (1784) considered that reproduction in reptiles and amphibians may be related to the environmental temperature and this still seems to be correct though light may also contribute. Licht (1972) has carefully analyzed the role of temperature in controlling reproduction in reptiles and considers that it supplies the most important stimulus. Such stimuli could be acting at several sites.

(*a*) A direct action on the brain could influence the release of hormones from the median eminence.

(*b*) Temperature could be exerting a direct action on gonadotrophin formation and release in the pituitary itself.

(*c*) When the temperature is increased it has been shown that the responsiveness of the target tissues to gonadotrophins increases. This is shown in Fig. 9.3 where the responses of the ovaries and oviducts of the lizard, *Xantusia vigilis*, can be seen to increase considerably at higher temperatures.

(*d*) It is possible that changes in body temperature may indirectly alter the levels of hormones by changing the rate of their inactivation.

Temperature has also been shown to influence the reproductive cycle in fishes.

In poikilotherms the effect of temperature may be of a 'permissive' nature for in the presence of a low body temperature metabolism is depressed and could be at such a low level that an action of light, or other stimulating factors, may be ineffective.

The availability of food and water can have dramatic effects on the breeding cycle. Many birds that live in the dry desert areas of Africa and

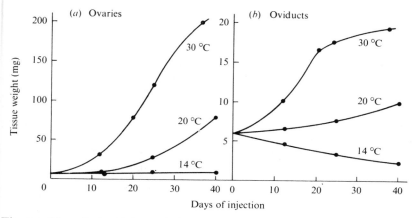

Fig. 9.3. The effects of the environmental temperature on the responses of the ovaries and oviducts of lizards (*Xantusia vigilis*) to the injections (on alternate days) of ovine FSH. It can be seen that at 14 °C there was little change in the weight of the tissues, there was a rather small effect at 20 °C while at 30 °C the growth of the ovaries and oviduct were marked. (From Licht, 1972.)

Australia (so-called xerophilous species) rapidly come into breeding condition following unpredictable seasonal rains. Breeding in most amphibians, even those from temperate regions, is also finally determined by rain and the availability of water in their breeding ponds. The South African toad *Xenopus laevis*, is thought to be unresponsive to light; reproduction is determined by an optimal nutritional condition and the availability of water. Domestic animals such as sheep are often fed a special protein-rich diet to bring them into breeding condition. It should be remembered, however, that not all species breed when they are in their best physiological condition as this may occur shortly after prolonged periods of hibernation or estivation, as seen commonly in amphibians and lungfishes, or at the end of a prolonged fast that follows a migration, such as in salmon and lampreys. At present it is not known how such a nutritional state and the availability of food and water influence breeding.

The breeding cycle of vertebrates is also influenced by a variety of ill-defined factors that for want of better knowledge are sometimes called psychological effects. These can be seen quite dramatically in many animals kept in captivity where they do not breed despite the fact that they otherwise appear to be in excellent physiological condition. This deficiency may be the result of the absence of certain environmental 'cues' such as sufficient social contact with other members of the species and an inability to perform a ritual courtship display. Social influences can be very important and it has been seen that reproduction is promoted in colonies of sea-birds when the numbers grow past a critical level. The mechanism for such effects is unknown but would appear to be mediated by the central nervous system and the hypothalamus.

While the hypothalamus and median eminence usually exert a major influence in controlling reproduction, as referred to earlier, this does not appear to occur in all vertebrates. In lampreys, the pituitary is essential for reproduction but it can be transplanted to other parts of the body, away from the region of the hypothalamus and breeding can still occur (Larsen, 1973). There is similarly no evidence that the hypothalamus controls reproduction in the chondrichthyes though gonadotrophins from the ventral lobe of the pars distalis are essential (Dodd, 1972*a*).

The activity of the pineal gland may also influence reproductive cycles though in this instance the evidence is principally confined to the laboratory rat. The rat pineal produces melatonin during the hours of darkness and this hormone can exert an inhibitory effect on reproduction (see Chapters 2 and 3). Pinealectomy (see Reiter and Sorrentino, 1970; Quay, 1970; Wurtman, Axelrod and Kelly, 1968) in young rats thus hastens their sexual maturation and in adults may increase the weight of the gonads. When hamsters that are normally exposed to long-day photoperiods are placed in darkness, their testes normally decrease in weight, from 3000 mg to 500 mg and this regression can be prevented by pinealectomy. The effects of pinealectomy on gonadal function in birds have been inconsistent, possibly reflecting the surgical trauma associated with this operation (Ralph, 1970). Recent experiments (Oishi and Lauber, 1974) on Japanese quail have failed to demonstrate any effect of removing the pineal on the growth of the gonads. Goldfish exposed to long-day photoperiods show an increase in the weight of the gonads in the months of January to May (but not at other times) and this effect is increased more than two-fold when the fish are pinealectomized (Fenwick, 1970). On the other hand, pinealectomy delays the maturation of the gonads in lampreys where pineal secretion may have a progonadotrophic action! (Joss, 1973).

Melatonin, that is secreted by the pineal, when administered to rats, mice and weasels decreases the responsiveness of the gonads to light stimulation. This gonadal effect has also been observed in the Japanese killifish (Urasaki, 1972), the domestic fowl and quail. The pineal may thus, through the action of secreted melatonin, exert an antigonadotrophic effect. Its site of action is uncertain but is probably the brain and this may lead to a decreased release of LH/FSH-RH from the median eminence. More direct effects, however, have not been excluded. Considerable differences exist in the responses of vertebrates to pinealectomy or the administration of melatonin (the results have been called 'inconsistent') so that at this time one cannot make a general statement as to the pineal's role in vertebrates. The daily rhythmical changes in the synthesis of melatonin, however, suggest that it could function as a 'biological clock' mediating daily or seasonal rhythms including reproduction. The pineal could thus add to or modify the role of the median eminence. It must be emphasized that at present the evidence for such an effect is equivocal. A particularly discordant note are the observations of Brown-Grant and Östberg (1974). They found that, in laboratory rats, denervation of the pineal, which abolishes its cyclical activity, did not interfere with the rats' normal ovarian cycles. They suggest that previous results, which they were unable to confirm, could have been the result of surgical trauma to the animals.

The nature of the stimuli that control reproduction are complex and we do not yet fully understand how they exert their effects. The endocrines, in close association with the brain, principally mediate the response of the reproductive system to such stimuli. The eminent British physiologist, F. H. A. Marshall, was the first to emphasize the importance of such an interrelationship in controlling breeding. Some years ago, he summarized the situation (Marshall, 1956) as follows: 'that (the) generative activity in animals occurs only as a result of definite stimuli, which are partly external and partly internal, while the precise nature of the necessary stimuli varies considerably in different kinds of animals according to the species, and still more according to the group to which the species belong'.

Maturation of the gametes – the gonadal cycles

As we have seen, animals come into breeding condition at different times of the year depending on the stimuli they receive, and react to, both from the external and their internal environments. If these 'cues' are sufficiently appropriate and are processed correctly, then breeding will be attempted. This process involves a complex series of changes in the body that are, to a considerable extent, mediated by altering the concentrations of hormones in the blood. The sperm and the ova then mature, or ripen, in preparation for their eventual union. As these preparations are proceeding, the changing levels of hormones contribute to the other physiological changes that are necessary to assure the fertilization of the ovum and, if this process is successful, the continued development of the egg and the embryo.

Such cycles in gonadal activity are relatively simple in the male when compared to those in the female. Sperm that can fertilize the ovum may be continually available for a period of many weeks, or even, as in man and feral pigeons, at all times of the year. The female, however, only produces ova available for fertilization periodically and, if not fertilized, they usually survive for less than a day. Such a periodic production of ova is an important event as it may not then occur again for many months. To mark this somewhat unique occurrence and make it clear to the male that he is at last acceptable, the female may send out various external signals and even actively seek male company. These 'signs' include 'calling', as in the cat, the production of a scent, as in the urine of the bitch, and the adoption of certain inviting sexual postures.

In mammals this period of sexual receptivity by the female is commonly called 'heat', or by physiologists, *estrus*. The preparatory period which precedes this is proestrus but if the animal is in a quiescent state, when no ova are being produced that are available for fertilization, it is called anestrus. The period during which the ova are being specially prepared for fertilization is called the *estrous cycle* which varies from four days in the laboratory rat to 27 days in kangaroos and (in its equivalent form, the human menstrual cycle) 28 days in women.

Many animals only experience a single estrous cycle in a year (called monoestrous) while others may have several such waves of ova production (polyestrous) spread out over several months of the breeding season or even for the entire year. Whether or not a single estrous cycle will be succeeded by another often depends on whether or not fertilization has occurred. If not, then there may be (though not always) another chance for successful reproduction within the over-all range of the general breeding season.

Testicular cycles in vertebrates

While certain male domestic animals exhibit continual spermatogenesis and sexual readiness throughout the year, this is not usual except in vertebrates from tropical regions and man. Seasonal breeding in a species is accompanied by a periodic maturation of the sperm (as well as the ova) along with such accessory and secondary sexual characters that facilitate its delivery on an appropriate occasion. Sperm may be available at all times during the reproductive season or mature in a single or several succeeding waves. The cystic type of spermatogenesis, where large numbers of sperm develop in unison inside envelopes that eject their contents into the seminiferous tubules, is most usual in amphibians and fishes (anamniotes) and is especially suited to those species where massive numbers of sperm are suddenly required for external fertilization. In reptiles, birds and mammals (amniotes), sperm mature from cells in the lining of the seminiferous tubules and this may be a more or less continuous process though it may also occur in waves. This acystic spermatogenesis is thought to be more suited to internal fertilization which may be attempted several times during a breed season.

The maturation of the sperm may proceed in several different ways which are dictated by whether or not the species is a seasonal breeder and whether it is poikilothermic or homeothermic.

Post-nuptial spermatogenesis is the more usual situation in seasonal poikilothermic breeders. This is illustrated by the frog *Rana esculenta*. Spermiation normally occurs in March, in Northern Europe and this is associated with a decline in testicular weight. Soon after this, however, the weight of the testis again increases and spermatogenesis proceeds throughout the summer but is halted during hibernation in winter (see Fig. 9.4) though it gradually increases again in the spring. The major spermatogenetic events thus occur in the summer preceding the breeding season and following the nuptial pairing in the spring of that year. Such a pattern of testicular activity is seen in many fishes and reptiles though considerable variations can occur. In some instances, sperm may mature fully prior to the winter hibernation, in other species, spermatogenesis may be halted at some

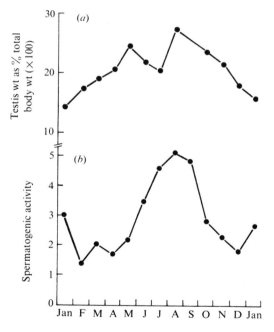

Fig. 9.4. Seasonal changes in the testicular weight (*a*) and spermatogenetic activity (*b*) in the European frog *Rana esculenta*. The decline in testicular weight that commences in May reflects spermiation during the breeding season. This sperm is that formed during the previous summer. Subsequently to this, spermatogenesis proceeds during the succeeding summer months but declines with the onset of winter hibernation. (From Lofts, 1964.)

intermediate stage of development and go on later, in the spring, or again sometimes it merely slows down in winter and proceeds more slowly.

In homeotherms, *prenuptial spermatogenesis* is usual. Testicular activity following the breeding season, during the winter months, may be slight but there is a rapid increase in activity when the spring nuptials become imminent. This pattern is usual in mammals and birds that breed periodically, though some species (such as bats) may store mature sperm in the epididymis for several months; during a period of hibernation for instance. Most birds exhibit characteristic 'refractory' periods following the breeding season, when the testes fail to respond to photoperiodic stimuli or administered gonadotrophins. The reptiles show a considerable diversity in testicular cycles. Chelonians usually exhibit amphibian-like post-nuptial spermatogenesis but the Lacertilia have several different testicular cycles (Fig. 9.5) and a pre-nuptial spermatogenesis is common.

The cyclical patterns of spermatogenesis described above are also termed *discontinuous spermatogenesis* in contrast to *continuous spermatogenesis*. The latter, apart from being present in some domestic temperate species, is common in animals that live in tropical areas where climatic conditions are relatively favorable at all times of the year. The frog, *Rana esculenta*, indeed

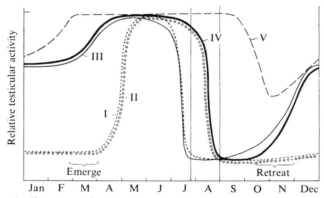

Fig. 9.5. A diagrammatic representation of the various patterns in seasonal development of the testes of lizards.

I through IV represents variations in the relative testicular activity of lacertilians that live in temperate regions: V, some tropical *Anolis* lizards.

'Emerge' and 'retreat' indicate the times that temperate species leave and enter winter hibernation.

The vertical lines indicate the period when most temperate lacertilians show no spermatogenetic activity.

It can be seen that pre-nuptial spermatogenesis occurs in types I and II (in spring) but in types III and IV spermatogenetic activity commences in the autumn. (From Licht, 1972.)

has a continuous spermatogenetic cycle in warm Mediterranean regions while, as described above, it has a discontinuous cycle in the more northern parts of Europe. This frog has thus been classified as a *potentially continuous breeder* or a continuo–discontinuous type. The environmental temperature determines which pattern will persist in such species. It should be noted, however, that it is not possible to alter a discontinuous spermatogenetic cycle to a continuous one simply by raising the temperature; it will not, for instance, change in *Rana temporaria* where the tissues appear to undergo an inherent rhythm in their ability to respond to hormonal stimuli. Variations that occur in the patterns of spermatogenetic activity are illustrated in Table 9.1 which summarizes differences among amphibians from different geographic areas.

The testicular cycle (like the ovarian cycle) is controlled by the adenohypophysis. Removal of the pituitary abolishes such cyclical activity and results in a regression of the testis that involves both the germ cells, in the seminiferous tubules, as well as the endocrine interstitial tissue (Leydig cells). In mammals, this is thought to involve the action of FSH on the seminiferous tubules and LH (in this instance more appropriately called ICSH) on the interstitial tissue. As we have seen (Chapter 3) in reptiles, amphibians and fishes a single gonadotrophin, incorporating both of these activities, may be present. While LH stimulates the production and release of testosterone the mode of action of FSH is less certain. It is usually necessary for the full maturation of the sperm but this may not be a direct effect. Hypophysectomized mammals, birds and fishes, in which the testes atrophy, can produce sperm following the administration of testosterone. It is surprising, however, that testosterone apparently cannot restore spermatogenetic activity in amphibians or at least in *Rana pipiens* (see Basu, 1969; Lofts, 1968).

It should be pointed out that the administration of testosterone to intact animals has often been observed to result in testicular regression and an inhibition of spermatogenesis. This paradox is apparently due to an inhibition by the androgen of the release of endogenous gonadotrophins. A parallel direct effect on the seminiferous tubules has not, however, been excluded. The inhibitory effects of testosterone on spermatogenesis thus appear to reflect an overabundance of this steroid.

Testosterone is, nevertheless, usually necessary for the maturation of the sperm but it is not yet clear whether FSH acts solely by stimulating the production of an androgen. Unfortunately the spermatogenetic effects of the administration of testosterone are often variable. It seems likely that FSH may act on the Sertoli cells to produce androgens that in turn mediate the maturation of the sperm (see Lofts, 1968).

Spermatogenesis is a prolonged and complex process that requires pre-

TABLE 9.I. *The types of spermatogenetic cycles exhibited by anuran amphibians that live in different geographical regions.* (From Basu, 1969)

Species	Habitat	Remarks
Continuous type of spermatogenesis		
Bufo arenarum	S. America	
Bufo paracnemis	S. America	
Bufo granulosus d'orbignyi	S. America	
Bufo melanostictus	India, Java	Lunar periodicity from Java reported
Telmatobius schreiteri	Andes mountains (high altitude)	Low winter temperature cannot affect the cycle
Hyla raddiana andina	Andes mountains (high altitude)	
Rana erythraea	India	
Rana grahami	India	
Rana hexadactyla	India (Pondicherry)	
Leptodactylus ocellatus reticulatus	S. America	
Leptodactylus prognathus	S. America	
Leptodactylus laticeps	S. America	
Physalaemus fascomaculatus	S. America	
Pseudis paradoxa	S. America	
Pseudis mantidactyla	S. America	
Rana cancrivora	Java	
Discontinuous type of spermatogenesis		
Rana temporaria	Europe	
Leptodactylus asper	S. America	
Leptodactylus bufonis	S. America	
Phyllomedusa sauvagii	S. America	
Rana pipiens	USA	High temperature causes spermatogenetic continuity
Hyla crucifer	USA	
Pleurodema bufonina	S. America (Patagonia), Australia	
Continuo–discontinuous type of spermatogenesis		
Rana esculenta	Europe	In winter spermatogenesis goes only up to spermatid formation
Rana gracea	S. America	
Rana ocellatus typica	S. America	
Rana tigrina	India (Calcutta)	
Rana nigromaculata	Japan (Niigata), China	

Species	Habitat	Remarks
Leptodactylus ocellatus typica	S. America	Two interruptions in spermatogenesis during cold winter and high summer
Variable spermatogenetic cycle as per geographic distribution		
Rana esculenta	Europe	Discontinuous cycle
ridibunda	Mediterranean region	Continuous cycle
Discoglossus pictus	Europe	Discontinuous cycle
	Mediterranean region	Continuous cycle

and postnatal maturation of the gonacytes, mitotic divisions of the spermatogonia and meiotic reduction divisions to form the spermatocytes, spermatids and the final (spermiogenesis) differentiation of spermatozoa. Androgens, and possibly FSH, are required for certain of these steps to proceed in a normal manner but there is considerable interspecies variation as to the stages of sperm maturation at which these hormones act. The endocrinology of gametogenesis is an important subject about which we know little. Dodd (1960, 1972b) has summarized what is known about this process in vertebrates. In the rat, testosterone may be necessary for early pre- and postnatal development of the gonacytes and it also promotes the meiotic division of the spermatocytes later on. FSH is required for the maturation of the spermatids. This pattern is, however, not the same even among the mammals and the information that is available is rather meager. In lampreys (Cyclostomata), hypophysectomy has little effect on the final stages of the maturation of the sperm. When this operation is performed in late winter or spring spermiation still occurs, but if hypophysectomy is carried out earlier, in October for instance, there is a considerable delay and spermiation may not take place at all (Larsen, 1973). In chondrichthyean fishes, hypophysectomy also inhibits the earlier stages (meiotic divisions of the spermatogonia) of sperm maturation and the same situation seems to apply among the teleosts. It seems likely that such effects of hypophysectomy are mediated by insufficient androgens though the lack of a direct effect of FSH may also be important. One cannot, with the limited and varied information available, make any generalization as to which stages of spermiogenesis are hormone-dependent in vertebrates. There are instances in fishes, as well as reptiles, birds and mammals, where the later stages of maturation are apparently dependent on endocrine stimulation. The situation in amphibians is especially confusing as in some instances spermatogenesis appears to be occurring at a time when the endogenous production of testosterone is low and exogenous testosterone may exert a direct inhibitory effect on the early stages of spermatogenesis. The comparative endocrinology of gametogenesis needs, and certainly merits, further exploration.

Little direct information is available about the circulating levels of testosterone and gonadotrophins in seasonally breeding animals. Changes in the concentrations of such hormones are inferred from histological examination of secondary sexual characters. The Leydig cells, and their analogues the boundary cells show a seasonal pattern in their histological appearance (see Lofts, 1968). In the periods that precede breeding, these cells enlarge and accumulate lipids and cholesterol. These cells become depleted of these materials at the height of the breeding season and this is thought to reflect the secretion of androgens which utilize lipids as their substrates. These histological changes are associated with breeding behavior, the development of secondary sex characters and can be imitated by the injection of gonadotrophins. Such changes have been observed in fishes, amphibians, reptiles, birds and mammals. An example of this can be seen in Fig. 9.6 where the height of the thumb-pad epithelia in the frog *Rana esculenta* can be seen to decline in June when the lipid and cholesterol content of the interstitial tissue is greatest. A seasonal pattern in the ability

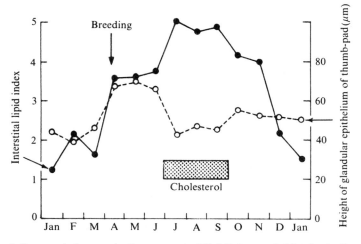

Fig. 9.6. Seasonal changes in the amount of lipid observed, histologically, in the interstitial cells of the testis of the frog *Rana esculenta*. This reaches a maximum in mid-summer, after breeding has occurred, when the cellular cholesterol levels are also greatest. These changes are thought to reflect a decline in the synthesis of androgens (which utilize the lipids as substrates for their formation). This change is consistent with the decline in the development of the thumb-pad which is under androgenic control. (From Lofts, 1964.)

of the testis of the cobra to convert progesterone to androgens, *in vitro*, is shown in Fig. 9.7. This androgen synthesis reaches an initial maximum during breeding in May but drops subsequently as the testes atrophy.

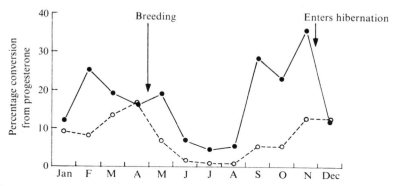

Fig. 9.7. Seasonal changes in the ability of the testis of a snake, the cobra, to convert (*in vitro*) progesterone (which acts as a substrate) to androgens. Testosterone production declines following breeding in May but rises again in late summer and autumn, during post-nuptial spermatogenesis, only to decrease once more as the snakes go into winter hibernation: ●, testosterone; ○, androstenedione. (From Lofts, 1969.)

When spermatogenesis is again initiated in the autumn the rate of progesterone to androgen conversion again increases but declines again with the onset of winter hibernation. Direct measurements of the plasma androgen concentrations have been made in the Australian lizard *Trachysaurus* (*Tiliqua*) *rugosa* (Bourne and Seamark, 1973). These reptiles breed in spring when the testicular weight is about 1300 mg, compared to 180 mg in summer. During the breeding season, the androgen concentration in the plasma is 33 ng/ml but it is only 10 ng/ml at other times of the year. A 10-fold increase in the plasma testosterone levels has also been observed in starlings (*Sturnus vulgaris*) during the breeding season and this was associated with an increased activity of the testicular interstitial cells (Temple, 1974). A periodic decrease in the hormone-secretory interstitial, as well as the spermatogenetic, tissue occurs in all the non-mammals that breed periodically. In mammals, however, there is usually a permanent hormone-secretory tissue in the testis.

The Sertoli tissue, which has been identified in all groups of vertebrates, has for a long time excited speculation as to its function. The histological appearance of this tissue shows changes in parallel to those of the Leydig cells (see Lofts, 1968) and spermatogenesis. An accumulation of lipids, in the Sertoli cells, follows spermiation but these materials are depleted when spermatogenesis is occurring. In animals that normally breed continually, like laboratory rats, hypophysectomy results in an accumulation of lipids in the Sertoli cells and this is thought to reflect a lack of their stimulation by FSH. It is now widely accepted that the Sertoli cells produce androgenic steroids that may influence spermatogenesis, and FSH probably acts to stimulate the secretion of such hormones. The cyclical changes that occur in the appearance of the Sertoli cells thus presumably reflect changes in the endogenous gonadotrophin levels in the blood.

Ovarian cycles in vertebrates

The maturation of the ovum in the ovary and its extrusion (ovulation) and passage into the oviduct or uterus involves the coordinated activity of FSH, LH, sometimes prolactin, and the secretion of estrogens, progesterone and, possibly, even small amounts of androgens from the ovary. The ovarian cycle results from increases and declines in the circulating concentrations of these hormones and this is largely the result of their interactions in stimulating or inhibiting each other's release, through a negative- and positive-feedback to the median eminence and hypothalamus.

These hormonal rhythms have only been closely analyzed in mammals and even these results are usually confined to more domesticated species.

Placental mammals

Three general patterns have been identified in the ovarian cycle of placental, or eutherian, mammals and these have been described (*a*) in the sheep, pigs and cattle, (*b*) in the laboratory rat and (*c*) in man.

Sheep

The ewe usually comes into estrus in the autumn, as a result of stimulation by shortening periods of daylight, and if pregnancy does not occur will continually produce ova at intervals of about 16 or 17 days until the following spring. Some breeds of sheep, like the merino, may breed for longer periods of the year. The estrous cycle of the ewe lasts for about 17 days and the hormonal changes that occur are summarized in Fig. 9.8. The onset of estrus is taken as time zero in the ovarian cycle and this lasts for about 24 hours, ovulation occurring towards the end of this time. Following ovulation, the blood supply to the ruptured Graafian follicle increases and the granulosa cells luteinize to form the corpus luteum. This structure reaches a maximum size on about day 8. Luteinization of the follicle is initiated by the action of LH and the secretion of progesterone is also stimulated by this hormone. LH is luteotrophic, an effect that is seen in most mammals. In some species, including the rat, mouse, rabbit and possibly the sheep, prolactin may also have a luteotrophic effect. Sometimes the two hormones act in conjunction with each other. Progesterone secretion from the corpus luteum rises until about day 11 of the cycle and then on day 13 undergoes a precipitous decline.

Accompanying these events is the development of the Graafian follicles and the maturation of the ova. This process proceeds under the influence of FSH and the estrogens that are secreted by the follicular cells which are

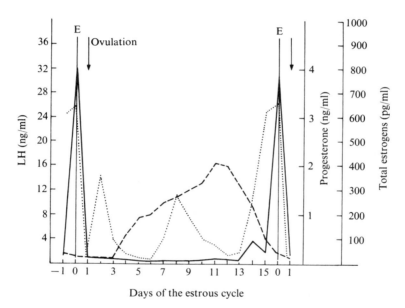

Days of the estrous cycle

Fig. 9.8. The estrous cycle of the ewe. Estrus (E) occurs at time *zero* and is followed by ovulation. The concentrations of plasma progesterone (from the jugular), estrogens (ovarian vein) and LH (from the jugular or ovarian vein) are shown in relation to these events. It can be seen that on day 12 there is a decline in progesterone which is accompanied by climb in estrogen concentration that initiates a 'surge' in release of LH that results in ovulation: dashed line, progesterone; dotted line, total estrogens; solid line, luteinizing hormone (jugular or ovarian vein). (From Hansel and Echternkamp, 1972.)

also stimulated by LH. LH thus appears to have a general steroidogenic effect on the ovarian tissues. During the preovulation phase of the cycle, estrogen levels are moderate but as can be seen in Fig. 9.8 they may display some periodic changes. The LH level is low but sufficient to maintain the secretion of steroid hormones. The estrogens and progesterone that are produced act on the accessory sex organs, especially the uterus and vagina, to get them into 'tip-top' condition for the prospective fertilization, the implantation of the egg, and pregnancy. The release of LH is kept low in the preovulatory period as a result of a negative-feedback inhibition of its release that is exerted by progesterone on the hypothalamus.

Between days 13 and 16 of the cycle dramatic changes take place in the hormonal concentrations that result in ovulation. There is a rapid decline in progesterone that reflects a breakdown of the corpus luteum. LH levels are still adequate to maintain this tissue but it loses its sensitivity to the hormone. Estrogen levels then climb upwards and by a positive-feedback action on the hypothalamus bring about a massive release of LH that causes the follicle to rupture and extrude its ovum. The effect of the estrogen via the median eminence is reflected in a decline of stored luteinizing hormone-releasing activity in the ewe's hypothalamus (Crighton, Hartley and Lamming, 1973).

The hormonal basis for estrous behavior has recently been questioned. It had commonly been assumed that it was solely a reflection of the actions of estrogens. The estrogen level, however, usually drops considerably just prior to estrus; the preovulatory surge is in fact rather temporary. There is now evidence to indicate that not only estrogen but also progesterone, as well as a small but significant release of an androgen, androstenedione, from the ovary, may contribute to estrous behavior.

After ovulation the LH stimulates the follicle granulosa cells to luteinize and if fertilization does not occur the cycle will then recommence. In the event of fertilization and an ensuing pregnancy, the corpus luteum, as we shall see later, will persist for a much longer time and contribute to the events of the gestational period.

The corpus luteum can thus be seen to play a commanding role in the estrous cycle and it has been called 'the clock'. The reason for the decline in the activity of the corpus luteum during the latter part of the estrous cycle has only recently been elucidated. It has been known for many years that, when the uterus of guinea-pigs is removed, the corpus luteum persists for a much longer period of time. This effect can also be seen in the ewe, as well as the cow and sow, but not in women, the rhesus monkey, dog, badger nor marsupials (Anderson, 1973). The non-pregnant uterus, in some species, appears to produce a substance that has been called a '*luteolysin*' that causes the corpus luteum to atrophy. There is some evidence to suggest that this may be a prostaglandin. Whatever its nature, it is interesting that this effect is not seen if the ovary is transplanted to a region that is distant from the uterus, such as the neck. The ovarian arterial blood and the uterine venous blood pass by each other in closely apposed vessels and it seems that this special vascular arrangement functions as a unique pathway by which the luteolysin can get to the ovary before it becomes diluted, or destroyed, in the general circulation. It is important, however, to remember that this effect is not seen in all species nor has such a role for a luteolysin been accepted by all (see Nalbandov, 1973). Instead, it has been proposed that the death of the corpus luteum results from a lack of LH due to competition for this trophic hormone by newly developing ovarian follicles.

Finally, before leaving the ewe, some comment should be made about the modern techniques that have made such investigations possible. For many years information about the estrous cycles in animals depended on histological examination of the ovary and its accessory tissues, the uterus and vagina. It was also possible to measure urinary steroid excretion but identification and measurement of blood steroid concentrations were not generally feasible or were unreliable. Applications of the science of immunology to endocrinology, however, changed all this. The basic technique for the radioimmunoassay of hormones, including the sex hormones, was developed initially by Solomon Berson and Rosalyn Yalow in New York. This procedure, which uses radioactively labelled antibodies to various hormones, made it possible accurately to identify and measure the small amounts of a variety of hormones present in the blood. In addition, antisera to many hormones have been developed, including anti-LH and anti-progesterone, which, by their ability to block, or not, certain processes in the reproductive cycle, facilitate understanding the gonadal mechanisms that are coordinated by the pituitary and steroid hormones.

The laboratory rat

The female rat has an ovarian cycle that is broadly similar to that of the ewe but there are some notable differences (see Fig. 9.9).

The rat estrous cycle lasts for four days and the events are normally regulated on the basis of a diurnal rhythm. This facilitates experiments on these animals as it is known that ovulation always occurs just after midnight and other changes can also be timed with remarkable accuracy (Fig. 9.10).

The adoption of such a rhythm is vital to the rat as the corpus luteum, which, as we have seen, acts as a 'clock' in many other mammals, is small and does not persist for long during its estrous cycle. Progesterone is present throughout the estrous cycle but it does not appear that changes in its levels contribute to the timing of ovulation. Instead there appears to be a 'timed' estrogen release on the morning of proestrus sometime before 10.00 a.m. This steroid promotes, as in other mammals, LH release but in contrast to other species this is immediately followed by a marked elevation in the plasma progesterone concentration. As this precedes the formation of the corpus luteum it presumably arises as a result of a luteotrophic effect

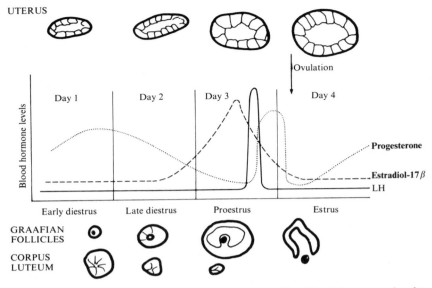

Fig. 9.9. The estrous cycle of the laboratory rat. The blood hormone levels; progesterone, estradiol-17β and LH are shown in relation to estrus and ovulation.

Also included are a representation of changes in the stages of development of the uterus, Graafian follicles and corpus luteum. It can be seen that the corpus luteum does not persist throughout the entire estrous cycle of the rat and that the preovulatory increase in progesterone is due to the secretion of this hormone by the ovarian interstitial tissue.

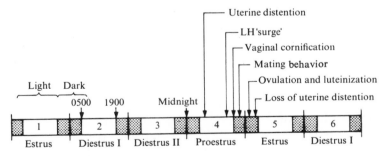

Fig. 9.10 The principal events in the rat estrous cycle in relation to the time of the day.

This cycle is precisely timed on the basis of a diurnal rhythm. Ovulation can be seen to occur shortly after midnight. Other events including; mating behavior, the LH 'surge' and the development of the uterus. (From Armstrong and Kennedy, 1972.)

of the LH on the ovarian interstitial tissue. This progesterone is vital to the onset of estrus and subsequent changes that occur in the uterus, which becomes less distended while the endometrium becomes more glandular. Progesterone does not appear to be important for ovulation which cannot be prevented by anti-progesterone serum.

The corpus luteum persists only if pregnancy or pseudopregnancy (as a result of copulation without fertilization) occurs, otherwise it does not have a significant role in controlling the rat ovarian cycle.

Man

The human ovarian, or menstrual, cycle lasts for 28 days and is quite distinct from that in non-primate mammals. A similar ovarian cycle also occurs in monkeys and apes. The corpus luteum persists for a more prolonged period of the cycle than in the rat but not for the whole of it, as in the ewe, cow or sow. The timing of the events of the human ovarian cycle is arbitrarily taken from the initiation of menstruation. This process is due to the discharge of superfluous structural remnants and secretions of the endometrium and contains some blood. In effect, menstruation represents the termination of the previous ovarian cycle and the life of the corpus luteum and lasts for about 4 to 5 days.

The preovulatory period of the human ovarian cycle thus takes place in the absence of a corpus luteum so that progesterone secretion is relatively small. 17α-OH-progesterone levels rise but this metabolite has little progestin activity. The follicle ripens under the influence of FSH and secretes estradiol which controls the release of this gonadotrophin by a negative-feedback inhibition in the hypothalamus. As in other mammals, a sudden surge in LH, initiated by the secreted estrogen, results in ovulation, usually on about day 16. There is also a sudden rise in FSH release at this time which may contribute to ovulation. No precise period of estrous behavior exists in the human female. She is receptive to the male at any time of the cycle. The ruptured follicle starts to luteinize after ovulation and progesterone secretion, due to the action of LH, rises but subsequently declines when the corpus luteum later degenerates and menstruation then occurs. In the event of fertilization, however, the corpus luteum persists. The reason for the premenstrual decline in the activity of the human corpus luteum is unknown and this degenerative process can proceed normally following hysterectomy; apparently it does not involve the action of a uterine luteolysin.

At least three different types of ovarian cycles thus exist among placental mammals. The principal differences involving the role of the corpus luteum and progesterone.

Ovulation

The mechanisms of initiation of ovulation, however, may also differ among the mammals. In the examples described above, ovulation takes place in response to an internal programming that controls hormone release so that ovulation is then said to be *spontaneous*. In other mammals, however, ovulation can be *induced* as a result of copulation and sexual excitement. This latter type of ovulation is known to occur in such species as the rabbit, cat, ferret, mink and racoon and it is suspected that it may also sometimes occur even in women. In such species, estrogen is released from the developing ovarian follicles which are under the influence of FSH (see Schwartz, 1973). This estrogen indicates when the follicles are ripe and results in mating behavior. The latter is in contrast to spontaneous ovulators in which progesterone is also necessary. If copulation takes place, this initiates a surge of LH release, as a result of neural stimulation of the hypothalamus and pituitary, and ovulation occurs. This event is accompanied by a rise in progesterone levels and takes place several hours after coitus when the sperm are ensconced in the oviduct. In non-mammals, the situation is less clear, however, the mere presence of the male or even some substitute may be all that is necessary to initiate ovulation. Apart from gallinacious birds like the domestic fowl, as well as domestic geese and ducks, most birds do not produce eggs in the absence of the male. It has, however, been reported that some birds, such as pet parrots, will lay eggs if suitably stroked and tickled. Copulation may thus not always be necessary and courting behavior and sexual display may be effective stimulants of ovulation.

Following parturition, several species of eutherians including the rabbit, ferret, mink and racoon come into a post-partum heat when they copulate and this, as indicated above, results in ovulation. Copulation not always needed to precipitate ovulation in these circumstances for, as we shall see in the next section, post-partum ovulation is common in marsupials where it is a spontaneous event and occurs at a time that merely reflects an extension of the normal estrous cycle.

Delayed implantation

Pregnancy usually persists for a precise and predictable period of time. Some interesting and, at first, mystifying exceptions have, however, been encountered. Animals that conceive in the autumn and deliver their young in spring can, on some occasions, such as when the length of the daylight period is artificially increased, produce their young much earlier. There have been other instances described, especially in kangaroos, where a female has been taken into captivity and without any contact with a male has, many months later, given birth to a young one. Faced with the necessity for an explanation, some people were even forced to consider the possibility of virgin birth! The cause is, nevertheless, quite a reasonable one. In a number of mammals especially the mustelid Carnivora (such as weasels and sable) and macropod marsupials (kangaroos), development of the fertilized egg can sometimes cease when a blastocyst, containing about 100 cells, has been formed. This blastocyst lies dormant for a time that may extend for several months, but can be subsequently stimulated to continue development. The delay is called an *obligatory* one when it is determined by external conditions, such as light, as seen in badgers, pine-marten, weasels and the roe deer. In other species, such as the mouse, rat and macropod marsupials it is *facultative* and controlled by more physiological events. As will be described in more detail on p. 344, this inhibition results from the effects of suckling and lactation.

Pregnancy

An excellent account of the role of hormones in this process is given by Heap (1972) and Heap, Perry and Challis (1973). When the fertilized egg is retained in the oviduct or uterus and the subsequent development of the young occurs at this site, within the female, pregnancy is said to be occurring. This term is usually assumed to include the viviparous condition but may also encompass ovoviviparity. The internal incubation of the young is also called *gestation*. The condition of pregnancy appears to have reached its highest state of organization in placental mammals though little information is available about this process in non-mammals. Pregnancy is not a uniquely mammalian phenomenon as it occurs in some chondrichthyeans, teleosts, reptiles and amphibians, though not in birds. Gestation may occur for quite long periods of time in placental mammals but this is not unique as it may extend for two years in some viviparous sharks and is of four years duration in the ovoviviparous urodele, *Salamandra atra*.

As we have seen, the hormonal preparation of the mammalian uterus for the reception, fertilization and implantation of the egg is initially stimulated by estrogens and progesterone, the latter usually having the subsequent dominant action, though both steroids act in simultaneous collaboration. Subsequently during pregnancy, these favorable uterine conditions need to be maintained and even modified from time to time as the fetus grows and is eventually delivered to the outside world. The necessary supplies of hormones are then not only altered qualitatively but increased quantities may also be required. These added needs have been met in various ways by the placental mammals and principally involve the function of the pituitary, the ovary, the placenta and the uterus.

Progesterone, to use an oft-quoted phrase, is called 'the hormone of pregnancy' but substantial, though usually smaller, amounts of estrogens are also used during gestation. These gonadal steroids maintain the endometrium and contribute to the considerable expansion that occurs in the myometrium during pregnancy. The hypertrophy of these muscles results from the stretching of the walls of the uterus and the induction, by estrogens, of new contractile proteins. Contractions of the uterus are not usually desirable during pregnancy and the responsiveness of the myometrium to stimulation is reduced by progesterone. The contractile effects of oxytocin are, for instance, usually reduced by pretreatment of the uterus with progesterone while estrogens have the opposite effect and enhance the responses to this neurohypophysial hormone. Such effects have not been demonstrated in all species but are very reproducible in some, like the rabbit. A most important role of progesterone in pregnancy in placentals is the inhibition of the estrous cycle and ovulation. This effect results from a negative-feedback inhibition of the release of LH from the pituitary and may be required when the periods of gestation exceed the length of the normal estrous cycle. Corpora lutea also persist in many viviparous and ovoviviparous non-mammals and although their precise role is uncertain it is suspected that they may also have a comparable role in such animals.

The problem of how to supply the added hormonal requirements of pregnancy has been met in various ways by different species of placental mammals. Estrogens and progesterone are typically secreted by the vertebrate ovary. The corpus luteum is usually the principal ovarian source of progesterone but normally this structure does not persist for longer than the estrous cycle. As we shall see, this situation even occurs in pregnant Australian marsupials. The period of gestation in these animals is similar to that of their estrous cycles so that a prolongation of the life of the corpus luteum is unnecessary. In the placental mammals, which have relatively longer periods of gestation, the corpus luteum persists for a much longer time and often remains functioning throughout the entire period of pregnancy. This extended survival is the result, in some species, of an inhibition of the effects of uterine luteolysins, due to the presence of extra material in the uterus and the stimulating actions of mixtures of luteotrophic hormones. These hormonal combinations may consist of FSH, LH, prolactin, and gonadotrophins that may be produced by the placenta. The precise hormonal content of this so-called '*luteotrophic complex*' differs considerably from species to species. Its function is to extend the normal lifetime of the corpus luteum and to promote the secretion of progesterone.

The production of progesterone by the ovary may be facilitated in various ways. In some species (the horse) additional corpora lutea may form, but in others (human and cattle) only a single corpus luteum is usually present. Animals that produce several young at a time have a correspondingly greater number of corpora lutea available for the production of progesterone. During pregnancy, the secretion of progesterone by individual corpora lutea may be increased by the action of the luteotrophic complex. In addition, the amount of available progesterone is the net result of its rate of production and destruction. As described in Chapter 4, proteins that bind steroid hormones are present in the plasma and when they are in such a bound condition the rate of the destruction of these hormones is reduced. During pregnancy, the formation of such steroid hormone-binding proteins in the liver may be increased, probably as a result of stimulation by estrogens. There are considerable interspecific differences in the physiological patterns that ensure adequate progesterone in pregnancy.

In some species, such as the rabbit, ovariectomy during pregnancy always results in prompt abortion. In other species, such as the sheep, guinea-pig, rat and human this operation does not necessarily result in a loss of the fetus. The placenta in these species produces sufficient gonadal steroids to support the uterus, though the supply may be inadequate during early pregnancy. There are considerable interspecific differences in the ability of the placenta to produce hormones. The placenta of the rabbit and goat, for instance, does not produce any steroid hormones, or luteotrophins, while the human placenta produces large quantities of all these materials. The pig placenta produces estrogen but not progesterone, while the sheep produces large amounts of progesterone.

The appearance of the placenta as a temporary endocrine organ that helps to supply the hormonal requirements of pregnancy is a fascinating physiological adaptation. Such a role has not been described in non-mammals or even in marsupial mammals. It is not possible to draw any orderly phyletic line as to the distribution of this hormone-secreting tissue in placentals and it could have evolved separately on several occasions to suit the needs of each particular species. In recent years, it has become apparent that tumorous tissues in mammals may produce a variety of hormones that normally arise from discrete endocrine glands. Perhaps there is some analogy between such tumors and the evolution of an endocrine placenta!

Parturition

The delivery of the young is a very precisely timed event that, although it undoubtedly involves hormonal changes is not very well understood. During pregnancy, the progesterone-dominated uterus is in a relatively quiescent state and it is reasonable to suspect that removal of such a progesterone-block may precipitate contractures that result in parturition. Plasma progesterone levels are quite low at birth in some animals, like sheep and ferrets, but in others, like women and guinea-pigs, this is not so. Estrogen levels often rise dramatically on the approach of parturition and this may sensitize the uterus and oppose the progesterone-block. Oxytocin is released from the neurohypophysis and stimulates contraction of the uterus. This hormone facilitates the delivery of the young but in some species parturition can still occur in the absence of oxytocin. Its role is therefore not always essential in mammals. Another polypeptide hormone, of uncertain chemical composition, *relaxin*, is released from the ovary and is also present in the placenta of rabbits and guinea-pigs. Relaxin promotes the relaxation of the ligaments of the pubic symphysis to allow passage of the young through what has been described as 'this triumphal arch!' This effect (on the pelvic ligaments) is detectable in most mammals but is most prominent in rabbits and guinea-pigs.

The desire to care for the young is also a hormonally mediated effect. The process of lactation from the mammary glands is normally (except it seems in man) an important part of this process in all mammals. The role of the hormones in lactation has been described in Chapter 5.

Marsupial mammals

The marsupials, that include the American opossum and large numbers of Australian mammals, like kangaroos, have a unique form of reproduction that is accompanied by some remarkable endocrine innovations. The initiation of the study of the reproductive endocrinology of the Australian marsupials was principally due to the efforts of H. Waring on the occasion of his academic migration to Australia in 1948.

Systematically, the marsupials are distinguished from the placentals by the absence of a true placenta; only a yolk-sac placenta is present so that the physiological connection with the parent is more tenuous than in placentals. Young marsupials are born in a relatively immature state comparable to that of embryos in the later part of the gestational period of placentals. The newborn young of marsupials are suckled on the teat where they undergo a considerable part of the development that would normally occur within the uterus of placentals. In many, but not all, marsupials this takes place in an external pouch or marsupium.

According to the opinion of G. B. Sharman, who is well informed in these matters, marsupials and placentals probably evolved from a common oviparous ancestor. Sharman's (1970) account of marsupial reproduction should be consulted by those who wish to extend their knowledge of this process. An even more comprehensive account has been provided by Tyndale-Biscoe (1973).

Australian marsupials usually breed from mid-summer to early winter: January to June in the Southern Hemisphere. This can, however, be modified so that, in periods of drought, reproduction will be inhibited while in favorable conditions it may occur at almost any time of the year. While there are many similarities between the endocrine control of reproduction in placental and marsupial mammals there are also some remarkable differences. The gonadal steroids, estrogens and progesterone, mediate the pre- and post-ovulatory changes in the reproductive tract during the estrous cycle of marsupials. Little is known about the nature of the pituitary gonadotrophins in marsupials except that some effects seen in

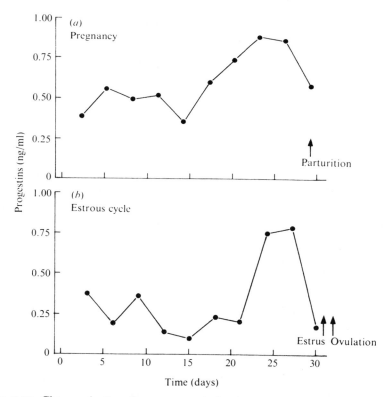

Fig. 9.11. Changes in the plasma progestin levels during pregnancy (*a*) and the estrous cycle (*b*) of a marsupial, the tammer wallaby *Macropus eugenii.*
The commencement of pregnancy or the estrous cycle was initiated by removing the suckling young from the pouch, thereby initiating the development of the fertilized blastocyst (see text) or the next reproductive cycle. Progesterone levels commenced to rise on about day 15 and declined just prior to estrus and ovulation, or parturition. (From Lemon, 1972.)

placentals can be mimicked by the injection of the placental hormone preparations. In marked contrast to placentals, pregnancy in marsupials does not interfere with the concurrent estrous cycle and the maturation and ovulation of the egg. This egg is usually produced at the normal time. Certain marsupials, the macropods or kangaroos, also display an interesting form of delayed implantation or more correctly called in this instance an *embryonic diapause* that differs from the process that is occasionally seen in placentals. The process of lactation in marsupials also has some rather unique features.

The estrous cycle of marsupials lasts for about 28 days and, as in placentals, consists of an initial period of follicular growth that is accompanied by the development of the uterus and vagina, at first under the influence of estrogens and then, in its secretory phase, by progesterone. Estrus follows a sudden decline in the level of progesterone (Fig. 9.11), reminiscent of that seen in some placentals, and lasts for several days during which ovulation occurs. The precise endocrine stimuli for ovulation have not been elucidated but it is spontaneous and not the result of any external sexual or copulatory stimuli. Fertilization is followed by the development of the egg into a blastocyst and if the animal is not already lactating, pregnancy will occur. A corpus luteum is formed in the ruptured follicle and persists for the period of time that is usual in the estrous cycle; its life is *not* prolonged by the pregnancy. An extended life for the corpus luteum is not necessary in marsupials as the period of gestation is usually nearly identical to the time of the normal estrous cycle (which continues to occur concurrently with the pregnancy!); nevertheless, the progesterone levels in pregnancy are greater than those in the normal estrous cycle (Fig. 9.11) which seems to reflect a hypersecretion from the ovary.

Ovulation of the egg, that ripens during pregnancy, occurs at various times in relation to parturition. The relationships of the estrous cycle and pregnancy are summarized in Fig. 9.12. Ovulation may occur *prior* to parturition, as in the swamp wallaby, *Wallabia bicolor*, where the period of gestation is 35 days compared to only 32 days for the estrous cycle. In this marsupial, pre-parturition ovulation is followed by copulation. If fertilization takes place, a blastocyst develops which if, lactation then occurs, lies dormant (see later). In other species like *Megaleia rufa*, parturition is closely succeeded by ovulation, post-partum copulation, and the formation of a blastocyst. In the grey kangaroo, *Macropus giganteus*, the period of gestation is much shorter than the estrous cycle, just as seen in the Australian brush possum, *Trichosurus*, and other non-kangaroos, and pre-scheduled future ovulation is then inhibited by the suckling stimulus provided by the young. If, however, the young is removed, ovulation follows nine days later. In the latter part of lactation of the grey

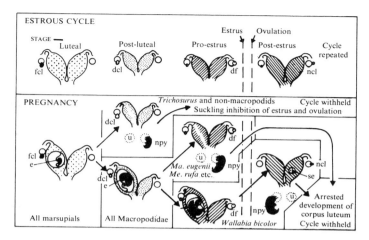

Fig. 9.12. The estrous cycle and pregnancy in marsupials. A diagrammatic summary of the size and functional relationships of the ovary and the uterus.

Estrous cycle: fcl, functional corpus luteum; dcl, degenerating corpus luteum; df, developing Graafian follicle; ncl, new corpus luteum.

Pregnancy (additional abbreviations): e, intrauterine embryo; npy, newborn pouch young attached to teat; se, segmenting egg.

Three different patterns in the reproductive cycle of the marsupials are shown; non-macropods like *Trichosurus* (Australian possum) and macropods (kangaroos) which have two types of cycle shown by; *Macropus eugenii* (the tammar wallaby and *Megaleia rufa* (the red kangaroo), and *Wallabia bicolor* (the swamp wallaby).

For detailed discussion see the text. (From Sharman, 1970. Copyright © 1970, by the American Association for the Advancement of Science.)

kangaroo this inhibition may decline so that ovulation and fertilization may occur, though while the young is in the pouch, the fertilized egg does not develop further than the blastocyst stage.

When the young kangaroo leaves the pouch the development of a dormant blastocyst can then proceed and pregnancy thus continues. The young kangaroos, however, remain with the mother and continue to suckle from outside the pouch; thus, the female kangaroo may have one young in the pouch, and another, much older young, 'at heel'. The two young then feed from different teats and the composition of the milk that each feeds on is quite different notwithstanding the fact that the endocrine secretions that are available to both glands are identical.

The delayed implantation in macropod marsupials follows the division of the fertilized egg to a stage when 80 cells are present. This blastocyst, in contrast to the placental one, is surrounded by a shell membrane and a layer of albumin; in which state it can survive for several months. It lies in the uterus, in the branch opposite to that where the preceding pregnancy occurred. The temporary inhibition of the development of the blastocyst depends on the suckling stimulus from the young kangaroo in the pouch. Once suckling declines the blastocyst then starts to develop further. The nature of the inhibitory stimulus is thought to result from neural stimulation of the pituitary, as a result of the suckling. Ovariectomy does not have any effect on the dormant blastocyst but the injection of estrogen and, especially, progesterone can initiate its development. It appears that the corpus luteum of lactation, that is formed from the follicle that gave rise to the dormant blastocyst, is relatively quiescent during lactation and its subsequent development and rapid secretion initiates the succeeding pregnancy. Secreted progesterone appears to accomplish this change by initiating, and so synchronizing, both the further development of the blastocyst and the luteal phase of the uterus; the latter providing an environment that is necessary for the growth of the embryo. The nature of the inhibition of the corpus luteum is uncertain but it is interesting that the injection of oxytocin, which is normally released in response to suckling, can prevent the development of the corpus luteum and the blastocyst in kangaroos that have been deprived of their suckling young. Oxytocin may thus have evolved a physiological role that has not been described in other vertebrates. It is, however, interesting that injected oxytocin shortens the life of the corpus luteum in cows and this effect depends on the presence of an intact uterus (Anderson, 1973).

The suppression of the normal estrous cycle that characteristically occurs in lactating marsupials also is related to the suckling stimulus (Fig. 9.13). In non-macropods, like *Trichosurus* (and *Macropus giganteus* in the early stages of lactation) this inhibition is due to a direct inhibitory action on the ovary that is probably mediated through the pituitary. In most macropod marsupials, there is an interesting deviation from this pattern as the corpus luteum of lactation appears to be essential for the response. It is thought that, following suckling, a release of a pituitary hormone stimulates the corpus luteum which releases a secretion that inhibits the ovary. It is uncertain what this secretion may be; if it is progesterone it presumably must be a minimal release so as to not disturb the dormant blastocyst. The nature of the pituitary stimulus is uncertain; it cannot be mimicked by the injection of eutherian LH or prolactin.

Parturition in marsupials does not appear to be such a dramatic event as it is in mammals which bear much larger young. It, nevertheless, appears to be hormone-dependent as it is prevented by ovariectomy. This effect may reflect the absence of estrogens, which in a sudden dramatic pre-parturition surge seem to contribute to the birth of the young in placentals. The progesterone concentration in the blood also increases, and then

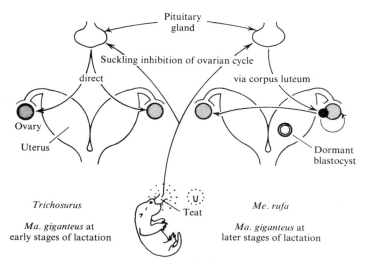

Fig. 9.13. The mechanism by which suckling may inhibit the ovarian cycle in marsupials.

Trichosurus vulpecula and *Macropus giganteus* in early stages of lactation, return to estrus soon after the young is removed from the pouch. In these animals inhibition seems to result from a direct inhibitory effect on the ovary, mediated by the suckling stimulus.

Megaleia rufa and *Macropus giganteus* at later stages of lactation do not return to estrus until about a month after the young is removed from the pouch. In these marsupials a functional corpus luteum is necessary for the inhibition to occur which, as a result of suckling–pituitary stimulation, releases an 'inhibitory factor'. (From Sharman, 1970. Copyright © 1970 by the American Association for the Advancement of Science.)

decreases, just before parturition (Lemon, 1972) and it is possible that this also has a role to play in delivery of the marsupial young. The circulating progesterone levels at parturition, however, may differ considerably, depending on the species, for, as we have seen, the length of gestation varies in relation to the estrous cycle so that the birth of the young occurs at various stages in the development of the corpus luteum.

Whether or not oxytocin is also involved in parturition, as in placentals, is unknown but it is present in the marsupial pituitary and it contracts the uterus of the wallaby, *Setonix brachyurus*, *in vitro* (Heller, 1973). This tissue is most sensitive in the late stages of pregnancy. Oxytocin, also promotes milk let-down when injected into kangaroos, an effect it also shares with the placentals.

The reproductive pattern in marsupials shows distinct differences from that of placental mammals and appears to be well adapted to their manner of life. Contrary to some popular opinion about the 'lowly' state of development of these animals, their reproduction is an extremely efficient process. The embryonic diapause of the kangaroos constitutes an excellent 'insurance' to continued reproduction so that if a young is lost, or when it is weaned, another pregnancy follows with little delay.

Monotremes

These mammals are confined to Australia and New Guinea and are remarkable as they produce large, shelled eggs which they care for. In the spiny anteater, *Tachyglossus*, the egg is lodged in a pouch for hatching while platypuses lay their eggs and tend them in burrows. The young are fed by lactation in a typical mammalian way and injected oxytocin, which is an homologous hormone in monotremes, initiates milk let-down (Griffiths, 1965). Little is known about the endocrine processes that control reproduction in these very interesting mammals. They are monoestrous. Like other mammals, but unlike birds, they possess a prominent corpus luteum. The egg undergoes some development while in the oviduct, equivalent to 38 to 40 hours' incubation in the chicken.

Non-mammals

Precise information about ovarian cycles in non-mammals is meager compared to that in mammals. Much of the available knowledge is based on morphological and histological observations on the ovaries and the accessory and secondary sexual characters, especially the oviduct. Such information is related to endocrine changes on the basis of the abilities of injected, exogenous, hormones to mimic or prevent such changes. These experimental approaches, while suffering from obvious limitations have, however, demonstrated that differences indeed exist between the ovarian cycles of different non-mammalian vertebrates. With newly available radioimmunoassay procedures for measuring hormone levels in the blood, the precise role of hormones in the reproductive life of non-mammals is now being investigated more rigorously. At the present time the birds have received the most attention but these new techniques will clearly also be extended to the reptiles, amphibians and fishes.

There are several salient areas about which endocrine information in non-mammals promises to be especially interesting. These include:

(*a*) The evolution and role of the corpus luteum, especially in viviparous and ovoviviparous species.

(*b*) The mechanism by which a single gonadotrophin (thought to be present in reptiles, amphibians and fishes) controls the ovarian cycle.

(*c*) The possible physiological role of the neurohypophysial peptides in influencing the contractility of the oviducts.

It is usually somewhat difficult to make a strict comparison between the ovarian cycles of mammals and non-mammals. This partly reflects a lack of information about the latter but the timing of the events also often differs rather radically. Thus, birds usually take many weeks of preparation to come into breeding condition when ovulation becomes possible. This latter process then occurs at regular intervals of about 24 hours which can proceed for several weeks, or in the domestic fowl, with some minor breaks, for up to 300 days of the year. This almost daily ovulation cannot be strictly compared to the entire estrous cycle of mammals but may be more synonymous with very short estrous cycles or rapidly successive periods of estrus. In other species of fish and amphibians, a single massive (sometimes referred to as 'explosive') ovulation may occur but in the meantime the eggs may be held in readiness for some time; ovulation thus does not always appear to be an irrevocable event in a strictly pre-timed program.

Birds

The ovarian cycle of most birds is primarily under photoperiodic control. The daily changes in light are the primary stimulus which directs the over-all endocrine preparations for the breeding season (see Chapter 4). As described earlier (see Fig. 4.15), in quail subjected to a long-day photoperiod, a release of gonadotrophin-releasing hormone, from the median eminence, results in a discharge of pituitary gonadotrophins. Plasma LH levels have been shown to increase in Japanese quail that are photoperiodically stimulated by long day-lengths (Nicholls, Scanes and Follett, 1973). It also seems likely that FSH is released during photoperiodic stimulation but this has not yet been directly measured. The changes in the levels of pituitary gonadotrophins indicate that a release occurs at a precise time each day, which, in the quail, takes place in the evening after dusk. This daily rhythmical release of gonadotrophins promotes the growth of the ovary and the maturation of the follicles. Estrogens are known to stimulate the growth of the avian oviduct (progesterone may also contribute to this increase) and secondary sexual characters and are released during such preparations for reproduction.

When the bird is finally ready to breed, ovulation may begin. In domestic fowl, ducks and geese, this is spontaneous but in other birds the presence of the male is usually necessary so that ovulation may then be said to be induced. There are several other factors that determine whether or not ovulation will occur in birds. If the newly laid eggs are continually removed from the nest some birds will continue to lay more eggs (*non-determinate layers*). A house sparrow has thus been stimulated to produce 51 eggs in a season; ovulation apparently continued until the ovary was exhausted of suitable follicles. The domestic fowl, that can produce 300 eggs in a year, is an even more dramatic example of this phenomenon. How such birds recognize the number of eggs in the 'clutch' is unknown but it has been suggested that this may be the result of a tactile stimulus or sight. Other types of birds (*determinate layers*) produce a set number of eggs and changing the number in the nest does not modify ovulation.

In the domestic fowl, LH, as in mammals, initiates ovulation but the mechanism controlling the release of this hormone is not clear. The injection of progesterone promotes ovulation while estrogens delay it; effects that are in direct contrast to those seen in mammals (Fraps, 1955). The normal rhythmical release of LH, which commences about eight hours prior to ovulation is, however, preceded by an increase in plasma estradiol (Fig. 9.14b) just as in mammals. To complicate the interpretation of this, the rise in LH is also accompanied by increased levels of progesterone and the release of the gonadotrophin never *precedes* that of the steroid (Fig. 9.14a). It is thus likely that both estrogens and progesterone are involved in the process of ovulation in birds; possibly LH release is initiated by estrogens but other processes that also determine the extrusion of the egg from the follicle may be influenced by both types of steroids in a manner that is reflected by the injection of these hormones.

It has been shown in the domestic fowl, that, as long as there is an egg in the oviduct, further ovulation is inhibited. This effect can be mimicked by placing an irritant, such as a piece of thread, in the oviduct. Such a condition can be prolonged for about three weeks and as no regression in the ovary or oviduct occurs secretion of FSH and estrogens is thought to be unimpaired. The inhibition of ovulation by the presence of an egg in the oviduct is thought to be the result of a neural stimulus which may inhibit LH release. The injection of progesterone or LH into such birds overcomes this inhibition and promotes ovulation.

The precise site of origin of the circulating progesterone in birds is uncertain. Birds do not possess a corpus luteum but the ovary nevertheless secretes progesterone. This steroid may be formed by the follicles themselves, the interstitial tissue or the corpora atretica. The role of progesterone in the ovarian cycle is also not clear. In mammals and other vertebrates, this steroid inhibits the release of LH and LH-like gonadotrophins by its negative-feedback inhibition of the hypothalamus. Such an effect would be unexpected in birds if, as suspected, progesterone stimulates the release of LH. As birds lack a corpus luteum, LH also cannot exert its usual luteinizing and luteotrophic actions though it is possible that it may have comparable effects at other sites in the ovary. There is need, at this stage,

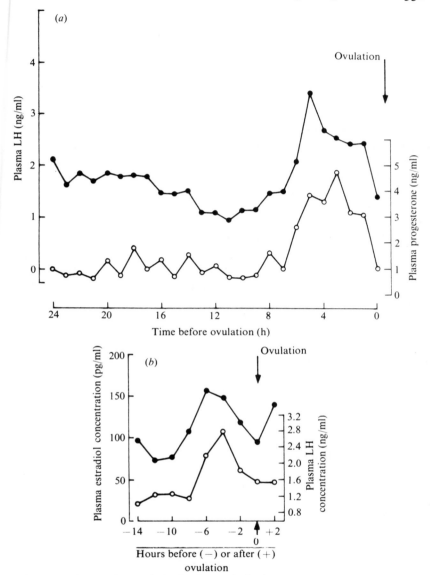

Fig. 9.14. The ovarian cycle in the domestic fowl.

(a) Changes in the plasma levels of LH (●) and progesterone (○) during the ovulatory cycle. The relationship between the rises in the levels of progesterone and LH are not clear; the release of LH apparently does not initiate a release of progesterone as it never precedes it. (From Furr *et al.*, 1973.)

(b) Changes in the levels of LH (○) and estradiol (●). The rise in the level of estradiol occurs about 2 h before that of LH. (From Senior and Cunningham, 1974.)

for a note of caution as it should be recalled that the endocrine observations on the avian ovarian cycle are nearly all confined to domestic species, especially *Gallus domesticus*.

The egg-laying cycle of the domestic fowl is thought to occur in the following manner (van Tienhoven and Planck, 1973). The eggs are laid in a clutch, or 'sequence', three to five in number, which are each produced at intervals of about 26 h. There is a period of 40 to 48 h between the laying of each clutch. Ovulation and oviposition are controlled by an endogenous rhythm lasting for 26 to 28 h the commencement of which is normally timed according to the photoperiod. Depending on such stimulation the length of the cycle can be retarded or advanced by about 2 h and so may vary from 24 to about 30 h. In continual light, other periodic events, such as the times of feeding and fluctuations in temperature, can be used to initiate the egg-laying cycle. Such external stimuli appear to sensitize regions of the hypothalamus and median eminence which, in response to stimulation by circulating progesterone, and possibly estrogens, secretes LH-releasing hormone. LH is then released from the pituitary which results in ovulation 8 h later. Subsequent formation of the egg takes place in the oviduct and the timing of the events there seems to depend on photoperiodic stimulation working in conjunction with the ruptured follicle. Removal of the latter tissue from the ovary results in a retention of the egg in the oviduct. Normally oviposition occurs 13 to 14 h after ovulation. It is possible that contractions of the oviduct that occur during oviposition are assisted by vasotocin which is released from the neurohypophysis.

Avian reproduction has certain unique features that do not occur in mammals and that have resulted in some special endocrine arrangements. As described earlier, oviparous vertebrates respond to estrogens by the formation, in the liver, of a special calcium-binding phospholipoprotein that is incorporated into the egg. This effect is especially important in species, like the birds, that produce eggs with large yolks. It is also usual for birds to make some special arrangements for the incubation of the eggs and, after hatching, for the care of the young. This maternal instinct, which is also often displayed by the male, is influenced by the endocrines. The development of 'brood patches' on the ventral surface of the skin can be promoted by the injection of prolactin and estrogens. These featherless, richly vascularized areas facilitate the transfer of heat from the parent to the eggs. 'Broodiness', or the desire to incubate the eggs and care for the young can also be promoted by injections of prolactin. This hormone suppresses gonadal function in birds and it is thought that broodiness may in fact be the result of a withdrawal of gonadal steroids (see Parkes and Marshall, 1960). At present, it is not clear whether or not prolactin normally exerts such an effect in hens. The action of prolactin in stimulating a secretion from the crop-sac of doves and pigeons (with which they feed their young) has been described earlier (Chapter 5).

Birds thus show some interesting deviations and novelties in the use of hormones for integrating their reproductive processes. An evolution of the role of certain hormones has clearly occurred in this interesting offshoot from a reptilian stock.

Reptiles

The Reptilia contain oviparous, ovoviviparous and viviparous species. Unlike in birds, a distinct corpus luteum is formed following ovulation and although the available evidence strongly suggests that it secretes progesterone it seems unlikely that this hormone contributes to the maintenance of pregnancy. A further distinction from birds and mammals is seen in the mechanism of ovarian control which apparently is mediated by a single gonadotrophic hormone. It has, however, recently been shown that two chemical principles, one with LH-type and the other FSH-type activity, can be separated in extracts from a chelonian (the snapping turtle) pituitary (Licht and Papkoff, 1974a). It remains possible that a single gonadotrophin exists in other groups of the reptiles and if so it apparently can perform the functions that are carried out by both of the mammalian gonadotrophins.

The changes that occur during the ovarian cycle of the ovoviviparous lizard, *Sceloporus cyanogenys*, are summarized in Fig. 9.15. The ovary starts to grow in October or November and this is accompanied by the development of the oviduct. These changes can be prevented by hypophysectomy. The gonadotrophin stimulates gonadal growth and the secretion of estrogen. Implantation of small pellets of estrogens into the region of the median eminence reduces the growth of the oviduct. This effect is probably the result of a lower rate of ovarian estrogen secretion, due to the inhibition of gonadotrophin release by a negative-feedback inhibition. Ovulation is also prevented by such an estrogen implant. Mammalian FSH has been shown to promote ovulation in several species of lizards (Licht, 1970) and the endogenous gonadotrophin no doubt also has this effect.

Following ovulation in *Sceloporus cyanogenys* the corpus luteum develops and this is correlated with a three-fold increase in the circulating progesterone concentration. This elevated hormone level persists in the plasma until parturition when it declines. A similar pattern in circulating progesterone levels has also been observed in the viviparous snake, *Natrix sipedon* (Chan, Ziegel and Callard, 1973). Direct evidence that reptilian corpora lutea can produce progesterone has been obtained following *in-vitro* incubation of such tissue obtained from the snapping turtle, *Chelydra*

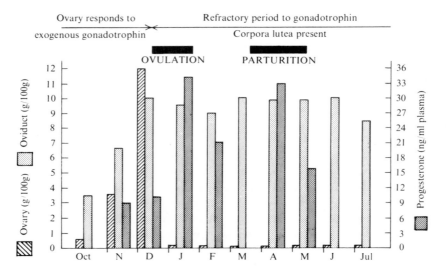

Fig. 9.15. The annual ovarian cycle of the ovoviviparous lizard *Sceloporus cyanogenys*.

The ovaries and oviducts start to develop (under the influence of gonado-trophin) in October and ovulation may occur in December to January. Gestation lasts for about 12 weeks and the young are delivered in late March to mid-May. Corpora lutea persist during pregnancy and the plasma progesterone levels rise, but then decline in late summer following parturition. (From Callard *et al.*, 1972.)

serpentina (Klicka and Mahmoud, 1972). In *Sceloporus cyanogenys* the circulating progesterone levels are reduced following hypophysectomy, suggesting that there is some pituitary control over this hormone, but in pregnant lizards relatively high concentrations continue to persist so that if a luteotrophic effect is present it is apparently not vital (Callard *et al.*, 1972). In addition, the implantation of pellets of progesterone into the region of the median eminence results in a depression of the circulating progesterone concentration (Callard and Doolittle, 1973). This suggests the presence of a negative-feedback inhibition of the release of a trophic hormone and is accompanied by a decrease in the growth of the ovary and oviduct. The latter effect suggests that ovarian estrogen secretion is also inhibited.

Inhibition of gonadotrophin release in reptiles can thus apparently be inhibited by both progesterone and estrogens but how this can be reconciled with the orderly release of a single gonadotrophin that controls several gonadal functions is unknown and it remains possible that a second hormone will be identified, as in the snapping turtle.

Corpora atretica, formed by the dissolution of unovulated follicles, may also contribute to the control of reptilian ovarian cycles. At the end of the summer breeding season the lizard *Anolis carolinensis* becomes refractory to the effects of photoperiodic stimulation and this can be related to the presence of corpora atretica in the ovary. In addition these lizards, at this time, respond poorly to injected gonadotrophins but the response to these hormones could be increased five-fold if the corpora atretica were removed. The nature of the latter's inhibitory effect on the female reproductive system is unknown (Crews and Licht, 1974).

Progesterone, as we have seen, plays an important role in maintaining pregnancy in mammals but there is no conclusive evidence to indicate that this occurs in reptiles. Ovariectomy or hypophysectomy do not affect the course of pregnancy in a variety of viviparous and ovoviviparous species of reptiles (see Yaron, 1972). Progesterone, nevertheless, attains high concentrations during a reptilian pregnancy; so what is its function? Callard and Doolittle (1973) have suggested that its action in reptiles may be to inhibit gonadal growth during gestation and this may represent a 'more primitive' role than the regulation of the uterine environment that is seen in mammals. Corpora lutea are also formed following ovulation in oviparous reptiles and it has been found that when this tissue is removed in gravid *Sceloporous undulatus* (an oviparous lizard) an earlier oviposition occurs, suggesting that progesterone may control the period of egg retention in such reptiles (Roth, Jones and Gerrard, 1973).

In reptiles, as also in birds, estrogen, possibly in conjunction with growth hormone, stimulates the production of phospholipoproteins by the liver and these are incorporated into the egg. Prolactin, when injected, has been shown to exert an antigonadal effect but again, as in birds, the significance of this inhibition is unknown *in vivo*. It is nevertheless interesting that these actions of estrogens and prolactin are shared with the birds.

Despite the valuable experiments that have already been performed much additional, and more precise, information is needed before an adequate account of the role of hormones in the reptilian ovarian cycle can be given.

Amphibians

Most amphibians are oviparous though there are a few species that have ovoviviparous and even viviparous habits. An excellent account of the ovarian cycle in amphibians is given by Redshaw (1972). Complete maturation of the oocytes usually takes several years while formation of the yolk, in species that live in temperate zones, commences in the summer preceding spawning. The development of the ova is controlled by the adenohypophysis and the hypothalamus. Hypophysectomy or transplantation of the pituitary, so that it is no longer in contact with the hypothalamus, interrupts oogenesis. The available evidence seems to indicate that only a single gonadotrophin is present in the amphibian adenohypophysis.[1] This hormone (or hormones?) regulates the development of the ovum and the secretion of ovarian steroid hormones.

Estrogens are produced by the ovarian follicles and these contribute to the development of other sexual characters, including the oviduct, as well as vitellogenesis.

Progesterone is apparently also produced by the ovary, though the precise site of its formation is uncertain as most amphibians (except for ovoviviparous and viviparous species) do not form a distinct corpus luteum after they ovulate. Whether or not either or both gonadal steroid hormones exert a negative-feedback inhibition on the release of gonadotrophin is unknown.

Ovulation can be readily promoted in amphibians by the injection of gonadotrophin. This hormone may be obtained from amphibian pituitaries, but exogenous hormones, from other species, are also effective. The latter hormonal effects are particularly well known as they are the basis for a convenient pregnancy test for women. Human chorionic gonadotrophin (HCG) that is secreted in the urine during pregnancy induces ovulation in frogs and toads. Mammalian LH is usually considered to be more effective than FSH in inducing ovulation in frogs and so may have a closer structural resemblance to the amphibian gonadotrophin. It has recently been shown (Licht, 1973) that the mammalian gonadotrophins differ in their ability to induce spermiation in male amphibians; thus, LH is more potent than FSH in *Rana pipiens* but FSH is about twice as potent as LH in *Hyla regilla* and *Eleutherodactylus coqui*. It therefore seems likely that mammalian gonadotrophins may show similar differences in their ability to induce ovulation in different species of female amphibians. Ovulation is often, though not always, induced at the time of sexual pairing. *Xenopus* seems to be on the verge of ovulation for prolonged periods of time while in *Rana temporaria* the eggs are stored in the oviduct, from which they are expelled when mating occurs.

The precise hormonal events that initiate ovulation and oviposition are not known. The injection of HCG into the toad *Bufo bufo* results in ovulation in about 24 hours and this is preceded by a release of a progesterone-like material into the blood (Fig. 9.16). It has also been shown, *in vitro*, that progesterone can induce ovulation. In addition, the injection of progesterone hastens ovulation while estrogen retards it; a situation reminis-

---

[1] Two distinct gonadotrophins, one with LH and the other with FSH activity, have been isolated from the bullfrog, *Rana catesbeiana* pituitary (Licht and Papkoff, 1974*b*).

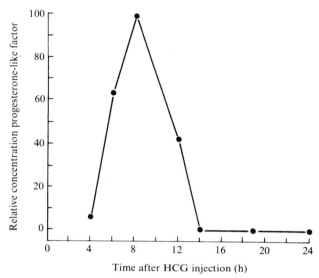

Fig. 9.16. The effects of injections of a gonadotrophin (human chorionic gonado-trophin, HCG) on the level of a progesterone-like factor in the plasma of female 'winter' toads, *Bufo bufo*.

The HCG results in ovulation in about 24 h and this is preceded by a rise and then a decline in this 'factor'. Injections of progesterone can induce ovulation in amphibians and it is possible that this is involved in the effect of the HCG (as well as mediating release of 'jelly' from glands in the oviduct). (From Thornton, 1972.)

cent of that which occurs in birds. It is to be hoped that the use of radio-immunoassay procedures will allow the measurement of amphibian gonadotrophin, progesterone and estrogens so that the natural events that occur during the ovarian cycle in amphibians can be more directly observed.

The oviduct undergoes a distinct annual cycle in *Bufo bufo* and attains its greatest size in the autumn (Jorgenson and Vijayakumar, 1970). A decline in the weight of the oviduct takes place during spawning in April. This decline is due to a loss of secretory contents that coat the eggs with a 'jelly'. The secretion of this jelly, like that of avidin in the fowl oviduct, is controlled by progesterone.

A diagrammatic summary of the role of hormones in controlling ovarian functions in amphibians is given in Fig. 9.17.

Some very interesting observations have been made on the effects of progesterone on gestation in a viviparous frog *Nectophrynoides occidentalis* (Xavier and Ozon, 1971; Zuber-Vogeli and Xavier, 1973; Xavier, 1974). This frog lives in West Africa where it is subjected to periods of seasonal drought during which it estivates in burrows. Following ovulation in October the fertilized eggs are retained in the oviduct where development

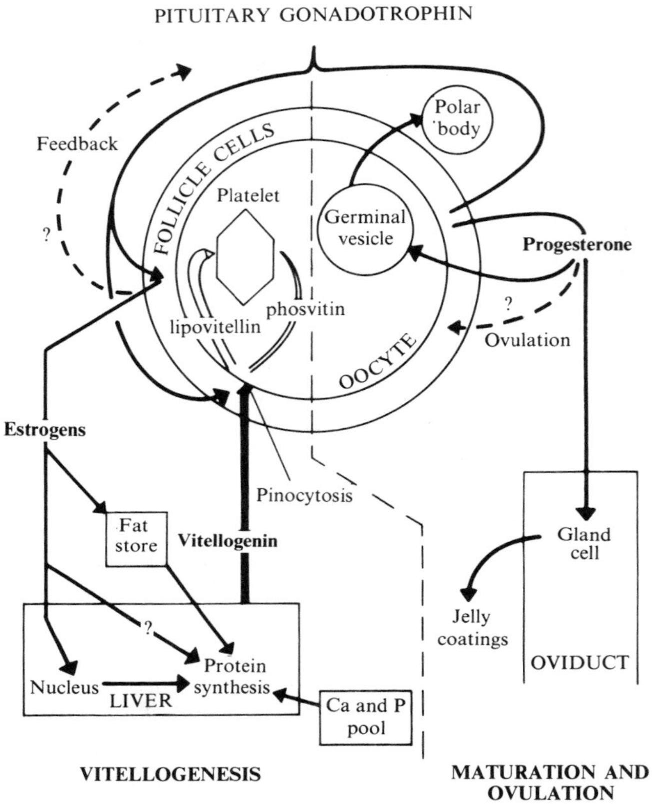

PITUITARY GONADOTROPHIN

Fig. 9.17. The role of hormones in the production of eggs in anuran amphibians. The pituitary gonadotrophin controls the release estrogens and progesterone by the ovary.

Left. The control of the process of *vitellogenesis*. Estrogen, formed by the follicular cells, induces the formation of vitellogenin in the liver, which is incorporated into the yolk of the developing oocytes. The uptake process is stimulated by the gonadotrophin.

Right. The *maturation of the oocyte* and ovulation. These processes are controlled by the pituitary gonadotrophin which mediates the formation of a 'maturation agent' that seems to be progesterone. The progesterone also stimulates the oviductal glands to secrete the coating of 'jelly' with which the eggs are coated.

This summary is principally based on experiments on *Xenopus laevis* and *Bufo bufo*. (From Follett and Redshaw, 1974.)

proceeds until parturition the following June. In November, these pregnant frogs estivate and do not emerge until April (see Fig. 9.18). Corpora lutea are formed following ovulation, which apparently secrete progesterone.

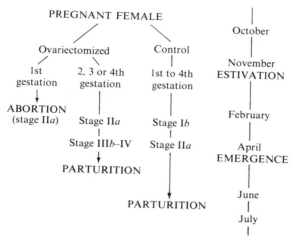

Fig. 9.18. Gestation in the viviparous frog, *Nectophrynoides occidentalis*, in relation to seasons.

Normally these frogs ovulate and become pregnant in October. The dry season commences in November when they estivate from which they emerge, with the onset of rain, in April. The young are born in June. If these frogs are ovariectomized early in pregnancy, they may either abort, if the animals are young (and this is their 1st pregnancy) or, if they are large and it is the second, third or fourth time of gestation, the development of the young is accelerated and they are born much earlier than usual. Ovarian progesterone is thought to delay the development of the young during the period of estivation. (From Zuber-Vogeli and Xavier, 1973.)

When the ovaries from pregnant frogs are incubated *in vitro* with the progesterone substrate, pregnenolone, they convert this steroid to progesterone. This ability to form progesterone declines as gestation progresses (Fig. 9.19). Following parturition, pregnenolone is converted to other steroids by the ovarian tissue and this process increases until ovulation again takes place. The preovulatory period is also the time when production of estrogens are thought to increase. If ovariectomy is performed early in gestation (see Fig. 9.18) of young frogs, during their first pregnancy, abortion occurs. In more mature frogs, however, development of the young is accelerated following ovariectomy and parturition takes place about three months earlier than usual. The implantation of progesterone into these frogs towards the end of gestation reduces the rate of growth of the embryos. Progesterone thus appears to slow the rate of development of the embryos during the prolonged period of estivation so that the young are delivered at a more appropriate and favorable time of the year. This is indeed a novel role for progesterone.

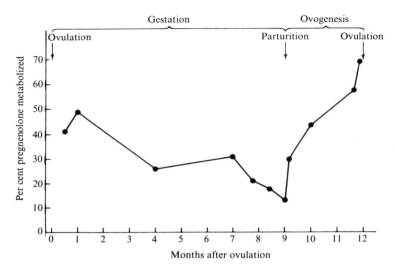

Fig. 9.19. The ability of the ovarian tissue of the viviparous frog *Nectophrynoïdes occidentalis* to metabolize pregnenolone (*in vitro*) at different stages of its ovarian cycle.

During gestation the principal steroid produced from the pregnenolone is progesterone but after parturition 17-hydroxyprogesterone, androstendione and testosterone are also formed. (From Xavier and Ozon, 1971.)

Fishes

Sporadically distributed information is available about the control of ovarian function in fishes. This is not unexpected considering the enormous numbers of piscine species, and the wide phyletic gaps that separate them. In addition, fish are usually somewhat diffident scientific collaborators.

Most fishes are oviparous but some species have evolved ovoviviparous and viviparous methods of reproduction. In teleosts the last two processes are usually rather different from the *in-utero* development common to many other vertebrates. The young teleosts thus may develop *in situ* in the follicle or be incubated in the hollow central cavity of the ovary. In some teleosts successive broods (superfetation) may develop in such follicles which are then delivered in waves. It would not be unexpected if such dramatic differences in the procedures for reproduction resulted in endocrine adaptations.

In teleosts the development of the oocytes and vitellogenesis are dependent on the pituitary. This gland appears to contain a single gonadotrophin which mediates these effects. The injection of homologous gonadotrophins can promote ovulation in teleosts. The roles of estrogens and progesterone

in this process are, however, unknown. The endogenous release of gonadotrophin in teleosts is under the influence of the hypothalamus.

In cyclostome and chondrichthyean fishes, the pituitary, via the action
of a gonadotrophin, also controls the development of the ova but this
process does not appear to be under hypothalamic control. It is rather a
mystery how cyclical control of reproduction is mediated in these vertebrates which are the only groups known to lack such a mechanism.

Little is known about the influence of gonadotrophin on gonadal steroid
production in fishes though it is generally considered that estrogen secretion
is controlled by such a hormone. The production of progesterone by the
ovary and the possible role of corpora lutea is contentious. Many teleosts
possess so-called 'pre-ovulatory corpora lutea' which are formed as a result
of atresia of unovulated follices and are more aptly called corpora atretica.
Post-ovulatory corpora lutea, as well as corpora atretica, are present in
many chondrichthyeans and there is considerable speculation as to whether
they contribute to successful gestation in ovoviviparous and viviparous
species (see Chieffi, 1967; Dodd, 1972a). Hypophysectomy does not
interrupt pregnancy, at least for the first three months, in the viviparous
shark, *Mustelus canis*, suggesting that an adenohypophysial control of
progesterone secretion is not vital. It is, however, unknown whether
progesterone contributes to gestation in ovoviviparous and viviparous
fishes. Hisaw in 1959 stated that 'the elimination of yolk during follicular
atresia and material from ruptured follicles at ovulation is a primitive
function of corpora lutea and endocrine functions such as luteinization of
the granulosa by pituitary luteinizing hormone and secretion of progesterone in response to pituitary luteotrophic hormone as seen in mammals, are more recent adaptations'. This interesting idea has, however, not
been unquestionably accepted.

In many teleost and chondrichthyean fishes, the thyroid gland displays
an increased activity during the breeding season. The latter is associated
with many physiological and environmental changes so that it is difficult
to be certain whether the endocrine events are primarily related to reproduction. Sage (1973) considers that it is likely that the thyroid is involved in
the reproductive process in fishes as it is necessary for gonadal maturation
in some species. Such a role for thyroxine could reflect a primeval endocrine
use of this hormone.

*Oviposition and parturition in non-mammals – a role for the
neurohypophysial hormones?*

The passage of eggs or young along the female gonaducts and their exit
into the outside world may be assisted by rhythmical contractions of the

muscles that surround these ducts. Such muscles are usually non-striated (smooth) muscles (though striated muscle may also be present in some fishes), which have an inherent ability to contract even in the absence of nerves or hormones. The rate and pattern of contractility of smooth muscles can, nevertheless, be modified by such stimuli. As we have seen in mammals, oxytocin can promote contractions and aid in the process of parturition. It should be remembered, however, that smooth muscle readily reacts to local stimuli, and this may include the presence of an egg or fetus, so that oviposition or parturition can occur even in the absence of neural or hormonal stimuli.

The neurohypophysial hormones have a special ability to contract mammalian uterine smooth muscle and this response has also been shown to occur (mainly *in vitro*) in many other species of birds, reptiles, amphibians and fishes (Heller, 1972). Such effects can usually be elicited by low con-

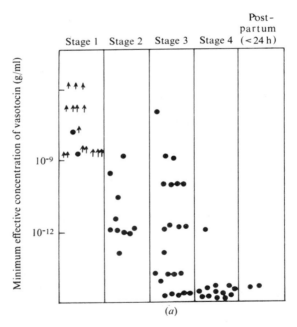

(a)

Fig. 9.20. Periodic changes in the responsiveness of the ability of the ovoviviparous ovary of a teleost fish *Poecilia*, and the oviduct of a urodele amphibian *Necturus maculosus*, to contract (*in vitro*) to vasotocin.

(a) *Poecilia* (the guppy); minimum effective concentration of vasotocin required to produce a contraction of the ovary during successive stages of gestation. The arrows indicate a lack of response; it can be seen that the preparations were most sensitive just prior to parturition (stage 4). (From Heller, 1972.)

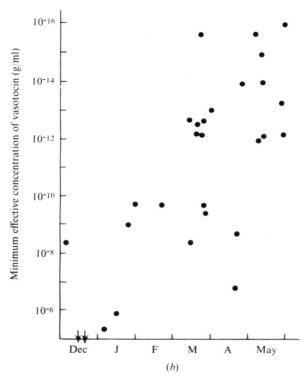

(*b*) *Necturus* (the mudpuppy); minimum effective concentration of vasotocin required to contract the oviduct at different seasons of the year. It can be seen that this was least in winter but progressively increased and was greatest in April and May. (From Heller, Ferreri and Leathers, 1970.)

centrations of such peptide hormones that represent only a small fraction of those stored in the neurohypophysis.

It is interesting that in poecilid teleosts that are ovoviviparous, the ovary contains smooth muscle and this is even more sensitive to the effects of vasotocin than the oviduct. The young in such fishes develop within the follicles so that their expulsion may conceivably be promoted by the contraction of these ovarian muscles.

Such contractile responses of the oviduct and teleost ovary to vasotocin can be seen to change at different stages of the sexual cycle and, like mammals, the sensitivity is greatest at the time of parturition or oviposition. This can be seen in the ovary of *Poecilia* (Fig. 9.20); an effect that can be mimicked by the implantation of gonadal steroids into these fish. The oviduct, *in vitro*, of the mudpuppy, *Necturus maculosus*, also shows seasonal changes in sensitivity to vasotocin (Fig. 9.20); the tissue may be as much as 100-fold more sensitive to this neurohypophysial hormone in May compared with its sensitivity in December and January.

Observations *in vitro*, however, must be interpreted with considerable caution as they may not take place *in vivo* and even if the latter does occur following injections of hormones it may not reflect a normal physiological response. In other words, we must be careful to distinguish the pharmacological from the physiological effects of these hormones on the oviduct and uterus. The problem of the evolution of the roles of the neurohypophysial hormones in vertebrates has intrigued endocrinologists for many years. As we have seen (Chapter 3), such hormones are present in all vertebrates. While the neurohypophysial hormones have a fairly well-characterized role in osmoregulation of tetrapods, their role in fishes is not at all clear. The neurohypophysial hormones can contract smooth muscle of the oviduct and uterus in representatives of all the main groups of vertebrates and it is tempting to speculate that these effects may be of physiological significance and even reflect a more ancient role for such hormones.

The evidence for this interesting endocrine hypothesis has been summarized by Heller (1972). H. Heller over a long scientific lifetime has made many fascinating contributions to the comparative endocrinology of the neurohypophysis of which the present interest is a more recent outcome. There have been sporadic reports, spread over many years, about the ability of injected neurohypophysial hormones to promote oviposition and parturition in different vertebrates. This effect has been observed in the domestic fowl, several species of lizards and the ovoviviparous fire-salamander. The injection of neurohypophysial hormones also stimulates spawning-like behavior in the killifish, *Fundulus heteroclitus*. It is interesting that stored isotocin disappears from the pituitaries of the female, but not the male, killifish during the breeding season in June (Sawyer and Pickford, 1963). This change probably reflects a release of this neurohypophysial hormone which could be involved in the reproductive process. The precise physiological significance of such observations, however, is uncertain.

Observations, *in vitro*, indicate that vasotocin is the most active of the neurohypophysial peptides in stimulating the contractility of the oviduct in non-mammals. An interesting exception is the oviduct of the dogfish, *Scyliorhinus canicula*, in which another neurohypophysial peptide present in these fish is the most active. It would thus seem that an evolution of the receptor sensitivity in the gonaducts can occur, that is related to the nature of the homologous hormones which are present. In mammals, oxytocin has a greater uterotonic effect than vasotocin, which is not an homologous hormone in this group of vertebrates. Such an evolution in the sensitivity of the gonaducts to the homologous neurohypophysial peptides also leads us to suspect that they may have a physiological role. We must not, however, carry this sort of thing too far!

If the neurohypophysial hormones do indeed contribute to the physiology of oviposition and parturition in non-mammals (and even ovulation in teleosts) it is probably just that – a contribution. The domestic hen can still lay an egg following neurohypophysectomy and ovoviviparous poecilid fish still produce young following hypophysectomy. As in mammals, such hormones could, however, facilitate parturition as well as oviposition.

In teleost fishes, it is possible that another neurosecretory hormone may be involved in eliciting contractions of the gonaducts. As described in Chapter 8, urotensin II, from the urophysis, exhibits an ability to contract smooth muscles from the urinary bladder and gonaducts of teleosts. This substance may have an hormonal role in the reproduction of these fishes, such as in assisting the process of spawning. Thus a decline in the stored urotensin II in the urophysis of the white sucker, *Catostomus commersoni*, has been observed following spawning in the male, but not the female, fish (Lederis, 1973).

The role of hormones in maturation and development of the young

Reproduction can only be considered complete when the young have attained independence from the parents and are themselves able to propagate the species. Growth, differentiation and maturation of the young, either in the egg or *in utero*, is a most remarkable process the intricacies of which were, it seems, at least until recently, more appreciated by biologists 50 years ago than in the succeeding period of time. The role of chemical substances in coordinating and directing such embryological processes is reminiscent of the action of hormones though such inductor substances are not usually classified as such and will not be dealt with here. There has, however, been speculation as to whether inductors that influence sexual differentiation are indeed identical to the gonadal steroid hormones.

It was appreciated more than 100 years ago that endocrine secretions could affect development (see Jost, 1971). The earliest observations were on the effects of congenital thyroid deficiency which is called cretinism in man. Such a thyroid deficiency results in inadequate development of the nervous system, skeleton and the reproductive organs. It seems that these hormones are, however, more important in early postnatal life than fetal development. Other hormones may be necessary earlier in embryonic development. In encephalectomized fetal rats and anencephalic human fetuses, the prenatal development of the adrenal cortex is retarded, apparently reflecting an absence of pituitary stimulation due to the lack of hypothalamic control. The parathyroids are also functional in the fetal rat and removal of these glands results in hypocalcemia. The stage of embryonic development when such hormones may become important varies a great deal. It should also be recalled that hormones such as thyroxine and the steroid hormones may cross the placenta in viviparous species so that the maternal endocrines may contribute to the development of the fetus. In extreme situations, such transfer of hormones across the placenta can result in fetal abnormalities such as masculinization of female human babies born to mothers to whom large doses of progesterone have been administered during pregnancy.

The effects of exogenous progesterone on sexual differentiation was to a considerable extent a predictable phenomenon. The observations of Lillie in 1917 on the free-martin effect in cattle led to considerable speculation as to the role of fetal sex hormones on sexual differentiation. Lillie observed that in some cows bearing twin fetuses of opposite sexes the sexual differentiation of the genetic female was changed so that it was born with testes and a male gonaduct system. The external genitalia remained female in character and the animal was infertile. This effect has been attributed to the passage, across the interdigitating fetal membranes of materials, possibly androgens, that effect the change. This interpretation as to the role of male sex hormones has not gone unchallenged and it has more recently been suggested that other factors may be involved.

These interesting observations, nevertheless, resulted in experimental testing of the ability of sex hormones to modify sexual differentiation in various other developing vertebrates. These experiments involve various techniques such as parabiotically joining, thus crossing, the circulation of embryos of the opposite sex, cross-grafting of fetal gonads, and the administration of gonadal steroid hormones. Such manipulations often resulted in considerable changes, even to the extent of reversing the recipient's predetermined genetic sex. A note of caution is, however, necessary as the results are usually not simple or predictable and the effects may depend on the age of the embryo, the dose of the steroidal hormones, the genetic sex of the recipient, and the particular species used.

Before describing some of these effects further, we should recall the patterns of sexual differentiation in embryonic mammals. The primordial gonad has the potential to develop into either a testis or an ovary and is divided into two distinct regions: a cortex, which is the definitive ovary, and a medulla that may become the testis. This segmentation of the primordial gonad applies to all vertebrates except cyclostomes and teleosts where a single structure is present. The ultimate predominance of one of these gonadal zones is normally determined genetically. Associated with the development of the gonads are their ducts (see Fig. 9.21): the Mullerian duct which may persist and develop into the oviduct or uterus, and the Wolffian duct which, in the male, becomes the vas deferens. The ultimate differentiation and persistence of the gonads, and their accessories, is dependent on the secretion of androgens or estrogens by the definitive

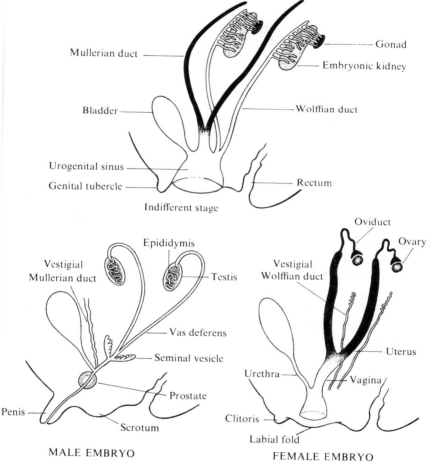

Fig. 9.21. Differentiation of the sexual organs in the embryonic mammal. The appropriate development of the genetic male is dependent on the presence of androgens and that of the genetic female on estrogens. This pattern can be changed by removal or antagonism of the natural hormones or by injecting hormones more typical of the opposite sex. (From Frye, 1967, by permission of Macmillan Publishing Co. Inc., New York. Copyright © 1967.)

gonad; thus, to some extent, one can manipulate their development by castration of the embryos and the injection of estrogens or androgens. It has recently become possible to distinguish such effects of hormones pharmacologically by administering a specific androgen antagonist, cyproterone. When this steroid is injected into male fetal rats (Elgar, Neumann and Berswordt-Wallrabe, 1971) differentiation of the Wolffian ducts and the vesicular and prostate glands is inhibited suggesting their normal dependence on androgens. The differentiation of the gonads and the regression of the embryonic Mullerian ducts is, however, not affected. The importance of androgens during the development of the male hypothalamic control mechanism of gonadotrophin release has already been described (Chapter 4).

The most extensive studies on experimental manipulation of embryonic sexual differentiation have been made in amphibians (see Dodd, 1960). Parabiotic union of male and female embryos of amphibians results in an inhibition of the growth or a masculinization of the ovary. This dominance of the testis over the ovary is typical in such experiments on amphibians. Parallel changes occur in the relative development of the Wolffian and Mullerian ducts. Normally in the male the latter become rudimentary but their growth can be stimulated by parabiosis with a female. Such effects were initially attributed to hypothetical inductor substances but can often be mimicked by administering gonadal steroid hormones. In some anurans (Ranidae), androgens have a masculinizing effect when they are administered to female embryos. Estrogens may have the opposite action and feminize male embryos but such effects of the female hormones are less predictable and pronounced. Other anurans and urodeles respond differently as the male embryos exhibit a stable feminizing response to administered estrogens; but androgens also have feminizing actions (paradoxal) and inhibit the medulla of the primordial gonad. These last two amphibian responses are similar to those observed in chondrichthyean fish (Chieffi, 1967). Estrogens and progesterone, as well as testosterone, have a feminizing effect on genetic males so that sex reversal is only possible in the female direction in these fish. In the domestic fowl, the injection of estrogens, in the early stages of incubation, into genetic males results in various degrees of feminization: they may become intersexual when the left testis becomes an ovo-testis, or even an ovary. The changes are accompanied by a persistence of the Mullerian ducts (see Parkes and Marshall, 1960). Such avian intersexes usually revert to their normal genetic sex later in life. Androgens may have the converse effects in birds but the results are rather variable and they may even have feminizing actions like those described above in amphibians and chondrichthyeans.

Sex-reversal (or sex-inversion) is a particularly interesting phenomenon in teleost fishes as it occurs normally during the life cycle of many species (see Reinbloth, 1970, 1972). This sex change may be from a male into a female (*protandry*) or more commonly a female into a male (*protogyny*). The stimuli that result in such sex inversions are not well understood but the removal of the male can initiate a protogynic sex change. The female fish then may become males that produce normal sperm. The injection of testosterone can mimic this transformation in wrasses (*Thalassoma bifasciatum*) but Reinbloth does not consider this to be proof that this is the normal mechanism mediating such a sex transformation. It is, however, an attractive hypothesis for the endocrinologist. Such a possibility is supported by the observation that in the protogynous symbranchid teleost *Monopterus albus*, the rice field eel, the gonads, *in vitro*, switch their steroid syntheses from a predominance of estrogens, in their female phase, to androgens in their male phase (Chan and Phillips, 1969).

True hermaphrodites, which can simultaneously produce both sperm and eggs and even be self-fertilizing have been described most commonly among the teleost fishes. Hermaphrodism is the normal situation in a fascinating oviparous teleost, *Rivulus marmoratus*, that lives in tidal-pluvial zones on the coasts of Florida and the West Indies (see Harrington, 1968). The differentiation of males can be promoted when embryonic development proceeds at temperatures below 20 °C, a situation that does not normally occur in this fish's native habitat. It is not known whether such sexual differentiation is mediated by endocrine changes under these conditions. The normal balance of sex hormones in hermaphroditic vertebrates constitutes rather an endocrine puzzle as it is difficult to conceive how different sex hormones can exist, be controlled, and act simultaneously within the same animal. This is an intriguing problem for the comparative endocrinologist.

The control of metamorphosis

Many fishes and amphibians exist in two or more distinct morphological and physiological forms during their life cycles. The transformation from one type to another is called metamorphosis. 'True' metamorphosis is considered to occur in preparation for life in a different habitat, such as fresh water (as opposed to the sea), or an aquatic compared to a terrestrial existence. These changes may involve a migration that is sometimes associated with sexual maturation and reproduction.

An interesting account of metamorphosis in fishes is given by Barrington (1968). Lampreys (Cyclostomata) undergo a prolonged period of larval development in fresh water which lasts for about $5\frac{1}{2}$ years. The metamorphosis of the ammocoete to the adult, which migrates to the sea, lasts for several weeks. Subsequently, lampreys again return to the rivers to breed and then undergo physiological changes, such as reflected by their inability to osmoregulate in sea-water. The environmental and physiological events that determine these metamorphic changes are unknown. Experimental manipulation of the lampreys' thyroid physiology, by placing them in solutions containing either thyroid hormones or anti-thyroid substances, have yielded inconclusive results.

Many teleost fish also undergo a metamorphosis. The best-known examples are seen in eels and salmon. The leptocephalus larval eel is transformed into the elver but little is known about the mechanism of this change that takes place in the sea and precedes migration into rivers. Salmon spawn in fresh water and the young parr, upon reaching a certain size, are transformed into smolt which migrate to the sea. Considerable endocrine changes occur at this time and these can be seen histologically in the pituitary and thyroid glands (Fontaine, 1954). The uptake of radio-iodine by the thyroid increases early in metamorphosis and the levels of 17-hydroxycorticosteroids in the plasma of the parr is five times greater than in the smolt. It is, however, not possible to decide whether such endocrine changes initiate metamorphosis or merely occur as a part of the general maturation process.

The possibility that changes in the endocrine glands, especially the thyroid, may initiate metamorphosis in fishes arose from the observation that thyroid hormones can initiate metamorphosis in most amphibians. The profound and dramatic morphological changes which accompany the metamorphosis of anuran tadpoles into adult frogs and toads have been a source of wonder to biologists for a long time. The transformation from a purely aquatic animal, with no limbs or lungs, into a terrestrial beast that breathes and hops about on four legs is also accompanied by many physiological and biochemical changes. The larval life and metamorphosis of amphibians may be relatively short, from several weeks in desert-dwelling species where water is available for only a short time to as long as three years in bullfrogs. The factors that determine the time of metamorphosis are not clear; they are partly genetic but they can also be modified by the environment. Bullfrog tadpoles from the tropical southern parts of the United States may metamorphose before the beginning of the first winter after hatching, while those in northern areas may endure three winters before this change occurs. Possible environmental factors that influence the time of metamorphosis include nutrition, temperature, the salinity and acidity of the water where they live, the relative proximity of other tadpoles ('crowding') and some experiments even suggest that light may stimulate this process (see Dent, 1968). One can foresee that such factors could exert their effects through the activation of endocrine glands, in this instance the thyroid through its hypothalamic and pituitary control mechanisms.

The feeding of thyroid gland extracts can produce metamorphosis in tadpoles far earlier than it would normally occur. Conversely the administration of anti-thyroid drugs prolongs, or even prevents, metamorphosis. Natural metamorphosis in tadpoles is accompanied by a sudden increase in thyroid gland activity as indicated by histological changes and an increase in the rate of uptake of radioactive iodine. There can be no doubt that the activity of the thyroid gland determines metamorphosis in tadpoles but this is only a part of the endocrine story. The thyroid in tadpoles, like that in other vertebrates, is under the control of TSH from the adenohypophysis. The injection of TSH into tadpoles thus also results in a premature metamorphosis. Hypophysectomized tadpoles do not metamorphose but grow, larger and larger, and attain 'giant' proportions. The hypothalamus and median eminence which are usually the next sites in the chain of thyroid control are also involved in metamorphosis for when the tadpole pituitary is transplanted to the tail, metamorphosis is prevented. Such tadpoles are dark in color due to an uncontrolled release of MSH, and they grow more rapidly than usual.

The latter effect on growth is an important clue which probably, at least partly, reflects a lack of the hypothalamic-inhibition of the release of prolactin. Injections of prolactin into bullfrog tadpoles have been shown to antagonize thyroxine-induced tail resorption and delay metamorphosis (Nicoll *et al.*, 1965; Etkin and Gona, 1967). The same effect has been achieved by grafts of tadpole pituitaries so that this effect probably also exists physiologically. Prolactin is thought to antagonize the peripheral actions of thyroxine and also exerts an inhibitory (goitrogenic) effect on the thyroid gland. Such effects are apparently confined to these amphibians and do not occur, for instance, in mammals.

Etkin (1970), after a careful assessment, has provided a description of how metamorphosis is normally regulated in tadpoles. This synthesis is summarized in Fig. 9.22 and is based on the observations already described which have been correlated with histological changes that occur in the hypothalamus, pituitary and thyroid gland. Metamorphosis is divided into three stages: (*a*) a period of rapid growth called premetamorphosis; (*b*) a time of reduced growth but increased differentiation called prometamorphosis and (*c*) metamorphic-climax when there are 'explosive changes'; the tail is resorbed and the frog emerges and takes up a terrestrial existence. Premetamorphosis is characterized endocrinologically as a time when thyroid hormone secretion is low, which reflects the anatomical immaturity of the hypothalamus–pituitary axis and a low rate cf TSH secretion. This condition is stabilized further by the presence of large amounts of prolactin, possibly reflecting an immaturity of the inhibitory

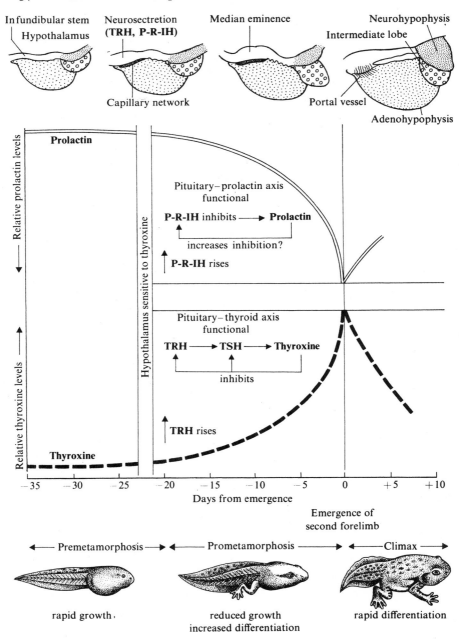

Fig. 9.22. The role of hormones in the growth and development of the tadpole of a frog.

influence of the hypothalamus (P-R-IH), which further inhibits any progress towards metamorphic change. With the progressive maturation of the hypothalamus–pituitary axis toward the beginning of prometamorphosis, TRH gradually increases and releases TSH. The thyroxine concentration thus rises progressively during prometamorphosis. The hypothalamus continues to mature under the influence of thyroxine (called a 'positive-feedback'), and when this is complete and the portal blood supply to the adenohypophysis is finally established, there is a massive stimulation of the thyroid, via TRH and TSH, and metamorphic-climax ensues. During this last period the levels of thyroxine are thought to be declining (due to the operation of the adult negative-feedback inhibition of TRH release).

The unequivocal proof of this theory of tadpole metamorphosis will depend on direct measurements of the hormone levels in tadpoles; a difficult, but with modern techniques, not an impossible task.

Newts and salamanders also undergo a metamorphic transformation but this is not as dramatic as in frogs and toads. Larval urodeles possess limbs and the most prominent morphological change is often the loss of the external gills. Other, less obvious changes nevertheless also occur. This metamorphosis is under pituitary–thyroid control and can be inhibited by prolactin (Gona and Etkin, 1970). A number of species of urodeles are neotenic; they retain their larval characters and never attain the normal adult morphology but can breed while in the larval form. Well-known examples of neoteny in urodeles are seen in axolotls (*Ambystoma mexicanum*) and mudpuppies (*Necturus maculosus*).

It was an event that caused some comment in the biological world when it was found that feeding thyroid glands to axolotls caused them to metamorphose into adult salamanders. The same effect can be elicited by TSH, indicating that the natural disability of these urodeles is due to a pituitary, rather than a thyroid, deficiency. These interesting experiments (see Dent, 1968) involved grafting of pituitaries from metamorphosing tiger salamanders (*Ambystoma tigrinum*) into axolotls which then metamorphosed themselves. The converse experiment, transplanting axolotl pituitaries into hypophysectomized tiger salamanders never resulted in metamorphosis of

---

Upper. The development of the pituitary, especially in relation to the establishment of its connections to the hypothalamus.

Lower. Changes in the activity and hormone concentrations of the pituitary–prolactin axis and the pituitary–thyroid axis. Major events are the acquisition by the hypothalamus of a sensitivity to thyroxine, which hastens its development, and the onset of the definitive roles of TRH and P-R-IH, so that TSH and thyroxine secretion increases while prolactin decreases. (Based on Etkin, 1970.)

the recipients which thereafter remained as larvae. Other neotenous urodeles, like the mudpuppy, however, do not metamorphose when given thyroid hormone; their tissues are not responsive to this hormone.

An interesting departure from the usual amphibian pattern is shown by the eastern spotted newt, *Notophthalmus* (*Diemictylus*) *viridescens*. This animal undergoes two metamorphoses during its life cycle. The first is from the aquatic larva to the adult, or red eft, that lives a terrestrial existence for one to three years, but undergoes a second metamorphosis when it returns to water to breed. This transformation is accompanied by morphological changes in the skin and the newt also loses its tongue. The second metamorphosis is thought to be due to a rise in prolactin levels which is called the 'eft water-drive effect' of this hormone (this has been referred to earlier). This change in the prolactin activity is accompanied by a decline in thyroid hormone (Gona, Pearlman and Etkin, 1970).

The dramatic effects of thyroxine on the development of amphibians has contributed considerably to our ideas about the role of the thyroid in mammalian development. It is, however, now generally considered that the two processes are not analogous and that the 'morphogenetic' effect of thyroid hormone in amphibians represents a special application of these hormones to their physiology. The aquatic and terrestrial phases in an amphibian's life cycle can be viewed as separate processes each of which has undergone evolutionary modification consistent with life in each environment. The transformation of one form to another has no parallel in other tetrapods. The use of the thyroid hormone, and probably also prolactin, to control such metamorphosis is an outstanding example of how adaptable the endocrine system is to the needs of evolutionary change.

Conclusions

Apart from nutrition, reproduction probably involves the most complex processes of humoral coordination that exists in vertebrates. It can also be considered as under 'multihormonal control'. Reproduction, and the preparations for this event, involve a variety of tissues, organs and several distinct, accurately timed, physiological events (for instance impregnation, ovulation, and parturition) and usually take a prolonged period of time to reach fruition. Hormones are especially suited to such needs for coordination. The nature of the reproductive process displays considerable morphological and physiological variation and certain types of mechanisms, such as viviparity in mammals and oviparity in birds, predominate in certain systematic groups, in which they are a feature, and involve special endocrine mechanisms. There are, however, many examples of what may be parallel evolution, such as viviparity in fishes and reptiles in which the special roles of hormones may have evolved independently but have a similar end result.

The diversity in reproductive processes does not appear to have involved many changes in the structure of the hormones themselves. The gonadal steroid hormones have the same structure in all vertebrates, though those from the pituitary show distinct differences which are probably of more consequence as regards limiting their action to a certain species than reflecting any functional predilection to coordinate novel processes. It is, however, of special note that pituitary gonadotrophin appears to exist as a single molecule in some vertebrates, especially the fishes, but in most tetrapods it now seems likely that two distinct hormones, one with LH and the other FSH activity, have emerged. This dichotomy presumably allows for the operation of a more specific and precise control mechanism but the physiological differences that, it would appear, must result are unknown. Another notable endocrine novelty has emerged in eutherian mammals and is the ability of the placenta to act as an additional site for steroid hormone synthesis and to form two pituitary-like hormones, chorionic gonadotrophin and somatomammotrophin. There is, however, considerable interspecific variability in the endocrine function of the eutherian placenta and it is suspected that this may have arisen on several separate evolutionary occasions and been perpetuated according to the requirements of the particular species involved.

Hormones contribute directly to the control of differentiation and growth of the embryo and behavioral and physiological processes concerned with the care of the young. The control of metamorphosis in amphibians is a unique and dramatic example of how endocrines can influence development but they also contribute more ubiquitously, especially to sexual differentiation, in all groups of vertebrates. The phylogenetically novel process of lactation in mammals is a clear example of the evolution of endocrine function, though hormones may also contribute to the process of parental care of the young in a variety of other vertebrates.

References

Abe, K., Robison, G. A., Liddle, G. W., Butcher, R. W., Nicholson, W. E. and Baird, C. E. (1969). Role of cyclic AMP in mediating the effects of MSH, norepinephrine and melatonin on frog skin color. *Endocrinology* **85**, 674–682.

Acher, R., Chauvet, J. and Chauvet, M. T. (1972). Phylogeny of the neuro-hypophysial hormones. Two new active peptides isolated from a cartilaginous fish, *Squalus acanthias*. *Eur. J. Biochem.* **29**, 12–19.

Agus, Z. S., Gardner, L. B., Beck, L. H. and Goldberg, M. (1973). Effects of parathyroid hormone on renal tubular reabsorption of calcium, sodium and phosphate. *Amer. J. Physiol.* **224**, 1143–1148.

Alvarado, R. H. and Johnson, S. R. (1966). The effects of neurohypophysial hormones on water and sodium balance in larval and adult bullfrogs (*Rana catesbeiana*). *Comp. Biochem. Physiol.* **18**, 549–561.

Amoroso, E. C. and Marshall, F. H. A. (1960). External factors in sexual periodicity. In *Marshalls Physiology of Reproduction* (edited by A. S. Parkes), vol. I (Pt 2) pp. 707–831. London: Longmans.

Anderson, L. L. (1973). Effects of hysterectomy and other factors on luteal function. In *Handbook of Physiology*, Section 7 *Endocrinology*, vol. II *Female reproductive system* (Pt. 2) pp. 69–86. Washington: American Physiological Society.

Anon (1970). Effects of sexual activity on beard growth in man. *Nature, Lond.* **226**, 869–870.

Ariëns Kappers, J. (1965). Survey of the innervation of the epiphysis cerebri and the accessory pineal organs of vertebrates. *Prog. Brain Res.* **10**, 87–151.

—— (1970). The pineal organ: An introduction. In *The Pineal Gland* (edited by G. E. W. Wolstenholme and J. Knight) pp. 3–25. Edinburgh and London: Churchill Livingstone.

Armstrong, D. T. and Kennedy, T. G. (1972). Role of luteinizing hormones in regulation of the rat estrous cycle. *Amer. Zool.* **12**, 245–255.

Augee, M. L. and McDonald, I. R. (1973). Role of the adrenal cortex in the adaptation of the monotreme *Tachyglossus aculeatus* to low environmental temperature. *J. Endocr.* **58**, 513–523.

Aurbach, G. D., Keitmann, H. T., Niall, H. D., Tregear, G. W., O'Riordan, J. L. H., Marcus, R., Marx, S. J. and Potts, J. T. (1972). Structure, synthesis, and mechanism of action of parathyroid hormone. *Rec. Prog. Hormone Res.* **28**, 353–392.

Axelrod, J. (1974). The pineal gland: a neurochemical transducer. *Science* **184**, 1341–1348.

Axelrod, J., Wurtman, R. J. and Snyder, S. H. (1965). Control of hydroxyindole *O*-methyltransferase activity in the rat pineal gland by environmental lighting. *J. biol. Chem.* **240**, 949–954.

Baber, E. C. (1876). Contributions to the minute anatomy of the thyroid gland of the dog. *Proc. Roy. Soc.* **24**, 240–241.

Babiker, M. M. and Rankin, J. C. (1973). Effects of neurohypophysial hormones on renal function in the freshwater- and sea-water-adapted eel (*Anguilla anguilla L.*) *J. Endocr.* **57**, xi–xii.

Bach, J-F., Dardenne, M., Papiernik, M., Barois, A., Levasseur, P. and Le Brigand, H. (1972). Evidence for a serum-factor secreted by the human thymus. *Lancet* **2**, 1056–1058.

Bagnara, J. T. (1969). Responses of pigment cells of amphibians to intermedin. *Colloques du C.N.R.S.* no. **177**, 153–158.

Bagnara, J. T. and Hadley, M. E. (1970). Endocrinology of the amphibian pineal. *Amer. Zool.* **10**, 201–216.

(1972). *Chromatophores and Color Change*. New Jersey: Prentice Hall.

Balazs, R., Cocks, W. A., Eayrs, J. T. and Kovacs, S. (1971). Biochemical effects of thyroid hormones on the developing brain. In *Hormones in Development* (edited by M. Hamburgh and E. J. W. Barrington), pp. 357–379. New York: Appleton–Century–Crofts.

Baldwin, R. L. (1969). Development of milk synthesis. *J. Dairy Sci.* **52**, 729–736.

Ball, J. N. and Baker, B. I. (1969). The pituitary gland: anatomy and histophysiology. In *Fish Physiology* (edited by W. S. Hoar and D. J. Randall), vol II *The Endocrine System*, pp. 1–110. New York: Academic Press.

Ball, J. N., Chester Jones, I., Forster, M. E., Hargreaves, G., Hawkins, E. F. and Milne, K. P. (1971). Measurement of plasma cortisol levels in the eel *Anguilla anguilla* in relation to osmotic adjustments. *J. Endocr.* **50**, 75–96.

Ball, J. N. and Ensor, D. M. (1965). Effect of prolactin on plasma sodium in the teleost, *Poecilia latipinna*. *J. Endocr.* **32**, 269–270.

(1967). Specific action of prolactin on plasma sodium levels in hypophysectomized *Poecilia latipinna* (Teleostei). *Gen. comp. Endocr.* **8**, 432–440.

Ball, J. N. and Ingleton, P. M. (1973). Adaptive variations in prolactin secretion in relation to external salinity in the teleost *Poecilia latipinna*. *Gen. comp. Endocr.* **20**, 312–325.

Bargmann, W. (1943). Die Epiphysis cerebri. *Handbuch der mikroskopischen Anatomie des Menschen*. Vol. VI (4). Berlin: Springer Verlag.

Barrington, E. J. W. (1942). Blood sugar and the follicles of Langerhans in the ammocoete larva. *J. exp. Biol.* **19**, 45–55.

(1962). Hormones and vertebrate evolution. *Experimentia* **18**, 201–210.

(1968). Metamorphosis in lower chordates. In *Metamorphosis, A Problem in Developmental Biology* (edited by W. Etkin and L. I. Gilbert), pp. 223–270. New York: Appleton–Century–Crofts.

Barrington, E. J. W. and Dockray, G. J. (1970). The effect of intestinal extracts of lampreys (*Lampetra fluviatilis* and *Petromyzon marinus*) on pancreatic secretion in the rat. *Gen. comp. Endocr.* **14**, 170–177.

(1972). Cholecystokinin–pancreozymin-like activity in the eel *Anguilla anguilla*. *Gen. comp. Endocr.* **19**, 80–87.

Basu, S. L. (1969). Effects of hormones on the salientian spermatogenesis *in vivo* and *in vitro*. *Gen. comp. Endocr. Suppl.* **2**, 203–213.

Bates, R. W., Miller, R. A. and Garrison, M. M. (1962). Evidence in the hypophysectomized pigeon of a synergism among prolactin, growth hormone, thyroxine, and prednisone upon weight of the body, digestive tract, kidney and fat stores. *Endocrinology* **71**, 345–360.

Bayliss, W. M. and Starling, E. H. (1902). The mechanism of pancreatic secretion. *J. Physiol., Lond.* **28**, 325–353.

(1903). On the uniformity of the pancreatic mechanism in vertebrata. *J. Physiol., Lond.* **29**, 174–180.

Bélanger, L. F., Dimond, M. T. and Copp, D. H. (1973). Histological observations on bone and cartilage of growing turtles treated with calcitonin, *Gen. comp. Endocr.* **20**, 297–304.

Bellamy, D. and Leonard, R. A. (1965). Effect of cortisol on the growth of chicks. *Gen. comp. Endocr.* **5**, 402–410.

Bentley, P. J. (1962). Studies on the permeability of the large intestine and urinary bladder of the tortoise (*Testudo graeca*) with special reference to the effects of neurohypophysial and adrenocortical hormones. *Gen. comp. Endocr.* **2**, 323–328.

(1966). Hyperglycaemic effect of neurohypophysial hormones in the chicken, *Gallus domesticus*. *J. Endocr.* **34**, 527–528.

(1969). Neurohypophysial function in Amphibia: hormone activity in the plasma. *J. Endocr.* **43**, 359–369.

(1971). *Endocrines and Osmoregulation. A Comparative Account of the Regulation of Water and Salt in Vertebrates.* New York, Berlin, Heidelberg: Springer Verlag.

(1972). Introductory remarks. Symposium on endocrinology and osmoregulation. *Fedn Proc.* **31**, 1583–1586.

(1973). Osmoregulation in the aquatic urodeles *Amphiuma means* (the congo eel) and *Siren lacertina* (the mud eel). Effects of vasotocin. *Gen. comp. Endocr.* **20**, 386–392.

Bentley, P. J. and Follett, B. K. (1963). Kidney function in a primitive vertebrate, the cyclostome *Lampetra fluviatilis*. *J. Physiol., Lond.* **169**, 902–918.

(1965). The effects of hormones on the carbohydrate metabolism of the lamprey *Lampetra fluviatilis*. *J. Endocr.* **31**, 127–137.

Berde, B. and Boissonnas, R. A. (1968). Basic pharmacological properties of synthetic analogues and homologues of the neurohypophysial hormones. In *Neurohypophysial Hormones and Similar Polypeptides* (edited by B. Berde), pp. 802–870. Berlin, Heidelberg, New York: Springer Verlag.

Berlind, A. (1972a). Teleost caudal neurosecretory system: release of urotensin II from isolated urophyses. *Gen. comp. Endocr.* **18**, 557–571.

Berlind, A. (1972b). Teleost caudal neurosecretory system: sperm duct contraction induced by urophysial material. *J. Endocr.* **52**, 567–574.

Berlind, A., Lacanilao, F. and Bern, H. A. (1972). Teleost caudal neurosecretory system: effects of osmotic stress on urophysial proteins and active factors. *Comp. Biochem. Physiol.* **42A**, 345–352.

Bern, H. A. (1972). Comparative endocrinology – the state of the field and art. *Gen. comp. Endocr. Suppl.* **3**, 751–761.

Bern, H. A. and Nicoll, C. S. (1968). The comparative endocrinology of prolactin. *Rec. Prog. Hormone Res.* **24**, 681–713.

(1969). The zoological specificity of prolactin. *Colloques du C.N.R.S.* **177**, 193–202.

Bewley, T. A. and Li, C. H. (1970). Primary structures of human pituitary growth hormone and sheep pituitary lactogenic hormone compared. *Science* **168**, 1361–1362.

Binkley, S., MacBride, S. E., Klein, D. C. and Ralph, C. L. (1973). Pineal enzymes: regulation of avian melatonin synthesis. *Science* **181**, 273–275.

Blair-West, J. R., Coghlan, J. P., Denton, D. A., Nelson, J. F., Orchard, E., Scoggins, B. A., Wright, R. D., Myers, K. and Junqueira, C. L. (1968). Physiological, morphological and behavioural adaptation to a sodium deficient environment by native Australian and introduced species of animals. *Nature, Lond.* **217**, 922–928.

Blum, J. J. (1967). An adrenergic control system in *Tetrahymena. Proc. natn. Acad. Sci., USA* **58**, 81–88.

Boehlke, K. W., Church, R. L., Tiemeier, O. W. and Eleftheriou, B. E. (1966). Diurnal rhythm in plasma glucocorticoid levels in the channel catfish (*Ictalurus punctatus*). *Gen. comp. Endocr.* **7**, 18–21.

Boelkins, J. N. and Kenny, A. D. (1973). Plasma calcitonin levels in Japanese quail. *Endocrinology* **92**, 1754–1760.

Bourne, A. R. and Seamark, R. F. (1973). Seasonal changes in testicular function in the lizard *Tiliqua rugosa. J. Endocr.* **57**, x.

Bower, A. and Hadley, M. E. (1973). Catecholamine control of melanophore stimulating hormone (MSH) secretion *in vitro. Amer. Zool.* **13**, 1277.

Bower, A., Hadley, M. E. and Hruby, V. J. (1974). Biogenic amines and control of melanophore stimulating hormone release. *Science* **184**, 70–72

Bradshaw, S. D. (1972). The endocrine control of water and electrolyte metabolism in desert reptiles. *Gen. comp. Endocrin. Suppl.* **3**, 360–373.

Bradshaw, S. D., Shoemaker, V. H. and Nagy, K. A. (1972). The role of adrenal corticosteroids in the regulation of kidney function in the desert lizard *Dipsosaurus dorsalis. Comp. Biochem. Physiol.* **43A**, 621–635.

Bradshaw, S. D. and Waring, H. (1969). Comparative studies on the biological activity of melanin-dispersing hormone (MDH). *Colloques du C.N.R.S.* **177**, 135–151.

Braun, E. J. and Dantzler, W. H. (1972). Functions of mammalian-type and reptilian-type nephrons in kidney of desert quail. *Amer. J. Physiol.* **222**, 617–629.

(1974). Effects of ADH on single-nephron glomerular filtration rates in the avian kidney. *Amer. J. Physiol.* **226**, 1–28.

Bromer, W. W. (1972). Chemistry of glucagon and gastrin. *Handbook of Physiology*, Section 7, *Endocrinology*, vol I *Endocrine pancrease*, pp. 133–138. Washington: American Physiological Society.

Brooks, C. J. W., Brooks, R. V., Fotherby, K., Grant, J. K., Klopper, A. and Klyne, W. (1970). The identification of steroids. *J. Endocr.* **47**, 265–272.

Brown, P. S. and Brown, S. C. (1973). Prolactin and thyroid hormone interactions in salt and water balance in the newt *Notophththalmus viridescens. Gen. comp. Endocr.* **20**, 456–466.

Brown-Grant, K. and Ostberg, A. J. C. (1974). Lack of effect of pineal denervation on the responses of the female albino rat to exposure to constant light. *J. Endocr.* **62**, 45–50.

Browning, H. C. (1969). Role of prolactin in regulation of reproductive cycles. *Gen. comp. Endocr. Suppl.* **2**, 42–54.

Bullough, W. S. (1971). The actions of chalones. *Ag. Actions* **2**, 1–7.

Burgers, A. C. J. (1963). Melanophore-stimulating hormones in vertebrates. *Ann. N.Y. Acad. Sci.* **100**, 669–677.

Burzawa-Gerard, E. and Fontaine, Y. A. (1972). The gonadotropins of lower vertebrates. *Gen. comp. Endocr. Suppl.* **3**, 715–728.

Butler, D. G. (1966). Effect of hypophysectomy on osmoregulation in the European eel (*Anguilla anguilla* L.). *Comp. Biochem. Physiol.* **18**, 773–781.

(1969). Corpuscles of Stannius and renal physiology in the eel (*Anguilla rostrata*). *J. Fish. Res. Bd Can.* **26**, 639–654.

Butler, D. G. and Carmichael, F. J. (1972). (Na$^+$–K$^+$)-ATPase activity in eel (*Anguilla rostrata*) gills in relation to changes in environmental salinity: role of adrenocortical steroids. *Gen. comp. Endocr.* **19**, 421–427.

Butler, D. G., Clarke, W. C., Donaldson, E. M. and Langford, R. W. (1969). Surgical adrenalectomy of a teleost fish (*Anguilla rostrata* LESUEUR): effect on plasma cortisol and tissue electrolyte and carbohydrate concentrations. *Gen. comp. Endocr.* **12**, 503–514.

Cahill, G. F., Aoki, T. T. and Marliss, E. B. (1972). Insulin and muscle protein. *Handbook of Physiology*, Section 7 *Endocrinology*, vol. I *Endocrine pancreas*, pp. 563–577. Washington: American Physiological Society.

Callard, I. P. and Doolittle, J. P. (1973). The influence of intrahypothalamic injections of progesterone on ovarian growth and function in the ovoviviparous iguanid lizard *Sceloperus cyanogenys*. *Comp. Biochem. Physiol.* **44A**, 625–629.

Callard, I. P., Doolittle, J., Banks, W. L. and Chan, S. W. C. (1972). Recent studies on the control of the reptilian ovarian cycle. *Gen. comp. Endocr. Suppl.* **3**, 65–75.

Capelli, J. P., Wesson, L. G. and Aponte, G. E. (1970). A phylogenetic study of the renin–angiotensin system. *Amer. J. Physiol.* **218**, 1171–1178.

Celis, M. E., Hase, S. and Walter, R. (1972). Structure-activity studies of MSH-release-inhibiting hormone. *FEBS letters* **27**, 327–330.

Celis, M. E., Taleisnik, S. and Walter, R. (1971). Regulation of formation and proposed structure of the factor inhibiting the release of melanocyte-stimulating-hormone. *Proc. natn. Acad. Sci., USA* **68**, 1428–1433.

Chadwick, C. S. and Jackson, H. R. (1948). Acceleration of skin growth and molting in the red eft of *Triturus viridescens* by means of prolactin injections. *Anat. Rec.* **101**, 718.

Chan, D. K. O. (1972). Hormonal regulation of calcium balance in teleost fish. *Gen. comp. Endocr. Suppl.* **3**, 411–420.

Chan. D. K. O., Chester Jones, I., Henderson, I. W. and Rankin, J. C. (1967). Studies on the experimental alteration of water and electrolyte composition of the eel (*Anguilla anguilla* L.). *J. Endocr.* **37**, 297–317.

Chan, D. K. O., Phillips, J. G. and Chester Jones, I. (1967). Studies on electrolyte changes in the lip-shark, *Hemiscyllium plagiosum* (Bennett), with special reference to the hormonal influence on the rectal gland. *Comp. Biochem. Physiol.* **23**, 185–198.

Chan, S. T. H. and Phillips, J. G. (1969). The biosynthesis of steroids by the gonads of the ricefield eel, *Monopterus albus* at various stages during natural sex-reversal. *Gen. comp. Endocr.* **12**, 619–636.

Chan, S. W. C. and Phillips, J. G. (1971). Seasonal variations in production *in vitro* of corticosteroids by the frog (*Rana rugulosa*) adrenal. *J. Endocr.* **50**, 1–17.

Chan, S. W. C., Ziegel, S. and Callard, I. P. (1973). Plasma progesterone in snakes. *Comp. Biochem. Physiol.* **44A**, 631–637.

Channing, C. P., Licht, P., Papkoff, H. and Donaldson, E. M. (1974). Comparative activities of mammalian, reptilian and piscine gonadotropins in monkey granulosa cell cultures. *Gen. comp. Endocr.* **22**, 137–145.

Chavin, W., Kim, K. and Tchen, T. T. (1963). Endocrine control of pigmentation. *Ann. N. Y. Acad. Sci.* **100**, 678–685.

Chester Jones, I., Bellamy, D., Chan, D. K. O., Follett, B. K., Henderson, I. W., Phillips, J. G. and Snart, R. S. (1972). Biological actions of steroid hormones on nonmammalian vertebrates. In *Steroids in Nonmammalian Vertebrates* (edited by D. R. Idler), pp. 414–480. New York and London: Academic Press.

Chester Jones, I., Henderson, I. W., Chan, D. K. O., Rankin, J. C., Mosley, W., Brown, J. J., Lever, A. F., Robertson, J. I. S. and Tree, M. (1966). Pressor activity in extracts of the corpuscles of Stannius from the European eel (*Anguilla anguilla* L.). *J. Endocr.* **34**, 393–408.

Chieffi, G. (1967). The reproductive system of elasmobranchs: developmental and endocrinological aspects. In *Sharks, Skates and Rays* (edited by P. W. Gilbert, R. F. Mathewson and D. P. Rall), pp. 553–580. Baltimore: Johns Hopkins.

Chiu, K. W. and Lynn, W. G. (1972). Observations on thyroidal control of sloughing in the garter snake, *Thamnophis sirtalis*, *Copeia* 1972 (no. 1), 158–163.

Chiu, K. W. and Phillips, J. G. (1971a). The effect of hypophysectomy and of injections of thyrotrophin and corticotrophin into hypophysectomized animals on the sloughing cycle of the lizard *Gekko gecko* L. *J. Endocr.* **49**, 611–618.

(1971b). The role of prolactin in the sloughing cycle in the lizard *Gekko gecko* L. *J. Endocr.* **49**, 625–634.

Clark, N. B. (1967). Influence of estrogens upon serum calcium, phosphate and protein concentrations of fresh-water turtles. *Comp. Biochem. Physiol.* **20**, 823–834.

(1972). Calcium regulation in reptiles. *Gen. comp. Endocr. Suppl.* **3**, 430–440.

Clark, N. B. and Dantzler, W. H. (1972). Renal tubular transport of calcium and phosphate in snakes: role of parathyroid hormone. *Amer. J. Physiol.* **223**, 1455–1464.

Clarke, W. C., Bern, H. A., Li, C. H. and Cohen, D. C. (1973). Somatotropic and sodium-retaining effects of human growth hormone and placental lactogen in lower vertebrates. *Endocrinology* **93**, 960–964.

Cockburn, F., Hull, D. and Walton, I. (1968). The effect of lipolytic hormones and theophylline on heat production in brown adipose tissue in vivo. *Brit. J. Pharmacol.* **31**, 568–577.

Cofré, G. and Crabbé, J. (1965). Stimulation by aldosterone of active sodium transport by the isolated colon of the toad *Bufo marinus*. *Nature, Lond.* **207**, 1299–1300.

Collins, K. J. and Weiner, J. S. (1968). Endocrinological aspects of exposure to high environmental temperatures. *Physiol. Rev.* **48**, 785–839.

Colombo, L., Bern, H. A. and Pieprzyk, J. (1971). Steroid transformations by the corpuscles of Stannius and the body of *Salmo gairdnerii* (Teleostei). *Gen. comp. Endocr.* **16**, 74–84.

Cooper, W. E. and Ferguson, G. W. (1972). Steroids and color change during gravidity in the lizard *Crotaphytus collaris*. *Gen. comp. Endocr.* **18**, 69–72.

Coote, J. H., Johns, E. J., Macleod, V. H. and Singer, B. (1972). Effect of renal nerve stimulation, renal blood flow and adrenergic blockade on plasma renin activity in the cat. *J. Physiol., Lond.* **226**, 15–36.

Copp, D. H. (1969). The ultimobranchial glands and calcium regulation. In *Fish Physiology* (edited by W. S. Hoar and D. J. Randall), vol. II *The Endocrine System*, pp. 377–398. New York: Academic Press.

—— (1972). Calcium regulation in birds. *Gen. comp. Endocr. Suppl.* **3**, 441–447.

Copp, D. H., Cameron, E. C., Cheney, B. A., Davidson, A. G. F. and Henze, K. G. (1962). Evidence for calcitonin – a new hormone from the parathyroid that lowers blood calcium. *Endocrinology* **70**, 638–649.

Copp, D. H., Cockcroft, D. W. and Keuk, Y. (1967*a*). Calcitonin from ultimobranchial glands of dogfish and chickens. *Science* **158**, 924–926.

—— (1967*b*). Ultimobranchial origin of calcitonin, hypocalcemic effect of extracts from chicken glands. *Can. J. Physiol. Pharmacol.* **45**, 1095–1099.

Cortelyou, J. R. (1967). The effect of commercially prepared parathyroid extracts on plasma and urine calcium levels in *Rana pipiens*. *Gen. comp. Endocr.* **9**, 234–240.

Cowie, A. T. (1972). Lactation and its hormonal control. In *Hormones in Reproduction* (edited by C. R. Austin and R. V. Short), pp. 106–143. London: Cambridge University Press.

Cowie, A. T. and Tindal, J. S. (1971). *The Physiology of Lactation*. Baltimore: Williams and Wilkins.

Crabbé, J. and De Weer, P. (1964). Action of aldosterone on the bladder and skin of the toad. *Nature, Lond.* **202**, 278–279.

Crews, D. and Licht, P. (1974). Inhibition by corpora atretica of ovarian sensitivity and hormonal stimulation in the lizard, *Anolis carolinensis*. *Endocrinology* **95**, 102–106.

Crighton, D. B., Hartley, B. M. and Lamming, G. E. (1973). Changes in the luteinizing hormone releasing activity of the hypothalamus, and in the pituitary gland and plasma luteinizing hormone during the oestrous cycle of the sheep. *J. Endocr.* **58**, 377–385.

Crocker, A. D. and Holmes, W. N. (1971). Intestinal absorption in ducklings (*Anas platyrhynchos*) maintained on fresh water and hypertonic saline. *Comp. Biochem. Physiol.* **40A**, 203–211.

Daughaday, W. H. (1971). Sulfation factor regulation of skeletal growth. *Amer. J. Med.* **50**, 277–280.

Daughaday, W. H., Hall, K., Raben, M. S., Salmon, W. D., Van den Brande, J. L. and Van Wyke, J. J. (1972). Somatomedin: proposed designation for sulphation factor. *Nature, Lond.* **235**, 107.

Davis, P. J., Gregerman, R. I. and Poole, W. E. (1969). Thyroxine-binding proteins in the serum of the grey kangaroo. *J. Endocr.* **45**, 477–478.

Davis, P. J. and Jurgelski, W. (1973). Thyroid hormone-binding in opossum serum: evidence for polymorphism and relationship to haptoglobin polymorphism. *Endocrinology* **92**, 822–832.

DeLuca, H. F. (1971). The role of vitamin D and its relationship to parathyroid hormone and calcitonin. *Rec. Prog. Hormone Res.* **27**, 479–510.

DeLuca, H. F., Morii, H. and Melancon, M. J. (1968). The interaction of vitamin D, parathyroid hormone and thyrocalcitonin. In *Parathyroid Hormone and Thyrocalcitonin (Calcitonin)* (edited by R. V. Talmage and F. F. Belanger), pp. 448–454. Amsterdam: Excerpta Mecia Foundation.

DeLuise, M., Martin, T. J., Greenberg, P. B. and Michelangeli, V. (1972). Metabolism of porcine, human and salmon calcitonin in the rat. *J. Endocr.* **53**, 475–482.

Dent, J. N. (1968). Survey of amphibian metamorphosis. In *Metamorphosis, a Problem in Developmental Biology* (edited by W. Etkin and L. I. Gilbert), pp. 271–311. New York: Appleton–Century–Crofts.

DeRoos, R. and DeRoos, C. C. (1972). Comparative effects of the pituitary-adrenocortical axis and catecholamines on carbohydrate metabolism in elasmobranch fish. *Gen. comp. Endocr. Suppl.* **3**, 192–197.

Desranleau, R., Gilardeau, C. and Chrétien, M. (1972). Radioimmunoassay of ovine beta-lipotropic hormone. *Endocrinology* **91**, 1004–1010.

Dharmamba, M., Mayer-Gostan, N., Maetz, J. and Bern, H. A. (1973). Effect of prolactin on sodium movement in *Tilapia mossambica* adapted to sea water. *Gen. com. Endocr.* **21**, 179–187.

Dicker, S. E. and Elliott, A. B. (1973). Neurohypophysial hormones and homeostasis in the crab-eating frog, *Rana cancrivora*. *Hormone Res.* **4**, 224–260.

Dodd, J. M. (1960). Gonadal and gonadotrophic hormones in lower vertebrates. In *Marshall's Physiology of Reproduction* (edited by A. S. Parkes), vol. I (Pt 2), pp. 417–582. London: Longmans.

(1972a). Ovarian control in cyclostomes and elasmobranchs. *Amer. Zool.* **12**, 325–339.

(1972b). The endocrine regulation of gametogenesis and gonad maturation in fishes. *Gen. comp. Endocr. Suppl.* **3**, 675–687.

Dodd, J. M. and Dodd, M. H. I. (1969). Phylogenetic specificity of thyroid stimulating hormone with special reference to the Amphibia. *Colloques du C.N.R.S.* **177**, 277–285.

Donaldson, E. M., Yamzaki, F., Dye, H. M. and Philleo, W. W. (1972). Preparation of gonadotropin from salmon (*Oncorhynchus tshawytscha*) pituitary glands. *Gen. comp. Endocr.* **18**, 469–481.

Donoso, A. O. and Segura, E. T. (1965). Seasonal variations of plasma adrenaline and noradrenaline in toads. *Gen. comp. Endocr.* **5**, 440–443.

Douglas, W. W. (1968). Stimulus–secretion coupling: the concept and clues from chromaffin and other cells. *Brit. J. Pharmacol.* **34**, 451–474.

Dousa, T., Hechter, O., Schwartz, I. L. and Walter, R. (1971). Neurohypophyseal hormone-responsive adenylate cyclase from mammalian kidney. *Proc. natn. Acad. Sci., USA* **68**, 1693–1697.

Dousa, T., Walter, R., Schwartz, I. L., Sands, H. and Hechter, O. (1972). Role of cyclic AMP in the action of neurohypophyseal hormones on kidney. *Advances in Cyclic Nucleotide Research* (edited by P. Greengard and G. A. Robison), **I**, 121–135. New York: Raven Press.

Ebling, F. J. and Hale, P. A. (1970). The control of the mammalian molt. *Mem. Soc. Endocr.* **18**, 215–235.

Eddy, J. M. P. and Strahan, R. (1968). The role of the pineal complex in the pigmentary effector system of lampreys, *Mordacia mordax* (Richardson) and *Geotria australis* Gray. *Gen. comp. Endocr.* **11**, 528–534.

Egami, N. and Ishii, S. (1962). Hypophysial control of reproductive functions in teleost fishes. *Gen. comp. Endocr. Suppl.* **1**, 248–253.

Elger, W., Neumann, F. and von Berswordt-Wallrabe, R. (1971). The influence of androgen antagonists and progestogens on the sex differentiation of different mammalian species. In *Hormones in Development* (edited by M. Hamburgh and E. J. W. Barrington), pp. 651–667. New York: Appleton–Century–Crofts.

Elliott, A. B. (1968). Effects of adrenaline on water uptake in *Bufo melanostictus*. *J. Physiol., Lond.* **197**, 87–88P.

Ensor, D. M. and Ball, J. N. (1972). Prolactin and osmoregulation in fishes. *Fedn Proc.* **31**, 1615–1623.

Ensor, D. M., Edmondson, M. R. and Phillips, J. G. (1972). Prolactin and dehydration in rats. *J. Endocr.* **53**, lix–lx.

Ensor, D. M., Simons, I. M. and Phillips, J. G. (1973). The effect of hypophysectomy and prolactin replacement therapy on salt and water metabolism in *Anas platyrhynchos*. *J. Endocr.* **57**, xi.

Epple, A. (1969). The endocrine pancreas. In *Fish Physiology* (edited by W. S. Hoar and D. J. Randall), vol. II *The Endocrine System*, pp. 275–319. New York: Academic Press.

Epstein, F. H., Cynamon, M. and McKay, W. (1971). Endocrine control of Na–K-ATPase and seawater adaptation in *Anguilla rostrata*. *Gen. comp. Endocr.* **16**, 323–328.

Epstein, F. H., Katz, A. I. and Pickford, G. E. (1967). Sodium- and potassium-activated adenosine triphosphatase of gills: role in adaptation of teleosts to salt water. *Science* **156**, 1245–1247.

Estler, C. J. and Ammon, H. P. T. (1969). The importance of the adrenergic beta-receptors for thermogenesis and survival of acutely cold-exposed mice. *Can. J. Physiol. Pharmacol.* **47**, 427–434.

Etkin, W. (1970). The endocrine mechanism of amphibian metamorphosis, an evolutionary achievement. *Mem. Soc. Endocri.* **18**, 137–153.

Etkin, W. and Gona, A. G. (1967). Antagonism between prolactin and thyroid hormone in amphibian development. *J. exp. Zool.* **165**, 249–258.

Fagerlund, U. H. M. (1967). Plasma cortisol concentration in relation to stress in adult sockeye salmon during the freshwater stage in their life cycle. *Gen. comp. Endocr.* **8**, 197–207.

Falkmer, S. and Patent, G. J. (1972). Comparative and embryological aspects of the pancreatic islets. In *Handbook of Physiology*, Section 7 *Endocrinology*, vol. I *Endocrine pancreas*, pp. 1–23. Washington: American Physiological Society.

Farer, L. S., Robbins, J., Blumberg, B. S. and Rall, J. E. (1962). Thyroxine-serum protein complexes in various animals. *Endocrinology* **70**, 686–696.

Fenwick, J. C. (1970). The pineal organ: photoperiod and reproductive cycles in the goldfish *Carassius auratus L. J. Endocr.* **46**, 101–111.

Fenwick, J. C. and Forster, M. E. (1972). Effects of Stanniectomy and hypophysectomy on total plasma cortisol levels in the eel (*Anguilla anguilla* L). *Gen. comp. Endocr.* **19**, 184–191.

Ferguson, D. R. and Heller, H. (1965). Distribution of neurohypophysial hormones in mammals. *J. Physiol., Lond.* **180**, 846–863.

Ferguson, G. W. and Chen, C. L. (1973). Steroid hormones, color change and ovarian cycling in free-living female collard lizards, *Crotaphytus collaris*. *Amer. Zool.* **13**, 1277.

Fernholm, B. (1972). Neurohypophysial–adenohypophysial relations in hagfish (Myxinoidea, Cyclostomata). *Gen. comp. Endocr. Suppl.* **3**, 1–10.

Fitzsimons, J. T. (1972). Thirst. *Physiol. Rev.* **52**, 468–561.

Fleming, W. R., Brehe, J. and Hanson, R. (1973). Some complicating factors in the study of calcium metabolism in teleosts. *Amer. Zool.* **13**, 793–797.

Fleming, W. R., Stanley, J. G. and Meier, A. H. (1964). Seasonal effects of external calcium, estradiol, and ACTH on the serum calcium and sodium levels of *Fundulus kansae*. *Gen. comp. Endocr.* **4**, 61–67.

Foà, P. P. (1972). The secretion of glucagon. *Handbook of Physiology*, Section 7 *Endocrinology*, vol. I, *Endocrine pancreas*, pp. 261–277. Washington: American Physiological Society.

Follett, B. K. (1963). Mole ratios of the neurohypophysial hormones in the vertebrate neural lobe. *Nature, Lond.* **198**, 693–694.

Follett, B. K. and Redshaw, M. R. (1974). The physiology of vitellogenesis. In *Physiology of the Amphibia* (edited by B. Lofts), vol. II, pp. 219–298. New York: Academic Press.

Follett, B. K. and Riley, J. (1967). Effect of the length of the daily photoperiod on thyroid activity in the female Japanese quail (*Coturnix coturnix japonica*). *J. Endocr.* **39**, 615–616.

Follett, B. K. and Sharp, P. J. (1969). Circadian rhythmicity in photoperiodically induced gonadotrophin release and gonadal growth in the quail. *Nature, Lond.* **223**, 968–971.

Fontaine, M. (1954). Du déterminisme physiologique des migrations. *Biol. Rev.* **29**, 390–418.

—— (1964). Corpuscules de Stannius et régulation ionique (Ca, K, Na) du milieu interiéur de l'Anguille (*Anguilla anguilla* L.). *C. R. Acad. Sci., Paris* **259**, 875–878.

Fontaine, M., Callamand, O. and Olivereau, M. (1949). Hypophyse et euryhalinité chez l'anguille. *C. R. Acad. Sci., Paris* **228**, 513–514.

Fontaine, Y-A. (1964). Characteristics of the zoological specificity of some protein hormones from the anterior pituitary. *Nature, Lond.* **202**, 1296–1298.

—— (1969a). La spécificité zoologique des protéines hypophysaires capables de stimuler la thyroide. *Acta Endocrin., Kobn, Suppl.* **136**, 1–154.

—— (1969b). La spécifité zoologique d'action des hormones thyréotropes. *Colloque du C.N.R.S.* **177**, 267–275.

Forrest, J. N., Cohen, A. D., Schon, D. A. and Epstein, F. H. (1973a). Na transport and Na–K-ATPase in gills during adaptation to seawater: effects of cortisol. *Amer. J. Physiol.* **224**, 709–713.

Forrest, J. N., MacKay, W. C., Gallagher, B. and Epstein, F. H. (1973b). Plasma cortisol response to saltwater adaptation in the American eel *Anguilla rostrata*. *Amer. J. Physiol.* **224**, 714–717.

Frantz, A. G., Kleinberg, D. L. and Noel, G. L. (1972). Studies on prolactin in man. *Rec. Prog. Hormone Res.* **28**, 527–573.

Fraps, R. M. (1955). Egg production and fertility in poultry. In *Progress in the Physiology of Farm Animals* (edited by J. Hammond) vol. II, pp. 661–740. London: Butterworths.

Freeman, H. C. and Idler, D. R. (1973). Effects of corticosteroids on liver transaminases in two salmonids, the rainbow trout (*Salmo gairdnerii*) and the brook trout (*Salvelinus fontinalis*). *Gen. comp. Endocr.* **20**, 69–75.

Fridberg, G. and Bern, H. A. (1968). The urophysis and the caudal neurosecretory system of fishes. *Biol. Rev.* **43**, 175–199.

Fritz, I. B. (1972). Insulin actions on carbohydrate and lipid metabolism. In *Biochemical Actions of Hormones* (edited by G. Litwack), Vol. II, pp. 165–214. New York and London: Academic Press.

Fritz, I. B. and Lee, L. P. K. (1972). Fat mobilization and ketogenesis. *Handbook of Physiology*, Section 7 *Endocrinology*, vol. I *Endocrine pancreas*, pp. 579–596. Washington: American Physiological Society.

Frye, B. E. (1967). *Hormonal Control in Vertebrates*, p. 104. New York: The Macmillan Co.

Frye, B. E., Brown, P. S. and Snyder, B. W. (1972). Effects of prolactin and somatotropin on growth and metamorphosis of amphibians. *Gen. comp. Endocr. Suppl.* 3, 209–220.

Funder, J. W., Feldman, D. and Edelman, I. S. (1973). The roles of plasma binding and receptor specificity in the mineralocorticoid action of aldosterone. *Endocrinology* 92, 994–1004.

Furr, B. J. A., Bonney, R. C., England, R. J. and Cunningham, F. J. (1973). Luteinizing hormone and progesterone in peripheral blood during the ovulatory cycle in the hen, *Gallus domesticus. J. Endocr.* 57, 159–169.

Garabedian, M., Tanaka, Y., Holick, M. F. and DeLuca, H. F. (1974). Response of intestinal calcium transport and bone calcium mobilization to 1,25-dihydroxyvitamin D_3 in thyroparathyroidectomized rats. *Endocrinology* 94, 1022–1027.

Geschwind, I. I. (1967). Growth hormone activity in the lungfish pituitary. *Gen. comp. Endocr.* 8, 82–83.

——— (1969). The main lines of evolution of the pituitary hormones. *Colloques du C.N.R.S.* 177, 385–400.

Geschwind, I. I., Huseby, R. A. and Nishioka, R. (1972). The effect of melanocyte-stimulating hormone on coat color in the mouse. *Rec. Prog. Hormone Res.* 28, 91–129.

Gibbs, J., Young, R. C. and Smith, G. P. (1973). Cholecystokinin elicits satiety in rats with open gastric fistulas. *Nature, Lond.* 245, 323–325.

Ginsburg, M. (1968). Production, release, transportation, and elimination of the neurohypophysial hormone. In *Neurohypophysial Hormones and similar Polypeptides* (edited by B. Berde), pp. 286–371. Berlin, Heidelberg and New York: Springer Verlag.

Godet, M. (1961). Le problème hydrique et son controle hypophysaire chez le Protptère. *Ann. Faculty Sciences de l'Université Dakar* 6, 183–201.

Goldman, J. M. and Hadley, M. E. (1969). The beta adrenergic receptor and cyclic 3′-5′-adenosine monophosphate: possible roles in the regulation of melanophore responses of the spadefoot toad, *Scaphiopus couchi. Gen. comp. Endocr.* 13, 151–163.

Goldstein, A. L., Hooper, J. A., Schulof, R. S., Cohen, G. H., Thurman, G. B., McDaniel, M. C., White, A. and Dardenne, M. (1974). Thymosin and the immunopathology of aging. *Fedn Proc.* 33, 2053–2056.

Gona, A. G. and Etkin, W. (1970). Inhibition of metamorphosis in *Ambystoma tigrinum* by prolactin. *Gen. comp. Endocr.* 14, 589–591.

Gona, O. and Gona, A. G. (1973). Action of human placental lactogen on second metamorphosis in the newt *Notophthalmus viridescens. Gen. comp. Endocr.* 21, 377–380.

Gona, A. G., Pearlman, T. and Etkin, W. (1970). Prolactin–thyroid interaction in the newt, *Diemictlylus viridescens. J. Endocr.* 48, 585–590.

Goodridge, A. G. (1964). The effect of insulin, glucagon and prolactin on lipid synthesis and related metabolic activity in migratory and non-migratory finches. *Comp. Biochem. Physiol.* 13, 1–26.

Gorbman, A. (1940). Suitability of the common goldfish for assay of thyrotropic hormone. *Proc. Soc. exp. Biol. Med., New York* 45, 772–773.

Gorbman, A. and Bern, H. A. (1962). *A Textbook of Comparative Endocrinology*, p. 220. New York: Wiley.

Gorbman, A. and Hyder, M. (1973). Failure of mammalian TRH to stimulate thyroid function in the lungfish. *Gen. comp. Endocr.* **20**, 588–589.

Gotshall, R. W., Davis, J. O., Shade, R. E., Spielman, W., Johnson, J. A. and Braverman, B. (1973). Effects of renal denervation on renin release in sodium-depleted dogs. *Amer. J. Physiol.* **225**, 344–349.

Goy, R. W. and Goldfoot, D. A. (1973). Hormonal influences on sexually dimorphic behavior. *Handbook of Physiology*, Section 7 *Endocrinology*, vol. II *Female reproductive system* (Pt 1), pp. 169–186. Washington: American Physiological Society.

Greenwood, A. W. and Blyth, J. S. S. (1935). Variation in plumage response of brown leghorn breast feather and its reaction to oestrone. *Proc. Zool. Soc. Lond. Ser. A* **109**, 247–288.

Greer, M. A. and Haibach, H. (1974). Thyroid secretion. *Handbook of Physiology*, Section 7 *Endocrinology*, vol. III *Thyroid*, pp. 135–146. Washington: American Physiological Society.

Gregory, R. A. (1962). *Secretory Mechanisms of the Gastrointestinal Tract*, p. 153. London: Edward Arnold.

Griffiths, M. (1965). Rate of growth and intake of milk in a suckling echidna. *Comp. Biochem. Physiol.* **16**, 383–392.

Guillemin, R. and Burgus, R. (1972). The hormones of the hypothalamus. *Scientific American* **227** (November) 24–33.

Habener, J. F., Singh, F. R., Deftos, L. J., Neer, R. M. and Potts, J. T. (1971). Explanation for unusual potency of salmon calcitonin. *Nature New Biol.* **232**, 91–92.

Hadley, M. E. (1972). Functional significance of vertebrate integumental pigmentation. *Amer. Zool.* **12**, 63–76.

Hall, P. F. (1969). Hormonal control of melanin synthesis in birds. *Gen. comp. Endocr. Suppl.* **2**, 451–458.

Hanaoka, T. (1953). Effect of melanophore hormone on regeneration of visual purple in solution. *Nature, Lond.* **172**, 866.

Handler, J. S., Bensinger, R. and Orloff, J. (1968). Effects of adrenergic agents on toad bladder response to ADH, 3′,5′-AMP, and theophylline. *Amer. J. Physiol.* **215**, 1024–1031.

Hansel, W. and Echternkamp, S. E. (1972). Control of ovarian function in domestic animals. *Amer. Zool.* **12**, 225–243.

Hanstrom, B. (1966). Gross anatomy of the hypophysis in mammals. In *The Pituitary Gland* (edited by G. W. Harris and B. T. Donovan), vol. I, pp. 1–57. Berkeley and Los Angeles: University of California.

Harmeyer, J. and DeLuca, H. F. (1969). Calcium-binding protein and calcium absorption after vitamin D administration. *Arch. Biochem. Biophys.* **133**, 247–254.

Harper, A. A. and Raper, H. S. (1943). Pancreozymin, a stimulant of the secretion of pancreatic enzymes in extracts of the small intestine. *J. Physiol., Lond.* **102**, 115–125.

Harper, C. and Toverud, S. U. (1973). Ability of thyrocalcitonin to protect against hypercalcemia in adult rats. *Endocrinology* **93**, 1354–1359.

Harri, M. N. E. (1972). Effect of season and temperature acclimation on the tissue catecholamine level and utilization in the frog *Rana temporaria*. *Comp. gen. Pharmacol.* **3**, 101–112.

Harri, M. and Hedenstam, R. (1972). Calorigenic effect of adrenaline and nor-adrenaline in the frog, *Rana temporaria*. *Comp. Biochem. Physiol.* **41***A*, 409–419.

Harrington, R. W. (1968). Delimitation of the thermolabile phenocritical period of sex determination and differentiation in the ontogeny of the normally hermaphroditic fish *Rivulus marmoratus*, Poey. *Physiol. Zool.* **41**, 447–459.

Hartman, F. A. and Brownell, K. A. (1949). *The Adrenal Gland*. London: Henry Kimpton.

Hasan, S. H. and Heller, H. (1968). The clearance of neurohypophysial hormones from the circulation of non-mammalian vertebrates. *Brit. J. Pharmacol.* **33**, 523–530.

Hayashida, T. (1970). Immunological studies with rat pituitary growth hormone (RGH). 11. Comparative immunochemical investigation of GH from representatives of various vertebrates classes with monkey antiserum to RGH. *Gen. comp. Endocr.* **15**, 432–452.

(1971). Biological and immunochemical studies with growth hormone in pituitary extracts of holostean and chondrostean fishes. *Gen. comp. Endocr.* **17**, 275–280.

(1973). Biological and immunochemical studies with growth hormone in pituitary extracts of elasmobranchs. *Gen. comp. Endocr.* **20**, 377–385.

Hayashida, T. and Lagios, M. D. (1969). Fish growth hormone: a biological, immunochemical, and ultrastructural study of sturgeon and paddlefish pituitaries. *Gen. comp. Endocr.* **13**, 403–411.

Hayashida, T., Licht, P. and Nicoll, C. S. (1973). Amphibian pituitary growth hormone and prolactin: immunochemical relatedness to rat growth hormone. *Science* **182**, 169–171.

Hazelwood, R. L. (1973). The avian endocrine pancreas. *Amer. Zool.* **13**, 699–709.

Hazelwood, R. L., Turner, S. D., Kimmel, J. R. and Pollock, H. G. (1973). Spectrum effects of a new polypeptide (third hormone?) isolated from chicken pancreas. *Gen. comp. Endocr.* **21**, 485–497.

Heap, R. B. (1972). Role of hormones in pregnancy. In *Hormones in Reproduction* (edited by C. R. Austin and R. V. Short), pp. 73–105. London: Cambridge University Press.

Heap, R. B., Perry, J. S. and Challis, J. R. G. (1973). Hormonal maintenance of pregnancy. *Handbook of Physiology*, Section 7 *Endocrinology*, vol. II *Female reproductive system* (Pt 2), pp. 217–260. Washington: American Physiological Society.

Heding, L. G. (1971). Radioimmunological determination of pancreatic and gut glucagon in plasma. *Diabetologia* **7**, 10–19.

Heins, J. N., Garland, J. T. and Daughaday, W. H. (1970). Incorporation of ^{35}S-sulfate into rat cartilage explants *in vitro*: effects of aging on responsiveness to stimulation by sulfation factor. *Endocrinology* **87**, 688–692.

Heller, H. (1941). Differentiation of an (amphibian) water balance principle from the antidiuretic principle of the posterior pituitary gland. *J. Physiol., Lond.* **100**, 125–141.

(1966). The hormone content of the vertebrate hypothalamo–neurohypophysial system. *Brit. Med. Bull.* **22**, 227–231.

(1972). The effect of neurohypophysial hormones on the female reproductive tract of lower vertebrates. *Gen. comp. Endocr. Suppl.* **3**, 703–714.

(1973). The effects of oxytocin and vasopressin during the oestrous cycle and pregnancy on the uterus of a marsupial species, the quokka (*Setonix brachyurus*). *J. Endocr.* **58**, 657–671.

——— (1974). Molecular aspects of comparative endocrinology. *Gen. comp. Endocr.* **22**, 315–332.

Heller, H., Ferreri, E. and Leathers, D. H. G. (1970). The effect of neurohypophysial hormones on the amphibian oviduct *in vitro*, with some remarks on the histology of this organ. *J. Endocr.* **47**, 495–509.

Heller, J. (1961). The physiology of the antidiuretic hormone VIII. The antidiuretic activity in the plasma of the mouse, guinea-pig, cat, rabbit and dog. *Physiol. Bohemoslov.* **10**, 167–172.

Heller, J. and Štulc, J. (1960). The physiology of the antidiuretic hormone. III. The antidiuretic activity of plasma in normal and dehydrated rats. *Physiol. Bohemslov.* **9**, 93–98.

Henderson, I. W. and Chester Jones, I. (1967). Endocrine influences on the net extrarenal fluxes of sodium and potassium in the European eel (*Anguilla anguilla* L.). *J. Endocr.* **37**, 319–325.

Henderson, I. W. and Wales, N. A. M. (1974). Renal diuresis and anti-diuresis after injections of arginine vasotocin in the fresh-water eel (*Anguilla anguilla* L.). *J. Endocr.* **41**, 487–500.

Henderson, J. R. (1969). Why are the Islets of Langerhans? *Lancet* ii, 469–470.

Hill, C. W. and Fromm, P. O. (1968). Response of the interrenal gland of rainbow trout (*Salmo gairdneri*) to stress. *Gen. comp. Endocr.* **11**, 69–77.

Hirano, T. (1969). Effects of hypophysectomy and salinity change on plasma cortisol concentration in the Japanese eel, *Anguilla japonica. Endocr. japon.* **16**, 557–560.

Hirsch, P. F. and Munson, P. L. (1969). Thyrocalcitonin. *Physiol. Rev.* **49**, 548–622.

Hisaw, F. L. (1959). The corpora lutea of elasmobranch fishes. *Anat. Rec.* **133**, 289.

Hogben, L. T. (1924). *The Pigmentary Effector System*, p. 67. Edinburgh: Oliver and Boyd.

——— (1942). Chromatic behaviour. *Proc. Roy. Soc. Lond. B* **131**, 111–136.

Hoffman, R. A. (1964). Terrestrial animals in cold: hibernators. *Handbook of Physiology*, Section 4 *Adaptation to the Environment*, pp. 379–403. Washington: American Physiological Society.

Holmes, R. L. and Ball, J. N. (1974). *The Pituitary Gland. A Comparative Account.* London: Cambridge University Press.

Holmes, W. N. (1972). Regulation of electrolyte balance in marine birds with special reference to the role of the pituitary–adrenal axis in the duck (*Anas platyrhynchos*) *Fedn Proc.* **31**, 1587–1598.

Holmes, W. N., Butler, D. G. and Phillips, J. G. (1961). Observations on the effects of maintaining glaucous-winged gulls (*Larus glaucescens*) on fresh water and sea water for long periods. *J. Endocr.* **23**, 53–61.

Horrobin, D. F., Burstyn, P. G., Lloyd, I. J., Durkin, N., Lipton, A. and Muiruri, K. L. (1971). Actions of prolactin on human renal function. *Lancet* ii, 352–354.

Howe, A. (1973). The mammalian pars intermedia: a review of its structure and function. *J. Endocr.* **59**, 385–409.

Humbel, R. E., Bosshard, H. R. and Zahn, H. (1972). Chemistry of insulin. *Handbook of Physiology*, Section 7 *Endocrinology*, vol. I *Endocrine pancreas*, pp. 111–132. Washington: American Physiological Society.

Idler, D. R. (editor). (1972). *Steroids in Nonmammalian Vertebrates*. New York and London: Academic Press.

Idler, D. R., Sangalang, G. B. and Truscott, B. (1972). Corticosteroids in the South American lungfish. *Gen. comp. Endocr. Suppl.* **3**, 238–244.

Idler, D. R. and Truscott, B. (1972). Corticosteroids in fish. In *Steroids in Non-mammalian Vertebrates* (edited by D. R. Idler), pp. 126–252. New York and London: Academic Press.

Ireland, M. P. (1969). Effect of urophysectomy in *Gasterosteus aculeatus* on survival in fresh water and sea-water. *J. Endocr.* **43**, 133–134.

— (1973). Effects of arginine vasotocin on sodium and potassium metabolism in *Xenopus laevis* after skin gland stimulation and sympathetic blockade. *Comp. Biochem. Physiol* **44A**, 487–493.

Ivy, A. C. and Oldberg, E. (1928). A hormone mechanism for gall bladder contraction and evacuation. *Amer. J. Physiol.* **86**, 599–613.

Jackson, I. M. D. and Reichlin, S. (1974). Thyrotropin-releasing hormone distribution in hypothalamic and extrahypothalamic brain tissues of mammalian and submammalian chordates. *Endocrinology* **95**, 854–862.

Jackson, R. G. and Sage, M. (1973). A comparison of the effects of mammalian TSH on the thyroid glands of the teleost *Galeichthys felis* and the elasmobranch *Dasyatis sabina. Comp. Biochem. Physiol.* **44A**, 867–870.

Janský, L. (1973). Non-shivering thermogenesis and its thermoregulatory significance. *Biol. Rev.* **48**, 85–132.

Janssens, P. A. (1964). The metabolism of the aestivating African lungfish. *Comp. Biochem. Physiol.* **11**, 105–117.

— (1967). Interference of metyrapone with the actions of cortisol in *Xenopus laevis* Daudin and the laboratory rat. *Gen. comp. Endocr.* **8**, 94–100.

Janssens, P. A., Vinson, G. P., Chester Jones, I. and Mosley, W. (1965). Amphibian characteristics of the adrenal cortex of the African lungfish (*Protopterus sp.*) *J. Endocr.* **32**, 373–382.

Jensen, E. V. and DeSombre, E. R. (1972). Estrogens and progestins. In *Biochemical Actions of Hormones* (edited by G. Litwack), vol. II pp. 215–255. New York and London: Academic Press.

— (1973). Estrogen–receptor interaction. *Science* **182**, 126–134.

Joel, C. D. (1965). The physiological role of brown adipose tissue. *Handbook of Physiology*, Section 5 *Adipose Tissue*, pp. 59–85. Washington: American Physiological Society.

John, T. M. and George, J. C. (1973). Influence of glucagon and neurohypophysial hormones on plasma free fatty acid levels in the pigeon. *Comp. Biochem. Physiol.* **45A**, 541–547.

Johnston, C. I., Davis, J. O., Wright, F. S. and Howards, S. S. (1967). Effects of renin and ACTH on adrenal steroid secretion in the American bullfrog. *Amer. J. Physiol.* **213**, 393–399.

Jorgenson, C. B., Larsen, L. O. and Rosenkilde, P. (1965). Hormonal dependency of molting in amphibians: effect of radiothyroidectomy in the toad *Bufo bufo* L. *Gen. comp. Endocr.* **5**, 248–251.

Jorgenson, C. B. and Vijayakumar, S. (1970). Annual oviduct cycle and its control in the toad *Bufo bufo* L. *Gen. comp. Endocr.* **14**, 404–411.

Jorpes, E. and Mutt, V. (1966). Cholecystokinin and pancreozymin, one single molecule? *Acta physiol. scand.* **66**, 196–202.

Joss, J. M. P. (1973). Pineal–gonad relationships in the lamprey *Lampetra fluviatilus. Gen. comp. Endocr.* **21**, 118–122.

Jost, A. (1971). Hormones in development; past and present prospects. In *Hormones and Development* (edited by M. Hamburgh and E. J. W. Barrington), pp. 1–18. New York: Appleton–Century–Crofts.

Kamiya, M. (1972). Sodium–potassium-activated adenosinetriphatase in isolated chloride cells from eel gills. *Comp. Biochem. Physiol.* **43B**, 611–617.

Keller, N., Richardson, U. I. and Yates, F. E. (1969). Protein binding and the biological activity of corticosteroids: *in vivo* induction of hepatic and pancreatic alanine amino-transferases by corticosteroids in normal and estrogen-treated rats. *Endocrinology* **84**, 49–62.

Kenny, A. D. (1971). Determination of calcitonin in plasma by bioassay. *Endocrinology* **89**, 1005–1013.

Kenny, A. D. and Dacke, C. G. (1974). The hypercalcaemic response to parathyroid hormone in Japanese quail. *J. Endocr.* **62**, 15–23.

Kerkof, P. R., Boschwitz, D. and Gorbman, A. (1973). The response of hagfish thyroid tissue to thyroid inhibitors and to mammalian thyroid-stimulating hormone. *Gen. comp. Endocr.* **21**, 231–240.

King, J. R. and Farner, D. S. (1965). Studies of fat deposition in migratory birds. *Ann. N. Y. Acad. Sci.* **131**, 422–440.

Kirshner, N. and Viveros, O. H. (1972). The secretory cycle of the adrenal medulla. *Pharm. Revs.* **24**, 385–398.

Kleiber, M. (1961). *The Fire of Life. An Introduction to Animal Energetics*, pp. 312. New York: Wiley.

Klicka, J. and Mahmoud, I. Y. (1972). Conversion of pregenolone-4^{14}C to progesterone-4^{14}C by turtle corpus luteum. *Gen. comp. Endocr.* **19**, 367–369.

Krieger, D. T. (1971). The hypothalamus and neuroendocrinology. *Hospital Practice* September, 87–99.

—— (1972). Circadian corticosteroid periodicity: critical period for abolition by neonatal injection of corticosteroid. *Science* **178**, 1205–1207.

Krishna, G., Hynie, S. and Brodie, B. B. (1968). Effects of thyroid hormones on adenyl cyclase in adipose tissue and on free fatty acid mobilization. *Proc. natn. Acad. Sci., USA* **59**, 884–889.

Krishnamurthy, V. G. and Bern, H. A. (1969). Correlative histological study of the corpuscles of Stannius and the juxtaglomerular cells of teleost fishes. *Gen. comp. Endocr.* **13**, 313–335.

Kumar, M. A. and Sturtridge, W. C. (1973). The physiological role of calcitonin assessed through chronic calcitonin deficiency in rats. *J. Physiol., Lond.* **233**, 33–43.

Lam, T. J, (1972). Prolactin and hydromineral metabolism in fishes. *Gen. comp. Endocr. Suppl.* **3**, 328–338.

LaPointe, J. L. and Jacobson, E. R. (1974). Hyperglycemic effect of neurohypophysial hormones in the lizard, *Klauberina riversiana. Gen. comp. Endocrin.* **22**, 135–136.

Larsen, L. O. (1965). Effects of hypophysectomy in the cyclostome, *Lampetra fluviatilis* (L) Gray. *Gen. comp. Endocr.* **5**, 16–30.

—— (1969). Effects of gonadectomy in the cyclostome, *Lampetra fluviatilis. Gen. comp. Endocr.* **13**, 516–517.

—— (1973). Development in adult, freshwater river lampreys and its hormonal control, Thesis: University of Copenhagen.

Larsen, L. O. and Rosenkilde, P. (1971). Iodine metabolism in normal, hypophysectomized, and thyrotropin-treated river lampreys, *Lampetra fluviatilis* (Gray) L. (Cyclostomata). *Gen. comp. Endocr.* **17**, 94–104.

Larsson, A. L. (1973). Metabolic effects of epinephrine and norepinephrine in the eel *Anguilla anguilla* L. *Gen. comp. Endocr.* **20**, 155–167.

Larsson, A. and Lewander, K. (1972). Effects of glucagon administration to eels (*Anguilla anguilla* L.). *Comp. Biochem. Physiol.* **43A**, 831–836.

Lawson, D. E. M., Fraser, D. R., Kodicek, E., Morris, H. R. and Williams, D. H. (1971). Identification of 1,25-dihydroxycholecalciferol, a new kidney hormone controlling calcium metabolism. *Nature, Lond.* **230**, 228–230.

LeBrie, S. J. (1972). Endocrines and water and electrolyte balance in reptiles. *Fedn Proc.* **31**, 1599–1608.

Lederis, K. (1973). Current studies on urotensin. *Amer. Zool.* **13**, 771–773.

Lee, A. K. and Mercer, E. H. (1967). Cocoon surrounding desert-dwelling frogs. *Science* **157**, 87–88.

Lee, T. H., Lee, M. S. and Lu, M-Y. (1972). Effects of α-MSH on melanogenesis and tyrosinase in B-16 melanoma. *Endocrinology* **91**, 1180–1188.

LeFevre, M. D. (1973). Effects of aldosterone on the isolated substrate-depleted turtle bladder. *Amer. J. Physiol.* **225**, 1252–1256.

Leibson, L. and Plisetskaya, E. M. (1968). Effect of insulin on blood sugar level and glycogen content in organs of some cyclostomes and fish. *Gen. comp. Endocr.* **11**, 381–392.

Leloup, J. and Fontaine, M. (1960). Iodine metabolism in lower vertebrates. *Ann. N. Y. Acad. Sci.* **86**, 316–353.

Leloup-Hatey, J. (1970). Influence de l'ablation des corpuscules de Stannius sur le fonctionnment de l'interrenal de l'anguille (*Anguilla anguilla* L.). *Gen. comp. Endocr.* **15**, 388–397.

Lemon, M. (1972). Peripheral plasma progesterone during pregnancy and the oestrous cycle in the tammar wallaby, *Macropus eugenii*. *J. Endocr.* **55**, 63–71.

Lerner, A. B. and McGuire, J. S. (1961). Effect of alpha- and beta-melanocyte stimulating hormone on the skin colour of man. *Nature, Lond.* **189**, 176–179.

Li, C. H. (1969). Recent studies on the chemistry of human growth hormone. *Colloque du C.N.R.S.* **177**, 175–179.

— (1972). Recent knowledge of the chemistry of lactogenic hormones. In *Lactogenic Hormones* (edited by G. E. W. Wolstenholme and J. Knight), pp. 7–22. Edinburgh and London: Churchill.

Li, C. H., Barnafi, L., Chrétien, M. and Chung, D. (1965). Isolation and amino-acid sequence of β-LPH from sheep pituitary glands. *Nature, Lond.* **208**, 1093–1094.

Licht, P. (1970). Effects of mammalian gonadotropins (ovine FSH and LH) in female lizards. *Gen. comp. Endocr.* **14**, 98–106.

— (1972). Environmental physiology of reptilian breeding cycles: role of temperature. *Gen. comp. Endocr. Suppl.* **3**, 477–487.

— (1973). Induction of spermiation in anurans by mammalian pituitary gonadotrophins and their subunits. *Gen. comp. Endocr.* **20**, 522–529.

Licht, P. and Hoyer, H. (1968). Somatotropic effects of exogenous prolactin and growth hormone in juvenile lizards (*Lacerta s. sicula*). *Gen. comp. Endocr.* **11**, 338–346.

Licht, P. and Papkoff, H. (1974*a*). Separation of two distinct gonadotropins from the pituitary gland of the snapping turtle (*Chelydra serpentina*). *Gen. comp. Endocr.* **22**, 218–237.

— (1974*b*). Separation of two distinct gonadotropins from the pituitary gland of the bullfrog, *Rana catesbeiana*. *Endocrinology* **94**, 1587–1594.

Licht, P. and Stockell Hartree, A. (1971). Actions of mammalian, avian and piscine gonadotrophins in the lizard. *J. Endocr.* **49**, 113–124.

Lillie, F. R. (1917). The free-martin; a study of the actions of sex hormones in the foetal life of cattle. *J. exp. Biol.* **23**, 371–452.

Ling, J. K. (1972). Adaptive functions of vertebrate molting cycles. *Amer. Zool.* **12**, 77–93.

Lockett, M. F. and Nail, B. (1965). A comparative study of the renal actions of growth and lactogenic hormones in rats. *J. Physiol. Lond.* **180**, 147–156.

Lofts, B. (1964). Seasonal changes in the functional activity of the interstitial and spermatogenetic tissues of the green frog *Rana esculenta. Gen. comp. Endocr.* **4**, 550–562.

(1968). Patterns of testicular activity. In *Perspectives in Endocrinology. Hormones in the Lives of Lower Vertebrates* (edited by E. J. W. Barrington and C. B. Jorgenson), pp. 239–304. London and New York: Academic Press.

(1969). Seasonal cycles in reptilian testes. *Gen. comp. Endocr. Suppl.* **2**, 147–155.

Lofts, B. and Bern, H. A. (1972). The functional morphology of steroidogenic tissues. In *Steriods in Nonmammalian Vertebrates* (edited by D. R. Idler), pp. 37–125. New York and London: Academic Press.

Lofts, B., Follett, B. K. and Murton, R. K. (1970). Temporal changes in the pituitary gonadal axis. *Mem. Soc. Endocr.* **18**, 545–575.

Lofts, B., Murton, R. K. and Thearle, R. J. P. (1973). The effects of testosterone propionate and gonadotropins on the bill pigmentation and testes of the House sparrow (*Passer domesticus*). *Gen. comp. Endocr.* **21**, 202–209.

Lofts, B., Phillips, J. G. and Tam, W. H. (1971). Seasonal changes in the histology of the adrenal gland of the cobra, *Naja naja. Gen. comp. Endocr.* **16**, 121–131.

Lowry, P. J. and Chadwick, A. (1970). Purification and amino acid sequence of melanocyte stimulating hormone from the dogfish *Squalus acanthias. Biochem. J.* **118**, 713–718.

Luckey, T. D. (1973). Perspective of thymic hormones. In *Thymic Hormones* (edited by T. D. Luckey), pp. 275–314. Baltimore, London, Tokyo: University Park Press.

Lutherer, L. O., Fregly, M. J. and Anton, A. H. (1969). An interrelationship between theophylline and catecholamines in the hypothyroid rat acutely exposed to cold. *Fedn Proc.* **28**, 1238–1242.

Lyons, W. R. (1958). Hormonal synergism in mammary growth. *Proc. Roy. Soc. Lond. B.* **149**, 303–325.

MacLeod, R. M. and Lehmeyer, J. E. (1974). Studies on the mechanism of the dopamine-mediated inhibition of prolactin secretion. *Endocrinology* **94**, 1077–1085.

Maderson, P. F. A., Chiu, K. W. and Phillips, J. G. (1970). Endocrine–epidermal relationships in squamate reptiles. *Mem. Soc. Endocr.* **18**, 259–284.

Maderson, P. F. A. and Licht, P. (1967). Epidermal morphology and sloughing frequency in normal and prolactin treated *Anolis carolinensis* (Iquanidae, Lacertilia). *J. Morphol.* **123**, 157–172.

Maetz, J. (1969). Observations on the role of the pituitary–interrenal axis in the ion regulation of the eel and other teleosts. *Gen. comp. Endocr. Suppl.* **2**, 299–316.

(1971). Fish gills: mechanisms of salt transfer in fresh water and sea water. *Phil. Trans. Roy. Soc. Lond. B.* **262**, 209–249.

Maetz, J. and Rankin, J. C. (1969). Quelques aspects du rôle biologique des hormones neurohypophysaires chez les poissons. *Colloques du C.N.R.S.* **177**, 45–54.

Manning, M. and Sawyer, W. H. (1970). 4-Threonine-oxytocin: a more active and specific oxytocic agent than oxytocin. *Nature, Lond.* **227**, 715–716.

Manns, J. G., Boda, J. M. and Willes, R. F. (1967). Probable role of propionate and butyrate in control of insulin secretion in sheep. *Amer. J. Physiol.* **212**, 756–764.

Maher, M. J. (1965). The role of the thyroid gland in the oxygen consumption of lizards. *Gen. comp. Endocr.* **5**, 320–325.

Marshall, F. H. A. (1956). The breeding season. In *Marshall's Physiology of Reproduction* (edited by A. S. Parkes), vol. I (Pt 1), pp. 1–42. London: Longmans.

Marx, S. J., Woodward, C. J. and Aurbach, G. D. (1972). Calcitonin receptors in kidney and bone. *Science* **178**, 999–1001.

Mayer, N., Maetz, J., Chan, D. K. O., Forster, M. and Chester Jones, I. (1967). Cortisol, a sodium excreting factor in the eel (*Anguilla anguilla* L.) adapted to sea water. *Nature, Lond.* **214**, 1118–1120.

McClanahan, L. (1967). Adaptations of the spadefoot toad *Scaphiopus couchi* to desert environments. *Comp. Biochem. Physiol.* **20**, 73–99.

McMillian, J. E. and Wilkinson, R. F. (1972). The effect of pancreatic hormones on blood glucose in *Ambystoma annulatum*. *Copeia* 1972 (no. 4), 664–668.

McNabb, R. A. (1969). The effects of thyroxine on glycogen stores and oxygen consumption in the leopard frog, *Rana pipiens*. *Gen. comp. Endocr.* **12**, 276–281.

McNatty, K. P., Cashmore, M. and Young, A. (1972). Diurnal variation in plasma cortisol levels in sheep. *J. Endocr.* **54**, 361–362.

Medica, P. A., Turner, F. B. and Smith, D. D. (1973). Hormonal induction of color change in female leopard lizards *Crotaphytus wislizenii*. *Copeia* 1973 (no. 4), 658–661.

Meier, A. H. (1970). Thyroxin phases the circadian fattening response to prolactin. *Proc. Soc. exp. Biol. Med., New York* **133**, 1113–1116.

Meier, A. H. and Farner, D. S. (1964). A possible endocrine basis for premigratory fattening in the white-crowned sparrow, *Zonotrichia leucophrys gambelii* (Nuttall). *Gen. comp. Endocr.* **4**, 584–595.

Meier, A. H., Trobec, T. N., Joseph, M. M. and John, T. M. (1971). Temporal synergism of prolactin and adrenal steroids in the regulation of fat stores. *Proc. Soc. exp. Biol. Med., New York* **137**, 408–415.

Meier, S. and Solursh, M. (1972). The comparative effects of several mammalian growth hormones on sulfate incorporation into acid mucopolysaccharides by cultured chick embryo chondrocytes. *Endocrinology* **90**, 1447–1451.

Minick, M. C. and Chavin, W. (1973). Effects of catecholamines upon serum FFA levels in normal and diabetic goldfish, *Carassius auratus* L. *Comp. Biochem. Physiol.* **44A**, 1003–1008.

Mirsky, I. A. (1965). Effect of biologically active peptides on adipose tissue. In *Handbook of Physiology*, Section 5 *Adipose Tissue*, pp. 407–415. Washington: American Physiology Society.

Mitnick, M. and Reichlin, S. (1972). Enzymatic synthesis of thyrotropin-releasing hormone (TRH) by hypothalamic 'TRH synthetase'. *Endocrinology* **91**, 1145–1153.

Monod, J. (1966). On the mechanism of molecular interactions in the control of cellular metabolism. *Endocrinology* **78**, 412–425.

Mueller, W. J., Brubaker, R. L., Gay, C. V. and Boelkins, J. N. (1973). Mechanisms of bone resorption in laying hens. *Fedn Proc.* **32**, 1951–1954.

Meuller, W. J., Hall, K. L., Maurer, C. A. and Joshua, I. G. (1973). Plasma calcium and inorganic phosphate response of laying hens to parathyroid hormone. *Endocrinology* **92**, 853–856.

Munday, K. A. (1957). The relation of endogenous melanophore-expanding hormone to hyperglycaemia in *Xenopus laevis. J. Endocr.* **15**, 190–198.

Myant, N. B. (1971). The role of thyroid hormone in the fetal and postnatal development of mammals. In *Hormones in Development* (edited by M. Hamburgh and E. J. Barrington), pp. 465–471. New York: Appleton–Century–Crofts.

Nalbandov, A. V. (1969). Specificity of action of gonadotrophic hormones. *Colloque du C.N.R.S.* **177**, 335–342.

(1973). Control of luteal function in mammals. In *Handbook of Physiology*, Section 7 *Endocrinology*, vol. II *Female reproductive system* (Pt I), pp. 153–167. Washington: American Physiological Society.

Nature (1973). Reference to newt in Siberia, **242**, 369.

Niall, H. D., Hogan, M. L., Sauer, R., Rosenblum, I. Y. and Greenwood, F. C. (1971). Sequences of pituitary and placental lactogenic and growth hormones: evolution from a primordial peptide by gene reduplication. *Proc. natn. Acad. Sci., USA* **68**, 866–869.

Nicholls, T. J., Scanes, C. G. and Follett, B. K. (1973). Plasma pituitary luteinizing hormone in Japanese quail during photoperiodically induced gonadal growth and regression. *Gen. comp. Endocr.* **21**, 84–98.

Nichols, C. W. (1973). Somatotropic effects of prolactin and growth hormone in juvenile snapping turtles (*Chelydra serpentina*). *Gen. comp. Endocr.* **21**, 219–224.

Nicoll, C. S., Bern, H. A., Dunlop, D. and Strohman, R. C. (1965). Prolactin, growth hormone, thyroxine and growth in tadpoles of *Rana catesbeiana. Amer. Zool.* **5**, 738–739.

Nicoll, C. S. and Licht, P. (1971). Evolutionary biology of prolactins and somatotropins. ii. Electrophoretic comparison of tetrapod somatotropins. *Gen. comp. Endocr.* **17**, 490–507.

Nilsson, A. (1970). Gastrointestinal hormones in the holocephalian fish *Chimaera monstrosa* (L.). *Comp. Biochem. Physiol.* **32**, 387–390.

Nishimura, H., Ogawa, M. and Sawyer, W. H. (1973). Renin–angiotensin system in primitive bony fishes and a holocephalian. *Amer. J. Physiol.* **224**, 950–956.

Nishimura, H., Oguri, M., Ogawa, M., Sokabe, H. and Imai, M. (1970). Absence of renin in kidneys of elasmobranchs and cyclostomes. *Amer. J. Physiol.* **218**, 911–915.

Nolly, H. L. and Fasciola, J. C. (1973). The specificity of the renin–angiotensinogen reaction through the phylogenetic scale. *Comp. Biochem. Physiol.* **44A**, 639–645.

Novales, R. R. (1972). Recent studies of the melanin-dispersing effect of MSH on melanophores. *Gen. comp. Endocr. Suppl.* **3**, 125–135.

(1973). Discussion of 'Endocrine regulation of pigmentation' by Frank S. Abbott. *Amer. Zool.* **13**, 895–897.

O'Connor, J. M. (1972). Pituitary gonadotropin release patterns in pre-spawning brook trout, *Salvelinus fontinalis*, rainbow trout *Salmo gairdneri* and leopard frogs, *Rana pipiens. Comp. Biochem. Physiol.* **43A**, 739–746.

Odum, E. P. (1965). Adipose tissue in migratory birds. In *Handbook of Physiology*, Section 5 *Adipose Tissue*, pp. 37–43. Washington: American Physiology Society.

Ogawa, M., Oguri, M., Sokabe, H. and Nishimura, H. (1972). Juxtaglomerular apparatus in vertebrates. *Gen. comp. Endocr. Suppl.* **3**, 374–380.

Ogawa, M., Yagasaki, M. and Yamazaki, J. (1973). The effect of prolactin on water influx in isolated gills of the goldfish *Carassius auratus* L. *Comp. Biochem. Physiol.* **44A**, 1177–1183.

Oguro, C. (1973). Parathyroid gland and serum calcium concentration in the giant salamander, *Megalobatrachus davidianus*. *Gen. comp. Endocr.* **21**, 565–568.

Oguro, C. and Tomisawa, A. (1972). Effects of parathyroidectomy on serum calcium concentration of the turtle *Geoclemys reevesii*. *Gen. comp. Endocr.* **19**, 587–588.

Oishi, T. and Lauber, J. K. (1974). Pineal control of photo-endocrine responses in growing Japanese quail. *Endocrinology* **94**, 1731–1734.

Oksche, A. (1965). Survey of the development and comparative morphology of the pineal organ. *Prog. Brain Res.* **10**, 3–28.

Olivereau, M. (1967). Observations sur l'hypophyse de l'anguille femelle en particulier lors de la maturation sexuelle. *Z. Zellforsch. mikrosk. Anat.* **80**, 286–306.

O'Malley, B. W. and Means, A. R. (1974). Female steroid hormones and target cells nuclei. *Science* **183**, 610–620.

Oyer, P. E., Cho, S., Peterson, J. D. and Steiner, D. F. (1971). Studies on human proinsulin. *J. biol. Chem.* **246**, 1375–1386.

Ozon, R. (1972). Androgens in fishes, amphibians, reptiles and birds. In *Steroids in Nonmammalian Vertebrates* (edited by D. R. Idler), pp. 329–389. New York and London: Academic Press.

Pang, P. K. T. (1973). Endocrine control of calcium metabolism in teleosts. *Amer. Zool.* **13**, 775–792.

Pang, P. K. T., Pang, R. K. and Sawyer, W. H. (1973). Effects of environmental calcium and replacement therapy on the killifish, *Fundulus heteroclitus*, after the surgical removal of the corpuscles of Stannius. *Endocrinology* **93**, 705–710.

—— (1974). Environmental calcium and the sensitivity of the killifish (*Fundulus heteroclitus*) in bioassays for the hypocalcemic response to Stannius corpuscles from killifish and cod (*Gadus morhua*). *Endocrinology* **94**, 548–555.

Pang, P. K. T. and Sawyer, W. H. (1974). Effects of prolactin on hypophysectomized mud puppies *Necturus maculosus*. *Amer. J. Physiol.* **226**, 458–462.

Papkoff, H. (1972). Subunit interrelationships among the pituitary glycoprotein hormones. *Gen. comp. Endocr. Suppl.* **3**, 609–616.

Parkes, A. S. and Marshall, A. J. (1960). The reproductive hormones in birds. In *Marshall's Physiology of Reproduction* (edited by A. S. Parkes), vol. I (Pt 2), pp. 583–706. London: Longmans.

Patent, G. J. (1970). Comparison of some hormonal effects on carbohydrate metabolism in an elasmobranch (*Squalus acanthias*) and a holocephalan (*Hydrolagus colliei*). *Gen. comp. Endocr.* **14**, 215–242.

Pavel, S., Dorcescu, M., Petrescu-Holban, R. and Ghinea, E. (1973). Biosynthesis of a vasotocin-like peptide in cell cultures from pineal glands of human fetuses. *Science* **181**, 1252–1253.

Payan, P. and Maetz, J. (1971). Balance hydrique chez les elasmobranches: arguments en faveur d'un contrôle endocrinien. *Gen. comp. Endocr.* **16**, 535–554.

Peaker, M. (1971). Avian salt glands. *Phil. Trans. Roy. Soc. Lond. B* **262**, 289–300.

Penhos, J. C. and Ramey, E. (1973). Studies on the endocrine pancreas of amphibians and reptiles. *Amer. Zool.* **12**, 667–698.

Peter, R. E. (1971). Feedback effects of thyroxine on the hypothalamus and pituitary of the goldfish, *Carassius auratus. J. Endocr.* **51**, 31–39.

Phillips, J. G. and Ensor, D. M. (1972). The significance of environmental factors in the hormone mediated changes of nasal (salt) gland activity in birds. *Gen. comp. Endocr. Suppl.* **3**, 393–404.

Pic, P., Mayer-Gostan, N. and Maetz, J. (1973). Sea-water teleosts: presence of α- and β-adrenergic receptors in the gill regulating salt extrusion and water permeability. In *Comparative Physiology* (edited by L. Bolis, K. Schmidt-Nielsen and S. H. P. Maddrell), pp. 292–322. Amsterdam: North-Holland.

Pickering, A. D. (1972). Effects of hypophysectomy on the activity of the endostyle and thyroid gland in the larval and adult river lamprey, *Lampetra fluviatilis L. Gen. comp. Endocr.* **18**, 335–343.

Pickford, G. E. and Kosto, B. (1957). Hormonal induction of melanogenesis in hypophysectomized killifish (*Fundulus heteroclitus*). *Endocrinology* **61**, 177–196.

Pickford, G. E., Pang, P. K. T., Weinstein, E., Torretti, J., Hendler, E. and Epstein, F. H. (1970). The response of the hypophysectomized Cyprinodont, *Fundulus heteroclitus*, to replacement therapy with cortisol: effects on blood serum and sodium-potassium activated adenosine triphosphatase in the gills, kidney, and intestinal mucosa. *Gen. comp. Endocr.* **14**, 524–534.

Pickford, G. E. and Phillips, J. G. (1959). Prolactin, a factor in promoting survival of hypophysectomized killifish in fresh water. *Science* **130**, 454–455.

Pictet, R. and Rutter, W. J. (1972). Development of the embryonic endocrine pancreas. In *Handbook of Physiology*, Section 7 *Endocrinology*, vol. I *Endocrine pancreas*, pp. 25–66. Washington: American Physiological Society.

Pohorecky, L. A. and Wurtman, R. J. (1971). Adrenocortical control of epinephrine synthesis. *Pharmacol. Rev.* **23**, 1–35.

Potts, J. T., Keutmann, H. T., Niall, H. D., Habener, J. F. and Tregear, G. W. (1972). Comparative biochemistry of parathyroid hormone. *Gen. comp. Endocr. Suppl.* **3**, 405–410.

Prigge, W. F. and Grande, F. (1971). Effects of glucagon, epinephrine and insulin on *in vitro* lipolysis of adipose tissue from mammals and birds. *Comp. Biochem. Physiol.* **39B**, 69–82.

Quay, W. B. (1970). Endocrine effects on the mammalian pineal. *Amer. Zool.* **10**, 237–246.

—— (1972). Integument and the environment: glandular composition, function and evolution. *Amer. Zool.* **12**, 95–108.

Quevedo, W. C. (1972). Epidermal melanin units: melanocyte-keratinocyte interactions. *Amer. Zool.* **12**, 35–41.

Rall, J. E., Robbins, J. and Lewallen, C. G. (1964). The thyroid. In *The Hormones* (edited by G. Pincus, K. V. Thimann and E. B. Astwood), vol. V, pp. 159–439. New York: Academic Press.

Ralph, C. L. (1970). Structure and alleged functions of avian pineals. *Amer. Zool.* **10**, 217–235.

Ramsey, D. H. and Bern, H. A. (1972). Stimulation by ovine prolactin of fluid transfer in everted sacs of rat small intestine. *J. Endocr.* **53**, 453–459.

Randle, P. J. and Hales, C. N. (1972). Insulin release mechanisms. In *Handbook of Physiology*, Section 7 *Endocrinology*, vol. I *Endocrine pancreas*, pp. 219–235. Washington: American Physiological Society.

Rankin, J. C. and Maetz, J. (1971). A perfused teleostean gill preparation: vascular actions of neurohypophysial hormones and catecholamines. *J. Endocr.* **51**, 621–635.

Rasquin, P. and Rosenbloom, L. (1954). Endocrine imbalance and tissue hyperplasia in teleosts maintained in darkness. *Bull. Amer. Mus. nat. Hist.* **104**, 359–420.

Redshaw, M. R. (1972). The hormonal control of the amphibian ovary. *Amer. Zool.* **12**, 289–306.

Reinbloth, R. (1970). Intersexuality in fishes. *Mem. Soc. Endocr.* **18**, 515–541.

— (1972). Hormonal control of the teleost ovary. *Amer. Zool.* **12**, 307–324.

Reiter, R. J. and Sorrentino, S. (1970). Reproductive effects of the mammalian pineal. *Amer. Zool.* **10**, 247–258.

Rippel, R. H., Johnson, E. S., White, W. F., Fujino, M., Yamazaki, I. and Nakayama, R. (1973). Ovulating and LH-releasing activity of a highly potent analog of synthetic gonadotropin-releasing hormone. *Endocrinology* **93**, 1449–1452.

Robertshaw, D., Taylor, C. R. and Mazzia, L. M. (1973). Sweating in primates: role of secretion of the adrenal medulla during exercise. *Amer. J. Physiol.* **224**, 678–681.

Robertson, D. R. (1968). The ultimobranchial gland in *Rana pipiens*. IV. Hypercalcemia and glandular hypertrophy. *Z. Zellforsch. mikroskop. Anat.* **85**, 441–542.

— (1969a). The ultimobranchial body of *Rana pipiens*. VIII. Effects of extirpation upon calcium distribution and bone cell types. *Gen. comp. Endocr.* **12**, 479–490.

— (1969b). The ultimobranchial body in *Rana pipiens*. IX. Effects of extirpation and transplantation on urinary calcium excretion. *Endocrinology* **84**, 1174–1178.

— (1971). Cytological and physiological activity of ultimobranchial gland in the premetamorphic anuran *Rana catesbeiana*. *Gen. comp. Physiol.* **16**, 329–341.

Robertson, O. H., Krupp, M. A., Thomas, S. F., Favour, C. B., Hane, S. and Wexler, B. C. (1961). Hyperadrenocorticoidism in spawning migratory and nonmigratory rainbow trout (*Salmo gairdnerii*); comparison with Pacific salmon (Genus *Oncorhynchus*). *Gen. comp. Endocr.* **1**, 473–484.

Robertson, O. H. and Wexler, B. C. (1959). Histological changes in the organs and tissues of migrating and spawning Pacific salmon (Genus *Oncorhynchus*). *Endocrinology* **66**, 222–239.

Robinson, K. W. and MacFarlane, W. V. (1957). Plasma antidiuretic activity of marsupials during exposure to heat. *Endocrinology* **60**, 679–680.

Robison, G. A., Butcher, R. W. and Sutherland, E. W. (1971). *Cyclic AMP.* New York and London: Academic Press.

— (1972). The catecholamines. In *Biochemical Actions of Hormones* (edited by G. Litwack), vol. II, pp. 81–111. New York and London: Academic Press.

Roth, J. J., Jones, R. E. and Gerrard, A. M. (1973). Corpora lutea and oviposition in the lizard *Sceloporus undulatus*. *Gen. comp. Endocr.* **21**, 569–572.

Rowan, W. (1925). Relation of light to bird migration and developmental changes. *Nature, Lond.* **115**, 494–495.

Rubin, B., Engel, S. L., Drungis, A. M., Dzelzkalns, M., Grigas, E. O., Waugh, M. H. and Yiacas, E. (1969). Cholecystokinin-like activities in guinea pigs and in dogs of the *C*-terminal octapeptide (SQ 19,884) of cholecystokinin. *J. Pharmac. Sci.* **58**, 955–959.

Rudinger, J. (1968). Synthetic analogues of oxytocin: an approach to problems of hormone action. *Proc. Roy. Soc., Lond. B* **170**, 17–26.

Rust, C. C. and Meyer, R. K. (1968). Effects of pituitary autografts on hair color in the short-tailed weasel. *Gen. comp. Endocr.* **11**, 548–551.

(1969). Hair color, molt, and testis size in male, short-tailed weasels treated with melatonin. *Science* **165**, 921–922.

Sage, M. (1973). The evolution of thyroidal function in fishes. *Amer. Zool.* **13**, 899–905.

Samols, E., Tyler, J., Megyesi, C. and Marks, V. (1966). Immunochemical glucagon in human pancreas, gut, and plasma. *Lancet* **ii**, 727–729.

Sandor, T. (1969). A comparative survey of steroids and steroidogenic pathways throughout the vertebrates. *Gen. comp. Endocr. Suppl.* **2**, 284–298.

Sandor, T. and Idler, D. R. (1972). Steroid methodology. In *Steroids in Non-mammalian Vertebrates* (edited by D. R. Idler), pp. 6–36. New York and London: Academic Press.

Sassin, J. F., Frantz, A. G., Weiztman, E. D. and Kapen, S. (1972). Human prolactin: 24-hour pattern with increased release during sleep. *Science* **177**, 1205–1207.

Sawyer, W. H. (1972a). Lungfishes and amphibians: endocrine adaptation and the transition from aquatic to terrestrial life. *Fedn Proc.* **31**, 1609–1614.

(1972b). Neurohypophysial hormones and water and sodium excretion in African lungfish. *Gen. comp. Endocr. Suppl.* **3**, 345–349.

Sawyer, W. H. and Pickford, G. E. (1963). Neurohypophyseal principles of *Fundulus heteroclitus*: characteristics and seasonal changes. *Gen. comp. Endocr.* **3**, 439–445.

Scanes, C. G., Dobson, S., Follett, B. K. and Dodd, J. M. (1972). Gonadotrophic activity in the pituitary gland of the dogfish (*Scyliorhinus canicula*). *J. Endocr.* **54**, 343–344.

Scanes, C. G., Follett, B. K. and Goos, H. J. Th. (1972). Cross-reaction in a chicken LH radioimmunoassay with plasma and pituitary extracts from various species. *Gen. comp. Endocr.* **19**, 596–600.

Schally, A. V., Arimura, A. and Kastin, A. J. (1973). Hypothalamic regulatory hormones. *Science* **179**, 341–350.

Schreibman, M. P. and Kallman, K. D. (1969). The effect of hypophysectomy on freshwater survival in teleosts of the order Antheriniformes. *Gen. comp. Endocr.* **13**, 27–38.

Schwartz, N. B. (1973). Mechanisms controlling ovulation in small mammals. In *Handbook of Physiology*, Section 7 *Endocrinology*, vol. II *Female reproductive system* (Pt 1), pp. 125–141. Washington: American Physiology Society.

Seal, U. S. and Doe, R. P. (1963). Corticosteroid-binding globulin: species distribution and small-scale purification. *Endocrinology* **73**, 371–376.

Sellers, E. A., Flattery, K. V. and Steiner, G. (1974). Cold acclimation in hypothyroid rats. *Amer. J. Physiol.* **226**, 290–294.

Senior, B. E. and Cunningham, F. J. (1974). Oestradiol and luteinizing hormone during the ovulatory cycle of the hen. *J. Endocr.* **60**, 201–202.

Shafrir, E. and Wertheimer, E. (1965). Comparative physiology of adipose tissue in different sites and in different species. In *Handbook of Physiology*, Section 5 *Adipose Tissue*, pp. 417–429. Washington: American Physiological Society.

Shapiro, M., Nicholson, W. E., Orth, D. N., Mitchel, W. M., Island, D. P. and Liddle, G. W. (1972). Preliminary characterization of the pituitary melanocyte stimulating hormones of several vertebrate species. *Endocrinology* **90**, 249–256.

Sharman, G. B. (1970). Reproductive physiology of marsupials. *Science* **167**, 1221–1228.

Shire, J. G. M. (1970). Genetic variation in adrenal structure: quantitative measurements on the cortex and medulla in hybrid mice. *J. Endocr.* **48**, 419–431.

Shoemaker, V. H., Nagy, K. A. and Bradshaw, S. D. (1972). Studies on the control of electrolyte excretion by the nasal gland of the lizard *Dipsosaurus dorsalis*. *Comp. Biochem. Physiol.* **42**A, 749–757.

Simpson, P. A. and Blair-West, J. R. (1972). Estimation of marsupial renin using marsupial renin-substrate. *J. Endocr.* **53**, 125–130.

Skadhauge, E. (1969). Activités biologiques des hormones neurohypophysaires chez les oiseaux et les reptiles. *Colloque du C.N.R.S.* **177**, 63–68.

Smith, H. W. (1930). Metabolism of the lungfish, *Protopterus aethiopicus*. *J. biol. Chem.* **88**, 97–130.

Smith, L. F. (1966). Species variation in the amino acid sequence of insulin. *Amer. J. Med.* **40**, 662–666.

Smith, P. M. and Follett, B. K. (1972). Luteinizing hormone releasing factor in the quail hypothalamus. *J. Endocr.* **53**, 131–138.

Sokabe, H. and Nakajima, T. (1972). Chemical structure and role of angiotensins in the vertebrates. *Gen. comp. Endocr. Suppl.* **3**, 382–392.

Sokabe, H., Nishimura, H., Ogawa, M. and Oguri, M. (1970). Determination of renin in the corpuscles of Stannius of the teleost. *Gen. comp. Endocr.* **14**, 510–516.

Sokabe, H., Nishimura, H., Kawabe, K., Tenmoku, S. and Arai, T. (1972). Plasma renin activity in varying hydrated states in the bullfrog. *Amer. J. Physiol.* **222**, 142–146.

Sokabe, H., Oide, H., Ogawa, M. and Utida, S. (1973). Plasma renin activity in Japanese eels (*Anguilla japonica*) adapted to sea-water or in dehydration. *Gen. comp. Endocr.* **21**, 160–167.

Spallanzani (1784). *Dissertations Relative to the Natural History of Animals and Vegetables* 2. Trans. from the Italian, London. Quoted by F. H. A. Marshall, 1956.

Speers, G. M., Perey, D. Y. E. and Brown, D. M. (1970). Effect of ultimobranchialectomy in the laying hen. *Endocrinology* **87**, 1292–1297.

Srivastava, A. K. and Meier, A. H. (1972). Daily variation in concentration of cortisol in plasma in intact and hypophysectomized gulf killifish. *Science* **177**, 185–187.

Stannius, H. (1839). Die Nebennieren bei Knochenfischen. *Arch. Anat. Physiol.* **97**, 97–101.

Steiner, D. F., Kemmler, W., Clark, J. L., Oyer, P. E. and Rubinstein, A. H. (1972). The biosynthesis of insulin. In *Handbook of Physiology*, Section 7

Endocrinology, vol. I *Endocrine pancreas*, pp. 175–198. Washington: American Physiological Society.

Sterling, K., Brenner, M. A. and Saldanha, V. F. (1973). Conversion of thyroxine to triiodothyronine by cultured human cells. *Science* **179**, 1000–1001.

Stetson, M. H. and Erickson, J. E. (1972). Hormonal control of photoperiodically induced fat deposition in white-crowned sparrows. *Gen. comp. Endocr.* **19**, 355–362.

Stewart, A. D. (1968). Genetic variation in the neurohypophysial hormones of the mouse. *J. Endocr.* **41**, xix–xx.

— (1972). Genetic determination of the storage of vasopressin and oxytocin in neural lobes of mice. *J. Physiol., Lond.* **222**, 157P.

— (1973). Sensitivity of mice to (8-arginine)- and (8-lysine)- vasopressins as antidiuretic hormones. *J. Endocr.* **59**, 195–196.

Stewart, J., Fraser, R., Papaioannou, V. and Tait, A. (1972). Aldosterone production and the zona glomerulosa: a genetic study. *Endocrinology* **90**, 968–972.

Strauss, J. S. and Ebling, F. J. (1970). Control and function of skin glands in mammals. *Mem. Soc. Endocr.* **18**, 341–368.

Sutherland, E. W. (1972). Studies on the mechanism of hormone action. *Science* **177**, 401–408.

Suzuki, S. and Kondo, Y. (1973). Thyroidal morphogenesis and biosynthesis of thyroglobulin before and after metamorphosis in the lamprey, *Lampetra reissneri*. *Gen. comp. Endocr.* **21**, 451–460.

Swift, D. R. and Pickford, G. E. (1965). Seasonal variations in the hormone content of the pituitary gland of the perch *Perca fluviatilis* L. *Gen. comp. Endocr.* **5**, 354–365.

Swaminathan, R., Bates, R. F. L. and Care, A. R. (1972). Fresh evidence for a physiological role for calcitonin in calcium homeostasis. *J. Endocr.* **54**, 525–526.

Swaminathan, R., Ker, J. and Care, A. D. (1974). Calcitonin and intestinal calcium absorption. *J. Endocr.* **61**, 83–94.

Takasugi, N. and Bern, H. A. (1962). Experimental studies on the caudal neurosecretory system in *Tilapia mossambica*. *Comp. Biochem. Physiol.* **6**, 289–303.

Tanabe, Y., Ishii, T. and Tamaki, Y. (1969). Comparison of thyroxine-binding plasma proteins of various vertebrates and their evolutionary aspects. *Gen. comp. Endocr.* **13**, 14–21.

Tanaka, Y., Frank, H. and DeLuca, H. F. (1973). Intestinal calcium transport: stimulation by low phosphorus diets. *Science* **181**, 564–566.

Tanner, J. M. (1972). Human growth hormone. *Nature, Lond.* **237**, 433–439.

Tashjian, A. H., Levine, L. and Wilhelmi, A. E. (1965). Immunochemical relatedness of porcine, bovine, ovine and primate growth hormones. *Endocrinology* **77**, 563–573.

Taylor, J. D. and Bagnara, J. T. (1972). Dermal chromatophores. *Amer. Zool.* **12**, 43–62.

Taylor, R. E., Tu, T. and Barker, S. B. (1967). Thyroxine-like actions of 3′-*iso*propyl-3′,5′-dibromo-L-thyronine, a potent iodine-free analog. *Endocrinology* **80**, 1143–1147.

Temple, S. A. (1974). Plasma testosterone titers during the annual reproductive cycle of starlings (*Sturnus vulgaris*). *Gen. comp. Endocr.* **22**, 470–479.

Tepperman, J. and Tepperman, H. M. (1970). Gluconeogenesis, lipogenesis and the Sherringtonian metaphor. *Fedn Proc.* **29**, 1284-1293.

Tewary, P. D. and Farner, D. S. (1973). Effect of castration and estrogen administration on the plumage pigment of the male House Finch (*Carpdacus mexicanus*). *Amer. Zool.* **13**, 1278.

Thody, A. J. and Plummer, N. A. (1973). A radioimmunoassay for β-melanocyte stimulating hormone in human plasma. *J. Endocr.* **58**, 263-273.

Thornton, V. F. (1972). A progesterone-like factor detected by bioassay in the blood of the toad (*Bufo bufo*) shortly before induced ovulation. *Gen. comp. Endocr.* **18**, 133-139.

Torresani, J., Gorbman, A., Lachiver, F. and Lissitzky, S. (1973). Immunological cross-reactivity between thyroglobulins of mammals and reptiles. *Gen. comp. Endocr.* **21**, 530-535.

Torrey, T. W. (1971). *Morphogenesis of the Vertebrates* (3rd edition), pp. 44-45. New York, London, Sydney, Toronto: John Wiley.

Tracy, H. J. and Gregory, R. A. (1964). Physiological properties of a series of synthetic peptides structurally related to gastrin I. *Nature, Lond.* **204**, 935-938.

Tregear, G. W., Rietschoten, J. V., Greene, E., Keutmann, H. T., Niall, H. D., Reit, B., Parsons, J. A. and Potts, J. T. (1973). Bovine parathyroid hormone: minimum chain length of synthetic peptide required for biological activity. *Endocrinology* **93**, 1349-1353.

Turkington, R. W. (1972). Multiple hormonal interactions. The mammary gland. In *Biochemical Actions of Hormones* (edited by G. Litwack), vol. II, pp. 55-80. New York and London: Academic Press.

Tyndale-Biscoe, H. (1973). *Life of Marsupials.* New York: Elsevier.

Urasaki, H. (1972). Effects of restricted photoperiod and melatonin administration on gonadal weight in the Japanese killifish. *J. Endocr.* **55**, 619-620.

Urist, M. R. (1962). The bone-body fluid continuum: calcium and phosphorus in the skeleton and blood of extinct and living vertebrates. *Perspectus Biol. Med.* **6**, 75-115.

(1963). The regulation of calcium and other ions in the serums of hagfish and lampreys. *Proc. N. Y. Acad. Sci.* **109**, 294-311.

(1973). Testosterone-induced development of limb gills of the lungfish, *Lepidosiren paradoxa. Comp. Biochem. Physiol.* **44A**, 131-135.

Urist, M. R. and Scheide, A. O. (1961). Partition of calcium and proteins in the blood of oviparous vertebrates during estrus. *J. gen. Physiol.* **44**, 743-756.

Urist, M. R., Uyeno, S., King, E., Okada, M., and Applegate, S. (1972). Calcium and phosphorus in the skeleton and blood of the lungfish, *Lepidosiren paradoxa*, with comment on humoral factors in calcium homeostasis in the Osteichthyes. *Comp. Biochem. Physiol.* **42A**, 393-408.

Utida, S., Hirano, T., Oide, H., Ando, M., Johnson, D. W. and Bern, H. A. (1972). Hormonal control of the intestine and urinary bladder in teleost osmoregulation. *Gen. comp. Endocr. Suppl.* **3**, 317-327.

Uttenthal, L. O. and Hope, D. B. (1972). Neurophysins and posterior pituitary hormones in the Suiformes. *Proc. Roy. Soc. Lond. B* **182**, 73-87.

van Tienhoven, A. and Planck, R. J. (1973). The effect of light on avian reproductive activity. In *Handbook of Physiology*, Section 7 *Endocrinology*, vol. II, *Female reproductive tract* (Pt I), pp. 79-107. Washington: American Physiological Society.

van Tienhoven, A. and Schally, A. V. (1972). Mammalian luteinizing hormone-releasing hormone induces ovulation in the domestic fowl. *Gen. comp. Endocr.* **19**, 594–595.

Valtin, H., Sawyer, W. H. and Sokol, H. W. (1965). Neurohypophysial principles in rats homozygous and heterozygous for hypothalamic diabetes insipidus (Brattleboro strain). *Endocrinology* **77**, 701–706.

Vander, A. J. (1967). Control of renin release. *Physiol. Rev.* **47**, 359–382.

Vizsolyi, E. and Perks, A. M. (1969). New neurohypophysial principle in foetal mammals. *Nature, Lond.* **223**, 1169–1171.

Waldo, C. M. and Wislocki, G. B. (1951). Observations on the shedding of the antlers of the virginia deer (*Odocoileus virginianus borealis*). *Amer. J. Anat.* **88**, 351–395.

Waring, H. (1936). Colour changes in the dogfish (*Scyllium canicula*). *Proc. Liverpool Biol. Soc.* **49**, 17–64.

— (1938). Chromatic behaviour of elasmobranchs. *Proc. Roy. Soc. Lond.* B **125**, 264–282.

— (1942). The co-ordination of vertebrate melanophore responses. *Biol. Rev.* **17**, 120–150.

— (1963). *Color Change Mechanisms in Cold-blooded Vertebrates*. London and New York: Academic Press.

Weinstein, B. (1968). On the relationship between glucagon and secretin. *Experientia* **24**, 406–408.

Weisbart, M. and Idler, D. R. (1970). Re-examination of the presence of corticosteroids in two cyclostomes, the Atlantic hagfish (*Myxine glutinosa* L.) and the sea lamprey (*Petromyzon marinus* L.). *J. Endocr.* **46**, 29–43.

Weiss, M. and McDonald, I. R. (1965). Corticosteroid secretion in the monotreme *Tachyglossus aculeatus*. *J. Endocr.* **33**, 203–210.

Wenberg, G. M. and Holland, J. C. (1973). The circannual variations of some of the hormones of the woodchuck (*Marmota monax*). *Comp. Biochem. Physiol.* **46A**, 523–535.

West, G. B. (1955). The comparative pharmacology of the suprarenal medulla. *Quart. Rev. Biol.* **30**, 116–137.

Wilson, J. F. and Dodd, J. M. (1973a). The role of the pineal complex and lateral eyes in the colour change response of the dogfish, *Scyliorhinus canicula* L. *J. Endocr.* **58**, 591–598.

— (1973b). The role of melonophore-stimulating hormone in melanogenesis in the dogfish, *Scyliorhinus canicula* L. *J. Endocr.* **58**, 685–686.

Wingstrand, K. G. (1951). *The Structure and Development of the Avian Pituitary*. C. W. K. Gleerup: Lund.

— (1966). Comparative anatomy and evolution of the hypophysis. In *The Pituitary Gland* (edited by G. W. Harris and B. T. Donovan), vol. I, pp. 58–146. Berkeley and Los Angeles: University of California.

Wise, J. K., Hendler, R. and Felig, P. (1972). Obesity: evidence of decreased secretion of glucagon. *Science* **178**, 513–514.

Woodhead, P. M. J. (1969). Effect of oestradiol and thyroxine upon the plasma calcium content of a shark, *Scyliorhinus canicula*. *Gen. comp. Endocr.* **13**, 310–312.

Woolley, P. (1957). Colour change in a chelonian. *Nature, Lond.* **179**, 1255–1256.

Wright, A., Chester Jones, I. and Phillips, J. G. (1957). The histology of the adrenal gland of prototheria. *J. Endocr.* **15**, 100–107.

Wurtman, R. J. and Axelrod, J. (1966). A 24-hr rhythm in the content of nore-pinephrine in the pineal and salivary glands of the rat. *Life Sciences* **5**, 665–669.

Wurtman, R. J., Axelrod, J. and Kelly, D. E. (1968). *The Pineal*. New York and London: Academic Press.

Xavier, F. (1974). La pseudogestation chez *Nectophyrnoïdes occidentalis* ANGEL. *Gen. comp. Endocr.* **22**, 98–115.

Xavier, F. and Ozon, R. (1971). Recherches sur l'activité endocrine de l'ovaire de *Nectophrynoïdes occidentalis* ANGEL (amphibien anoure vivipare). ii. Synthèse *in vitro* de stéroids. *Gen. comp. Endocr.* **16**, 30–40.

Yagil, R., Etzion, Z. and Berlyne, G. M. (1973). The effect of *d*-aldosterone and spironolactone on the concentration of sodium and potassium in the milk of rats. *J. Endocr.* **59**, 633–636.

Yaron, Z. (1972). Endocrine aspects of gestation in viviparous snakes. *Gen. comp. Endocr. Suppl.* **3**, 663–673.

Young, J. Z. (1935). The photoreceptors of lampreys. ii. The function of the pineal complex. *J. exp. Biol.* **12**, 254–270.

Zelnik, P. R. and Lederis, K. (1973). Chromatographic separation of urotensins. *Gen. comp. Endocr.* **20**, 392–400.

Zimmerman, E. A., Carmel, P. W., Husain, M. K., Ferin, M., Tannenbaum, M., Frantz, A. G. and Robison, A. G. (1973). Vasopressin and neurophysin: high concentrations in monkey hypophyseal portal blood. *Science* **182**, 925–927.

Zinder, O., Hamosh, M., Fleck, T. R. C. and Scow, R. O. (1974). Effect of pro-lactin on lipoprotein lipase in mammary gland and adipose tissue of rats. *Amer. J. Physiol.* **226**, 744–748.

Zipser, R. D., Licht, P. and Bern, H. A. (1969). Comparative effects of mammalian prolactin and growth hormone on growth in the toads *Bufo boreas* and *Bufo marinus*. *Gen. comp. Endocr.* **13**, 382–391.

Zuber-Vogeli, M. and Xavier, F. (1973). Les modifications cytologique de l'hypophyse distale des femelles de *Nectophrynoïdes occidentalis* Angel après ovariectomie. *Gen. comp. Endocr.* **20**, 199–213.

Index

A textbook of comparative endocrinology emphasizing the role of hormones in the physiological coordination of vertebrates— mammals, birds, reptiles, amphibians, and fishes.

Departing from the traditional approach in endocrinology of studying each gland in succession, the author takes the view that a more logical approach is to deal with each endocrine process in a wider biological context by relating it to an animal's physiology, ecology, and evolution.

Comparative Vertebrate Endocrinology discusses the intimate physiology of the endocrine system itself and describes the role of hormones in the processes of nutrition, osmoregulation, color change, calcium metabolism, and reproduction. The evolution of the hormones and their various physiological uses is stressed.

It is now known that several endocrine glands may secrete hormones that act together to integrate physiological events. Dr Bentley argues persuasively that this knowledge makes the integrated approach more desirable than the traditional serial approach. No other textbook examines the subject from this phenomenological point of view.

Comparative Vertebrate Endocrinology is suitable as a text for senior undergraduate/ graduate courses in vertebrate endocrinology and comparative endocrinology and as background reading for courses in comparative animal physiology. First-year medical students will find it very useful in their required endocrinology courses, and endocrinology researchers can turn to it as a reference source. The text requires only a basic background knowledge of zoology and animal physiology.